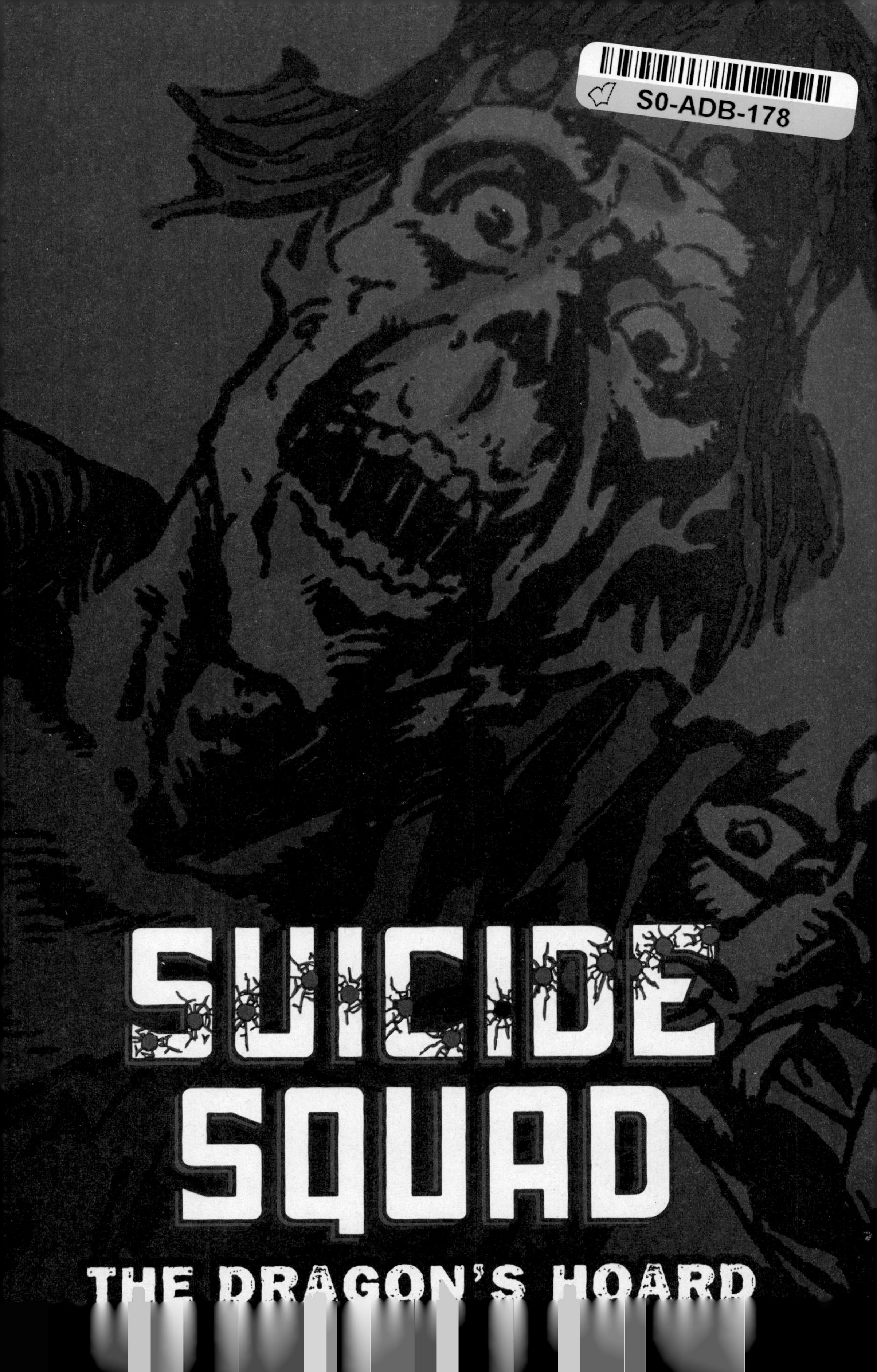
SUICIDE SQUAD
THE DRAGON'S HOARD

SUICIDE SQUAD

THE DRAGON'S HOARD

John OSTRANDER **Kim YALE**
writers

ROBERT CAMPANELLA **JIM FERN**
GEOF ISHERWOOD **KARL KESEL** **TOM MANDRAKE**
LUKE McDONNELL **GRANT MIEHM**
artists

Tom McCRAW
colorist

JOHN COSTANZA **Todd KLEIN**
letterers

collection cover artists
GEOF ISHERWOOD,
KARL KESEL and
ALLEN PASSALAQUA

AMANDA WALLER created by
JOHN OSTRANDER and **JOHN BYRNE**

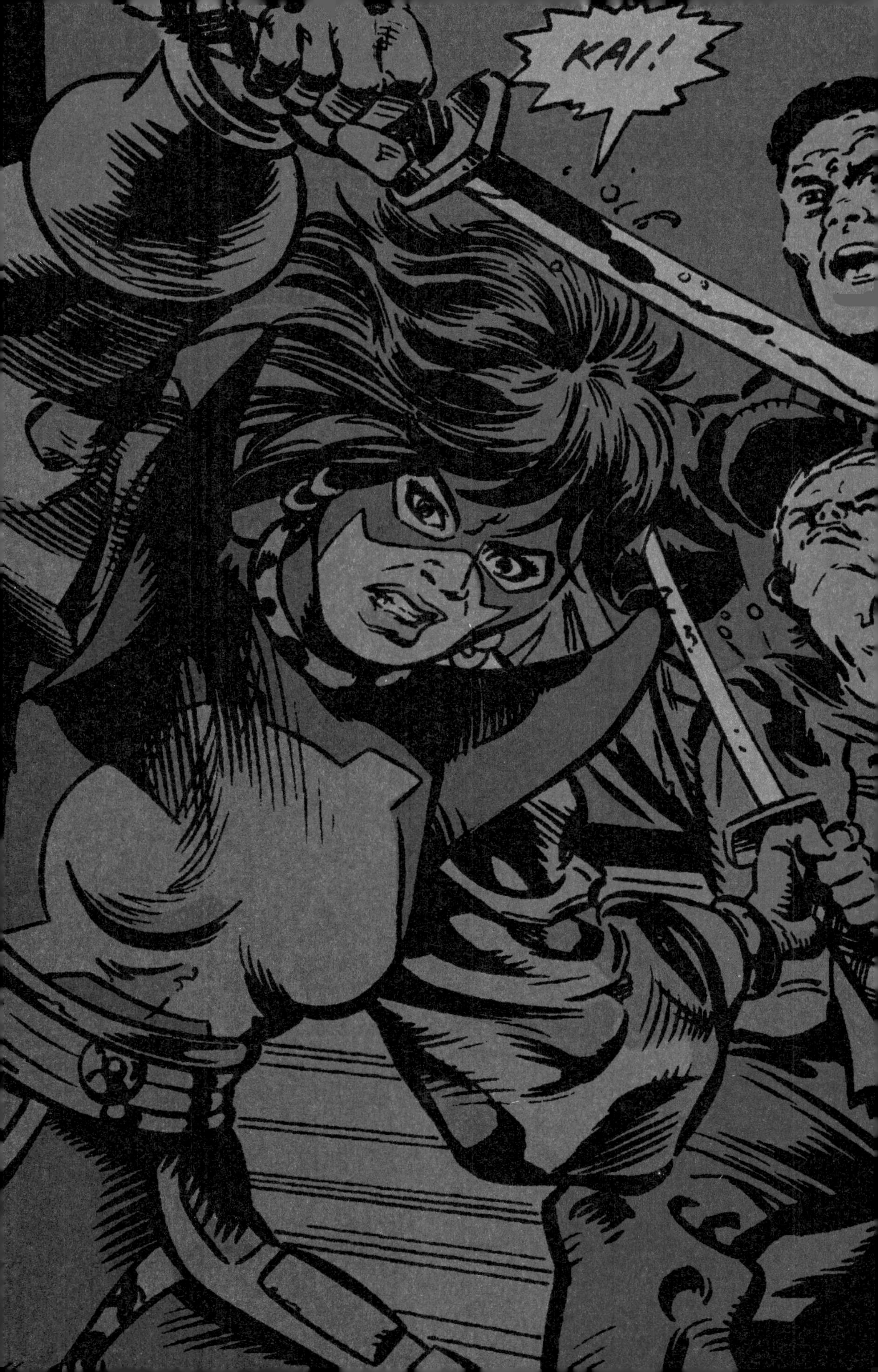
KAI!

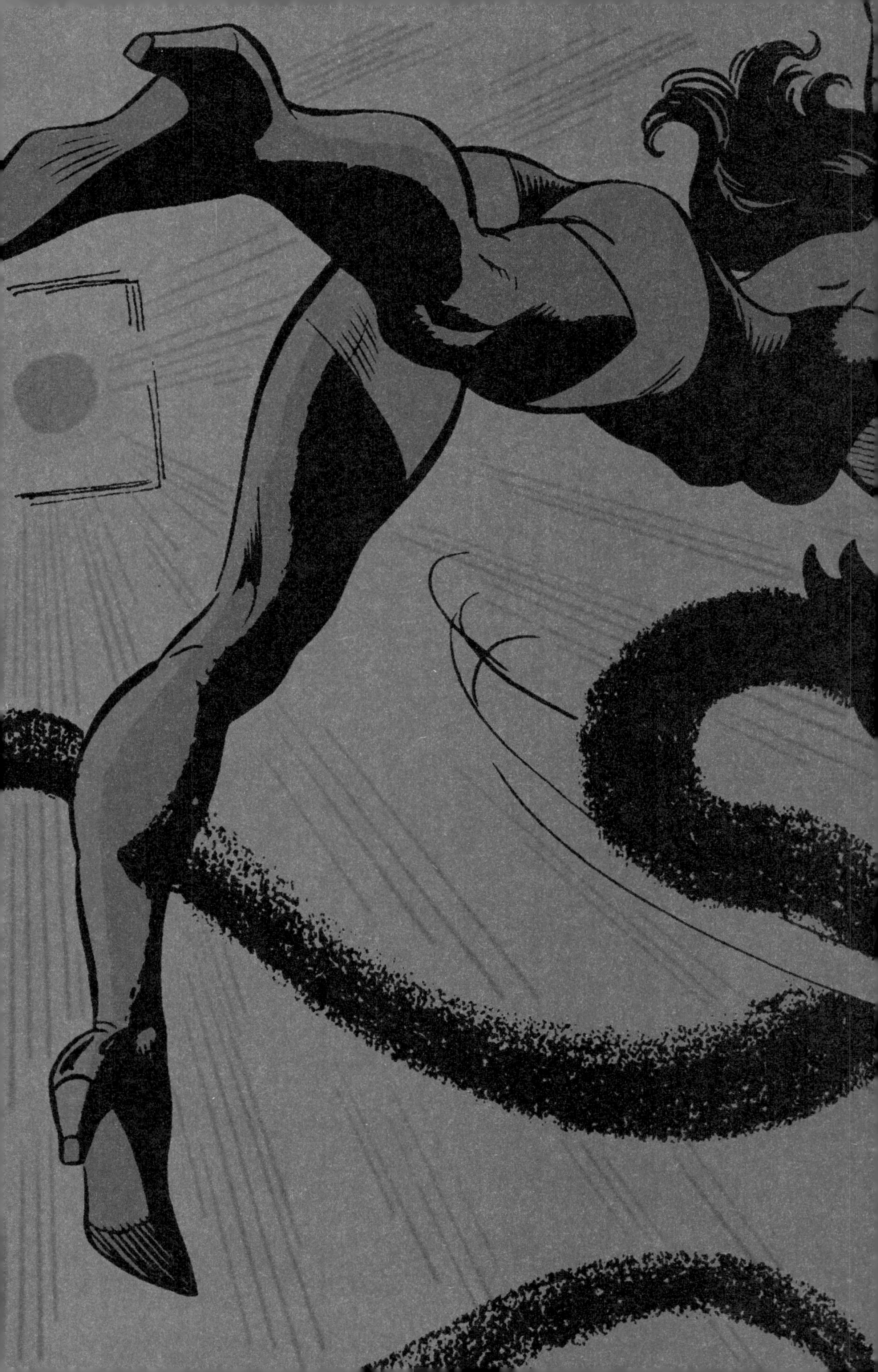

DEBT OF HONOR p7
FROM SUICIDE SQUAD #50, FEBRUARY 1991
Cover art by **GEOF ISHERWOOD** and **KARL KESEL**

FRACTURED IMAGE p46
From SUICIDE SQUAD #51, March 1991
Cover art by **LUKE McDONNELL** and **KARL KESEL**

THE DEATH AND LIFE AND DEATH AND LIFE AND DEATH AND LIFE OF DR. LIGHT p69
From SUICIDE SQUAD #52, April 1991
Cover art by **JIM FERN**

THE DRAGON'S HOARD PART ONE: DEAD EARNEST p92
FROM SUICIDE SQUAD #53, MAY 1991
Cover art by **GEOF ISHERWOOD** and **KARL KESEL**

THE DRAGON'S HOARD PART TWO: DIVINE WIND p115
From SUICIDE SQUAD #54, June 1991
Cover art by **GEOF ISHERWOOD** and **KARL KESEL**

THE DRAGON'S HOARD PART THREE: DEAD MAN'S HAND p138
FROM SUICIDE SQUAD #55, JULY 1991
Cover art by **GEOF ISHERWOOD** *and* **KARL KESEL**

THE DRAGON'S HOARD PART FOUR: DRAGON'S TEETH p161
From SUICIDE SQUAD #56, August 1991
Cover art by **GEOF ISHERWOOD** and **KARL KESEL**

THE DRAGON'S HOARD PART FIVE: DRAGON'S BLOOD p184
From SUICIDE SQUAD #57, September 1991
Cover art by **GEOF ISHERWOOD** and **KARL KESEL**

SUICIDE ATTACK! p207
From SUICIDE SQUAD #58, October 1991
Cover art by **GEOF ISHERWOOD** and **KARL KESEL**

DAN RASPLER EDITOR – ORIGINAL SERIES
JEB WOODARD GROUP EDITOR – COLLECTED EDITIONS
LIZ ERICKSON EDITOR – COLLECTED EDITION
STEVE COOK DESIGN DIRECTOR – BOOKS

BOB HARRAS SENIOR VP – EDITOR-IN-CHIEF, DC COMICS
PAT McCALLUM EXECUTIVE EDITOR, DC COMICS

DIANE NELSON PRESIDENT
DAN DiDIO PUBLISHER
JIM LEE PUBLISHER
GEOFF JOHNS PRESIDENT & CHIEF CREATIVE OFFICER
AMIT DESAI EXECUTIVE VP – BUSINESS & MARKETING STRATEGY,
          DIRECT TO CONSUMER & GLOBAL FRANCHISE MANAGEMENT
SAM ADES SENIOR VP & GENERAL MANAGER, DIGITAL SERVICES
BOBBIE CHASE VP & EXECUTIVE EDITOR, YOUNG READER & TALENT DEVELOPMENT
MARK CHIARELLO SENIOR VP – ART, DESIGN & COLLECTED EDITIONS
JOHN CUNNINGHAM SENIOR VP – SALES & TRADE MARKETING
ANNE DePIES SENIOR VP – BUSINESS STRATEGY, FINANCE & ADMINISTRATION
DON FALLETTI VP – MANUFACTURING OPERATIONS
LAWRENCE GANEM VP – EDITORIAL ADMINISTRATION & TALENT RELATIONS
ALISON GILL SENIOR VP – MANUFACTURING & OPERATIONS
HANK KANALZ SENIOR VP – EDITORIAL STRATEGY & ADMINISTRATION
JAY KOGAN VP – LEGAL AFFAIRS
JACK MAHAN VP – BUSINESS AFFAIRS
NICK J. NAPOLITANO VP – MANUFACTURING ADMINISTRATION
EDDIE SCANNELL VP – CONSUMER MARKETING
COURTNEY SIMMONS SENIOR VP – PUBLICITY & COMMUNICATIONS
JIM (SKI) SOKOLOWSKI VP – COMIC BOOK SPECIALTY SALES & TRADE MARKETING
NANCY SPEARS VP – MASS, BOOK, DIGITAL SALES & TRADE MARKETING
MICHELE R. WELLS VP – CONTENT STRATEGY

SUICIDE SQUAD VOLUME 7: THE DRAGON'S HOARD

DC COMICS, 2900 WEST ALAMEDA AVE., BURBANK, CA 91505
PRINTED BY LSC COMMUNICATIONS, OWENSVILLE, MO, USA. 11/3/17. FIRST PRINTING.
ISBN: 978-1-4012-7457-3

LIBRARY OF CONGRESS CATALOGING-IN-PUBLICATION DATA IS AVAILABLE.

PEFC Certified

Printed on paper from
sustainably managed
forests, controlled
sources

PEFC/29-31-337   www.pefc.org

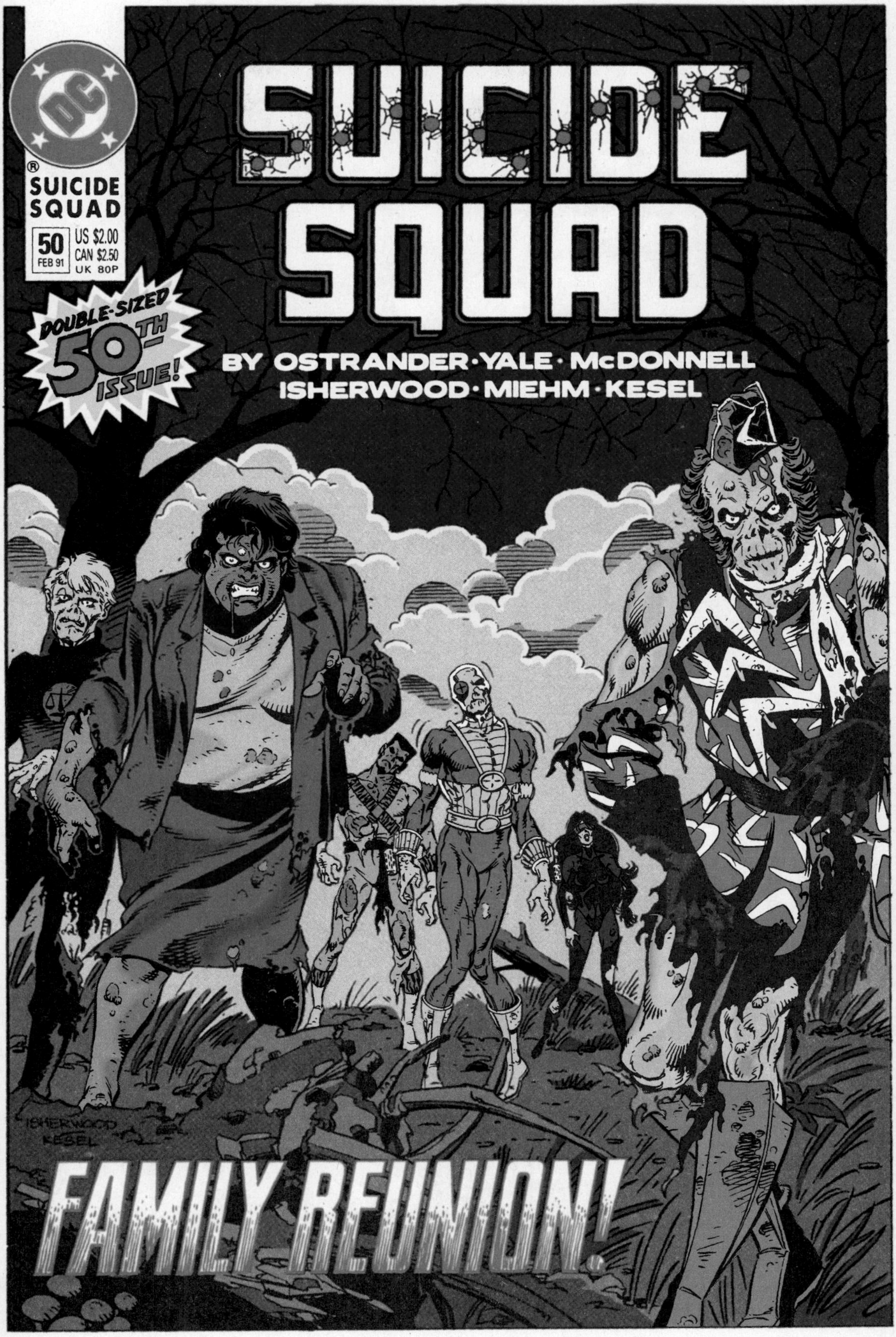
DC
SUICIDE SQUAD
50 FEB 91
US $2.00
CAN $2.50
UK 80P
DOUBLE-SIZED 50TH ISSUE!
SUICIDE SQUAD
BY OSTRANDER·YALE·McDONNELL
ISHERWOOD·MIEHM·KESEL
ISHERWOOD
KESEL
FAMILY REUNION!

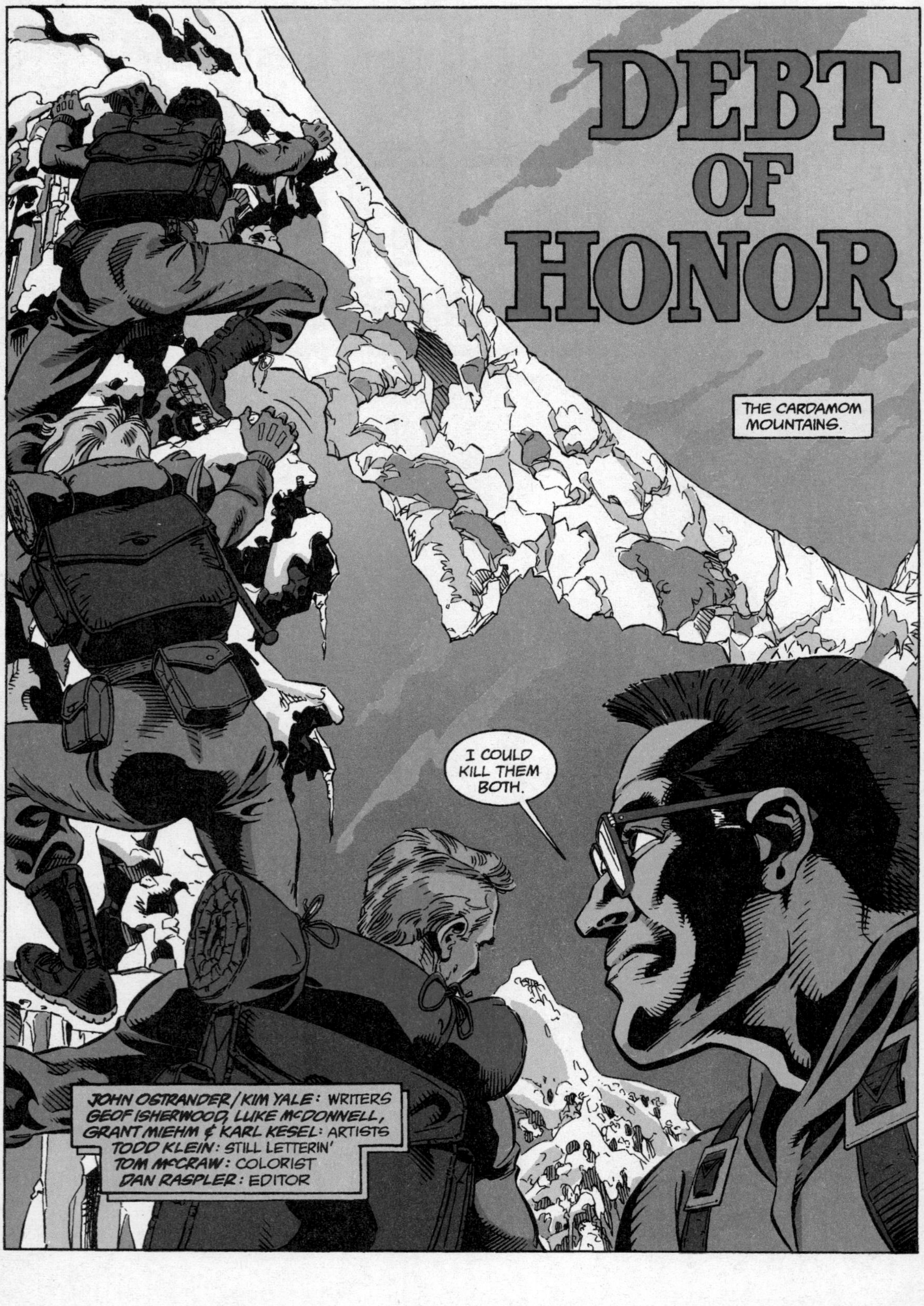
DEBT OF HONOR
THE CARDAMOM MOUNTAINS.
I COULD KILL THEM BOTH.
JOHN OSTRANDER / KIM YALE: WRITERS
GEOF ISHERWOOD, LUKE McDONNELL,
GRANT MIEHM & KARL KESEL: ARTISTS
TODD KLEIN: STILL LETTERIN'
TOM McCRAW: COLORIST
DAN RASPLER: EDITOR

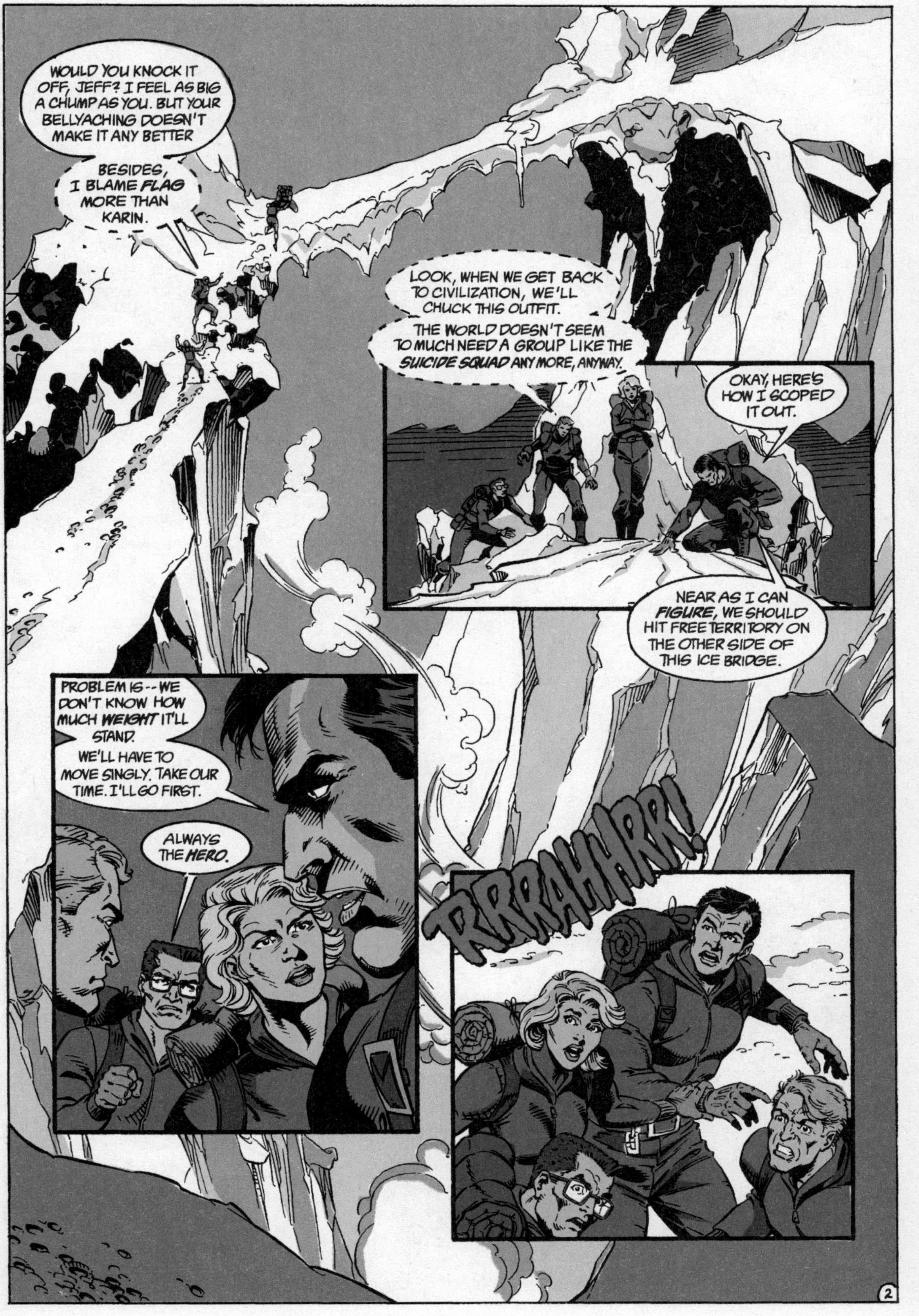
WOULD YOU KNOCK IT OFF, JEFF? I FEEL AS BIG A CHUMP AS YOU. BUT YOUR BELLYACHING DOESN'T MAKE IT ANY BETTER
BESIDES, I BLAME FLAG MORE THAN KARIN.
LOOK, WHEN WE GET BACK TO CIVILIZATION, WE'LL CHUCK THIS OUTFIT.
THE WORLD DOESN'T SEEM TO MUCH NEED A GROUP LIKE THE SUICIDE SQUAD ANY MORE, ANYWAY.
OKAY, HERE'S HOW I SCOPED IT OUT.
NEAR AS I CAN FIGURE, WE SHOULD HIT FREE TERRITORY ON THE OTHER SIDE OF THIS ICE BRIDGE.
PROBLEM IS--WE DON'T KNOW HOW MUCH WEIGHT IT'LL STAND.
WE'LL HAVE TO MOVE SINGLY. TAKE OUR TIME. I'LL GO FIRST.
ALWAYS THE HERO.
RRRAHHRR!
2

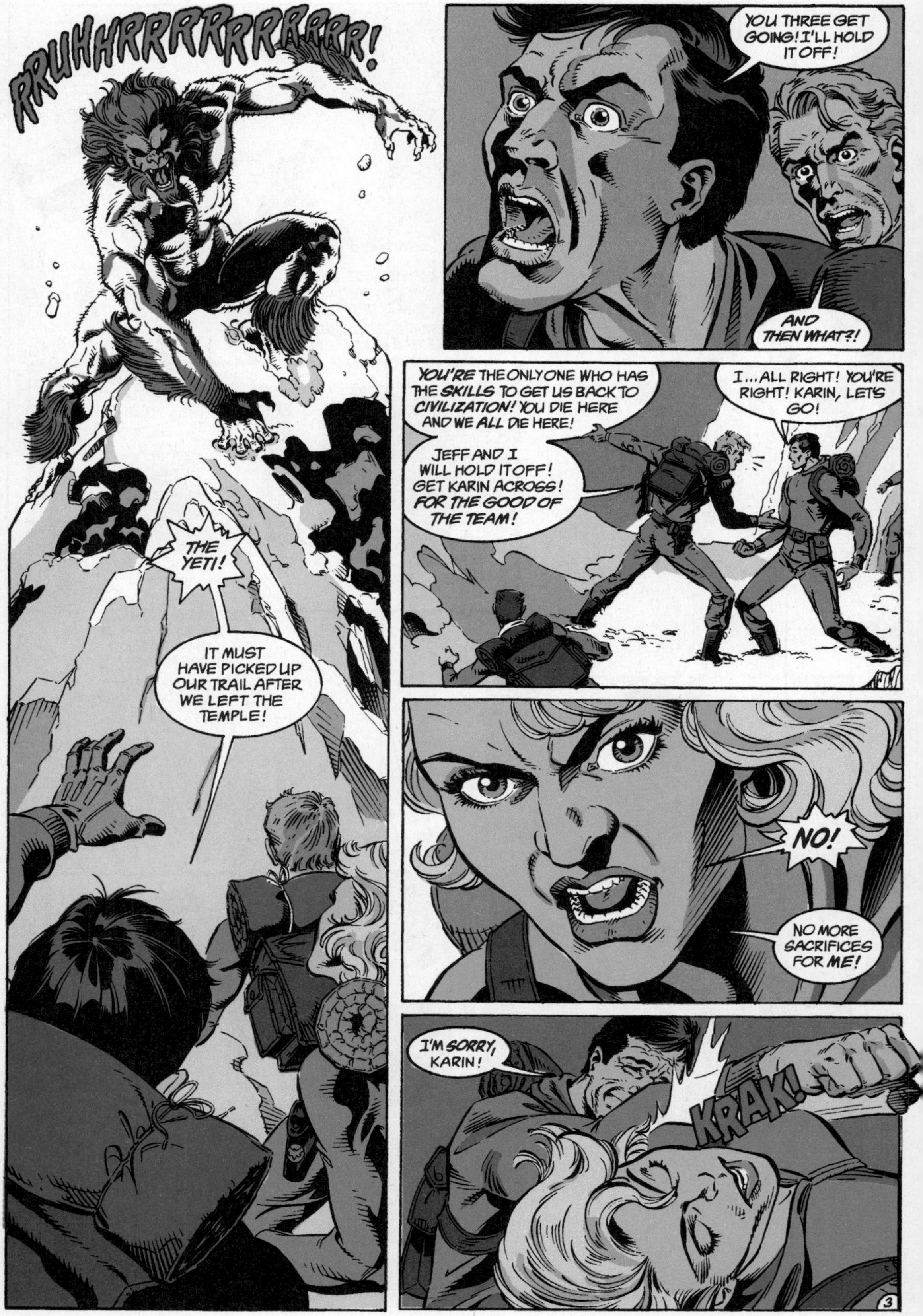

RRUHHRRRRRRRRRR!
THE YETI!
IT MUST HAVE PICKED UP OUR TRAIL AFTER WE LEFT THE TEMPLE!
YOU THREE GET GOING! I'LL HOLD IT OFF!
AND THEN WHAT?!
YOU'RE THE ONLY ONE WHO HAS THE SKILLS TO GET US BACK TO CIVILIZATION! YOU DIE HERE AND WE ALL DIE HERE!
JEFF AND I WILL HOLD IT OFF! GET KARIN ACROSS! FOR THE GOOD OF THE TEAM!
I... ALL RIGHT! YOU'RE RIGHT! KARIN, LET'S GO!
NO!
NO MORE SACRIFICES FOR ME!
I'M SORRY, KARIN!
KRAK!
3

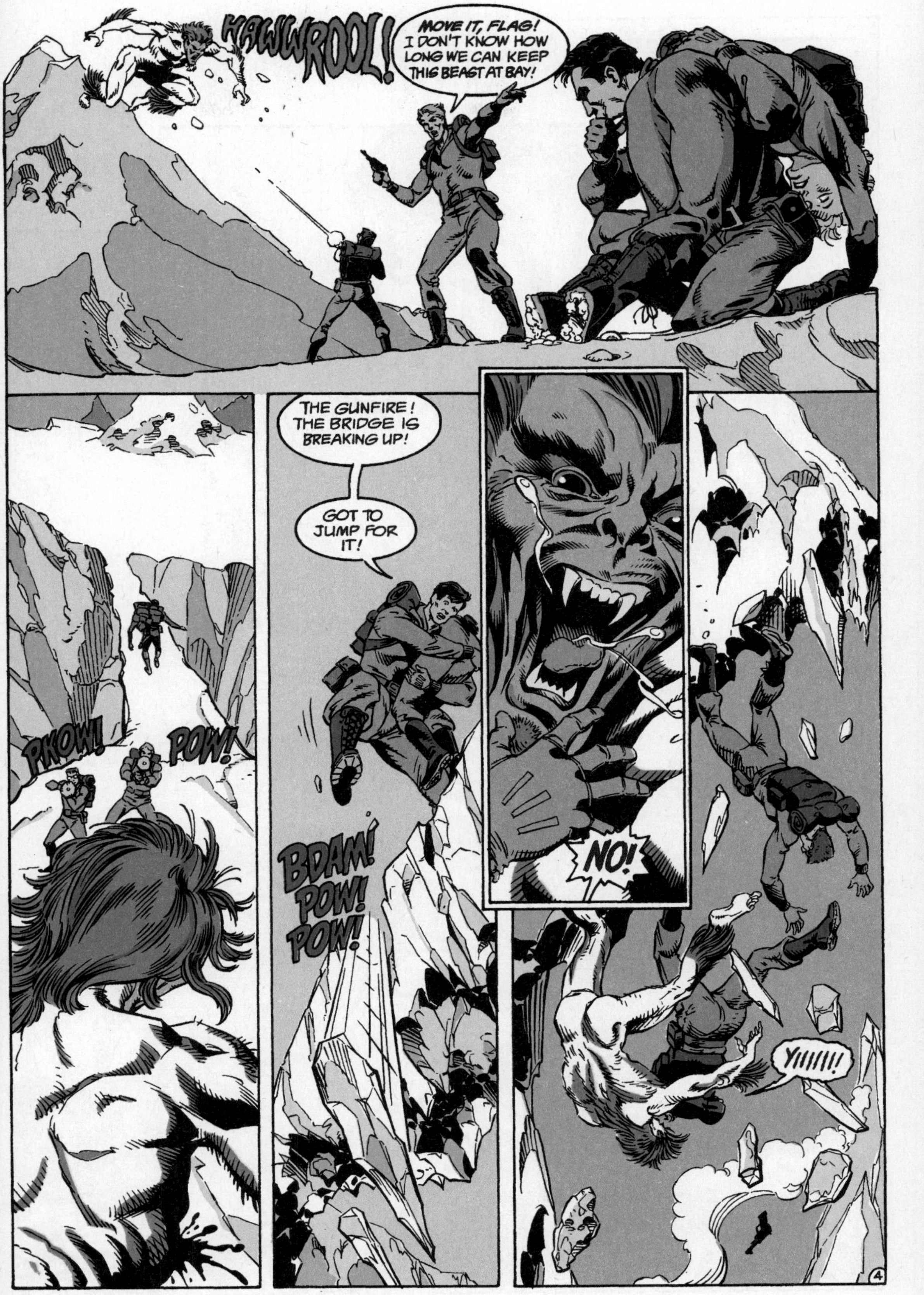
HAWWROOL!
MOVE IT, FLAG! I DON'T KNOW HOW LONG WE CAN KEEP THIS BEAST AT BAY!
PKOW!
POW!
THE GUNFIRE! THE BRIDGE IS BREAKING UP!
GOT TO JUMP FOR IT!
BDAM! POW! POW!
NO!
YIIIIII!
4

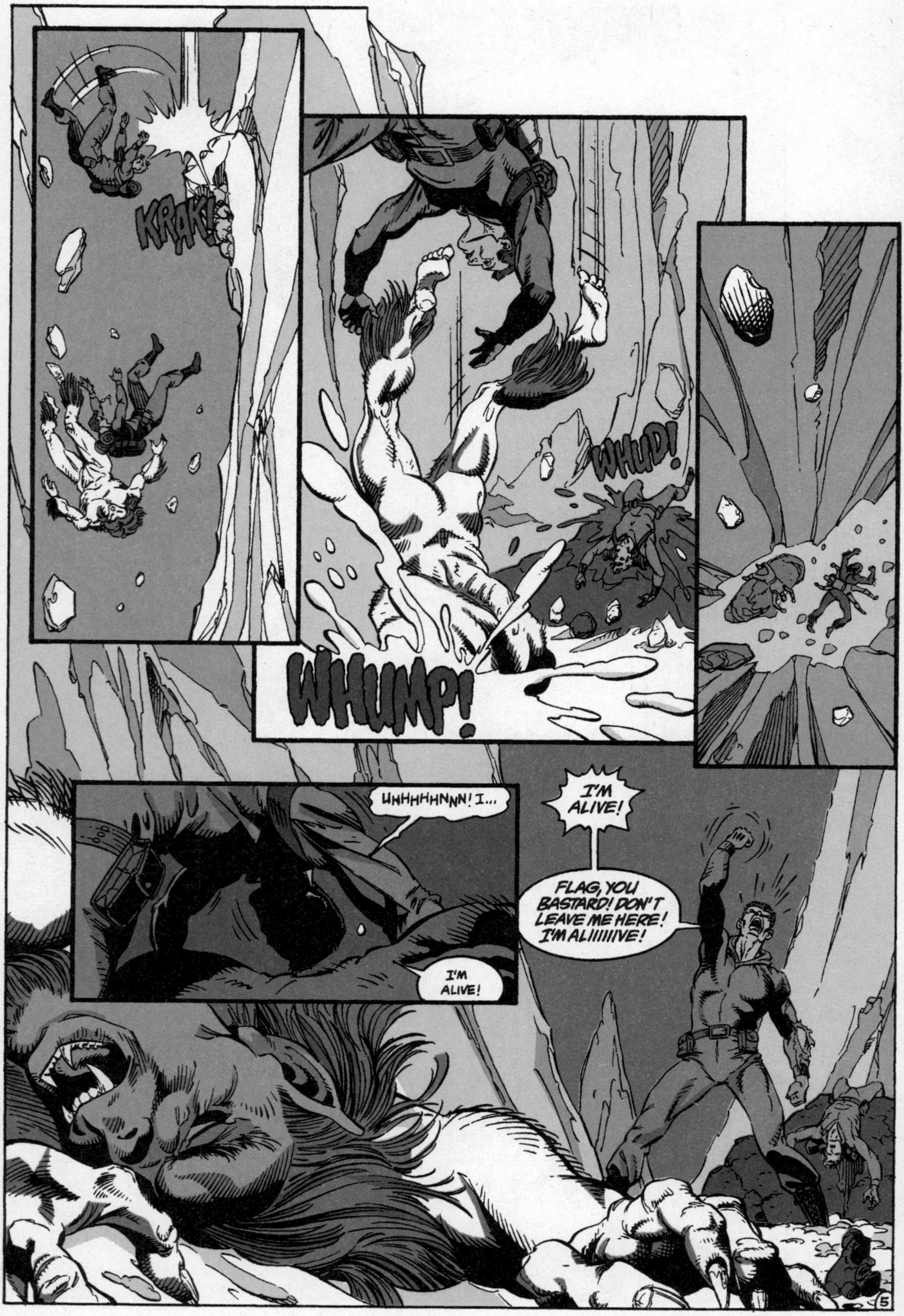
KRAK!
WHUD!
WHUMP!
UNHHHHNNN! I...
I'M ALIVE!
I'M ALIVE!
FLAG, YOU BASTARD! DON'T LEAVE ME HERE! I'M ALIIIIIIVE!
5

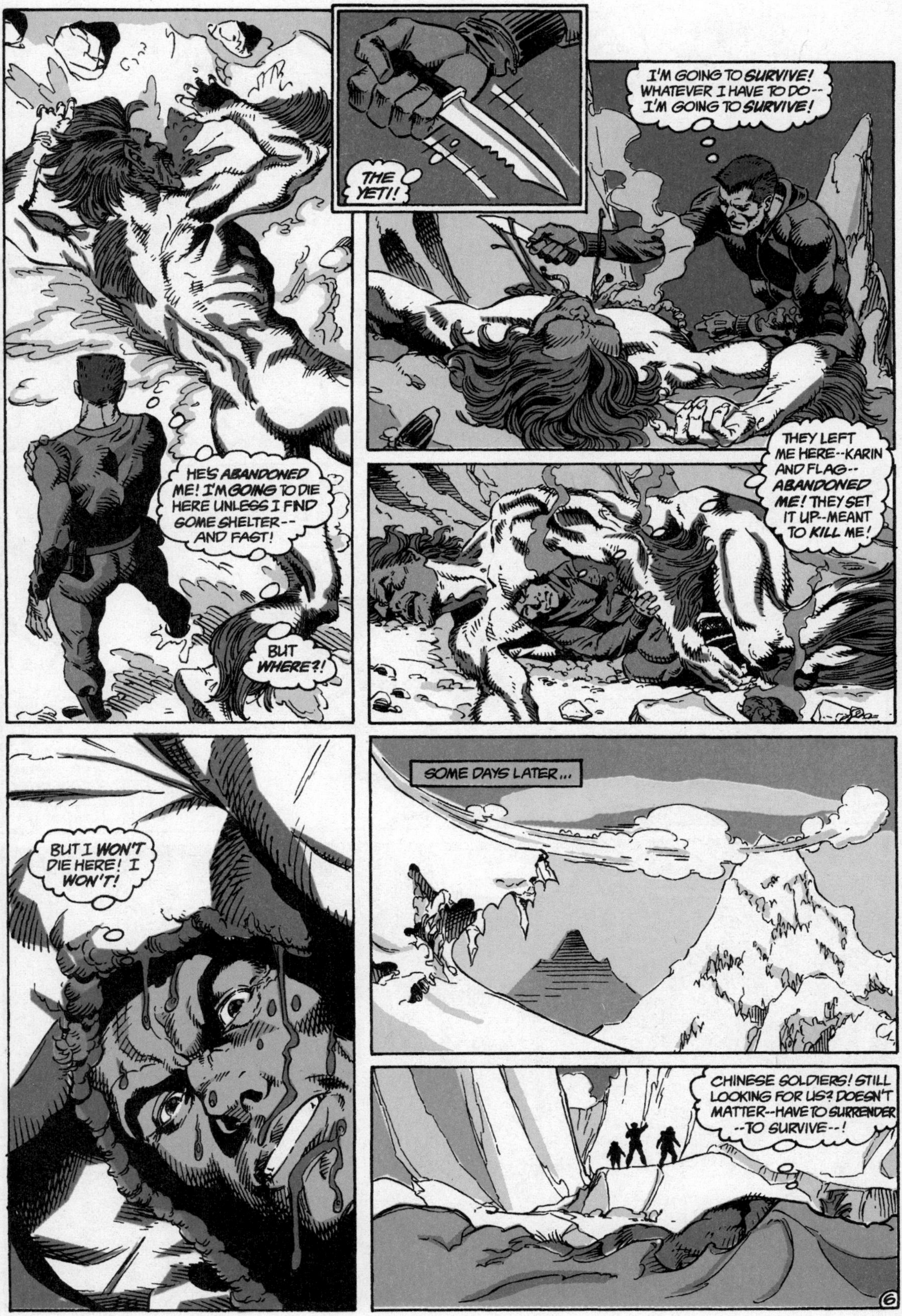

THE YETI!
I'M GOING TO SURVIVE! WHATEVER I HAVE TO DO-- I'M GOING TO SURVIVE!
HE'S ABANDONED ME! I'M GOING TO DIE HERE UNLESS I FIND SOME SHELTER-- AND FAST!
BUT WHERE?!
THEY LEFT ME HERE--KARIN AND FLAG-- ABANDONED ME! THEY SET IT UP--MEANT TO KILL ME!
BUT I WON'T DIE HERE! I WON'T!
SOME DAYS LATER...
CHINESE SOLDIERS! STILL LOOKING FOR US? DOESN'T MATTER--HAVE TO SURRENDER --TO SURVIVE--!
6

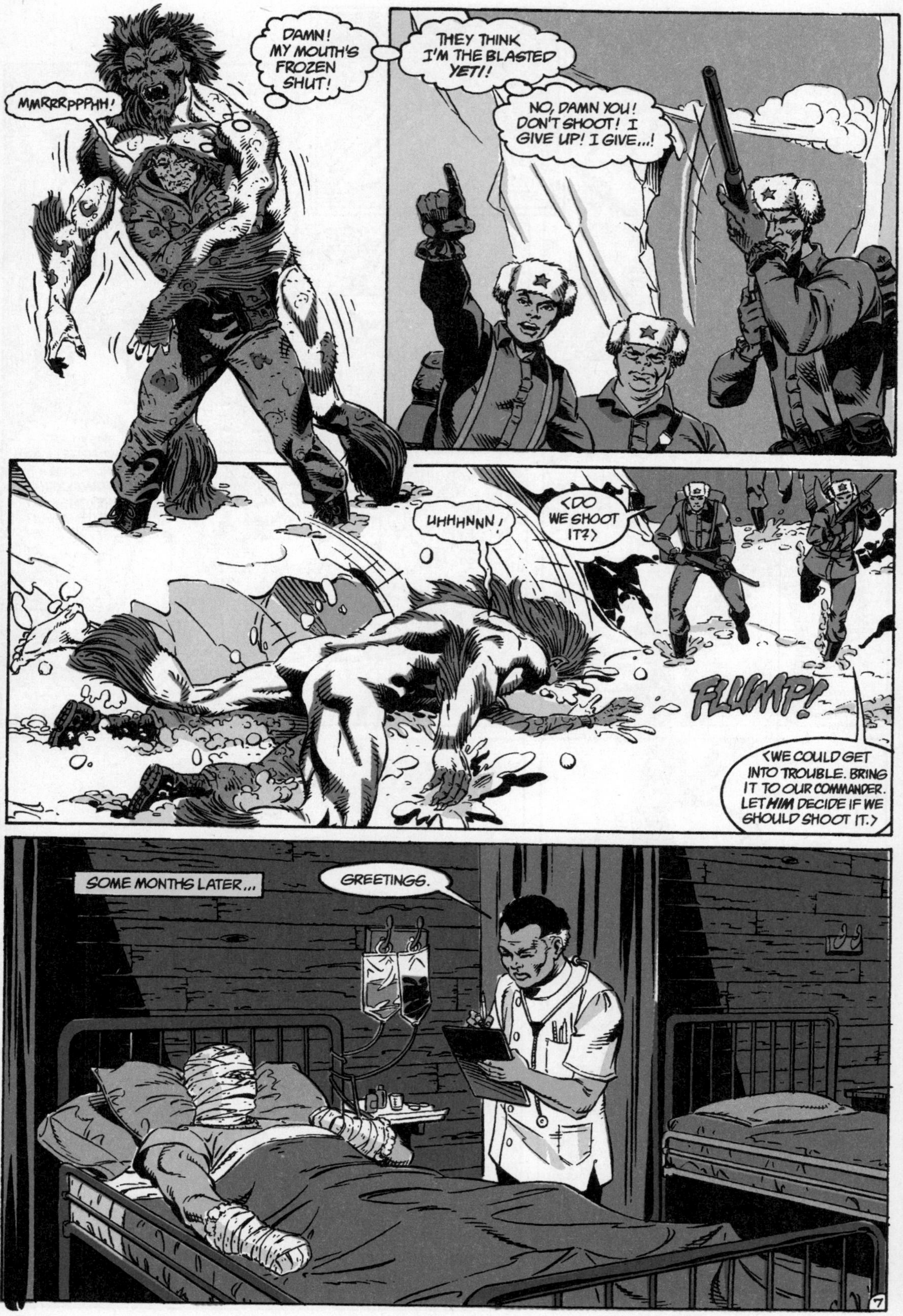

MMRRRPPPHH!
DAMN! MY MOUTH'S FROZEN SHUT!
THEY THINK I'M THE BLASTED YETI!
NO, DAMN YOU! DON'T SHOOT! I GIVE UP! I GIVE...!
UHHHNNN!
<DO WE SHOOT IT?>
FLUMP!
<WE COULD GET INTO TROUBLE. BRING IT TO OUR COMMANDER. LET HIM DECIDE IF WE SHOULD SHOOT IT.>
SOME MONTHS LATER...
GREETINGS.
7

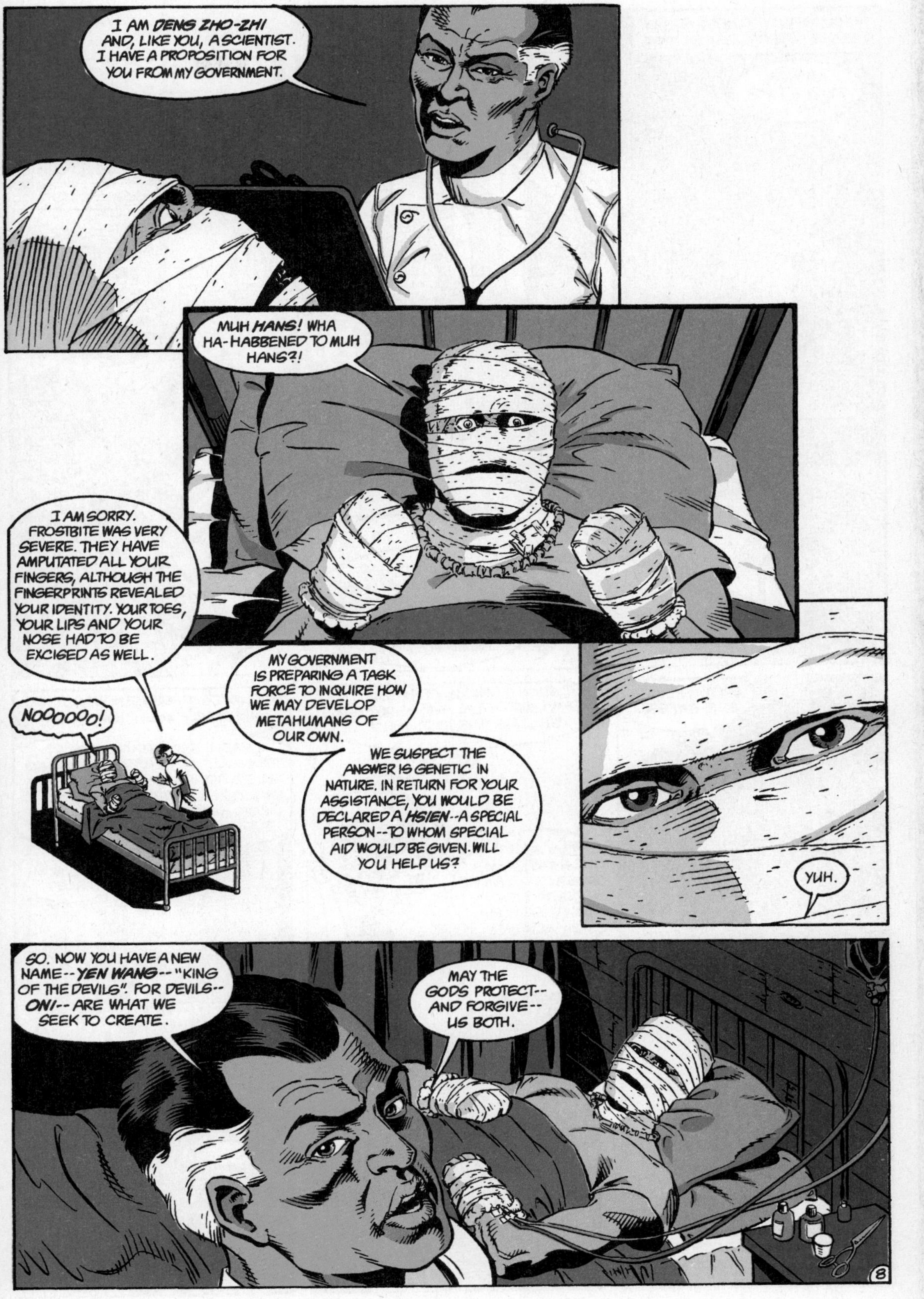
I AM DENG ZHO-ZHI AND, LIKE YOU, A SCIENTIST. I HAVE A PROPOSITION FOR YOU FROM MY GOVERNMENT.
MUH HANS! WHA HA-HABBENED TO MUH HANS?!
I AM SORRY. FROSTBITE WAS VERY SEVERE. THEY HAVE AMPUTATED ALL YOUR FINGERS, ALTHOUGH THE FINGERPRINTS REVEALED YOUR IDENTITY. YOUR TOES, YOUR LIPS AND YOUR NOSE HAD TO BE EXCISED AS WELL.
NOOOOOO!
MY GOVERNMENT IS PREPARING A TASK FORCE TO INQUIRE HOW WE MAY DEVELOP METAHUMANS OF OUR OWN.
WE SUSPECT THE ANSWER IS GENETIC IN NATURE. IN RETURN FOR YOUR ASSISTANCE, YOU WOULD BE DECLARED A HSIEN--A SPECIAL PERSON--TO WHOM SPECIAL AID WOULD BE GIVEN. WILL YOU HELP US?
YUH.
SO. NOW YOU HAVE A NEW NAME--YEN WANG--"KING OF THE DEVILS". FOR DEVILS--ONI--ARE WHAT WE SEEK TO CREATE.
MAY THE GODS PROTECT--AND FORGIVE--US BOTH.
8

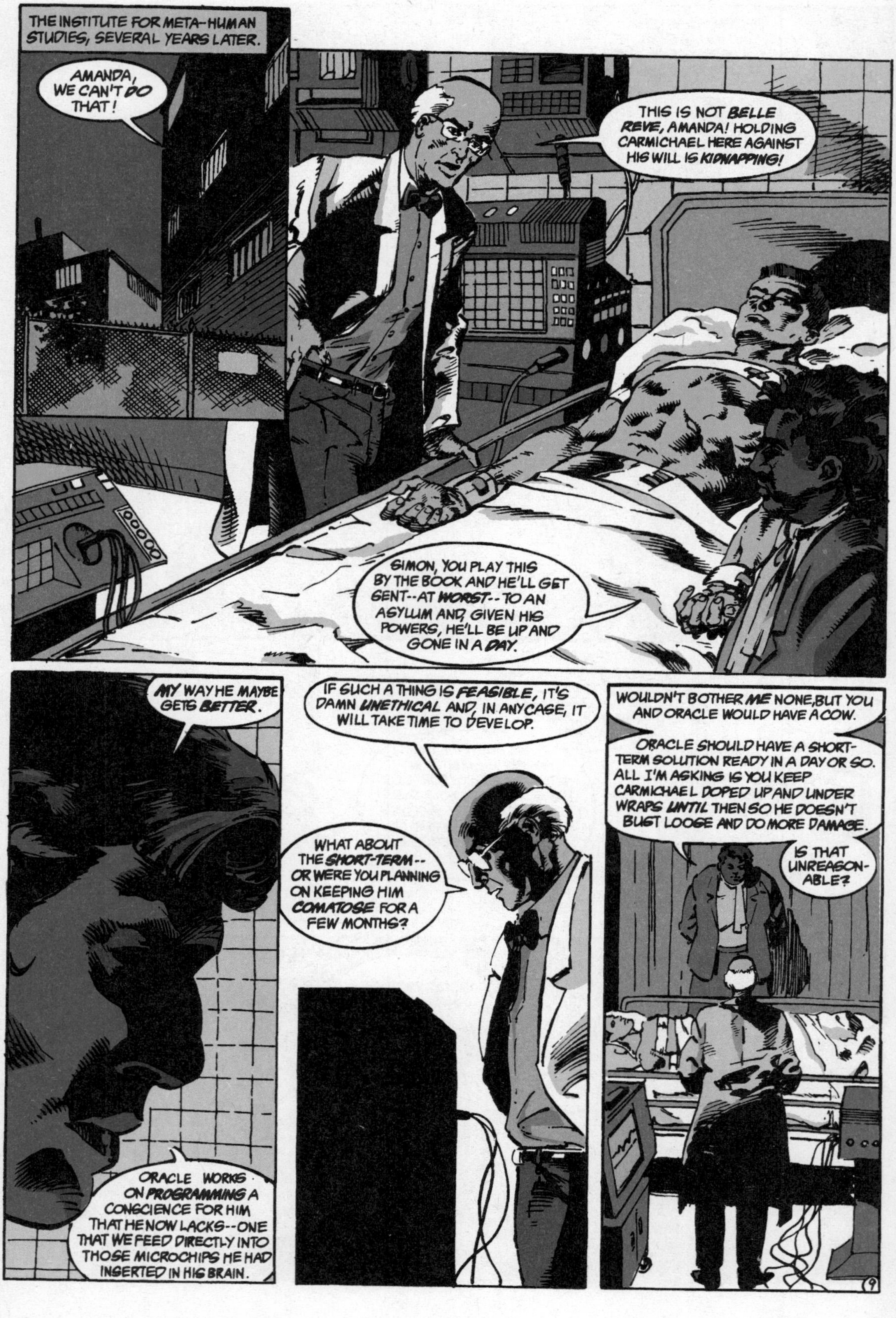
THE INSTITUTE FOR META-HUMAN STUDIES, SEVERAL YEARS LATER.
AMANDA, WE CAN'T DO THAT!
THIS IS NOT BELLE REVE, AMANDA! HOLDING CARMICHAEL HERE AGAINST HIS WILL IS KIDNAPPING!
SIMON, YOU PLAY THIS BY THE BOOK AND HE'LL GET SENT--AT WORST--TO AN ASYLUM AND, GIVEN HIS POWERS, HE'LL BE UP AND GONE IN A DAY.
MY WAY HE MAYBE GETS BETTER.
ORACLE WORKS ON PROGRAMMING A CONSCIENCE FOR HIM THAT HE NOW LACKS--ONE THAT WE FEED DIRECTLY INTO THOSE MICROCHIPS HE HAD INSERTED IN HIS BRAIN.
IF SUCH A THING IS FEASIBLE, IT'S DAMN UNETHICAL AND, IN ANY CASE, IT WILL TAKE TIME TO DEVELOP.
WHAT ABOUT THE SHORT-TERM--OR WERE YOU PLANNING ON KEEPING HIM COMATOSE FOR A FEW MONTHS?
WOULDN'T BOTHER ME NONE, BUT YOU AND ORACLE WOULD HAVE A COW.
ORACLE SHOULD HAVE A SHORT-TERM SOLUTION READY IN A DAY OR SO. ALL I'M ASKING IS YOU KEEP CARMICHAEL DOPED UP AND UNDER WRAPS UNTIL THEN SO HE DOESN'T BUST LOOSE AND DO MORE DAMAGE.
IS THAT UNREASON-ABLE?
9

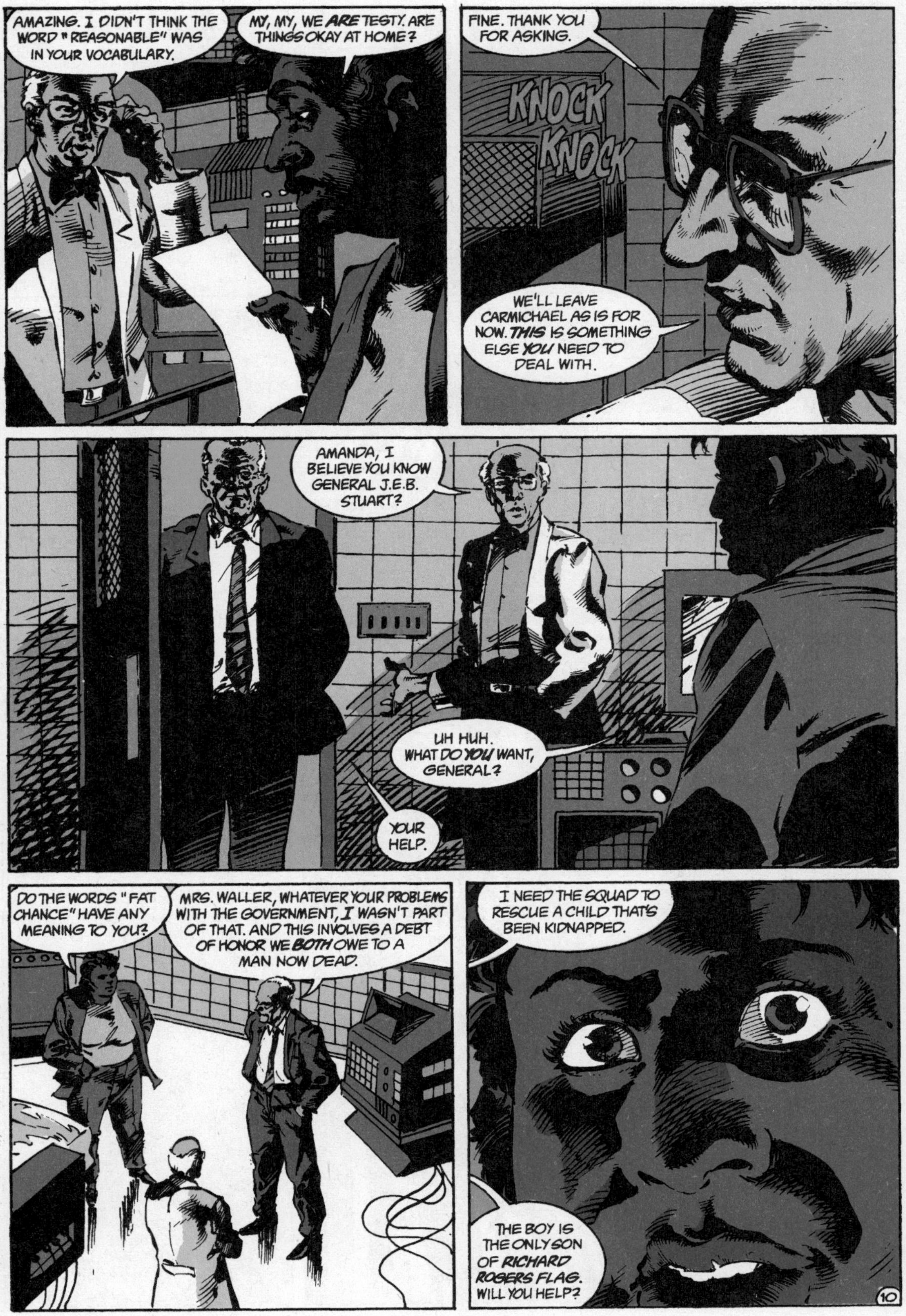
AMAZING. I DIDN'T THINK THE WORD "REASONABLE" WAS IN YOUR VOCABULARY.
MY, MY, WE ARE TESTY. ARE THINGS OKAY AT HOME?
FINE. THANK YOU FOR ASKING.
KNOCK KNOCK
WE'LL LEAVE CARMICHAEL AS IS FOR NOW. THIS IS SOMETHING ELSE YOU NEED TO DEAL WITH.
AMANDA, I BELIEVE YOU KNOW GENERAL J.E.B. STUART?
UH HUH. WHAT DO YOU WANT, GENERAL?
YOUR HELP.
DO THE WORDS "FAT CHANCE" HAVE ANY MEANING TO YOU?
MRS. WALLER, WHATEVER YOUR PROBLEMS WITH THE GOVERNMENT, I WASN'T PART OF THAT. AND THIS INVOLVES A DEBT OF HONOR WE BOTH OWE TO A MAN NOW DEAD.
I NEED THE SQUAD TO RESCUE A CHILD THAT'S BEEN KIDNAPPED.
THE BOY IS THE ONLY SON OF RICHARD ROGERS FLAG. WILL YOU HELP?
10

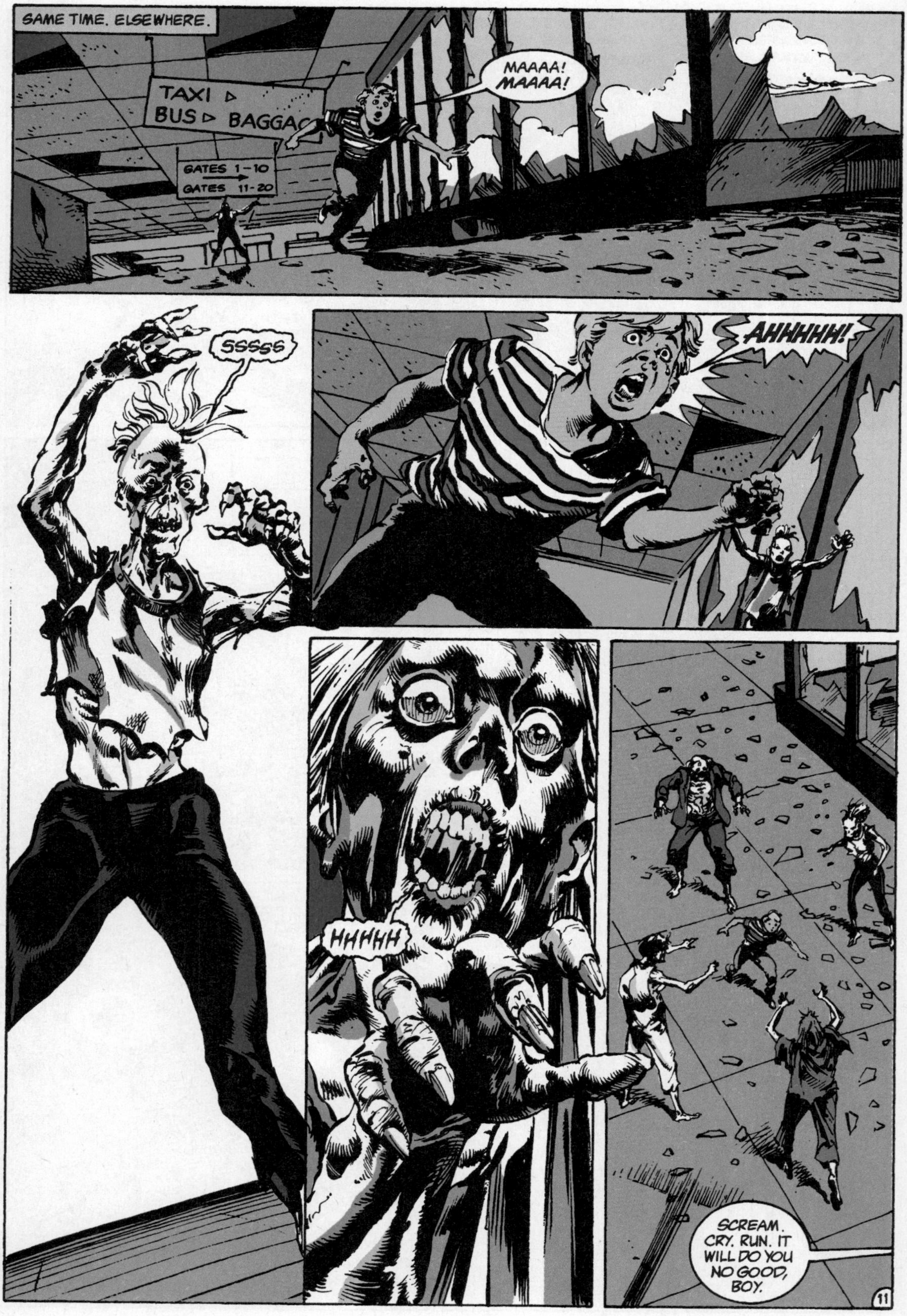
SAME TIME. ELSEWHERE.
TAXI ▷
BUS ▷ BAGGAG
GATES 1-10
GATES 11-20
MAAAA! MAAAA!
SSSSS
AHHHHH!
HHHHH
SCREAM. CRY. RUN. IT WILL DO YOU NO GOOD, BOY.
11

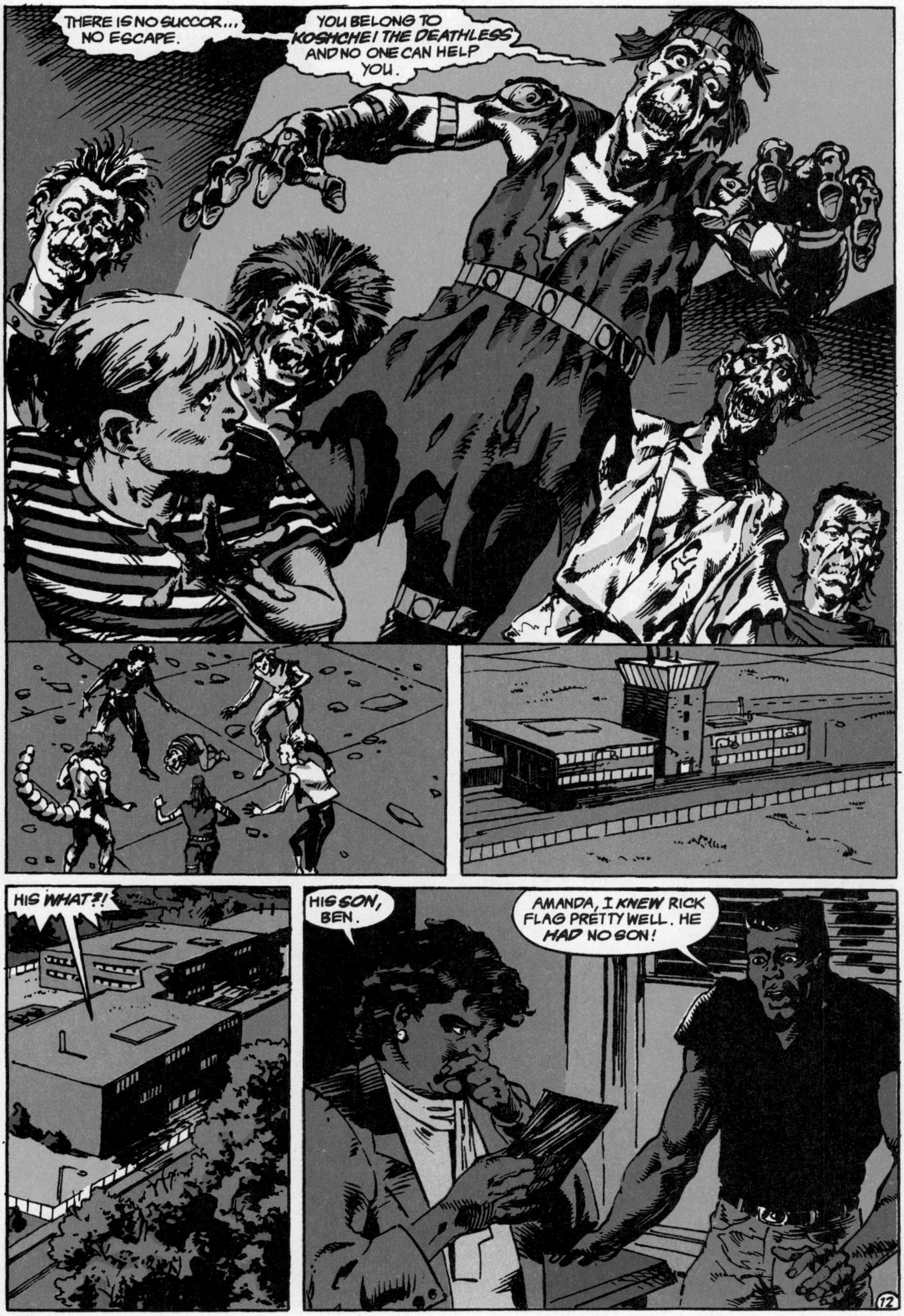
THERE IS NO SUCCOR... NO ESCAPE.
YOU BELONG TO KOSHCHEI THE DEATHLESS AND NO ONE CAN HELP YOU.
HIS WHAT?!
HIS SON, BEN.
AMANDA, I KNEW RICK FLAG PRETTY WELL. HE HAD NO SON!
12

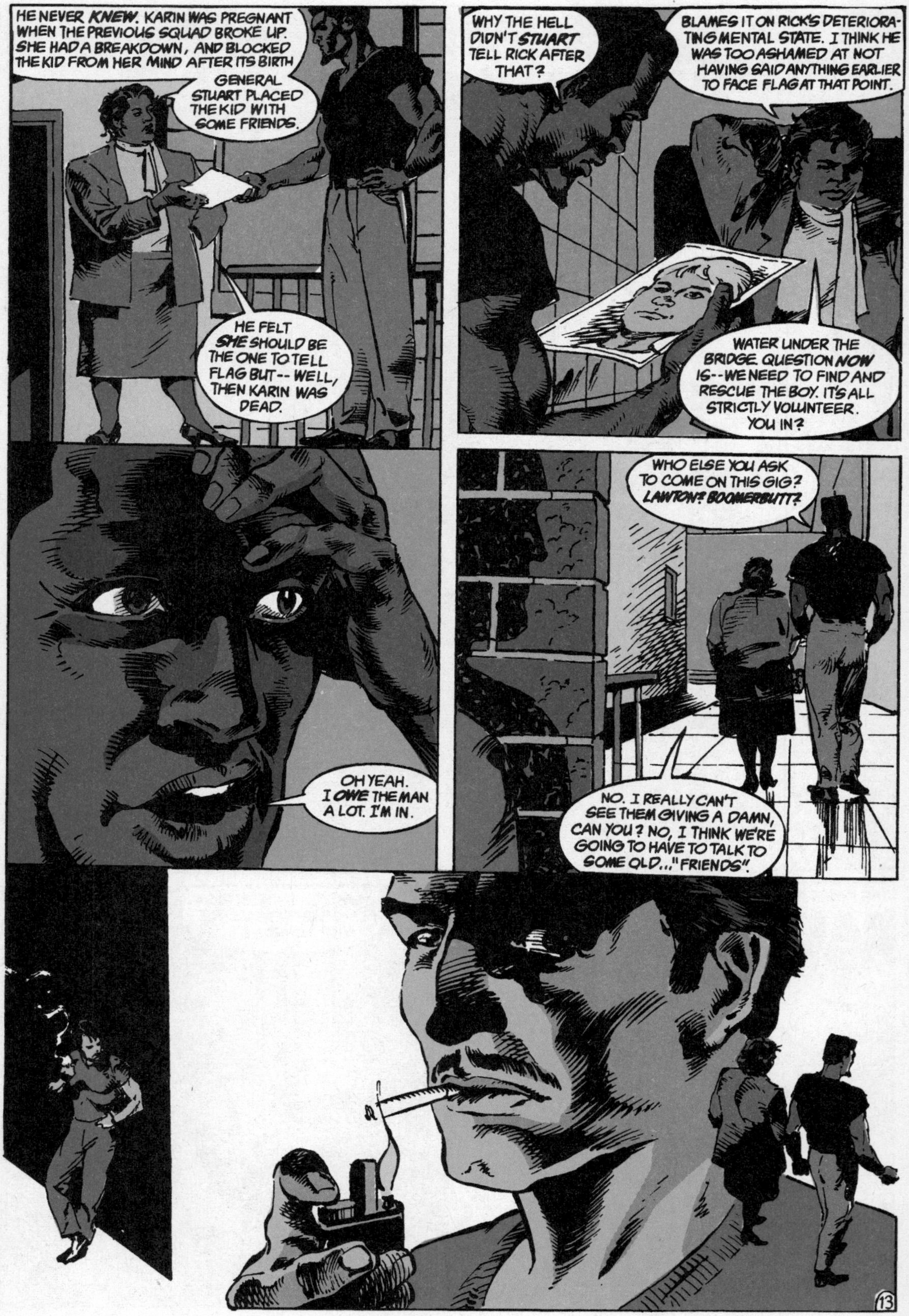
HE NEVER KNEW. KARIN WAS PREGNANT WHEN THE PREVIOUS SQUAD BROKE UP. SHE HAD A BREAKDOWN, AND BLOCKED THE KID FROM HER MIND AFTER ITS BIRTH
GENERAL STUART PLACED THE KID WITH SOME FRIENDS.
HE FELT SHE SHOULD BE THE ONE TO TELL FLAG BUT-- WELL, THEN KARIN WAS DEAD.
WHY THE HELL DIDN'T STUART TELL RICK AFTER THAT?
BLAMES IT ON RICK'S DETERIORATING MENTAL STATE. I THINK HE WAS TOO ASHAMED AT NOT HAVING SAID ANYTHING EARLIER TO FACE FLAG AT THAT POINT.
WATER UNDER THE BRIDGE. QUESTION NOW IS--WE NEED TO FIND AND RESCUE THE BOY. IT'S ALL STRICTLY VOLUNTEER. YOU IN?
OH YEAH. I OWE THE MAN A LOT. I'M IN.
WHO ELSE YOU ASK TO COME ON THIS GIG? LAWTON? BOOMERBUTT?
NO. I REALLY CAN'T SEE THEM GIVING A DAMN, CAN YOU? NO, I THINK WE'RE GOING TO HAVE TO TALK TO SOME OLD..."FRIENDS".
13

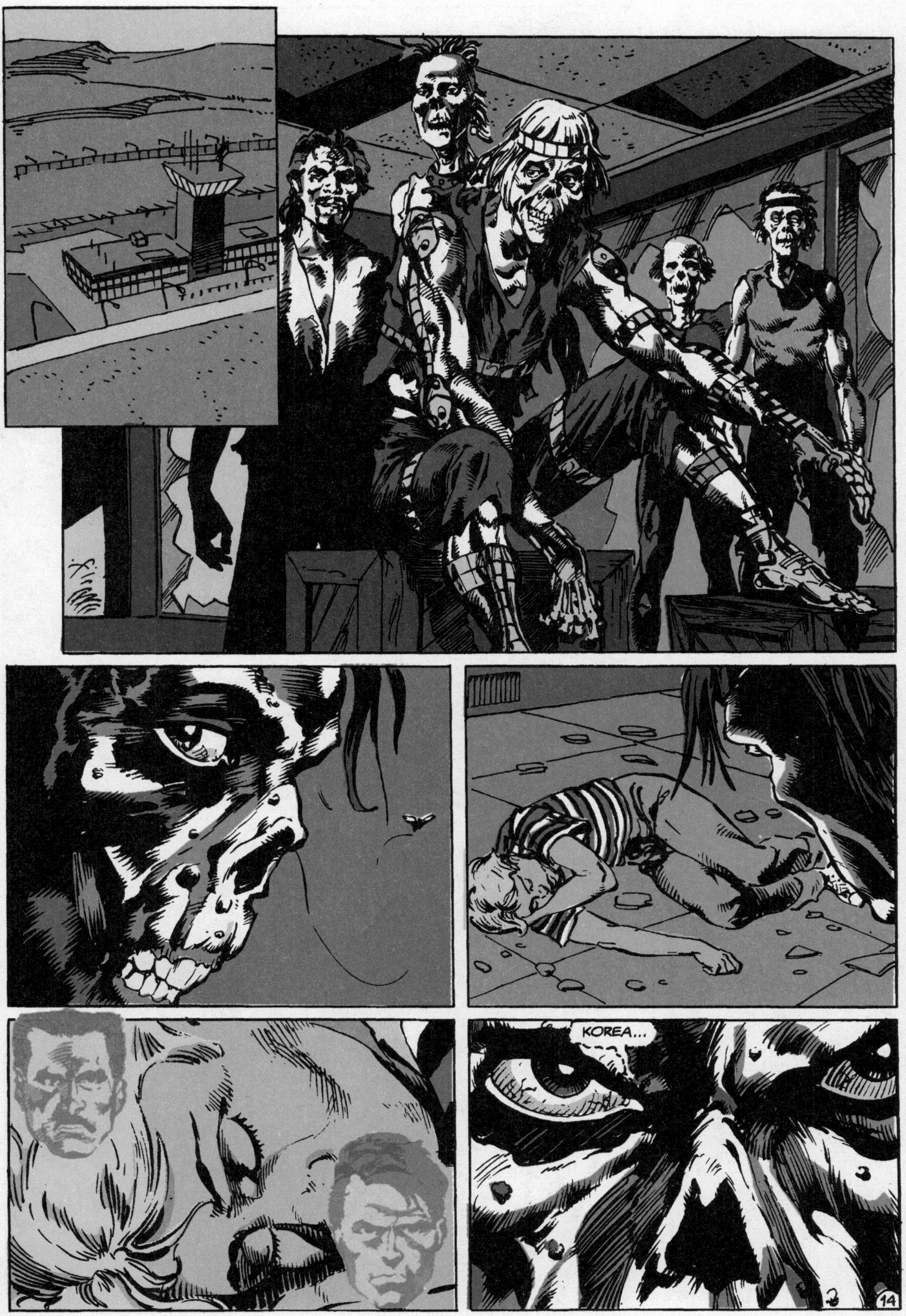
KOREA...
14

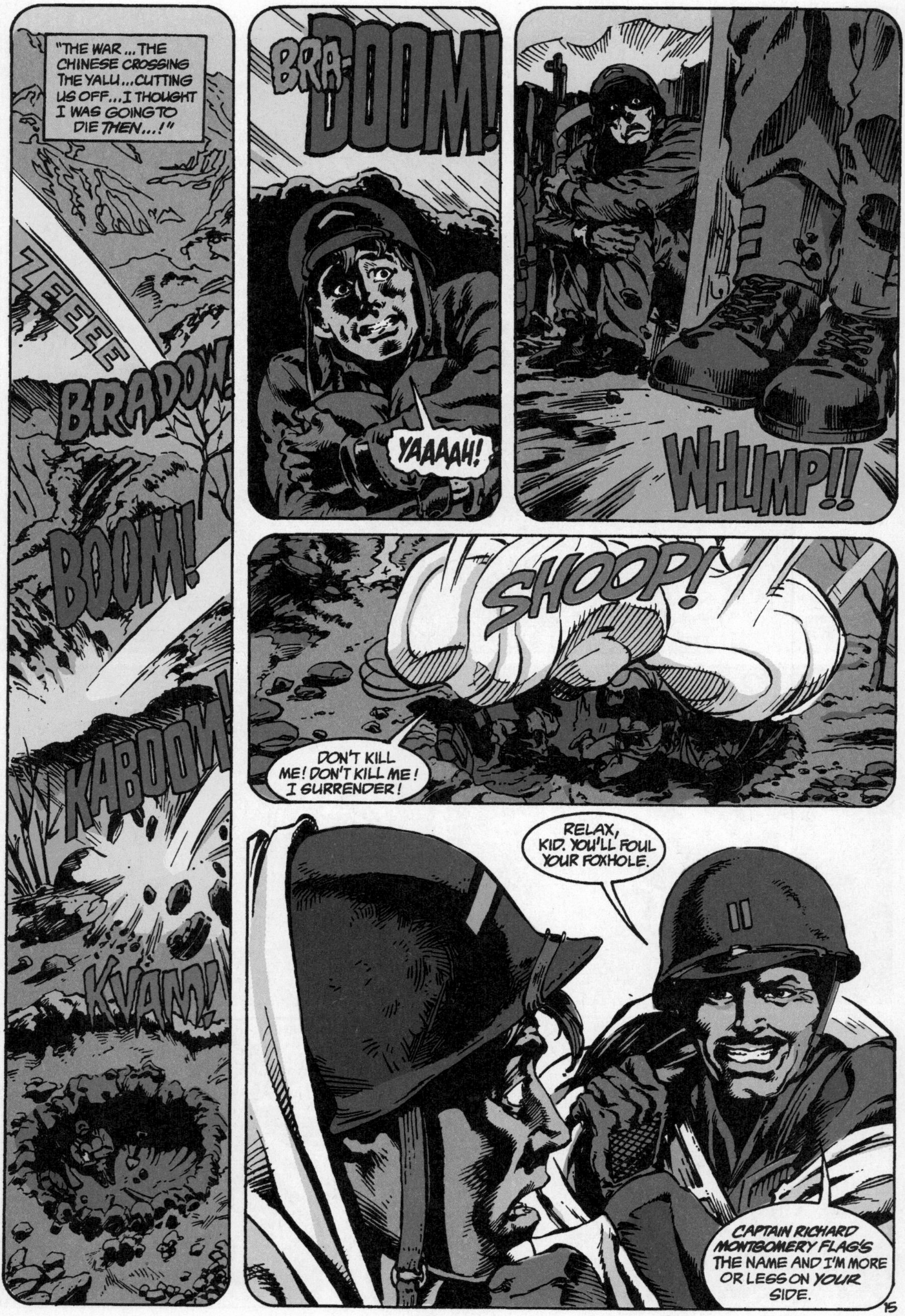

"THE WAR ... THE CHINESE CROSSING THE YALU ... CUTTING US OFF ... I THOUGHT I WAS GOING TO DIE THEN ... !"
ZEEEEE
BRADOW!
BOOM!
KABOOM!
KVAM!
BRA-DOOM!
YAAAAH!
WHUMP!!
SHOOP!
DON'T KILL ME! DON'T KILL ME! I SURRENDER!
RELAX, KID. YOU'LL FOUL YOUR FOXHOLE.
CAPTAIN RICHARD MONTGOMERY FLAG'S THE NAME AND I'M MORE OR LESS ON YOUR SIDE.
15

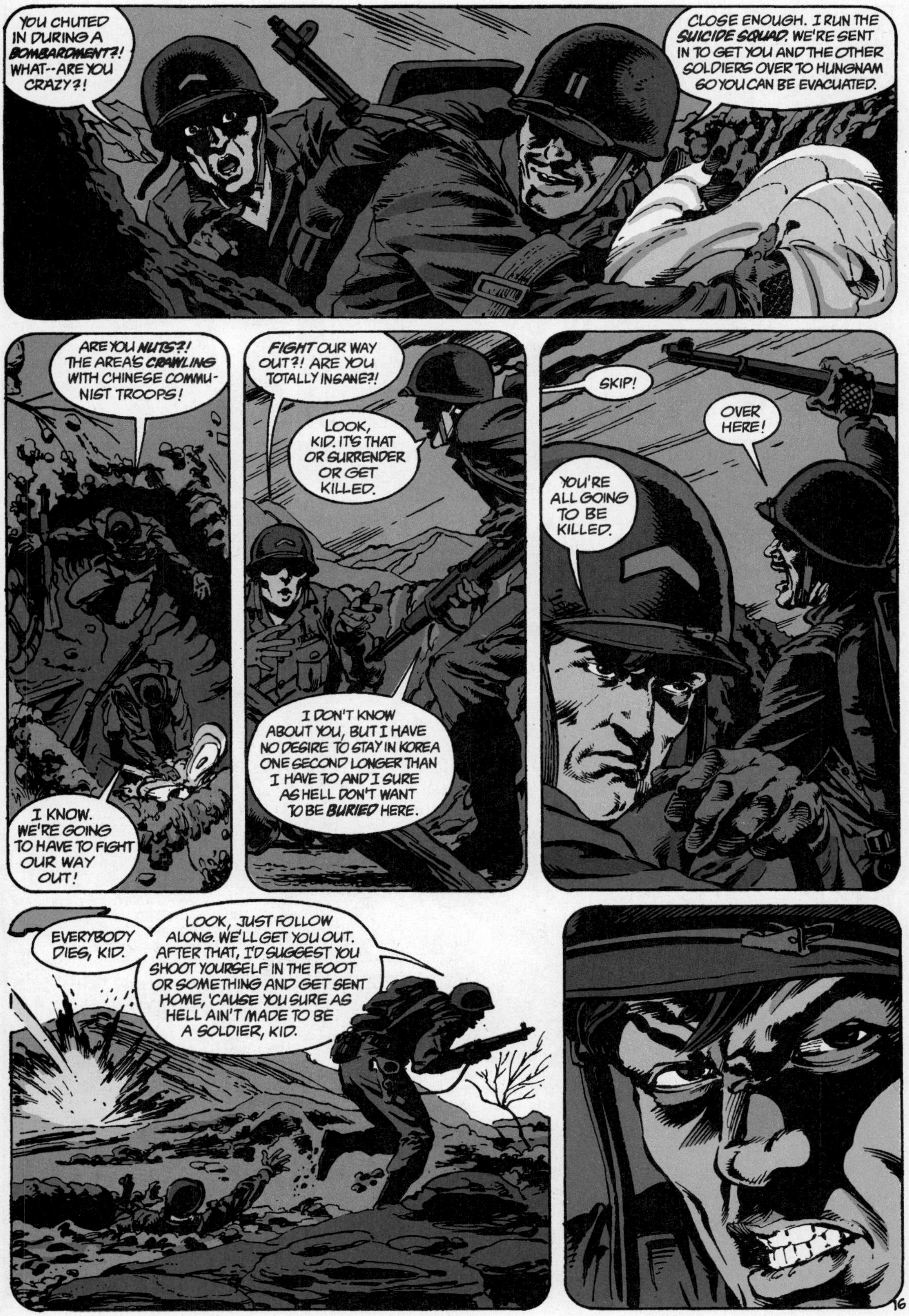
YOU CHUTED IN DURING A BOMBARDMENT?! WHAT--ARE YOU CRAZY?!
CLOSE ENOUGH. I RUN THE SUICIDE SQUAD. WE'RE SENT IN TO GET YOU AND THE OTHER SOLDIERS OVER TO HUNGNAM SO YOU CAN BE EVACUATED.
ARE YOU NUTS?! THE AREA'S CRAWLING WITH CHINESE COMMUNIST TROOPS!
I KNOW. WE'RE GOING TO HAVE TO FIGHT OUR WAY OUT!
FIGHT OUR WAY OUT?! ARE YOU TOTALLY INSANE?!
LOOK, KID. IT'S THAT OR SURRENDER OR GET KILLED.
I DON'T KNOW ABOUT YOU, BUT I HAVE NO DESIRE TO STAY IN KOREA ONE SECOND LONGER THAN I HAVE TO AND I SURE AS HELL DON'T WANT TO BE BURIED HERE.
SKIP!
OVER HERE!
YOU'RE ALL GOING TO BE KILLED.
EVERYBODY DIES, KID.
LOOK, JUST FOLLOW ALONG. WE'LL GET YOU OUT. AFTER THAT, I'D SUGGEST YOU SHOOT YOURSELF IN THE FOOT OR SOMETHING AND GET SENT HOME, 'CAUSE YOU SURE AS HELL AIN'T MADE TO BE A SOLDIER, KID.
16

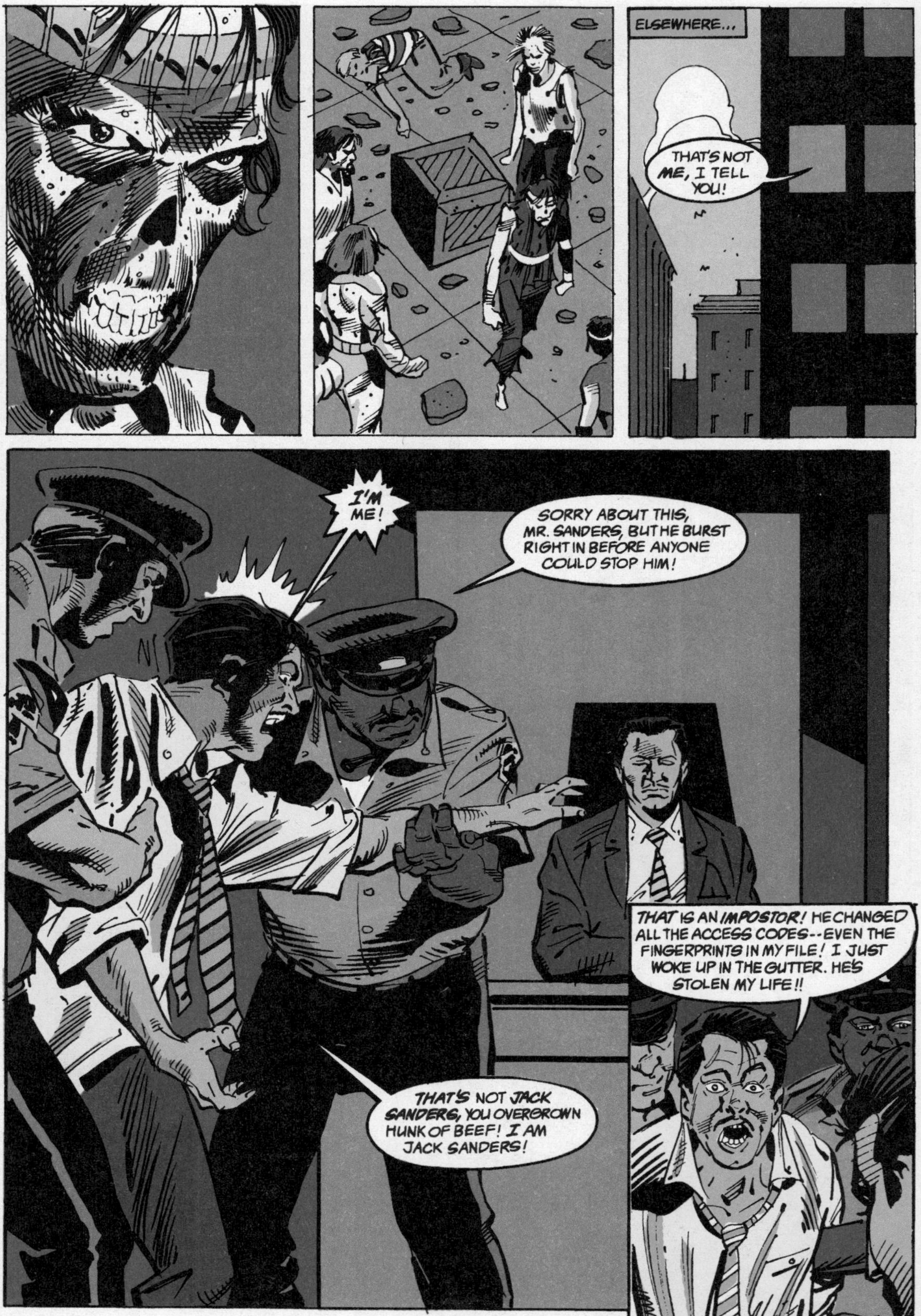

ELSEWHERE...
THAT'S NOT ME, I TELL YOU!
I'M ME!
SORRY ABOUT THIS, MR. SANDERS, BUT HE BURST RIGHT IN BEFORE ANYONE COULD STOP HIM!
THAT'S NOT JACK SANDERS, YOU OVERGROWN HUNK OF BEEF! I AM JACK SANDERS!
THAT IS AN IMPOSTOR! HE CHANGED ALL THE ACCESS CODES--EVEN THE FINGERPRINTS IN MY FILE! I JUST WOKE UP IN THE GUTTER. HE'S STOLEN MY LIFE!!

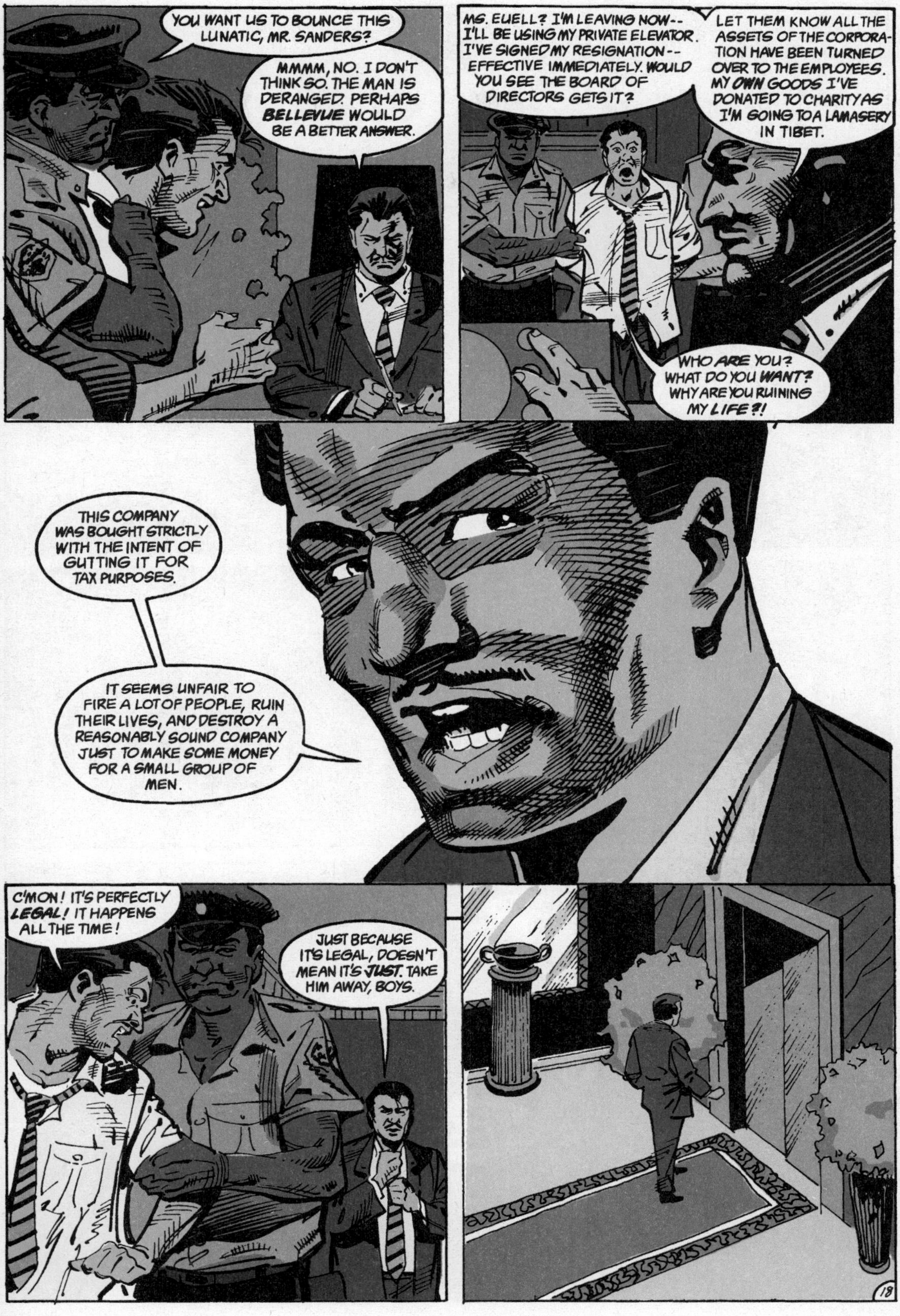
YOU WANT US TO BOUNCE THIS LUNATIC, MR. SANDERS?
MMMM, NO. I DON'T THINK SO. THE MAN IS DERANGED. PERHAPS BELLEVUE WOULD BE A BETTER ANSWER.
MS. EUELL? I'M LEAVING NOW-- I'LL BE USING MY PRIVATE ELEVATOR. I'VE SIGNED MY RESIGNATION-- EFFECTIVE IMMEDIATELY. WOULD YOU SEE THE BOARD OF DIRECTORS GETS IT?
LET THEM KNOW ALL THE ASSETS OF THE CORPORATION HAVE BEEN TURNED OVER TO THE EMPLOYEES. MY OWN GOODS I'VE DONATED TO CHARITY AS I'M GOING TO A LAMASERY IN TIBET.
WHO ARE YOU? WHAT DO YOU WANT? WHY ARE YOU RUINING MY LIFE?!
THIS COMPANY WAS BOUGHT STRICTLY WITH THE INTENT OF GUTTING IT FOR TAX PURPOSES.
IT SEEMS UNFAIR TO FIRE A LOT OF PEOPLE, RUIN THEIR LIVES, AND DESTROY A REASONABLY SOUND COMPANY JUST TO MAKE SOME MONEY FOR A SMALL GROUP OF MEN.
C'MON! IT'S PERFECTLY LEGAL! IT HAPPENS ALL THE TIME!
JUST BECAUSE IT'S LEGAL, DOESN'T MEAN IT'S JUST. TAKE HIM AWAY, BOYS.
18

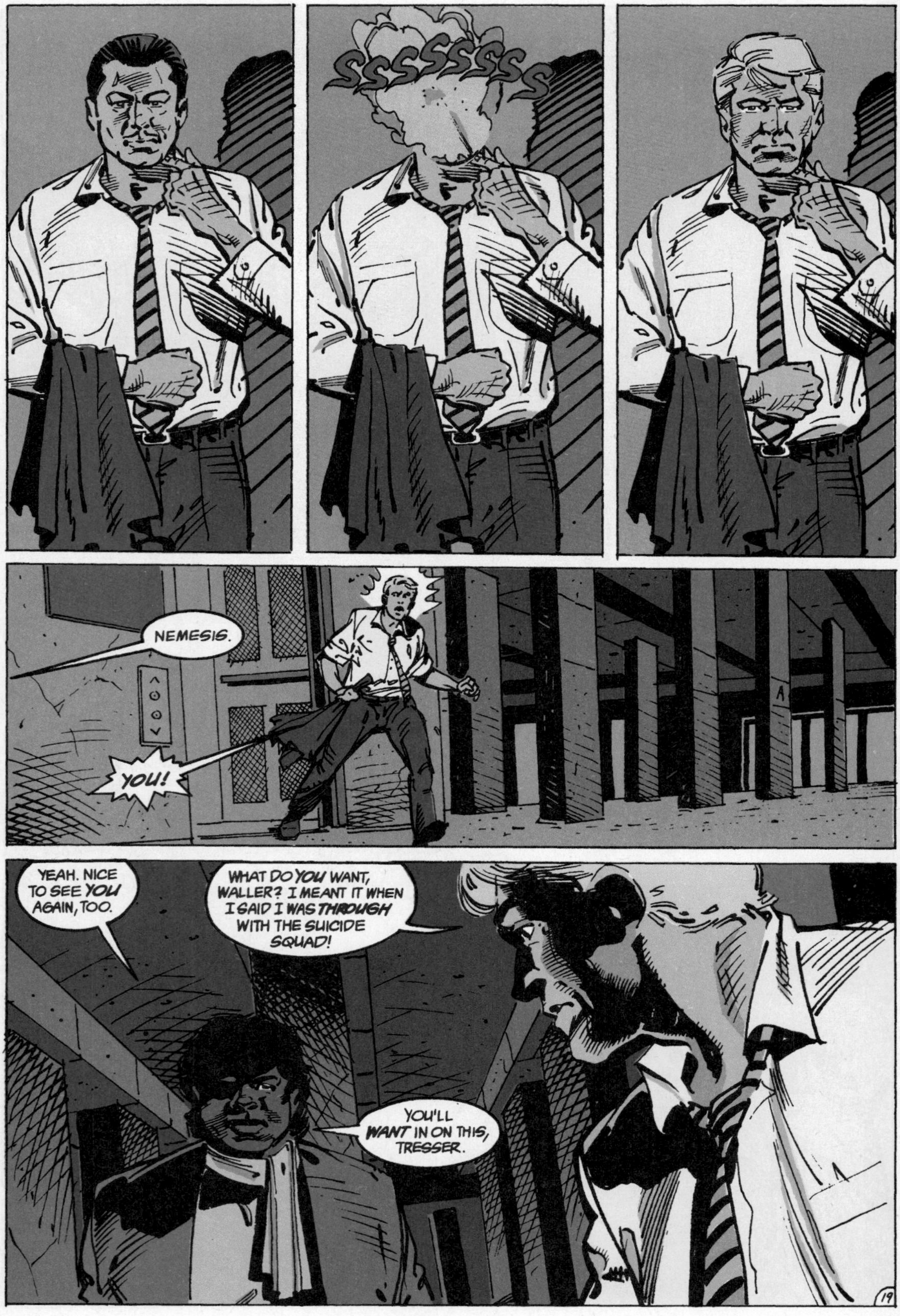
SSSSSSSS
NEMESIS.
YOU!
YEAH. NICE TO SEE YOU AGAIN, TOO.
WHAT DO YOU WANT, WALLER? I MEANT IT WHEN I SAID I WAS THROUGH WITH THE SUICIDE SQUAD!
YOU'LL WANT IN ON THIS, TRESSER.
19

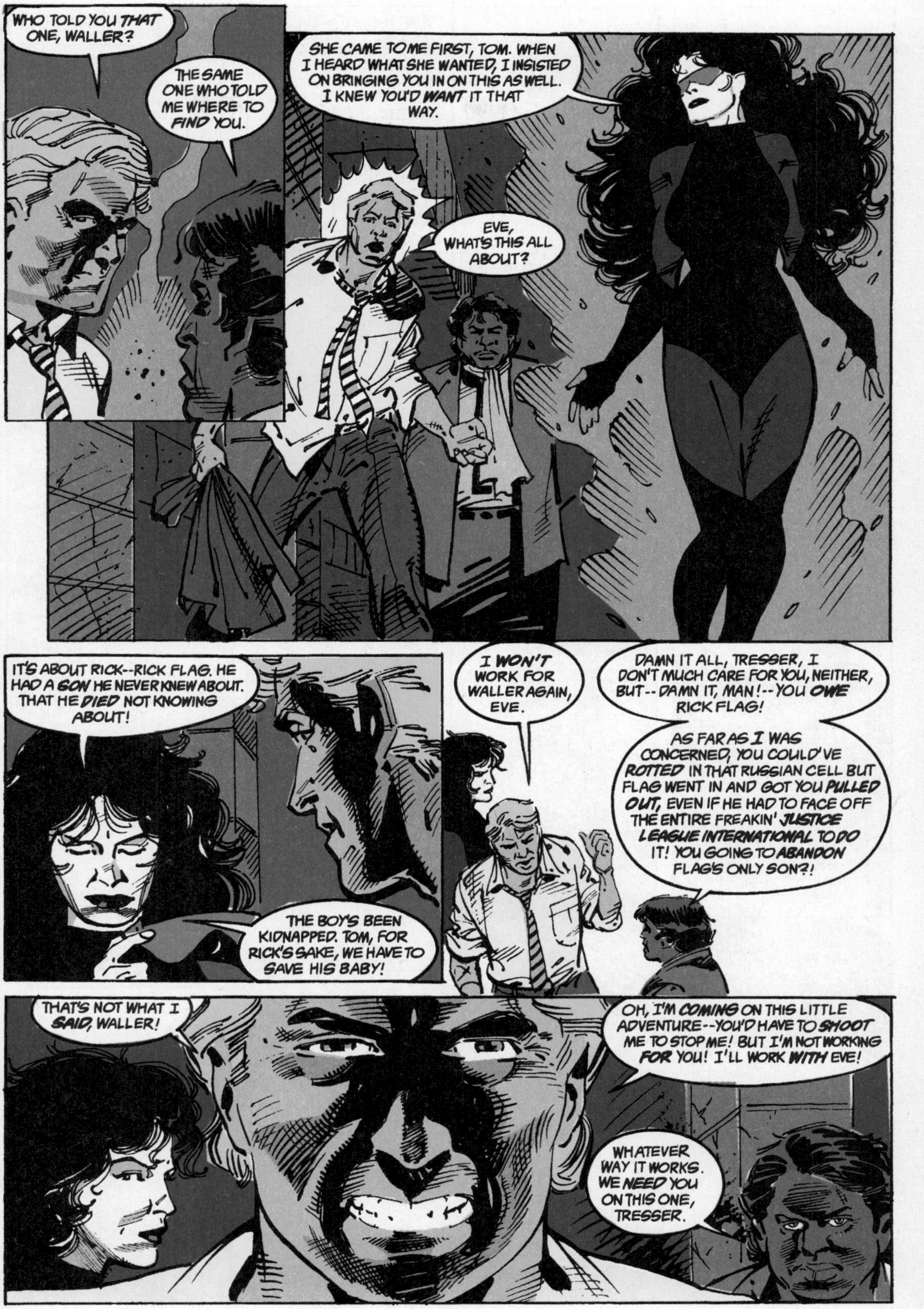
WHO TOLD YOU THAT ONE, WALLER?
THE SAME ONE WHO TOLD ME WHERE TO FIND YOU.
SHE CAME TO ME FIRST, TOM. WHEN I HEARD WHAT SHE WANTED, I INSISTED ON BRINGING YOU IN ON THIS AS WELL. I KNEW YOU'D WANT IT THAT WAY.
EVE, WHAT'S THIS ALL ABOUT?
IT'S ABOUT RICK--RICK FLAG. HE HAD A SON HE NEVER KNEW ABOUT. THAT HE DIED NOT KNOWING ABOUT!
THE BOY'S BEEN KIDNAPPED. TOM, FOR RICK'S SAKE, WE HAVE TO SAVE HIS BABY!
I WON'T WORK FOR WALLER AGAIN, EVE.
DAMN IT ALL, TRESSER, I DON'T MUCH CARE FOR YOU, NEITHER, BUT-- DAMN IT, MAN!--YOU OWE RICK FLAG!
AS FAR AS I WAS CONCERNED, YOU COULD'VE ROTTED IN THAT RUSSIAN CELL BUT FLAG WENT IN AND GOT YOU PULLED OUT, EVEN IF HE HAD TO FACE OFF THE ENTIRE FREAKIN' JUSTICE LEAGUE INTERNATIONAL TO DO IT! YOU GOING TO ABANDON FLAG'S ONLY SON?!
THAT'S NOT WHAT I SAID, WALLER!
OH, I'M COMING ON THIS LITTLE ADVENTURE--YOU'D HAVE TO SHOOT ME TO STOP ME! BUT I'M NOT WORKING FOR YOU! I'LL WORK WITH EVE!
WHATEVER WAY IT WORKS. WE NEED YOU ON THIS ONE, TRESSER.

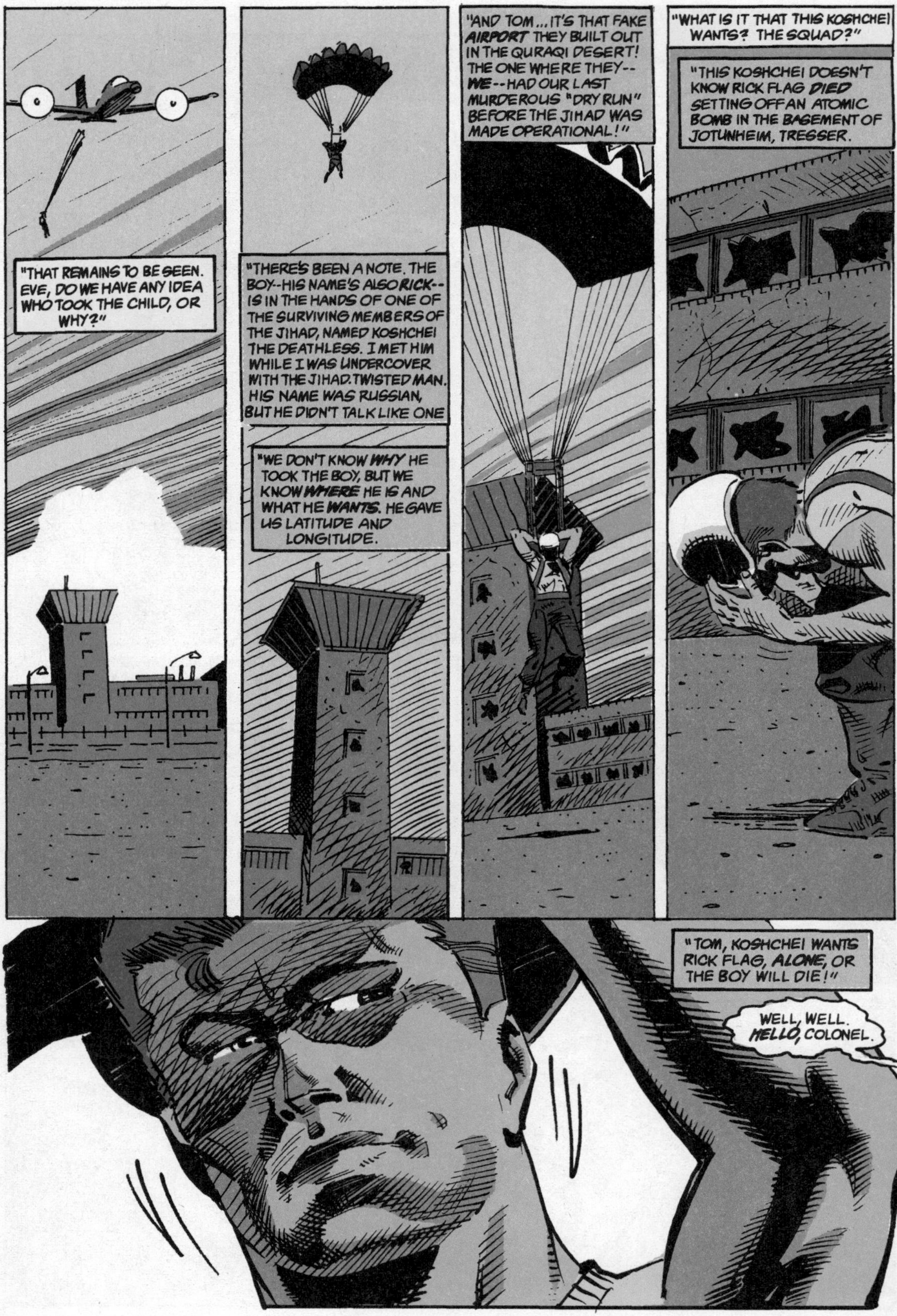
"THAT REMAINS TO BE SEEN. EVE, DO WE HAVE ANY IDEA WHO TOOK THE CHILD, OR WHY?"
"THERE'S BEEN A NOTE. THE BOY--HIS NAME'S ALSO RICK--IS IN THE HANDS OF ONE OF THE SURVIVING MEMBERS OF THE JIHAD, NAMED KOSHCHEI THE DEATHLESS. I MET HIM WHILE I WAS UNDERCOVER WITH THE JIHAD. TWISTED MAN. HIS NAME WAS RUSSIAN, BUT HE DIDN'T TALK LIKE ONE
"WE DON'T KNOW WHY HE TOOK THE BOY, BUT WE KNOW WHERE HE IS AND WHAT HE WANTS. HE GAVE US LATITUDE AND LONGITUDE.
"AND TOM... IT'S THAT FAKE AIRPORT THEY BUILT OUT IN THE QURAQI DESERT! THE ONE WHERE THEY--WE--HAD OUR LAST MURDEROUS "DRY RUN" BEFORE THE JIHAD WAS MADE OPERATIONAL!"
"WHAT IS IT THAT THIS KOSHCHEI WANTS? THE SQUAD?"
"THIS KOSHCHEI DOESN'T KNOW RICK FLAG DIED SETTING OFF AN ATOMIC BOMB IN THE BASEMENT OF JOTUNHEIM, TRESSER.
"TOM, KOSHCHEI WANTS RICK FLAG, ALONE, OR THE BOY WILL DIE!"
WELL, WELL. HELLO, COLONEL.

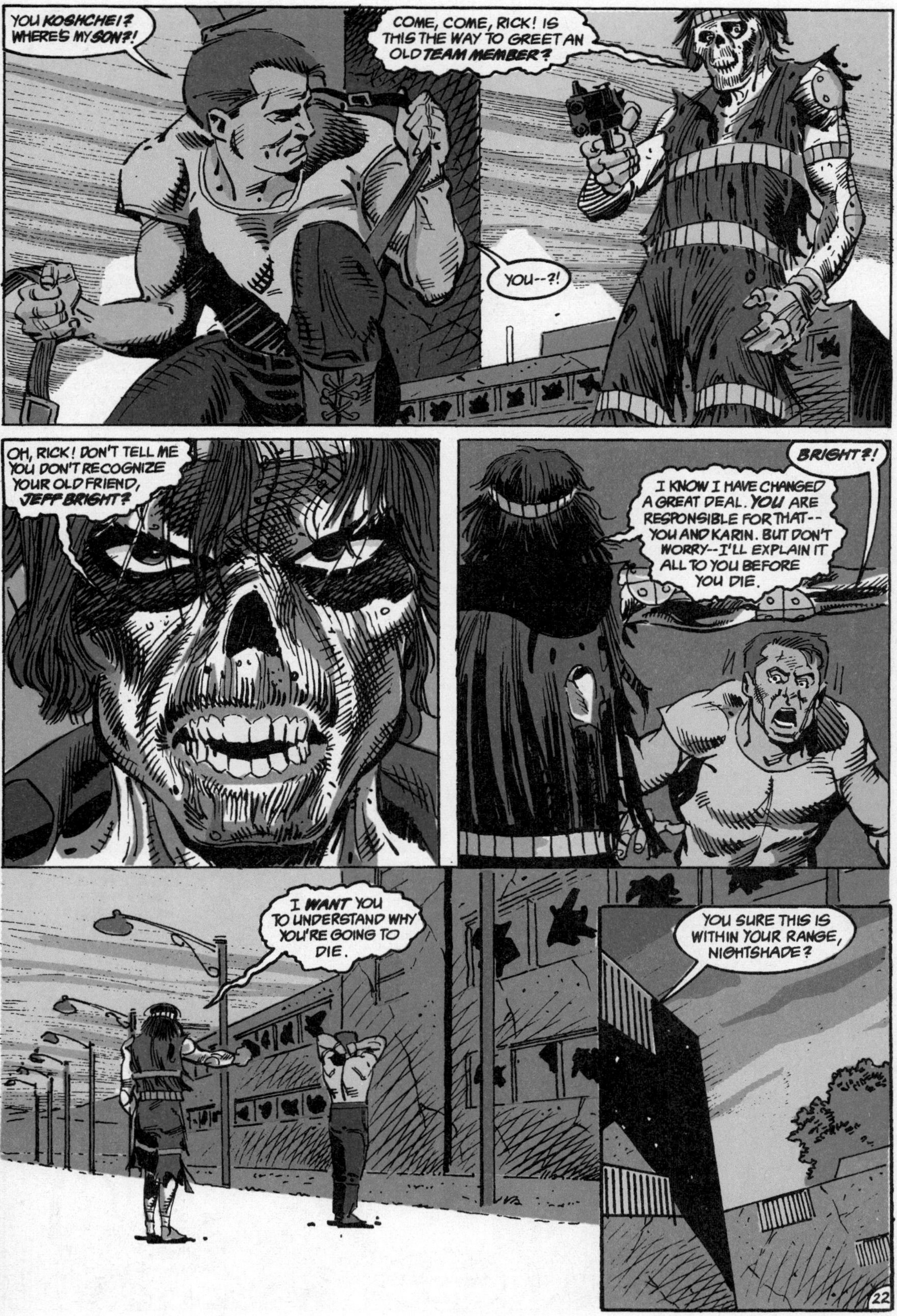
YOU KOSHCHEI? WHERE'S MY SON?!
COME, COME, RICK! IS THIS THE WAY TO GREET AN OLD TEAM MEMBER?
YOU--?!
OH, RICK! DON'T TELL ME YOU DON'T RECOGNIZE YOUR OLD FRIEND, JEFF BRIGHT?
BRIGHT?!
I KNOW I HAVE CHANGED A GREAT DEAL. YOU ARE RESPONSIBLE FOR THAT-- YOU AND KARIN. BUT DON'T WORRY--I'LL EXPLAIN IT ALL TO YOU BEFORE YOU DIE.
I WANT YOU TO UNDERSTAND WHY YOU'RE GOING TO DIE.
YOU SURE THIS IS WITHIN YOUR RANGE, NIGHTSHADE?
22

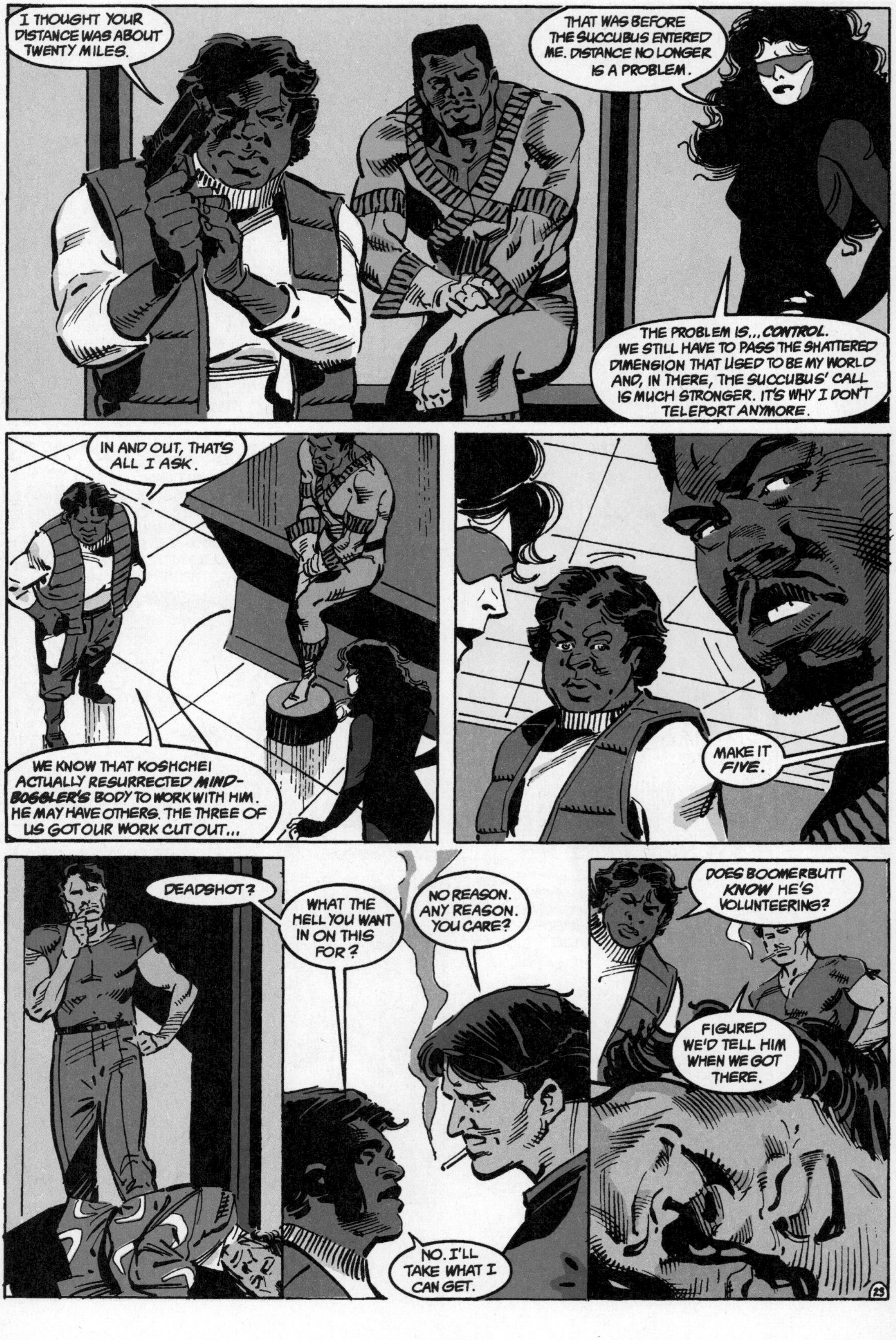
I THOUGHT YOUR DISTANCE WAS ABOUT TWENTY MILES.
THAT WAS BEFORE THE SUCCUBUS ENTERED ME. DISTANCE NO LONGER IS A PROBLEM.
THE PROBLEM IS... CONTROL. WE STILL HAVE TO PASS THE SHATTERED DIMENSION THAT USED TO BE MY WORLD AND, IN THERE, THE SUCCUBUS' CALL IS MUCH STRONGER. IT'S WHY I DON'T TELEPORT ANYMORE.
IN AND OUT, THAT'S ALL I ASK.
WE KNOW THAT KOSHCHEI ACTUALLY RESURRECTED MIND-BOGGLER'S BODY TO WORK WITH HIM. HE MAY HAVE OTHERS. THE THREE OF US GOT OUR WORK CUT OUT...
MAKE IT FIVE.
DEADSHOT?
WHAT THE HELL YOU WANT IN ON THIS FOR?
NO REASON. ANY REASON. YOU CARE?
NO. I'LL TAKE WHAT I CAN GET.
DOES BOOMERBUTT KNOW HE'S VOLUNTEERING?
FIGURED WE'D TELL HIM WHEN WE GOT THERE.
23

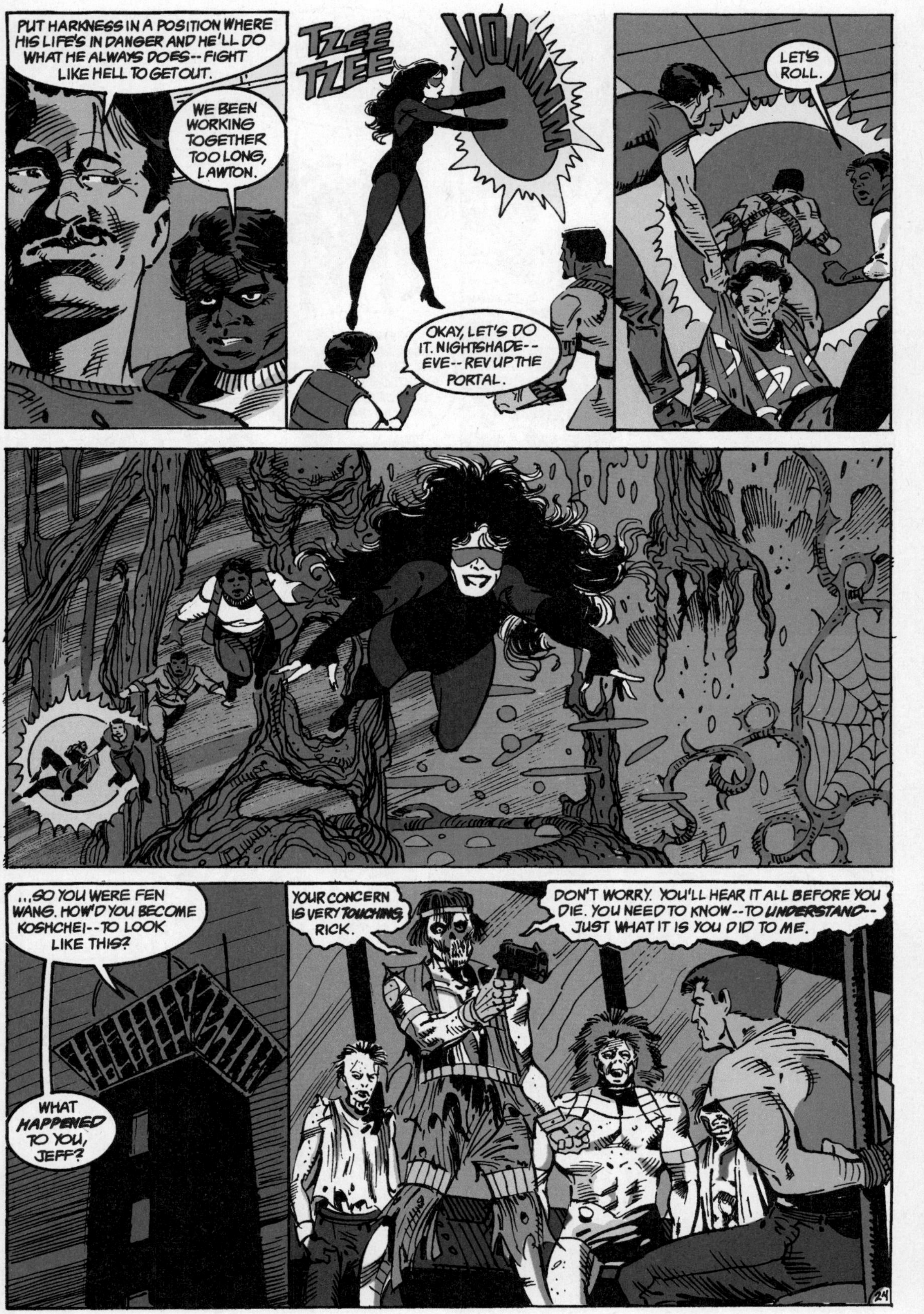
PUT HARKNESS IN A POSITION WHERE HIS LIFE'S IN DANGER AND HE'LL DO WHAT HE ALWAYS DOES--FIGHT LIKE HELL TO GET OUT.
WE BEEN WORKING TOGETHER TOO LONG, LAWTON.
TZEE TZEE
VOMMM
OKAY, LET'S DO IT. NIGHTSHADE--EVE--REV UP THE PORTAL.
LET'S ROLL.
...SO YOU WERE FEN WANG. HOW'D YOU BECOME KOSHCHEI--TO LOOK LIKE THIS?
WHAT HAPPENED TO YOU, JEFF?
YOUR CONCERN IS VERY TOUCHING, RICK.
DON'T WORRY. YOU'LL HEAR IT ALL BEFORE YOU DIE. YOU NEED TO KNOW--TO UNDERSTAND--JUST WHAT IT IS YOU DID TO ME.
24

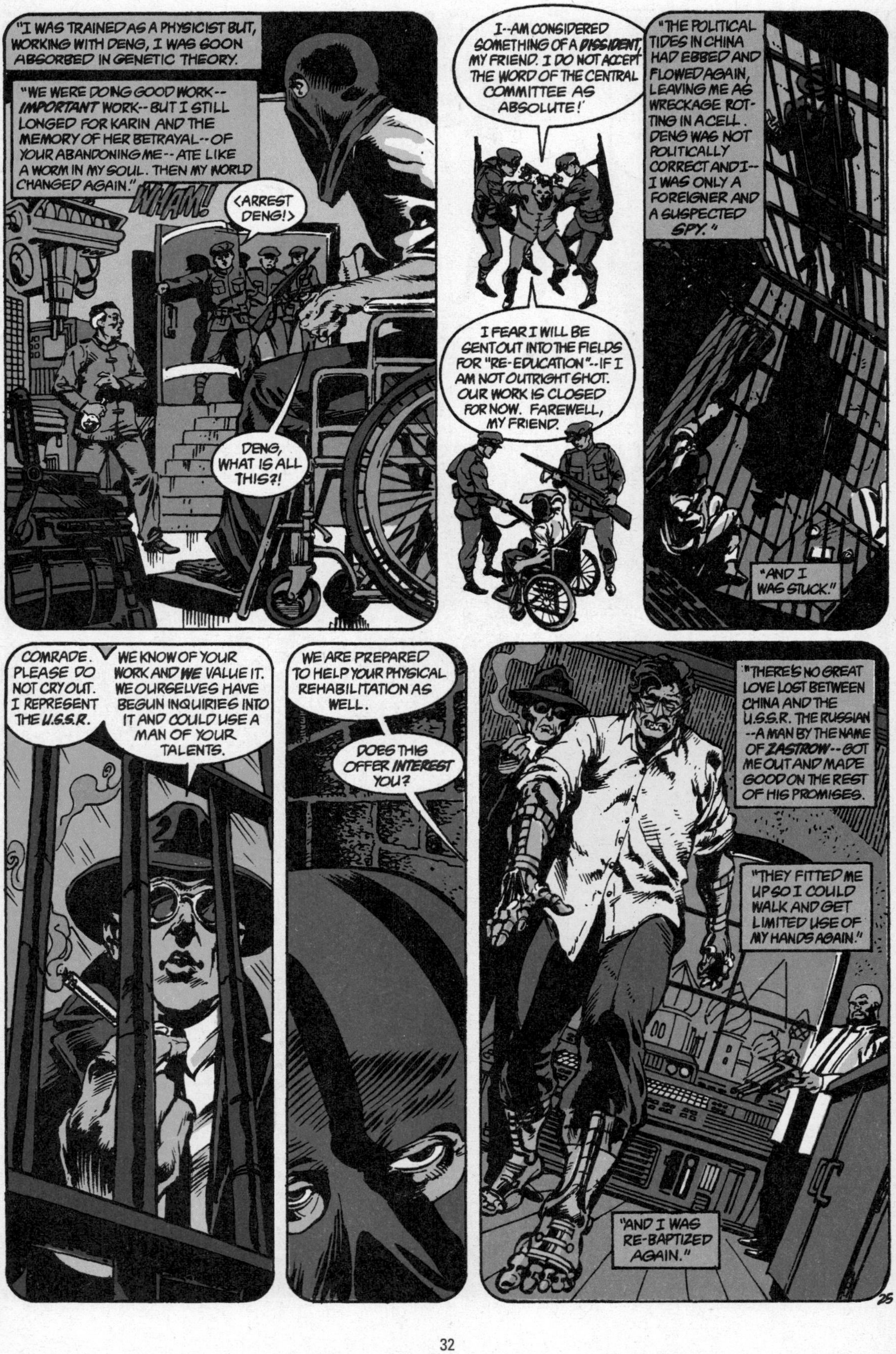
"I WAS TRAINED AS A PHYSICIST BUT, WORKING WITH DENG, I WAS SOON ABSORBED IN GENETIC THEORY.
"WE WERE DOING GOOD WORK--*IMPORTANT* WORK--BUT I STILL LONGED FOR KARIN AND THE MEMORY OF HER BETRAYAL--OF YOUR ABANDONING ME--ATE LIKE A WORM IN MY SOUL. THEN MY WORLD CHANGED AGAIN."
WHAM!
<ARREST DENG!>
DENG, WHAT IS ALL THIS?!
I--AM CONSIDERED SOMETHING OF A *DISSIDENT*, MY FRIEND. I DO NOT ACCEPT THE WORD OF THE CENTRAL COMMITTEE AS ABSOLUTE!
I FEAR I WILL BE SENT OUT INTO THE FIELDS FOR "RE-EDUCATION"--IF I AM NOT OUTRIGHT SHOT. OUR WORK IS CLOSED FOR NOW. FAREWELL, MY FRIEND.
"THE POLITICAL TIDES IN CHINA HAD EBBED AND FLOWED AGAIN, LEAVING ME AS WRECKAGE ROTTING IN A CELL. DENG WAS NOT POLITICALLY CORRECT AND I--I WAS ONLY A FOREIGNER AND A SUSPECTED *SPY*."
"AND I WAS STUCK."
COMRADE. PLEASE DO NOT CRY OUT. I REPRESENT THE *U.S.S.R.*
WE KNOW OF YOUR WORK AND *WE* VALUE IT. WE OURSELVES HAVE BEGUN INQUIRIES INTO IT AND COULD USE A MAN OF YOUR TALENTS.
WE ARE PREPARED TO HELP YOUR PHYSICAL REHABILITATION AS WELL.
DOES THIS OFFER *INTEREST* YOU?
"THERE'S NO GREAT LOVE LOST BETWEEN CHINA AND THE U.S.S.R. THE RUSSIAN--A MAN BY THE NAME OF *ZASTROW*--GOT ME OUT AND MADE GOOD ON THE REST OF HIS PROMISES.
"THEY FITTED ME UP SO I COULD WALK AND GET LIMITED USE OF MY HANDS AGAIN."
"AND I WAS RE-BAPTIZED AGAIN."
25

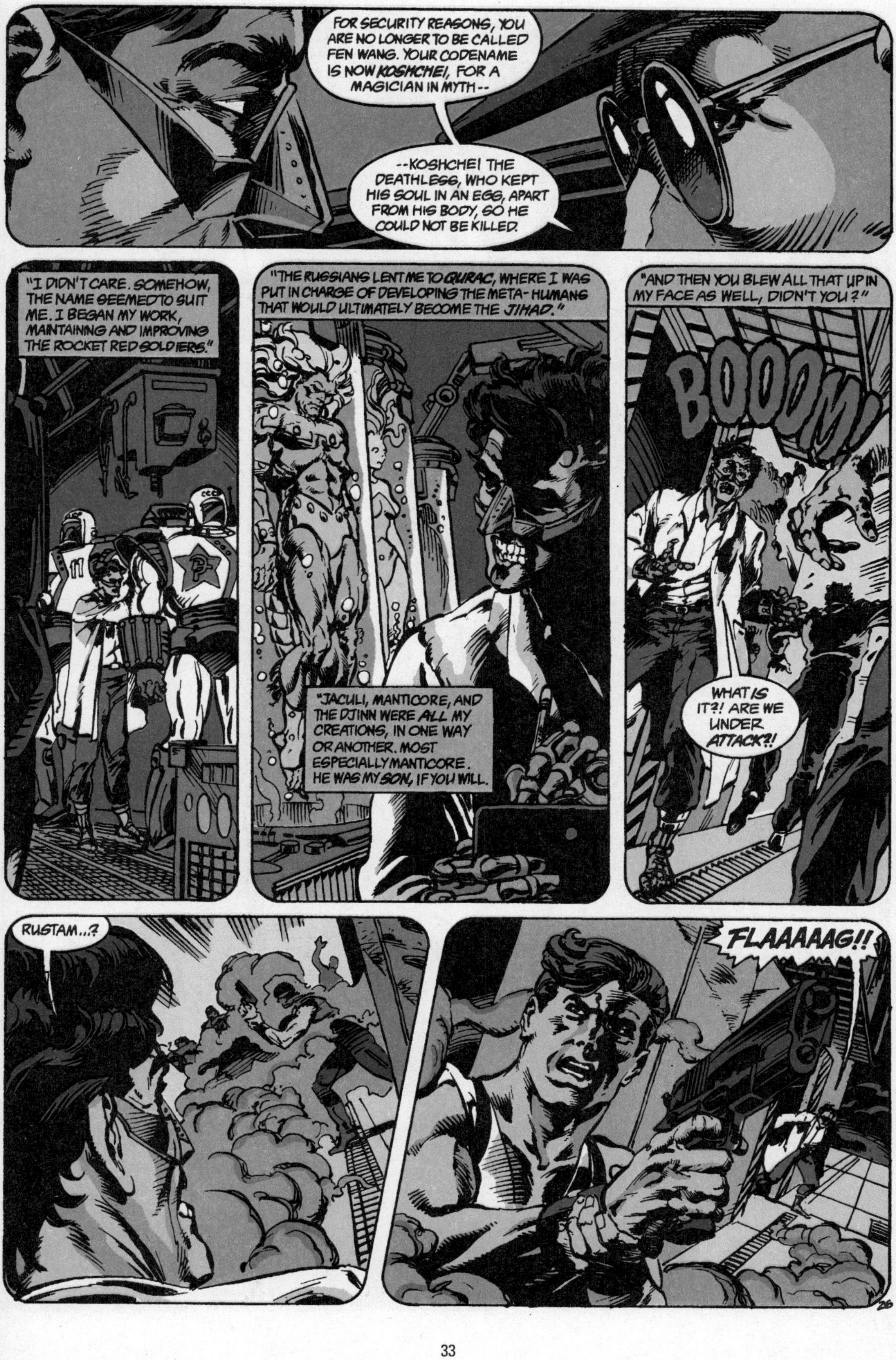

FOR SECURITY REASONS, YOU ARE NO LONGER TO BE CALLED FEN WANG. YOUR CODENAME IS NOW KOSHCHEI, FOR A MAGICIAN IN MYTH --
--KOSHCHEI THE DEATHLESS, WHO KEPT HIS SOUL IN AN EGG, APART FROM HIS BODY, SO HE COULD NOT BE KILLED.
"I DIDN'T CARE. SOMEHOW, THE NAME SEEMED TO SUIT ME. I BEGAN MY WORK, MAINTAINING AND IMPROVING THE ROCKET RED SOLDIERS."
"THE RUSSIANS LENT ME TO QURAC, WHERE I WAS PUT IN CHARGE OF DEVELOPING THE META-HUMANS THAT WOULD ULTIMATELY BECOME THE JIHAD."
"JACULI, MANTICORE, AND THE DJINN WERE ALL MY CREATIONS, IN ONE WAY OR ANOTHER. MOST ESPECIALLY MANTICORE. HE WAS MY SON, IF YOU WILL.
"AND THEN YOU BLEW ALL THAT UP IN MY FACE AS WELL, DIDN'T YOU?"
BOOOM!
WHAT IS IT?! ARE WE UNDER ATTACK?!
RUSTAM...?
FLAAAAAG!!
26

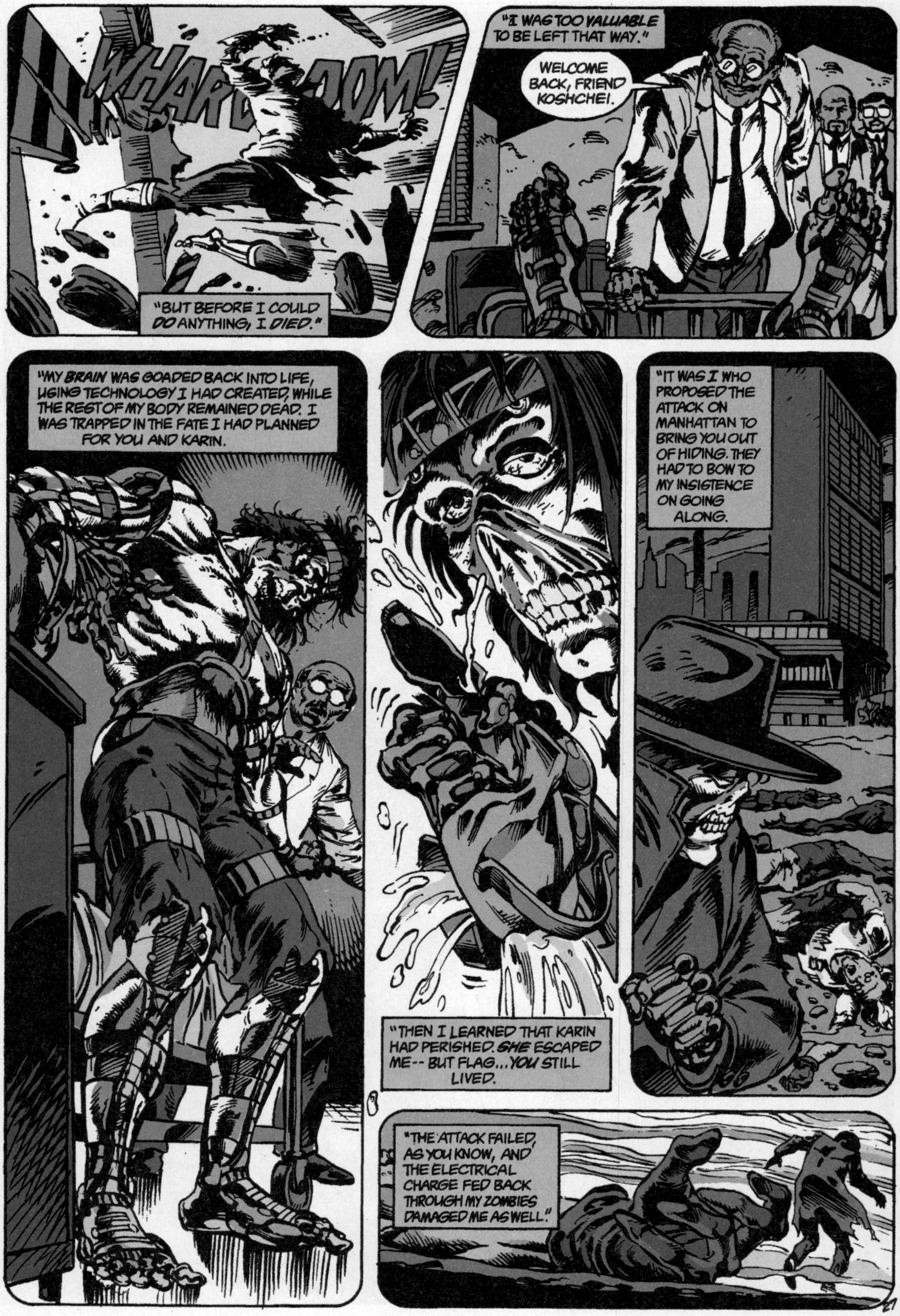
WHARDOOM!
"BUT BEFORE I COULD DO ANYTHING, I DIED."
"I WAS TOO VALUABLE TO BE LEFT THAT WAY."
WELCOME BACK, FRIEND KOSHCHEI.
"MY BRAIN WAS GOADED BACK INTO LIFE, USING TECHNOLOGY I HAD CREATED, WHILE THE REST OF MY BODY REMAINED DEAD. I WAS TRAPPED IN THE FATE I HAD PLANNED FOR YOU AND KARIN.
"THEN I LEARNED THAT KARIN HAD PERISHED. SHE ESCAPED ME-- BUT FLAG... YOU STILL LIVED.
"IT WAS I WHO PROPOSED THE ATTACK ON MANHATTAN TO BRING YOU OUT OF HIDING. THEY HAD TO BOW TO MY INSISTENCE ON GOING ALONG.
"THE ATTACK FAILED, AS YOU KNOW, AND THE ELECTRICAL CHARGE FED BACK THROUGH MY ZOMBIES DAMAGED ME AS WELL."
27

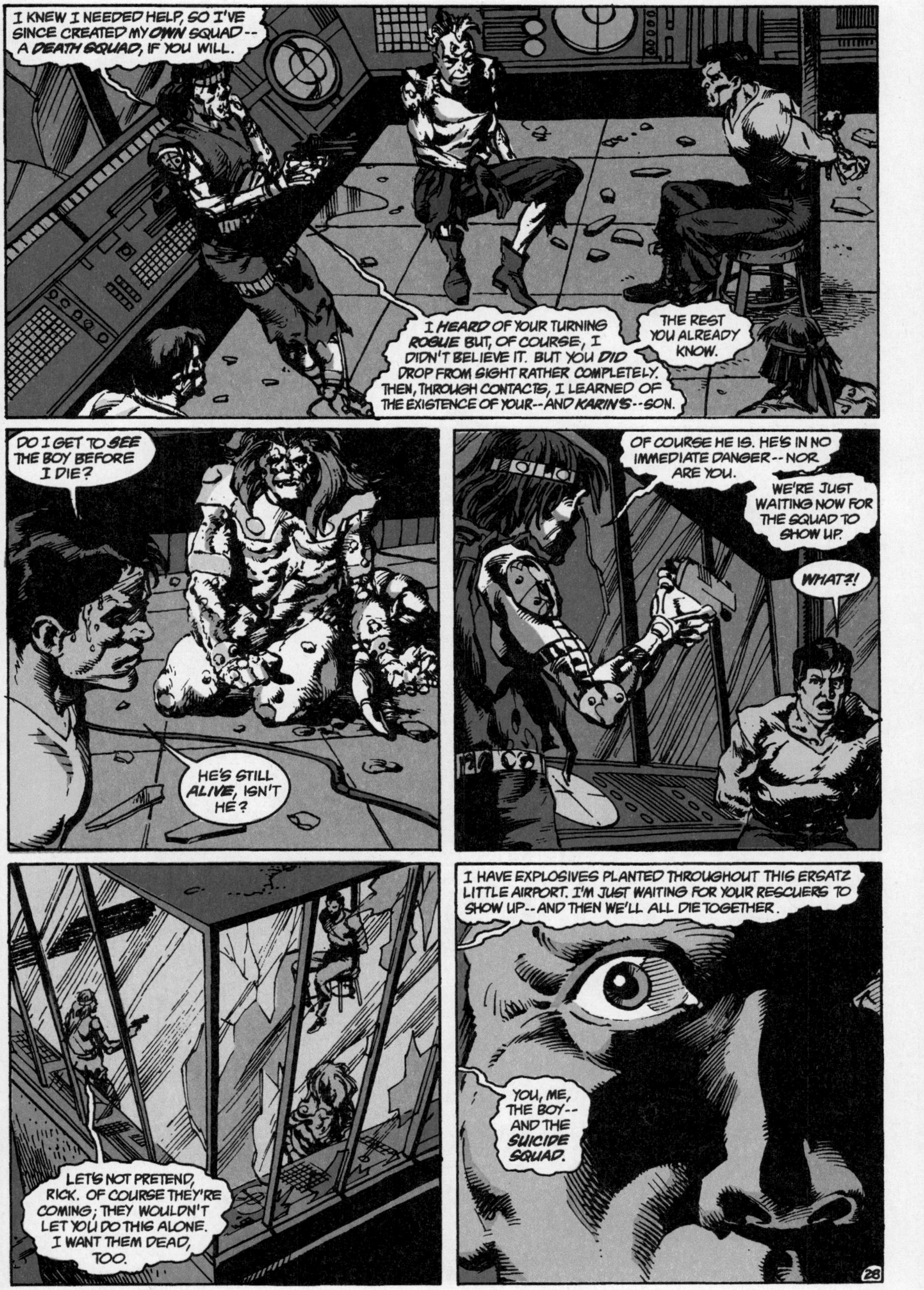
I KNEW I NEEDED HELP, SO I'VE SINCE CREATED MY OWN SQUAD-- A DEATH SQUAD, IF YOU WILL.
I HEARD OF YOUR TURNING ROGUE BUT, OF COURSE, I DIDN'T BELIEVE IT. BUT YOU DID DROP FROM SIGHT RATHER COMPLETELY. THEN, THROUGH CONTACTS, I LEARNED OF THE EXISTENCE OF YOUR--AND KARIN'S--SON.
THE REST YOU ALREADY KNOW.
DO I GET TO SEE THE BOY BEFORE I DIE?
HE'S STILL ALIVE, ISN'T HE?
OF COURSE HE IS. HE'S IN NO IMMEDIATE DANGER--NOR ARE YOU.
WE'RE JUST WAITING NOW FOR THE SQUAD TO SHOW UP.
WHAT?!
LET'S NOT PRETEND, RICK. OF COURSE THEY'RE COMING; THEY WOULDN'T LET YOU DO THIS ALONE. I WANT THEM DEAD, TOO.
I HAVE EXPLOSIVES PLANTED THROUGHOUT THIS ERSATZ LITTLE AIRPORT. I'M JUST WAITING FOR YOUR RESCUERS TO SHOW UP--AND THEN WE'LL ALL DIE TOGETHER.
YOU, ME, THE BOY--AND THE SUICIDE SQUAD.
28

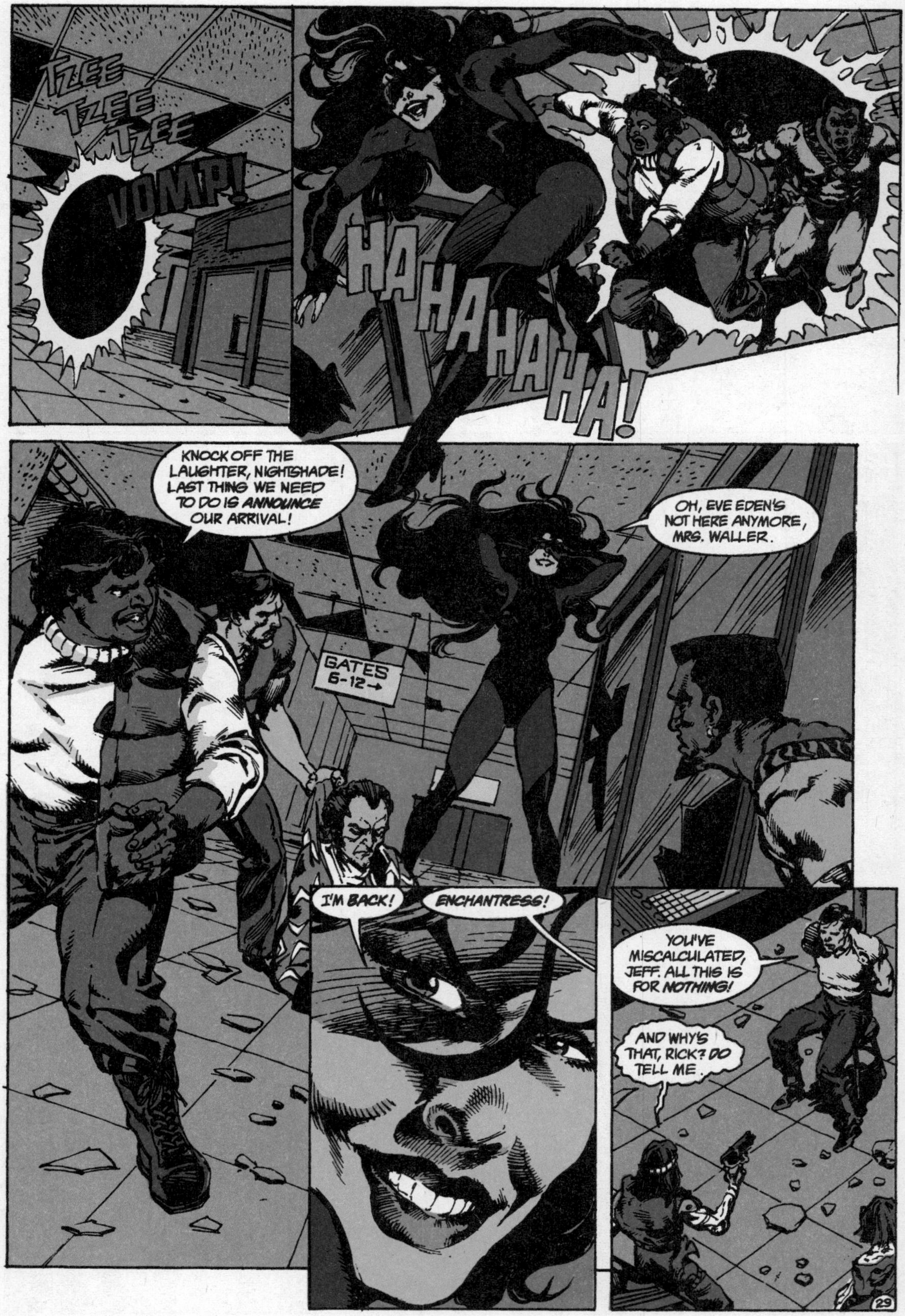
TZEE TZEE TZEE
VOMP!
HAHAHAHAHAHA!
KNOCK OFF THE LAUGHTER, NIGHTSHADE! LAST THING WE NEED TO DO IS ANNOUNCE OUR ARRIVAL!
OH, EVE EDEN'S NOT HERE ANYMORE, MRS. WALLER.
GATES 6-12 →
I'M BACK!
ENCHANTRESS!
YOU'VE MISCALCULATED, JEFF. ALL THIS IS FOR NOTHING!
AND WHY'S THAT, RICK? DO TELL ME.
29

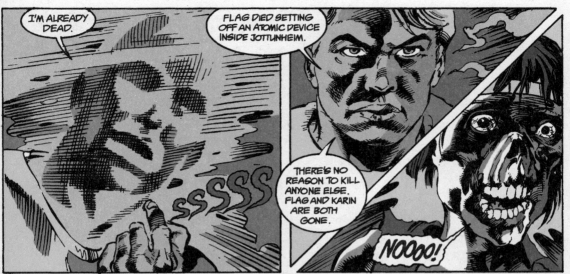

I'M ALREADY DEAD.

FLAG DIED SETTING OFF AN ATOMIC DEVICE INSIDE JOTTUNHEIM.

SSSSS

THERE'S NO REASON TO KILL ANYONE ELSE. FLAG AND KARIN ARE BOTH GONE.

NOOOO!

THERE'S THE *CHILD!* THERE'S THE *SQUAD!*

THERE'S *YOU!*

BLAM!

WHAM!

30

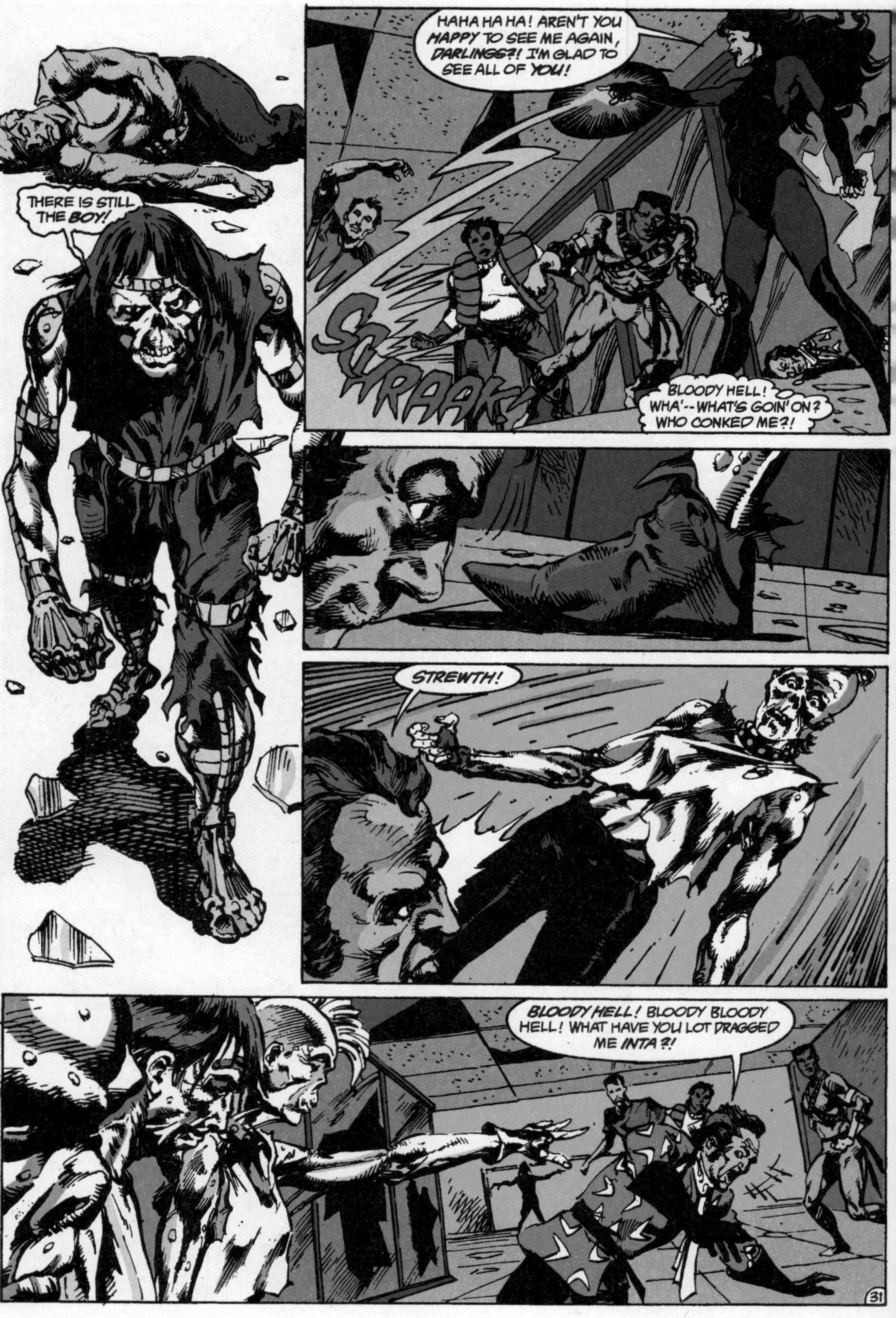
THERE IS STILL THE BOY!
HAHA HA HA! AREN'T YOU HAPPY TO SEE ME AGAIN, DARLINGS?! I'M GLAD TO SEE ALL OF YOU!
SCHRAAK!
BLOODY HELL! WHA'--WHAT'S GOIN' ON? WHO CONKED ME?!
STREWTH!
BLOODY HELL! BLOODY BLOODY HELL! WHAT HAVE YOU LOT DRAGGED ME INTA?!
31

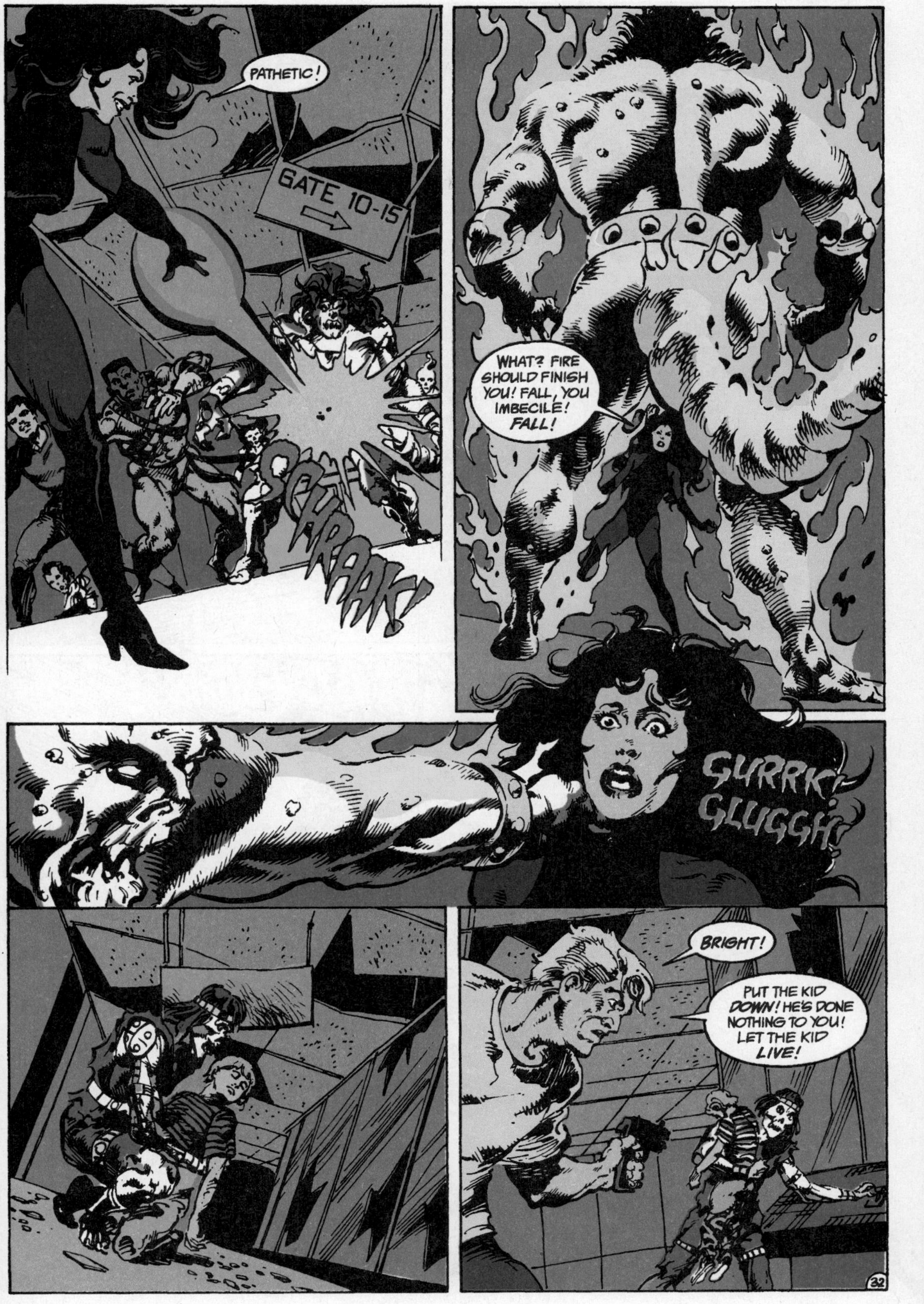
PATHETIC!
GATE 10-15
SCHRAAK!
WHAT? FIRE SHOULD FINISH YOU! FALL, YOU IMBECILE! FALL!
GURRK-GLUGGH
BRIGHT!
PUT THE KID DOWN! HE'S DONE NOTHING TO YOU! LET THE KID LIVE!
32

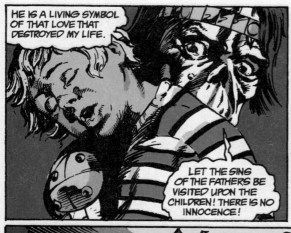

HE IS A LIVING SYMBOL OF THAT LOVE THAT DESTROYED MY LIFE.

LET THE SINS OF THE FATHERS BE VISITED UPON THE CHILDREN! THERE IS NO INNOCENCE!

DANGER

CK'EK!

B-RADOOM!

CHOOM!

BADOOM!

WHAROOM!

SSSSSSSSSS

RAVAN?!

33

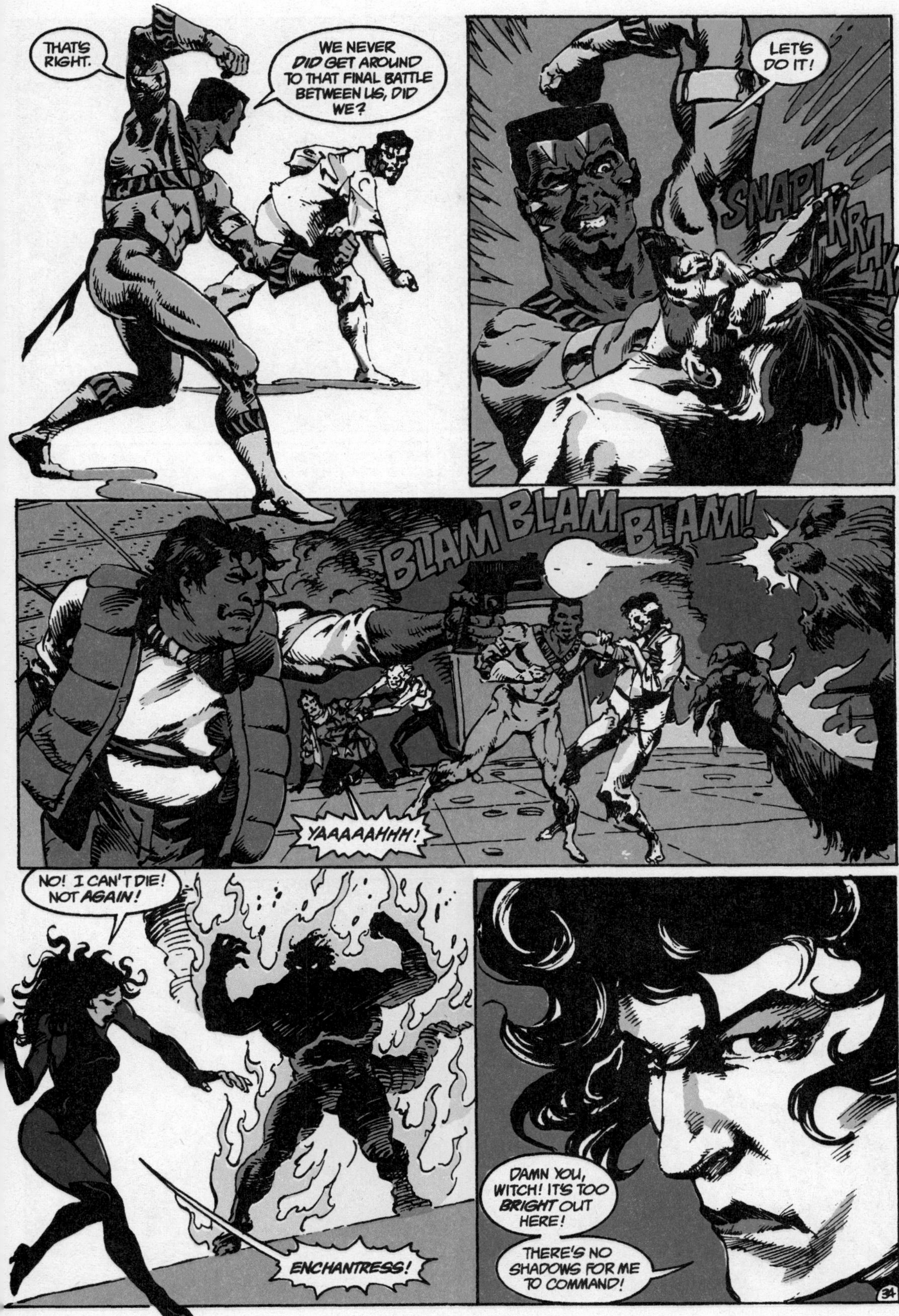
THAT'S RIGHT.
WE NEVER DID GET AROUND TO THAT FINAL BATTLE BETWEEN US, DID WE?
LET'S DO IT!
SNAP!
KRAK!
BLAM BLAM BLAM!
YAAAAAHHH!
NO! I CAN'T DIE! NOT AGAIN!
ENCHANTRESS!
DAMN YOU, WITCH! IT'S TOO BRIGHT OUT HERE!
THERE'S NO SHADOWS FOR ME TO COMMAND!
34

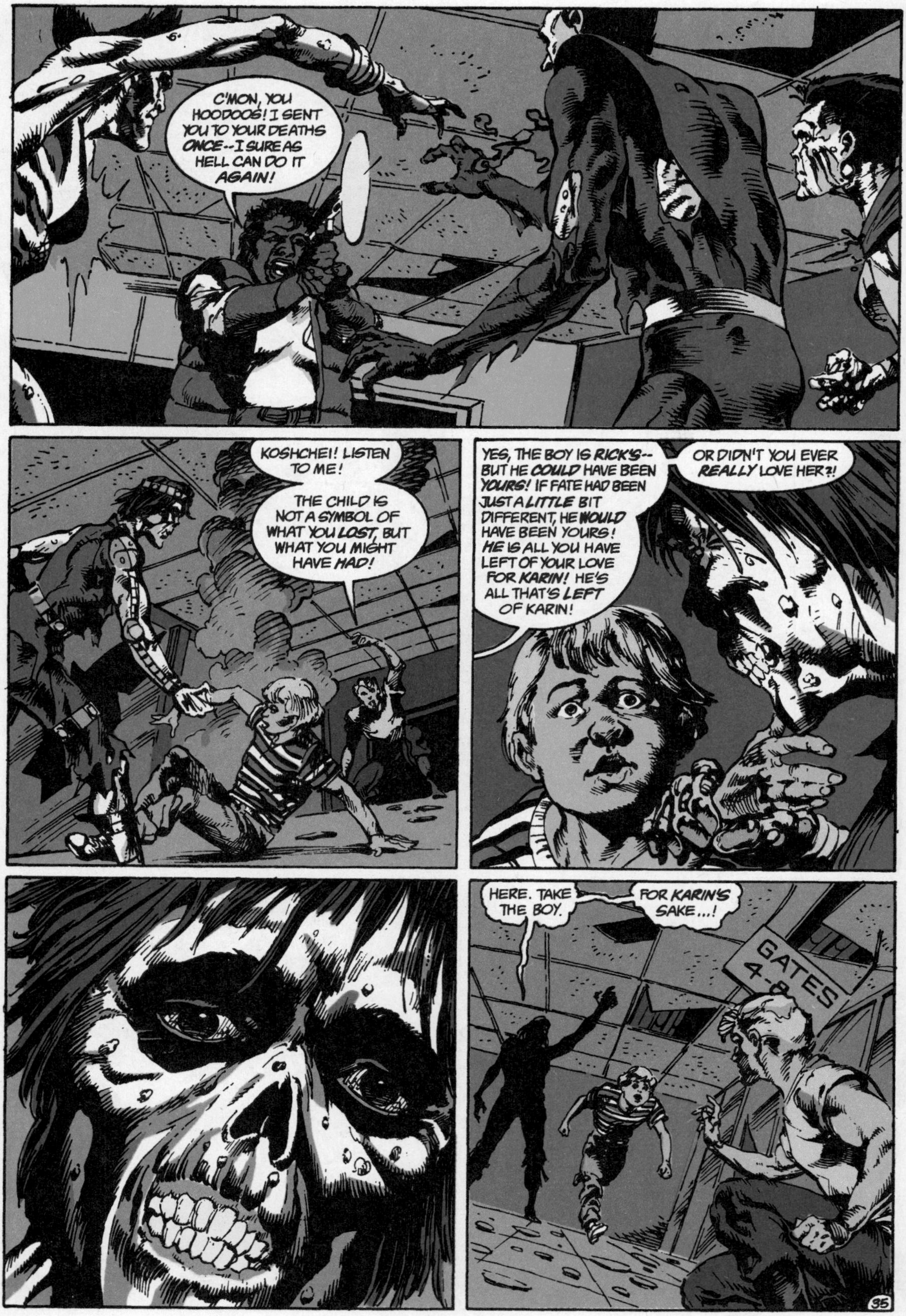
C'MON, YOU HOODOOS! I SENT YOU TO YOUR DEATHS ONCE--I SURE AS HELL CAN DO IT AGAIN!
KOSHCHEI! LISTEN TO ME!
THE CHILD IS NOT A SYMBOL OF WHAT YOU LOST, BUT WHAT YOU MIGHT HAVE HAD!
YES, THE BOY IS RICK'S-- BUT HE COULD HAVE BEEN YOURS! IF FATE HAD BEEN JUST A LITTLE BIT DIFFERENT, HE WOULD HAVE BEEN YOURS! HE IS ALL YOU HAVE LEFT OF YOUR LOVE FOR KARIN! HE'S ALL THAT'S LEFT OF KARIN!
OR DIDN'T YOU EVER REALLY LOVE HER?!
HERE. TAKE THE BOY.
FOR KARIN'S SAKE...!
GATES
35

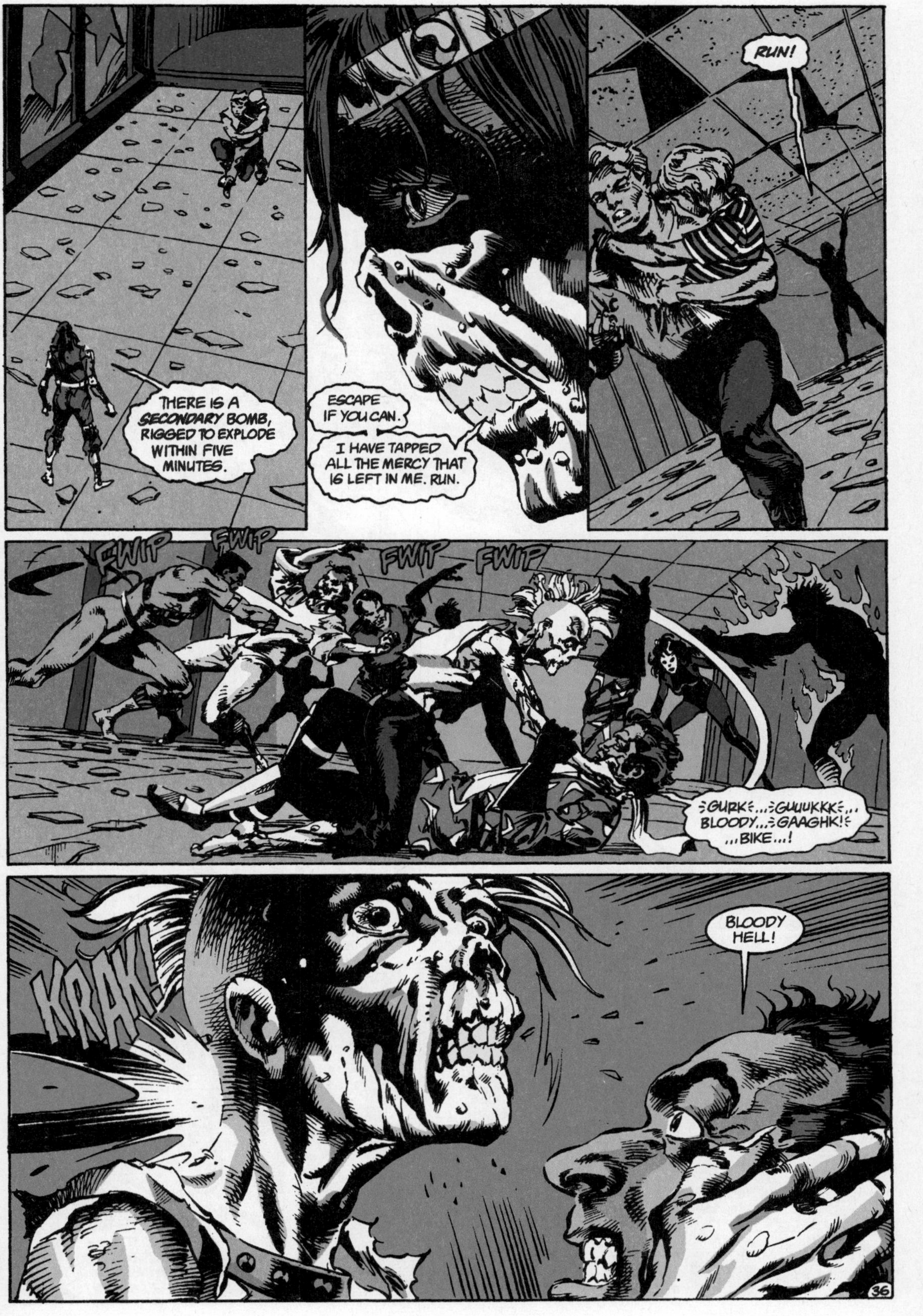
THERE IS A SECONDARY BOMB, RIGGED TO EXPLODE WITHIN FIVE MINUTES.
ESCAPE IF YOU CAN.
I HAVE TAPPED ALL THE MERCY THAT IS LEFT IN ME. RUN.
RUN!
FWIP
FWIP
FWIP
FWIP
GURK... GUUUKKK... BLOODY... GAAGHK! ...BIKE...!
KRAK!
BLOODY HELL!
36

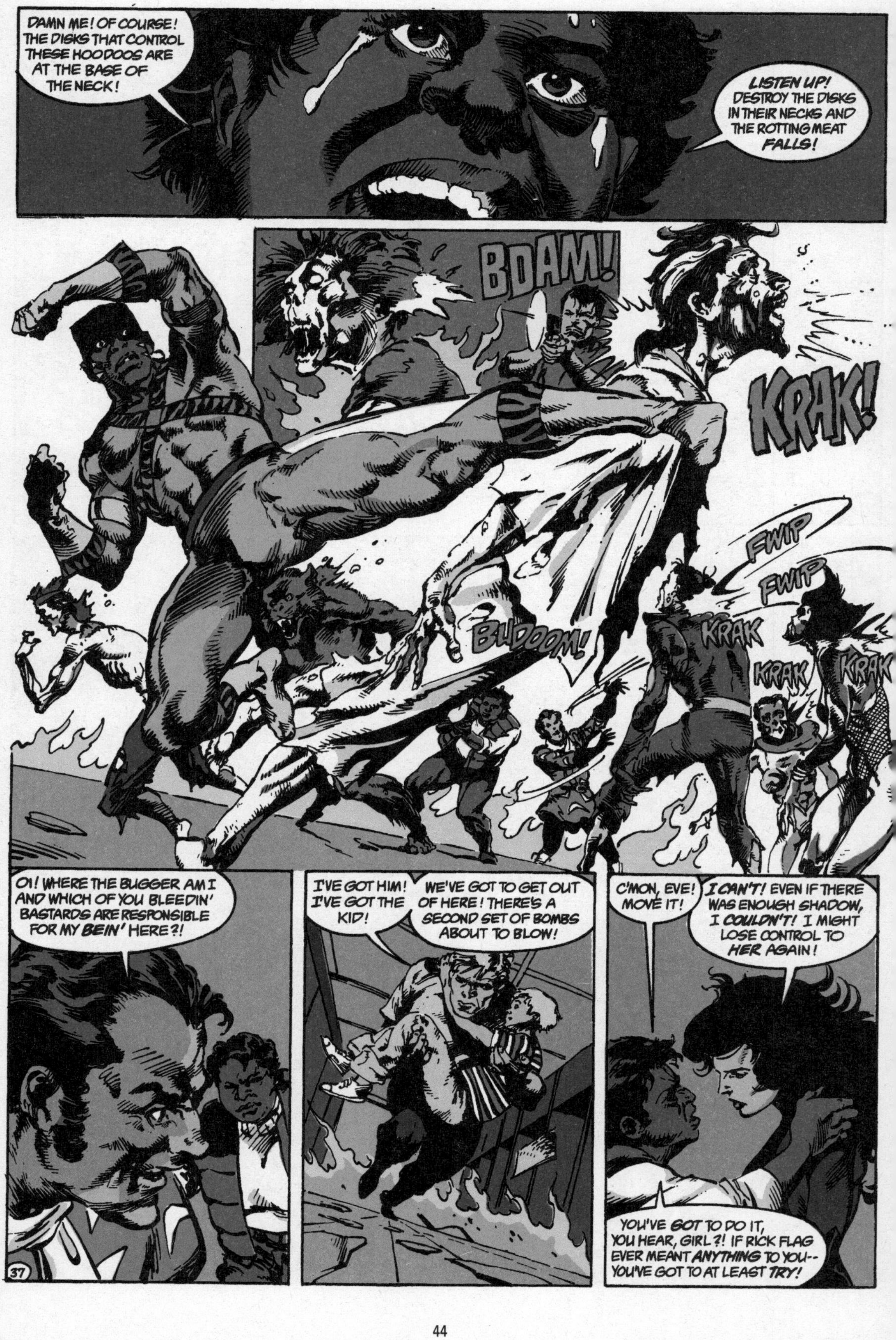

DAMN ME! OF COURSE! THE DISKS THAT CONTROL THESE HOODOOS ARE AT THE BASE OF THE NECK!
LISTEN UP! DESTROY THE DISKS IN THEIR NECKS AND THE ROTTING MEAT FALLS!
BDAM!
KRAK!
FWIP
FWIP
BUDOOM!
KRAK
KRAK
KRAK
OI! WHERE THE BUGGER AM I AND WHICH OF YOU BLEEDIN' BASTARDS ARE RESPONSIBLE FOR MY BEIN' HERE?!
I'VE GOT HIM! I'VE GOT THE KID!
WE'VE GOT TO GET OUT OF HERE! THERE'S A SECOND SET OF BOMBS ABOUT TO BLOW!
C'MON, EVE! MOVE IT!
I CAN'T! EVEN IF THERE WAS ENOUGH SHADOW, I COULDN'T! I MIGHT LOSE CONTROL TO HER AGAIN!
YOU'VE GOT TO DO IT, YOU HEAR, GIRL?! IF RICK FLAG EVER MEANT ANYTHING TO YOU-- YOU'VE GOT TO AT LEAST TRY!
37

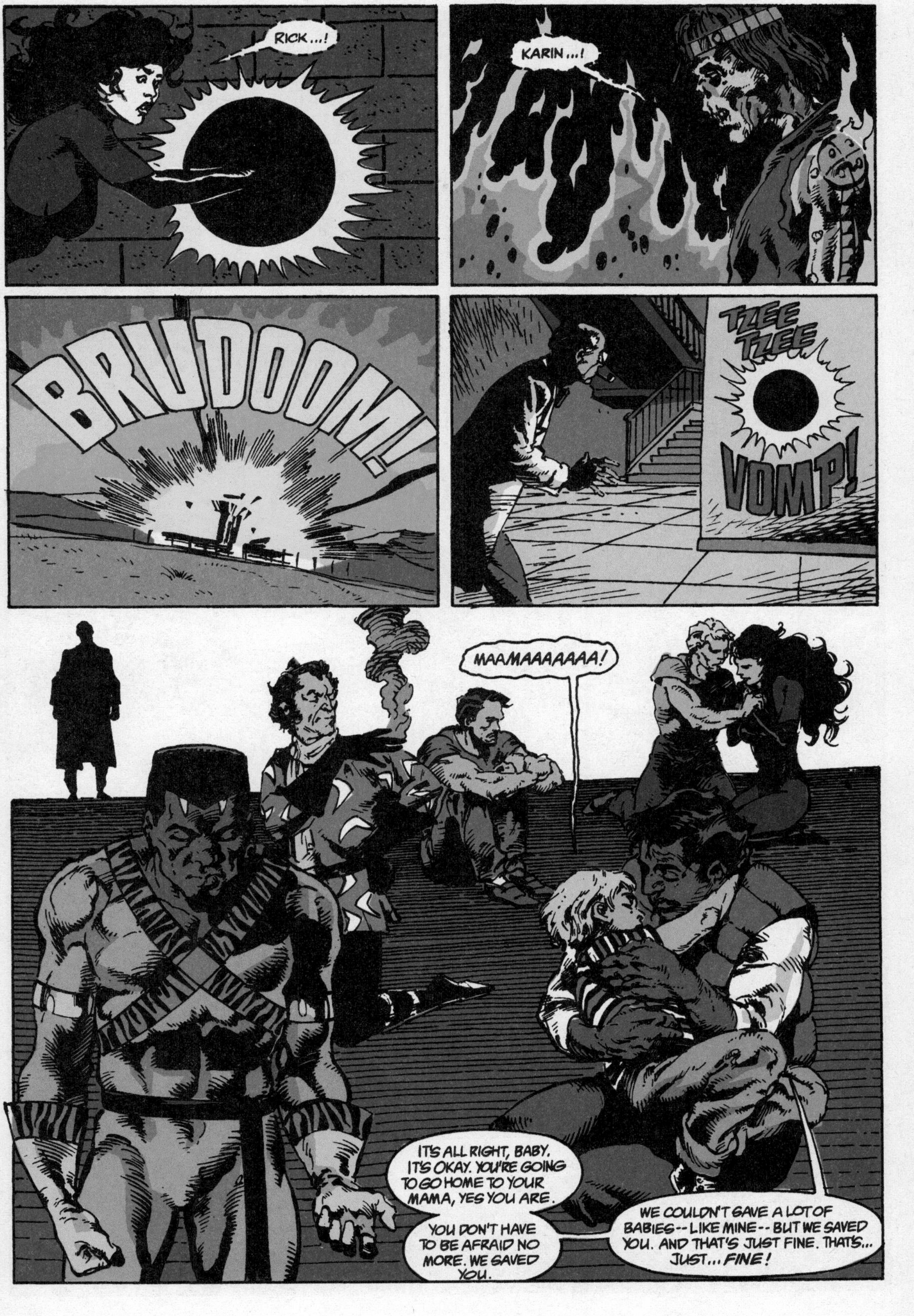
RICK...!
KARIN...!
BRUDOOM!!
TZEE TZEE
VOMP!
MAAMAAAAAAA!
IT'S ALL RIGHT, BABY. IT'S OKAY. YOU'RE GOING TO GO HOME TO YOUR MAMA, YES YOU ARE.
YOU DON'T HAVE TO BE AFRAID NO MORE. WE SAVED YOU.
WE COULDN'T SAVE A LOT OF BABIES-- LIKE MINE-- BUT WE SAVED YOU. AND THAT'S JUST FINE. THAT'S... JUST... FINE!

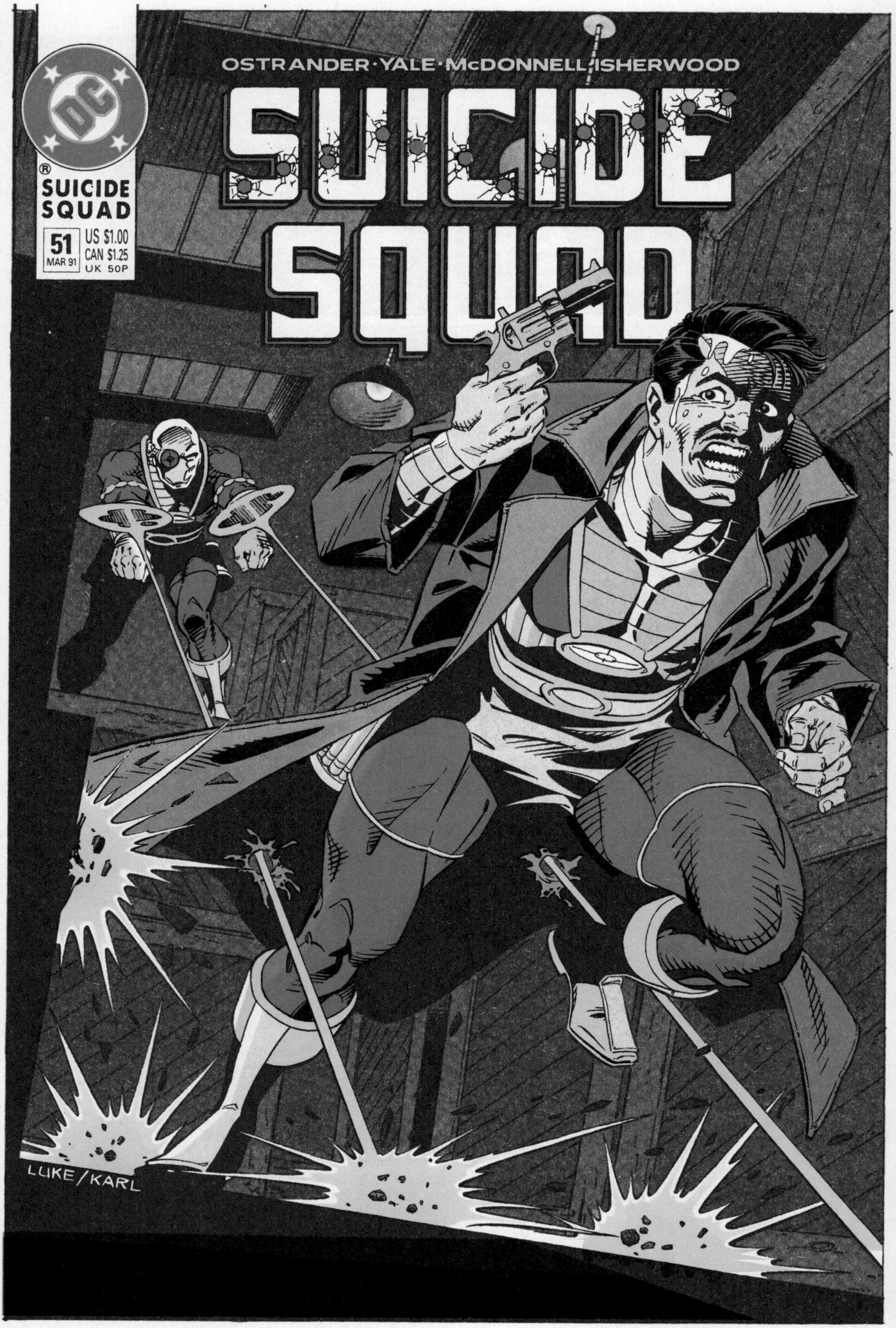
OSTRANDER·YALE·McDONNELL·ISHERWOOD
SUICIDE SQUAD
SUICIDE SQUAD
51
MAR 91
US $1.00
CAN $1.25
UK 50P
LUKE/KARL

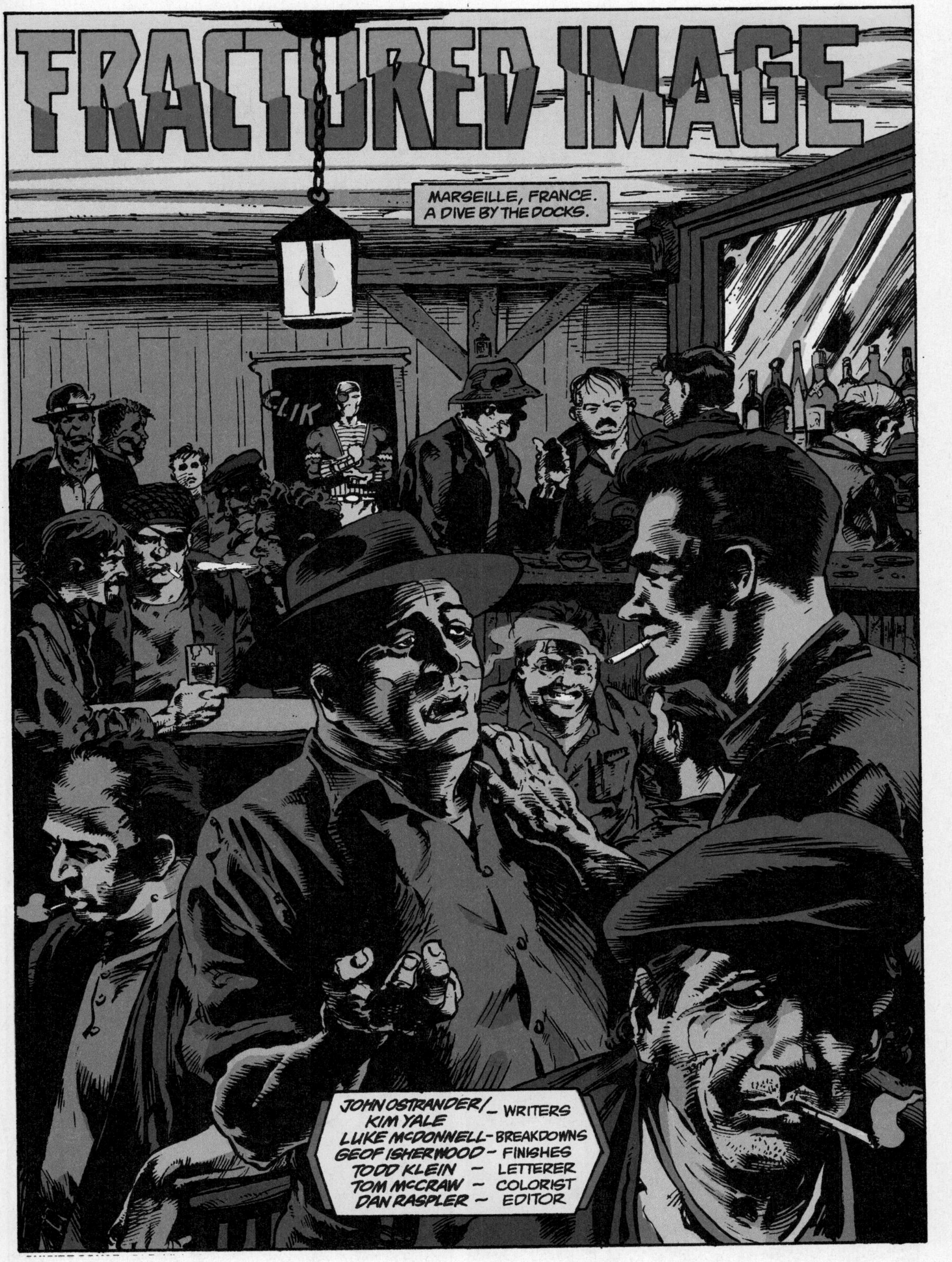
FRACTURED IMAGE
MARSEILLE, FRANCE. A DIVE BY THE DOCKS.
CLIK
JOHN OSTRANDER/ KIM YALE - WRITERS
LUKE McDONNELL - BREAKDOWNS
GEOF ISHERWOOD - FINISHES
TODD KLEIN - LETTERER
TOM McCRAW - COLORIST
DAN RASPLER - EDITOR

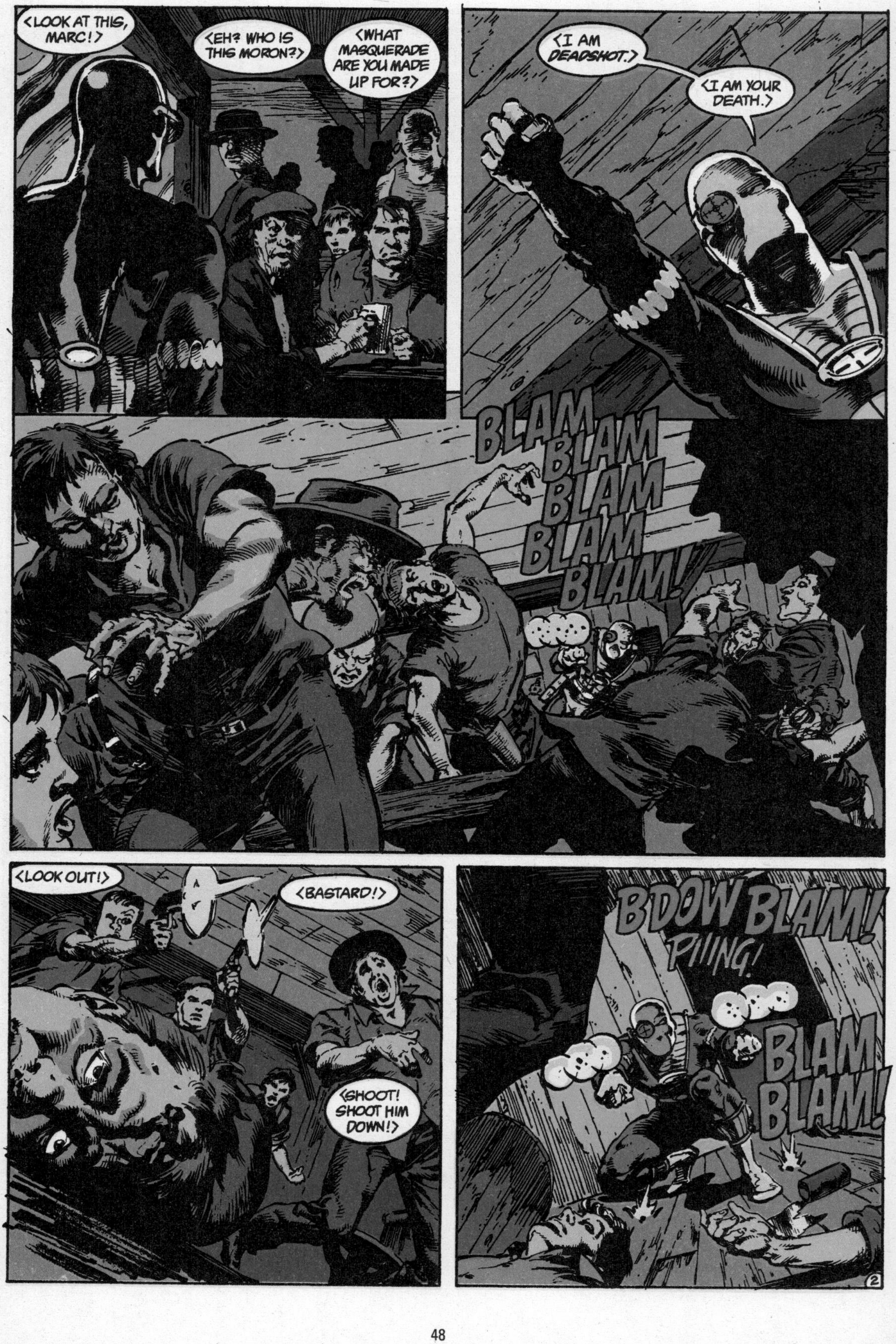
<LOOK AT THIS, MARC!>
<EH? WHO IS THIS MORON?>
<WHAT MASQUERADE ARE YOU MADE UP FOR?>
<I AM DEADSHOT.>
<I AM YOUR DEATH.>
BLAM BLAM BLAM BLAM BLAM!
<LOOK OUT!>
<BASTARD!>
<SHOOT! SHOOT HIM DOWN!>
BDOW BLAM!
PIIING!
BLAM BLAM!
2

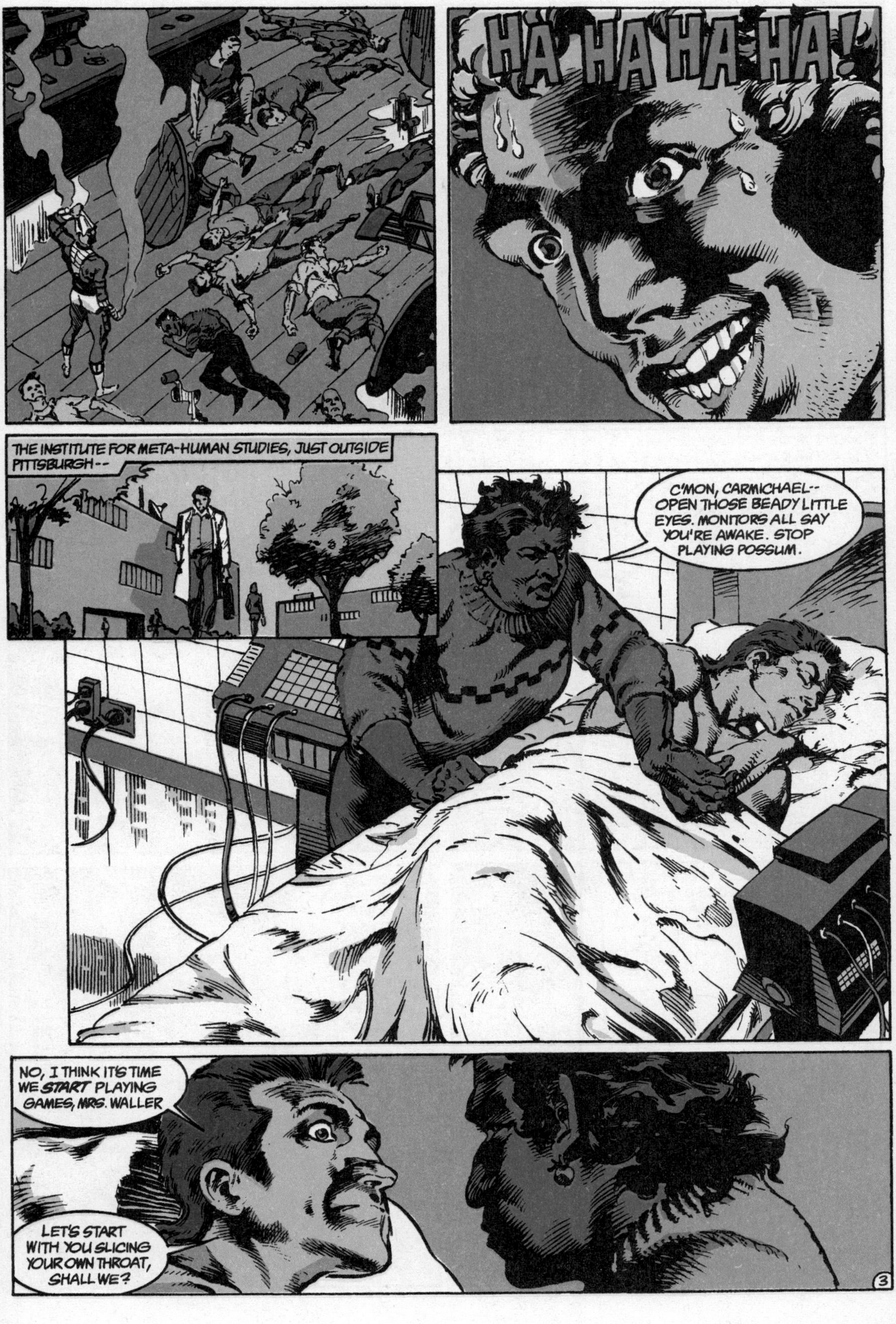
HA HA HA HA!
THE INSTITUTE FOR META-HUMAN STUDIES, JUST OUTSIDE PITTSBURGH--
C'MON, CARMICHAEL-- OPEN THOSE BEADY LITTLE EYES. MONITORS ALL SAY YOU'RE AWAKE. STOP PLAYING POSSUM.
NO, I THINK IT'S TIME WE *START* PLAYING GAMES, MRS. WALLER
LET'S START WITH YOU SLICING YOUR OWN THROAT, SHALL WE?
3

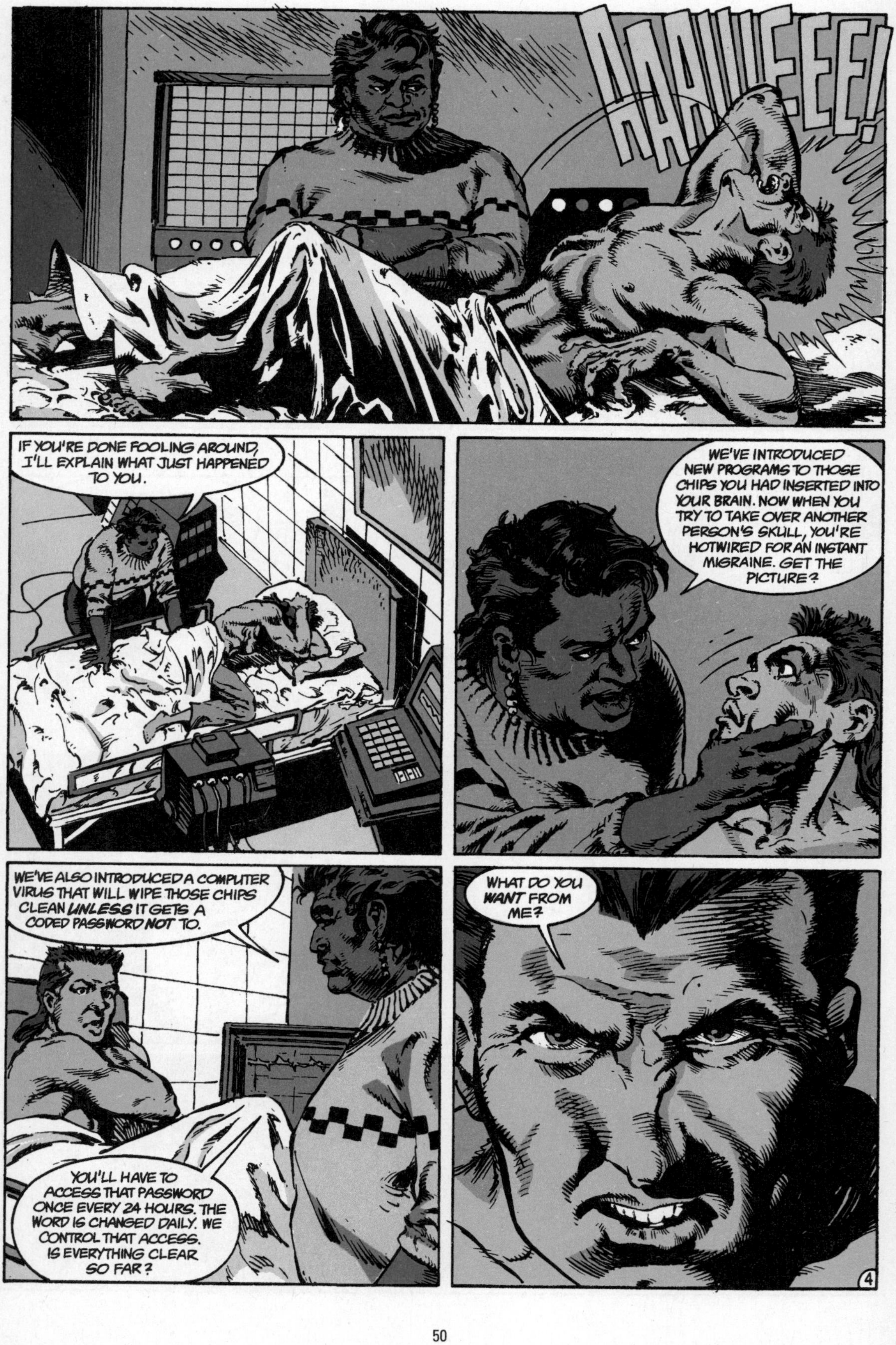
AAAIIIEEE!
IF YOU'RE DONE FOOLING AROUND, I'LL EXPLAIN WHAT JUST HAPPENED TO YOU.
WE'VE INTRODUCED NEW PROGRAMS TO THOSE CHIPS YOU HAD INSERTED INTO YOUR BRAIN. NOW WHEN YOU TRY TO TAKE OVER ANOTHER PERSON'S SKULL, YOU'RE HOTWIRED FOR AN INSTANT MIGRAINE. GET THE PICTURE?
WE'VE ALSO INTRODUCED A COMPUTER VIRUS THAT WILL WIPE THOSE CHIPS CLEAN UNLESS IT GETS A CODED PASSWORD NOT TO.
YOU'LL HAVE TO ACCESS THAT PASSWORD ONCE EVERY 24 HOURS. THE WORD IS CHANGED DAILY. WE CONTROL THAT ACCESS. IS EVERYTHING CLEAR SO FAR?
WHAT DO YOU WANT FROM ME?
4

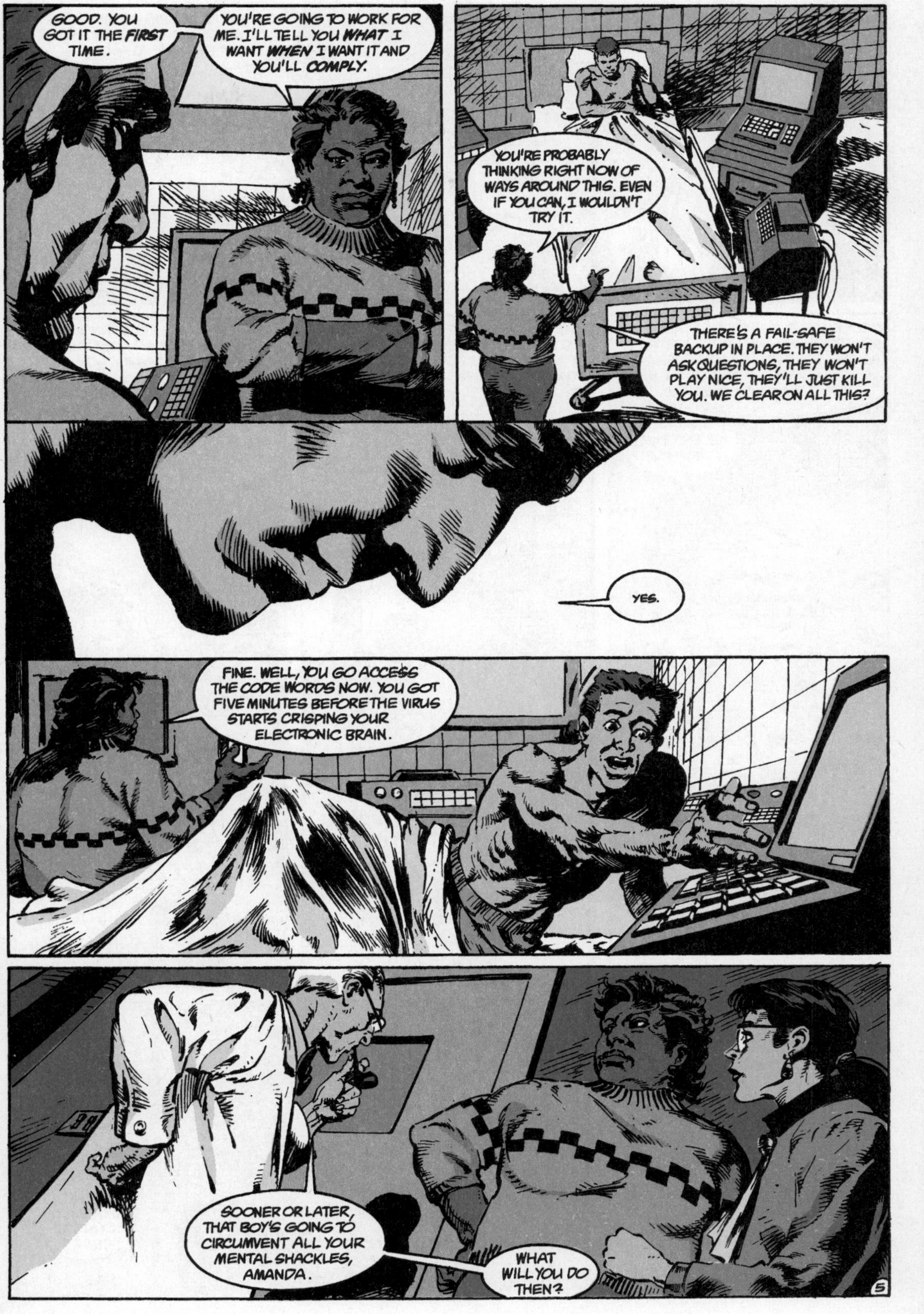
GOOD. YOU GOT IT THE FIRST TIME.
YOU'RE GOING TO WORK FOR ME. I'LL TELL YOU WHAT I WANT WHEN I WANT IT AND YOU'LL COMPLY.
YOU'RE PROBABLY THINKING RIGHT NOW OF WAYS AROUND THIS. EVEN IF YOU CAN, I WOULDN'T TRY IT.
THERE'S A FAIL-SAFE BACKUP IN PLACE. THEY WON'T ASK QUESTIONS, THEY WON'T PLAY NICE, THEY'LL JUST KILL YOU. WE CLEAR ON ALL THIS?
YES.
FINE. WELL, YOU GO ACCESS THE CODE WORDS NOW. YOU GOT FIVE MINUTES BEFORE THE VIRUS STARTS CRISPING YOUR ELECTRONIC BRAIN.
SOONER OR LATER, THAT BOY'S GOING TO CIRCUMVENT ALL YOUR MENTAL SHACKLES, AMANDA.
WHAT WILL YOU DO THEN?
5

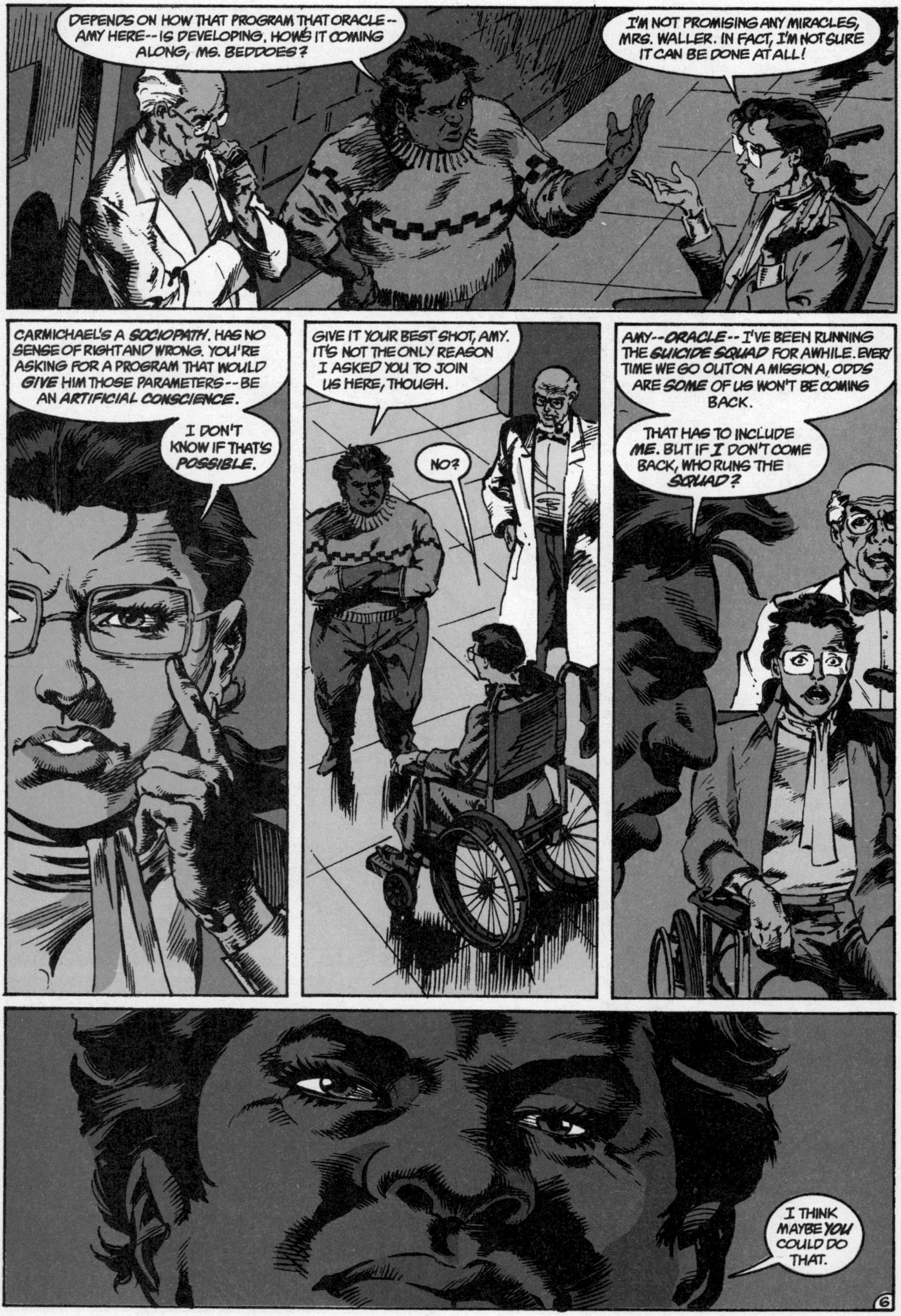
DEPENDS ON HOW THAT PROGRAM THAT ORACLE-- AMY HERE--IS DEVELOPING. HOW'S IT COMING ALONG, MS. BEDDOES?
I'M NOT PROMISING ANY MIRACLES, MRS. WALLER. IN FACT, I'M NOT SURE IT CAN BE DONE AT ALL!
CARMICHAEL'S A SOCIOPATH. HAS NO SENSE OF RIGHT AND WRONG. YOU'RE ASKING FOR A PROGRAM THAT WOULD GIVE HIM THOSE PARAMETERS--BE AN ARTIFICIAL CONSCIENCE.
I DON'T KNOW IF THAT'S POSSIBLE.
GIVE IT YOUR BEST SHOT, AMY. IT'S NOT THE ONLY REASON I ASKED YOU TO JOIN US HERE, THOUGH.
NO?
AMY--ORACLE--I'VE BEEN RUNNING THE SUICIDE SQUAD FOR AWHILE. EVERY TIME WE GO OUT ON A MISSION, ODDS ARE SOME OF US WON'T BE COMING BACK.
THAT HAS TO INCLUDE ME. BUT IF I DON'T COME BACK, WHO RUNS THE SQUAD?
I THINK MAYBE YOU COULD DO THAT.
6

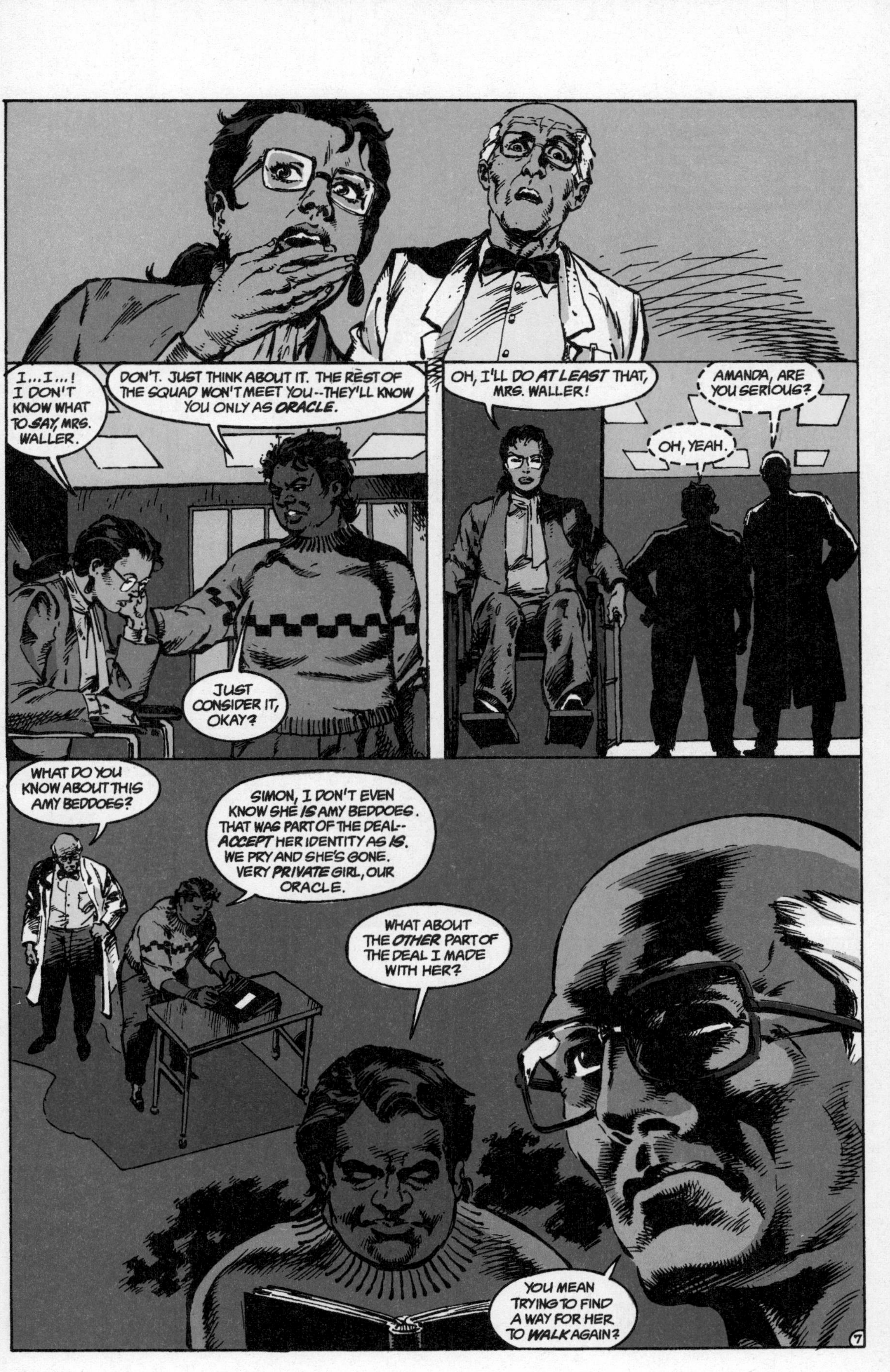
I...I...! I DON'T KNOW WHAT TO SAY, MRS. WALLER.
DON'T. JUST THINK ABOUT IT. THE REST OF THE SQUAD WON'T MEET YOU--THEY'LL KNOW YOU ONLY AS ORACLE.
JUST CONSIDER IT, OKAY?
OH, I'LL DO AT LEAST THAT, MRS. WALLER!
AMANDA, ARE YOU SERIOUS?
OH, YEAH.
WHAT DO YOU KNOW ABOUT THIS AMY BEDDOES?
SIMON, I DON'T EVEN KNOW SHE IS AMY BEDDOES. THAT WAS PART OF THE DEAL-- ACCEPT HER IDENTITY AS IS. WE PRY AND SHE'S GONE. VERY PRIVATE GIRL, OUR ORACLE.
WHAT ABOUT THE OTHER PART OF THE DEAL I MADE WITH HER?
YOU MEAN TRYING TO FIND A WAY FOR HER TO WALK AGAIN?
7

I'M *NOT* VERY OPTIMISTIC. THE TECHNOLOGY THAT LET *RAVAN* WALK IN SPITE OF A BROKEN BACK *WON'T* WORK WITH HER. PART OF HER SPINE IS ACTUALLY *MISSING* AND THERE'S BEEN EXTENSIVE *NEUROLOGICAL* DAMAGE.

DO WHAT YOU CAN. WHAT'S THE PROGRESS ON MARI AND COUNT VERTIGO?

"VIXEN IS IMPROVING. WHAT SHE NEEDS NOW MOSTLY IS SLEEP."

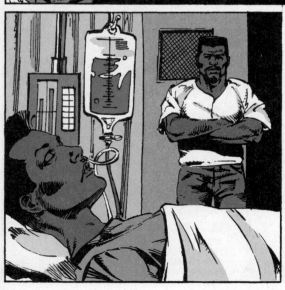

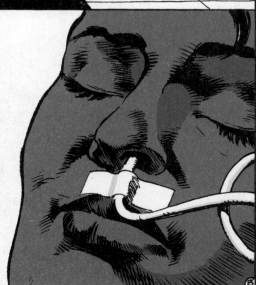

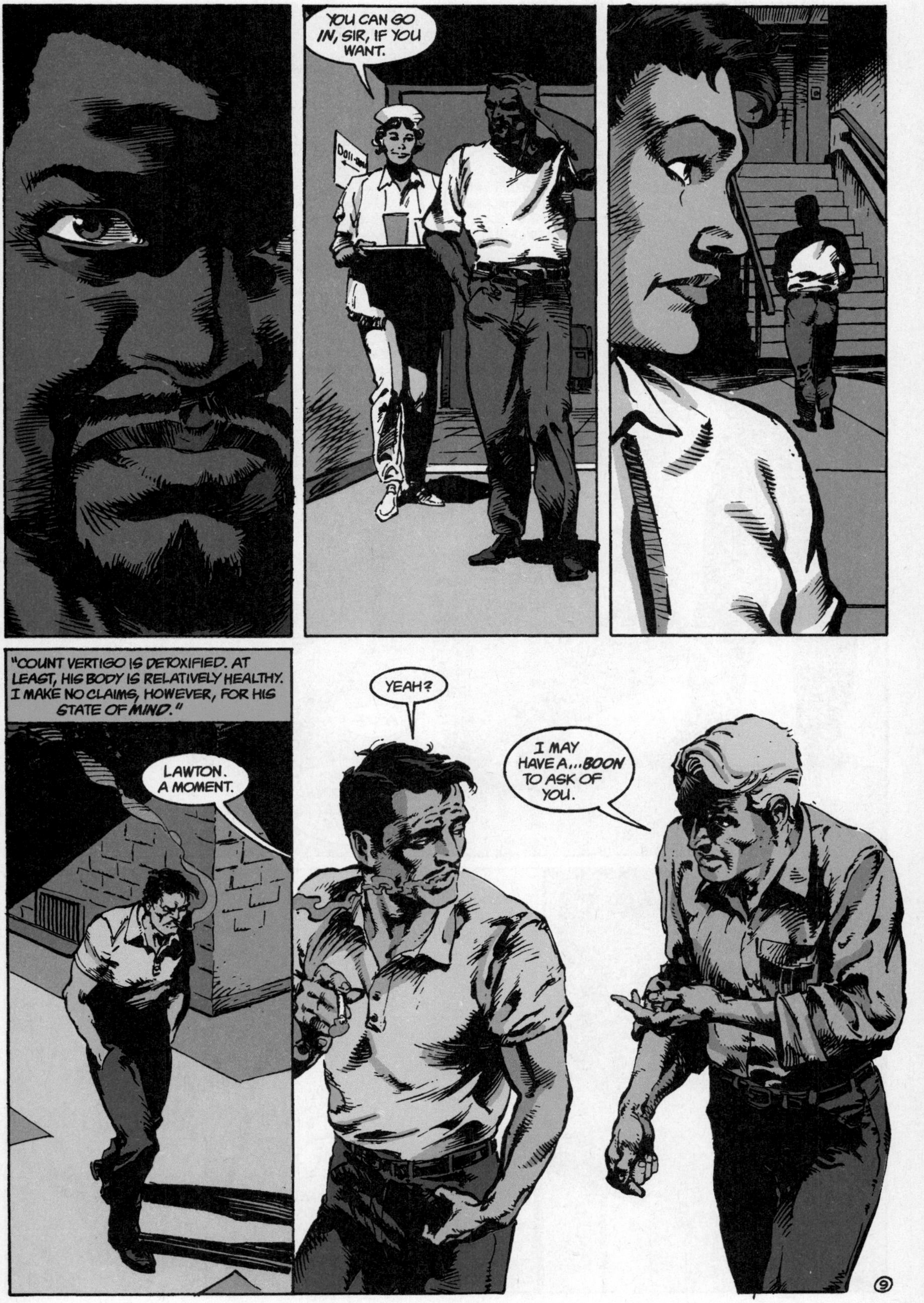
YOU CAN GO IN, SIR, IF YOU WANT.
"COUNT VERTIGO IS DETOXIFIED. AT LEAST, HIS BODY IS RELATIVELY HEALTHY. I MAKE NO CLAIMS, HOWEVER, FOR HIS STATE OF MIND."
LAWTON. A MOMENT.
YEAH?
I MAY HAVE A...BOON TO ASK OF YOU.
9

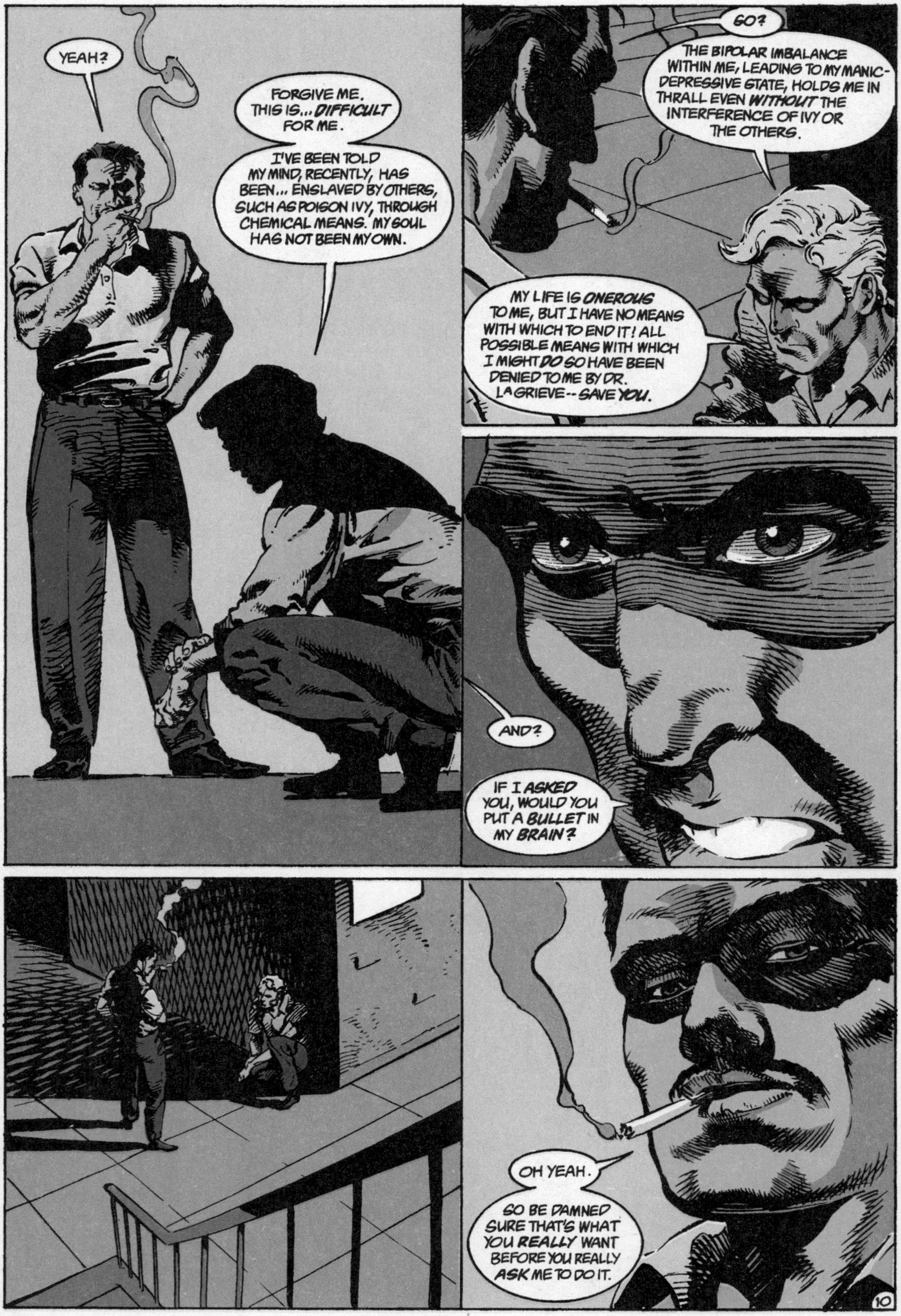
YEAH?
FORGIVE ME. THIS IS... DIFFICULT FOR ME.
I'VE BEEN TOLD MY MIND, RECENTLY, HAS BEEN... ENSLAVED BY OTHERS, SUCH AS POISON IVY, THROUGH CHEMICAL MEANS. MY SOUL HAS NOT BEEN MY OWN.
SO?
THE BIPOLAR IMBALANCE WITHIN ME, LEADING TO MY MANIC-DEPRESSIVE STATE, HOLDS ME IN THRALL EVEN WITHOUT THE INTERFERENCE OF IVY OR THE OTHERS.
MY LIFE IS ONEROUS TO ME, BUT I HAVE NO MEANS WITH WHICH TO END IT! ALL POSSIBLE MEANS WITH WHICH I MIGHT DO SO HAVE BEEN DENIED TO ME BY DR. LaGRIEVE-- SAVE YOU.
AND?
IF I ASKED YOU, WOULD YOU PUT A BULLET IN MY BRAIN?
OH YEAH.
SO BE DAMNED SURE THAT'S WHAT YOU REALLY WANT BEFORE YOU REALLY ASK ME TO DO IT.
10

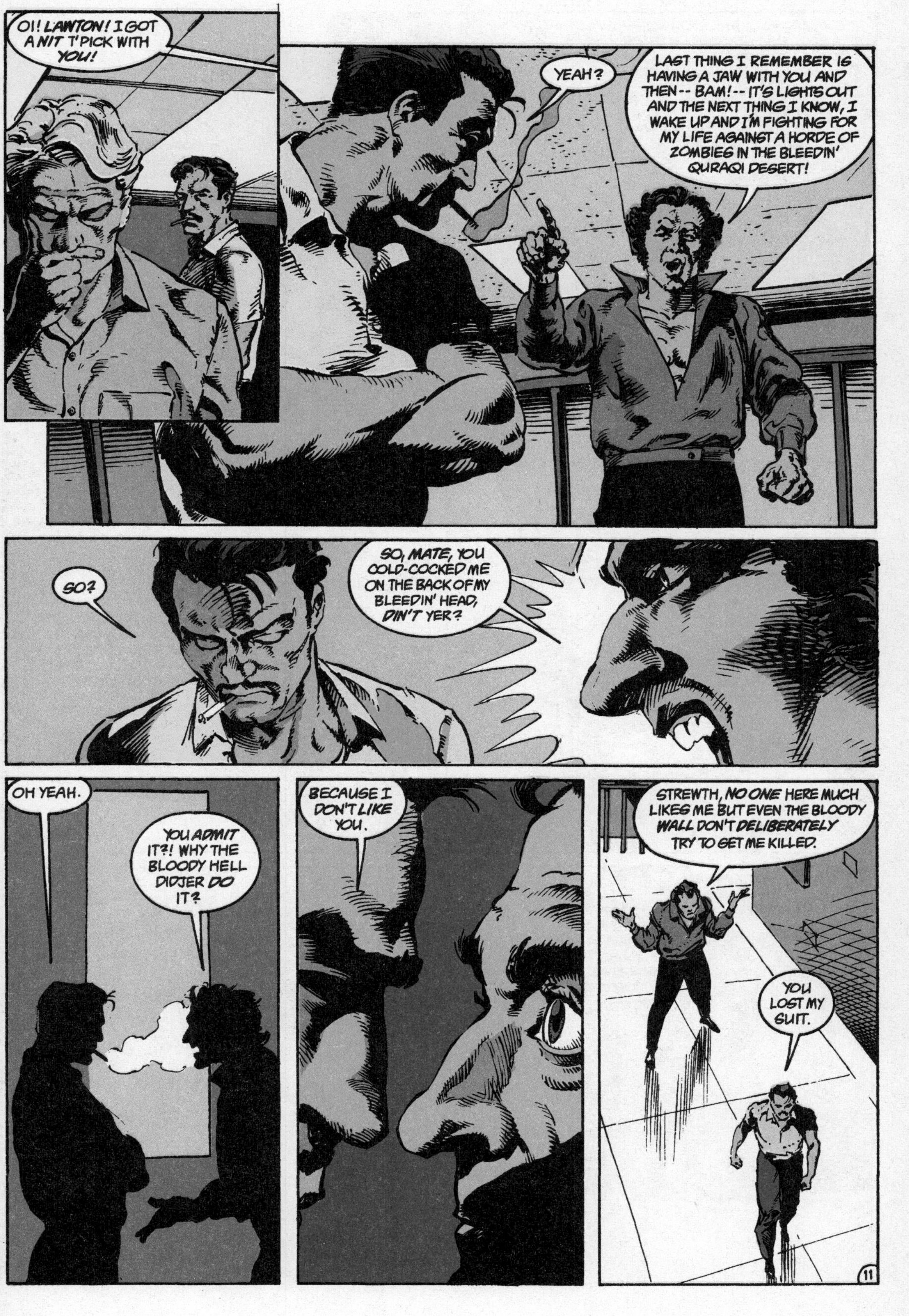
OI! LAWTON! I GOT A NIT T'PICK WITH YOU!
YEAH?
LAST THING I REMEMBER IS HAVING A JAW WITH YOU AND THEN -- BAM! -- IT'S LIGHTS OUT AND THE NEXT THING I KNOW, I WAKE UP AND I'M FIGHTING FOR MY LIFE AGAINST A HORDE OF ZOMBIES IN THE BLEEDIN' QURAQI DESERT!
SO?
SO, MATE, YOU COLD-COCKED ME ON THE BACK OF MY BLEEDIN' HEAD, DIN'T YER?
OH YEAH.
YOU ADMIT IT?! WHY THE BLOODY HELL DIDJER DO IT?
BECAUSE I DON'T LIKE YOU.
STREWTH, NO ONE HERE MUCH LIKES ME BUT EVEN THE BLOODY WALL DON'T DELIBERATELY TRY TO GET ME KILLED.
YOU LOST MY SUIT.
11

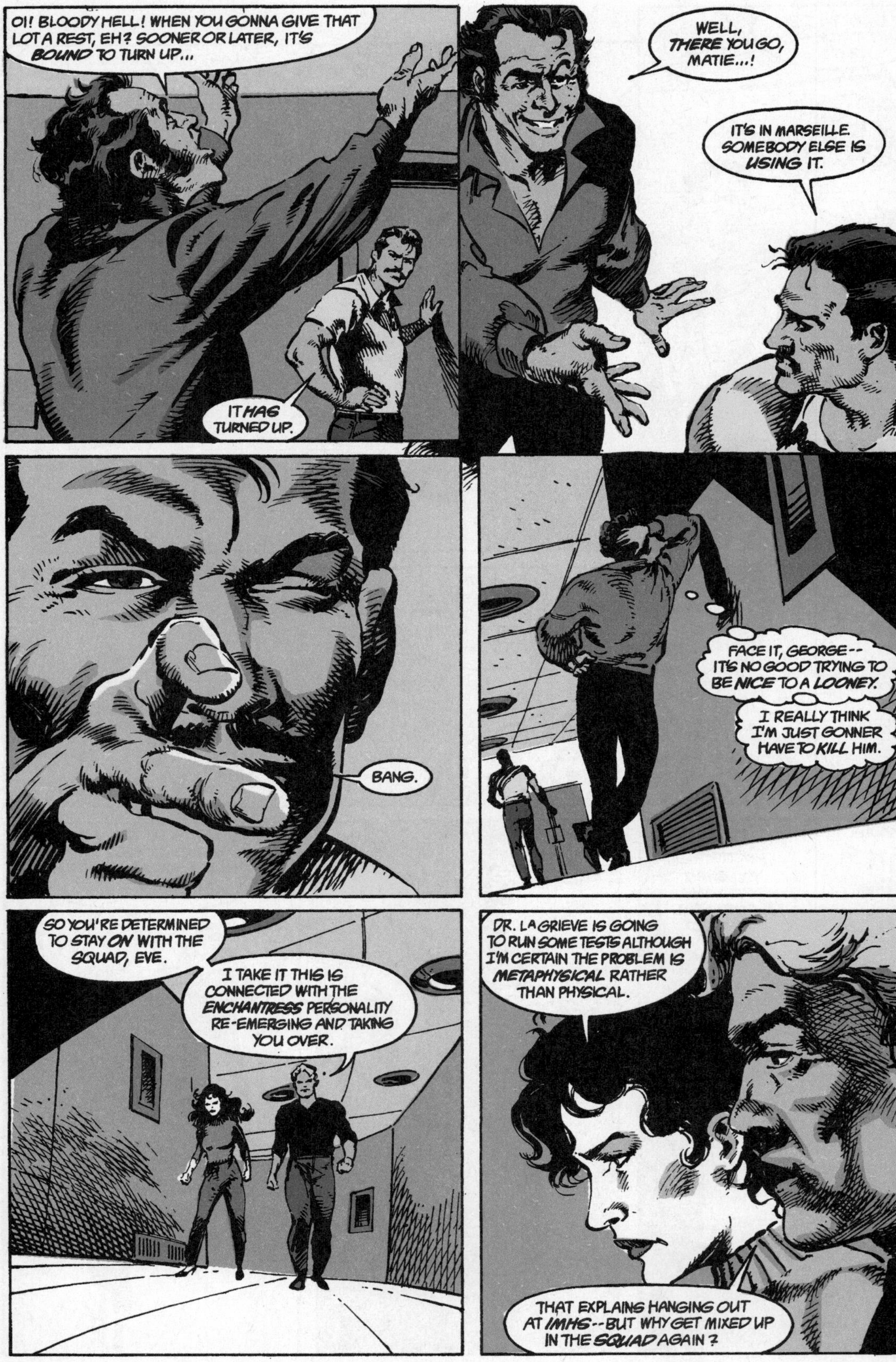
OI! BLOODY HELL! WHEN YOU GONNA GIVE THAT LOT A REST, EH? SOONER OR LATER, IT'S BOUND TO TURN UP...
IT HAS TURNED UP.
WELL, THERE YOU GO, MATIE...!
IT'S IN MARSEILLE. SOMEBODY ELSE IS USING IT.
BANG.
FACE IT, GEORGE-- IT'S NO GOOD TRYING TO BE NICE TO A LOONEY.
I REALLY THINK I'M JUST GONNER HAVE TO KILL HIM.
SO YOU'RE DETERMINED TO STAY ON WITH THE SQUAD, EVE.
I TAKE IT THIS IS CONNECTED WITH THE ENCHANTRESS PERSONALITY RE-EMERGING AND TAKING YOU OVER.
DR. LaGRIEVE IS GOING TO RUN SOME TESTS ALTHOUGH I'M CERTAIN THE PROBLEM IS METAPHYSICAL RATHER THAN PHYSICAL.
THAT EXPLAINS HANGING OUT AT IMHS--BUT WHY GET MIXED UP IN THE SQUAD AGAIN?
12

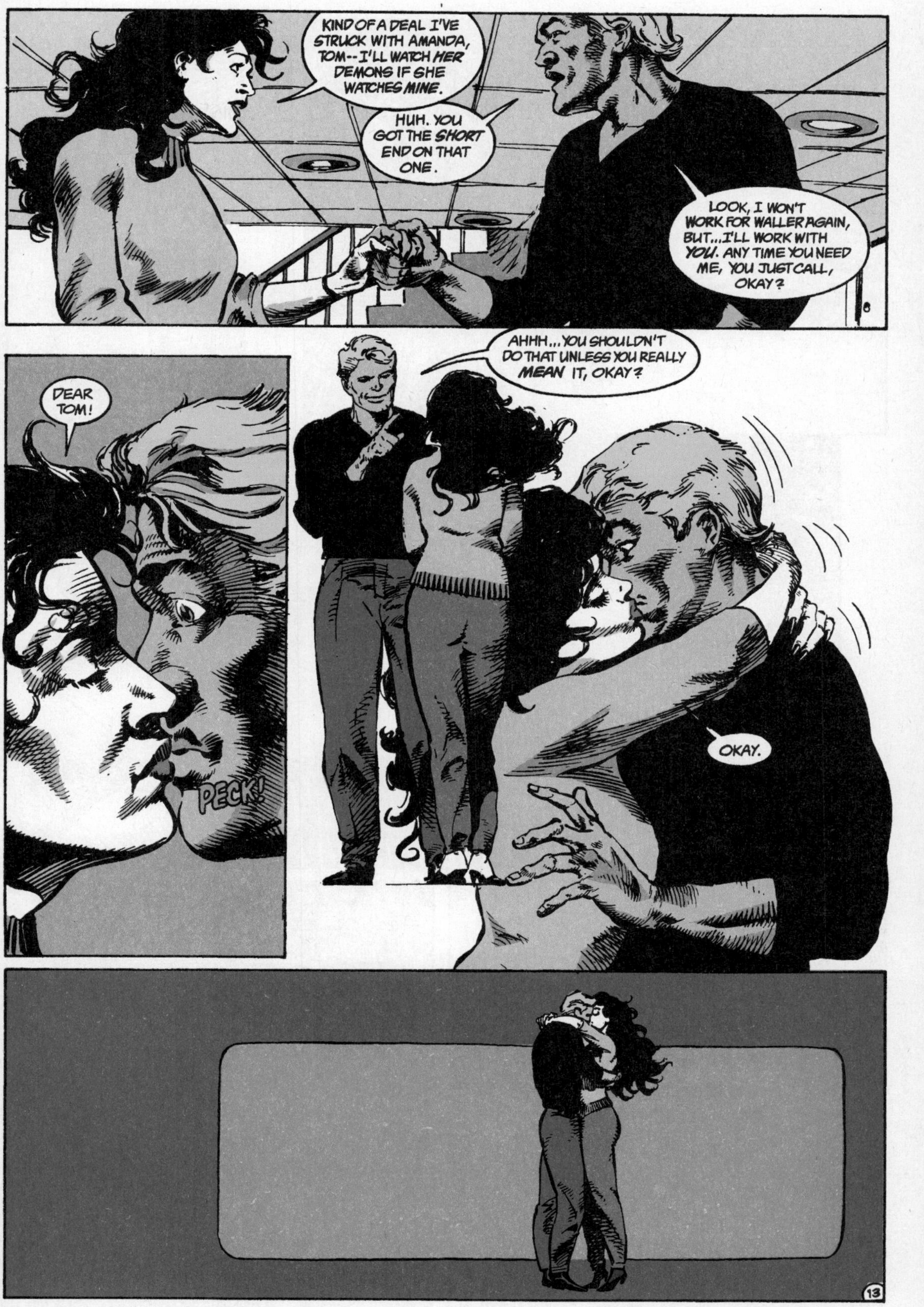
KIND OF A DEAL I'VE STRUCK WITH AMANDA, TOM--I'LL WATCH HER DEMONS IF SHE WATCHES MINE.
HUH. YOU GOT THE SHORT END ON THAT ONE.
LOOK, I WON'T WORK FOR WALLER AGAIN, BUT...I'LL WORK WITH YOU. ANY TIME YOU NEED ME, YOU JUST CALL, OKAY?
DEAR TOM!
PECK!
AHHH...YOU SHOULDN'T DO THAT UNLESS YOU REALLY MEAN IT, OKAY?
OKAY.
13

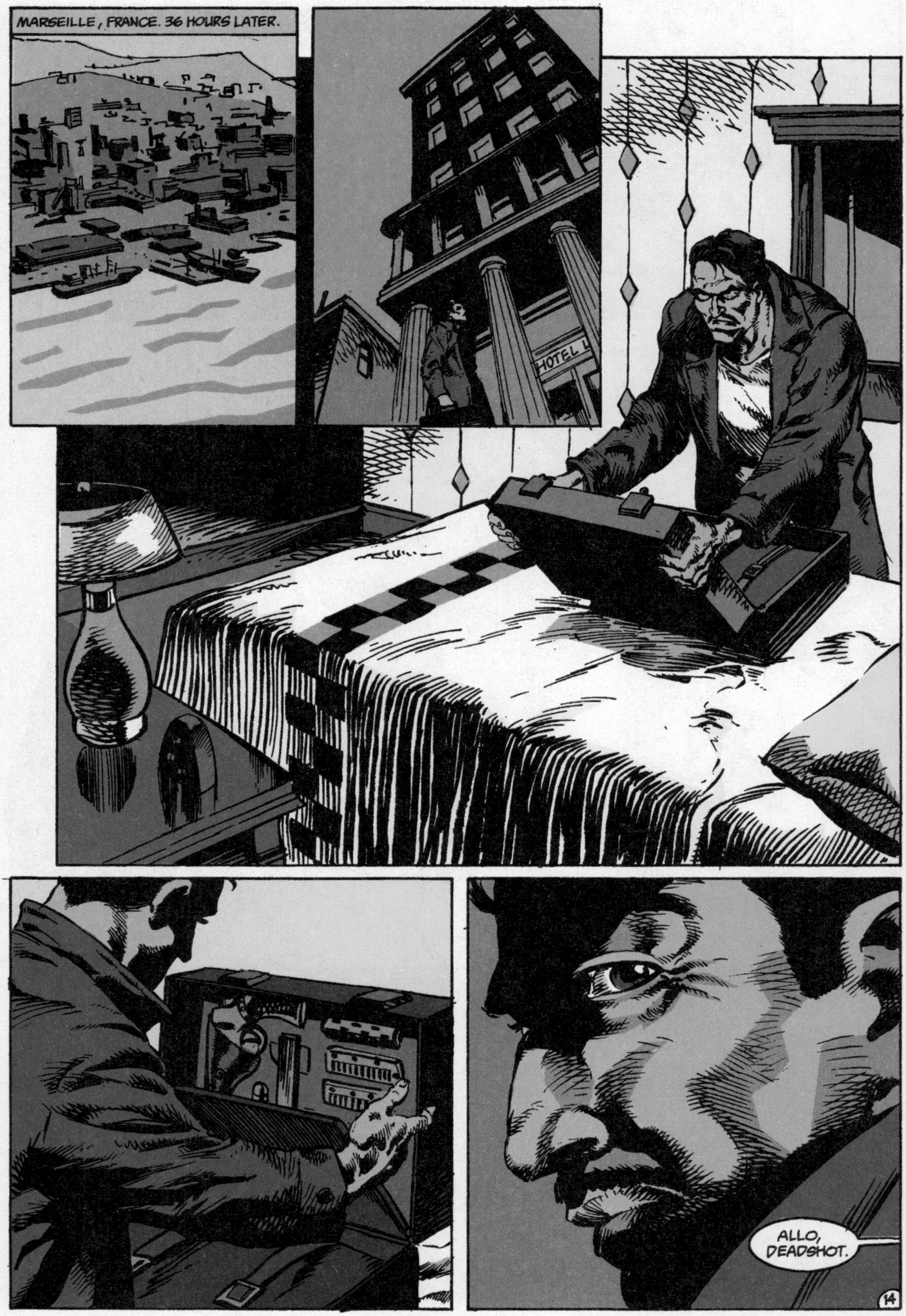
MARSEILLE, FRANCE. 36 HOURS LATER.
HOTEL
ALLO, DEADSHOT.
14

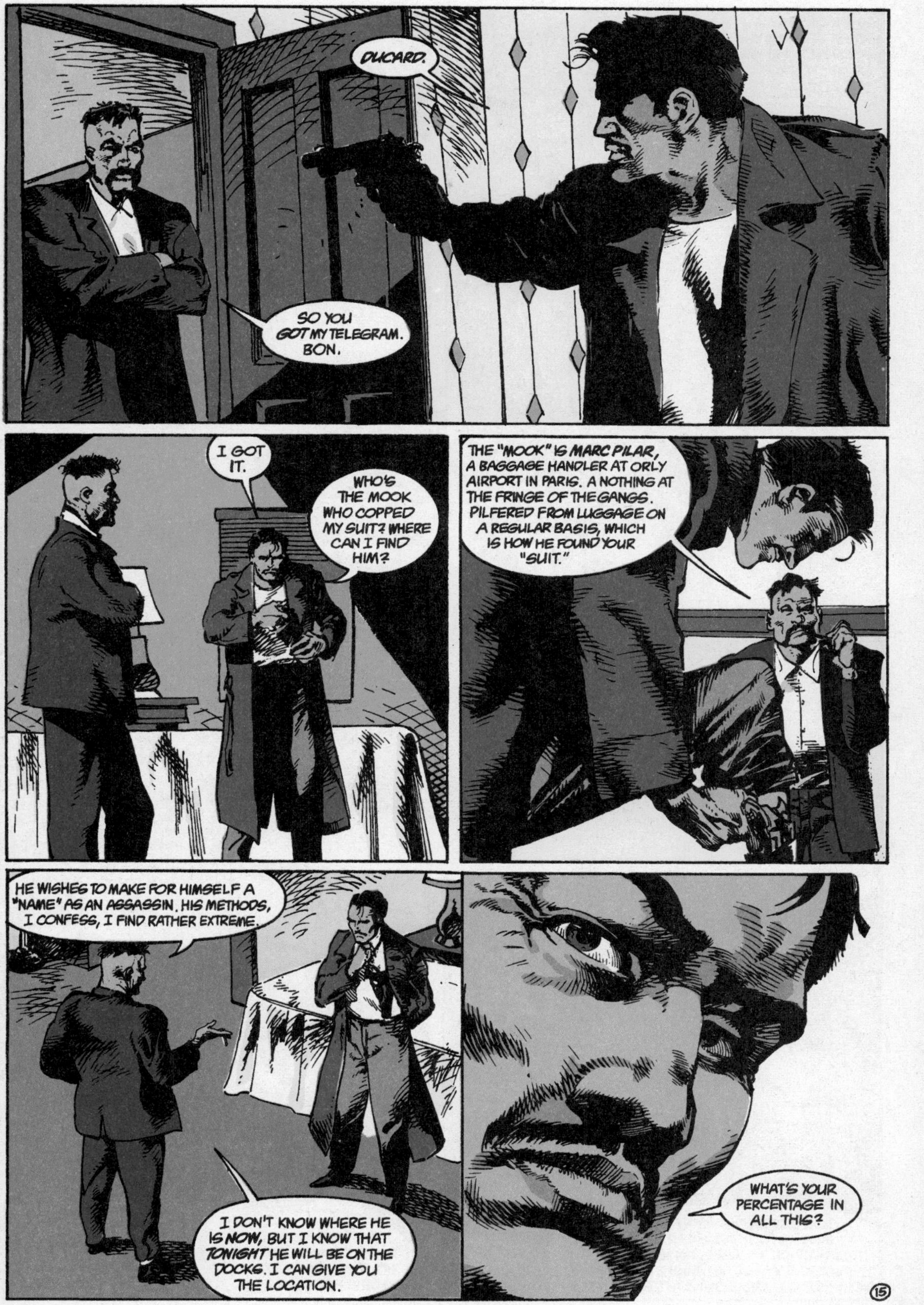
DUCARD.
SO YOU GOT MY TELEGRAM. BON.
I GOT IT.
WHO'S THE MOOK WHO COPPED MY SUIT? WHERE CAN I FIND HIM?
THE "MOOK" IS MARC PILAR, A BAGGAGE HANDLER AT ORLY AIRPORT IN PARIS. A NOTHING AT THE FRINGE OF THE GANGS. PILFERED FROM LUGGAGE ON A REGULAR BASIS, WHICH IS HOW HE FOUND YOUR "SUIT."
HE WISHES TO MAKE FOR HIMSELF A "NAME" AS AN ASSASSIN. HIS METHODS, I CONFESS, I FIND RATHER EXTREME.
I DON'T KNOW WHERE HE IS NOW, BUT I KNOW THAT TONIGHT HE WILL BE ON THE DOCKS. I CAN GIVE YOU THE LOCATION.
WHAT'S YOUR PERCENTAGE IN ALL THIS?
15

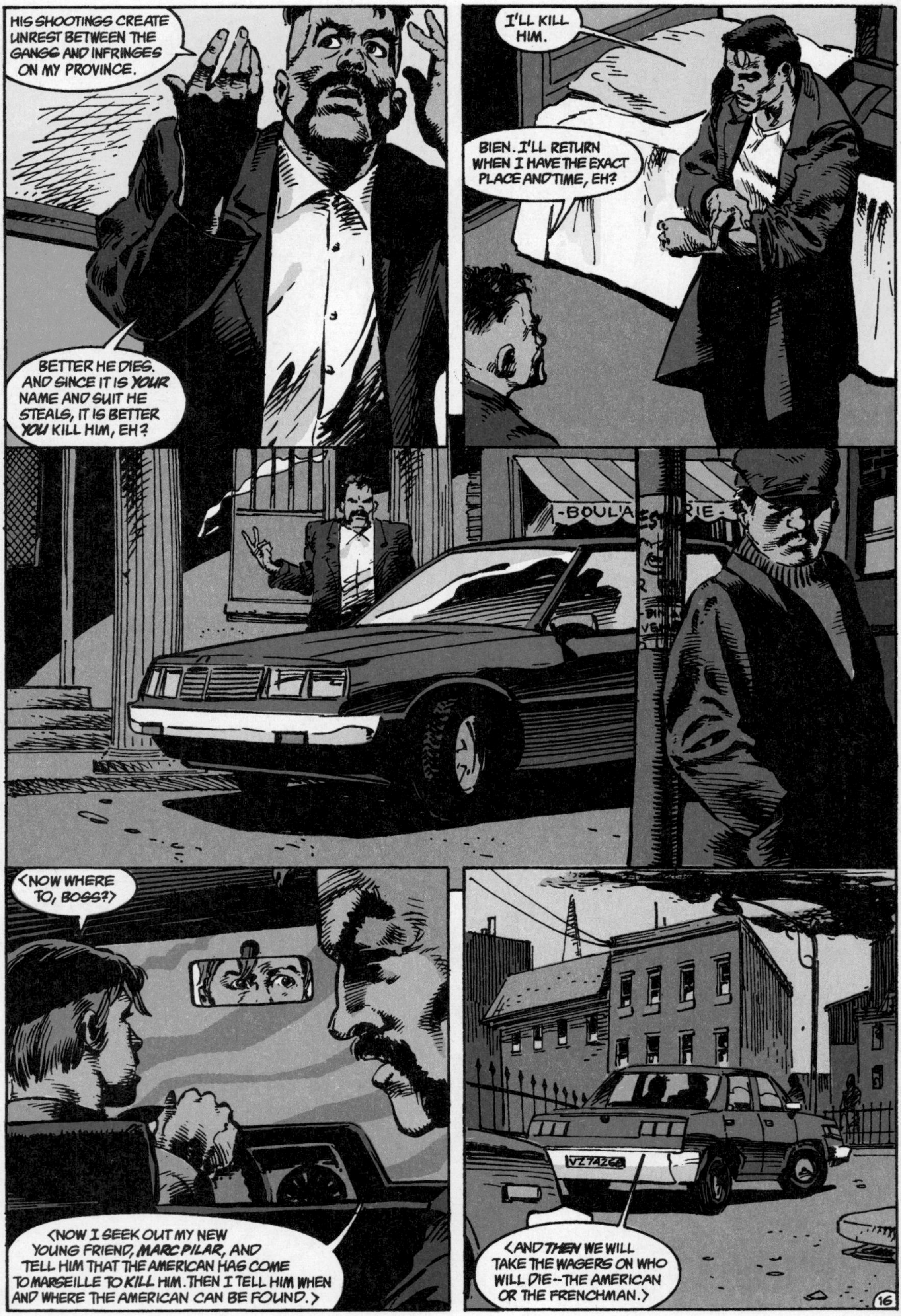
HIS SHOOTINGS CREATE UNREST BETWEEN THE GANGS AND INFRINGES ON MY PROVINCE.
BETTER HE DIES. AND SINCE IT IS YOUR NAME AND SUIT HE STEALS, IT IS BETTER YOU KILL HIM, EH?
I'LL KILL HIM.
BIEN. I'LL RETURN WHEN I HAVE THE EXACT PLACE AND TIME, EH?
-BOUL
<NOW WHERE TO, BOSS?>
<NOW I SEEK OUT MY NEW YOUNG FRIEND, MARC PILAR, AND TELL HIM THAT THE AMERICAN HAS COME TO MARSEILLE TO KILL HIM. THEN I TELL HIM WHEN AND WHERE THE AMERICAN CAN BE FOUND.>
VZ74Z68
<AND THEN WE WILL TAKE THE WAGERS ON WHO WILL DIE--THE AMERICAN OR THE FRENCHMAN.>
16

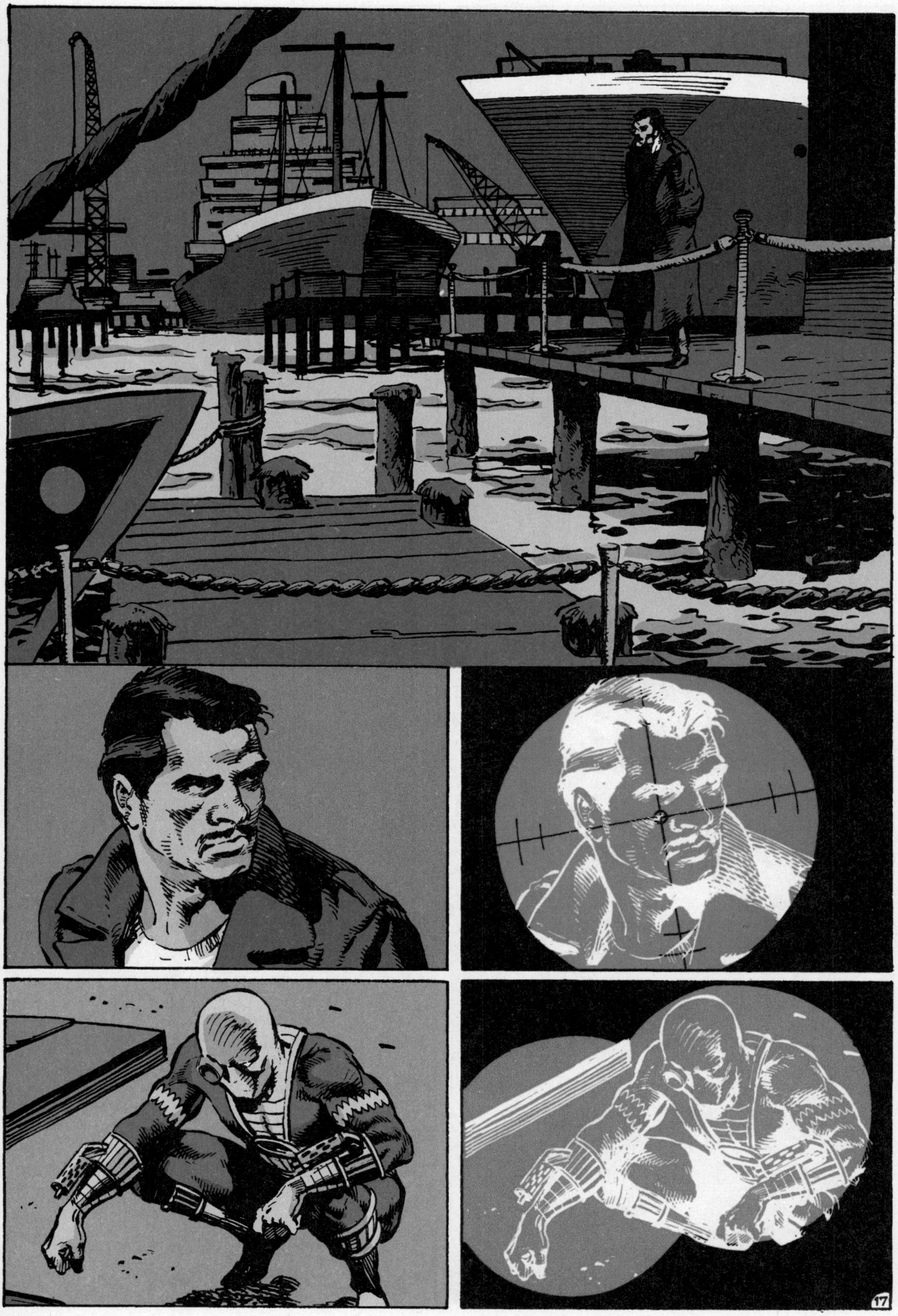
17

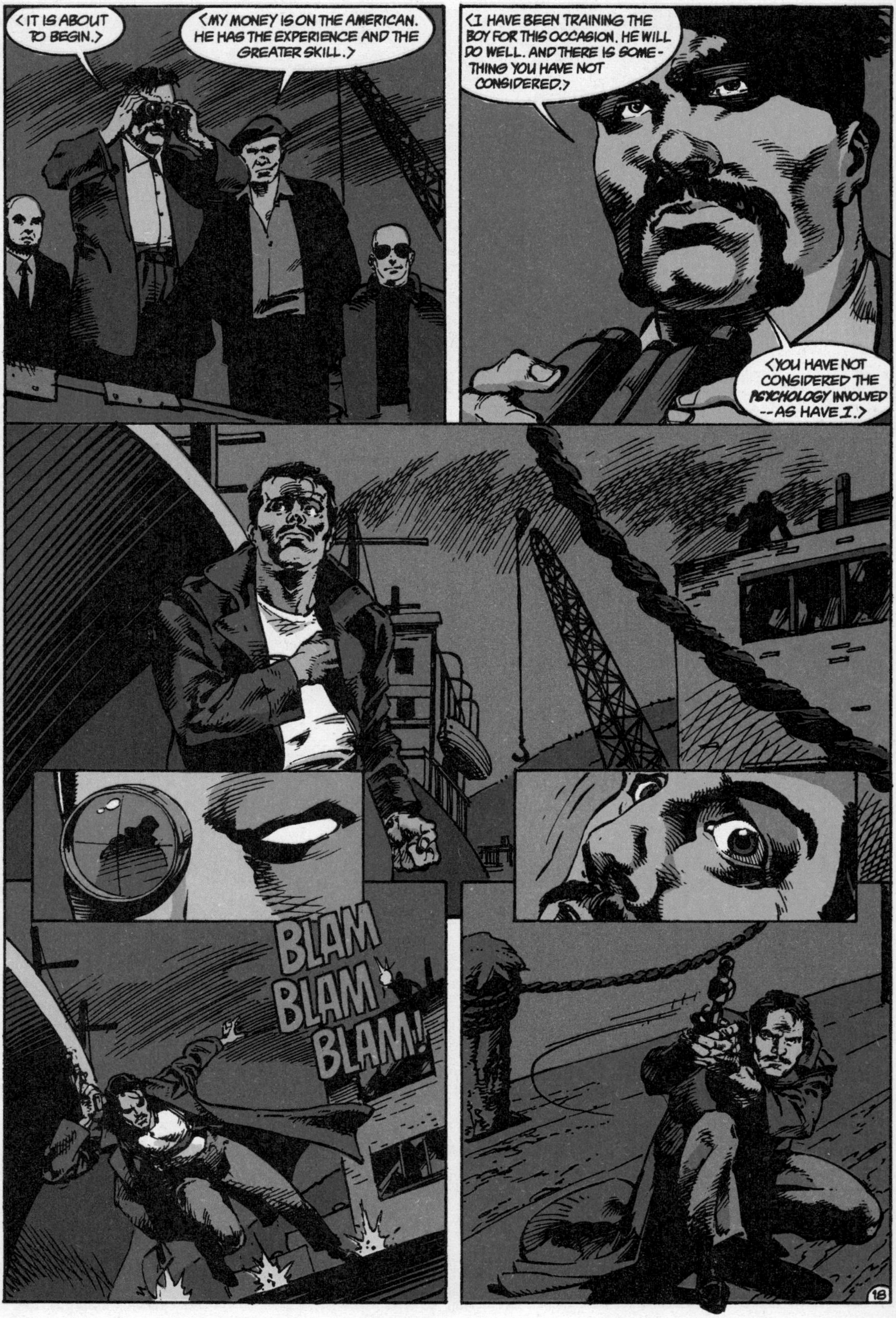
<IT IS ABOUT TO BEGIN.>
<MY MONEY IS ON THE AMERICAN. HE HAS THE EXPERIENCE AND THE GREATER SKILL.>
<I HAVE BEEN TRAINING THE BOY FOR THIS OCCASION. HE WILL DO WELL. AND THERE IS SOME-THING YOU HAVE NOT CONSIDERED.>
<YOU HAVE NOT CONSIDERED THE PSYCHOLOGY INVOLVED --AS HAVE I.>
BLAM
BLAM
BLAM!
18

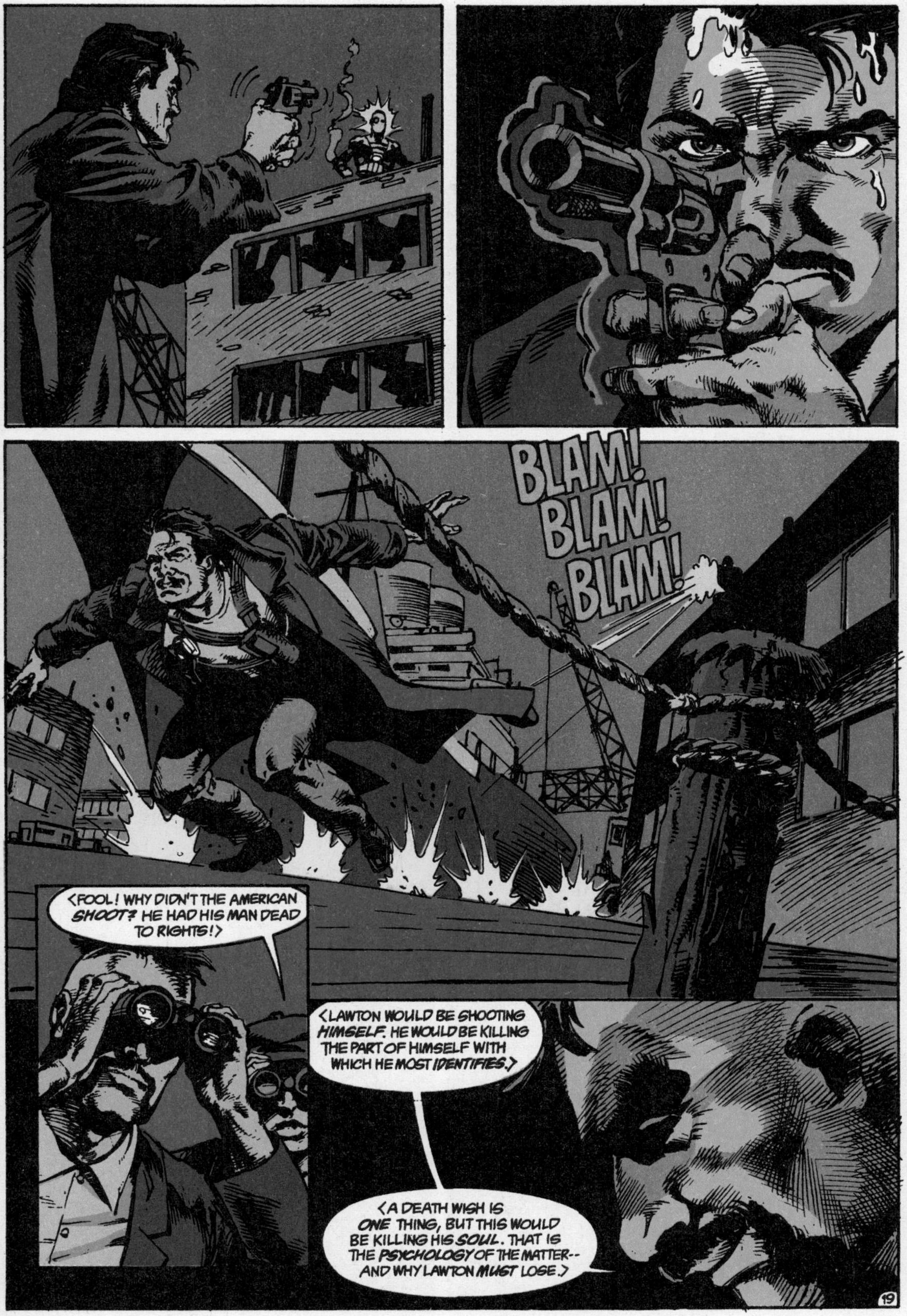
BLAM! BLAM! BLAM!
<FOOL! WHY DIDN'T THE AMERICAN SHOOT? HE HAD HIS MAN DEAD TO RIGHTS!>
<LAWTON WOULD BE SHOOTING HIMSELF. HE WOULD BE KILLING THE PART OF HIMSELF WITH WHICH HE MOST IDENTIFIES.>
<A DEATH WISH IS ONE THING, BUT THIS WOULD BE KILLING HIS SOUL. THAT IS THE PSYCHOLOGY OF THE MATTER-- AND WHY LAWTON MUST LOSE.>
19

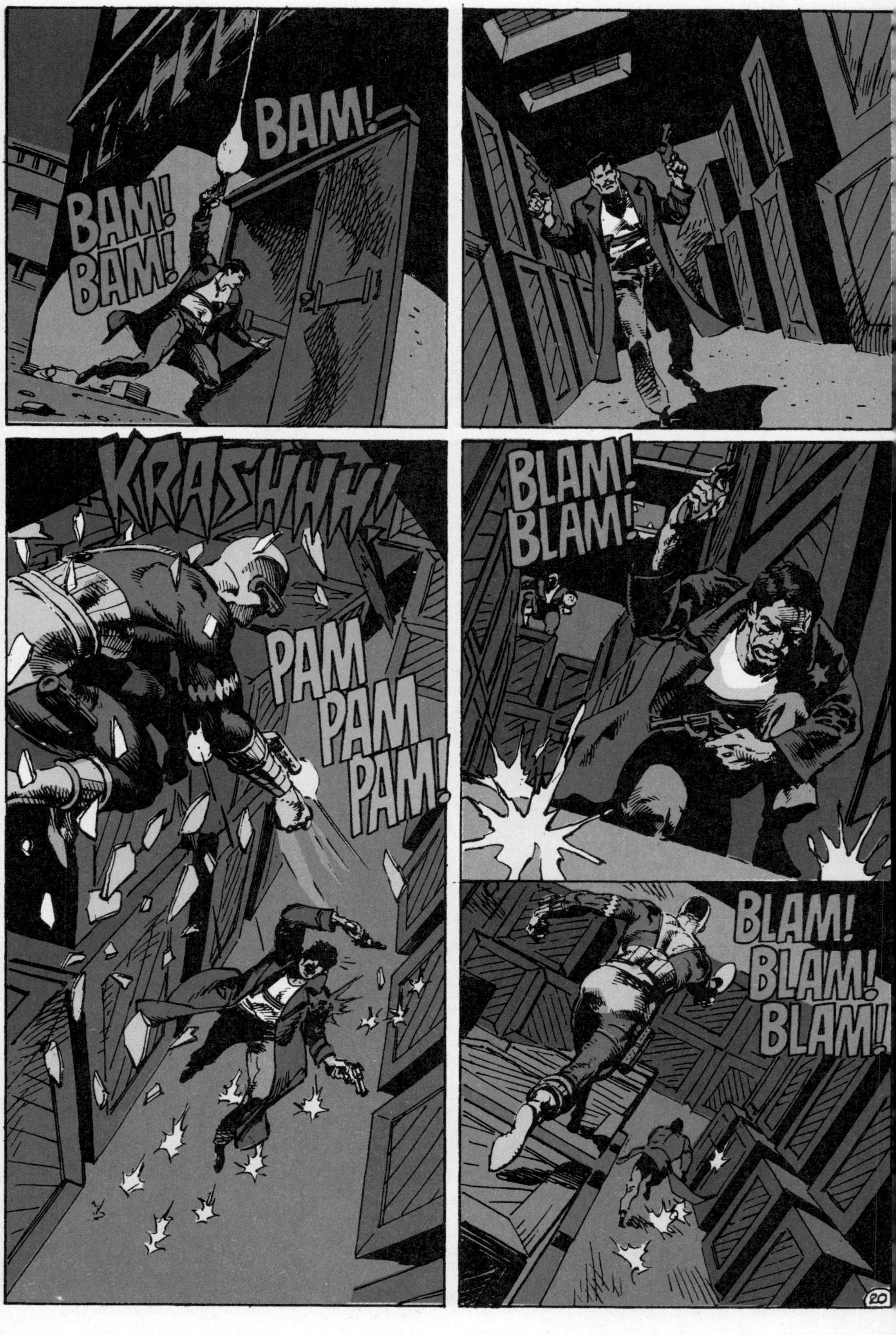
BAM!
BAM!
BAM!
KRASHHH!
PAM
PAM
PAM!
BLAM!
BLAM!
BLAM!
BLAM!
BLAM!
20

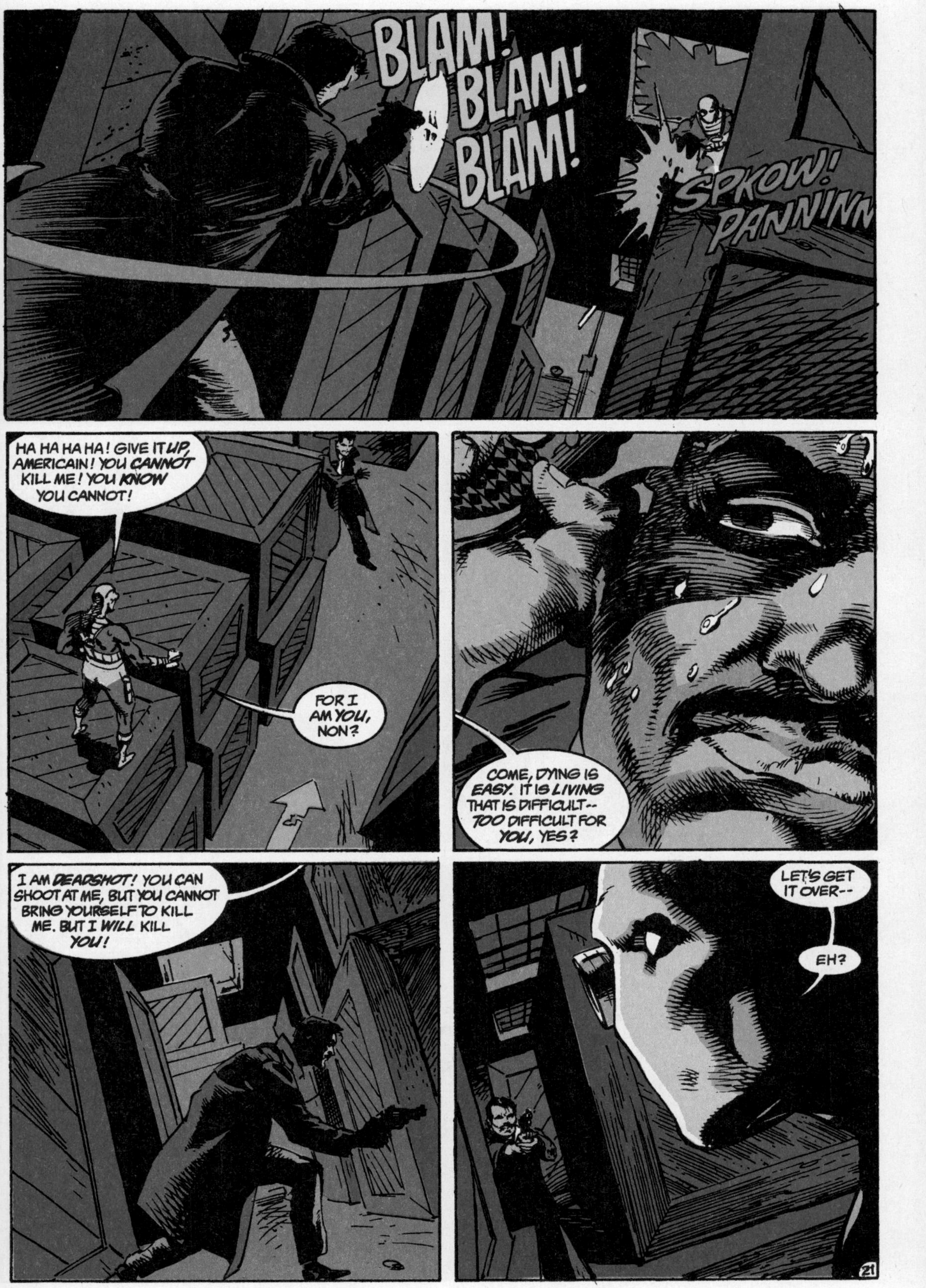

BLAM! BLAM! BLAM!
SPKOW! PANNINN
HA HA HA HA! GIVE IT UP, AMERICAIN! YOU CANNOT KILL ME! YOU KNOW YOU CANNOT!
FOR I AM YOU, NON?
COME, DYING IS EASY. IT IS LIVING THAT IS DIFFICULT-- TOO DIFFICULT FOR YOU, YES?
I AM DEADSHOT! YOU CAN SHOOT AT ME, BUT YOU CANNOT BRING YOURSELF TO KILL ME. BUT I WILL KILL YOU!
LET'S GET IT OVER--
EH?
21

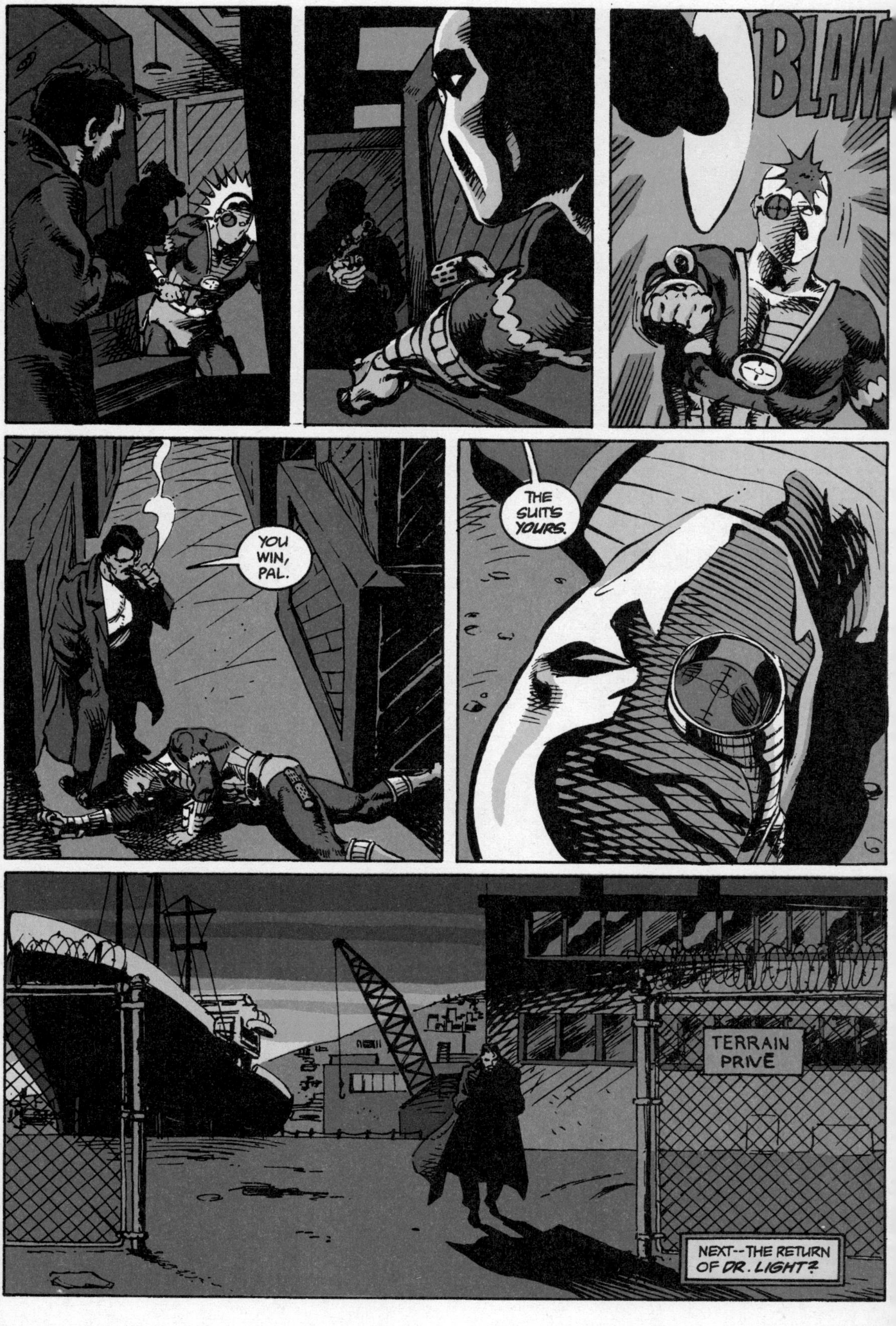
BLAM
YOU WIN, PAL.
THE SUIT'S YOURS.
TERRAIN PRIVÉ
NEXT--THE RETURN OF DR. LIGHT?

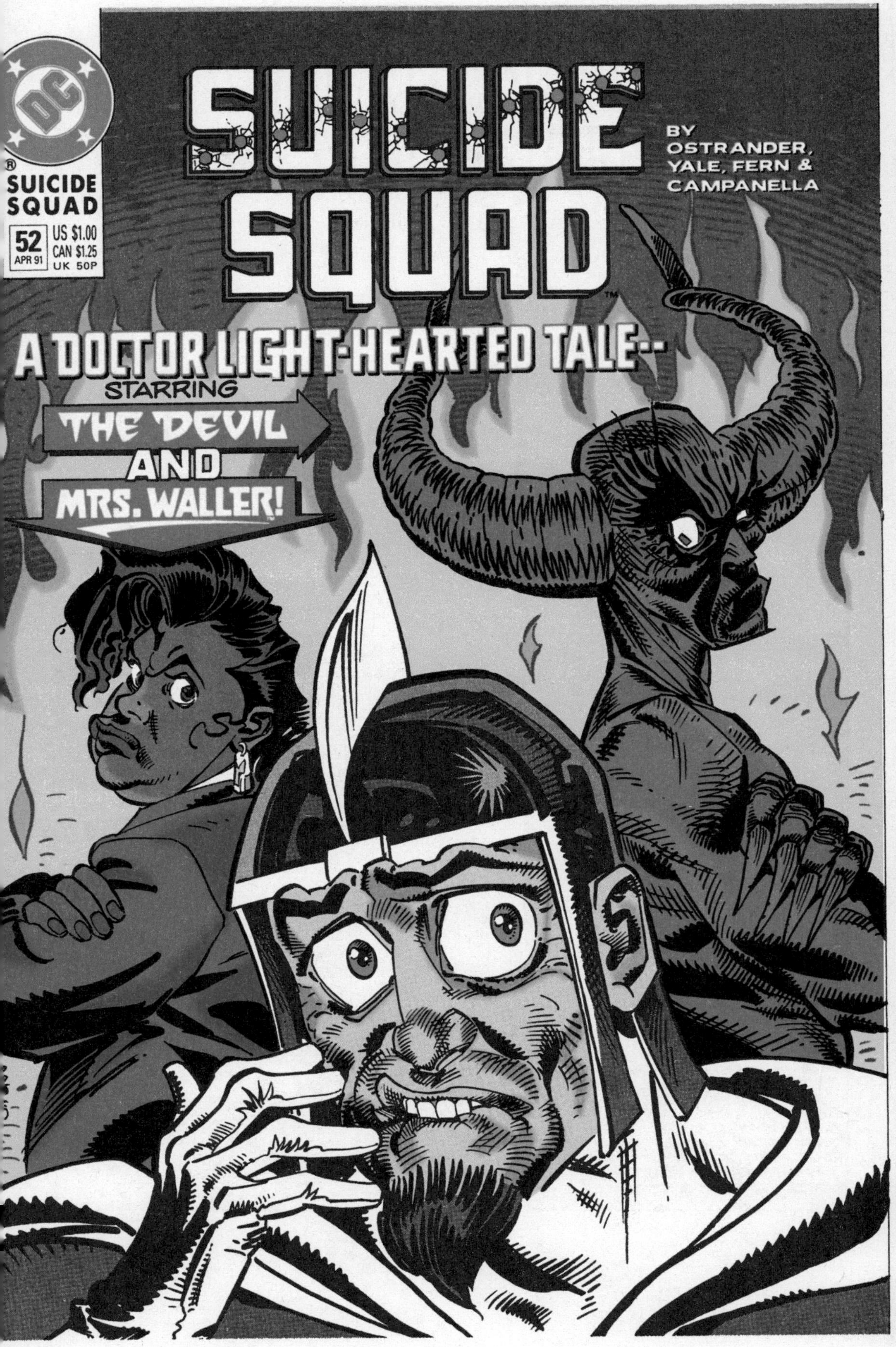

DC
SUICIDE SQUAD
52
APR 91
US $1.00
CAN $1.25
UK 50P
SUICIDE SQUAD
BY OSTRANDER, YALE, FERN & CAMPANELLA
A DOCTOR LIGHT-HEARTED TALE--
STARRING
THE DEVIL
AND
MRS. WALLER!

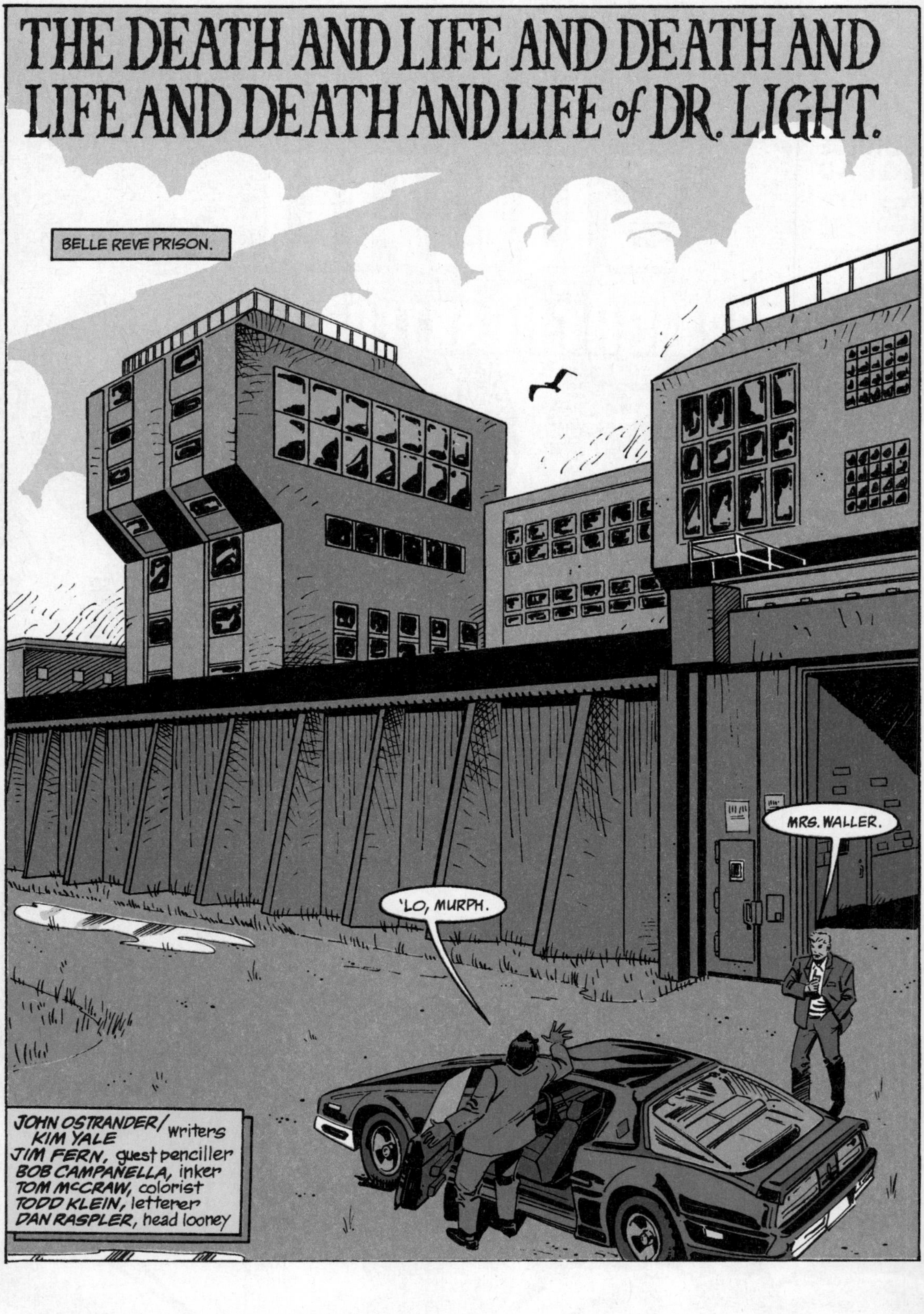
THE DEATH AND LIFE AND DEATH AND LIFE AND DEATH AND LIFE of DR. LIGHT.
BELLE REVE PRISON.
'LO, MURPH.
MRS. WALLER.
JOHN OSTRANDER/ KIM YALE writers
JIM FERN, guest penciller
BOB CAMPANELLA, inker
TOM McCRAW, colorist
TODD KLEIN, letterer
DAN RASPLER, head looney

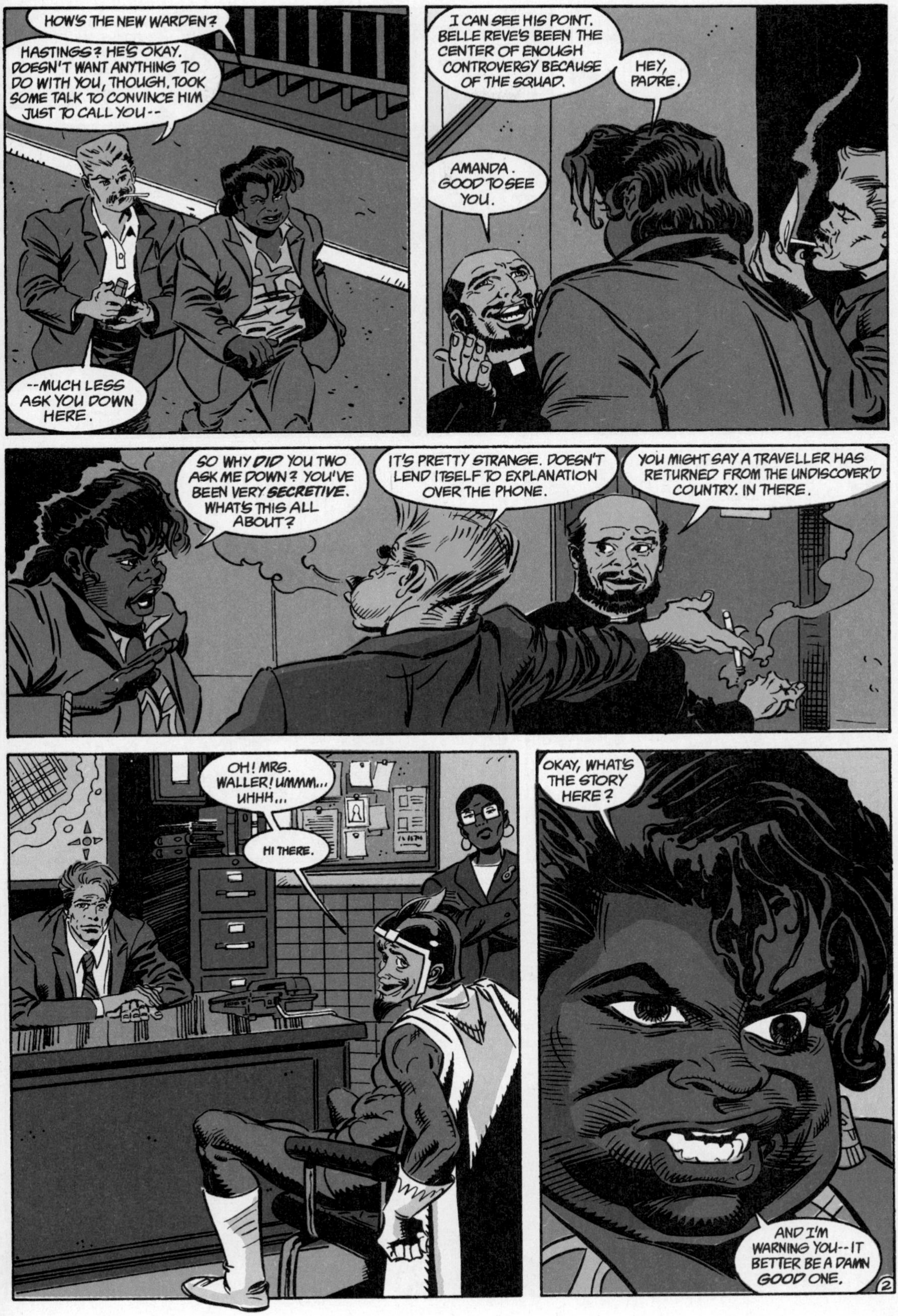
HOW'S THE NEW WARDEN?
HASTINGS? HE'S OKAY. DOESN'T WANT ANYTHING TO DO WITH YOU, THOUGH. TOOK SOME TALK TO CONVINCE HIM JUST TO CALL YOU--
--MUCH LESS ASK YOU DOWN HERE.
I CAN SEE HIS POINT. BELLE REVE'S BEEN THE CENTER OF ENOUGH CONTROVERSY BECAUSE OF THE SQUAD.
HEY, PADRE.
AMANDA. GOOD TO SEE YOU.
SO WHY DID YOU TWO ASK ME DOWN? YOU'VE BEEN VERY SECRETIVE. WHAT'S THIS ALL ABOUT?
IT'S PRETTY STRANGE. DOESN'T LEND ITSELF TO EXPLANATION OVER THE PHONE.
YOU MIGHT SAY A TRAVELLER HAS RETURNED FROM THE UNDISCOVER'D COUNTRY. IN THERE.
OH! MRS. WALLER! UMMM... UHHH...
HI THERE.
OKAY, WHAT'S THE STORY HERE?
AND I'M WARNING YOU--IT BETTER BE A DAMN GOOD ONE.
2

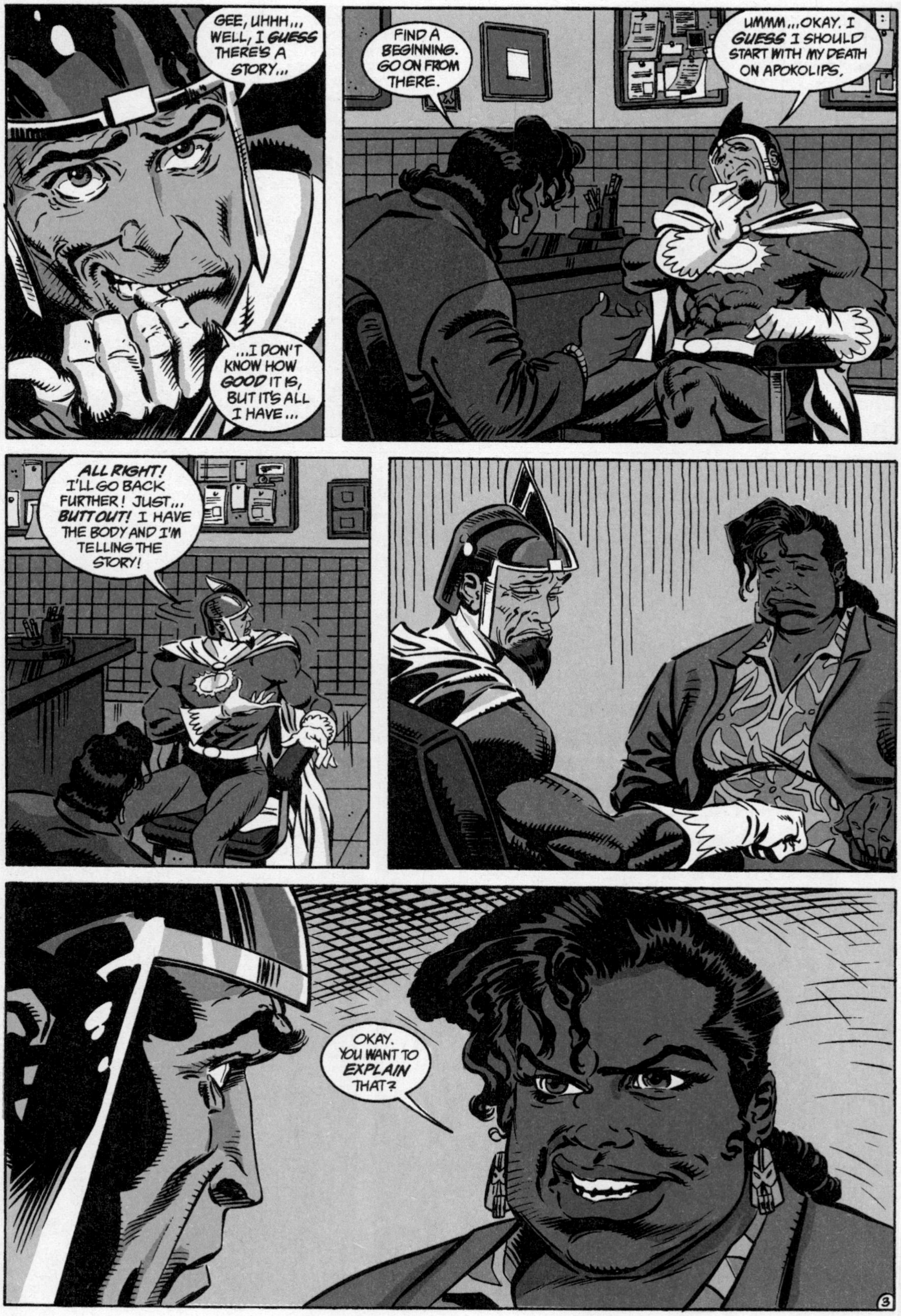
GEE, UHHH... WELL, I GUESS THERE'S A STORY...
...I DON'T KNOW HOW GOOD IT IS, BUT IT'S ALL I HAVE...
FIND A BEGINNING. GO ON FROM THERE.
UMMM...OKAY. I GUESS I SHOULD START WITH MY DEATH ON APOKOLIPS.
ALL RIGHT! I'LL GO BACK FURTHER! JUST... BUTT OUT! I HAVE THE BODY AND I'M TELLING THE STORY!
OKAY. YOU WANT TO EXPLAIN THAT?
3

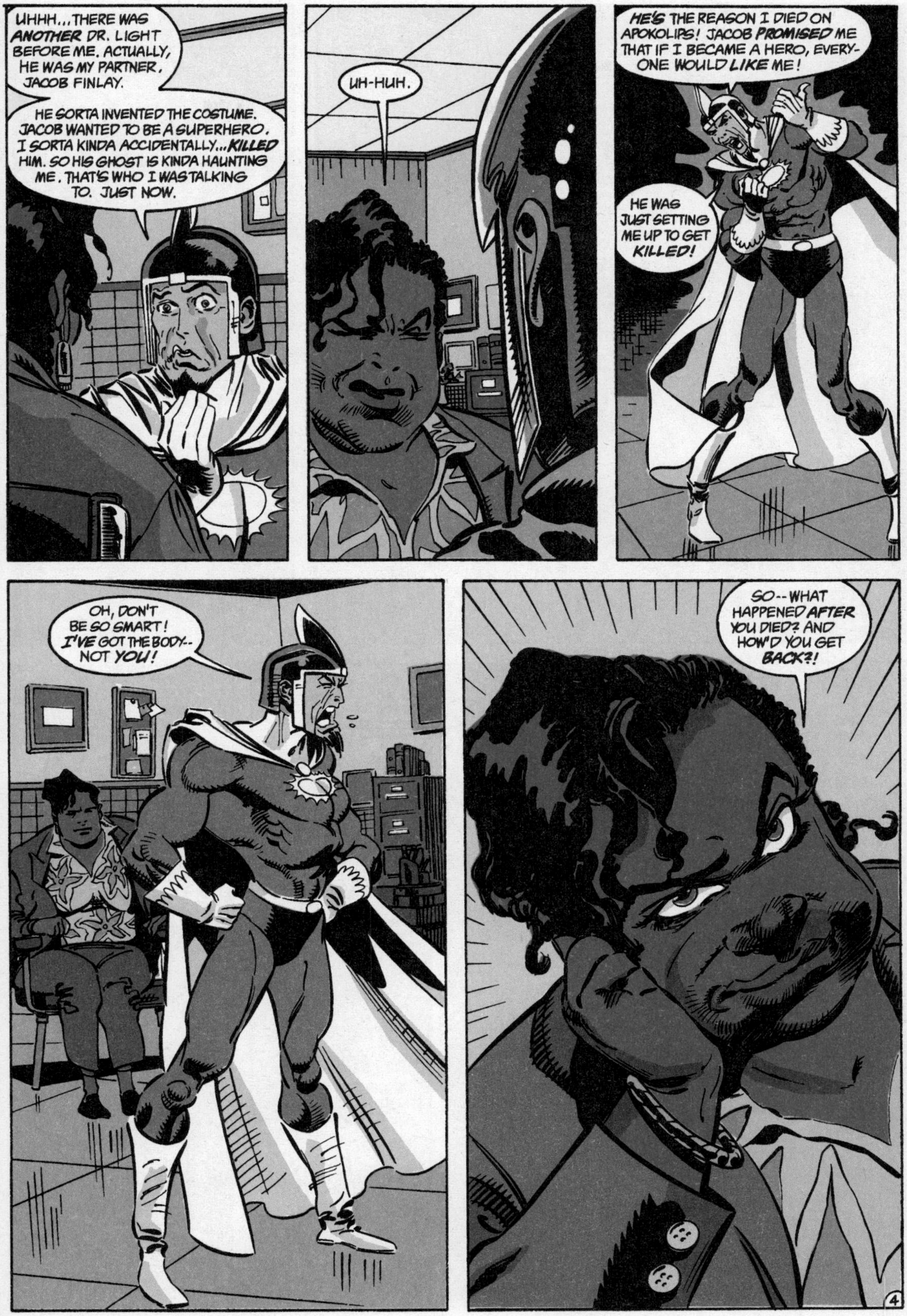
UHHH... THERE WAS ANOTHER DR. LIGHT BEFORE ME. ACTUALLY, HE WAS MY PARTNER. JACOB FINLAY.
HE SORTA INVENTED THE COSTUME. JACOB WANTED TO BE A SUPERHERO. I SORTA KINDA ACCIDENTALLY... KILLED HIM. SO HIS GHOST IS KINDA HAUNTING ME. THAT'S WHO I WAS TALKING TO. JUST NOW.
UH-HUH.
HE'S THE REASON I DIED ON APOKOLIPS! JACOB PROMISED ME THAT IF I BECAME A HERO, EVERY-ONE WOULD LIKE ME!
HE WAS JUST SETTING ME UP TO GET KILLED!
OH, DON'T BE SO SMART! I'VE GOT THE BODY-- NOT YOU!
SO--WHAT HAPPENED AFTER YOU DIED? AND HOW'D YOU GET BACK?!
4

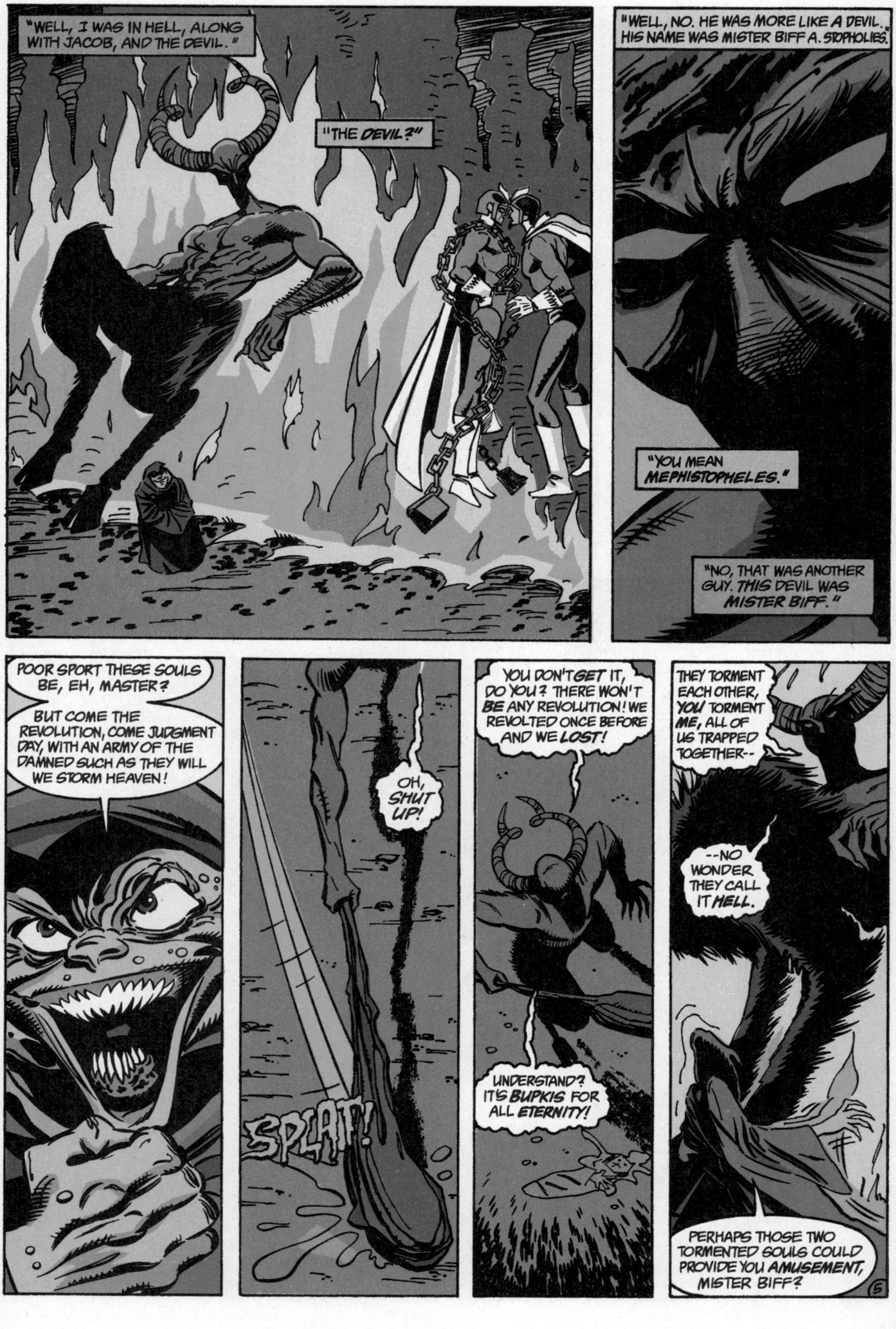
"WELL, I WAS IN HELL, ALONG WITH JACOB, AND THE DEVIL."
"THE DEVIL?"
"WELL, NO. HE WAS MORE LIKE A DEVIL. HIS NAME WAS MISTER BIFF A. STOPHOLIES."
"YOU MEAN MEPHISTOPHELES."
"NO, THAT WAS ANOTHER GUY. THIS DEVIL WAS MISTER BIFF."
POOR SPORT THESE SOULS BE, EH, MASTER?
BUT COME THE REVOLUTION, COME JUDGMENT DAY, WITH AN ARMY OF THE DAMNED SUCH AS THEY WILL WE STORM HEAVEN!
OH, SHUT UP!
SPLAT!
YOU DON'T GET IT, DO YOU? THERE WON'T BE ANY REVOLUTION! WE REVOLTED ONCE BEFORE AND WE LOST!
UNDERSTAND? IT'S BUPKIS FOR ALL ETERNITY!
THEY TORMENT EACH OTHER, YOU TORMENT ME, ALL OF US TRAPPED TOGETHER--
--NO WONDER THEY CALL IT HELL.
PERHAPS THOSE TWO TORMENTED SOULS COULD PROVIDE YOU AMUSEMENT, MISTER BIFF?
5

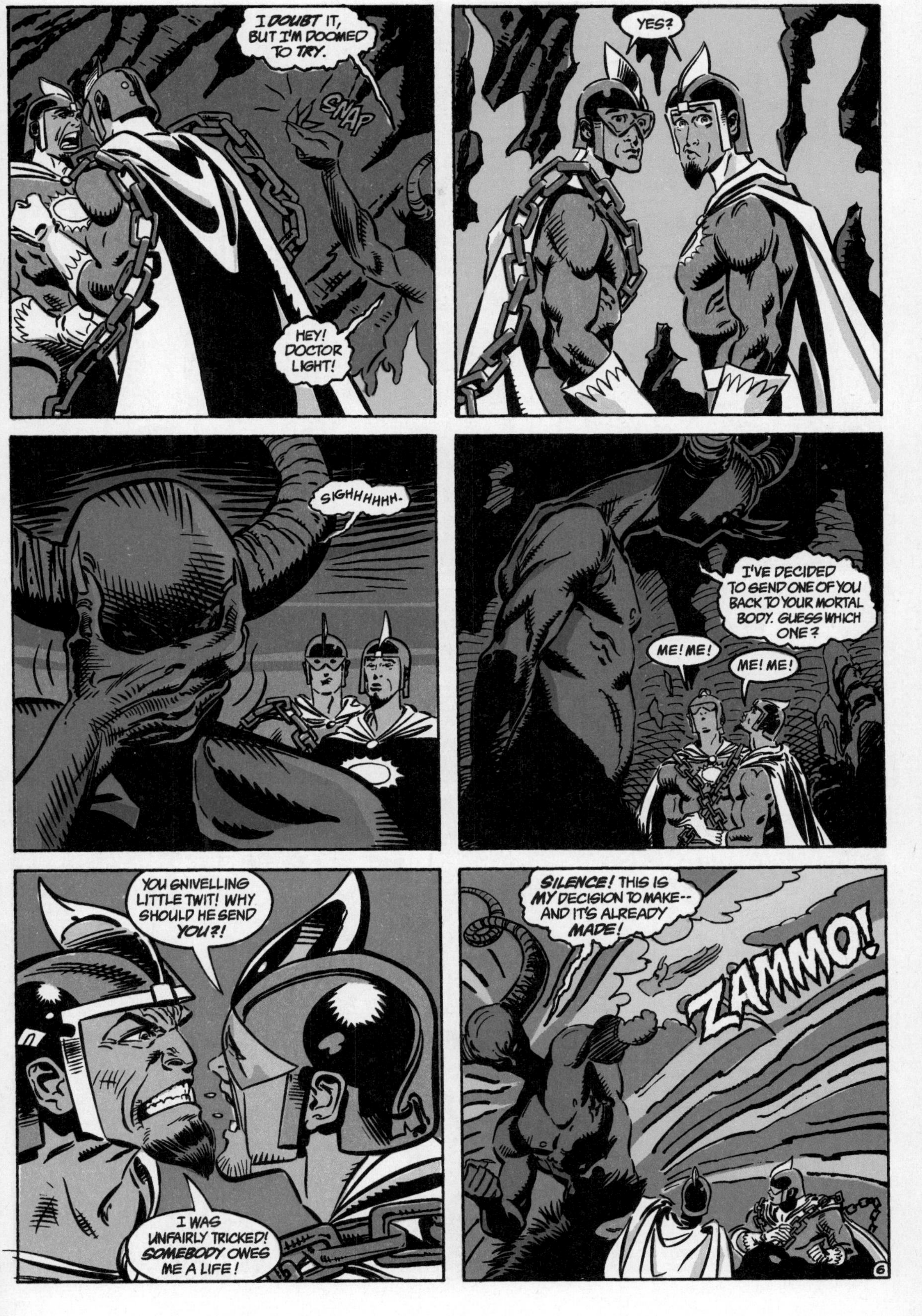
I DOUBT IT, BUT I'M DOOMED TO TRY.
SNAP
HEY! DOCTOR LIGHT!
YES?
SIGHHHHHH.
I'VE DECIDED TO SEND ONE OF YOU BACK TO YOUR MORTAL BODY. GUESS WHICH ONE?
ME! ME!
ME! ME!
YOU SNIVELLING LITTLE TWIT! WHY SHOULD HE SEND YOU?!
I WAS UNFAIRLY TRICKED! SOMEBODY OWES ME A LIFE!
SILENCE! THIS IS MY DECISION TO MAKE-- AND IT'S ALREADY MADE!
ZAMMO!
6

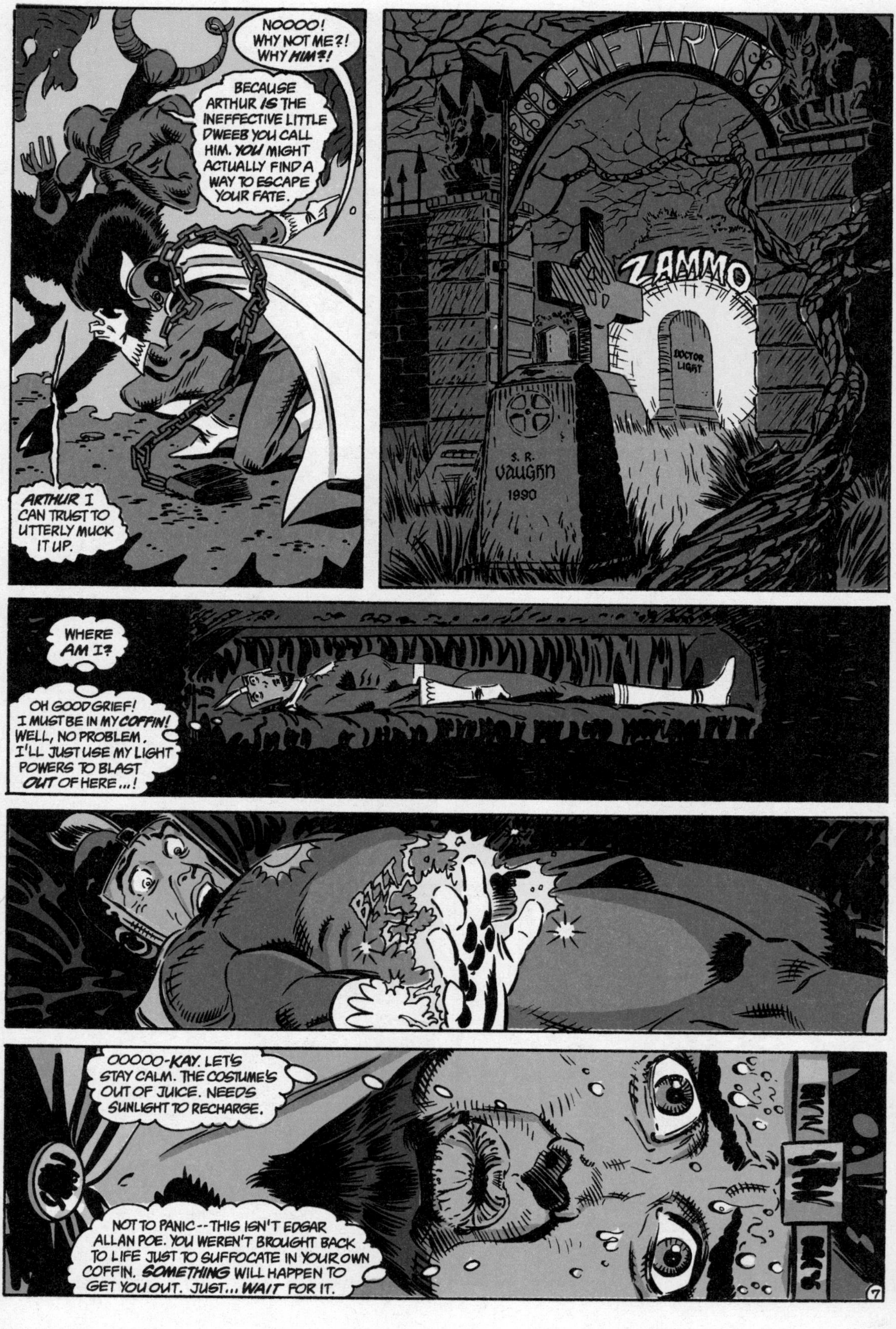
NOOOO! WHY NOT ME?! WHY HIM?!
BECAUSE ARTHUR IS THE INEFFECTIVE LITTLE DWEEB YOU CALL HIM. YOU MIGHT ACTUALLY FIND A WAY TO ESCAPE YOUR FATE.
ARTHUR I CAN TRUST TO UTTERLY MUCK IT UP.
CEMETARY
ZAMMO
DOCTOR LIGHT
S. R. VAUGHN 1990
WHERE AM I?
OH GOOD GRIEF! I MUST BE IN MY COFFIN! WELL, NO PROBLEM. I'LL JUST USE MY LIGHT POWERS TO BLAST OUT OF HERE...!
BZZT
OOOOO-KAY. LET'S STAY CALM. THE COSTUME'S OUT OF JUICE. NEEDS SUNLIGHT TO RECHARGE.
NOT TO PANIC--THIS ISN'T EDGAR ALLAN POE. YOU WEREN'T BROUGHT BACK TO LIFE JUST TO SUFFOCATE IN YOUR OWN COFFIN. SOMETHING WILL HAPPEN TO GET YOU OUT. JUST... WAIT FOR IT.
7

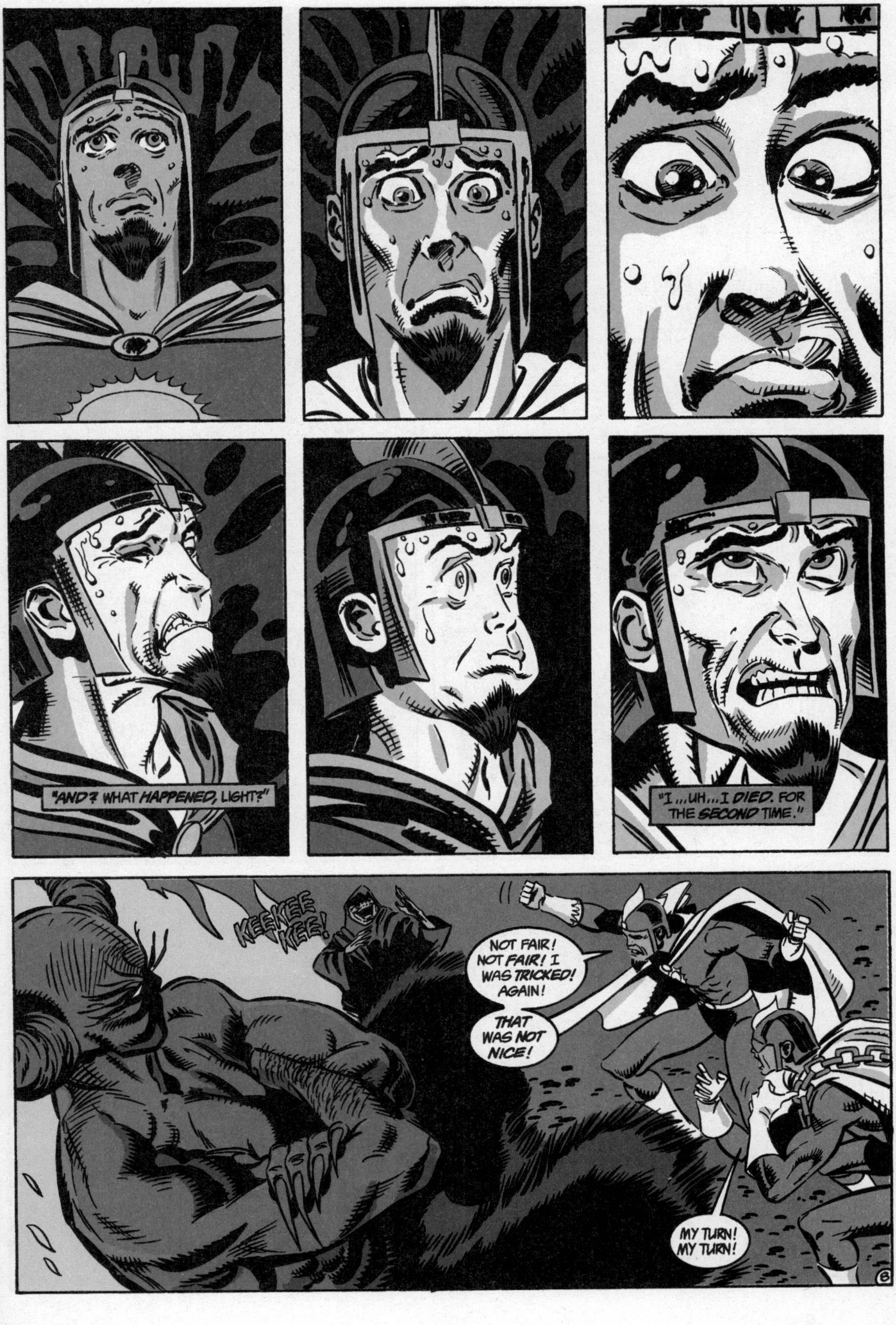
"AND? WHAT HAPPENED, LIGHT?"
"I ... UH ... I DIED. FOR THE SECOND TIME."
KEEKEE KEE!
NOT FAIR! NOT FAIR! I WAS TRICKED! AGAIN!
THAT WAS NOT NICE!
MY TURN! MY TURN!
8

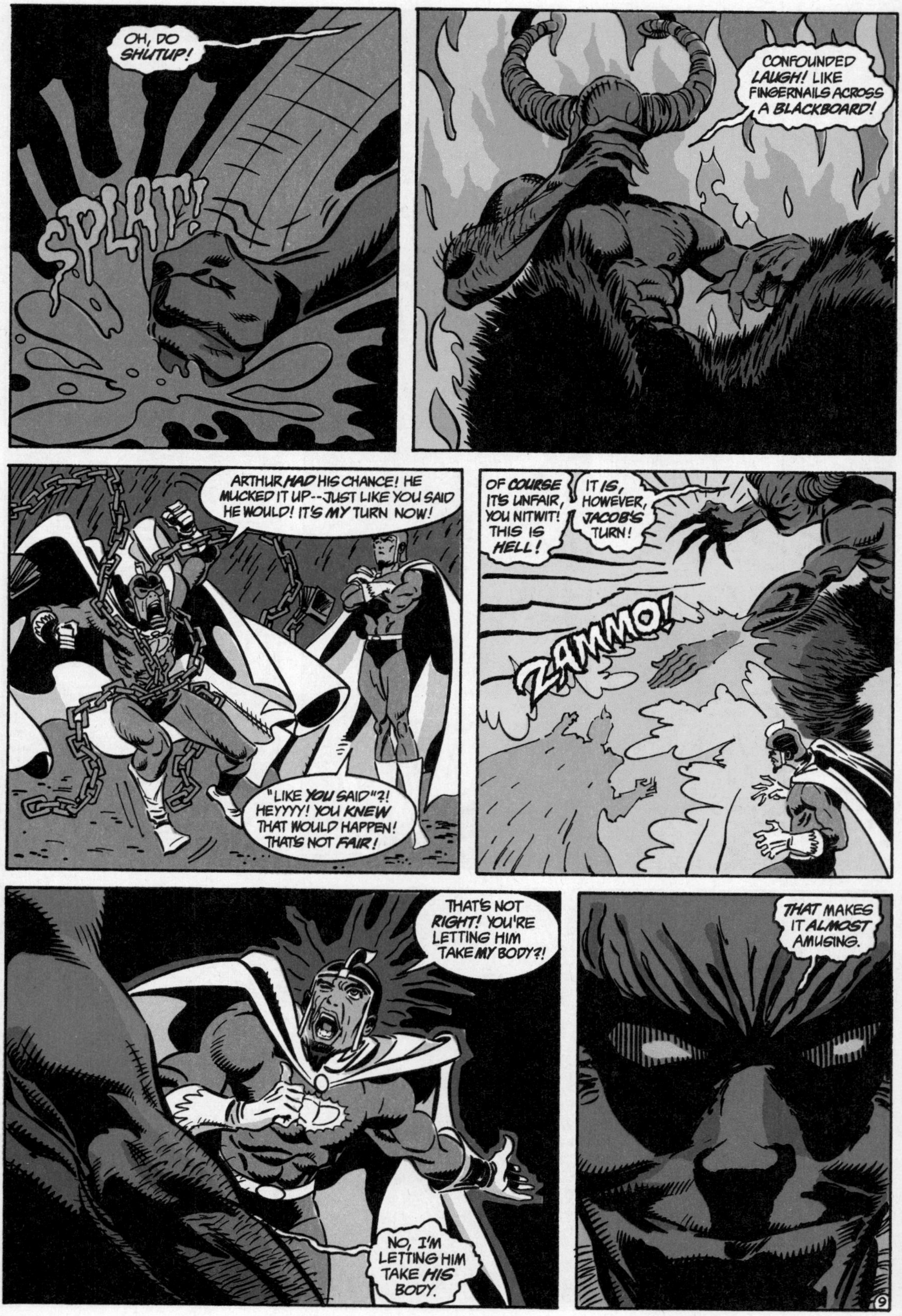
OH, DO SHUTUP!
SPLAT!
CONFOUNDED LAUGH! LIKE FINGERNAILS ACROSS A BLACKBOARD!
ARTHUR HAD HIS CHANCE! HE MUCKED IT UP--JUST LIKE YOU SAID HE WOULD! IT'S MY TURN NOW!
"LIKE YOU SAID"?! HEYYYY! YOU KNEW THAT WOULD HAPPEN! THAT'S NOT FAIR!
OF COURSE IT'S UNFAIR, YOU NITWIT! THIS IS HELL!
IT IS, HOWEVER, JACOB'S TURN!
ZAMMO!
THAT'S NOT RIGHT! YOU'RE LETTING HIM TAKE MY BODY?!
NO, I'M LETTING HIM TAKE HIS BODY.
THAT MAKES IT ALMOST AMUSING.
9

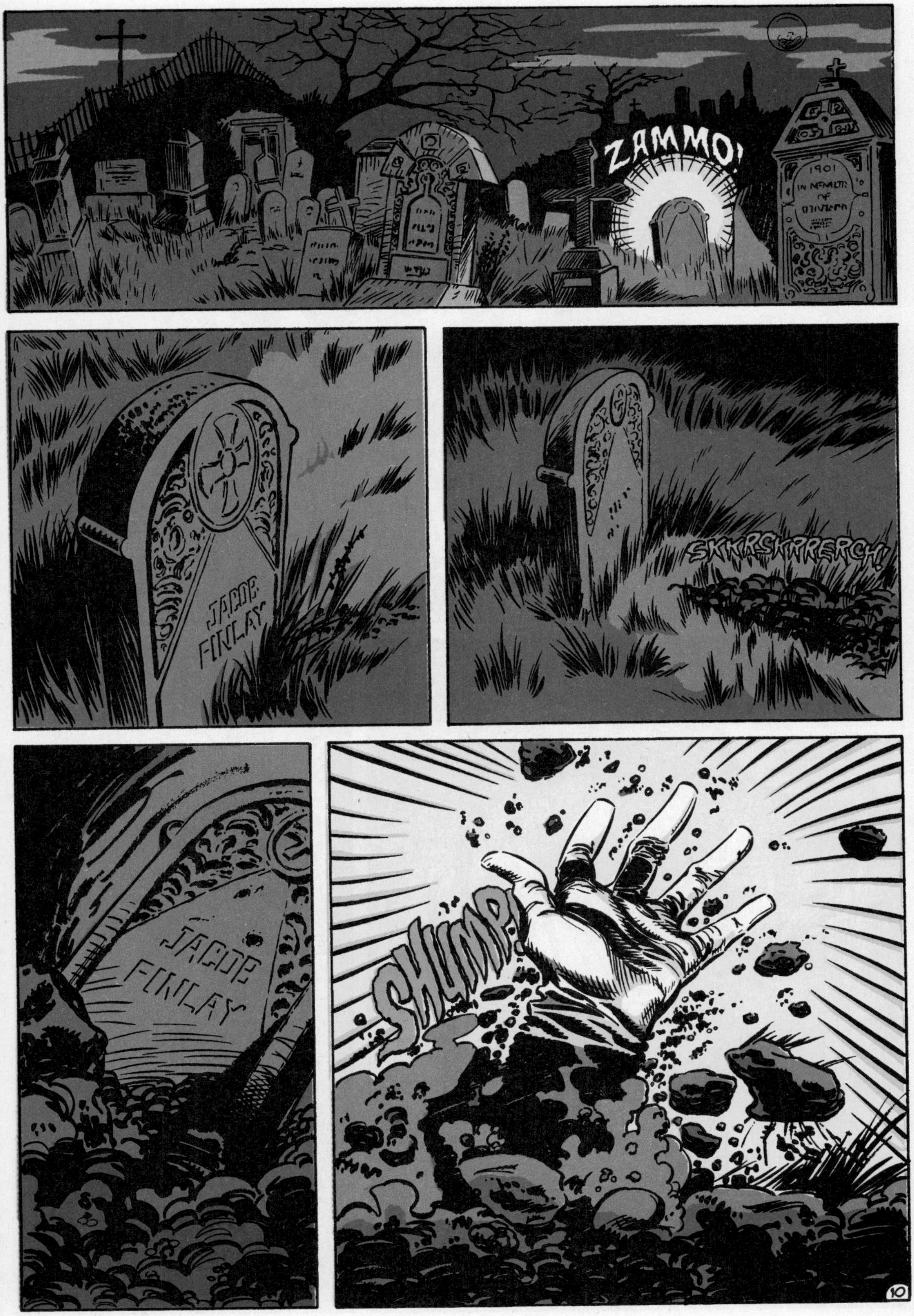
ZAMMO!
1901
IN MEMORY OF
JACOB FINLAY
SKKRSKRRRERCH!
JACOB FINLAY
SHUMP!
10

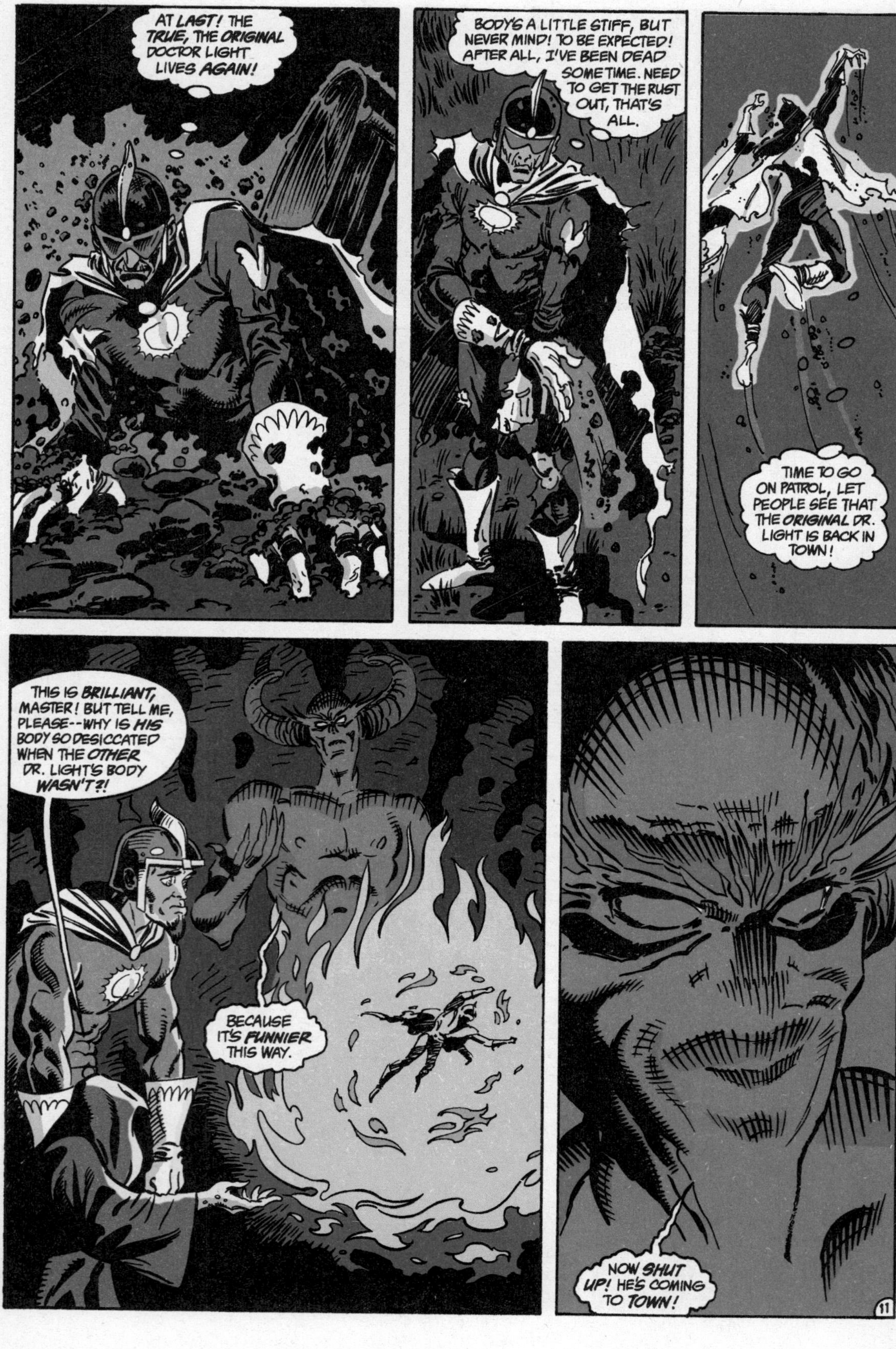
AT LAST! THE TRUE, THE ORIGINAL DOCTOR LIGHT LIVES AGAIN!
BODY'S A LITTLE STIFF, BUT NEVER MIND! TO BE EXPECTED! AFTER ALL, I'VE BEEN DEAD SOME TIME. NEED TO GET THE RUST OUT, THAT'S ALL.
TIME TO GO ON PATROL, LET PEOPLE SEE THAT THE ORIGINAL DR. LIGHT IS BACK IN TOWN!
THIS IS BRILLIANT, MASTER! BUT TELL ME, PLEASE--WHY IS HIS BODY SO DESICCATED WHEN THE OTHER DR. LIGHT'S BODY WASN'T?!
BECAUSE IT'S FUNNIER THIS WAY.
NOW SHUT UP! HE'S COMING TO TOWN!
11

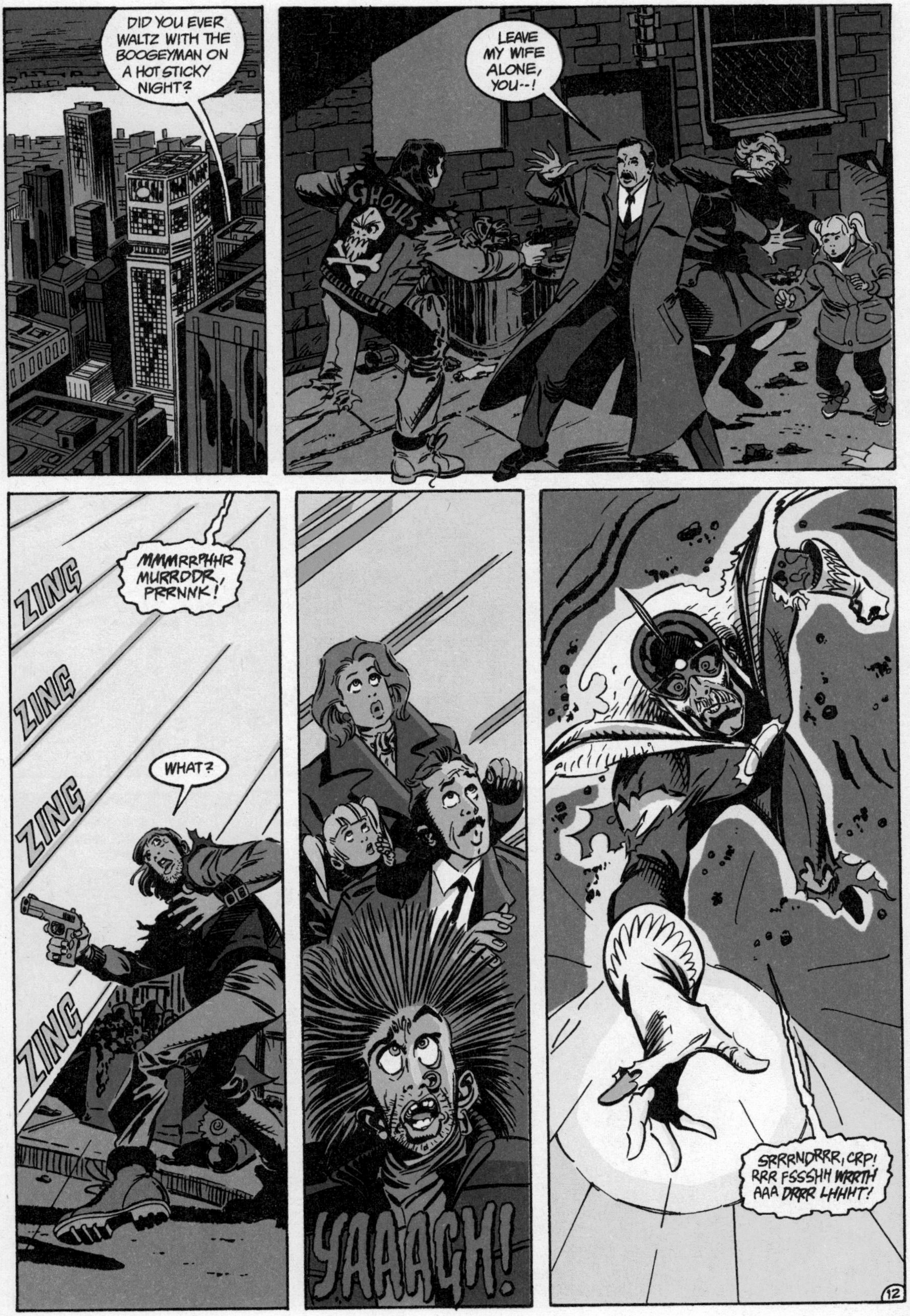
DID YOU EVER WALTZ WITH THE BOOGEYMAN ON A HOT STICKY NIGHT?
LEAVE MY WIFE ALONE, YOU--!
ZING
ZING
ZING
ZING
MMMRRPHHR MURRDDR, PRRNNK!
WHAT?
YAAAGH!
SRRRNDRRR, CRP! RRR FSSSHH WRRTH AAA DRRR LHHHT!
12

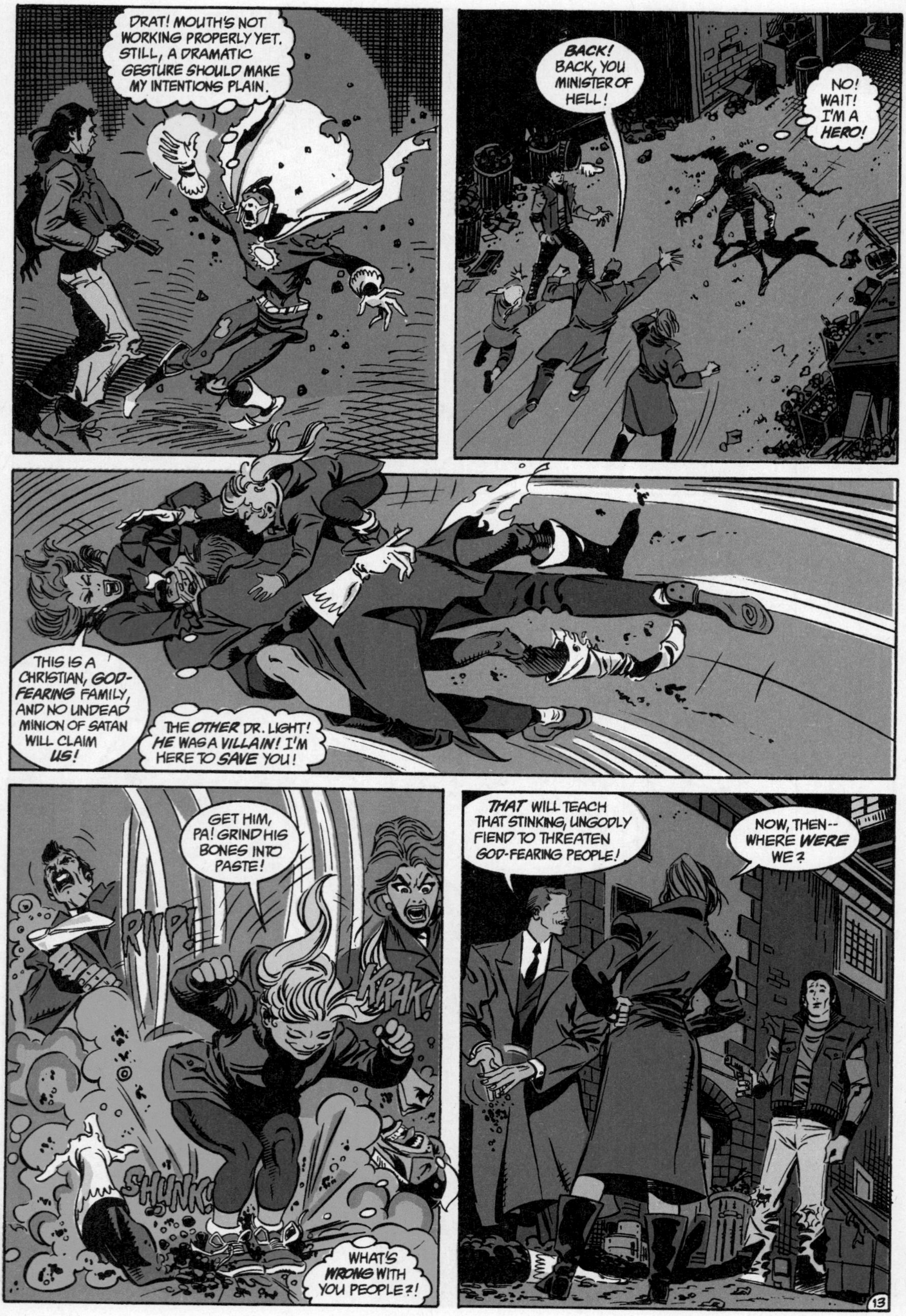
DRAT! MOUTH'S NOT WORKING PROPERLY YET. STILL, A DRAMATIC GESTURE SHOULD MAKE MY INTENTIONS PLAIN.
BACK! BACK, YOU MINISTER OF HELL!
NO! WAIT! I'M A HERO!
THIS IS A CHRISTIAN, GOD-FEARING FAMILY, AND NO UNDEAD MINION OF SATAN WILL CLAIM US!
THE OTHER DR. LIGHT! HE WAS A VILLAIN! I'M HERE TO SAVE YOU!
GET HIM, PA! GRIND HIS BONES INTO PASTE!
RIIP!
KRAK!
SHUNK!
WHAT'S WRONG WITH YOU PEOPLE?!
THAT WILL TEACH THAT STINKING, UNGODLY FIEND TO THREATEN GOD-FEARING PEOPLE!
NOW, THEN-- WHERE WERE WE?
13

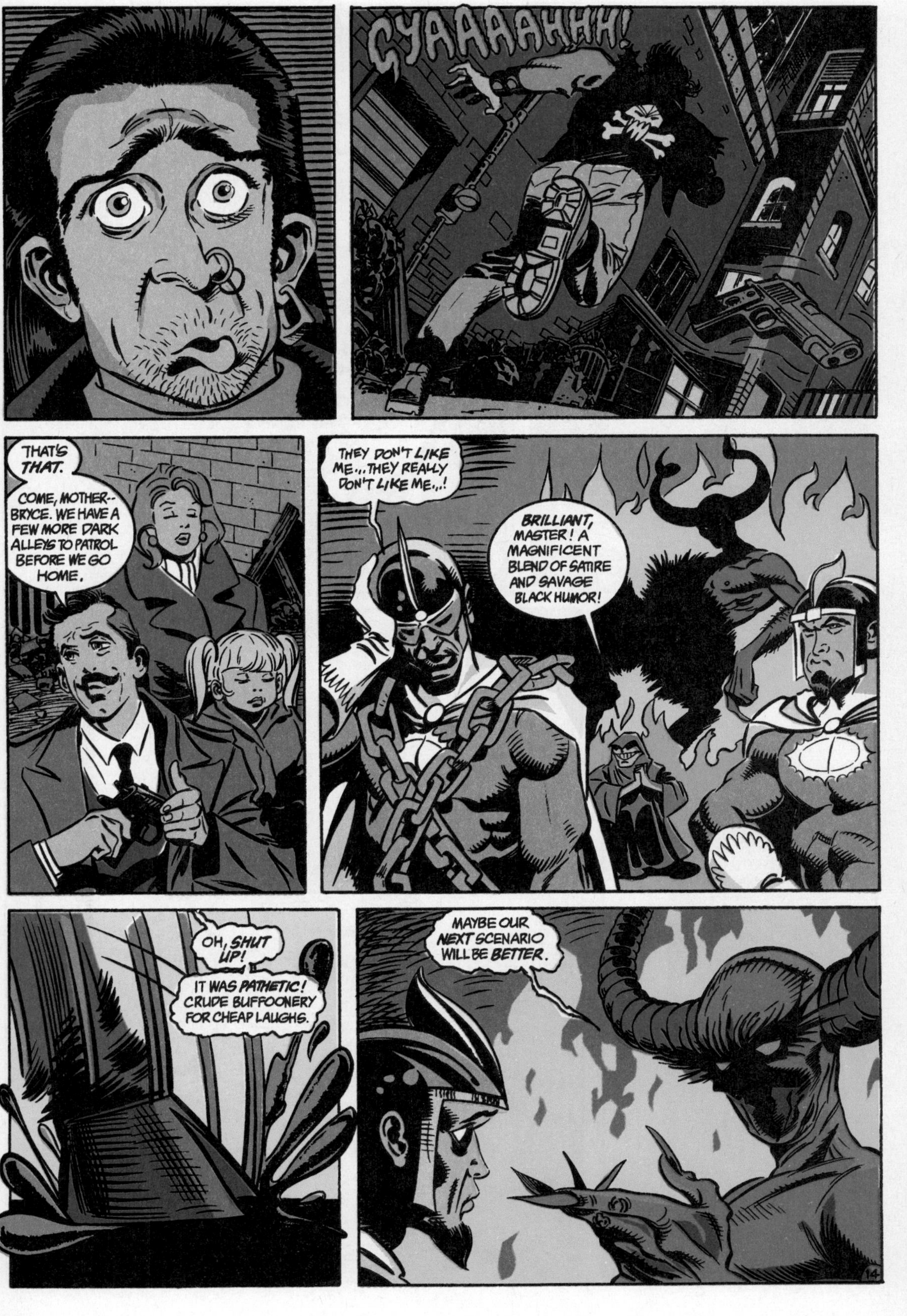
GYAAAAAHHH!
THAT'S THAT.
COME, MOTHER-- BRYCE. WE HAVE A FEW MORE DARK ALLEYS TO PATROL BEFORE WE GO HOME.
THEY DON'T LIKE ME... THEY REALLY DON'T LIKE ME...!
BRILLIANT, MASTER! A MAGNIFICENT BLEND OF SATIRE AND SAVAGE BLACK HUMOR!
OH, SHUT UP!
IT WAS PATHETIC! CRUDE BUFFOONERY FOR CHEAP LAUGHS.
MAYBE OUR NEXT SCENARIO WILL BE BETTER.
14

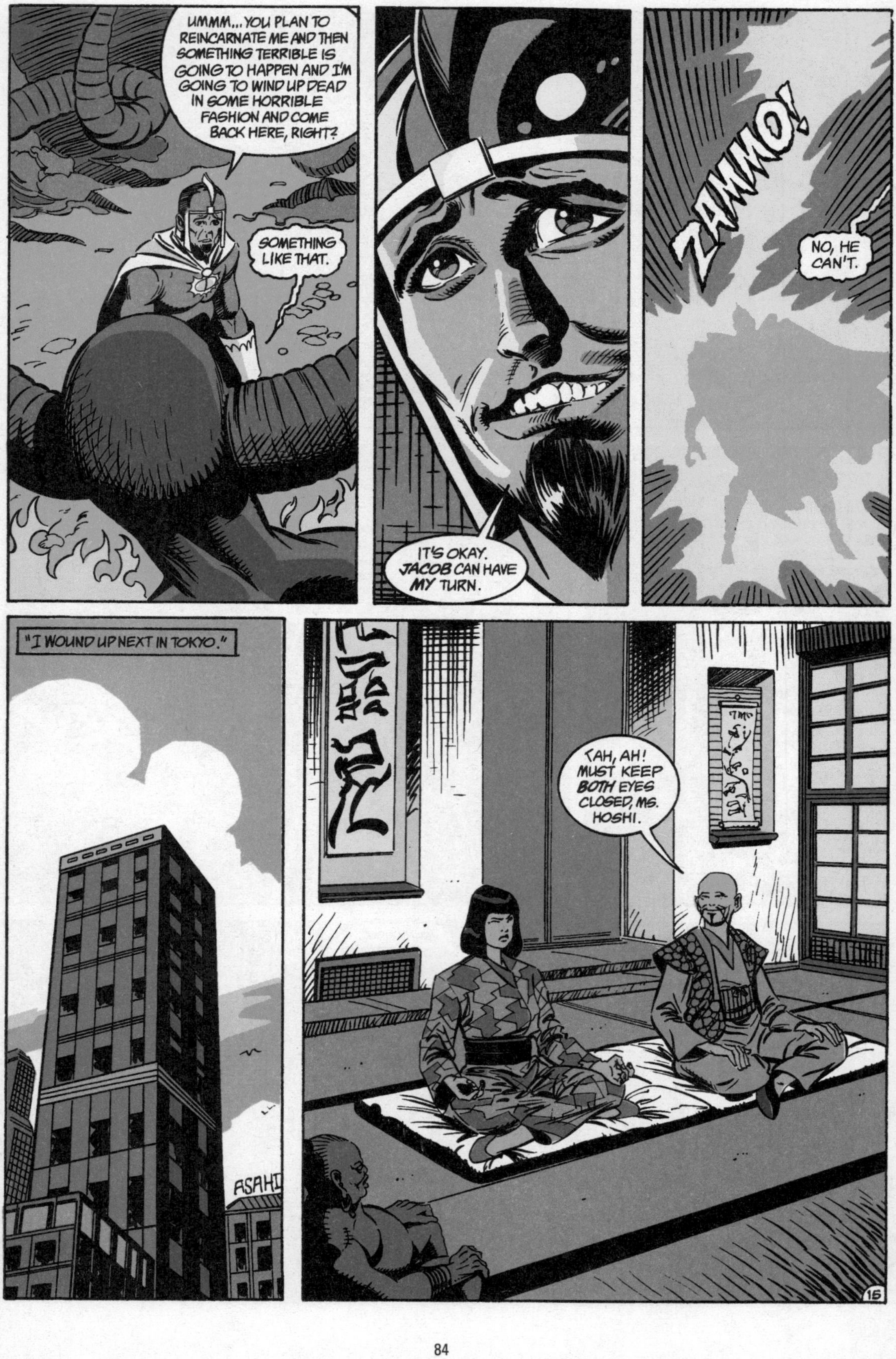
UMMM... YOU PLAN TO REINCARNATE ME AND THEN SOMETHING TERRIBLE IS GOING TO HAPPEN AND I'M GOING TO WIND UP DEAD IN SOME HORRIBLE FASHION AND COME BACK HERE, RIGHT?
SOMETHING LIKE THAT.
IT'S OKAY. JACOB CAN HAVE MY TURN.
ZAMMO!
NO, HE CAN'T.
"I WOUND UP NEXT IN TOKYO."
ASAHI
AH, AH! MUST KEEP BOTH EYES CLOSED, MS. HOSHI.
15

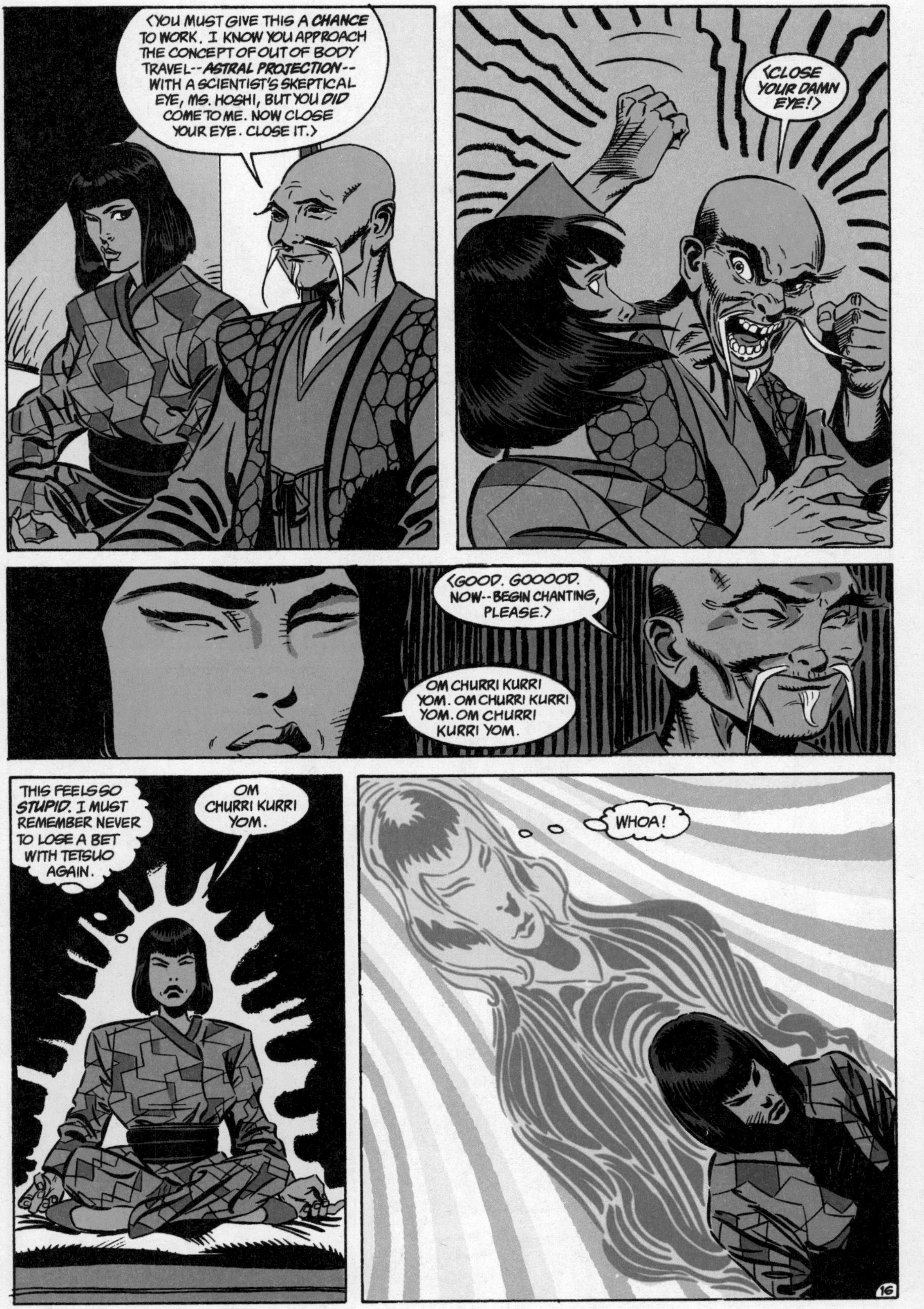

<YOU MUST GIVE THIS A CHANCE TO WORK. I KNOW YOU APPROACH THE CONCEPT OF OUT OF BODY TRAVEL--ASTRAL PROJECTION--WITH A SCIENTIST'S SKEPTICAL EYE, MS. HOSHI, BUT YOU DID COME TO ME. NOW CLOSE YOUR EYE. CLOSE IT.>
<CLOSE YOUR DAMN EYE!>
<GOOD. GOOOOD. NOW--BEGIN CHANTING, PLEASE.>
OM CHURRI KURRI YOM. OM CHURRI KURRI YOM. OM CHURRI KURRI YOM.
THIS FEELS SO STUPID. I MUST REMEMBER NEVER TO LOSE A BET WITH TETSUO AGAIN.
OM CHURRI KURRI YOM.
WHOA!
16

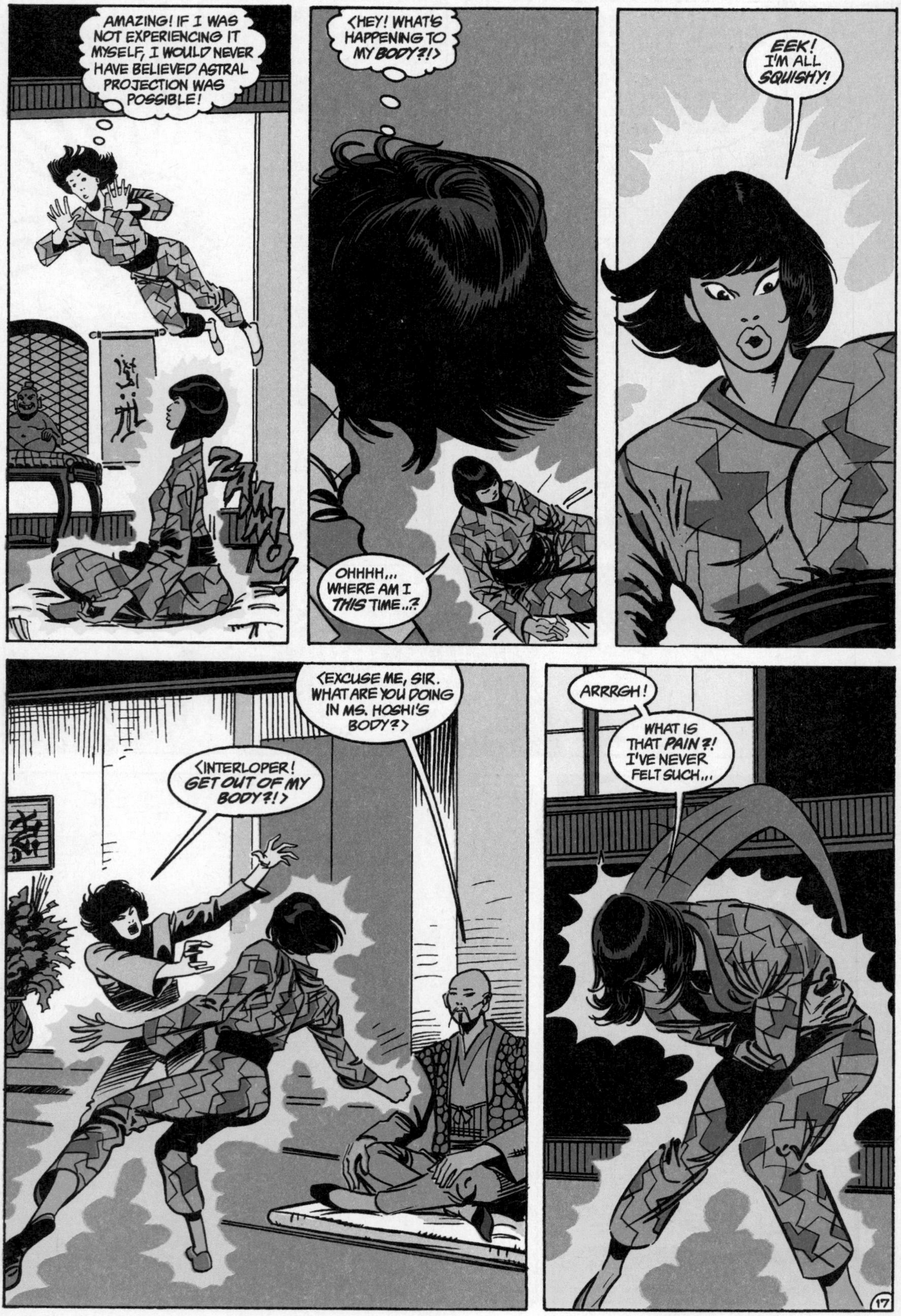
AMAZING! IF I WAS NOT EXPERIENCING IT MYSELF, I WOULD NEVER HAVE BELIEVED ASTRAL PROJECTION WAS POSSIBLE!
ZAMMO!
<HEY! WHAT'S HAPPENING TO MY BODY?!>
OHHHH... WHERE AM I THIS TIME...?
EEK! I'M ALL SQUISHY!
<EXCUSE ME, SIR. WHAT ARE YOU DOING IN MS. HOSHI'S BODY?>
<INTERLOPER! GET OUT OF MY BODY?!>
ARRRGH!
WHAT IS THAT PAIN?! I'VE NEVER FELT SUCH...
17

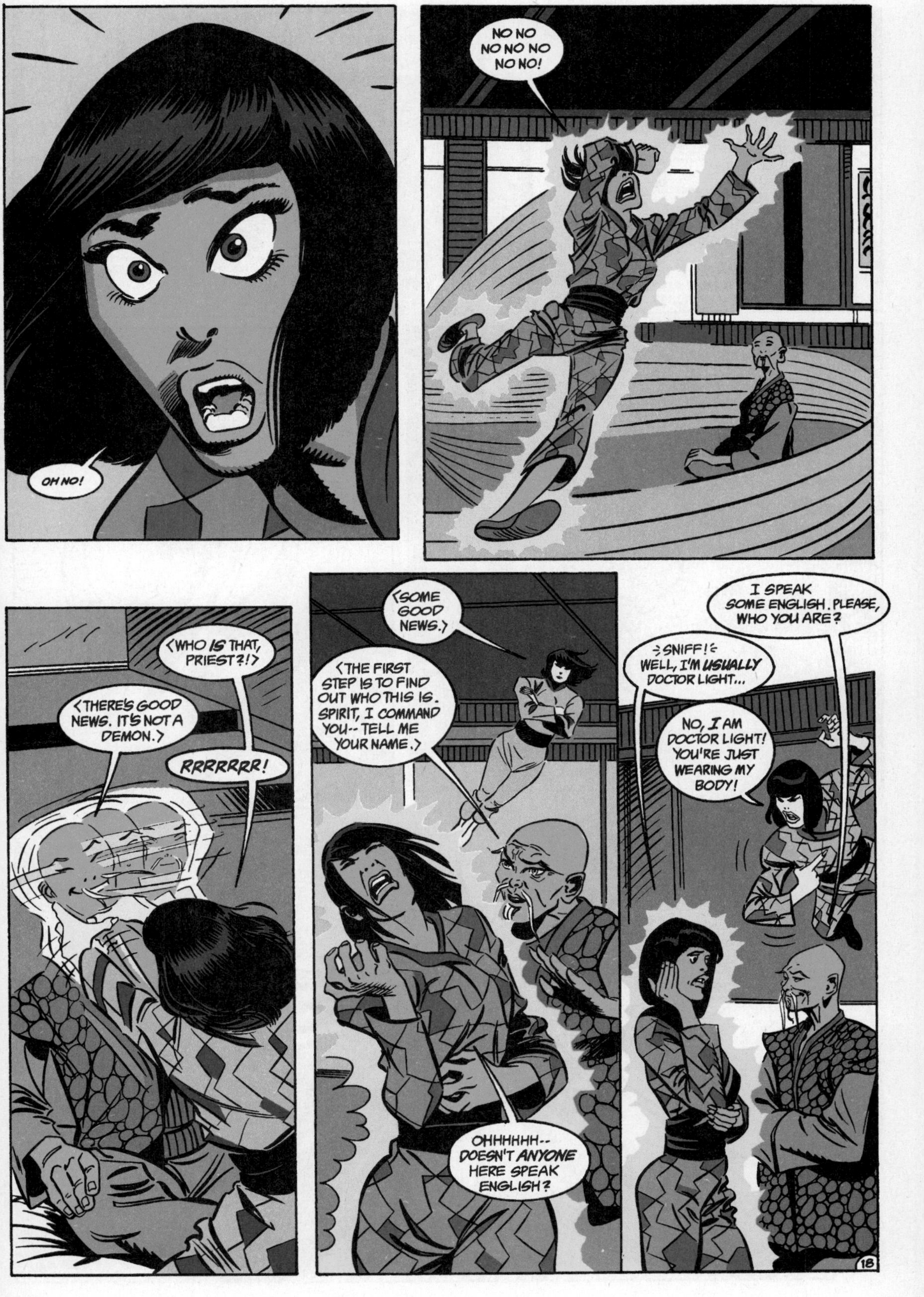
OH NO!
NO NO
NO NO NO
NO NO!
<WHO IS THAT, PRIEST?!>
<THERE'S GOOD NEWS. IT'S NOT A DEMON.>
RRRRRRR!
<SOME GOOD NEWS.>
<THE FIRST STEP IS TO FIND OUT WHO THIS IS. SPIRIT, I COMMAND YOU-- TELL ME YOUR NAME.>
OHHHHHH-- DOESN'T ANYONE HERE SPEAK ENGLISH?
I SPEAK SOME ENGLISH. PLEASE, WHO YOU ARE?
SNIFF! WELL, I'M USUALLY DOCTOR LIGHT...
NO, I AM DOCTOR LIGHT! YOU'RE JUST WEARING MY BODY!
18

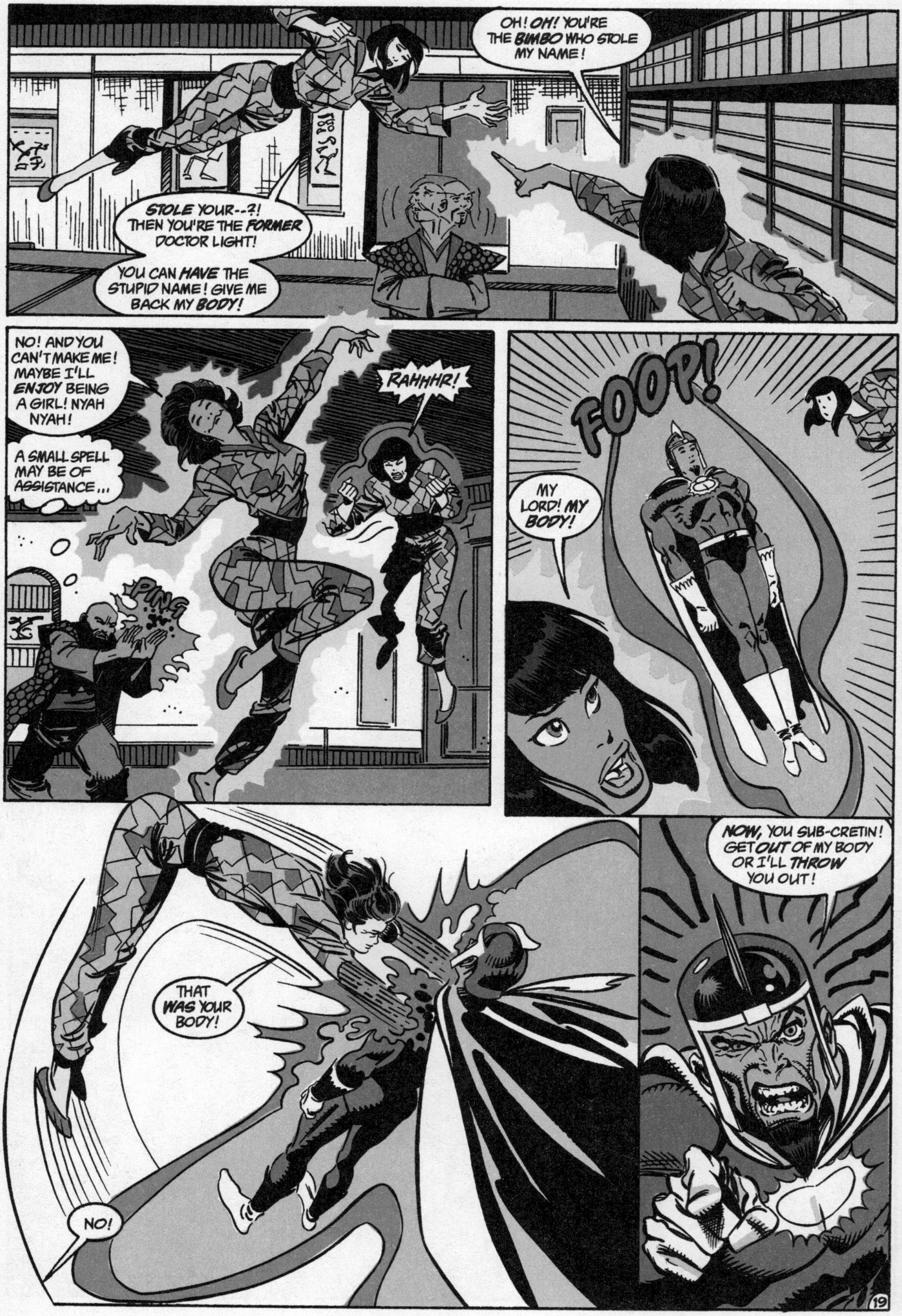
OH! OH! YOU'RE THE BIMBO WHO STOLE MY NAME!
STOLE YOUR--?! THEN YOU'RE THE FORMER DOCTOR LIGHT!
YOU CAN HAVE THE STUPID NAME! GIVE ME BACK MY BODY!
NO! AND YOU CAN'T MAKE ME! MAYBE I'LL ENJOY BEING A GIRL! NYAH NYAH!
A SMALL SPELL MAY BE OF ASSISTANCE...
RAHHHR!
PING
FOOP!
MY LORD! MY BODY!
THAT WAS YOUR BODY!
NO!
NOW, YOU SUB-CRETIN! GET OUT OF MY BODY OR I'LL THROW YOU OUT!
19

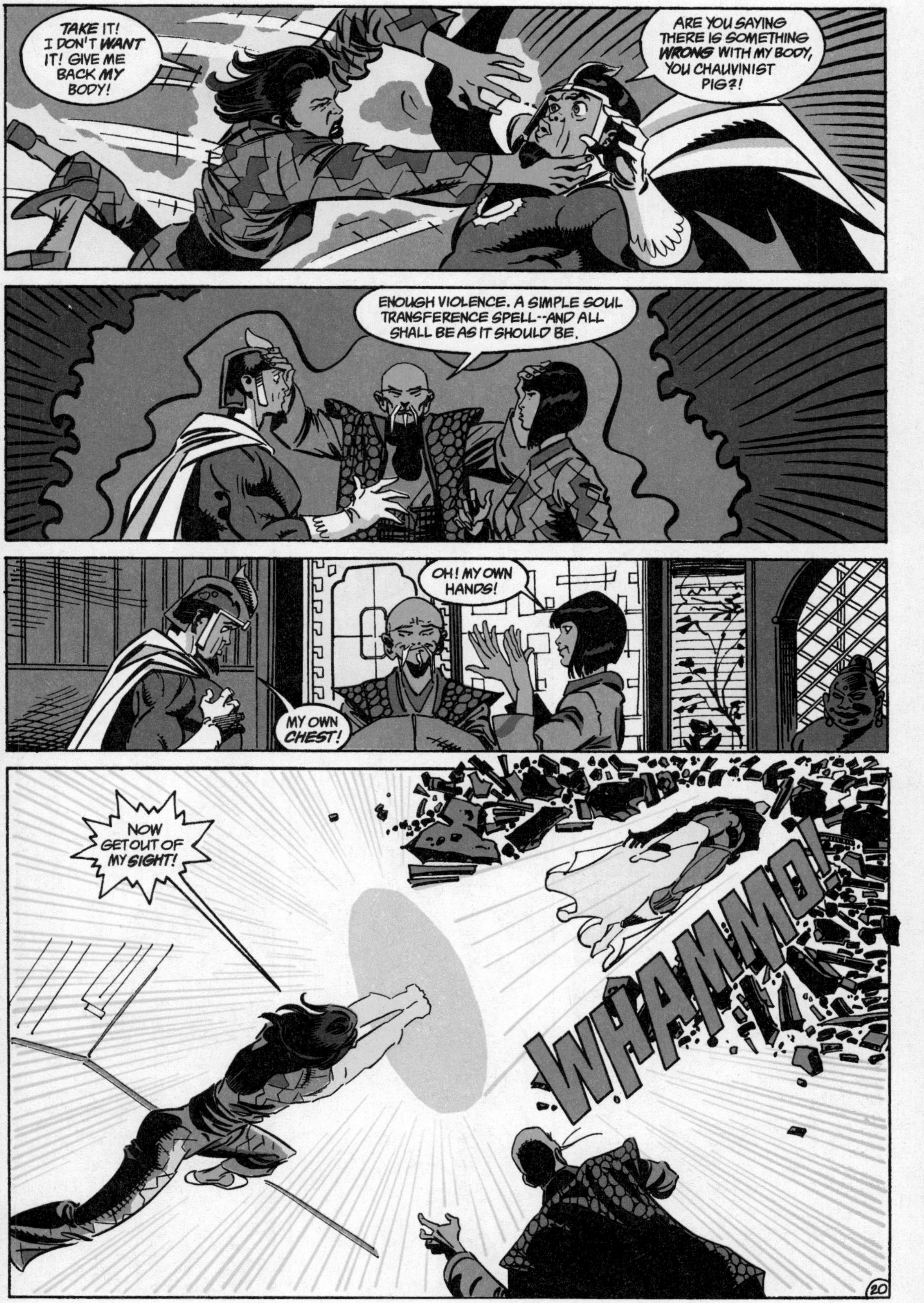
TAKE IT! I DON'T WANT IT! GIVE ME BACK MY BODY!
ARE YOU SAYING THERE IS SOMETHING WRONG WITH MY BODY, YOU CHAUVINIST PIG?!
ENOUGH VIOLENCE. A SIMPLE SOUL TRANSFERENCE SPELL--AND ALL SHALL BE AS IT SHOULD BE.
OH! MY OWN HANDS!
MY OWN CHEST!
NOW GET OUT OF MY SIGHT!
WHAMMO!
20

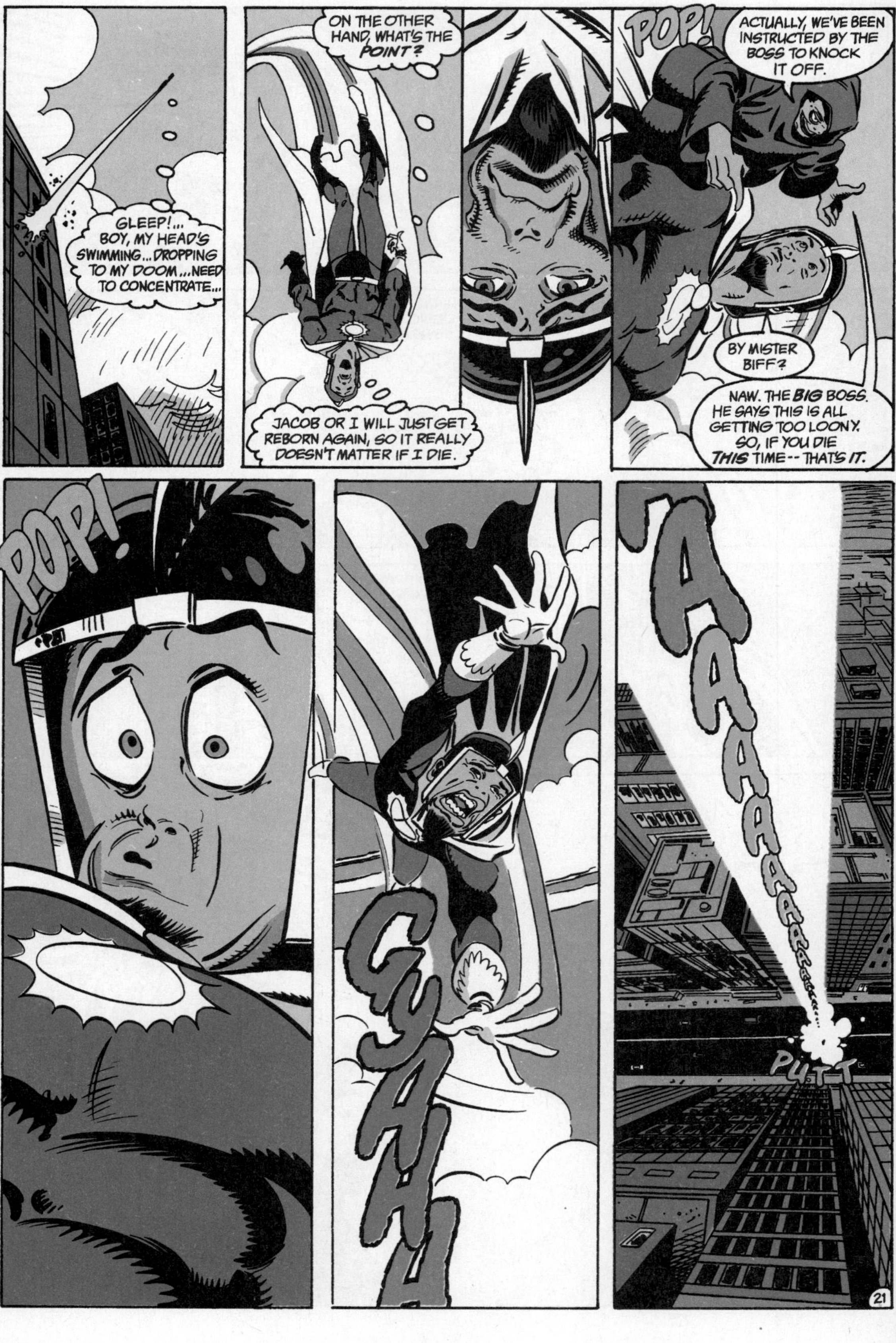

GLEEP!... BOY, MY HEAD'S SWIMMING...DROPPING TO MY DOOM...NEED TO CONCENTRATE...
ON THE OTHER HAND, WHAT'S THE POINT?
JACOB OR I WILL JUST GET REBORN AGAIN, SO IT REALLY DOESN'T MATTER IF I DIE.
POP!
ACTUALLY, WE'VE BEEN INSTRUCTED BY THE BOSS TO KNOCK IT OFF.
BY MISTER BIFF?
NAW. THE BIG BOSS. HE SAYS THIS IS ALL GETTING TOO LOONY. SO, IF YOU DIE THIS TIME-- THAT'S IT.
POP!
GYAAAH
AAAAAAAAAA
PUTT
21

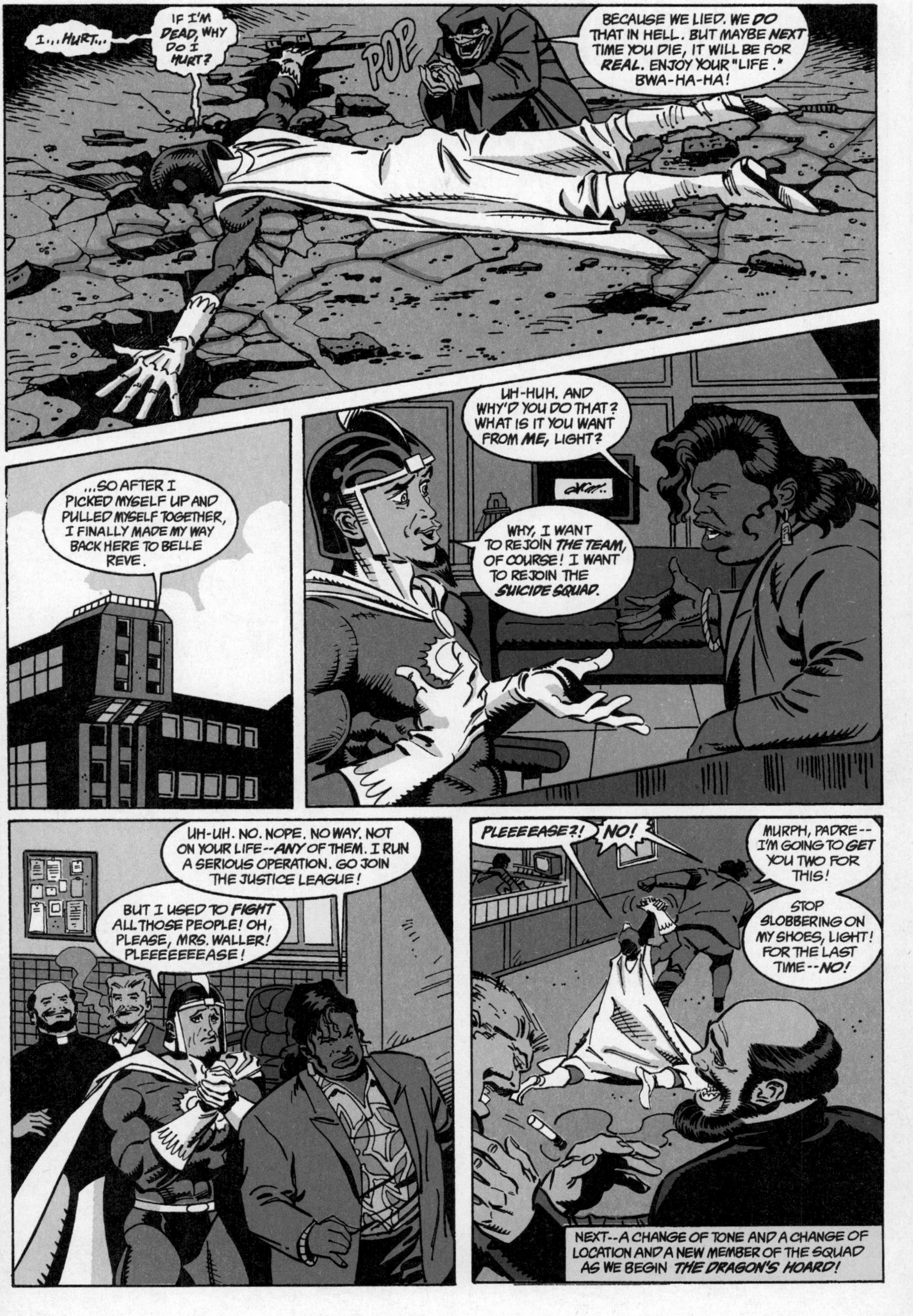

I... HURT...
IF I'M DEAD, WHY DO I HURT?
POP
BECAUSE WE LIED. WE DO THAT IN HELL. BUT MAYBE NEXT TIME YOU DIE, IT WILL BE FOR REAL. ENJOY YOUR "LIFE." BWA-HA-HA!
...SO AFTER I PICKED MYSELF UP AND PULLED MYSELF TOGETHER, I FINALLY MADE MY WAY BACK HERE TO BELLE REVE.
UH-HUH. AND WHY'D YOU DO THAT? WHAT IS IT YOU WANT FROM ME, LIGHT?
WHY, I WANT TO REJOIN THE TEAM, OF COURSE! I WANT TO REJOIN THE SUICIDE SQUAD.
UH-UH. NO. NOPE. NO WAY. NOT ON YOUR LIFE--ANY OF THEM. I RUN A SERIOUS OPERATION. GO JOIN THE JUSTICE LEAGUE!
BUT I USED TO FIGHT ALL THOSE PEOPLE! OH, PLEASE, MRS. WALLER! PLEEEEEEEASE!
PLEEEEASE?!
NO!
MURPH, PADRE-- I'M GOING TO GET YOU TWO FOR THIS!
STOP SLOBBERING ON MY SHOES, LIGHT! FOR THE LAST TIME--NO!
NEXT--A CHANGE OF TONE AND A CHANGE OF LOCATION AND A NEW MEMBER OF THE SQUAD AS WE BEGIN THE DRAGON'S HOARD!

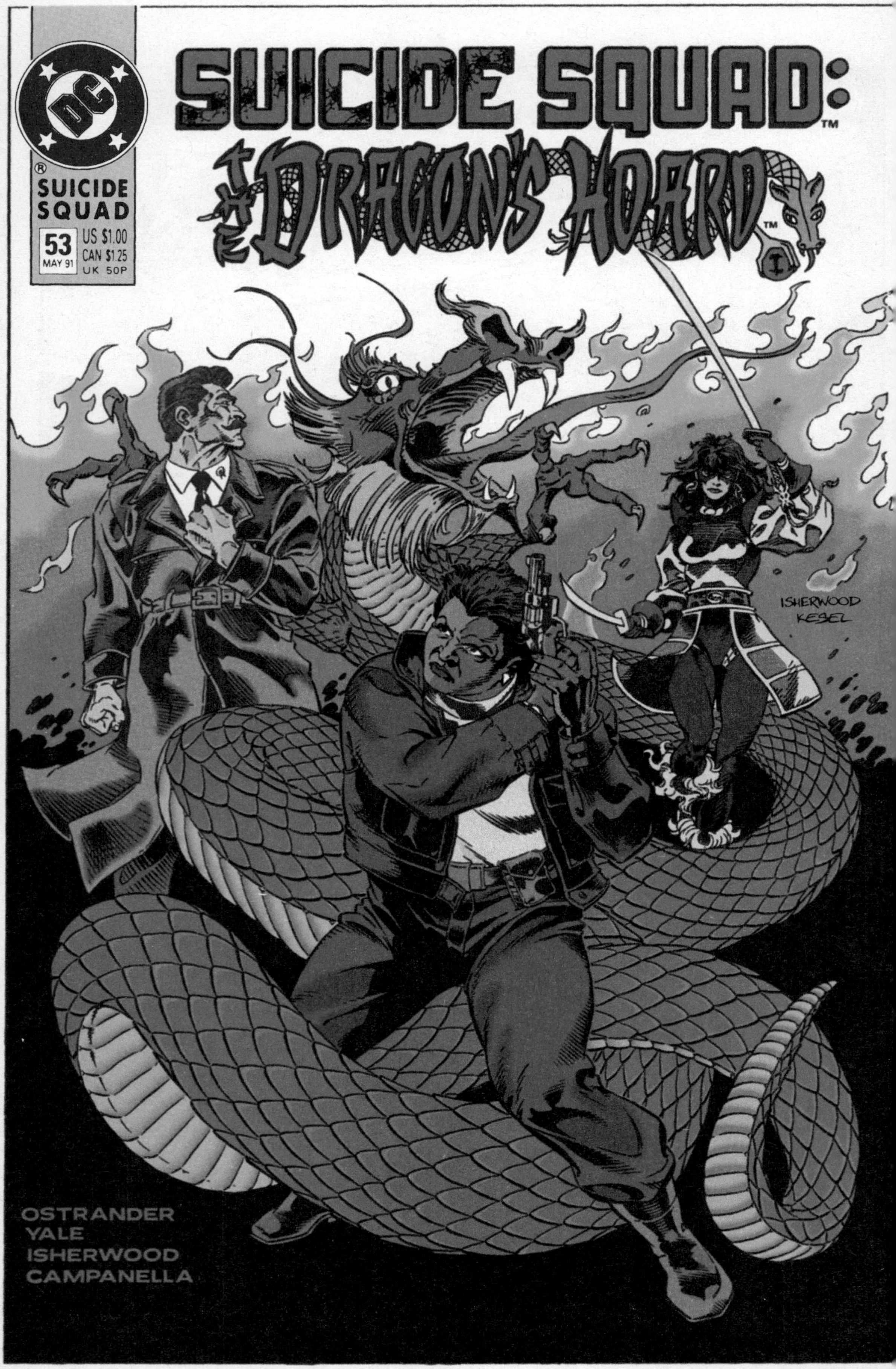
SUICIDE SQUAD:™
THE DRAGON'S HOARD™
SUICIDE SQUAD
53
MAY 91
US $1.00
CAN $1.25
UK 50P
ISHERWOOD
KESEL
OSTRANDER
YALE
ISHERWOOD
CAMPANELLA

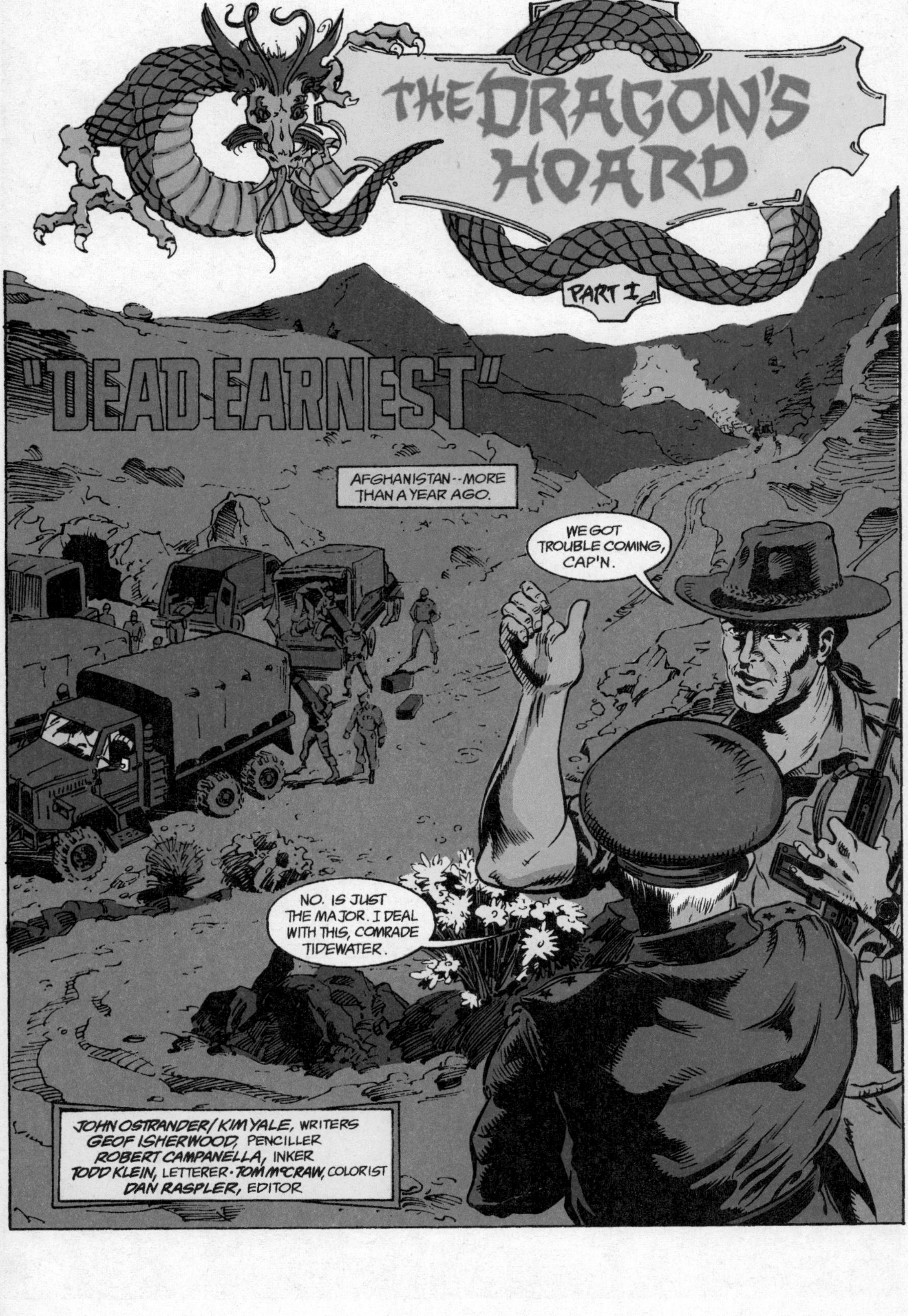
THE DRAGON'S HOARD
PART I
"DEAD EARNEST"
AFGHANISTAN--MORE THAN A YEAR AGO.
WE GOT TROUBLE COMING, CAP'N.
NO. IS JUST THE MAJOR. I DEAL WITH THIS, COMRADE TIDEWATER.
JOHN OSTRANDER/ KIM YALE, WRITERS
GEOF ISHERWOOD, PENCILLER
ROBERT CAMPANELLA, INKER
TODD KLEIN, LETTERER · TOM McCRAW, COLORIST
DAN RASPLER, EDITOR

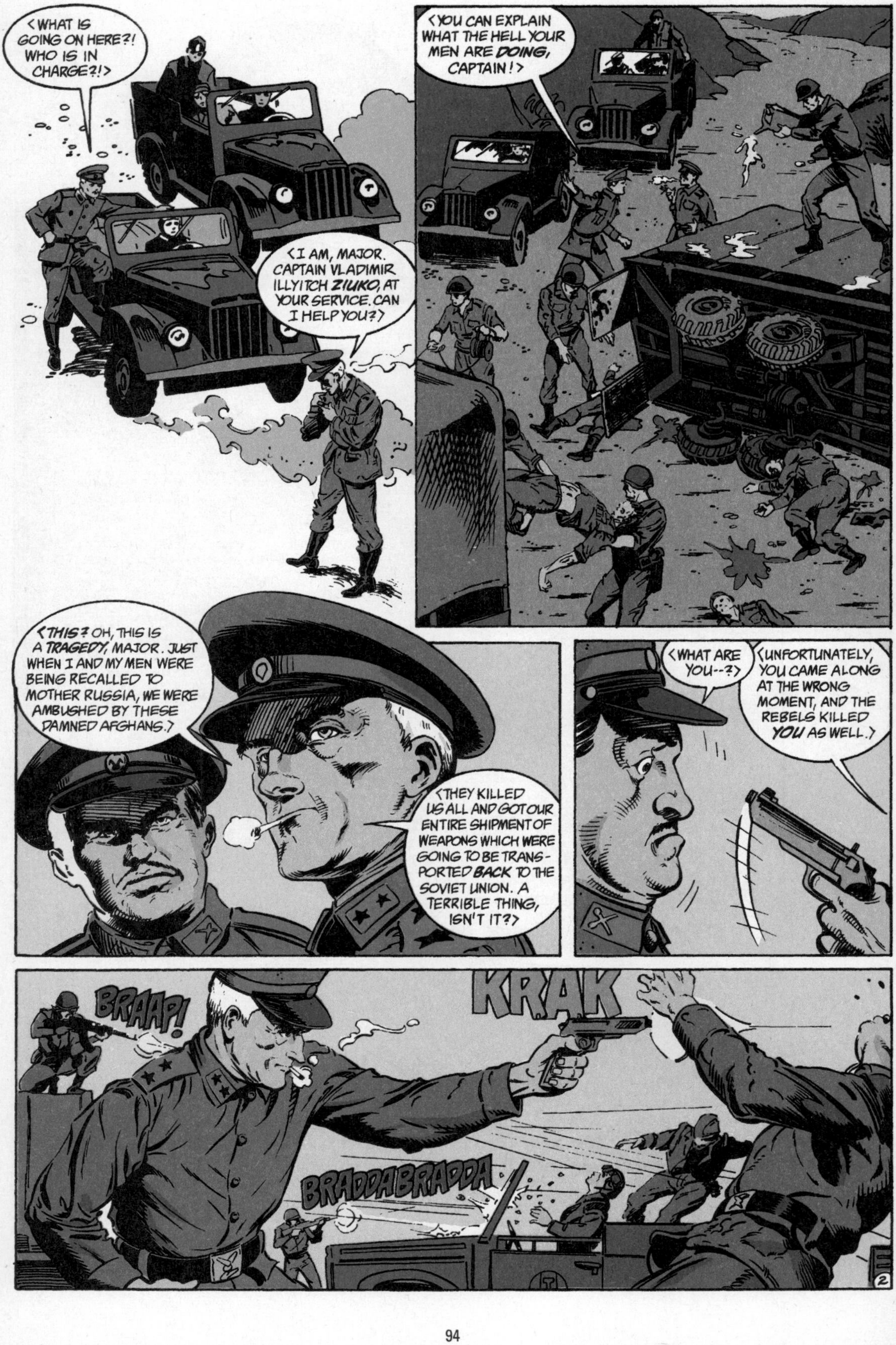

<WHAT IS GOING ON HERE?! WHO IS IN CHARGE?!>
<I AM, MAJOR. CAPTAIN VLADIMIR ILLYITCH ZIUKO, AT YOUR SERVICE. CAN I HELP YOU?>
<YOU CAN EXPLAIN WHAT THE HELL YOUR MEN ARE DOING, CAPTAIN!>
<THIS? OH, THIS IS A TRAGEDY, MAJOR. JUST WHEN I AND MY MEN WERE BEING RECALLED TO MOTHER RUSSIA, WE WERE AMBUSHED BY THESE DAMNED AFGHANS.>
<THEY KILLED US ALL AND GOT OUR ENTIRE SHIPMENT OF WEAPONS WHICH WERE GOING TO BE TRANS-PORTED BACK TO THE SOVIET UNION. A TERRIBLE THING, ISN'T IT?>
<WHAT ARE YOU--?>
<UNFORTUNATELY, YOU CAME ALONG AT THE WRONG MOMENT, AND THE REBELS KILLED YOU AS WELL.>
BRAAP!
KRAK
BRADDABRADDA
2

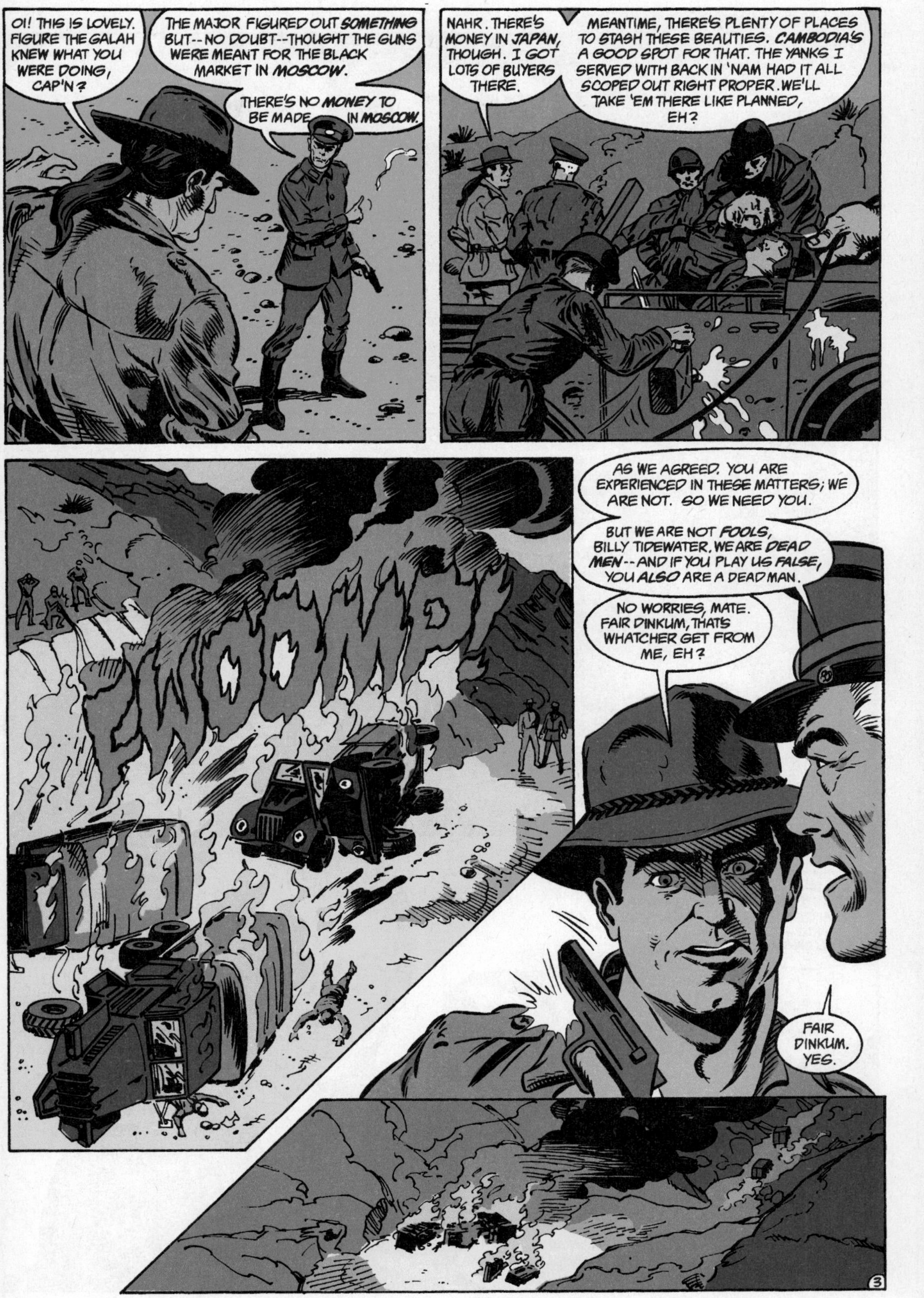

OI! THIS IS LOVELY. FIGURE THE GALAH KNEW WHAT YOU WERE DOING, CAP'N?
THE MAJOR FIGURED OUT SOMETHING BUT--NO DOUBT--THOUGHT THE GUNS WERE MEANT FOR THE BLACK MARKET IN MOSCOW.
THERE'S NO MONEY TO BE MADE IN MOSCOW.
NAHR. THERE'S MONEY IN JAPAN, THOUGH. I GOT LOTS OF BUYERS THERE.
MEANTIME, THERE'S PLENTY OF PLACES TO STASH THESE BEAUTIES. CAMBODIA'S A GOOD SPOT FOR THAT. THE YANKS I SERVED WITH BACK IN 'NAM HAD IT ALL SCOPED OUT RIGHT PROPER. WE'LL TAKE 'EM THERE LIKE PLANNED, EH?
AS WE AGREED. YOU ARE EXPERIENCED IN THESE MATTERS; WE ARE NOT. SO WE NEED YOU.
BUT WE ARE NOT FOOLS, BILLY TIDEWATER. WE ARE DEAD MEN--AND IF YOU PLAY US FALSE, YOU ALSO ARE A DEAD MAN.
NO WORRIES, MATE. FAIR DINKUM, THAT'S WHATCHER GET FROM ME, EH?
FAIR DINKUM. YES.
3

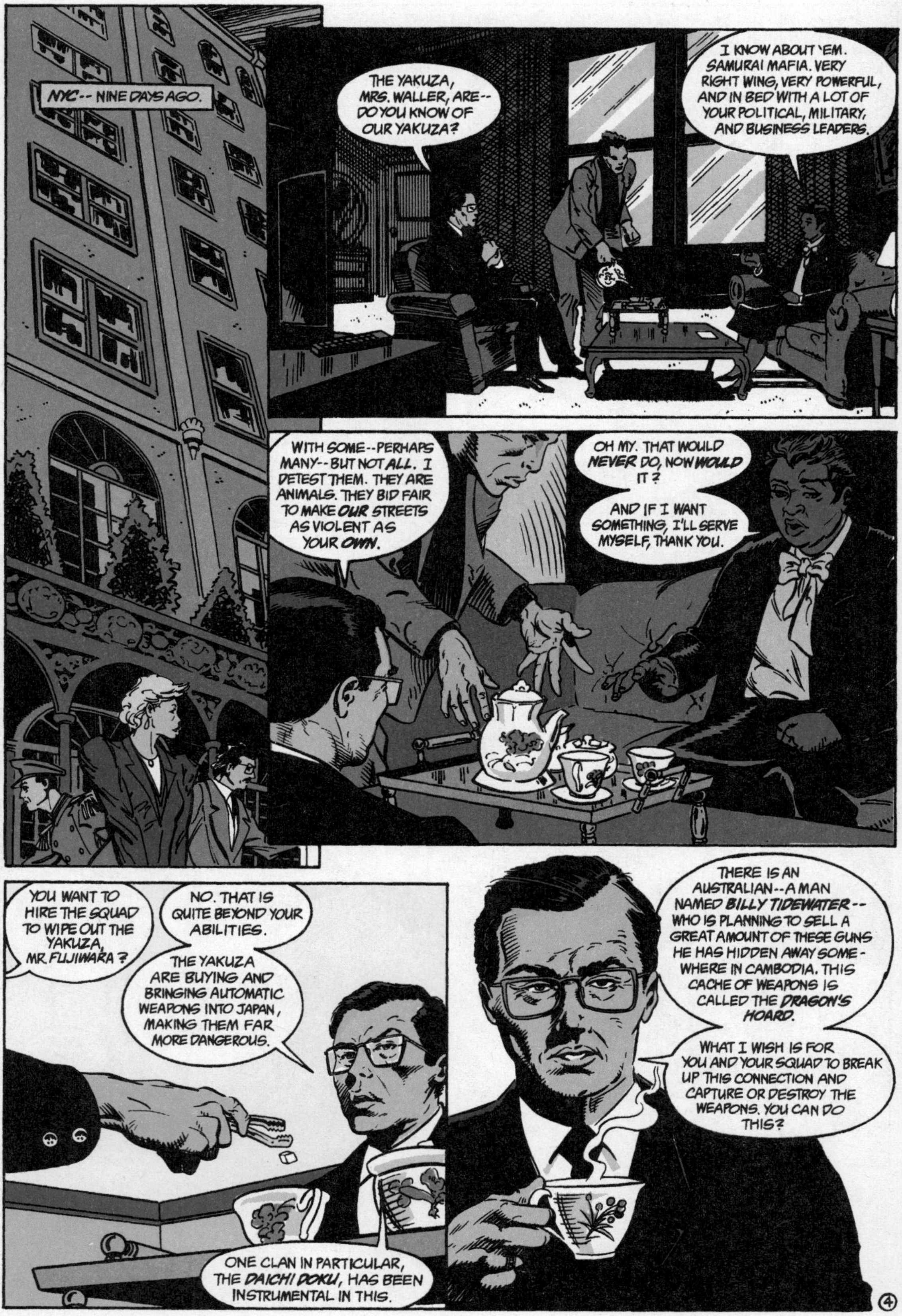
NYC -- NINE DAYS AGO.
THE YAKUZA, MRS. WALLER, ARE-- DO YOU KNOW OF OUR YAKUZA?
I KNOW ABOUT 'EM. SAMURAI MAFIA. VERY RIGHT WING, VERY POWERFUL, AND IN BED WITH A LOT OF YOUR POLITICAL, MILITARY, AND BUSINESS LEADERS.
WITH SOME--PERHAPS MANY--BUT NOT ALL. I DETEST THEM. THEY ARE ANIMALS. THEY BID FAIR TO MAKE OUR STREETS AS VIOLENT AS YOUR OWN.
OH MY. THAT WOULD NEVER DO, NOW WOULD IT?
AND IF I WANT SOMETHING, I'LL SERVE MYSELF, THANK YOU.
YOU WANT TO HIRE THE SQUAD TO WIPE OUT THE YAKUZA, MR. FUJIWARA?
NO. THAT IS QUITE BEYOND YOUR ABILITIES.
THE YAKUZA ARE BUYING AND BRINGING AUTOMATIC WEAPONS INTO JAPAN, MAKING THEM FAR MORE DANGEROUS.
ONE CLAN IN PARTICULAR, THE DAICHI DOKU, HAS BEEN INSTRUMENTAL IN THIS.
THERE IS AN AUSTRALIAN--A MAN NAMED BILLY TIDEWATER-- WHO IS PLANNING TO SELL A GREAT AMOUNT OF THESE GUNS HE HAS HIDDEN AWAY SOME-WHERE IN CAMBODIA. THIS CACHE OF WEAPONS IS CALLED THE DRAGON'S HOARD.
WHAT I WISH IS FOR YOU AND YOUR SQUAD TO BREAK UP THIS CONNECTION AND CAPTURE OR DESTROY THE WEAPONS. YOU CAN DO THIS?
4

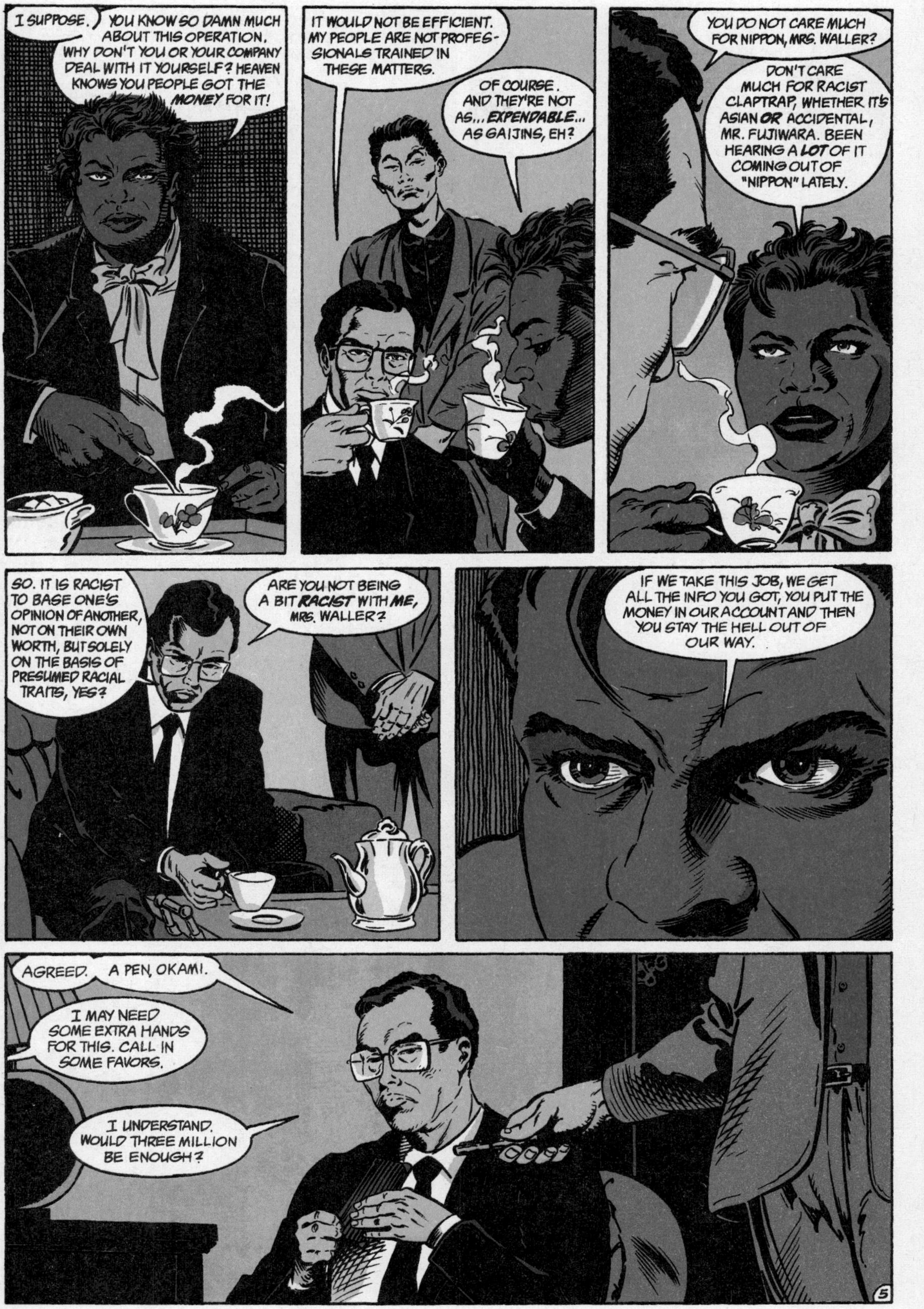
I SUPPOSE.
YOU KNOW SO DAMN MUCH ABOUT THIS OPERATION. WHY DON'T YOU OR YOUR COMPANY DEAL WITH IT YOURSELF? HEAVEN KNOWS YOU PEOPLE GOT THE MONEY FOR IT!
IT WOULD NOT BE EFFICIENT. MY PEOPLE ARE NOT PROFES-SIONALS TRAINED IN THESE MATTERS.
OF COURSE. AND THEY'RE NOT AS... EXPENDABLE... AS GAIJINS, EH?
YOU DO NOT CARE MUCH FOR NIPPON, MRS. WALLER?
DON'T CARE MUCH FOR RACIST CLAPTRAP, WHETHER IT'S ASIAN OR ACCIDENTAL, MR. FUJIWARA. BEEN HEARING A LOT OF IT COMING OUT OF "NIPPON" LATELY.
SO. IT IS RACIST TO BASE ONE'S OPINION OF ANOTHER, NOT ON THEIR OWN WORTH, BUT SOLELY ON THE BASIS OF PRESUMED RACIAL TRAITS, YES?
ARE YOU NOT BEING A BIT RACIST WITH ME, MRS. WALLER?
IF WE TAKE THIS JOB, WE GET ALL THE INFO YOU GOT, YOU PUT THE MONEY IN OUR ACCOUNT AND THEN YOU STAY THE HELL OUT OF OUR WAY.
AGREED.
A PEN, OKAMI.
I MAY NEED SOME EXTRA HANDS FOR THIS. CALL IN SOME FAVORS.
I UNDERSTAND. WOULD THREE MILLION BE ENOUGH?
5

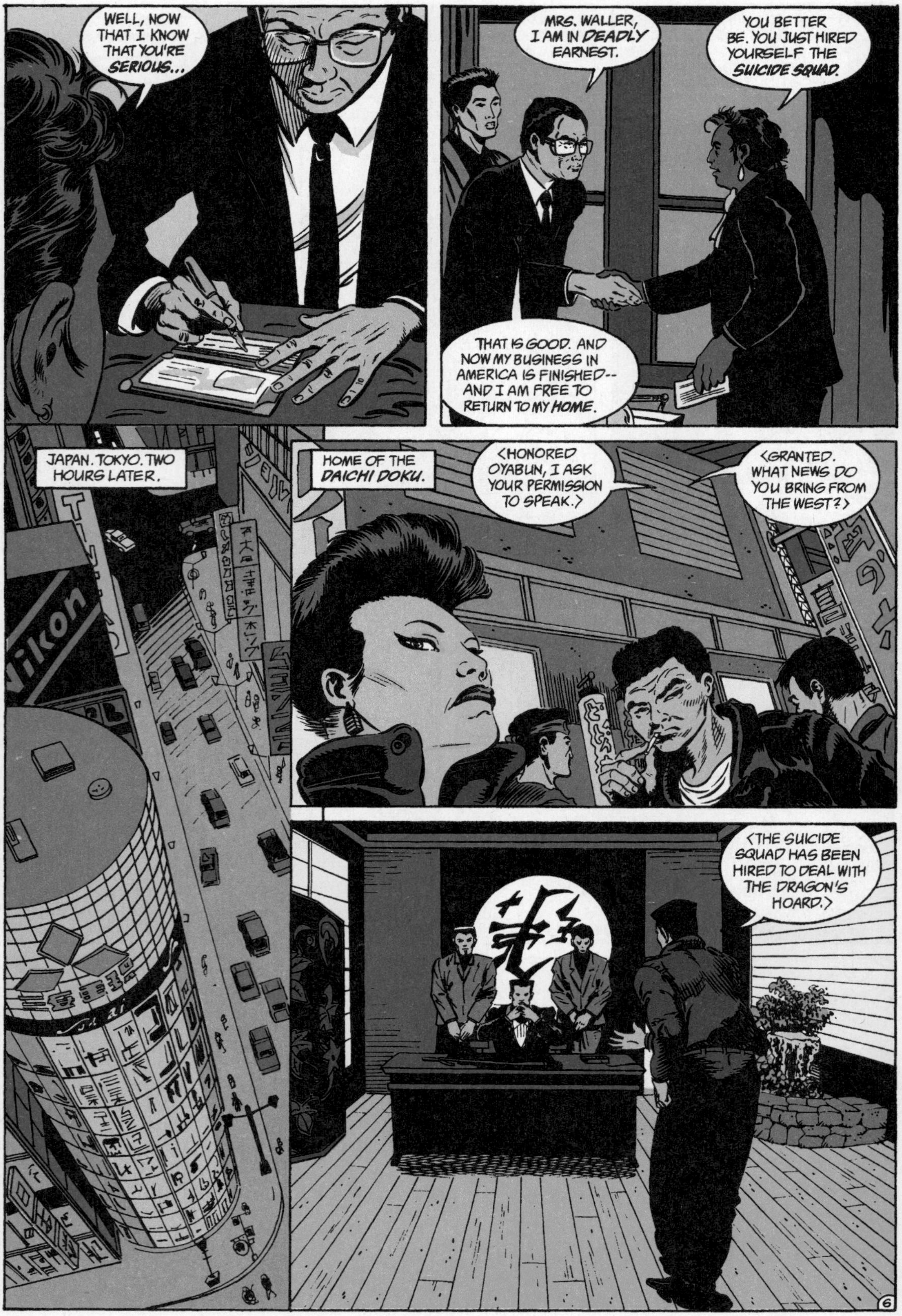
WELL, NOW THAT I KNOW THAT YOU'RE SERIOUS...
MRS. WALLER, I AM IN DEADLY EARNEST.
YOU BETTER BE. YOU JUST HIRED YOURSELF THE SUICIDE SQUAD.
THAT IS GOOD. AND NOW MY BUSINESS IN AMERICA IS FINISHED-- AND I AM FREE TO RETURN TO MY HOME.
JAPAN. TOKYO. TWO HOURS LATER.
Nikon
HOME OF THE DAICHI DOKU.
<HONORED OYABUN, I ASK YOUR PERMISSION TO SPEAK.>
<GRANTED. WHAT NEWS DO YOU BRING FROM THE WEST?>
<THE SUICIDE SQUAD HAS BEEN HIRED TO DEAL WITH THE DRAGON'S HOARD.>
6

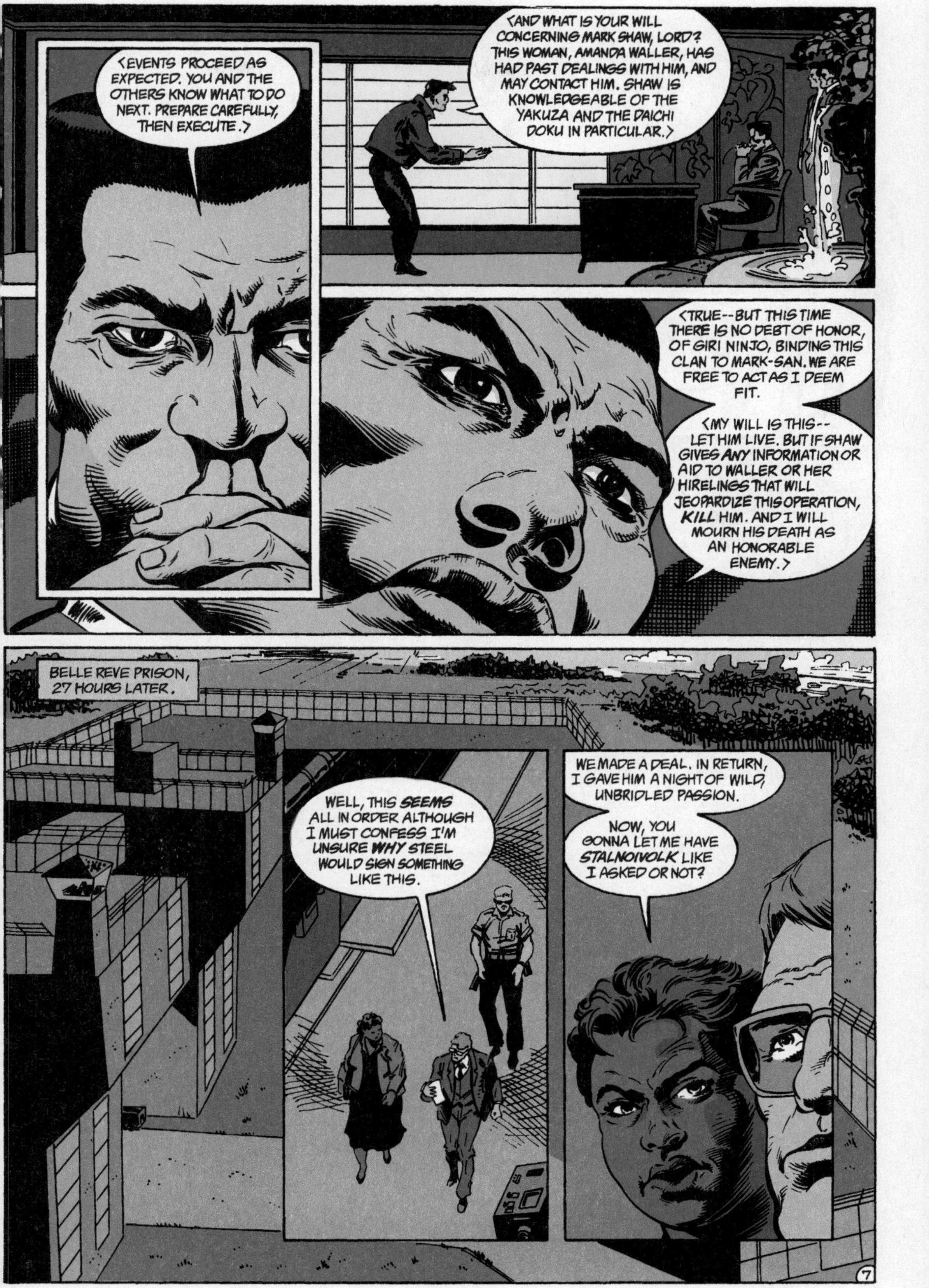

<EVENTS PROCEED AS EXPECTED. YOU AND THE OTHERS KNOW WHAT TO DO NEXT. PREPARE CAREFULLY, THEN EXECUTE.>
<AND WHAT IS YOUR WILL CONCERNING MARK SHAW, LORD? THIS WOMAN, AMANDA WALLER, HAS HAD PAST DEALINGS WITH HIM, AND MAY CONTACT HIM. SHAW IS KNOWLEDGEABLE OF THE YAKUZA AND THE DAICHI DOKU IN PARTICULAR.>
<TRUE--BUT THIS TIME THERE IS NO DEBT OF HONOR, OF GIRI NINJO, BINDING THIS CLAN TO MARK-SAN. WE ARE FREE TO ACT AS I DEEM FIT.
<MY WILL IS THIS--LET HIM LIVE. BUT IF SHAW GIVES ANY INFORMATION OR AID TO WALLER OR HER HIRELINGS THAT WILL JEOPARDIZE THIS OPERATION, KILL HIM. AND I WILL MOURN HIS DEATH AS AN HONORABLE ENEMY.>
BELLE REVE PRISON, 27 HOURS LATER.
WELL, THIS SEEMS ALL IN ORDER ALTHOUGH I MUST CONFESS I'M UNSURE WHY STEEL WOULD SIGN SOMETHING LIKE THIS.
WE MADE A DEAL. IN RETURN, I GAVE HIM A NIGHT OF WILD, UNBRIDLED PASSION.
NOW, YOU GONNA LET ME HAVE STALNOIVOLK LIKE I ASKED OR NOT?
7

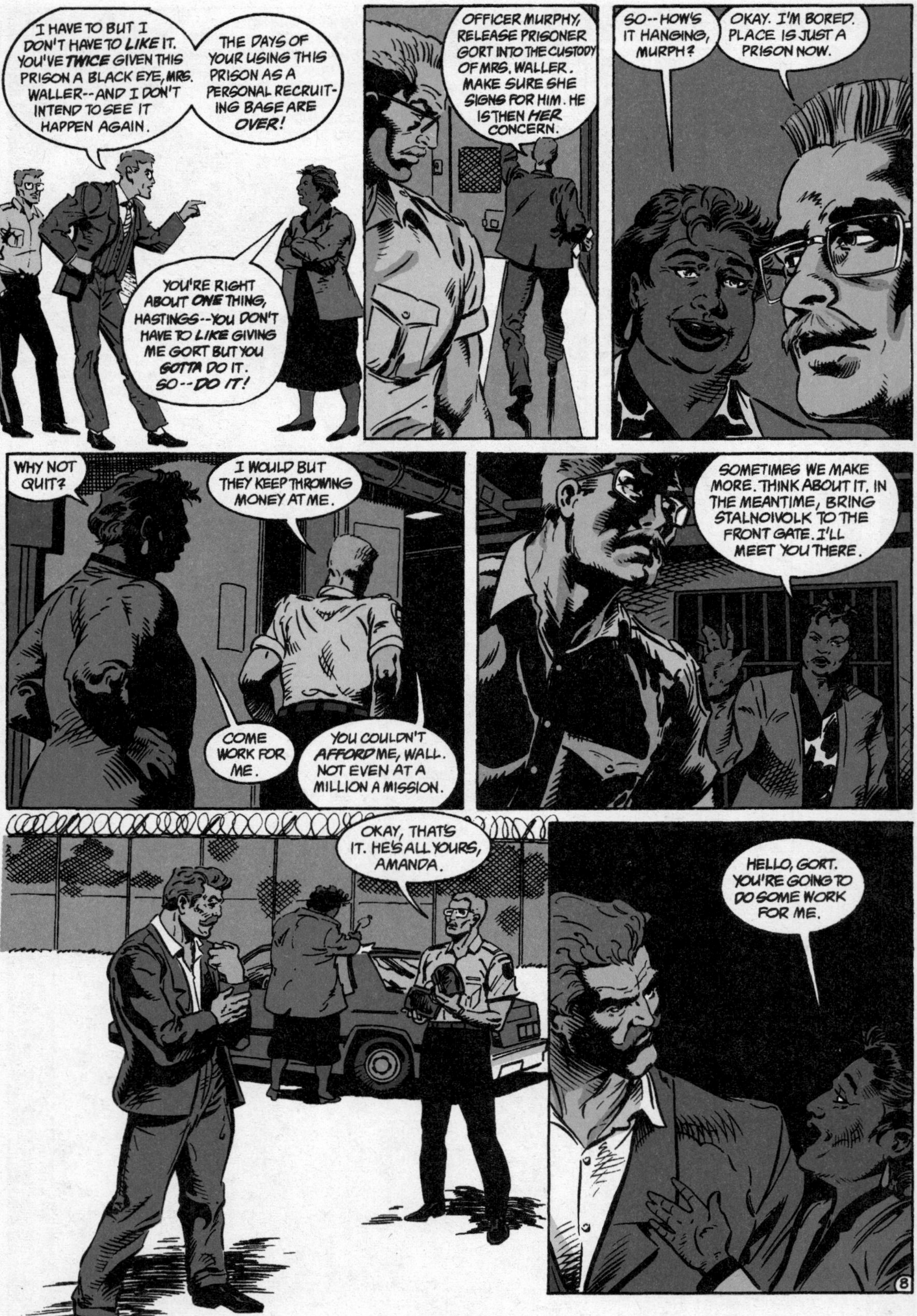
I HAVE TO BUT I DON'T HAVE TO LIKE IT. YOU'VE TWICE GIVEN THIS PRISON A BLACK EYE, MRS. WALLER--AND I DON'T INTEND TO SEE IT HAPPEN AGAIN.
THE DAYS OF YOUR USING THIS PRISON AS A PERSONAL RECRUITING BASE ARE OVER!
YOU'RE RIGHT ABOUT ONE THING, HASTINGS--YOU DON'T HAVE TO LIKE GIVING ME GORT BUT YOU GOTTA DO IT. SO--DO IT!
OFFICER MURPHY, RELEASE PRISONER GORT INTO THE CUSTODY OF MRS. WALLER. MAKE SURE SHE SIGNS FOR HIM. HE IS THEN HER CONCERN.
SO--HOW'S IT HANGING, MURPH?
OKAY. I'M BORED. PLACE IS JUST A PRISON NOW.
WHY NOT QUIT?
I WOULD BUT THEY KEEP THROWING MONEY AT ME.
COME WORK FOR ME.
YOU COULDN'T AFFORD ME, WALL. NOT EVEN AT A MILLION A MISSION.
SOMETIMES WE MAKE MORE. THINK ABOUT IT. IN THE MEANTIME, BRING STALNOIVOLK TO THE FRONT GATE. I'LL MEET YOU THERE.
OKAY, THAT'S IT. HE'S ALL YOURS, AMANDA.
HELLO, GORT. YOU'RE GOING TO DO SOME WORK FOR ME.
8

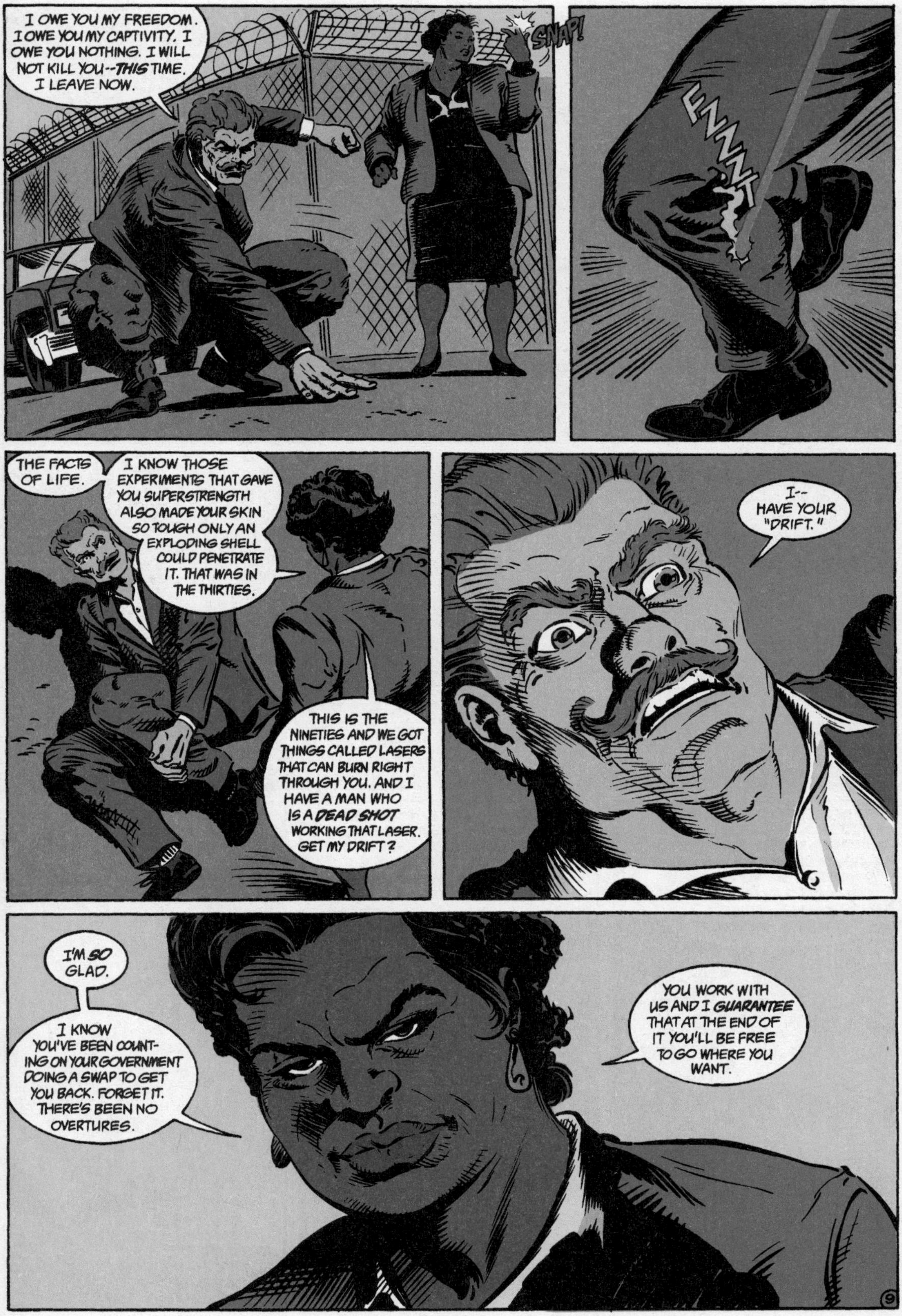
I OWE YOU MY FREEDOM. I OWE YOU MY CAPTIVITY. I OWE YOU NOTHING. I WILL NOT KILL YOU--THIS TIME. I LEAVE NOW.
SNAP!
FZZZZT
THE FACTS OF LIFE.
I KNOW THOSE EXPERIMENTS THAT GAVE YOU SUPERSTRENGTH ALSO MADE YOUR SKIN SO TOUGH ONLY AN EXPLODING SHELL COULD PENETRATE IT. THAT WAS IN THE THIRTIES.
THIS IS THE NINETIES AND WE GOT THINGS CALLED LASERS THAT CAN BURN RIGHT THROUGH YOU. AND I HAVE A MAN WHO IS A DEAD SHOT WORKING THAT LASER. GET MY DRIFT?
I-- HAVE YOUR "DRIFT."
I'M SO GLAD.
I KNOW YOU'VE BEEN COUNTING ON YOUR GOVERNMENT DOING A SWAP TO GET YOU BACK. FORGET IT. THERE'S BEEN NO OVERTURES.
YOU WORK WITH US AND I GUARANTEE THAT AT THE END OF IT YOU'LL BE FREE TO GO WHERE YOU WANT.
9

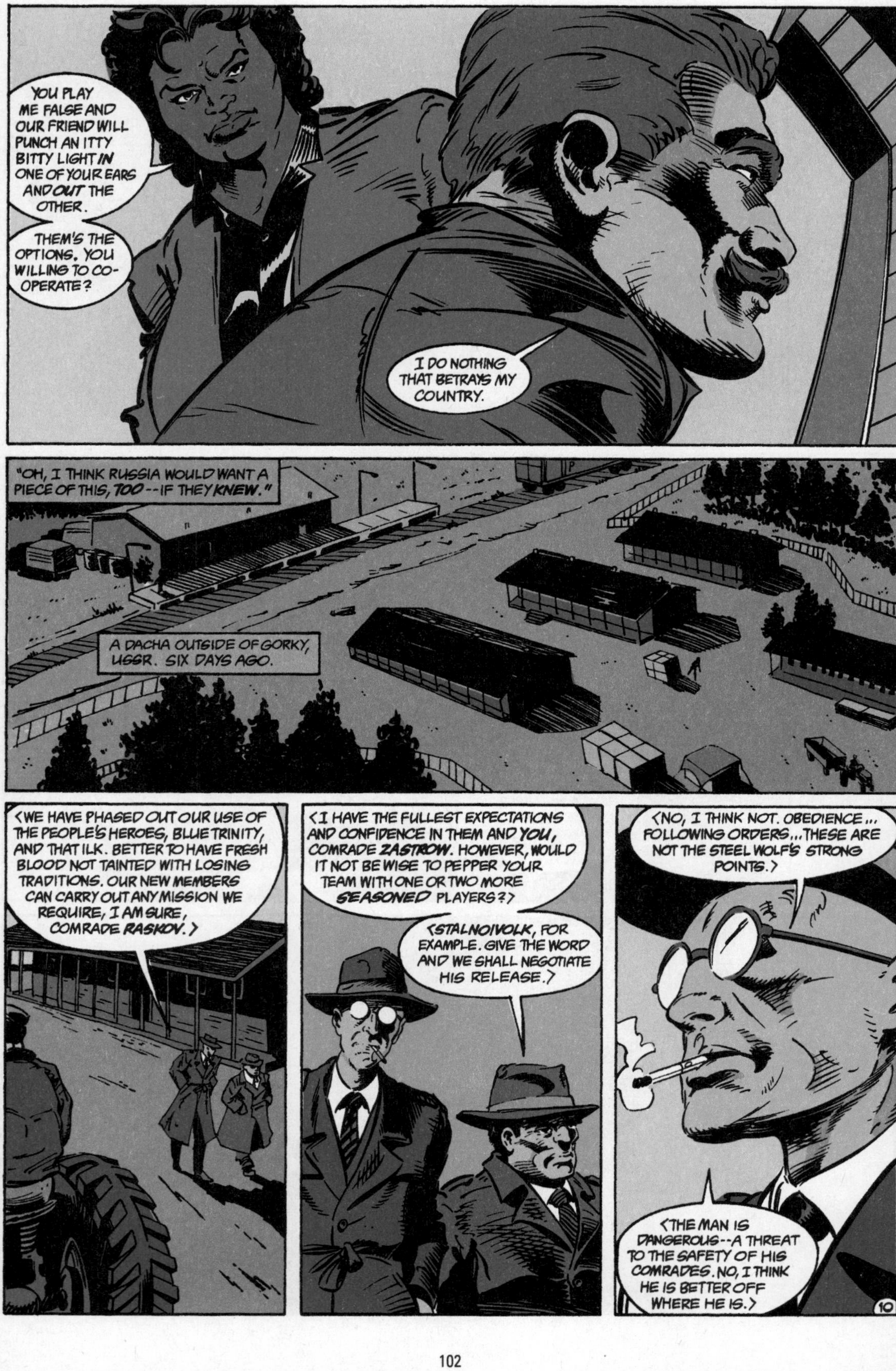
YOU PLAY ME FALSE AND OUR FRIEND WILL PUNCH AN ITTY BITTY LIGHT IN ONE OF YOUR EARS AND OUT THE OTHER.
THEM'S THE OPTIONS. YOU WILLING TO CO-OPERATE?
I DO NOTHING THAT BETRAYS MY COUNTRY.
"OH, I THINK RUSSIA WOULD WANT A PIECE OF THIS, TOO--IF THEY KNEW."
A DACHA OUTSIDE OF GORKY, USSR. SIX DAYS AGO.
<WE HAVE PHASED OUT OUR USE OF THE PEOPLE'S HEROES, BLUE TRINITY, AND THAT ILK. BETTER TO HAVE FRESH BLOOD NOT TAINTED WITH LOSING TRADITIONS. OUR NEW MEMBERS CAN CARRY OUT ANY MISSION WE REQUIRE, I AM SURE, COMRADE RASKOV.>
<I HAVE THE FULLEST EXPECTATIONS AND CONFIDENCE IN THEM AND YOU, COMRADE ZASTROW. HOWEVER, WOULD IT NOT BE WISE TO PEPPER YOUR TEAM WITH ONE OR TWO MORE SEASONED PLAYERS?>
<STALNOIVOLK, FOR EXAMPLE. GIVE THE WORD AND WE SHALL NEGOTIATE HIS RELEASE.>
<NO, I THINK NOT. OBEDIENCE... FOLLOWING ORDERS... THESE ARE NOT THE STEEL WOLF'S STRONG POINTS.>
<THE MAN IS DANGEROUS--A THREAT TO THE SAFETY OF HIS COMRADES. NO, I THINK HE IS BETTER OFF WHERE HE IS.>
10

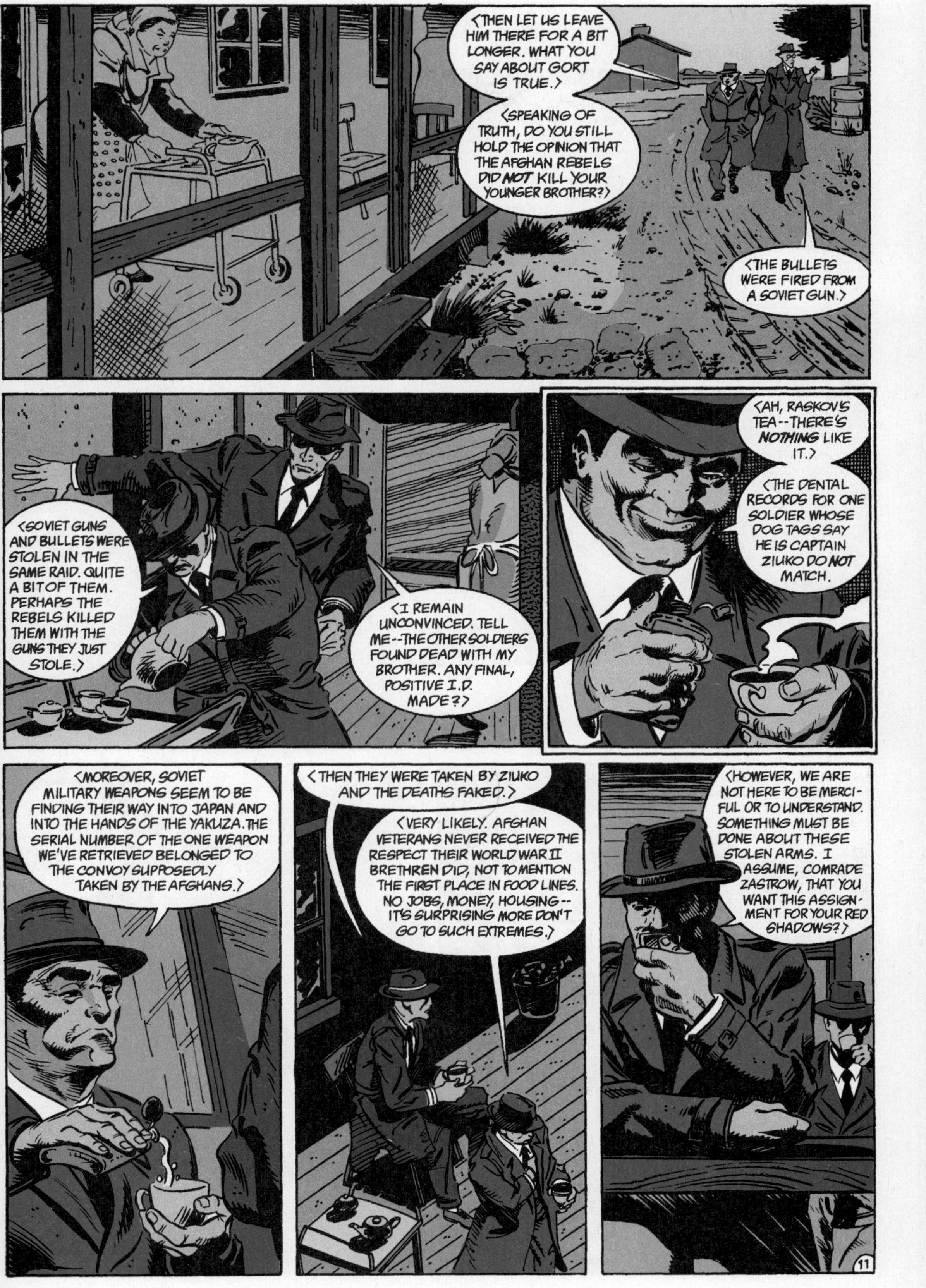
<THEN LET US LEAVE HIM THERE FOR A BIT LONGER. WHAT YOU SAY ABOUT GORT IS TRUE.>
<SPEAKING OF TRUTH, DO YOU STILL HOLD THE OPINION THAT THE AFGHAN REBELS DID NOT KILL YOUR YOUNGER BROTHER?>
<THE BULLETS WERE FIRED FROM A SOVIET GUN.>
<SOVIET GUNS AND BULLETS WERE STOLEN IN THE SAME RAID. QUITE A BIT OF THEM. PERHAPS THE REBELS KILLED THEM WITH THE GUNS THEY JUST STOLE.>
<I REMAIN UNCONVINCED. TELL ME--THE OTHER SOLDIERS FOUND DEAD WITH MY BROTHER. ANY FINAL, POSITIVE I.D. MADE?>
<AH, RASKOV'S TEA--THERE'S NOTHING LIKE IT.>
<THE DENTAL RECORDS FOR ONE SOLDIER WHOSE DOG TAGS SAY HE IS CAPTAIN ZIUKO DO NOT MATCH.
<MOREOVER, SOVIET MILITARY WEAPONS SEEM TO BE FINDING THEIR WAY INTO JAPAN AND INTO THE HANDS OF THE YAKUZA. THE SERIAL NUMBER OF THE ONE WEAPON WE'VE RETRIEVED BELONGED TO THE CONVOY SUPPOSEDLY TAKEN BY THE AFGHANS.>
<THEN THEY WERE TAKEN BY ZIUKO AND THE DEATHS FAKED.>
<VERY LIKELY. AFGHAN VETERANS NEVER RECEIVED THE RESPECT THEIR WORLD WAR II BRETHREN DID, NOT TO MENTION THE FIRST PLACE IN FOOD LINES. NO JOBS, MONEY, HOUSING--IT'S SURPRISING MORE DON'T GO TO SUCH EXTREMES.>
<HOWEVER, WE ARE NOT HERE TO BE MERCIFUL OR TO UNDERSTAND. SOMETHING MUST BE DONE ABOUT THESE STOLEN ARMS. I ASSUME, COMRADE ZASTROW, THAT YOU WANT THIS ASSIGNMENT FOR YOUR RED SHADOWS?>
11

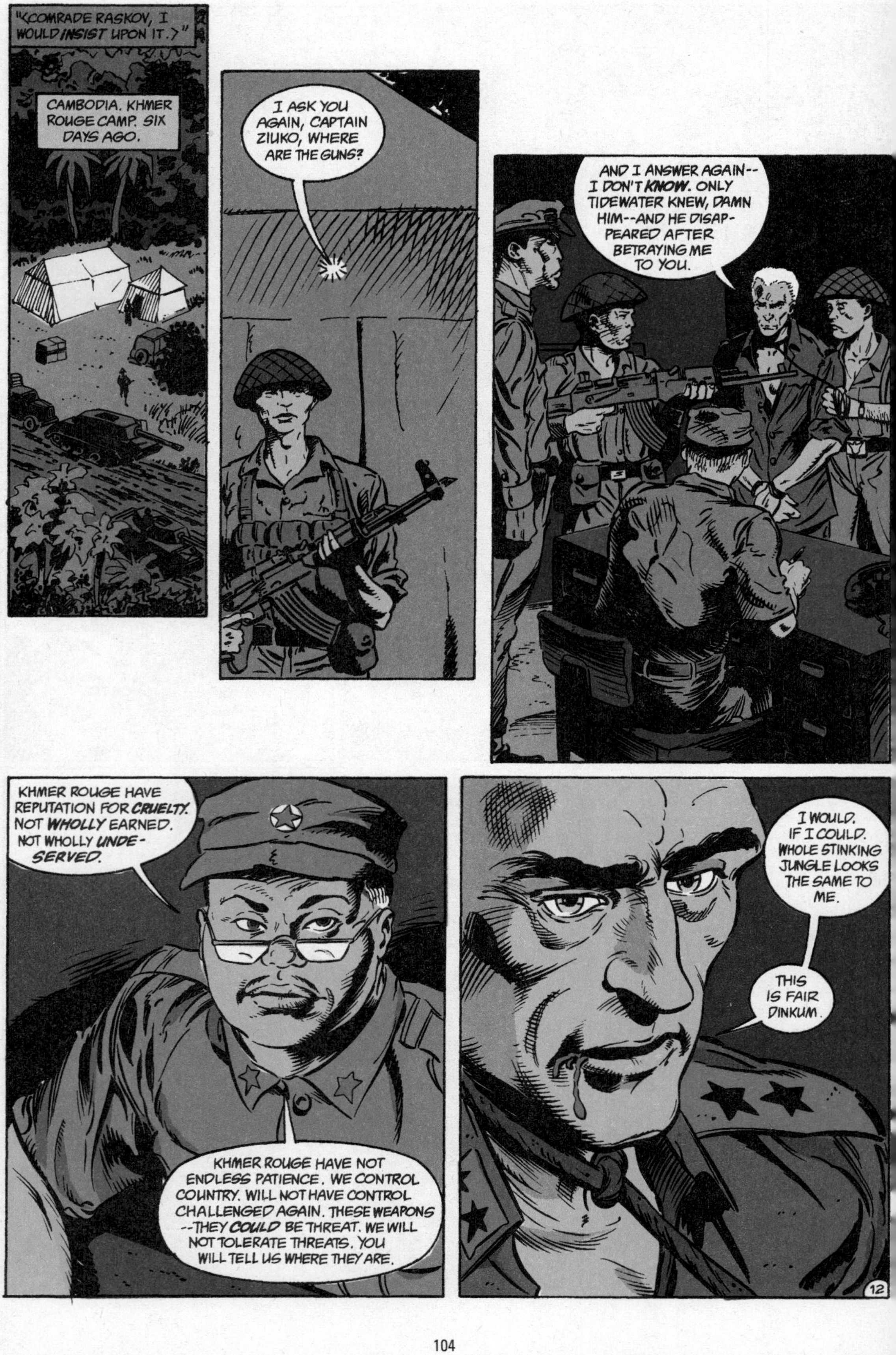

"<COMRADE RASKOV, I WOULD INSIST UPON IT.>"
CAMBODIA. KHMER ROUGE CAMP. SIX DAYS AGO.
I ASK YOU AGAIN, CAPTAIN ZIUKO, WHERE ARE THE GUNS?
AND I ANSWER AGAIN-- I DON'T KNOW. ONLY TIDEWATER KNEW, DAMN HIM--AND HE DISAPPEARED AFTER BETRAYING ME TO YOU.
KHMER ROUGE HAVE REPUTATION FOR CRUELTY. NOT WHOLLY EARNED. NOT WHOLLY UNDESERVED.
KHMER ROUGE HAVE NOT ENDLESS PATIENCE. WE CONTROL COUNTRY. WILL NOT HAVE CONTROL CHALLENGED AGAIN. THESE WEAPONS --THEY COULD BE THREAT. WE WILL NOT TOLERATE THREATS. YOU WILL TELL US WHERE THEY ARE.
I WOULD. IF I COULD. WHOLE STINKING JUNGLE LOOKS THE SAME TO ME.
THIS IS FAIR DINKUM.
12

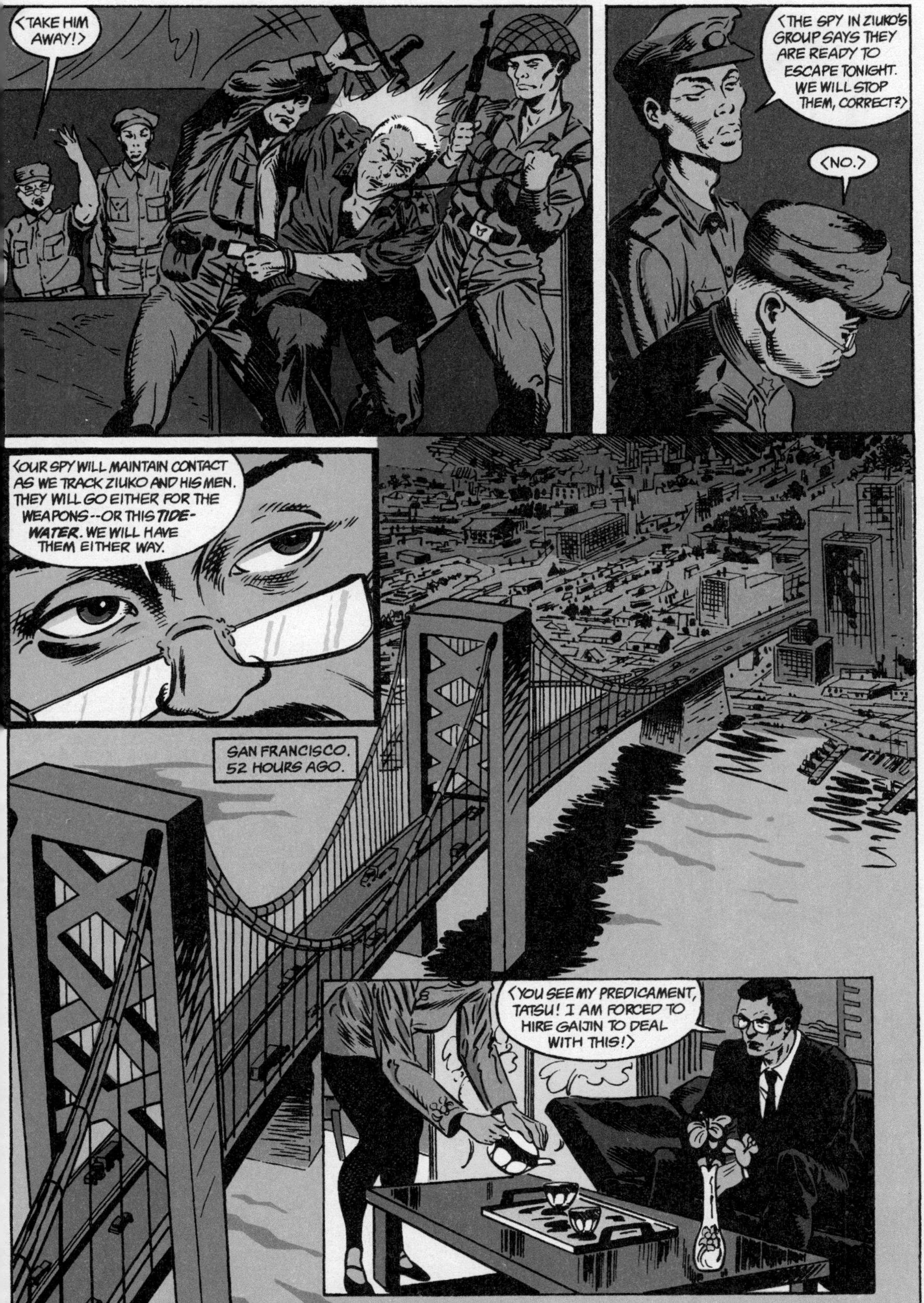

<TAKE HIM AWAY!>
<THE SPY IN ZIUKO'S GROUP SAYS THEY ARE READY TO ESCAPE TONIGHT. WE WILL STOP THEM, CORRECT?>
<NO.>
<OUR SPY WILL MAINTAIN CONTACT AS WE TRACK ZIUKO AND HIS MEN. THEY WILL GO EITHER FOR THE WEAPONS--OR THIS TIDE-WATER. WE WILL HAVE THEM EITHER WAY.
SAN FRANCISCO. 52 HOURS AGO.
<YOU SEE MY PREDICAMENT, TATSU! I AM FORCED TO HIRE GAIJIN TO DEAL WITH THIS!>
13

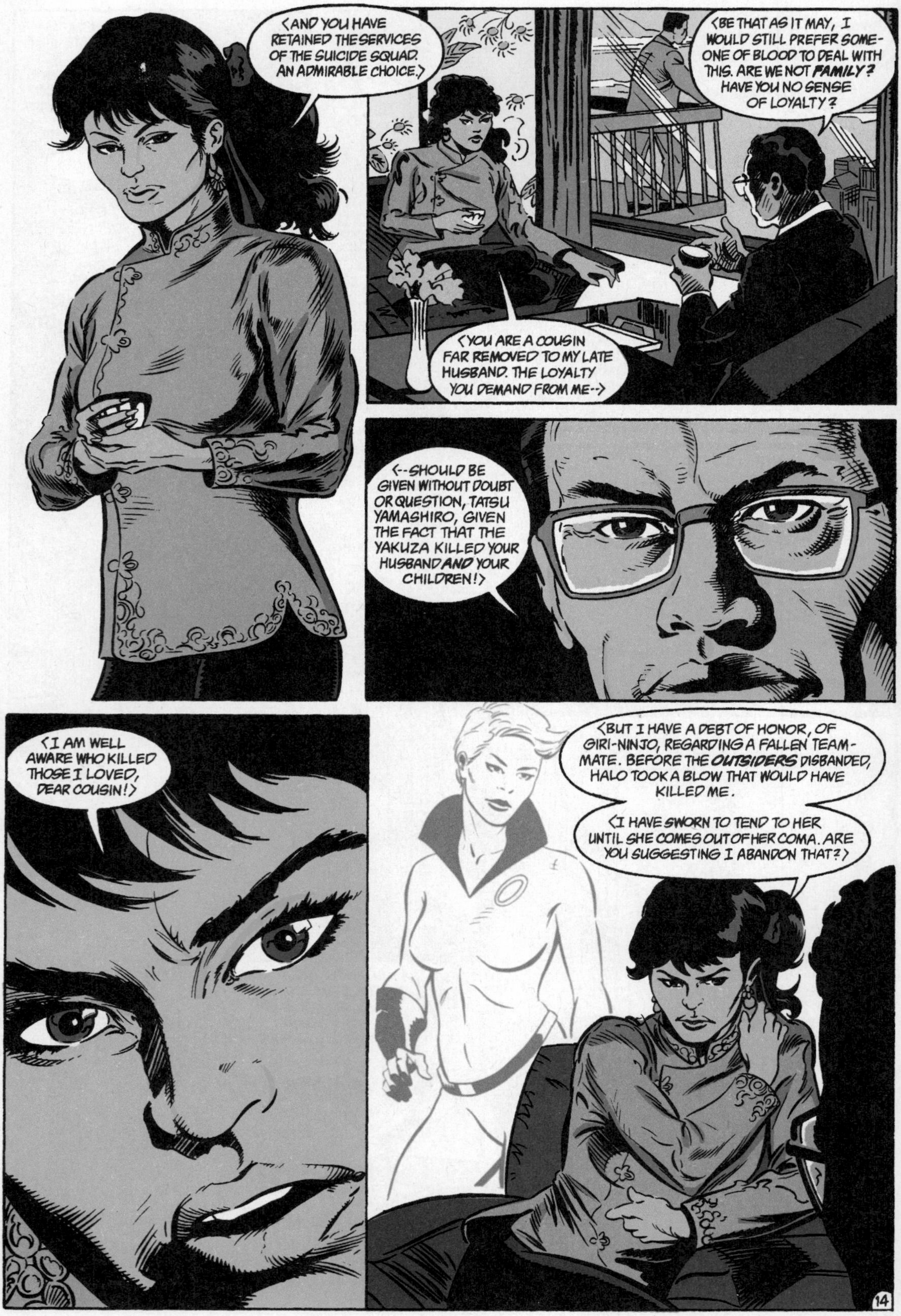

<AND YOU HAVE RETAINED THE SERVICES OF THE SUICIDE SQUAD. AN ADMIRABLE CHOICE.>
<BE THAT AS IT MAY, I WOULD STILL PREFER SOME-ONE OF BLOOD TO DEAL WITH THIS. ARE WE NOT FAMILY? HAVE YOU NO SENSE OF LOYALTY?
<YOU ARE A COUSIN FAR REMOVED TO MY LATE HUSBAND. THE LOYALTY YOU DEMAND FROM ME--
<--SHOULD BE GIVEN WITHOUT DOUBT OR QUESTION, TATSU YAMASHIRO, GIVEN THE FACT THAT THE YAKUZA KILLED YOUR HUSBAND AND YOUR CHILDREN!>
<I AM WELL AWARE WHO KILLED THOSE I LOVED, DEAR COUSIN!>
<BUT I HAVE A DEBT OF HONOR, OF GIRI-NINJO, REGARDING A FALLEN TEAM-MATE. BEFORE THE OUTSIDERS DISBANDED, HALO TOOK A BLOW THAT WOULD HAVE KILLED ME.
<I HAVE SWORN TO TEND TO HER UNTIL SHE COMES OUT OF HER COMA. ARE YOU SUGGESTING I ABANDON THAT?>
14

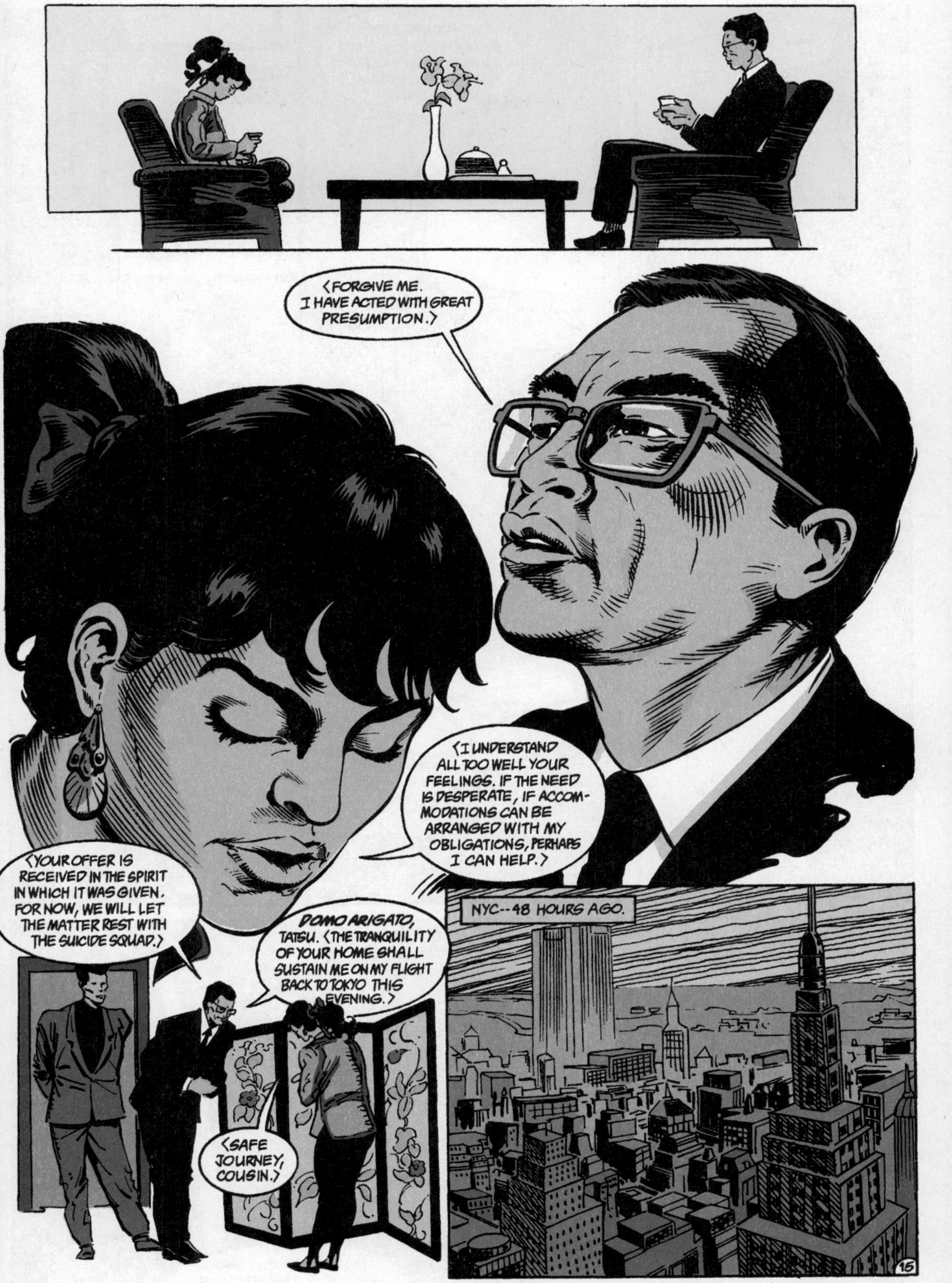

<FORGIVE ME. I HAVE ACTED WITH GREAT PRESUMPTION.>
<I UNDERSTAND ALL TOO WELL YOUR FEELINGS. IF THE NEED IS DESPERATE, IF ACCOMMODATIONS CAN BE ARRANGED WITH MY OBLIGATIONS, PERHAPS I CAN HELP.>
<YOUR OFFER IS RECEIVED IN THE SPIRIT IN WHICH IT WAS GIVEN. FOR NOW, WE WILL LET THE MATTER REST WITH THE SUICIDE SQUAD.>
DOMO ARIGATO, TATSU. <THE TRANQUILITY OF YOUR HOME SHALL SUSTAIN ME ON MY FLIGHT BACK TO TOKYO THIS EVENING.>
<SAFE JOURNEY, COUSIN.>
NYC--48 HOURS AGO.
15

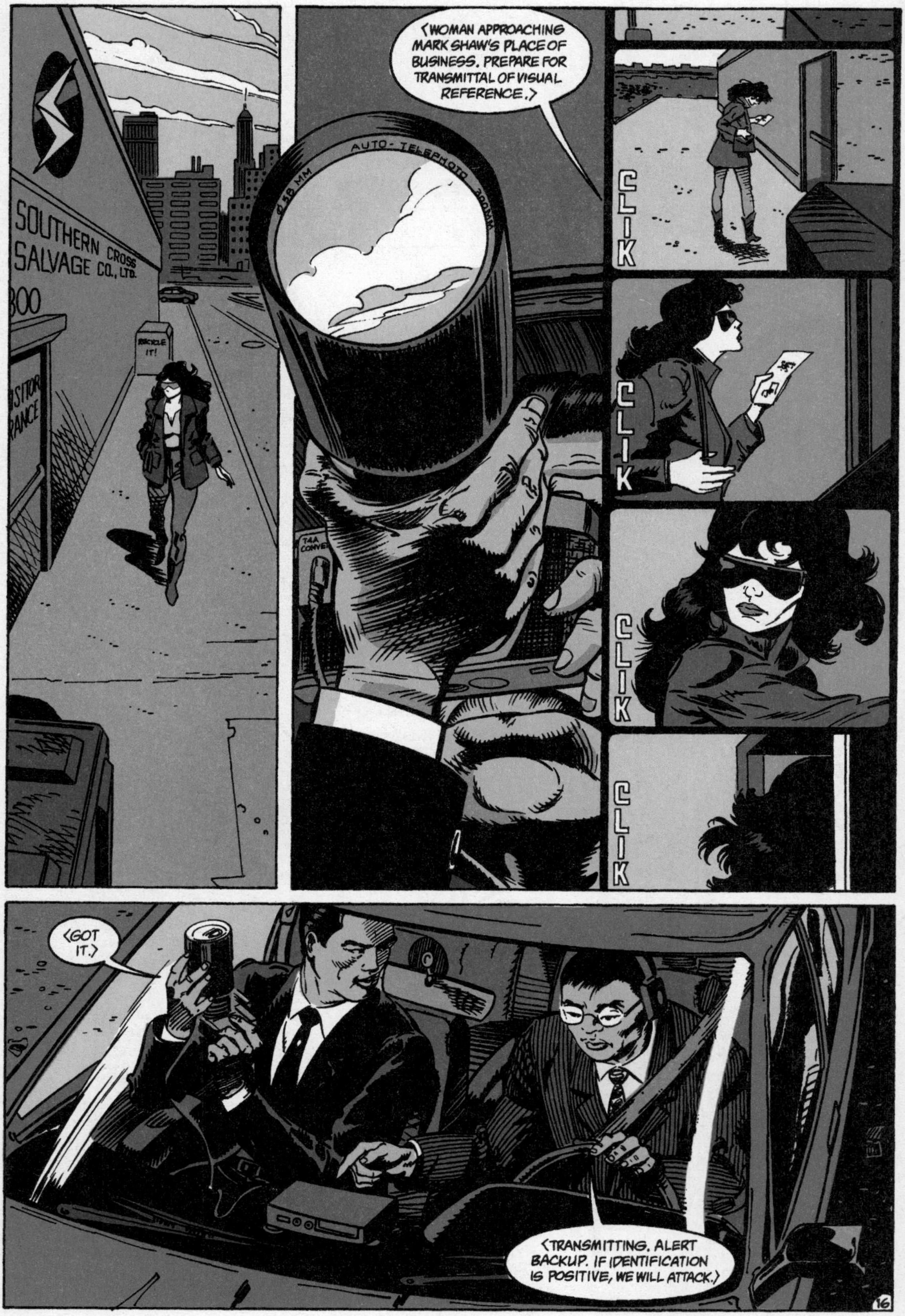

SOUTHERN CROSS SALVAGE CO., LTD.
800
RECYCLE IT!
‹WOMAN APPROACHING MARK SHAW'S PLACE OF BUSINESS. PREPARE FOR TRANSMITTAL OF VISUAL REFERENCE.›
AUTO-TELEPHOTO
CLIK
CLIK
CLIK
CLIK
‹GOT IT.›
‹TRANSMITTING. ALERT BACKUP. IF IDENTIFICATION IS POSITIVE, WE WILL ATTACK.›
16

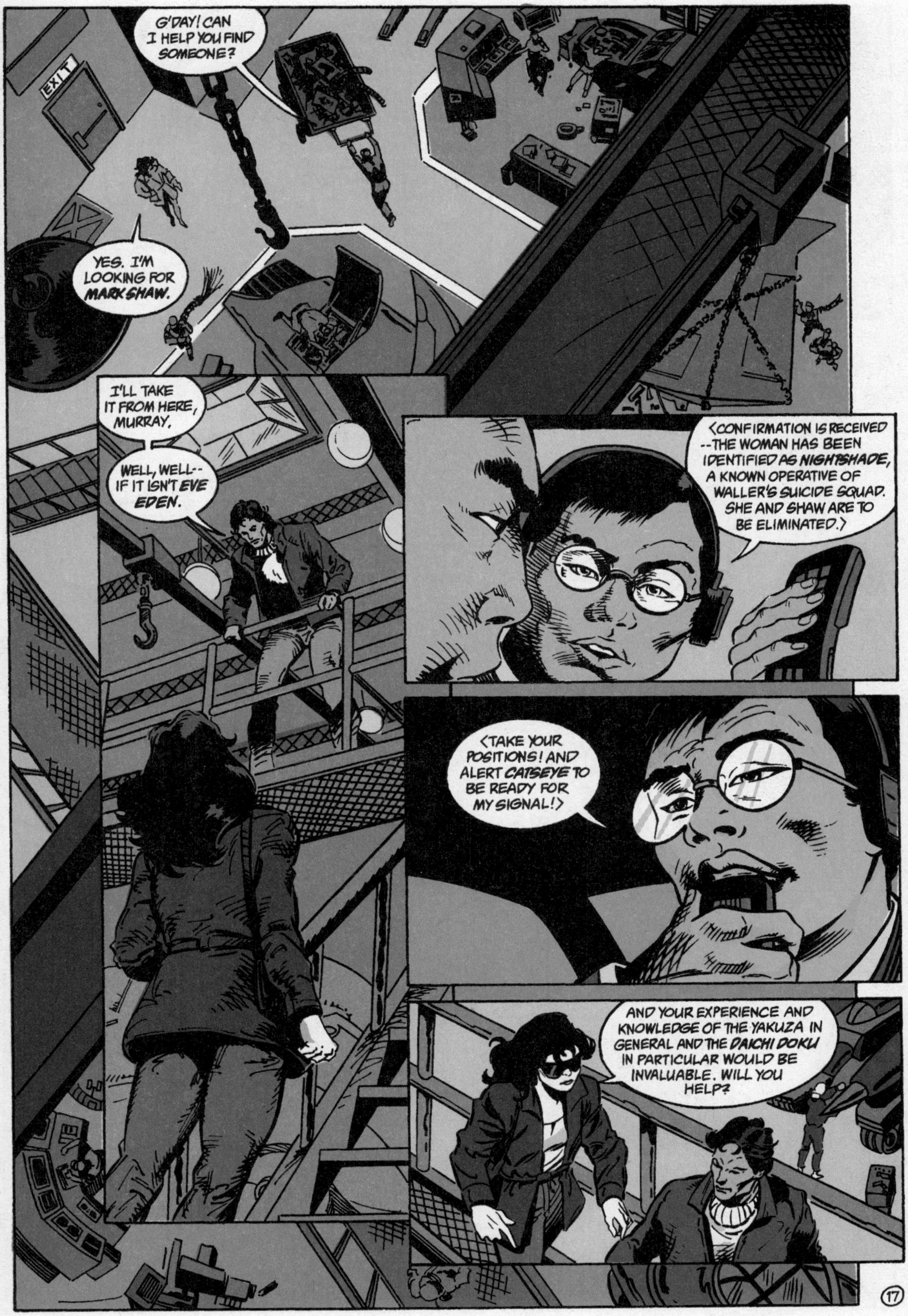
G'DAY! CAN I HELP YOU FIND SOMEONE?
YES. I'M LOOKING FOR MARK SHAW.
I'LL TAKE IT FROM HERE, MURRAY.
WELL, WELL-- IF IT ISN'T EVE EDEN.
<CONFIRMATION IS RECEIVED --THE WOMAN HAS BEEN IDENTIFIED AS NIGHTSHADE, A KNOWN OPERATIVE OF WALLER'S SUICIDE SQUAD. SHE AND SHAW ARE TO BE ELIMINATED.>
<TAKE YOUR POSITIONS! AND ALERT CATSEYE TO BE READY FOR MY SIGNAL!>
AND YOUR EXPERIENCE AND KNOWLEDGE OF THE YAKUZA IN GENERAL AND THE DAICHI DOKU IN PARTICULAR WOULD BE INVALUABLE. WILL YOU HELP?
17

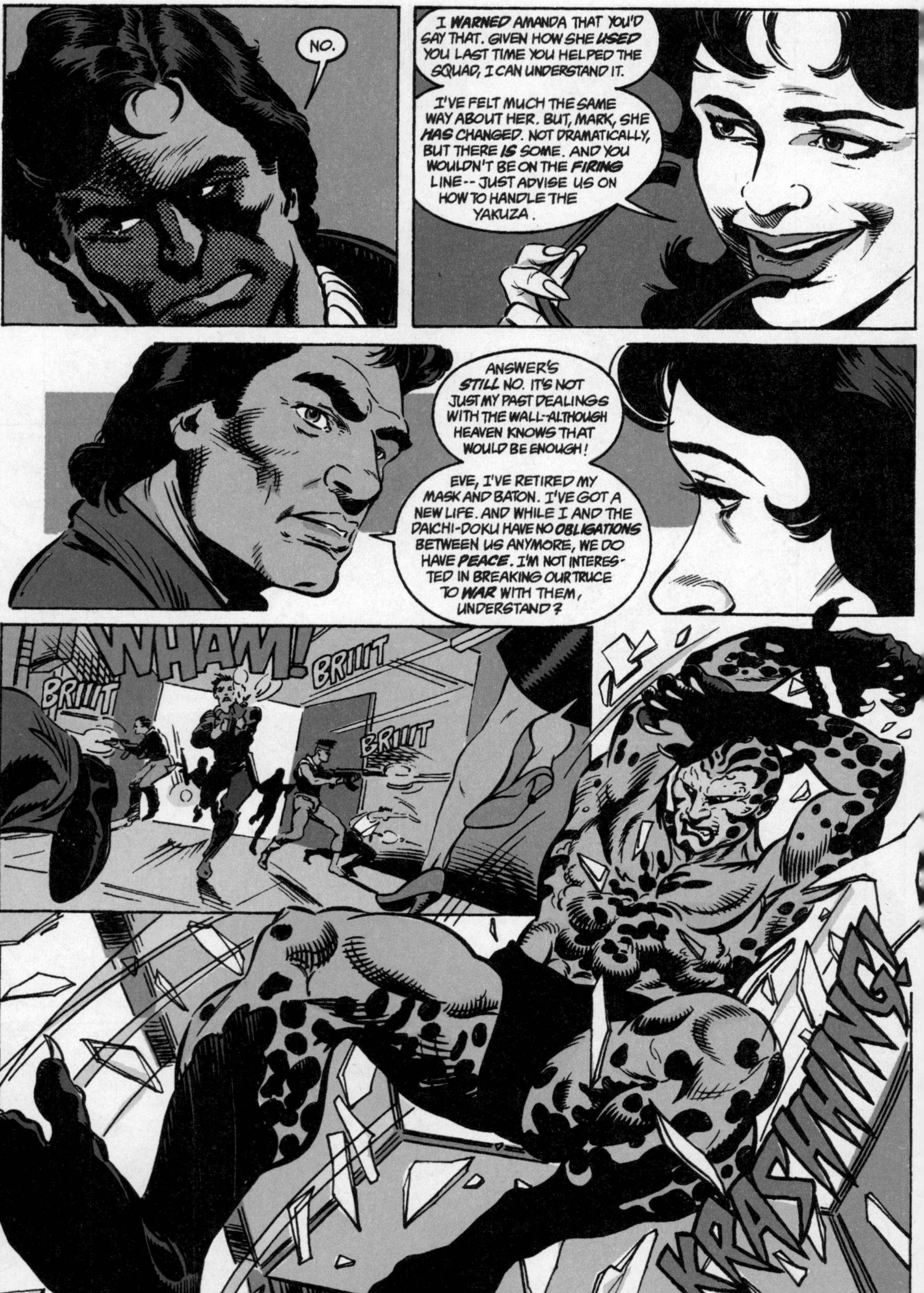
NO.
I WARNED AMANDA THAT YOU'D SAY THAT. GIVEN HOW SHE USED YOU LAST TIME YOU HELPED THE SQUAD, I CAN UNDERSTAND IT.
I'VE FELT MUCH THE SAME WAY ABOUT HER. BUT, MARK, SHE HAS CHANGED. NOT DRAMATICALLY, BUT THERE IS SOME. AND YOU WOULDN'T BE ON THE FIRING LINE-- JUST ADVISE US ON HOW TO HANDLE THE YAKUZA.
ANSWER'S STILL NO. IT'S NOT JUST MY PAST DEALINGS WITH THE WALL-ALTHOUGH HEAVEN KNOWS THAT WOULD BE ENOUGH!
EVE, I'VE RETIRED MY MASK AND BATON. I'VE GOT A NEW LIFE. AND WHILE I AND THE DAICHI-DOKU HAVE NO OBLIGATIONS BETWEEN US ANYMORE, WE DO HAVE PEACE. I'M NOT INTERESTED IN BREAKING OUR TRUCE TO WAR WITH THEM, UNDERSTAND?
WHAM!
BRIIIT
BRIIIT
BRIIIT
KRASHHNG!
18

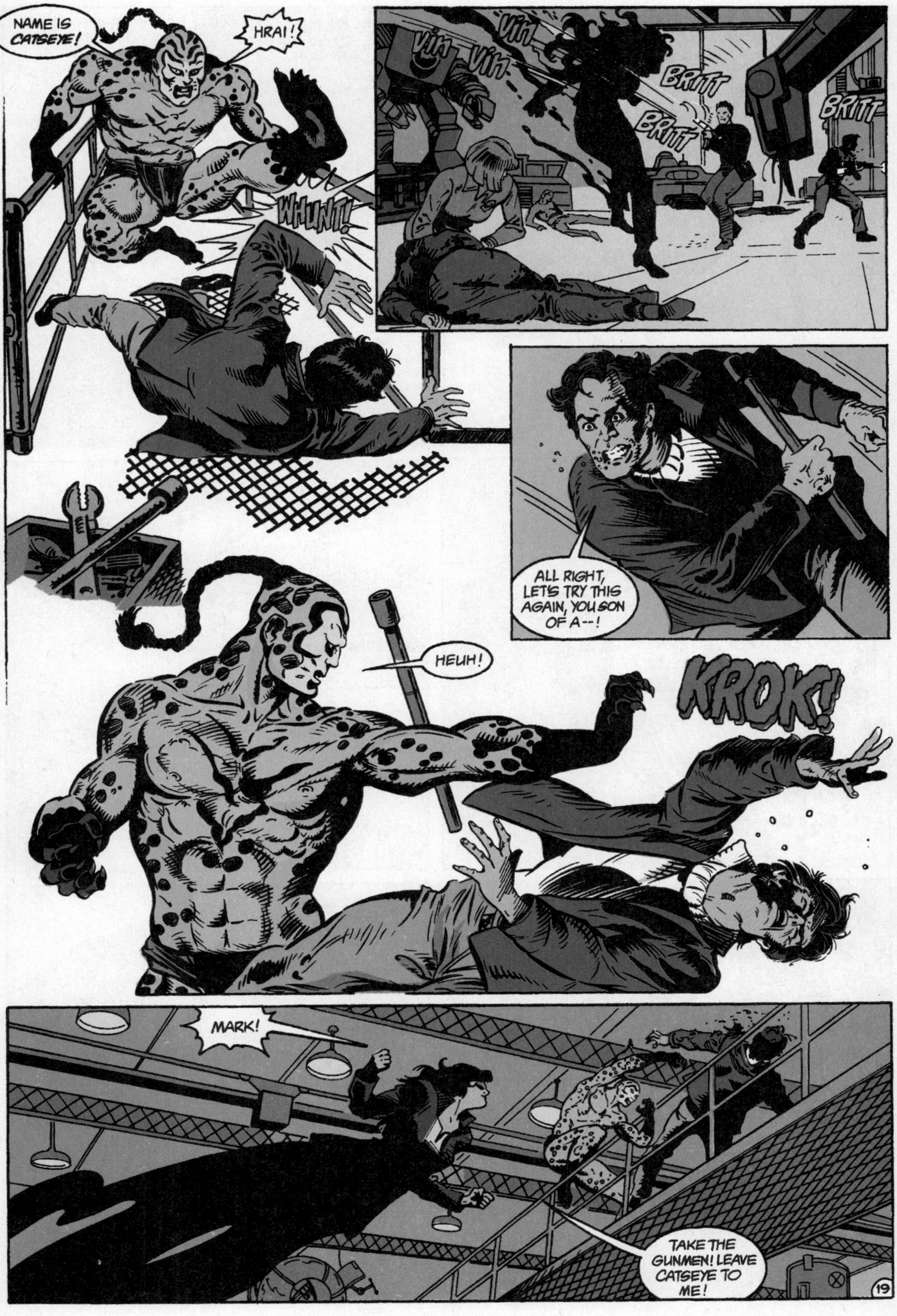
NAME IS CATSEYE!
HRAI!
WHUNT!
VIH
VIH
VIH
BRITT
BRITT
BRITT
ALL RIGHT, LET'S TRY THIS AGAIN, YOU SON OF A--!
HEUH!
KROK!
MARK!
TAKE THE GUNMEN! LEAVE CATSEYE TO ME!
19

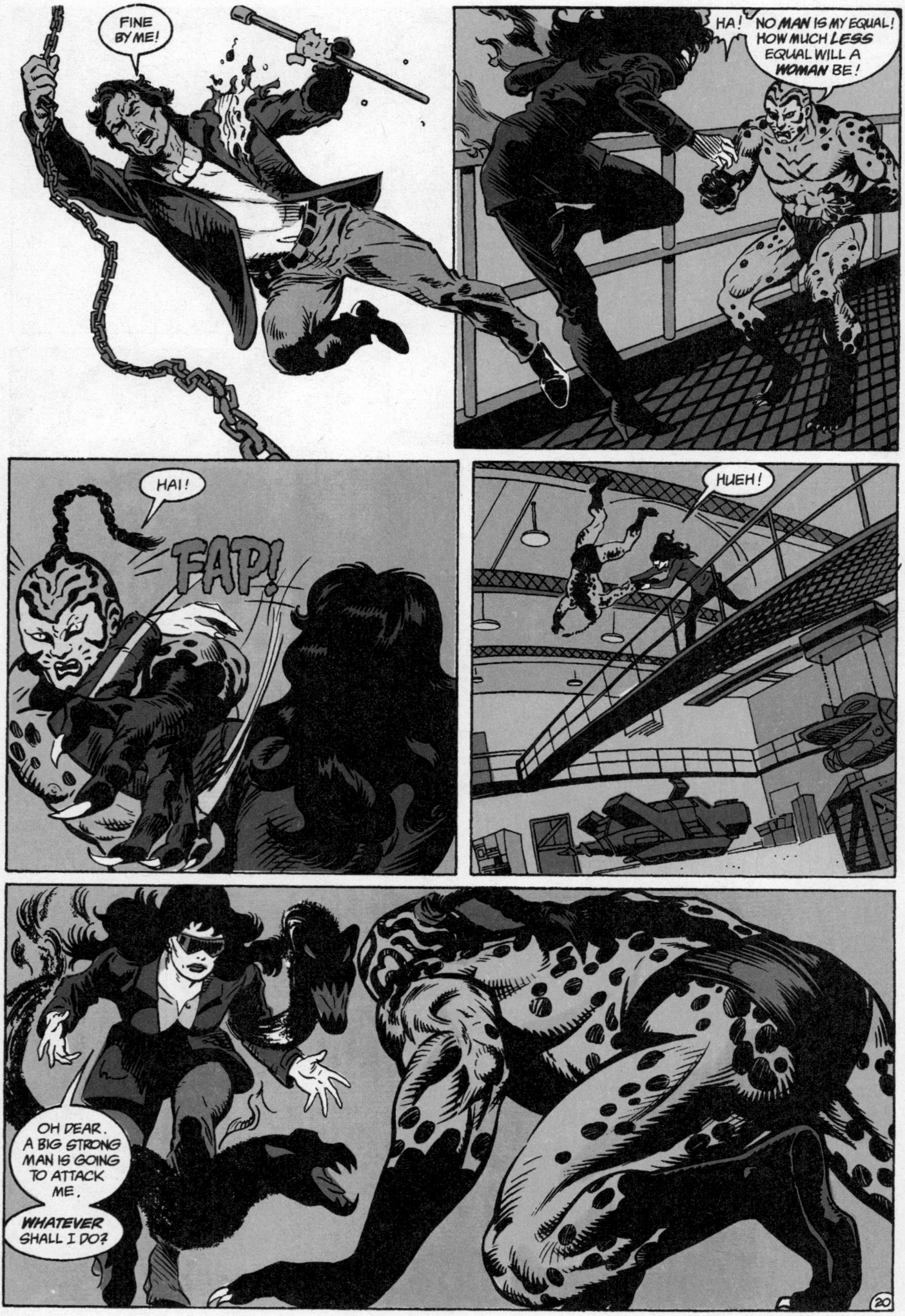

FINE BY ME!
HA!
NO MAN IS MY EQUAL! HOW MUCH LESS EQUAL WILL A WOMAN BE!
HAI!
FAP!
HUEH!
OH DEAR. A BIG STRONG MAN IS GOING TO ATTACK ME.
WHATEVER SHALL I DO?
20

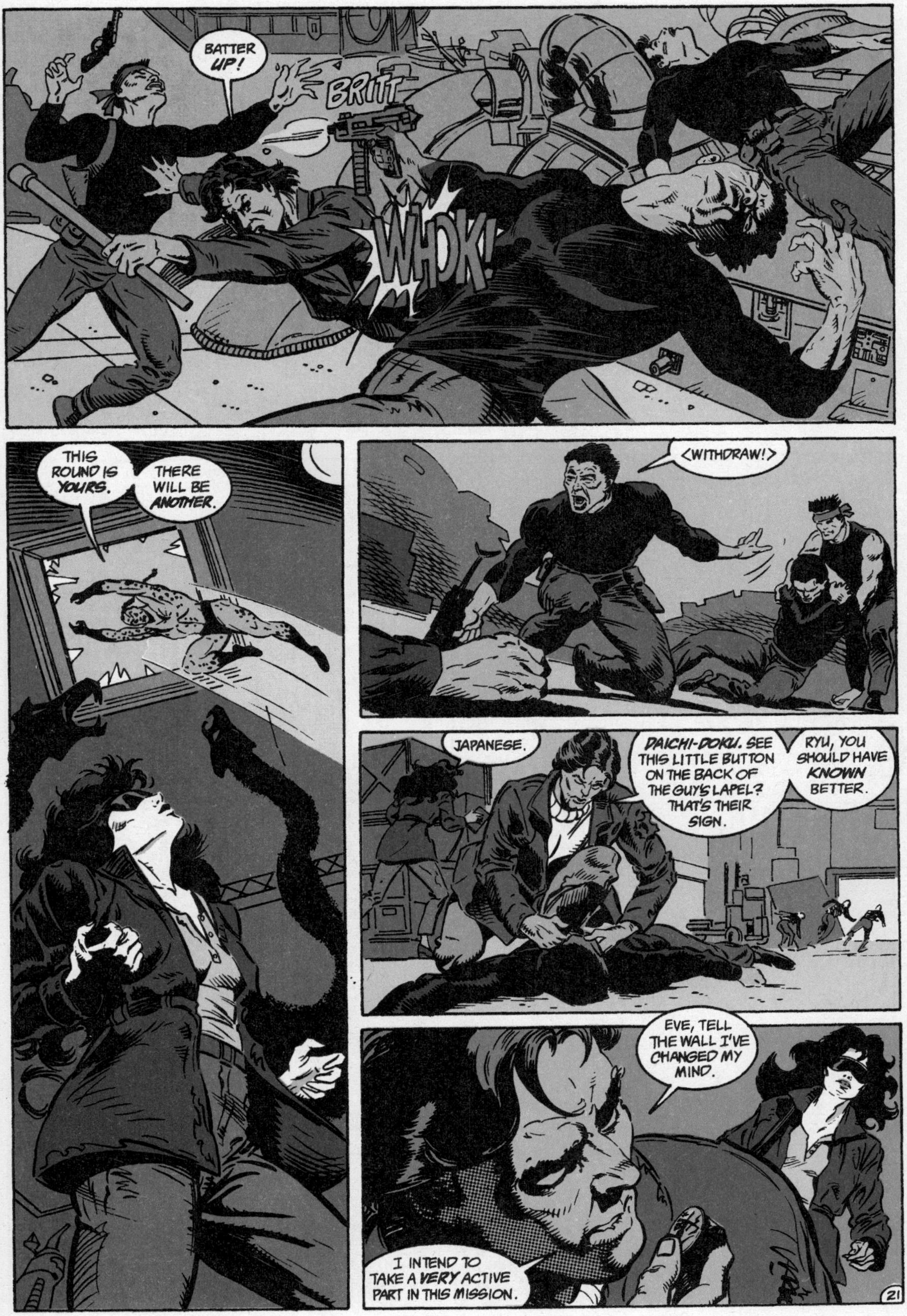
BATTER UP!
BRITT
WHOK!
THIS ROUND IS YOURS.
THERE WILL BE ANOTHER.
<WITHDRAW!>
JAPANESE.
DAICHI-DOKU. SEE THIS LITTLE BUTTON ON THE BACK OF THE GUY'S LAPEL? THAT'S THEIR SIGN.
RYU, YOU SHOULD HAVE KNOWN BETTER.
EVE, TELL THE WALL I'VE CHANGED MY MIND.
I INTEND TO TAKE A VERY ACTIVE PART IN THIS MISSION.
21

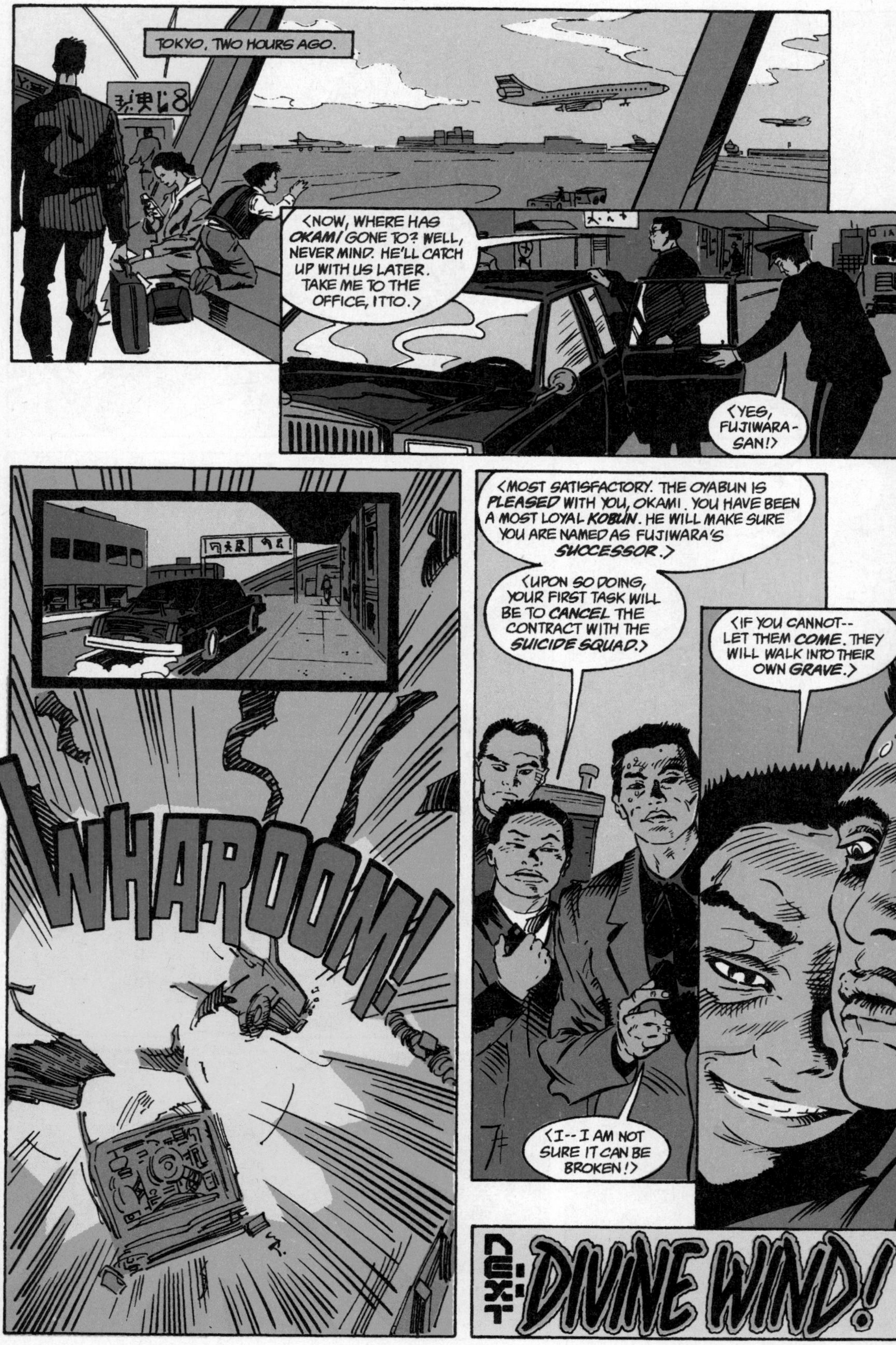
TOKYO, TWO HOURS AGO.
<NOW, WHERE HAS OKAMI GONE TO? WELL, NEVER MIND. HE'LL CATCH UP WITH US LATER. TAKE ME TO THE OFFICE, ITTO.>
<YES, FUJIWARA-SAN!>
WHAROOM!
<MOST SATISFACTORY. THE OYABUN IS PLEASED WITH YOU, OKAMI. YOU HAVE BEEN A MOST LOYAL KOBUN. HE WILL MAKE SURE YOU ARE NAMED AS FUJIWARA'S SUCCESSOR.>
<UPON SO DOING, YOUR FIRST TASK WILL BE TO CANCEL THE CONTRACT WITH THE SUICIDE SQUAD.>
<I-- I AM NOT SURE IT CAN BE BROKEN!>
<IF YOU CANNOT-- LET THEM COME. THEY WILL WALK INTO THEIR OWN GRAVE.>
NEXT: DIVINE WIND!

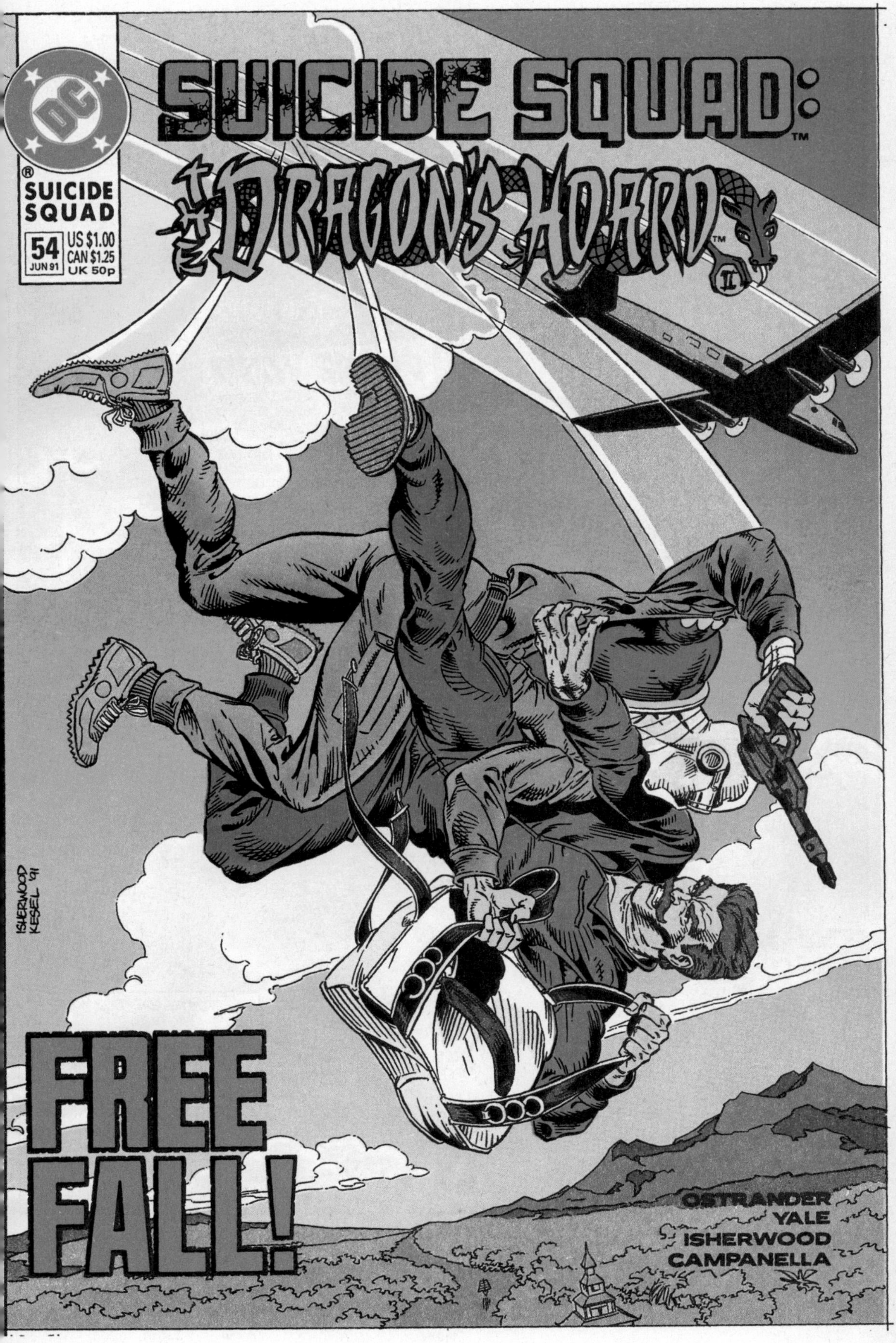
SUICIDE SQUAD:
THE DRAGON'S HOARD
DC
SUICIDE SQUAD
54
JUN 91
US $1.00
CAN $1.25
UK 50p
ISHERWOOD KESEL '91
FREE FALL!
OSTRANDER
YALE
ISHERWOOD
CAMPANELLA

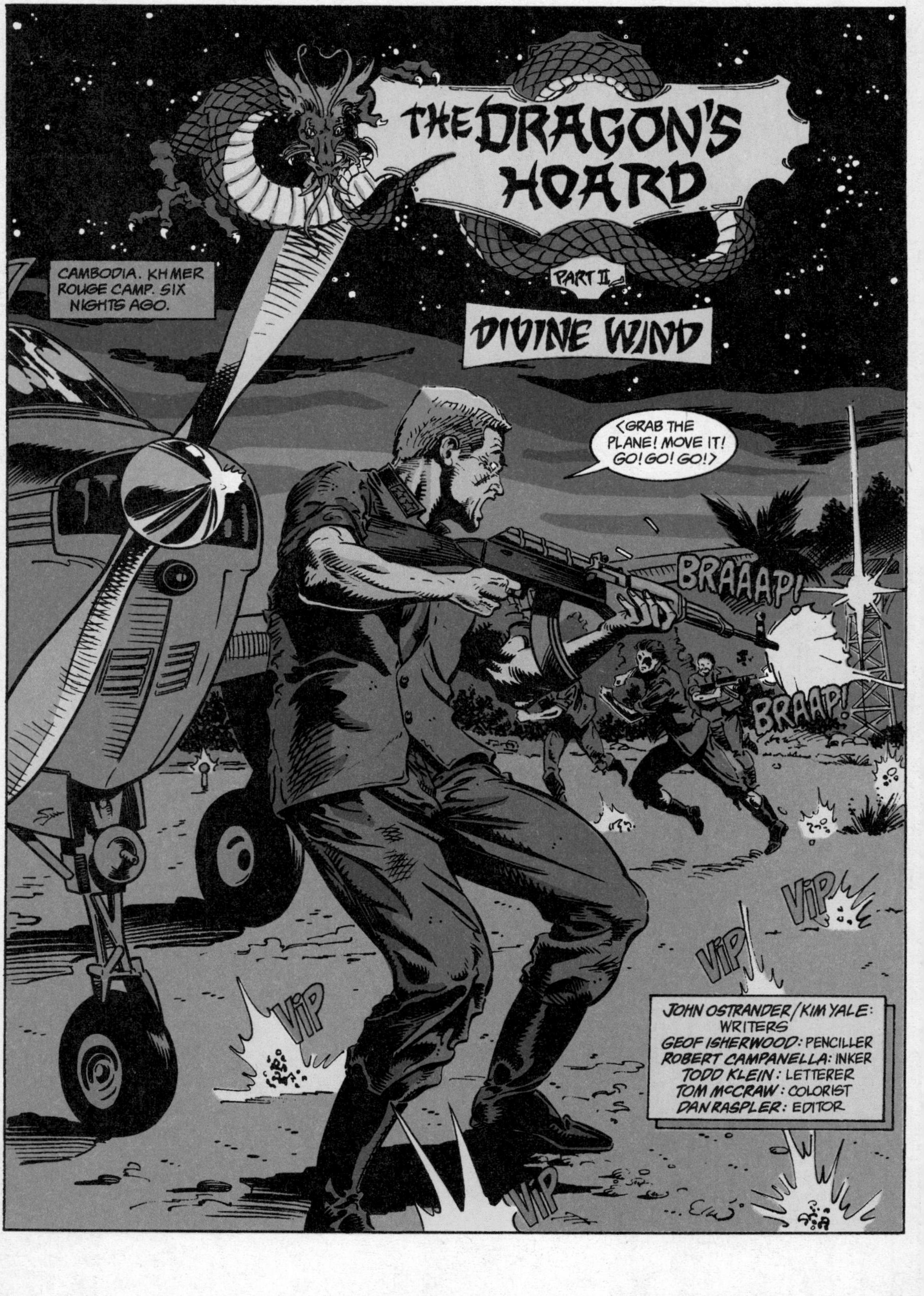
THE DRAGON'S HOARD
PART II
DIVINE WIND
CAMBODIA. KHMER ROUGE CAMP. SIX NIGHTS AGO.
<GRAB THE PLANE! MOVE IT! GO! GO! GO!>
BRAAAP!
BRAAP!
VIP
VIP
VIP
VIP
JOHN OSTRANDER/KIM YALE: WRITERS
GEOF ISHERWOOD: PENCILLER
ROBERT CAMPANELLA: INKER
TODD KLEIN: LETTERER
TOM McCRAW: COLORIST
DAN RASPLER: EDITOR

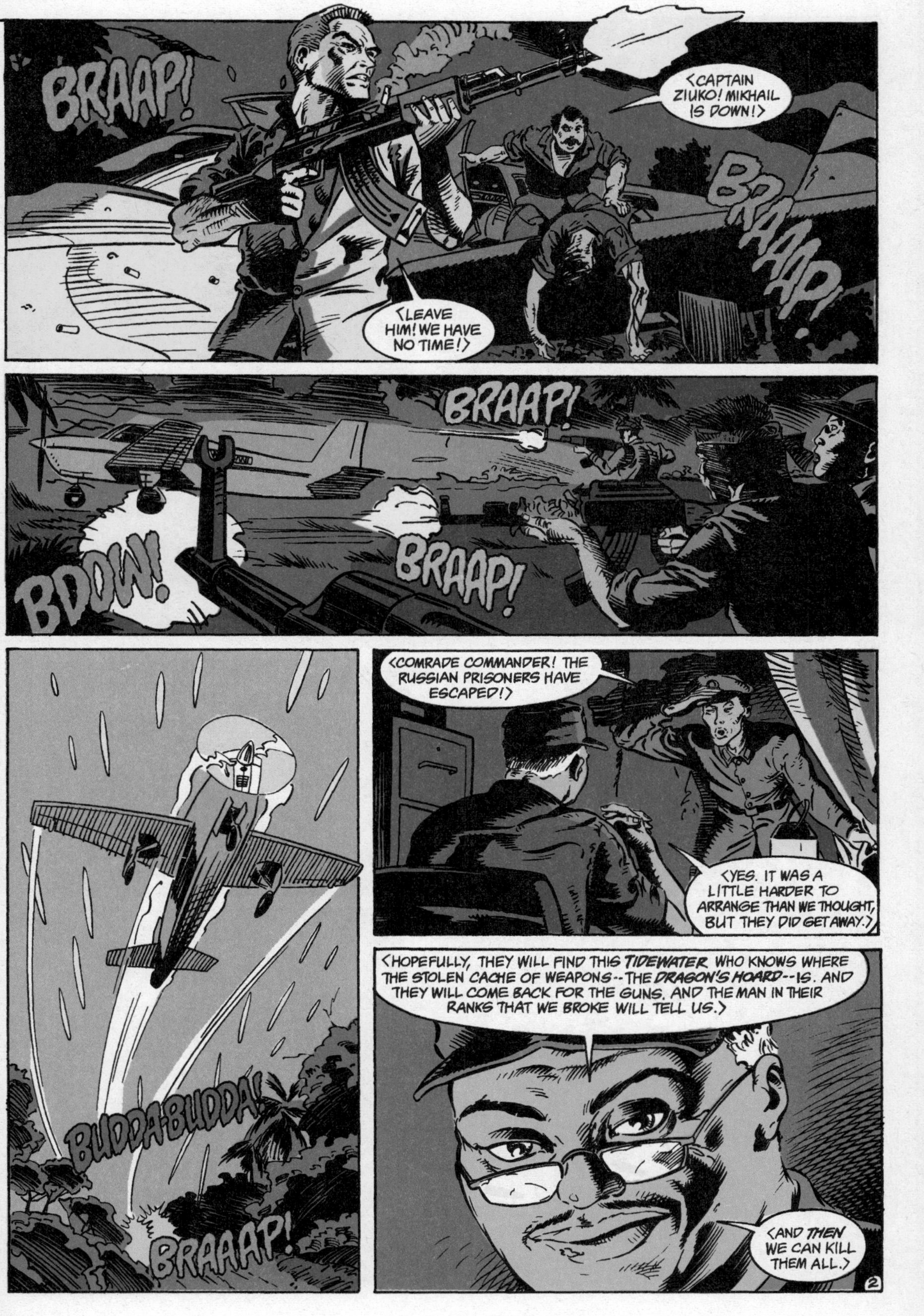
BRAAP!
<CAPTAIN ZIUKO! MIKHAIL IS DOWN!>
BRAAAP!
<LEAVE HIM! WE HAVE NO TIME!>
BRAAP!
BDOW!
BRAAP!
BUDDA BUDDA!
BRAAAP!
<COMRADE COMMANDER! THE RUSSIAN PRISONERS HAVE ESCAPED!>
<YES. IT WAS A LITTLE HARDER TO ARRANGE THAN WE THOUGHT, BUT THEY DID GET AWAY.>
<HOPEFULLY, THEY WILL FIND THIS TIDEWATER WHO KNOWS WHERE THE STOLEN CACHE OF WEAPONS--THE DRAGON'S HOARD--IS. AND THEY WILL COME BACK FOR THE GUNS. AND THE MAN IN THEIR RANKS THAT WE BROKE WILL TELL US.>
<AND THEN WE CAN KILL THEM ALL.>
2

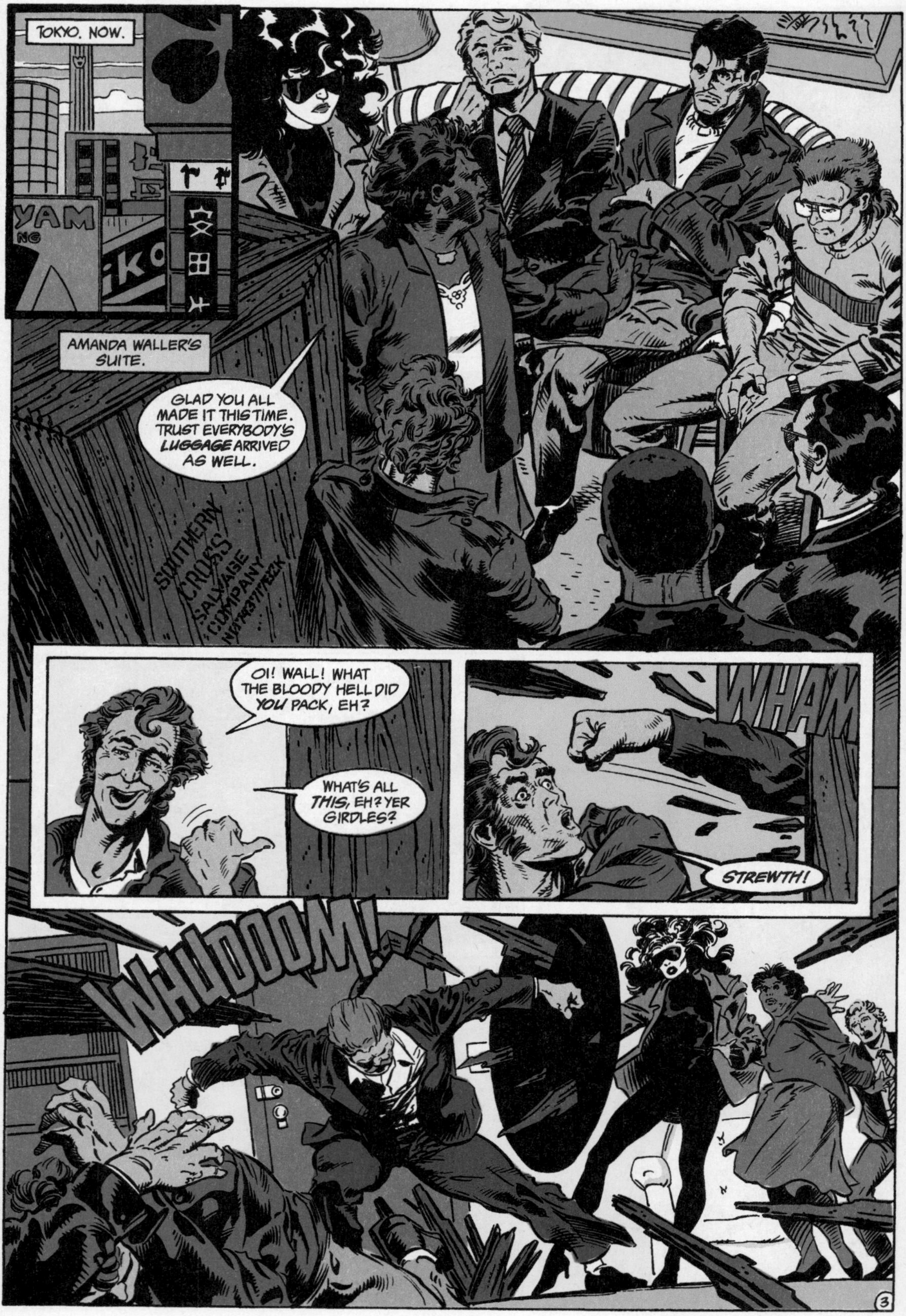
TOKYO. NOW.
AMANDA WALLER'S SUITE.
GLAD YOU ALL MADE IT THIS TIME. TRUST EVERYBODY'S LUGGAGE ARRIVED AS WELL.
SOUTHERN CROSS SALVAGE COMPANY
OI! WALL! WHAT THE BLOODY HELL DID YOU PACK, EH?
WHAT'S ALL THIS, EH? YER GIRDLES?
WHAM
STREWTH!
WHUDOOM!
3

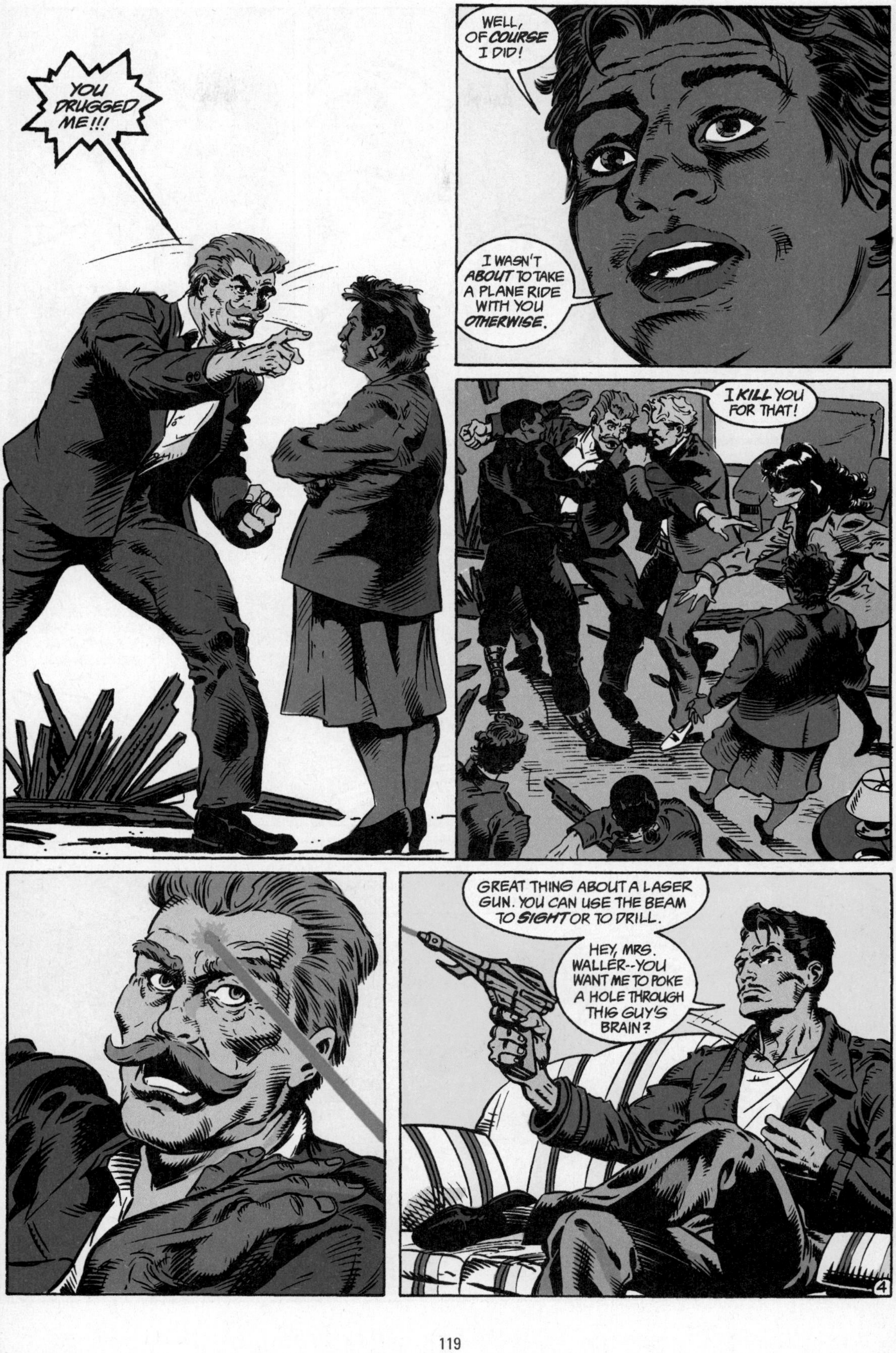
YOU DRUGGED ME!!!
WELL, OF COURSE I DID!
I WASN'T ABOUT TO TAKE A PLANE RIDE WITH YOU OTHERWISE.
I KILL YOU FOR THAT!
GREAT THING ABOUT A LASER GUN. YOU CAN USE THE BEAM TO SIGHT OR TO DRILL.
HEY, MRS. WALLER--YOU WANT ME TO POKE A HOLE THROUGH THIS GUY'S BRAIN?
4

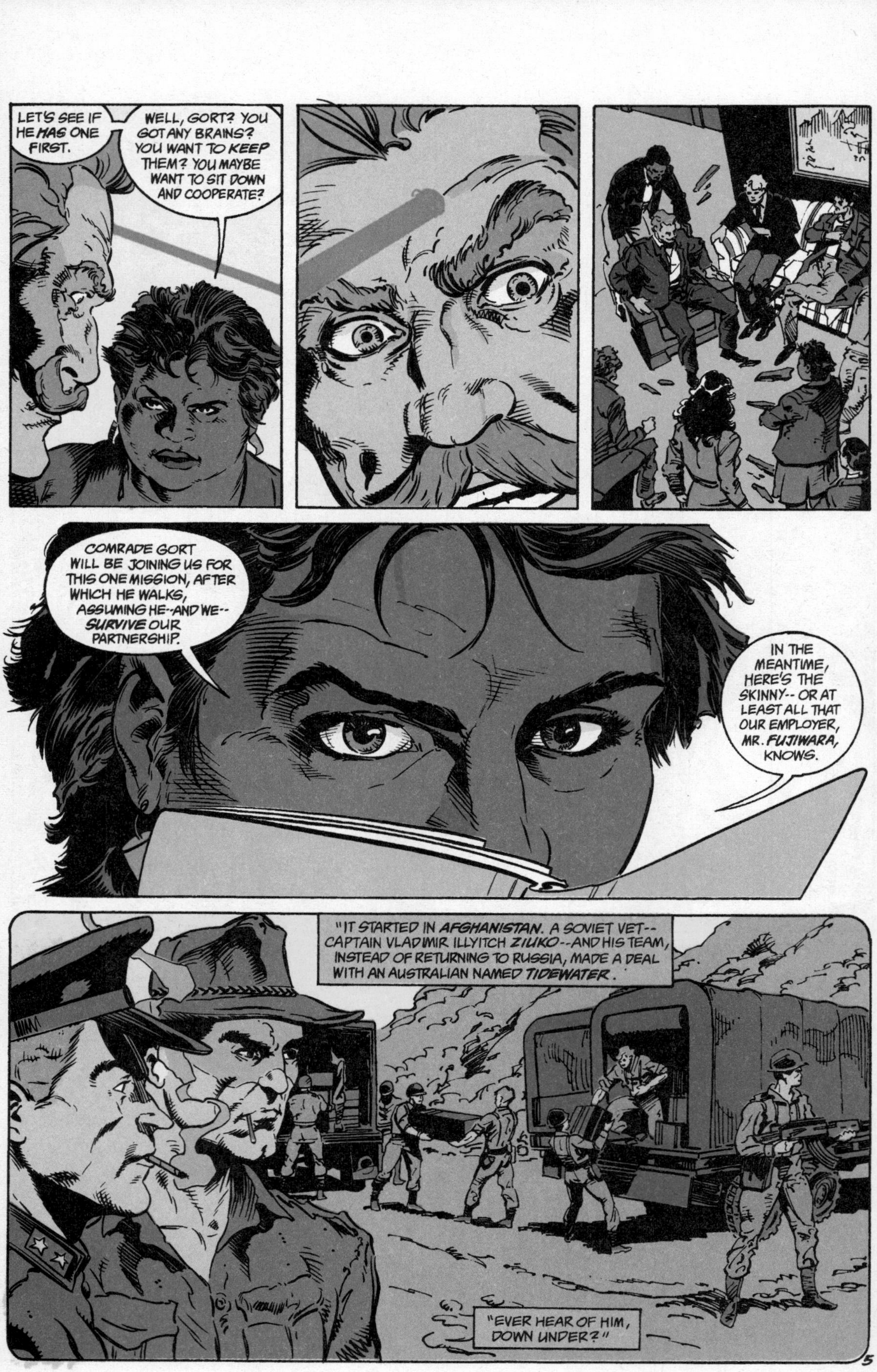
LET'S SEE IF HE HAS ONE FIRST.
WELL, GORT? YOU GOT ANY BRAINS? YOU WANT TO KEEP THEM? YOU MAYBE WANT TO SIT DOWN AND COOPERATE?
COMRADE GORT WILL BE JOINING US FOR THIS ONE MISSION, AFTER WHICH HE WALKS, ASSUMING HE--AND WE--SURVIVE OUR PARTNERSHIP.
IN THE MEANTIME, HERE'S THE SKINNY-- OR AT LEAST ALL THAT OUR EMPLOYER, MR. FUJIWARA, KNOWS.
"IT STARTED IN AFGHANISTAN. A SOVIET VET--CAPTAIN VLADIMIR ILLYITCH ZIUKO--AND HIS TEAM, INSTEAD OF RETURNING TO RUSSIA, MADE A DEAL WITH AN AUSTRALIAN NAMED TIDEWATER.
"EVER HEAR OF HIM, DOWN UNDER?"
5

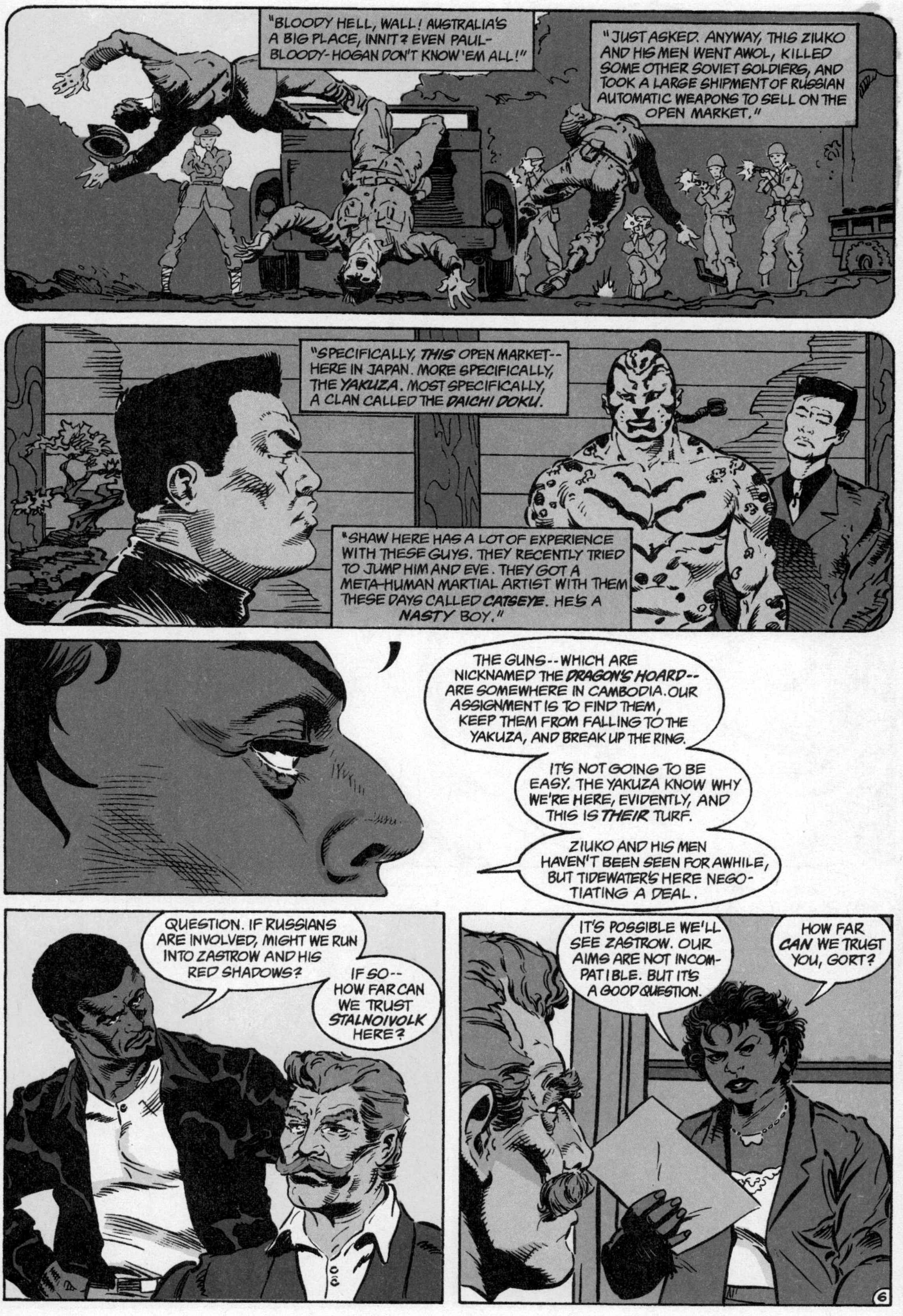
"BLOODY HELL, WALL! AUSTRALIA'S A BIG PLACE, INNIT? EVEN PAUL-BLOODY-HOGAN DON'T KNOW 'EM ALL!"
"JUST ASKED. ANYWAY, THIS ZIUKO AND HIS MEN WENT AWOL, KILLED SOME OTHER SOVIET SOLDIERS, AND TOOK A LARGE SHIPMENT OF RUSSIAN AUTOMATIC WEAPONS TO SELL ON THE OPEN MARKET."
"SPECIFICALLY, THIS OPEN MARKET--HERE IN JAPAN. MORE SPECIFICALLY, THE YAKUZA. MOST SPECIFICALLY, A CLAN CALLED THE DAICHI DOKU.
"SHAW HERE HAS A LOT OF EXPERIENCE WITH THESE GUYS. THEY RECENTLY TRIED TO JUMP HIM AND EVE. THEY GOT A META-HUMAN MARTIAL ARTIST WITH THEM THESE DAYS CALLED CATSEYE. HE'S A NASTY BOY."
THE GUNS--WHICH ARE NICKNAMED THE DRAGON'S HOARD--ARE SOMEWHERE IN CAMBODIA. OUR ASSIGNMENT IS TO FIND THEM, KEEP THEM FROM FALLING TO THE YAKUZA, AND BREAK UP THE RING.
IT'S NOT GOING TO BE EASY. THE YAKUZA KNOW WHY WE'RE HERE, EVIDENTLY, AND THIS IS THEIR TURF.
ZIUKO AND HIS MEN HAVEN'T BEEN SEEN FOR AWHILE, BUT TIDEWATER'S HERE NEGO-TIATING A DEAL.
QUESTION. IF RUSSIANS ARE INVOLVED, MIGHT WE RUN INTO ZASTROW AND HIS RED SHADOWS?
IF SO--HOW FAR CAN WE TRUST STALNOIVOLK HERE?
IT'S POSSIBLE WE'LL SEE ZASTROW. OUR AIMS ARE NOT INCOM-PATIBLE. BUT IT'S A GOOD QUESTION.
HOW FAR CAN WE TRUST YOU, GORT?
6

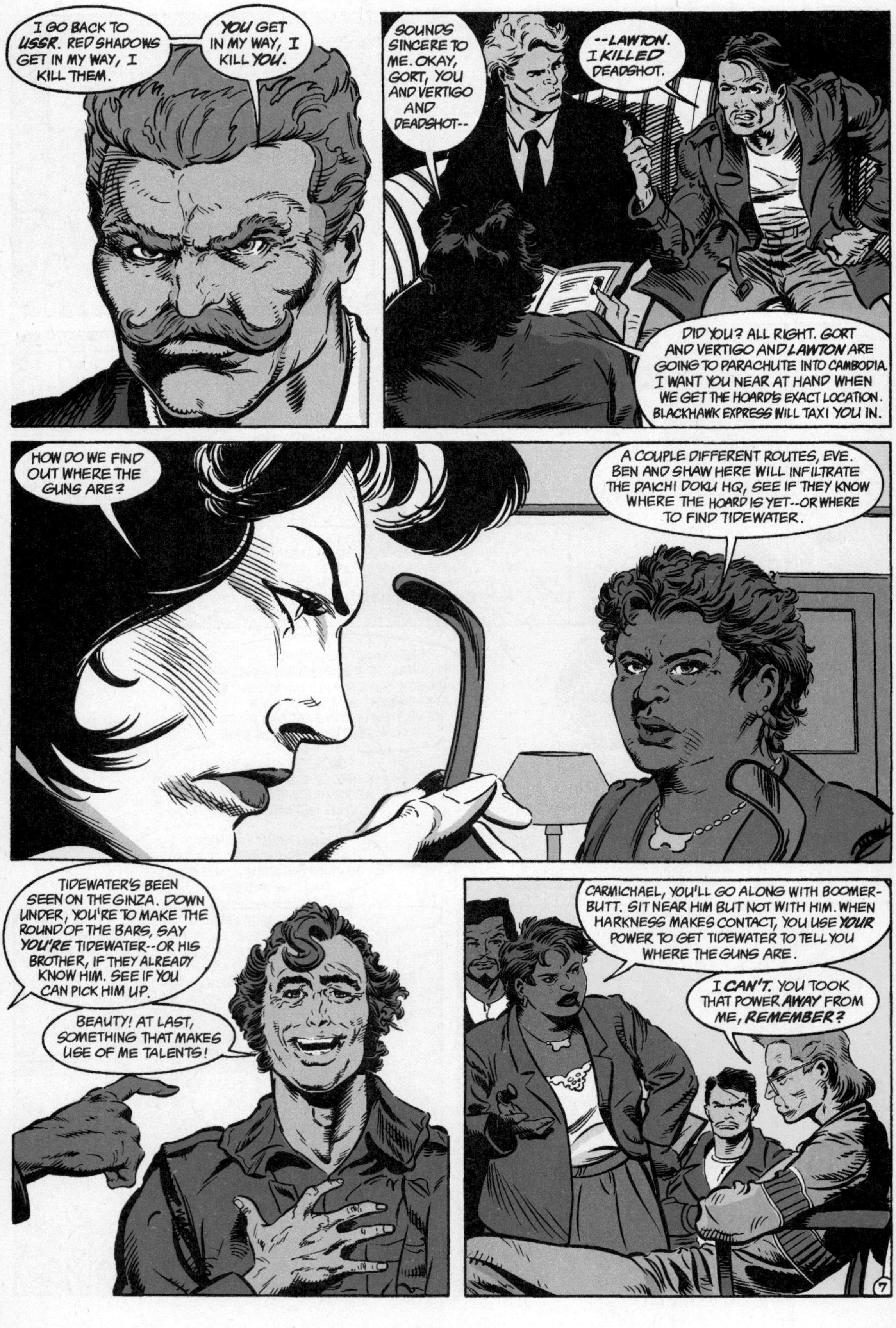
I GO BACK TO USSR. RED SHADOWS GET IN MY WAY, I KILL THEM.
YOU GET IN MY WAY, I KILL YOU.
SOUNDS SINCERE TO ME. OKAY, GORT, YOU AND VERTIGO AND DEADSHOT--
--LAWTON. I KILLED DEADSHOT.
DID YOU? ALL RIGHT. GORT AND VERTIGO AND LAWTON ARE GOING TO PARACHUTE INTO CAMBODIA. I WANT YOU NEAR AT HAND WHEN WE GET THE HOARD'S EXACT LOCATION. BLACKHAWK EXPRESS WILL TAXI YOU IN.
HOW DO WE FIND OUT WHERE THE GUNS ARE?
A COUPLE DIFFERENT ROUTES, EVE. BEN AND SHAW HERE WILL INFILTRATE THE DAICHI DOKU HQ, SEE IF THEY KNOW WHERE THE HOARD IS YET--OR WHERE TO FIND TIDEWATER.
TIDEWATER'S BEEN SEEN ON THE GINZA. DOWN UNDER, YOU'RE TO MAKE THE ROUND OF THE BARS, SAY YOU'RE TIDEWATER--OR HIS BROTHER, IF THEY ALREADY KNOW HIM. SEE IF YOU CAN PICK HIM UP.
BEAUTY! AT LAST, SOMETHING THAT MAKES USE OF ME TALENTS!
CARMICHAEL, YOU'LL GO ALONG WITH BOOMER-BUTT. SIT NEAR HIM BUT NOT WITH HIM. WHEN HARKNESS MAKES CONTACT, YOU USE YOUR POWER TO GET TIDEWATER TO TELL YOU WHERE THE GUNS ARE.
I CAN'T. YOU TOOK THAT POWER AWAY FROM ME, REMEMBER?
7

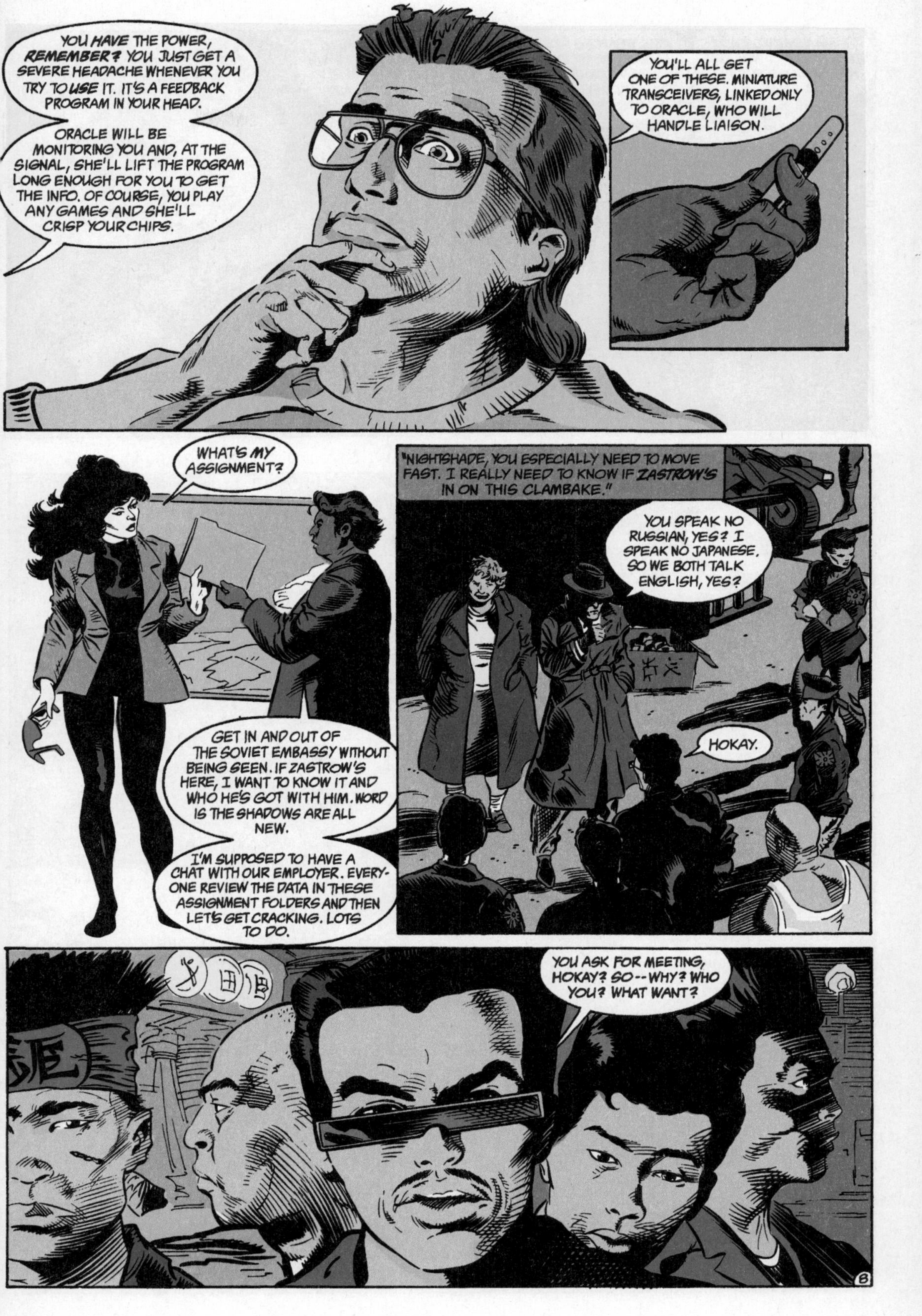

YOU HAVE THE POWER, REMEMBER? YOU JUST GET A SEVERE HEADACHE WHENEVER YOU TRY TO USE IT. IT'S A FEEDBACK PROGRAM IN YOUR HEAD.
ORACLE WILL BE MONITORING YOU AND, AT THE SIGNAL, SHE'LL LIFT THE PROGRAM LONG ENOUGH FOR YOU TO GET THE INFO. OF COURSE, YOU PLAY ANY GAMES AND SHE'LL CRISP YOUR CHIPS.
YOU'LL ALL GET ONE OF THESE. MINIATURE TRANSCEIVERS, LINKED ONLY TO ORACLE, WHO WILL HANDLE LIAISON.
WHAT'S MY ASSIGNMENT?
GET IN AND OUT OF THE SOVIET EMBASSY WITHOUT BEING SEEN. IF ZASTROW'S HERE, I WANT TO KNOW IT AND WHO HE'S GOT WITH HIM. WORD IS THE SHADOWS ARE ALL NEW.
I'M SUPPOSED TO HAVE A CHAT WITH OUR EMPLOYER. EVERY-ONE REVIEW THE DATA IN THESE ASSIGNMENT FOLDERS AND THEN LET'S GET CRACKING. LOTS TO DO.
"NIGHTSHADE, YOU ESPECIALLY NEED TO MOVE FAST. I REALLY NEED TO KNOW IF ZASTROW'S IN ON THIS CLAMBAKE."
YOU SPEAK NO RUSSIAN, YES? I SPEAK NO JAPANESE, SO WE BOTH TALK ENGLISH, YES?
HOKAY.
YOU ASK FOR MEETING, HOKAY? SO--WHY? WHO YOU? WHAT WANT?
8

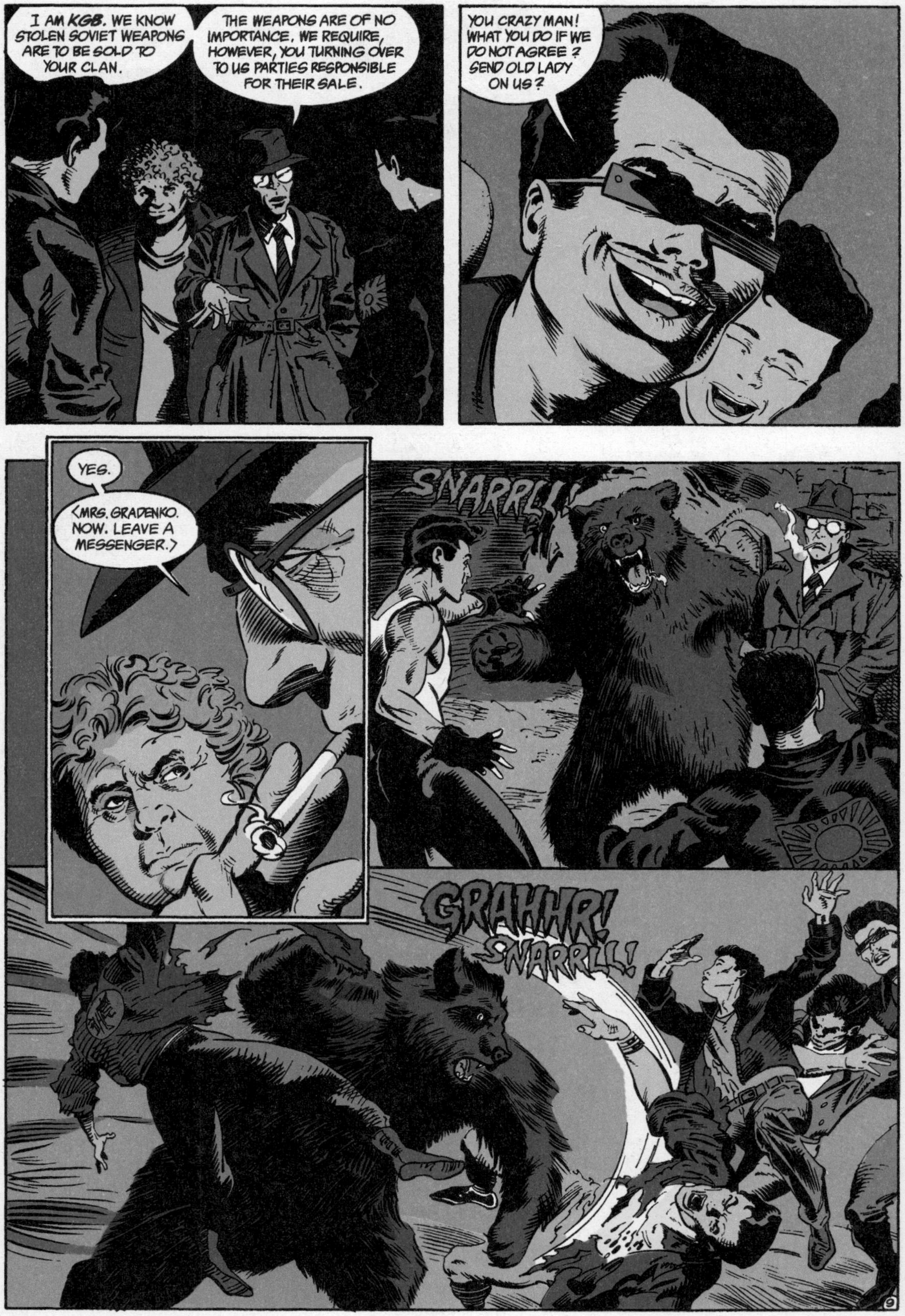
I AM KGB. WE KNOW STOLEN SOVIET WEAPONS ARE TO BE SOLD TO YOUR CLAN.
THE WEAPONS ARE OF NO IMPORTANCE. WE REQUIRE, HOWEVER, YOU TURNING OVER TO US PARTIES RESPONSIBLE FOR THEIR SALE.
YOU CRAZY MAN! WHAT YOU DO IF WE DO NOT AGREE? SEND OLD LADY ON US?
YES.
<MRS. GRADENKO. NOW. LEAVE A MESSENGER.>
SNARRLL!
GRAHHR!
SNARRLL!
9

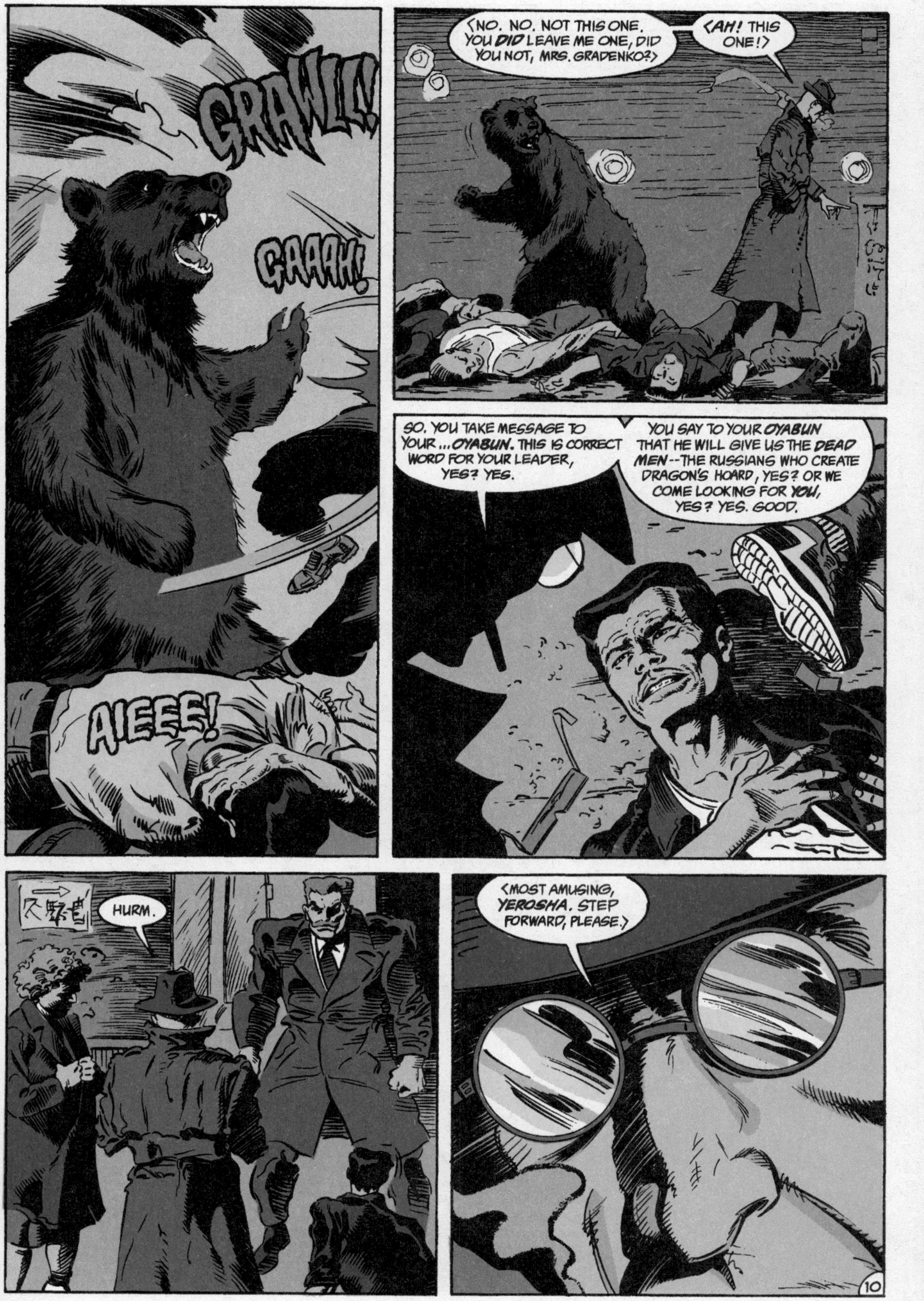
GRAWL!
GAAAH!
AIEEE!
<NO. NO. NOT THIS ONE. YOU DID LEAVE ME ONE, DID YOU NOT, MRS. GRADENKO?>
<AH! THIS ONE!>
SO. YOU TAKE MESSAGE TO YOUR ...OYABUN. THIS IS CORRECT WORD FOR YOUR LEADER, YES? YES.
YOU SAY TO YOUR OYABUN THAT HE WILL GIVE US THE DEAD MEN--THE RUSSIANS WHO CREATE DRAGON'S HOARD, YES? OR WE COME LOOKING FOR YOU, YES? YES. GOOD.
HURM.
<MOST AMUSING, YEROSHA. STEP FORWARD, PLEASE.>
10

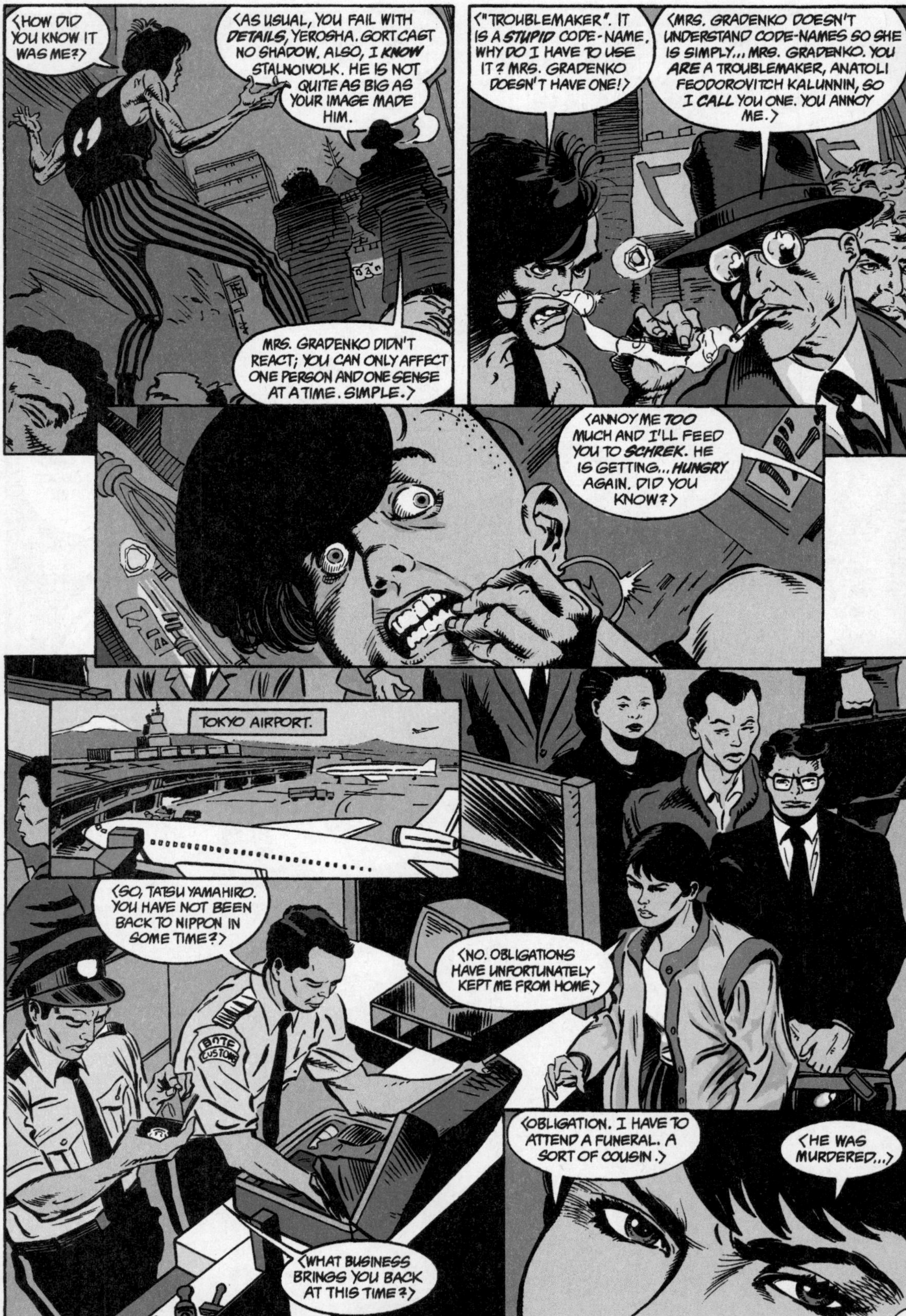
<HOW DID YOU KNOW IT WAS ME?>
<AS USUAL, YOU FAIL WITH DETAILS, YEROSHA. GORT CAST NO SHADOW. ALSO, I KNOW STALNOIVOLK. HE IS NOT QUITE AS BIG AS YOUR IMAGE MADE HIM.
MRS. GRADENKO DIDN'T REACT; YOU CAN ONLY AFFECT ONE PERSON AND ONE SENSE AT A TIME. SIMPLE.>
<"TROUBLEMAKER". IT IS A STUPID CODE-NAME. WHY DO I HAVE TO USE IT? MRS. GRADENKO DOESN'T HAVE ONE!>
<MRS. GRADENKO DOESN'T UNDERSTAND CODE-NAMES SO SHE IS SIMPLY... MRS. GRADENKO. YOU ARE A TROUBLEMAKER, ANATOLI FEODOROVITCH KALUNNIN, SO I CALL YOU ONE. YOU ANNOY ME.>
<ANNOY ME TOO MUCH AND I'LL FEED YOU TO SCHREK. HE IS GETTING... HUNGRY AGAIN. DID YOU KNOW?>
TOKYO AIRPORT.
<SO, TATSU YAMAHIRO. YOU HAVE NOT BEEN BACK TO NIPPON IN SOME TIME?>
<NO. OBLIGATIONS HAVE UNFORTUNATELY KEPT ME FROM HOME.>
<WHAT BUSINESS BRINGS YOU BACK AT THIS TIME?>
<OBLIGATION. I HAVE TO ATTEND A FUNERAL. A SORT OF COUSIN.>
<HE WAS MURDERED...>
11

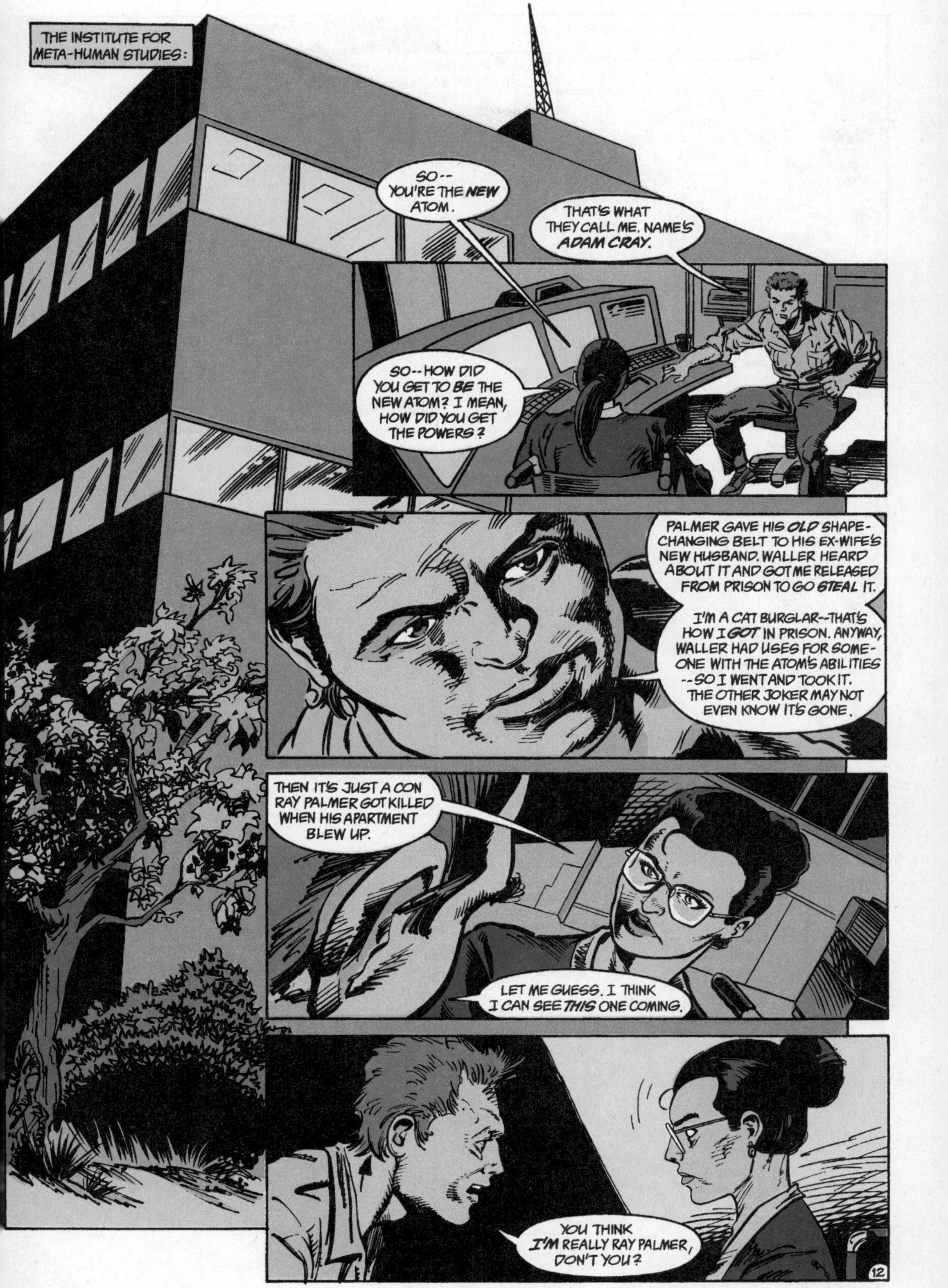
THE INSTITUTE FOR META-HUMAN STUDIES:
SO-- YOU'RE THE NEW ATOM.
THAT'S WHAT THEY CALL ME. NAME'S ADAM CRAY.
SO--HOW DID YOU GET TO BE THE NEW ATOM? I MEAN, HOW DID YOU GET THE POWERS?
PALMER GAVE HIS OLD SHAPE-CHANGING BELT TO HIS EX-WIFE'S NEW HUSBAND. WALLER HEARD ABOUT IT AND GOT ME RELEASED FROM PRISON TO GO STEAL IT.
I'M A CAT BURGLAR--THAT'S HOW I GOT IN PRISON. ANYWAY, WALLER HAD USES FOR SOME-ONE WITH THE ATOM'S ABILITIES --SO I WENT AND TOOK IT. THE OTHER JOKER MAY NOT EVEN KNOW IT'S GONE.
THEN IT'S JUST A CON RAY PALMER GOT KILLED WHEN HIS APARTMENT BLEW UP.
LET ME GUESS. I THINK I CAN SEE THIS ONE COMING.
YOU THINK I'M REALLY RAY PALMER, DON'T YOU?
12

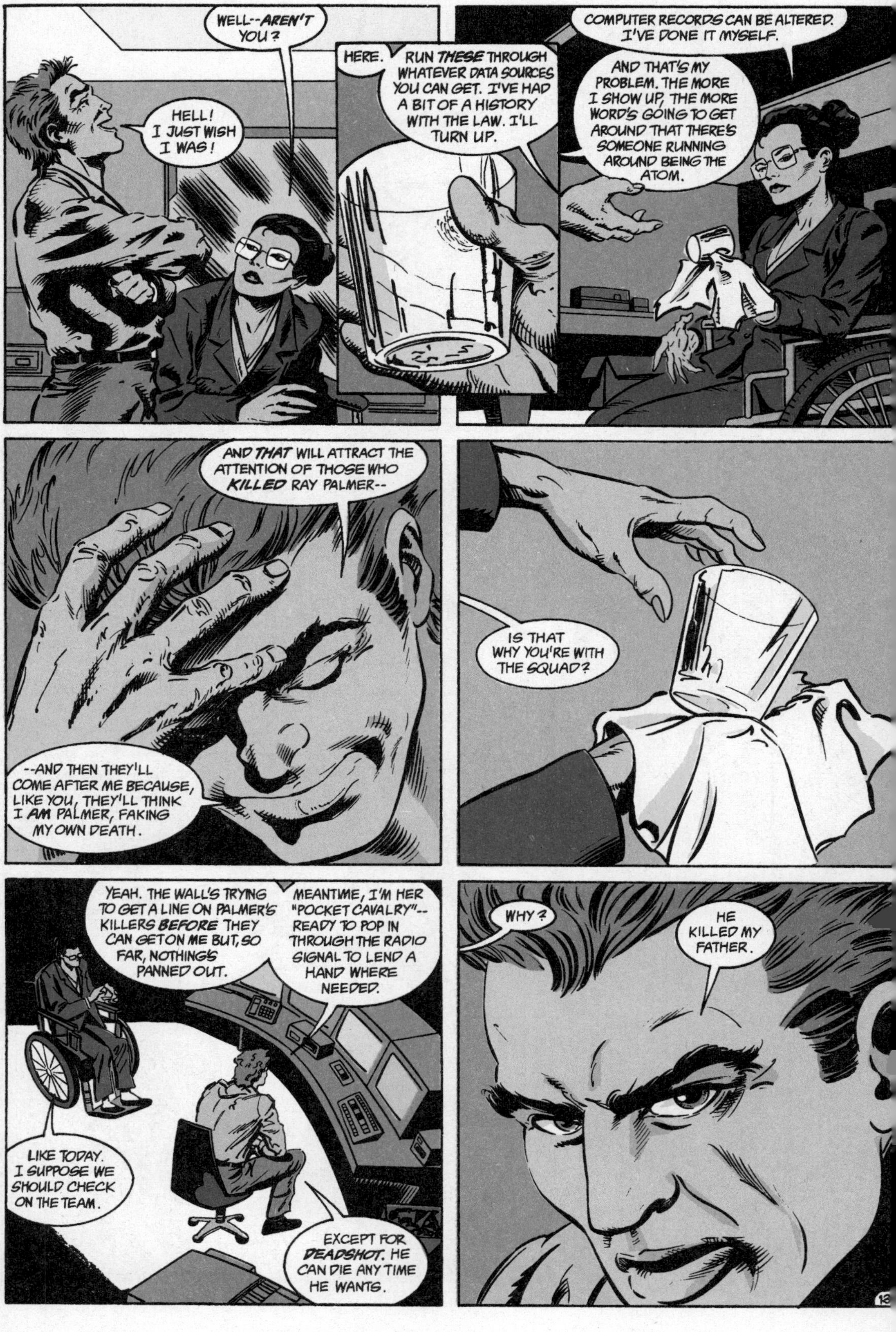
WELL--AREN'T YOU?
HELL! I JUST WISH I WAS!
HERE.
RUN THESE THROUGH WHATEVER DATA SOURCES YOU CAN GET. I'VE HAD A BIT OF A HISTORY WITH THE LAW. I'LL TURN UP.
COMPUTER RECORDS CAN BE ALTERED. I'VE DONE IT MYSELF.
AND THAT'S MY PROBLEM. THE MORE I SHOW UP, THE MORE WORD'S GOING TO GET AROUND THAT THERE'S SOMEONE RUNNING AROUND BEING THE ATOM.
AND THAT WILL ATTRACT THE ATTENTION OF THOSE WHO KILLED RAY PALMER--
--AND THEN THEY'LL COME AFTER ME BECAUSE, LIKE YOU, THEY'LL THINK I AM PALMER, FAKING MY OWN DEATH.
IS THAT WHY YOU'RE WITH THE SQUAD?
YEAH. THE WALL'S TRYING TO GET A LINE ON PALMER'S KILLERS BEFORE THEY CAN GET ON ME BUT, SO FAR, NOTHING'S PANNED OUT.
MEANTIME, I'M HER "POCKET CAVALRY"-- READY TO POP IN THROUGH THE RADIO SIGNAL TO LEND A HAND WHERE NEEDED.
LIKE TODAY. I SUPPOSE WE SHOULD CHECK ON THE TEAM.
EXCEPT FOR DEADSHOT. HE CAN DIE ANY TIME HE WANTS.
WHY?
HE KILLED MY FATHER.
13

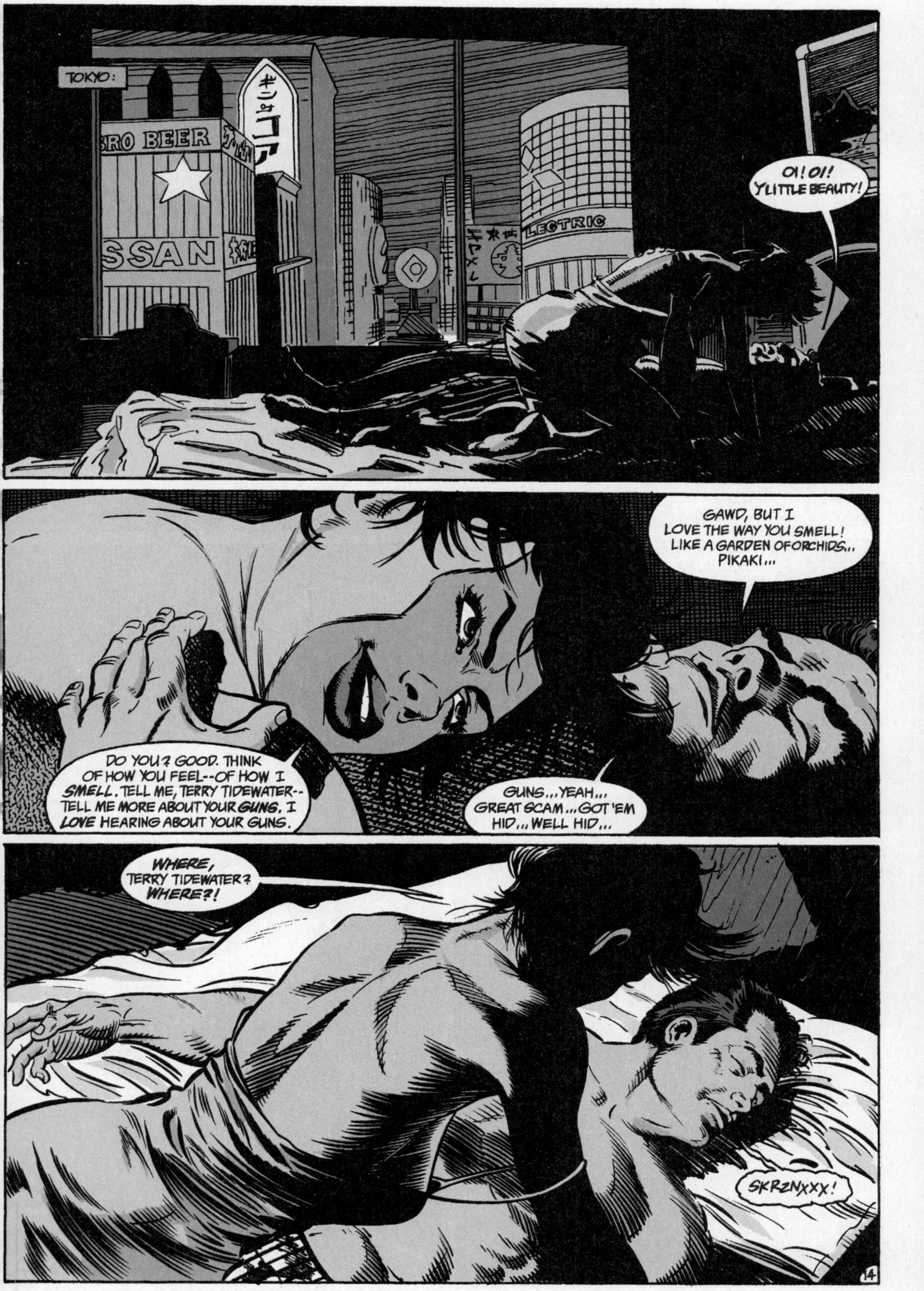
TOKYO:
BRO BEER
SSAN
LECTRIC
OI! OI! Y LITTLE BEAUTY!
GAWD, BUT I LOVE THE WAY YOU SMELL! LIKE A GARDEN OF ORCHIDS... PIKAKI...
DO YOU? GOOD. THINK OF HOW YOU FEEL--OF HOW I SMELL. TELL ME, TERRY TIDEWATER--TELL ME MORE ABOUT YOUR GUNS. I LOVE HEARING ABOUT YOUR GUNS.
GUNS... YEAH... GREAT SCAM... GOT 'EM HID... WELL HID...
WHERE, TERRY TIDEWATER? WHERE?!
SKRZNXXX!
14

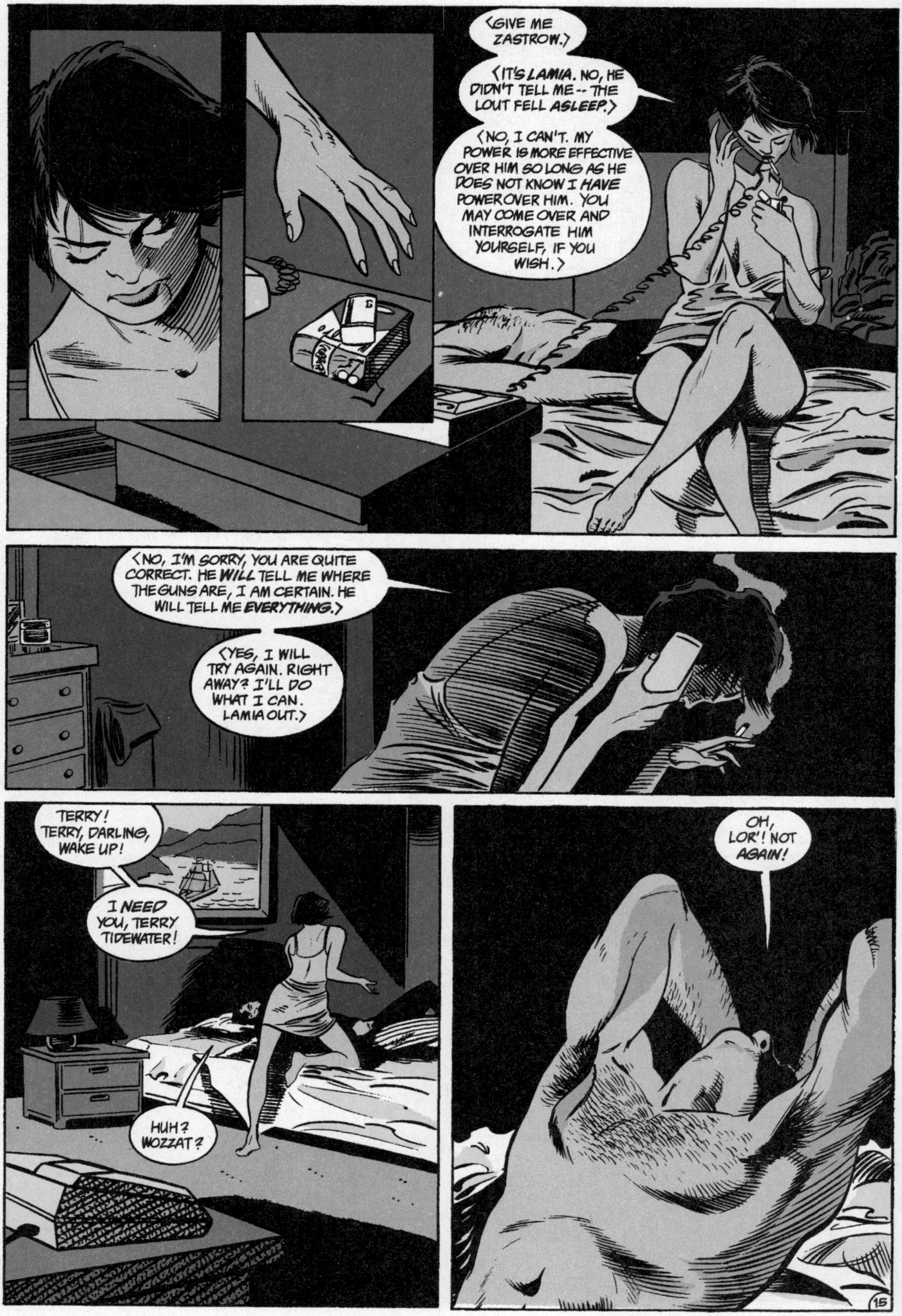

‹GIVE ME ZASTROW.›
‹IT'S LAMIA. NO, HE DIDN'T TELL ME -- THE LOUT FELL ASLEEP.›
‹NO, I CAN'T. MY POWER IS MORE EFFECTIVE OVER HIM SO LONG AS HE DOES NOT KNOW I HAVE POWER OVER HIM. YOU MAY COME OVER AND INTERROGATE HIM YOURSELF, IF YOU WISH.›
‹NO, I'M SORRY, YOU ARE QUITE CORRECT. HE WILL TELL ME WHERE THE GUNS ARE, I AM CERTAIN. HE WILL TELL ME EVERYTHING.›
‹YES, I WILL TRY AGAIN. RIGHT AWAY? I'LL DO WHAT I CAN. LAMIA OUT.›
TERRY! TERRY, DARLING, WAKE UP!
I NEED YOU, TERRY TIDEWATER!
HUH? WOZZAT?
OH, LOR'! NOT AGAIN!
15

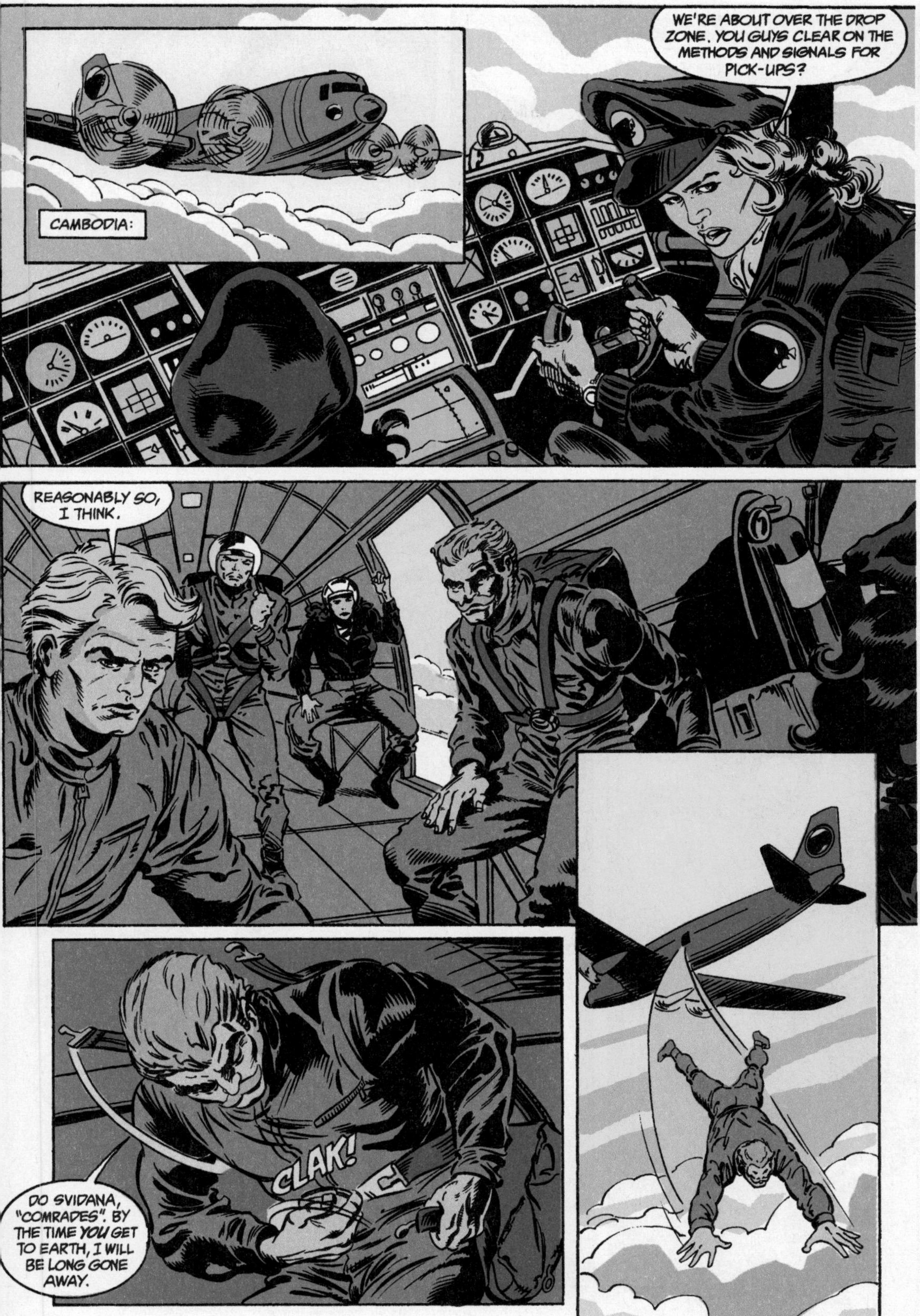
CAMBODIA:
WE'RE ABOUT OVER THE DROP ZONE. YOU GUYS CLEAR ON THE METHODS AND SIGNALS FOR PICK-UPS?
REASONABLY SO, I THINK.
CLAK!
DO SVIDANA, "COMRADES". BY THE TIME YOU GET TO EARTH, I WILL BE LONG GONE AWAY.
16

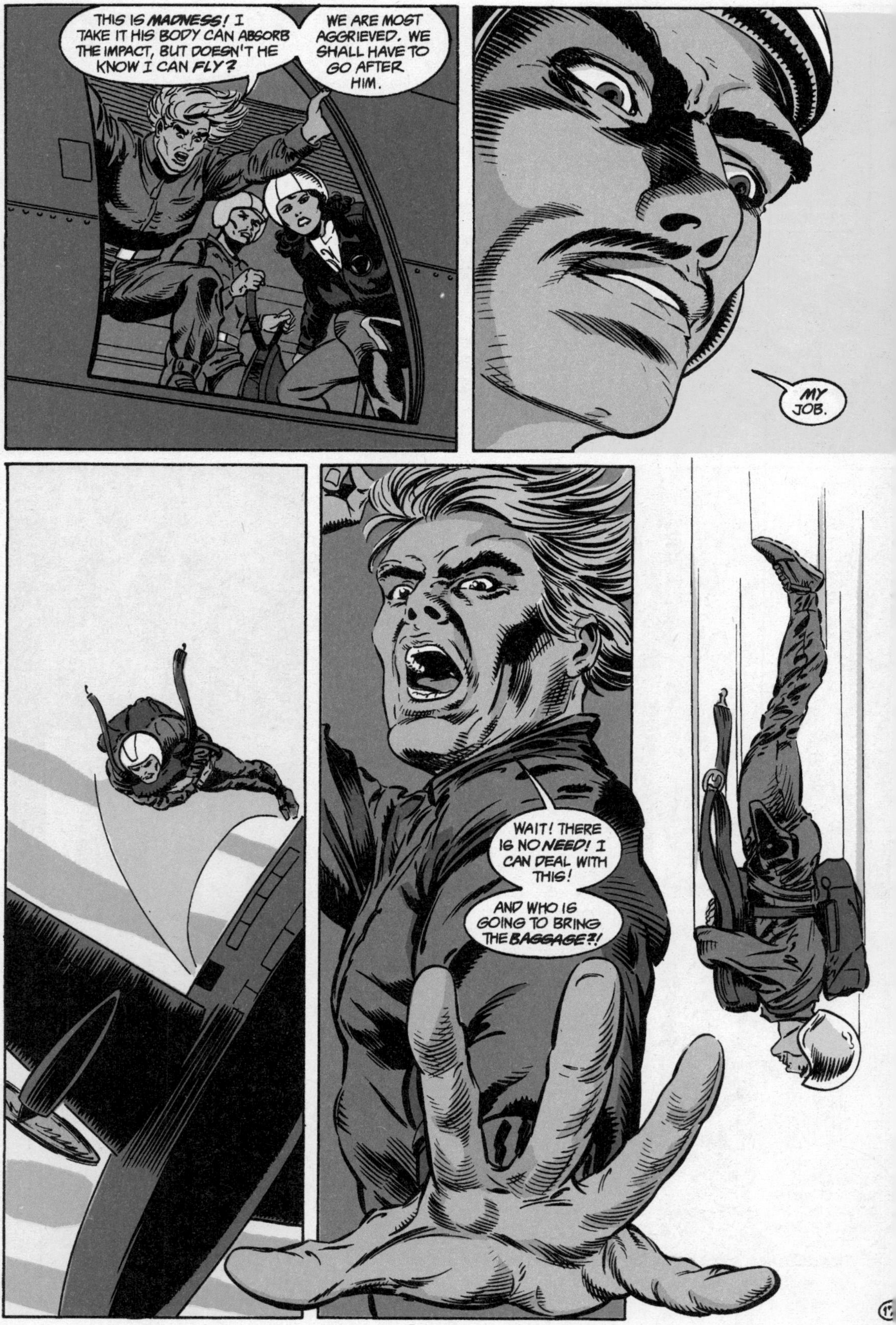
THIS IS MADNESS! I TAKE IT HIS BODY CAN ABSORB THE IMPACT, BUT DOESN'T HE KNOW I CAN FLY?
WE ARE MOST AGGRIEVED. WE SHALL HAVE TO GO AFTER HIM.
MY JOB.
WAIT! THERE IS NO NEED! I CAN DEAL WITH THIS!
AND WHO IS GOING TO BRING THE BAGGAGE?!

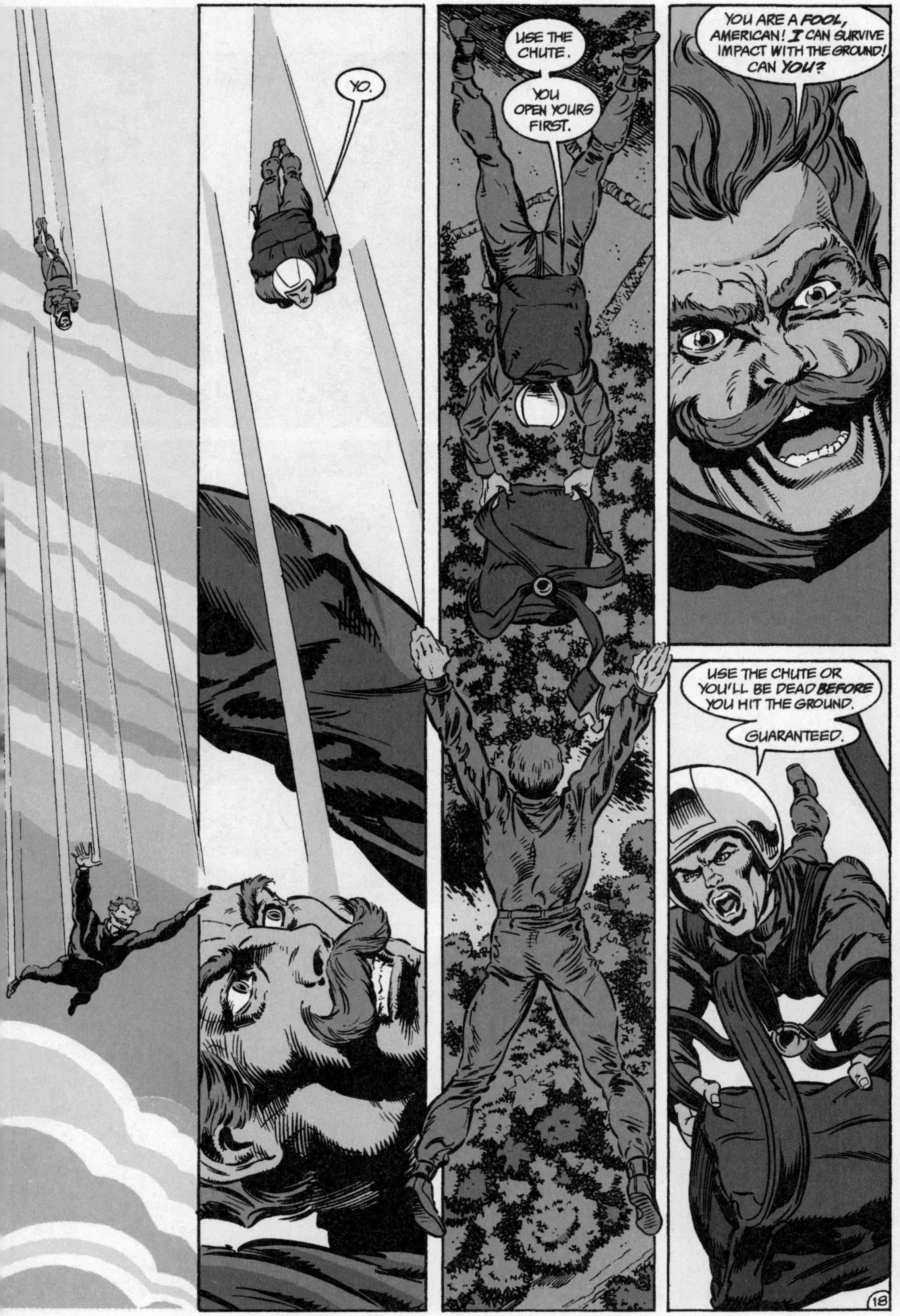
YO.
USE THE CHUTE.
YOU OPEN YOURS FIRST.
YOU ARE A FOOL, AMERICAN! I CAN SURVIVE IMPACT WITH THE GROUND! CAN YOU?
USE THE CHUTE OR YOU'LL BE DEAD BEFORE YOU HIT THE GROUND.
GUARANTEED.
18

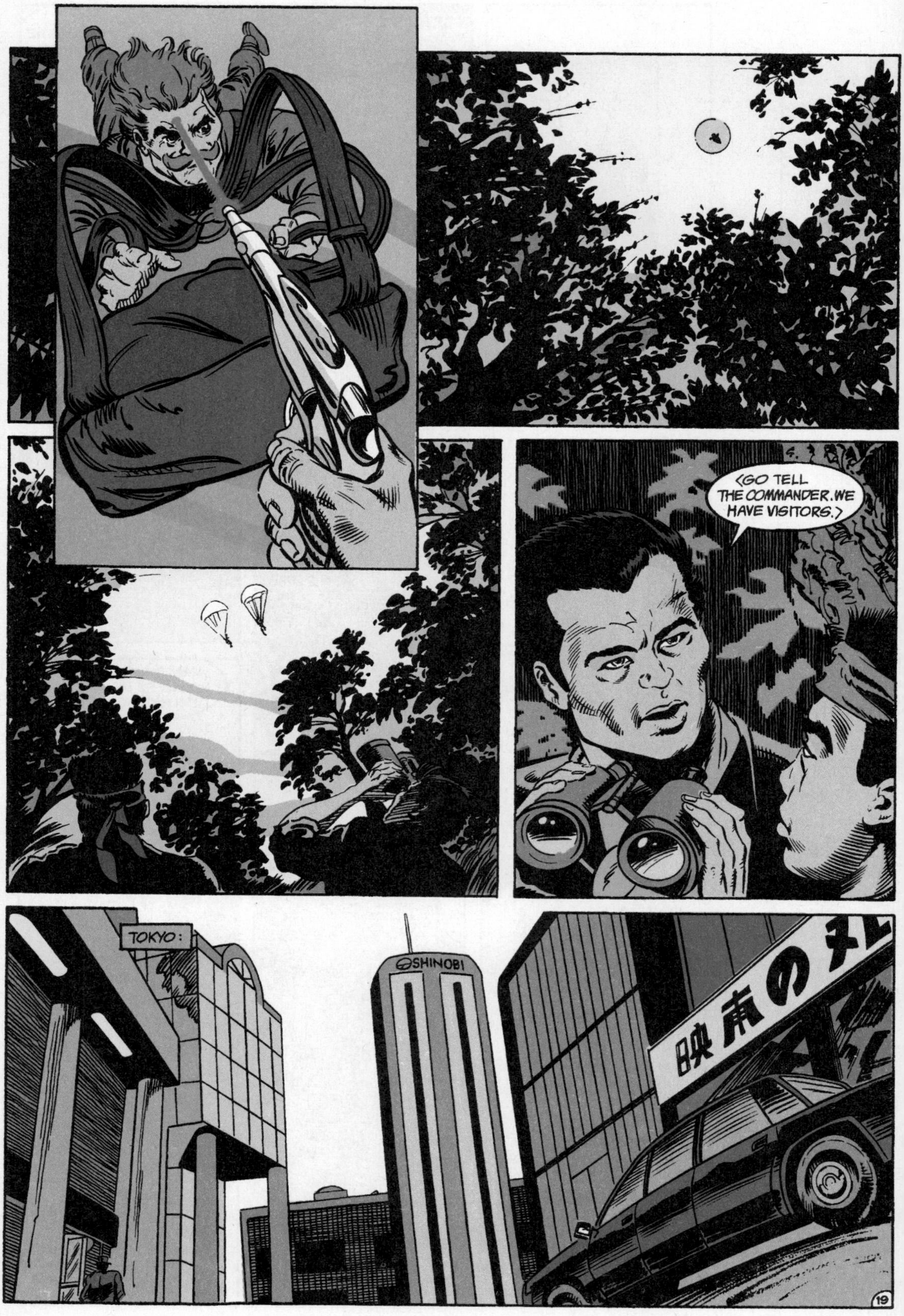

<GO TELL THE COMMANDER. WE HAVE VISITORS.>
TOKYO:
SHINOBI
映東の
19

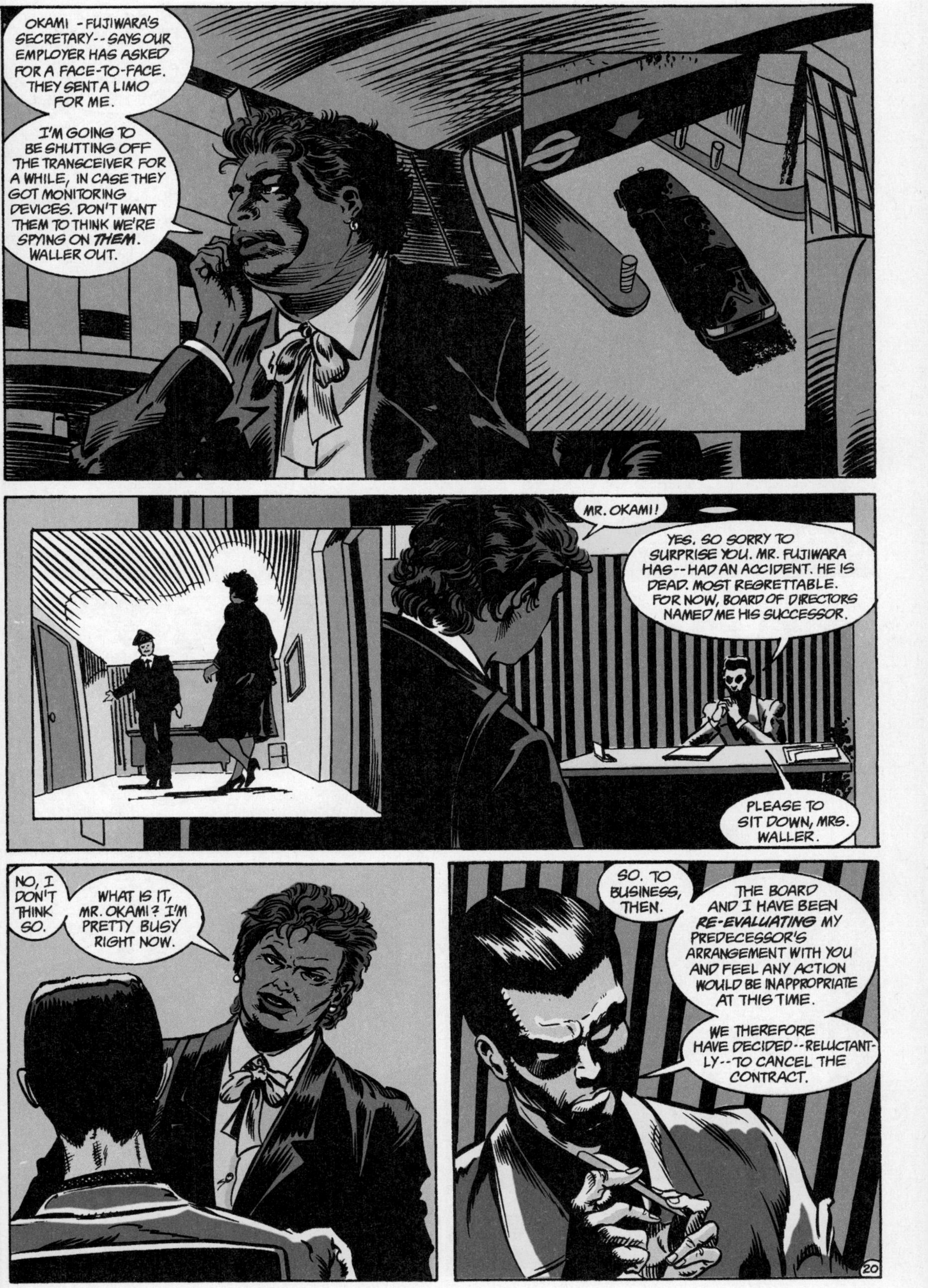
OKAMI - FUJIWARA'S SECRETARY-- SAYS OUR EMPLOYER HAS ASKED FOR A FACE-TO-FACE. THEY SENT A LIMO FOR ME.
I'M GOING TO BE SHUTTING OFF THE TRANSCEIVER FOR A WHILE, IN CASE THEY GOT MONITORING DEVICES. DON'T WANT THEM TO THINK WE'RE SPYING ON *THEM*. WALLER OUT.
MR. OKAMI!
YES. SO SORRY TO SURPRISE YOU. MR. FUJIWARA HAS--HAD AN ACCIDENT. HE IS DEAD. MOST REGRETTABLE. FOR NOW, BOARD OF DIRECTORS NAMED ME HIS SUCCESSOR.
PLEASE TO SIT DOWN, MRS. WALLER.
NO, I DON'T THINK SO.
WHAT IS IT, MR. OKAMI? I'M PRETTY BUSY RIGHT NOW.
SO. TO BUSINESS, THEN.
THE BOARD AND I HAVE BEEN *RE-EVALUATING* MY PREDECESSOR'S ARRANGEMENT WITH YOU AND FEEL ANY ACTION WOULD BE INAPPROPRIATE AT THIS TIME.
WE THEREFORE HAVE DECIDED--RELUCTANTLY--TO CANCEL THE CONTRACT.
20

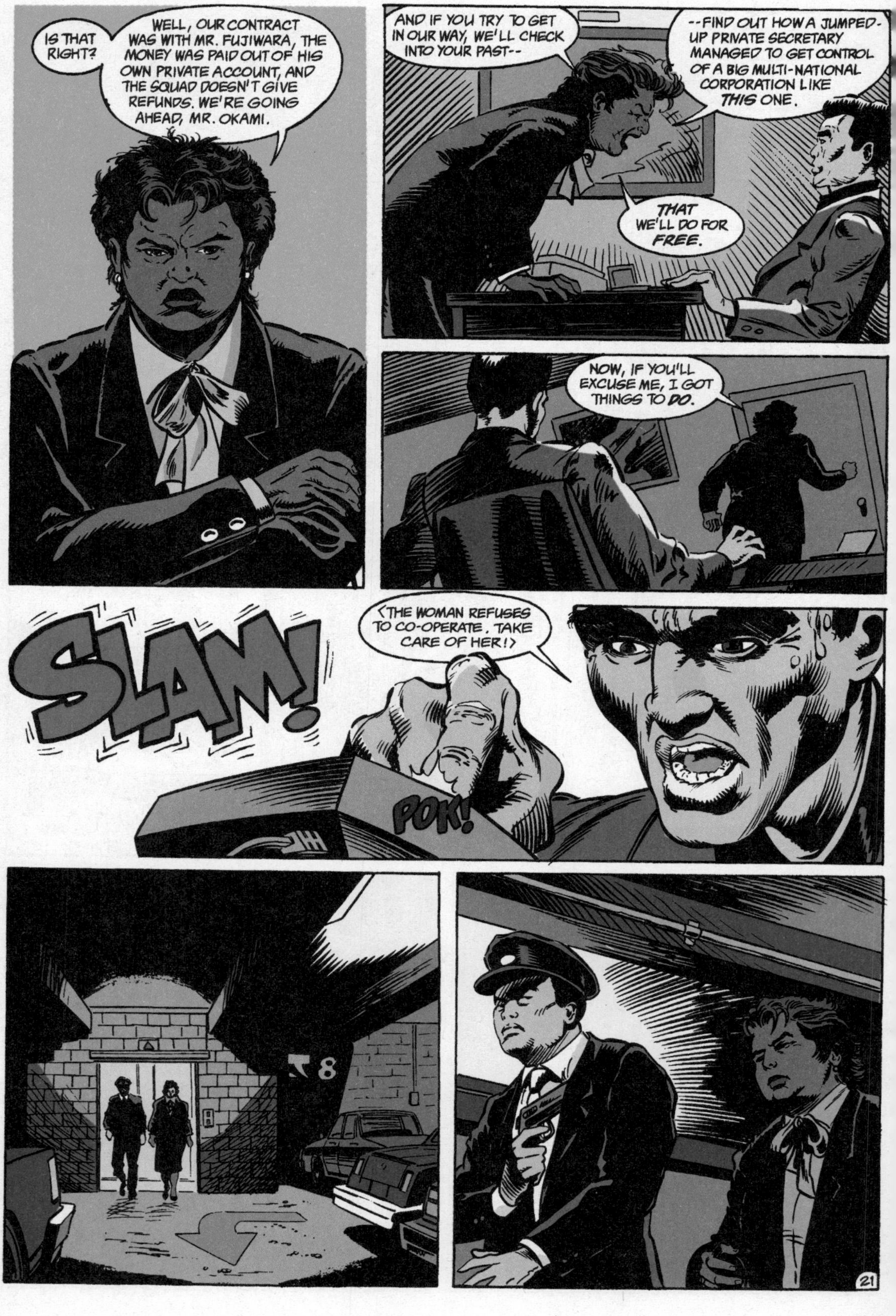
IS THAT RIGHT?
WELL, OUR CONTRACT WAS WITH MR. FUJIWARA, THE MONEY WAS PAID OUT OF HIS OWN PRIVATE ACCOUNT, AND THE SQUAD DOESN'T GIVE REFUNDS. WE'RE GOING AHEAD, MR. OKAMI.
AND IF YOU TRY TO GET IN OUR WAY, WE'LL CHECK INTO YOUR PAST--
--FIND OUT HOW A JUMPED-UP PRIVATE SECRETARY MANAGED TO GET CONTROL OF A BIG MULTI-NATIONAL CORPORATION LIKE THIS ONE.
THAT WE'LL DO FOR FREE.
NOW, IF YOU'LL EXCUSE ME, I GOT THINGS TO DO.
SLAM!
<THE WOMAN REFUSES TO CO-OPERATE. TAKE CARE OF HER!>
POK!
8
21

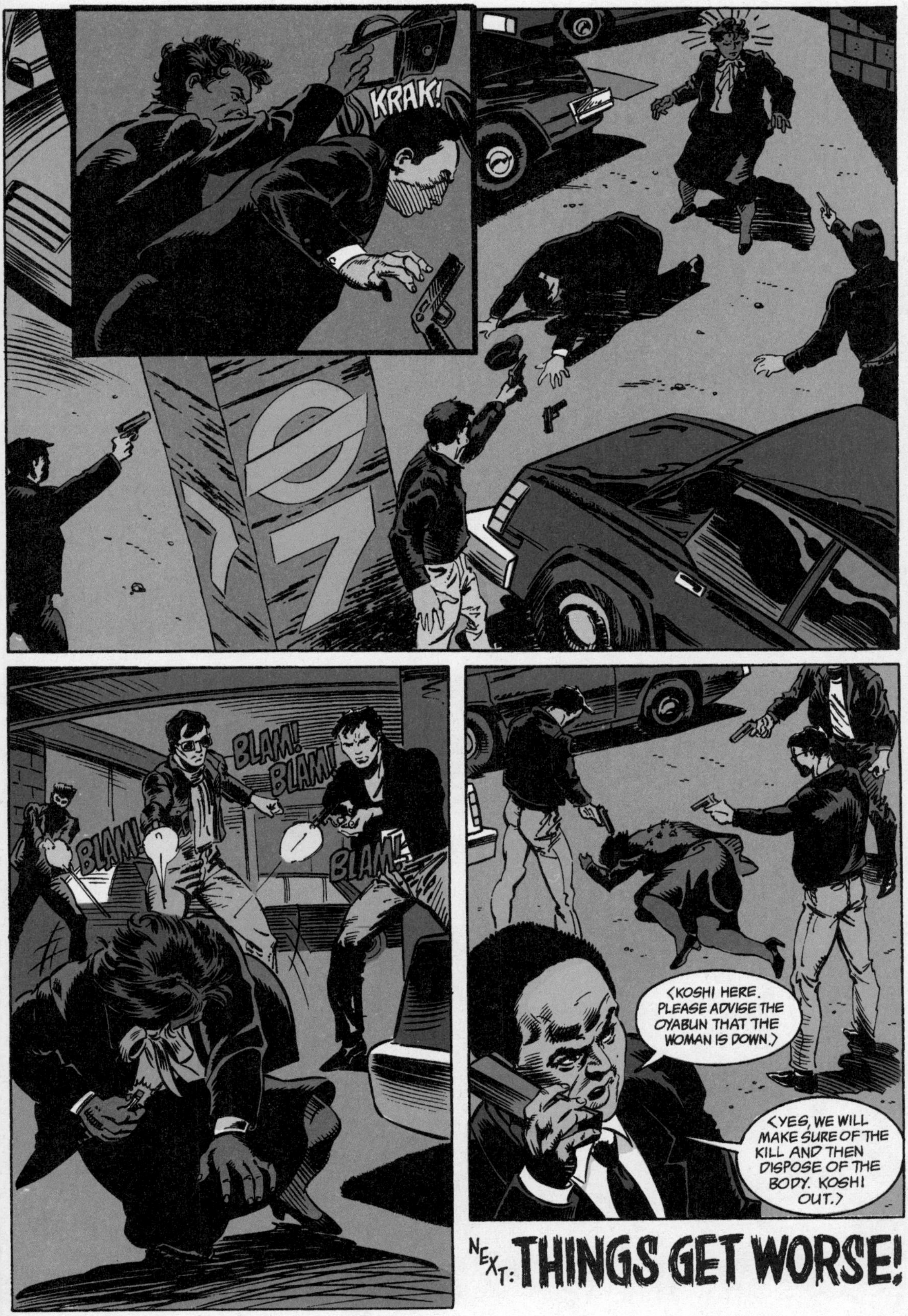
KRAK!
BLAM! BLAM!
BLAM!
BLAM!
<KOSHI HERE. PLEASE ADVISE THE OYABUN THAT THE WOMAN IS DOWN.>
<YES, WE WILL MAKE SURE OF THE KILL AND THEN DISPOSE OF THE BODY. KOSHI OUT.>
NEXT: THINGS GET WORSE!

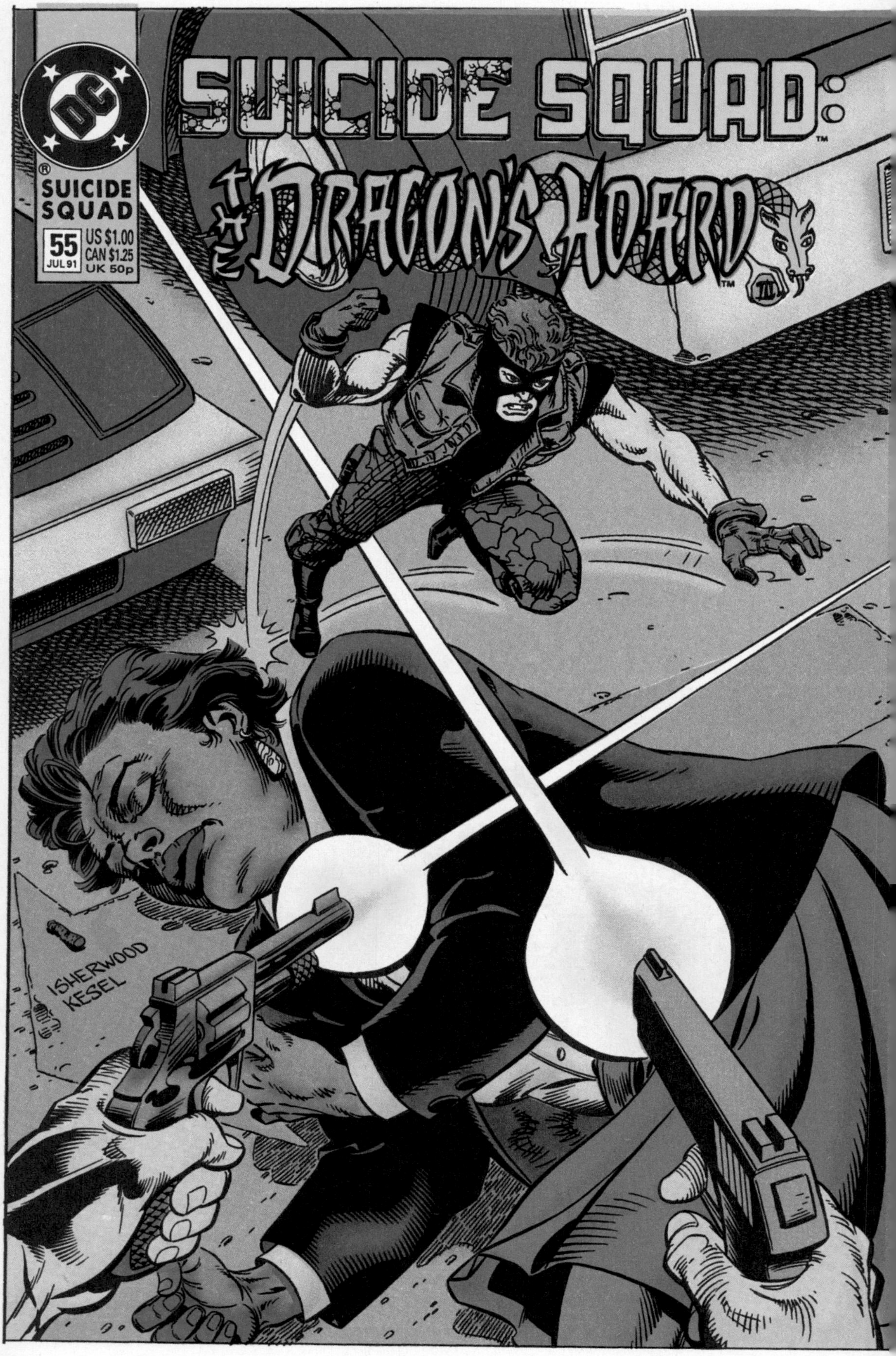

SUICIDE SQUAD:
THE DRAGON'S HOARD
DC
SUICIDE SQUAD
55
JUL 91
US $1.00
CAN $1.25
UK 50p
ISHERWOOD
KESEL

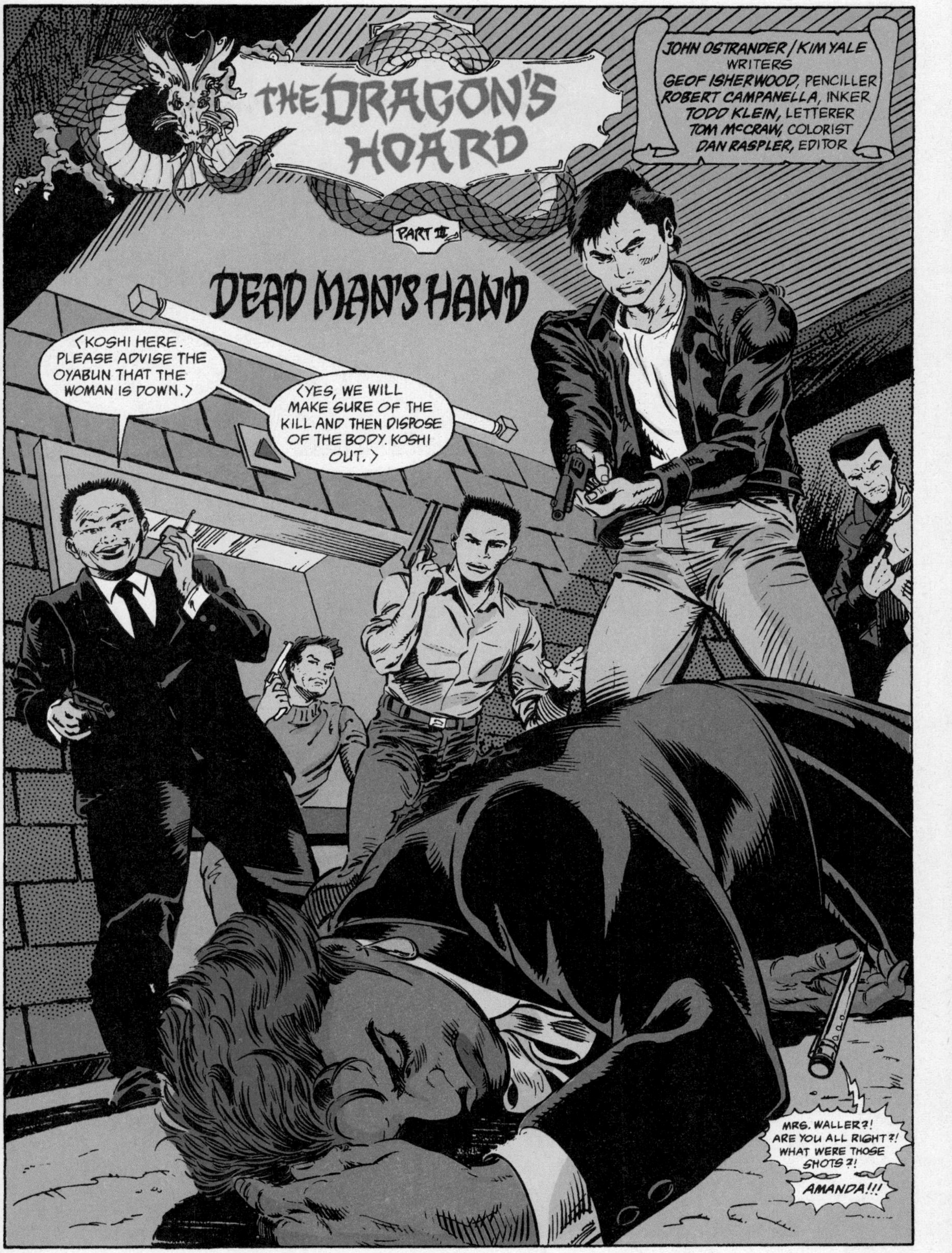
THE DRAGON'S HOARD
PART III
DEAD MAN'S HAND
JOHN OSTRANDER / KIM YALE WRITERS
GEOF ISHERWOOD, PENCILLER
ROBERT CAMPANELLA, INKER
TODD KLEIN, LETTERER
TOM McCRAW, COLORIST
DAN RASPLER, EDITOR
<KOSHI HERE. PLEASE ADVISE THE OYABUN THAT THE WOMAN IS DOWN.>
<YES, WE WILL MAKE SURE OF THE KILL AND THEN DISPOSE OF THE BODY. KOSHI OUT.>
MRS. WALLER?! ARE YOU ALL RIGHT?! WHAT WERE THOSE SHOTS?!
AMANDA!!!

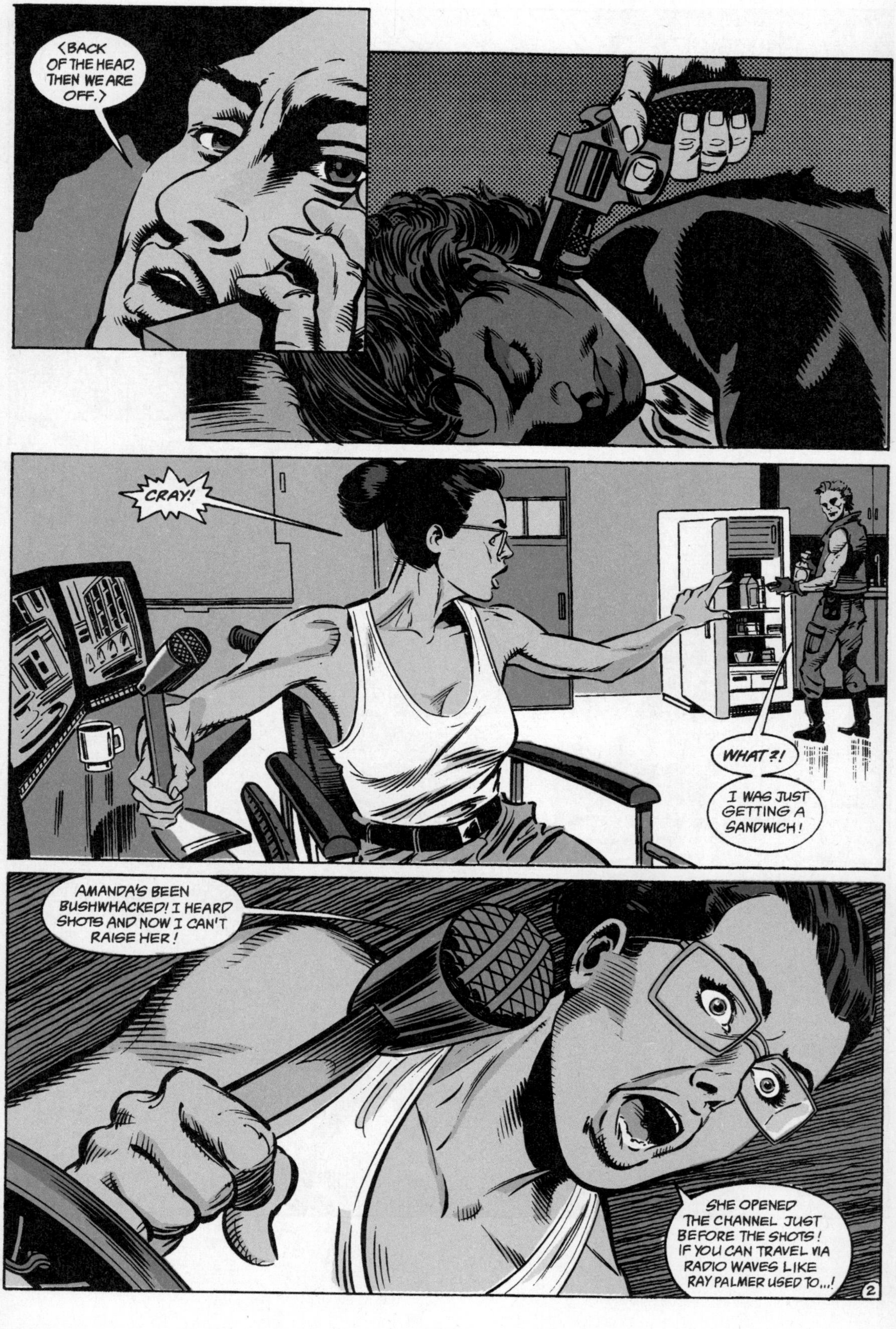

<BACK OF THE HEAD. THEN WE ARE OFF.>
CRAY!
WHAT?!
I WAS JUST GETTING A SANDWICH!
AMANDA'S BEEN BUSHWHACKED! I HEARD SHOTS AND NOW I CAN'T RAISE HER!
SHE OPENED THE CHANNEL JUST BEFORE THE SHOTS! IF YOU CAN TRAVEL VIA RADIO WAVES LIKE RAY PALMER USED TO...!
2

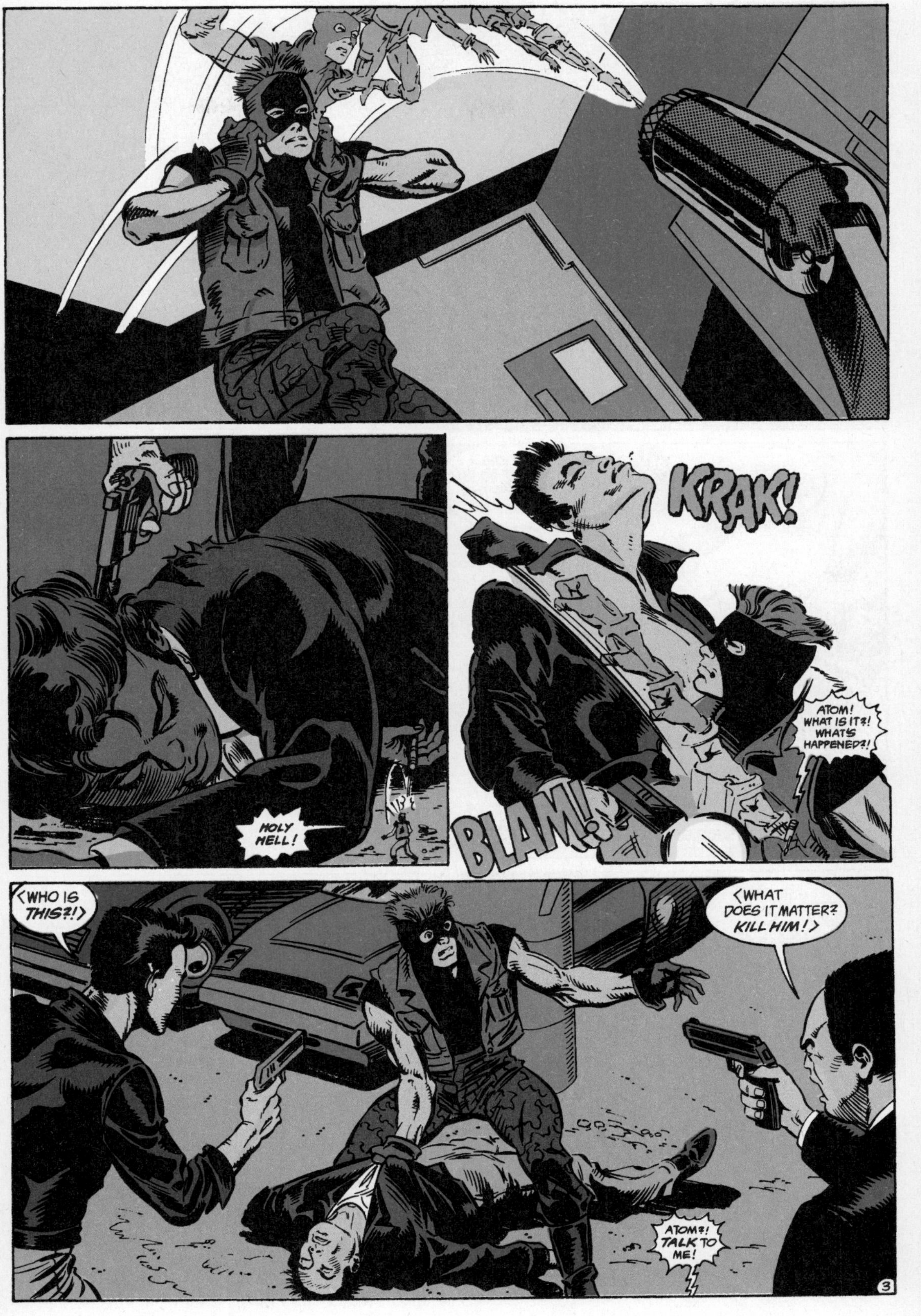
HOLY HELL!
KRAK!
ATOM! WHAT IS IT?! WHAT'S HAPPENED?!
BLAM!
<WHO IS THIS?!>
<WHAT DOES IT MATTER? KILL HIM!>
ATOM?! TALK TO ME!
3

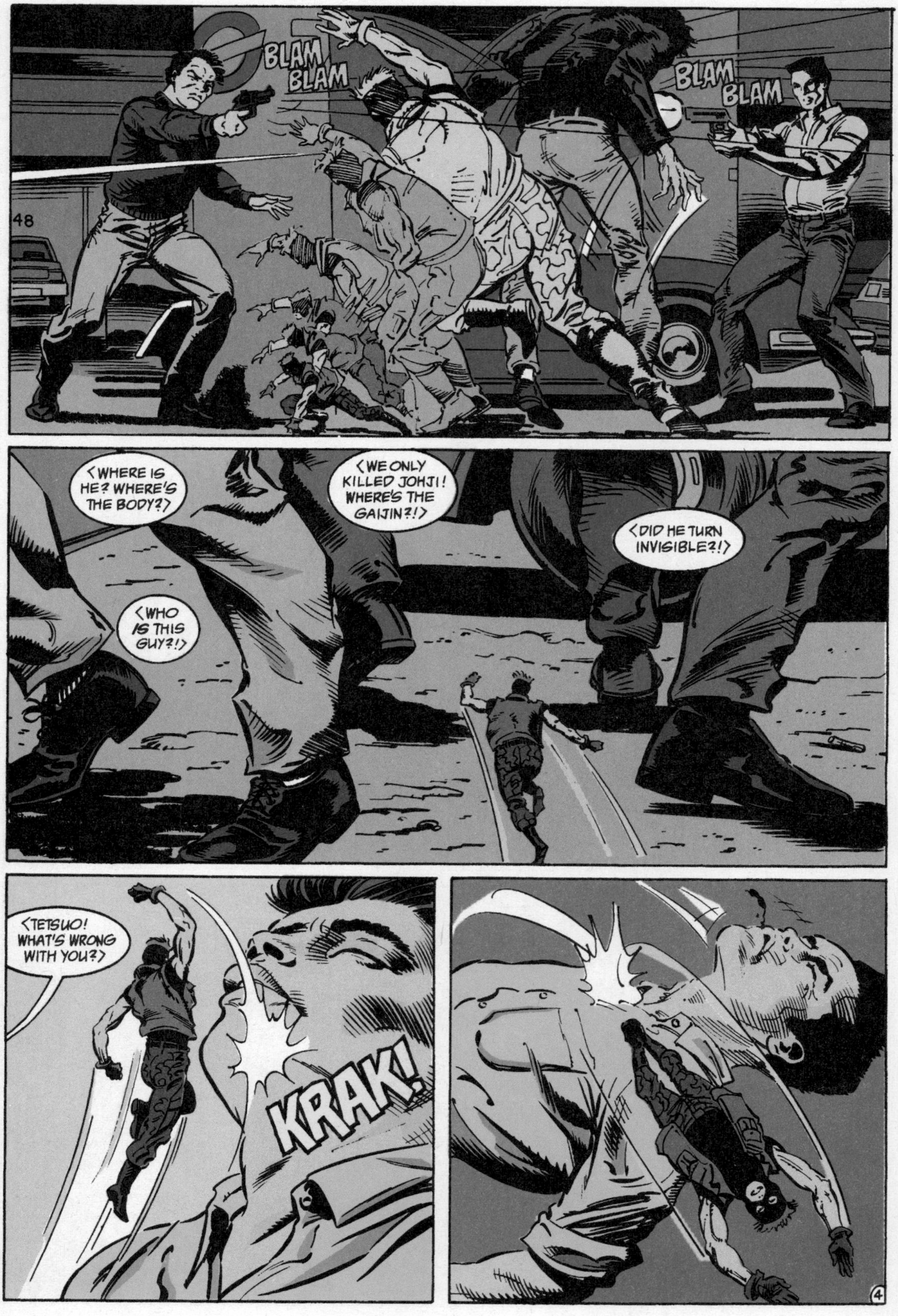
BLAM
BLAM
BLAM
BLAM
48
<WHERE IS HE? WHERE'S THE BODY?>
<WE ONLY KILLED JOHJI! WHERE'S THE GAIJIN?!>
<DID HE TURN INVISIBLE?!>
<WHO IS THIS GUY?!>
<TETSUO! WHAT'S WRONG WITH YOU?>
KRAK!
4

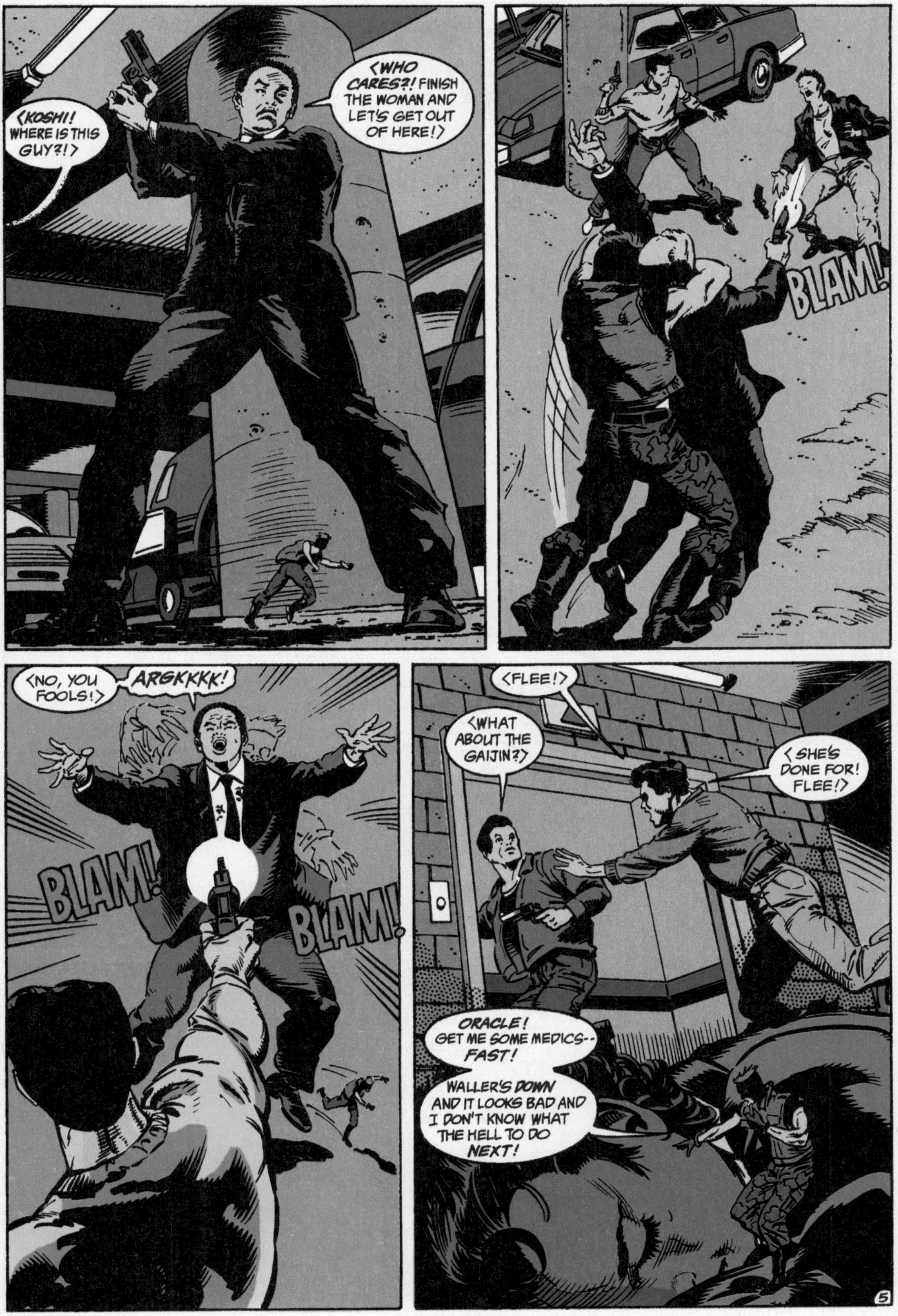

<KOSHI! WHERE IS THIS GUY?!>
<WHO CARES?! FINISH THE WOMAN AND LET'S GET OUT OF HERE!>
BLAM!
<NO, YOU FOOLS!>
ARGKKKK!
BLAM!
BLAM!
<FLEE!>
<WHAT ABOUT THE GAIJIN?>
<SHE'S DONE FOR! FLEE!>
ORACLE! GET ME SOME MEDICS-- FAST!
WALLER'S DOWN AND IT LOOKS BAD AND I DON'T KNOW WHAT THE HELL TO DO NEXT!
5

FACT IS -- SUDDENLY I DON'T FEEL SO GOOD MYSELF! IN FACT, I FEEL LIKE --

CRAY? ARE *YOU* ALL RIGHT?! CRAY?!

WHUMP!

AT THE SAME TIME, ON THE SHINJUKU, TOKYO'S CLUB DISTRICT...

HERE NOW. YOU OLD ENOUGH TO DRINK THAT, SPROUT?

NUKE YOURSELF.

I HATE THIS STUPID COUNTRY. I HATE THEIR BEER. I HATE THEIR WOMEN. I HATE THIS JOB AND EVERYONE ON IT.

OI! DROP OFF! YA KNOW WHAT YER WHOLE PROBLEM IS, SPORT? YER GOT AN *ATTITUDE* PROBLEM.

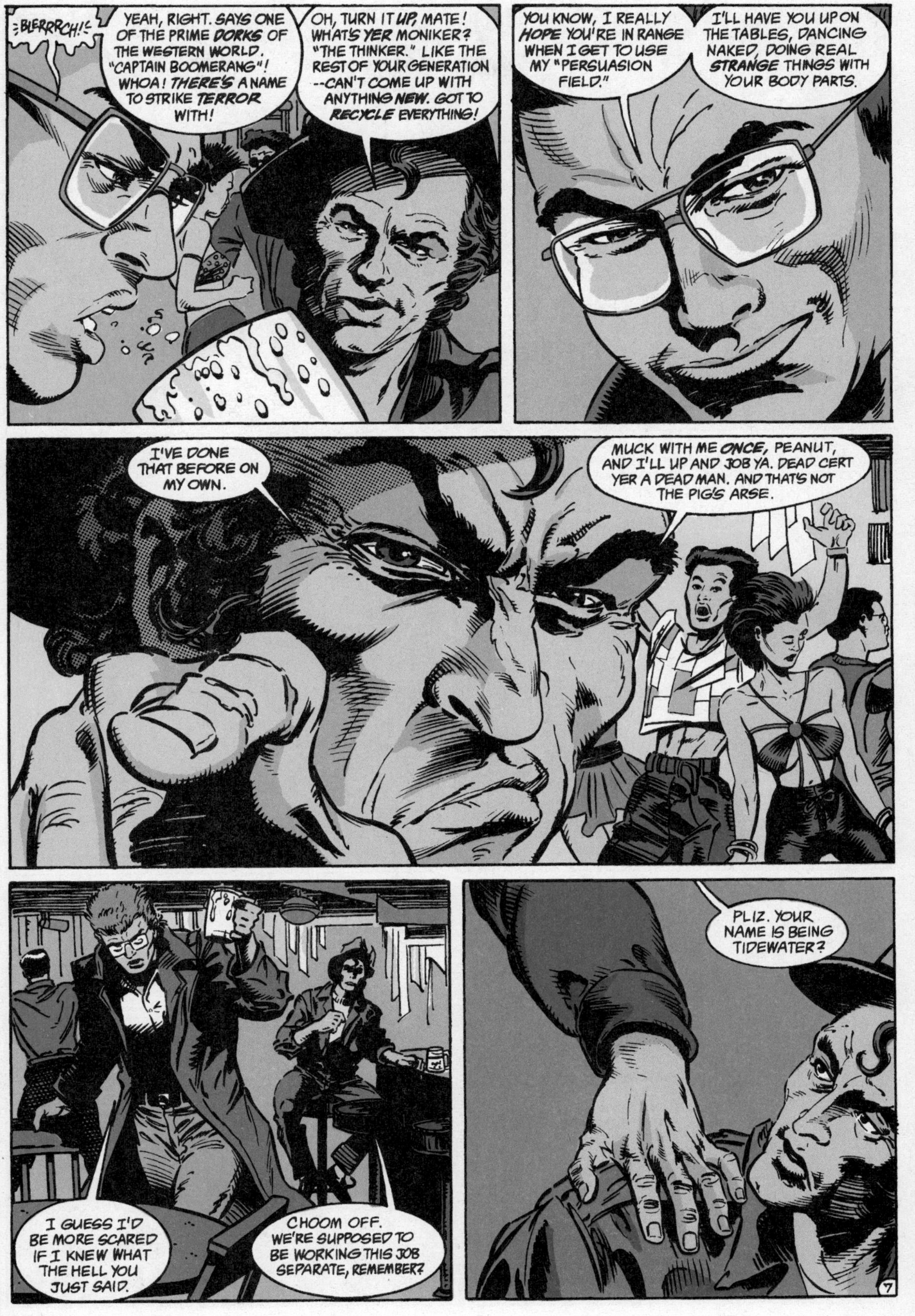
BLERRRCH!!
YEAH, RIGHT. SAYS ONE OF THE PRIME DORKS OF THE WESTERN WORLD. "CAPTAIN BOOMERANG"! WHOA! THERE'S A NAME TO STRIKE TERROR WITH!
OH, TURN IT UP, MATE! WHAT'S YER MONIKER? "THE THINKER." LIKE THE REST OF YOUR GENERATION --CAN'T COME UP WITH ANYTHING NEW. GOT TO RECYCLE EVERYTHING!
YOU KNOW, I REALLY HOPE YOU'RE IN RANGE WHEN I GET TO USE MY "PERSUASION FIELD."
I'LL HAVE YOU UP ON THE TABLES, DANCING NAKED, DOING REAL STRANGE THINGS WITH YOUR BODY PARTS.
I'VE DONE THAT BEFORE ON MY OWN.
MUCK WITH ME ONCE, PEANUT, AND I'LL UP AND JOB YA. DEAD CERT YER A DEAD MAN. AND THAT'S NOT THE PIG'S ARSE.
I GUESS I'D BE MORE SCARED IF I KNEW WHAT THE HELL YOU JUST SAID.
CHOOM OFF. WE'RE SUPPOSED TO BE WORKING THIS JOB SEPARATE, REMEMBER?
PLIZ. YOUR NAME IS BEING TIDEWATER?
7

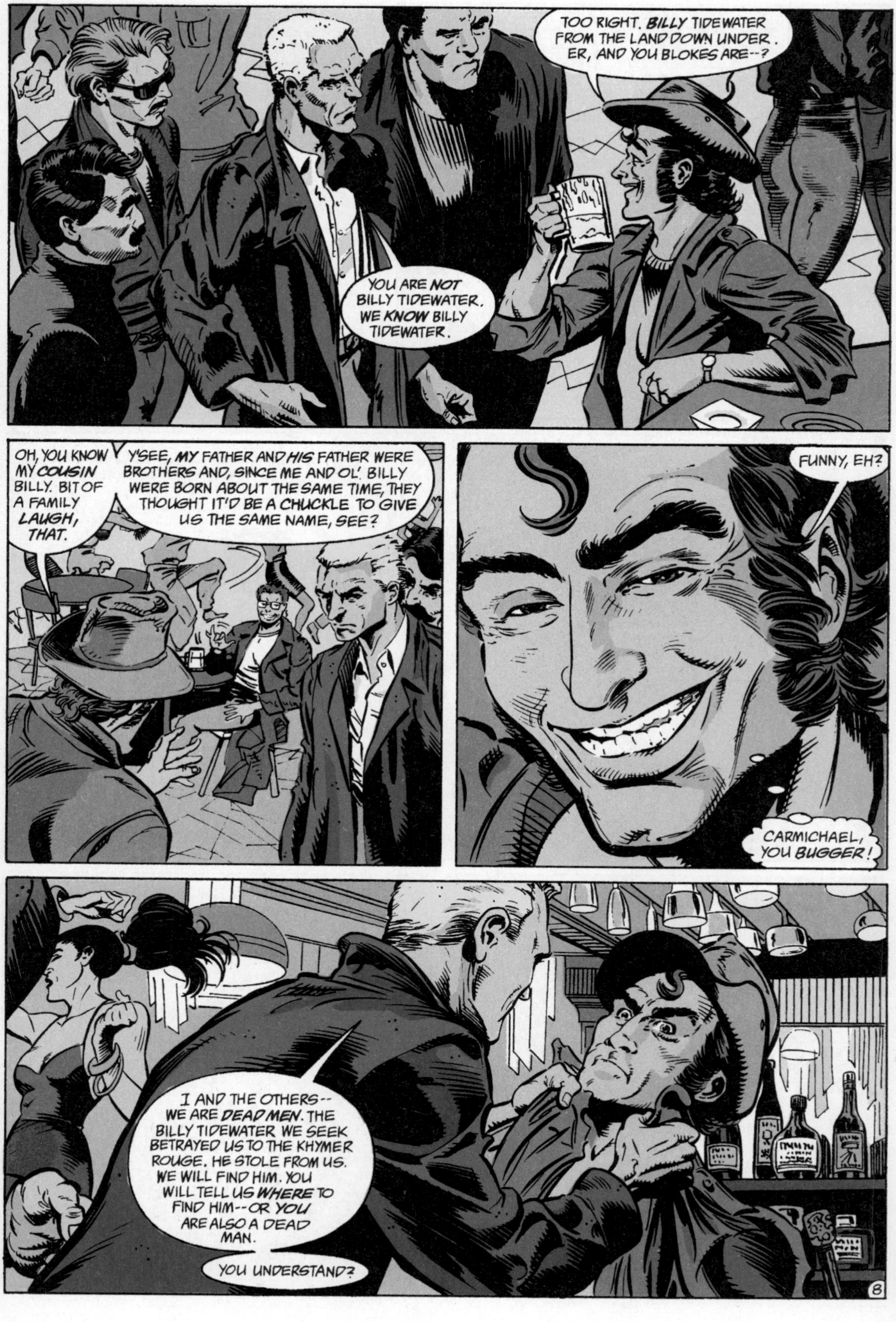
TOO RIGHT. BILLY TIDEWATER FROM THE LAND DOWN UNDER. ER, AND YOU BLOKES ARE--?
YOU ARE NOT BILLY TIDEWATER. WE KNOW BILLY TIDEWATER.
OH, YOU KNOW MY COUSIN BILLY. BIT OF A FAMILY LAUGH, THAT.
Y'SEE, MY FATHER AND HIS FATHER WERE BROTHERS AND, SINCE ME AND OL' BILLY WERE BORN ABOUT THE SAME TIME, THEY THOUGHT IT'D BE A CHUCKLE TO GIVE US THE SAME NAME, SEE?
FUNNY, EH?
CARMICHAEL, YOU BUGGER!
I AND THE OTHERS-- WE ARE DEAD MEN. THE BILLY TIDEWATER WE SEEK BETRAYED US TO THE KHYMER ROUGE. HE STOLE FROM US. WE WILL FIND HIM. YOU WILL TELL US WHERE TO FIND HIM--OR YOU ARE ALSO A DEAD MAN.
YOU UNDERSTAND?
8

TOO RIGHT! THE BUGGER'S STOLEN FROM ME AS WELL--KITH AND KIN AS I MAY BE! TELL YOU WHAT--WE'LL JOIN FORCES, YOU AND I! MATES, EH?

TO SHOW MY GOOD FAITH, I'LL LET YER IN ON SOMETHING FOR FREE.

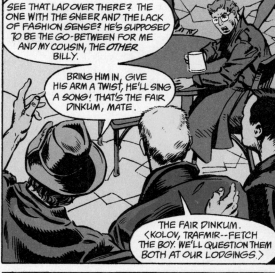

SEE THAT LAD OVER THERE? THE ONE WITH THE SNEER AND THE LACK OF FASHION SENSE? HE'S SUPPOSED TO BE THE GO-BETWEEN FOR ME AND MY COUSIN, THE *OTHER* BILLY.

BRING HIM IN, GIVE HIS ARM A TWIST, HE'LL SING A SONG! THAT'S THE FAIR DINKUM, MATE.

THE FAIR DINKUM. ⟨KOLOV, TRAFMIR--FETCH THE BOY. WE'LL QUESTION THEM BOTH AT OUR LODGINGS.⟩

HUL-LOOOO, AAAAMY. GOT A CONTACT, BABE. TWO UGLIES HEADING TOWARDS ME SO HOW ABOUT RELEASING MY HEAD SO I CAN SIC A LI'L MENTAL INFLUENCE ON 'EM?

WHAT SAY, AAAAAAMY?

HELLO, HELLO. CARMICHAEL TO BASE. WHERE *ARE* YOU, YOU STUPID COW?!

PLIZ. YOU TO COME WIZ US.

WHAM!

UNGHHHHH!

COME. WE TALK WITH BOY. WE TALK WITH YOU. WE TALK ABOUT YOUR "COUSIN." WE HAVE NICE *LONG* CHAT. COME.

WELL, *THAT* DIDN'T GO AS PLANNED! BLOODY HELL!

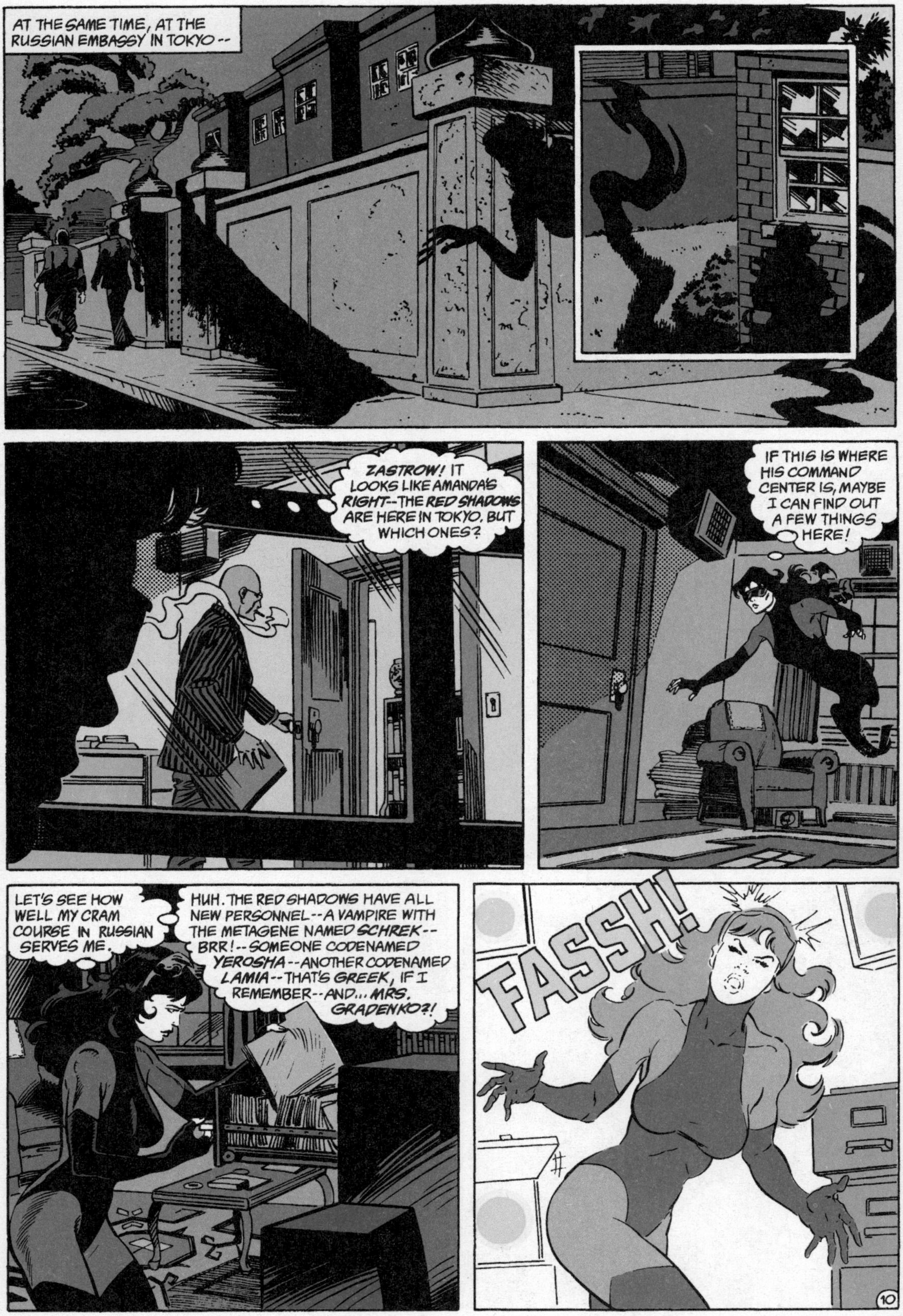
AT THE SAME TIME, AT THE RUSSIAN EMBASSY IN TOKYO --
ZASTROW! IT LOOKS LIKE AMANDA'S RIGHT--THE RED SHADOWS ARE HERE IN TOKYO, BUT WHICH ONES?
IF THIS IS WHERE HIS COMMAND CENTER IS, MAYBE I CAN FIND OUT A FEW THINGS HERE!
LET'S SEE HOW WELL MY CRAM COURSE IN RUSSIAN SERVES ME.
HUH. THE RED SHADOWS HAVE ALL NEW PERSONNEL--A VAMPIRE WITH THE METAGENE NAMED SCHREK--BRR!--SOMEONE CODENAMED YEROSHA--ANOTHER CODENAMED LAMIA--THAT'S GREEK, IF I REMEMBER--AND... MRS. GRADENKO?!
FASSH!
10

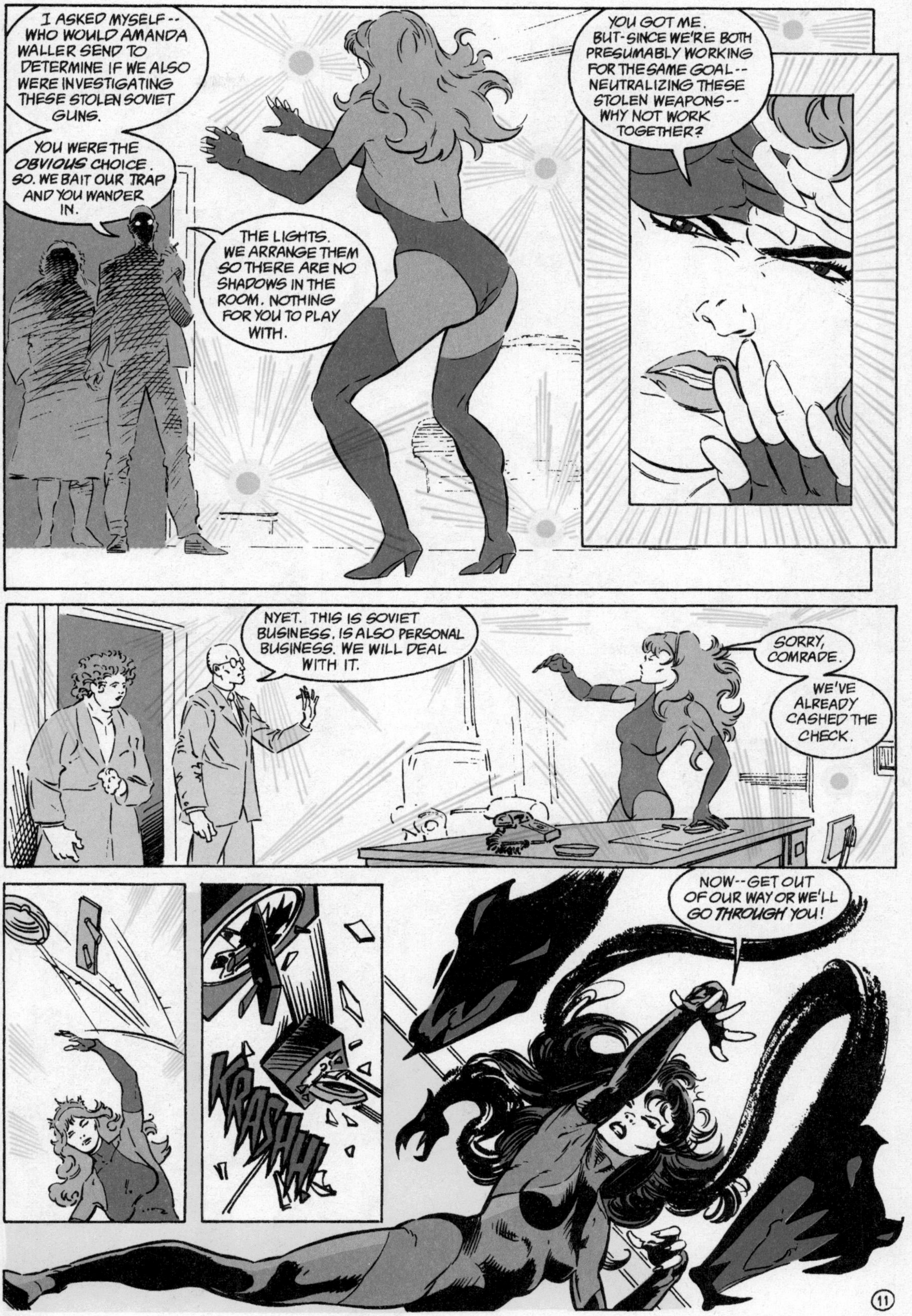
I ASKED MYSELF -- WHO WOULD AMANDA WALLER SEND TO DETERMINE IF WE ALSO WERE INVESTIGATING THESE STOLEN SOVIET GUNS.
YOU WERE THE OBVIOUS CHOICE. SO. WE BAIT OUR TRAP AND YOU WANDER IN.
THE LIGHTS. WE ARRANGE THEM SO THERE ARE NO SHADOWS IN THE ROOM. NOTHING FOR YOU TO PLAY WITH.
YOU GOT ME. BUT-SINCE WE'RE BOTH PRESUMABLY WORKING FOR THE SAME GOAL-- NEUTRALIZING THESE STOLEN WEAPONS-- WHY NOT WORK TOGETHER?
NYET. THIS IS SOVIET BUSINESS. IS ALSO PERSONAL BUSINESS. WE WILL DEAL WITH IT.
SORRY, COMRADE.
WE'VE ALREADY CASHED THE CHECK.
KRASHH!
NOW--GET OUT OF OUR WAY OR WE'LL GO THROUGH YOU!
11

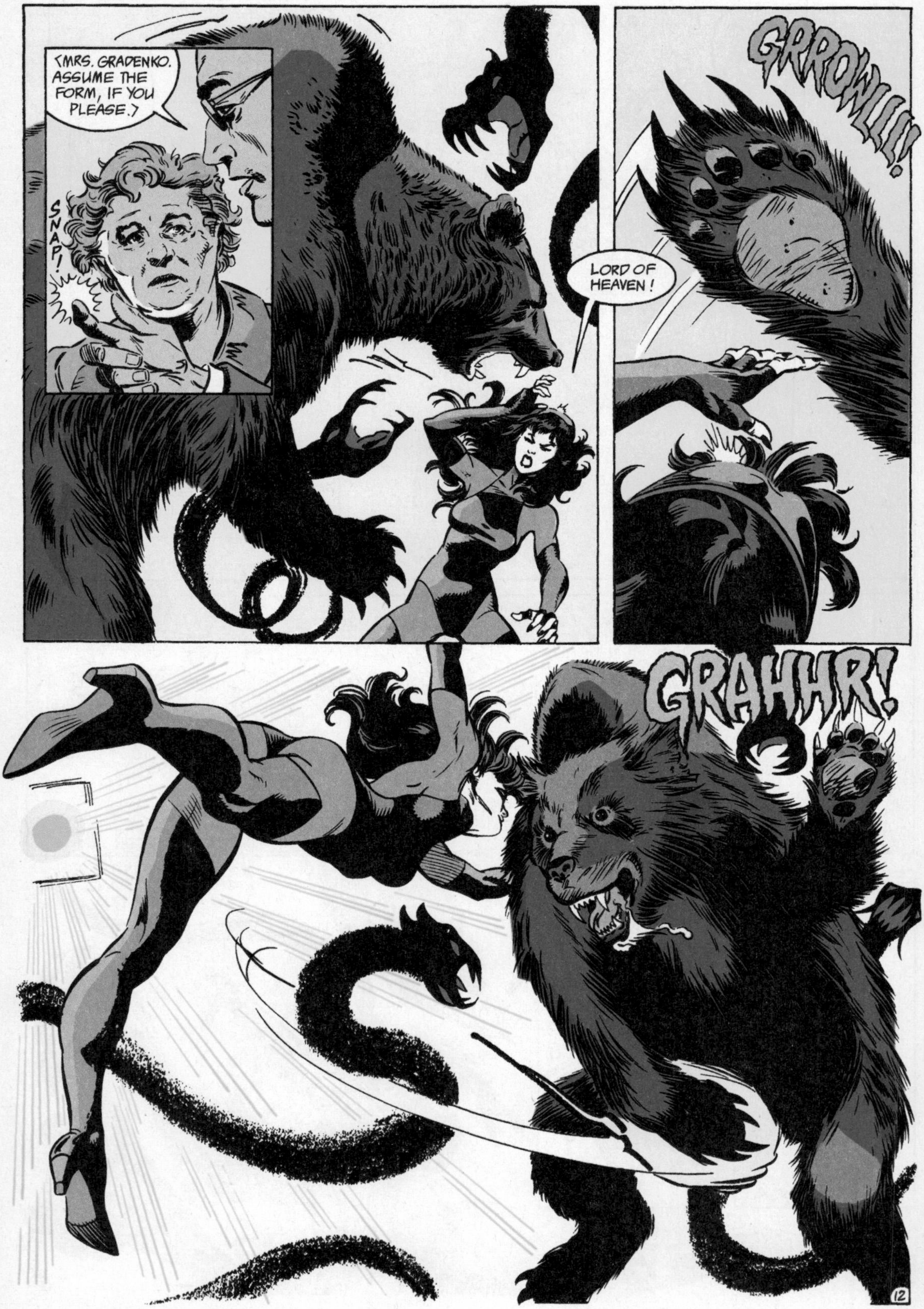

<MRS. GRADENKO. ASSUME THE FORM, IF YOU PLEASE.>
SNAP!
LORD OF HEAVEN!
GRROWLLL!
GRAHHR!
12

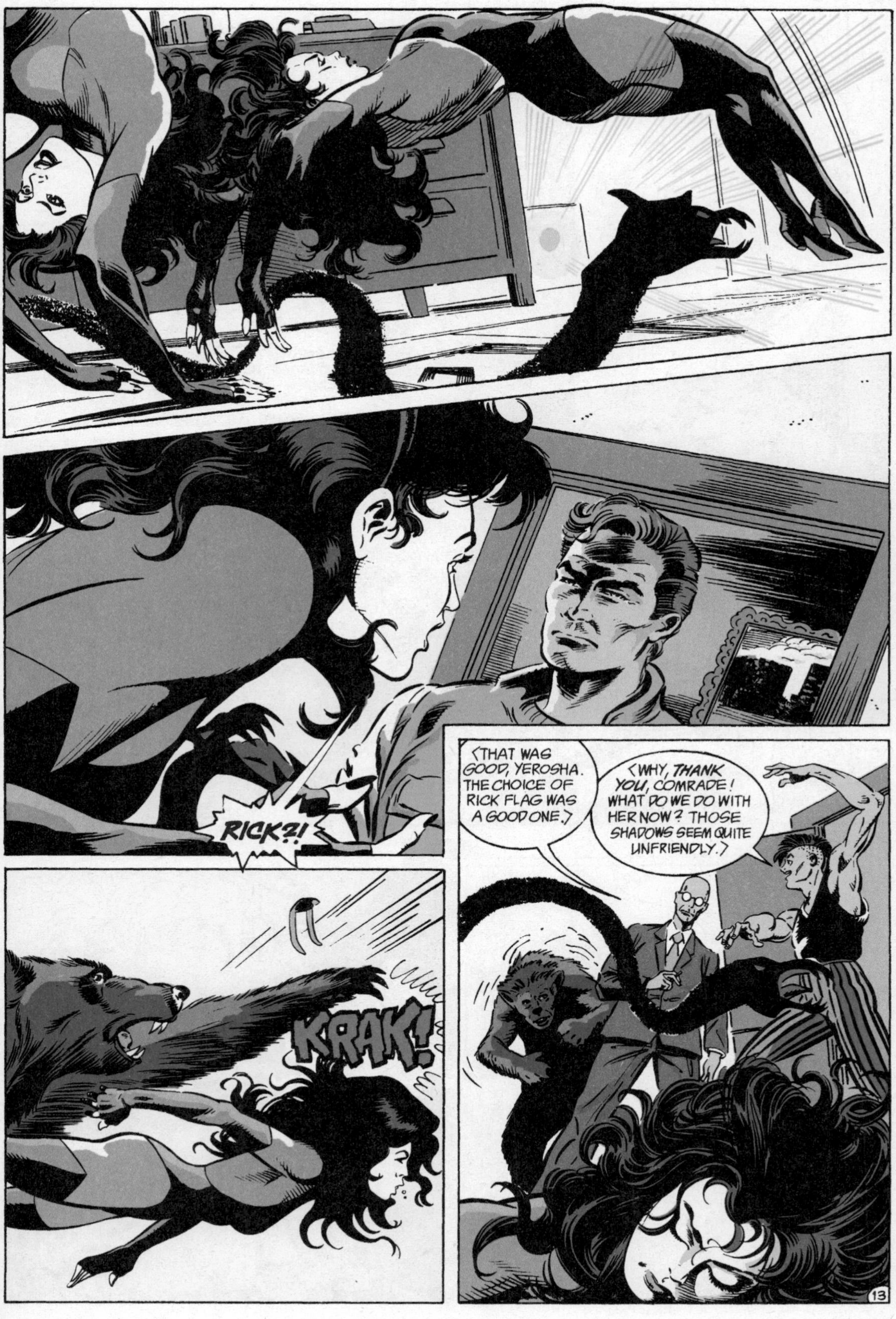
RICK?!
<THAT WAS GOOD, YEROSHA. THE CHOICE OF RICK FLAG WAS A GOOD ONE.>
<WHY, THANK YOU, COMRADE! WHAT DO WE DO WITH HER NOW? THOSE SHADOWS SEEM QUITE UNFRIENDLY.>
KRAK!
13

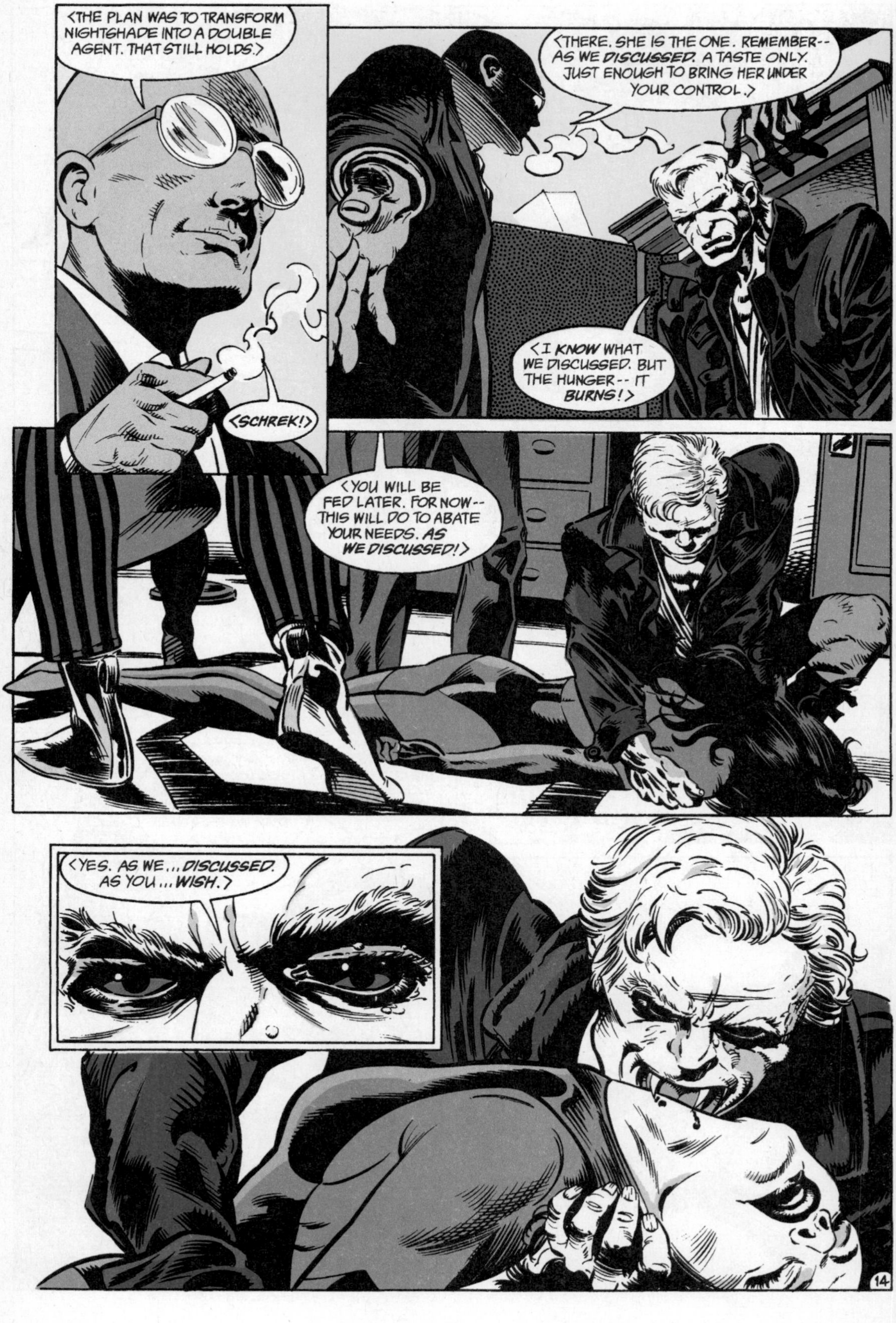
<THE PLAN WAS TO TRANSFORM NIGHTSHADE INTO A DOUBLE AGENT. THAT STILL HOLDS.>
<SCHREK!>
<THERE. SHE IS THE ONE. REMEMBER-- AS WE DISCUSSED. A TASTE ONLY. JUST ENOUGH TO BRING HER UNDER YOUR CONTROL.>
<I KNOW WHAT WE DISCUSSED. BUT THE HUNGER-- IT BURNS!>
<YOU WILL BE FED LATER. FOR NOW-- THIS WILL DO TO ABATE YOUR NEEDS. AS WE DISCUSSED!>
<YES. AS WE... DISCUSSED. AS YOU... WISH.>
14

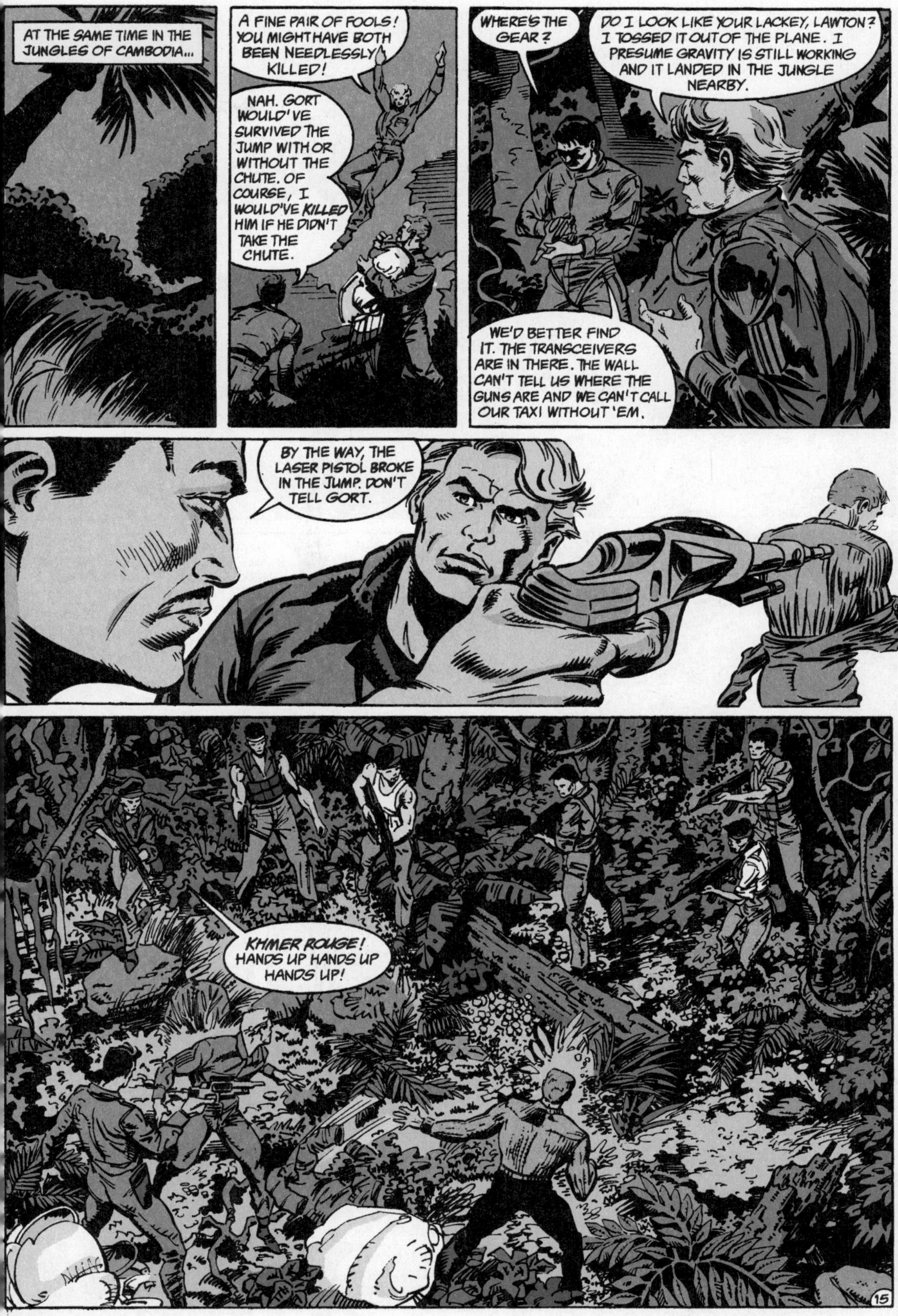
AT THE SAME TIME IN THE JUNGLES OF CAMBODIA...
A FINE PAIR OF FOOLS! YOU MIGHT HAVE BOTH BEEN NEEDLESSLY KILLED!
NAH. GORT WOULD'VE SURVIVED THE JUMP WITH OR WITHOUT THE CHUTE. OF COURSE, I WOULD'VE KILLED HIM IF HE DIDN'T TAKE THE CHUTE.
WHERE'S THE GEAR?
DO I LOOK LIKE YOUR LACKEY, LAWTON? I TOSSED IT OUT OF THE PLANE. I PRESUME GRAVITY IS STILL WORKING AND IT LANDED IN THE JUNGLE NEARBY.
WE'D BETTER FIND IT. THE TRANSCEIVERS ARE IN THERE. THE WALL CAN'T TELL US WHERE THE GUNS ARE AND WE CAN'T CALL OUR TAXI WITHOUT 'EM.
BY THE WAY, THE LASER PISTOL BROKE IN THE JUMP. DON'T TELL GORT.
KHMER ROUGE! HANDS UP HANDS UP HANDS UP!
15

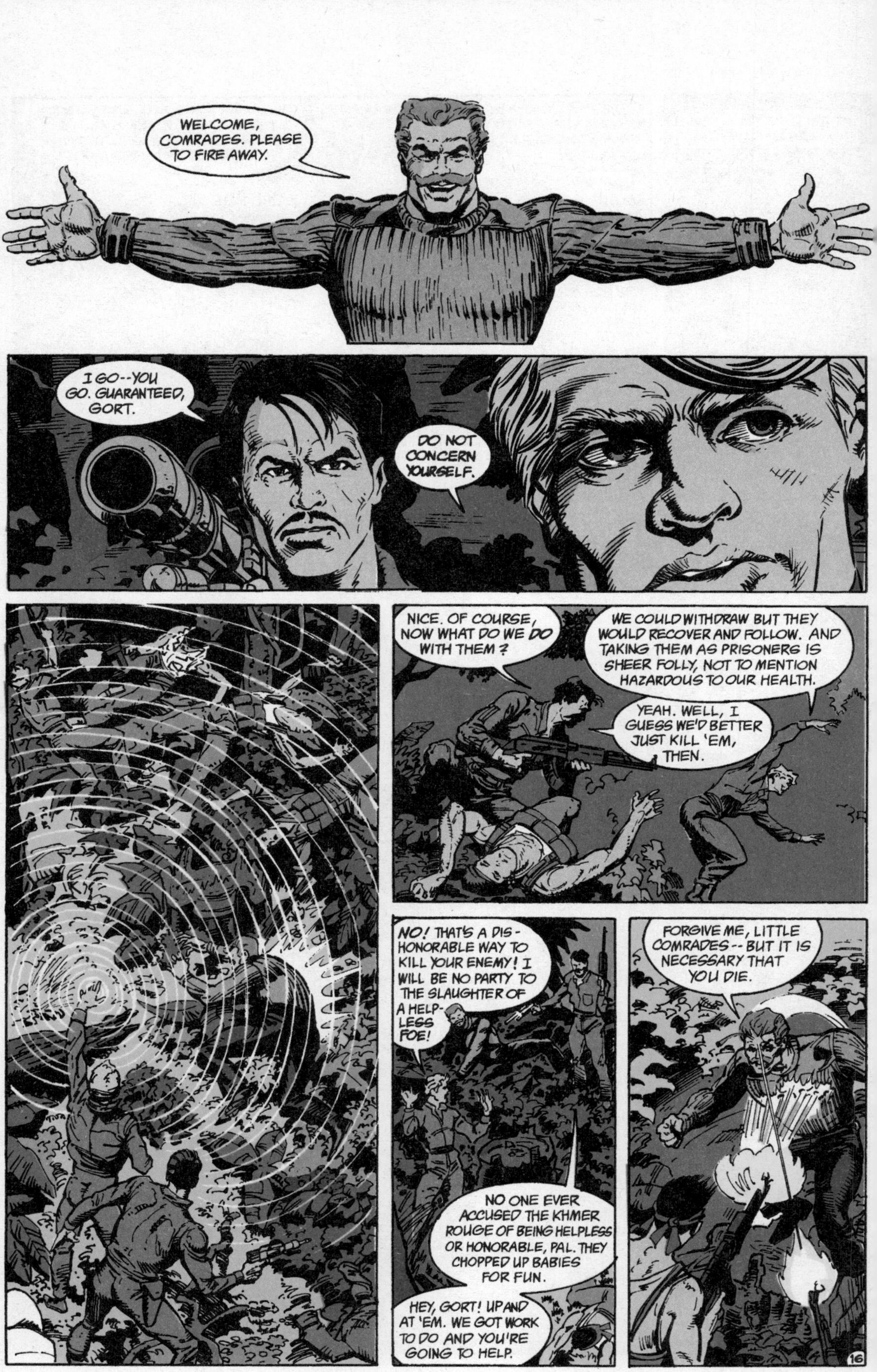
WELCOME, COMRADES. PLEASE TO FIRE AWAY.
I GO--YOU GO. GUARANTEED, GORT.
DO NOT CONCERN YOURSELF.
NICE. OF COURSE, NOW WHAT DO WE DO WITH THEM ?
WE COULD WITHDRAW BUT THEY WOULD RECOVER AND FOLLOW. AND TAKING THEM AS PRISONERS IS SHEER FOLLY, NOT TO MENTION HAZARDOUS TO OUR HEALTH.
YEAH. WELL, I GUESS WE'D BETTER JUST KILL 'EM, THEN.
NO! THAT'S A DIS-HONORABLE WAY TO KILL YOUR ENEMY! I WILL BE NO PARTY TO THE SLAUGHTER OF A HELP-LESS FOE!
NO ONE EVER ACCUSED THE KHMER ROUGE OF BEING HELPLESS OR HONORABLE, PAL. THEY CHOPPED UP BABIES FOR FUN.
HEY, GORT! UP AND AT 'EM. WE GOT WORK TO DO AND YOU'RE GOING TO HELP.
FORGIVE ME, LITTLE COMRADES -- BUT IT IS NECESSARY THAT YOU DIE.
16

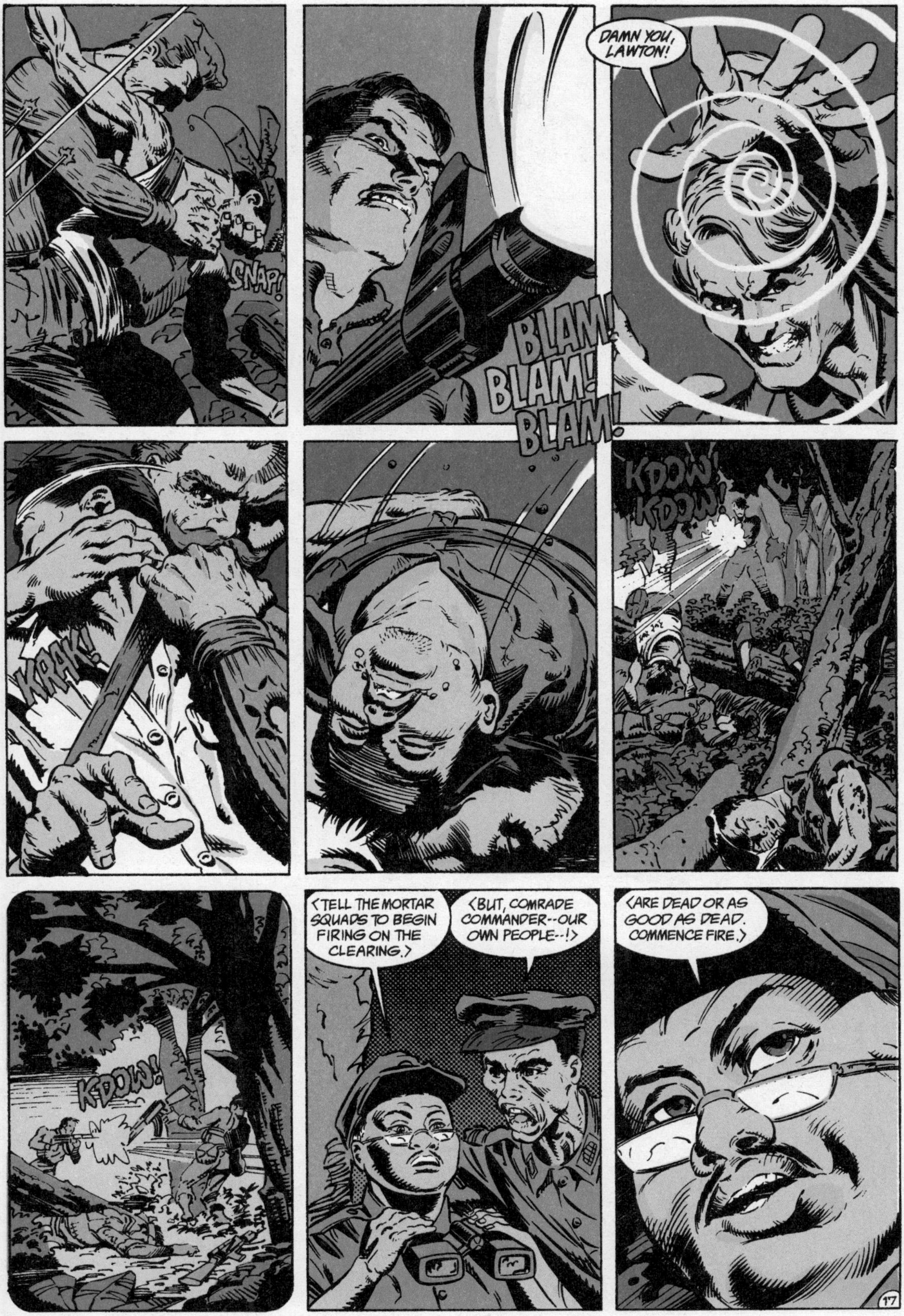
SNAP!
BLAM!
BLAM!
BLAM!
DAMN YOU, LAWTON!
KRAK!
KDOW!
KDOW!
KDOW!
<TELL THE MORTAR SQUADS TO BEGIN FIRING ON THE CLEARING.>
<BUT, COMRADE COMMANDER--OUR OWN PEOPLE--!>
<ARE DEAD OR AS GOOD AS DEAD. COMMENCE FIRE.>
17

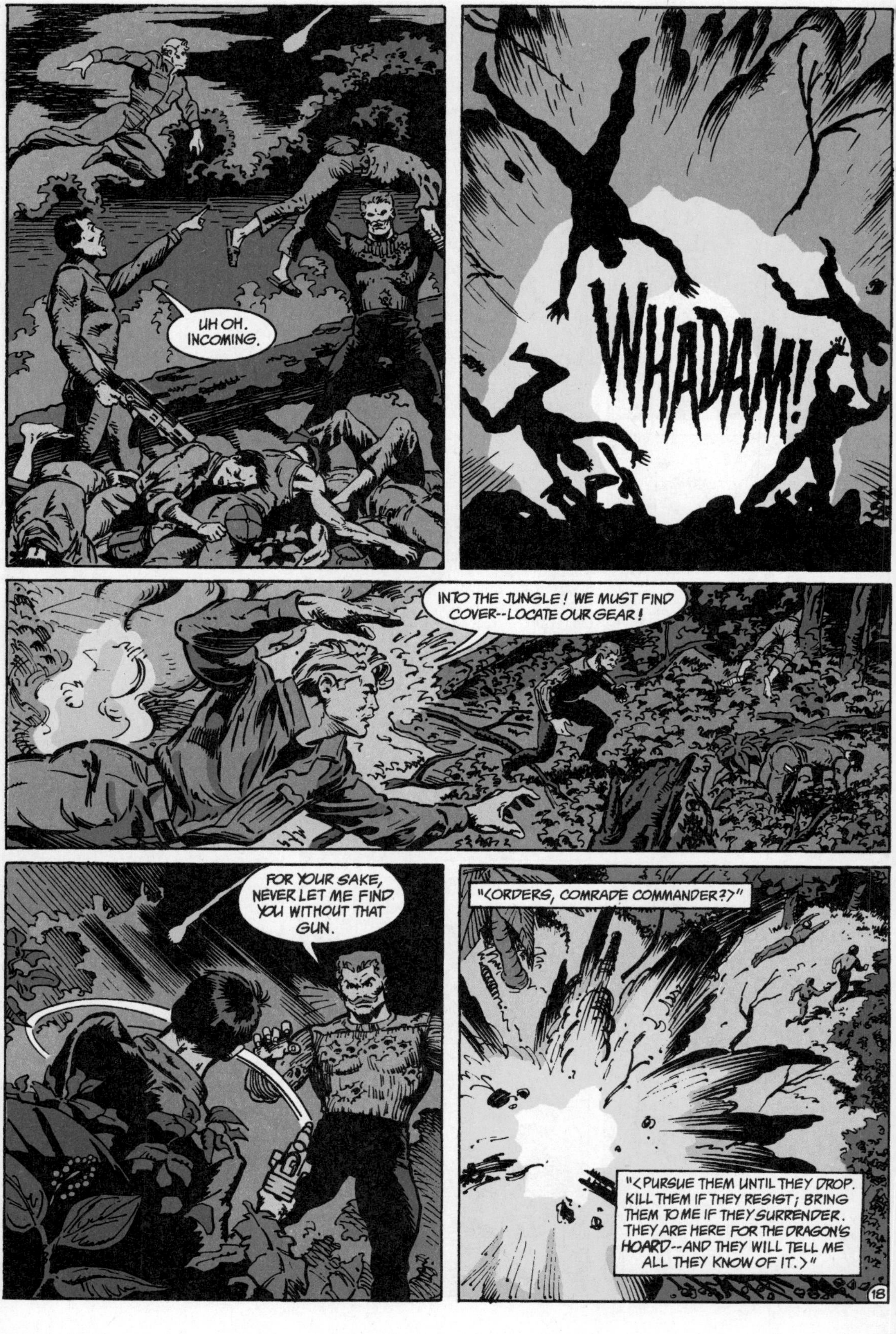
UH OH. INCOMING.
WHADAM!
INTO THE JUNGLE! WE MUST FIND COVER--LOCATE OUR GEAR!
FOR YOUR SAKE, NEVER LET ME FIND YOU WITHOUT THAT GUN.
"<ORDERS, COMRADE COMMANDER?>"
"<PURSUE THEM UNTIL THEY DROP. KILL THEM IF THEY RESIST; BRING THEM TO ME IF THEY SURRENDER. THEY ARE HERE FOR THE DRAGON'S HOARD--AND THEY WILL TELL ME ALL THEY KNOW OF IT.>"
18

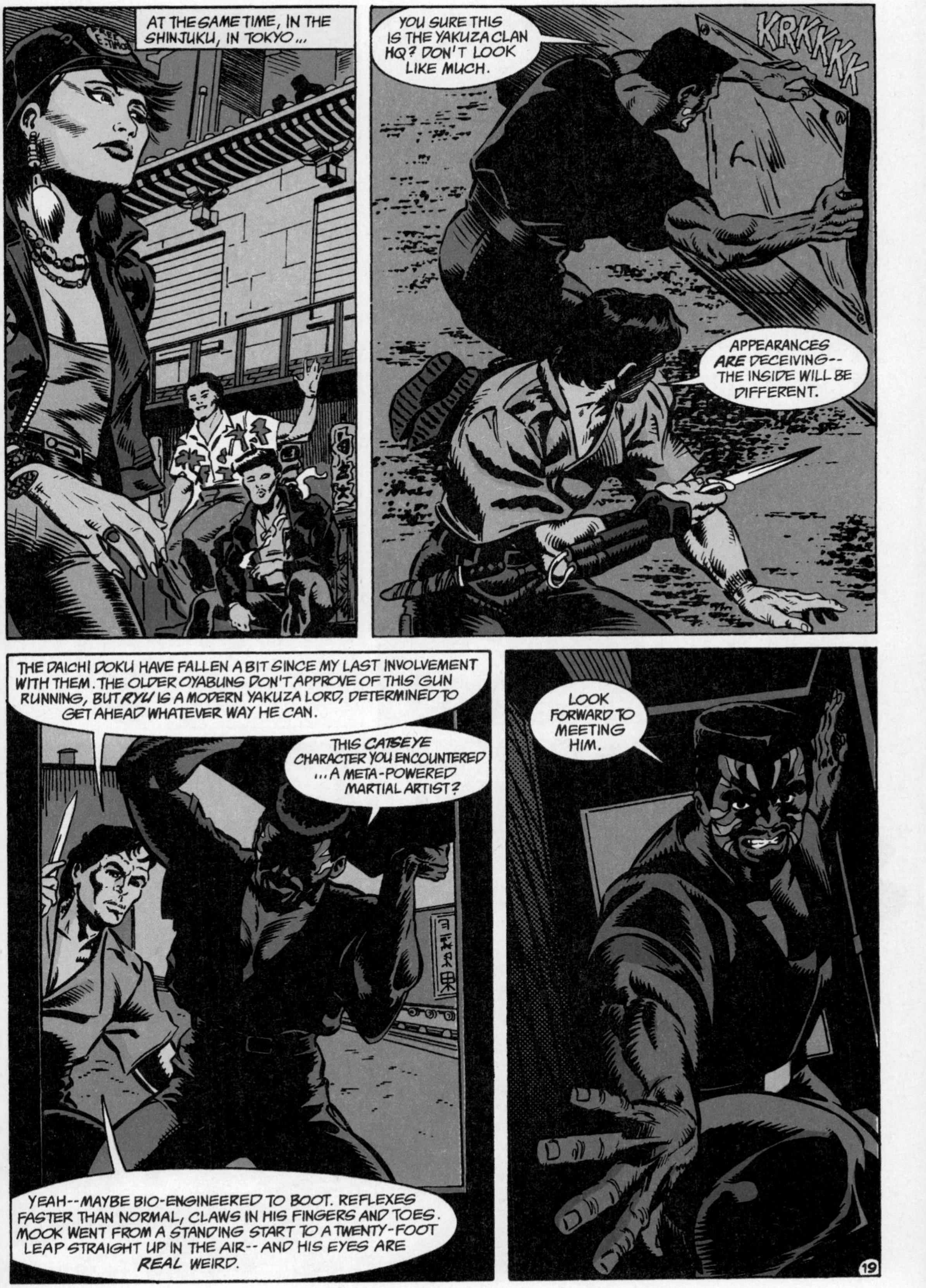
AT THE SAME TIME, IN THE SHINJUKU, IN TOKYO...
YOU SURE THIS IS THE YAKUZA CLAN HQ? DON'T LOOK LIKE MUCH.
KRKKKK
APPEARANCES ARE DECEIVING-- THE INSIDE WILL BE DIFFERENT.
THE DAICHI DOKU HAVE FALLEN A BIT SINCE MY LAST INVOLVEMENT WITH THEM. THE OLDER OYABUNS DON'T APPROVE OF THIS GUN RUNNING, BUT RYU IS A MODERN YAKUZA LORD, DETERMINED TO GET AHEAD WHATEVER WAY HE CAN.
THIS CATSEYE CHARACTER YOU ENCOUNTERED ...A META-POWERED MARTIAL ARTIST?
YEAH--MAYBE BIO-ENGINEERED TO BOOT. REFLEXES FASTER THAN NORMAL, CLAWS IN HIS FINGERS AND TOES. MOOK WENT FROM A STANDING START TO A TWENTY-FOOT LEAP STRAIGHT UP IN THE AIR-- AND HIS EYES ARE REAL WEIRD.
LOOK FORWARD TO MEETING HIM.
19

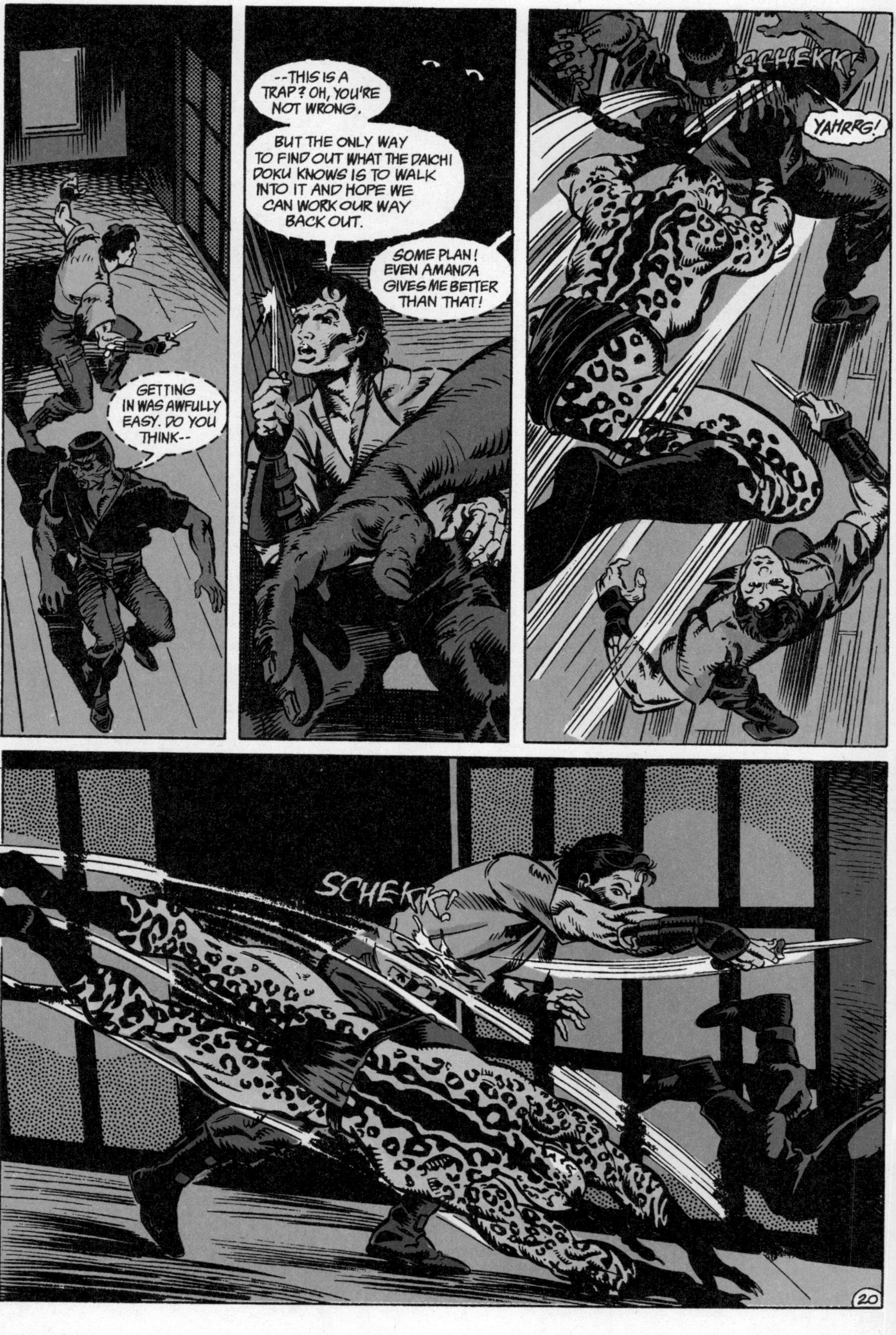
GETTING IN WAS AWFULLY EASY. DO YOU THINK--
--THIS IS A TRAP? OH, YOU'RE NOT WRONG.
BUT THE ONLY WAY TO FIND OUT WHAT THE DAICHI DOKU KNOWS IS TO WALK INTO IT AND HOPE WE CAN WORK OUR WAY BACK OUT.
SOME PLAN! EVEN AMANDA GIVES ME BETTER THAN THAT!
SCHEKK!
YAHRRG!
SCHEKK!
20

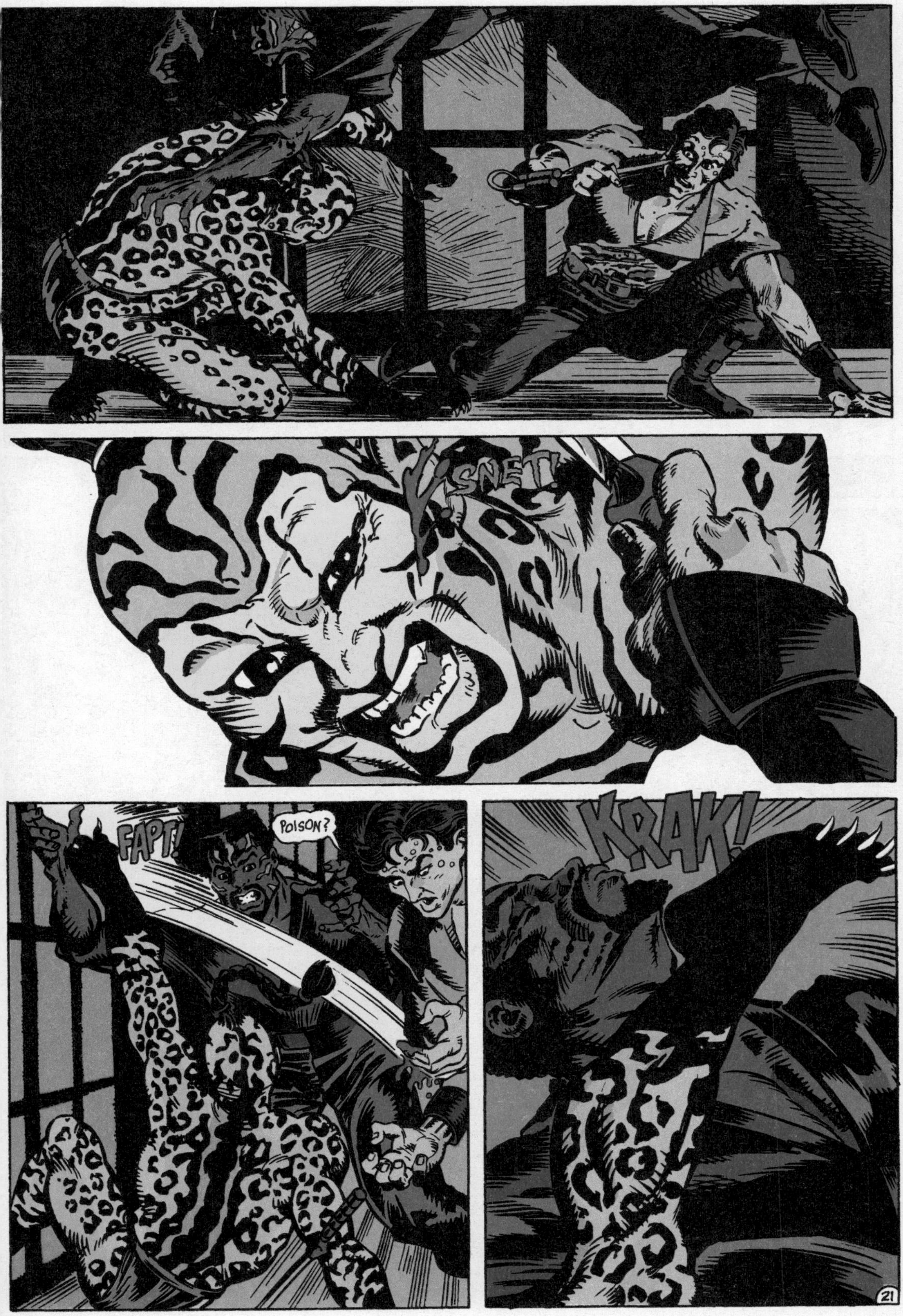
SNET!
FAPT!
POISON?
KRAK!
21

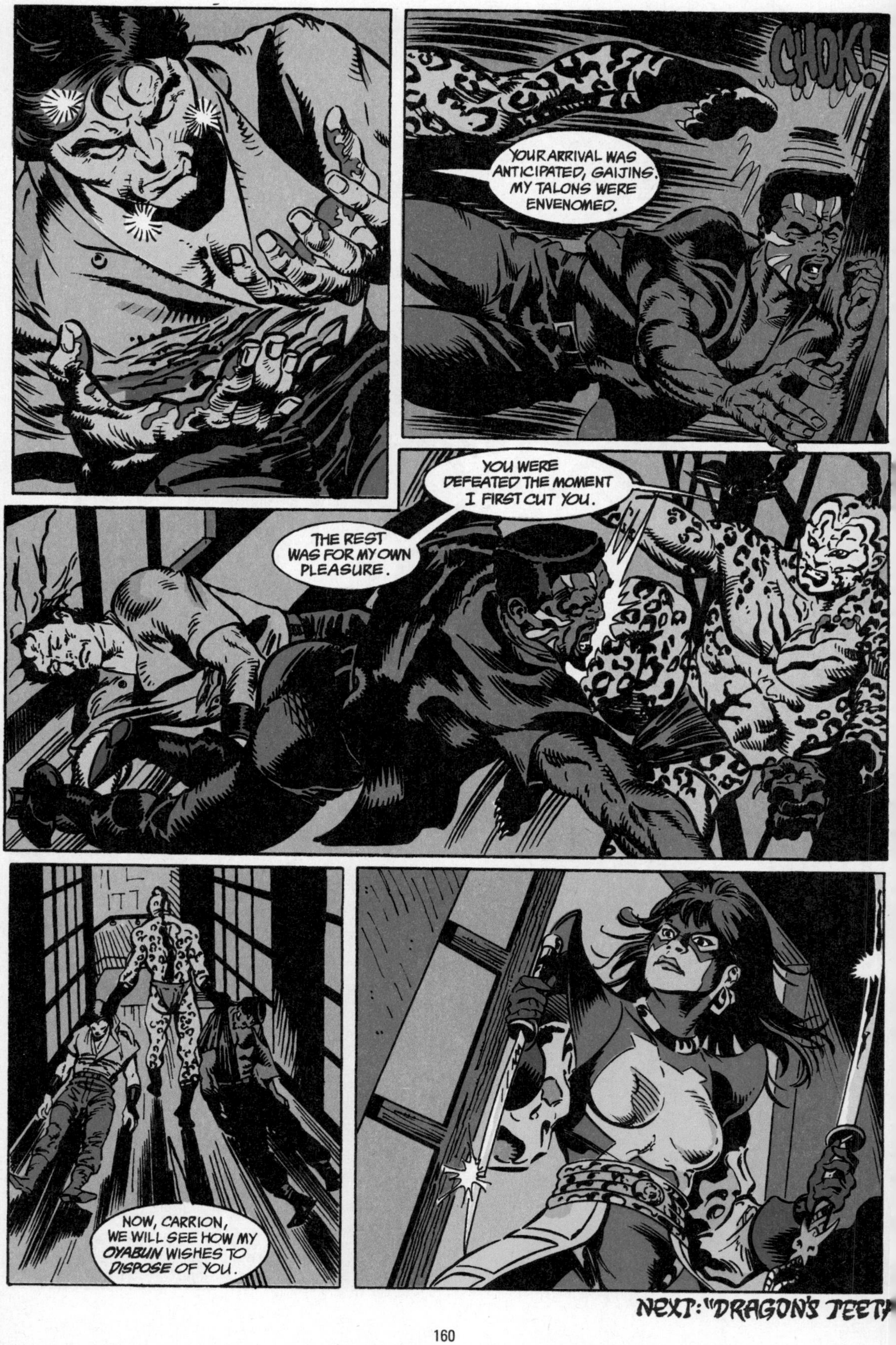
CHOK!
YOUR ARRIVAL WAS ANTICIPATED, GAIJINS. MY TALONS WERE ENVENOMED.
YOU WERE DEFEATED THE MOMENT I FIRST CUT YOU.
THE REST WAS FOR MY OWN PLEASURE.
NOW, CARRION, WE WILL SEE HOW MY OYABUN WISHES TO DISPOSE OF YOU.
NEXT: "DRAGON'S TEETH

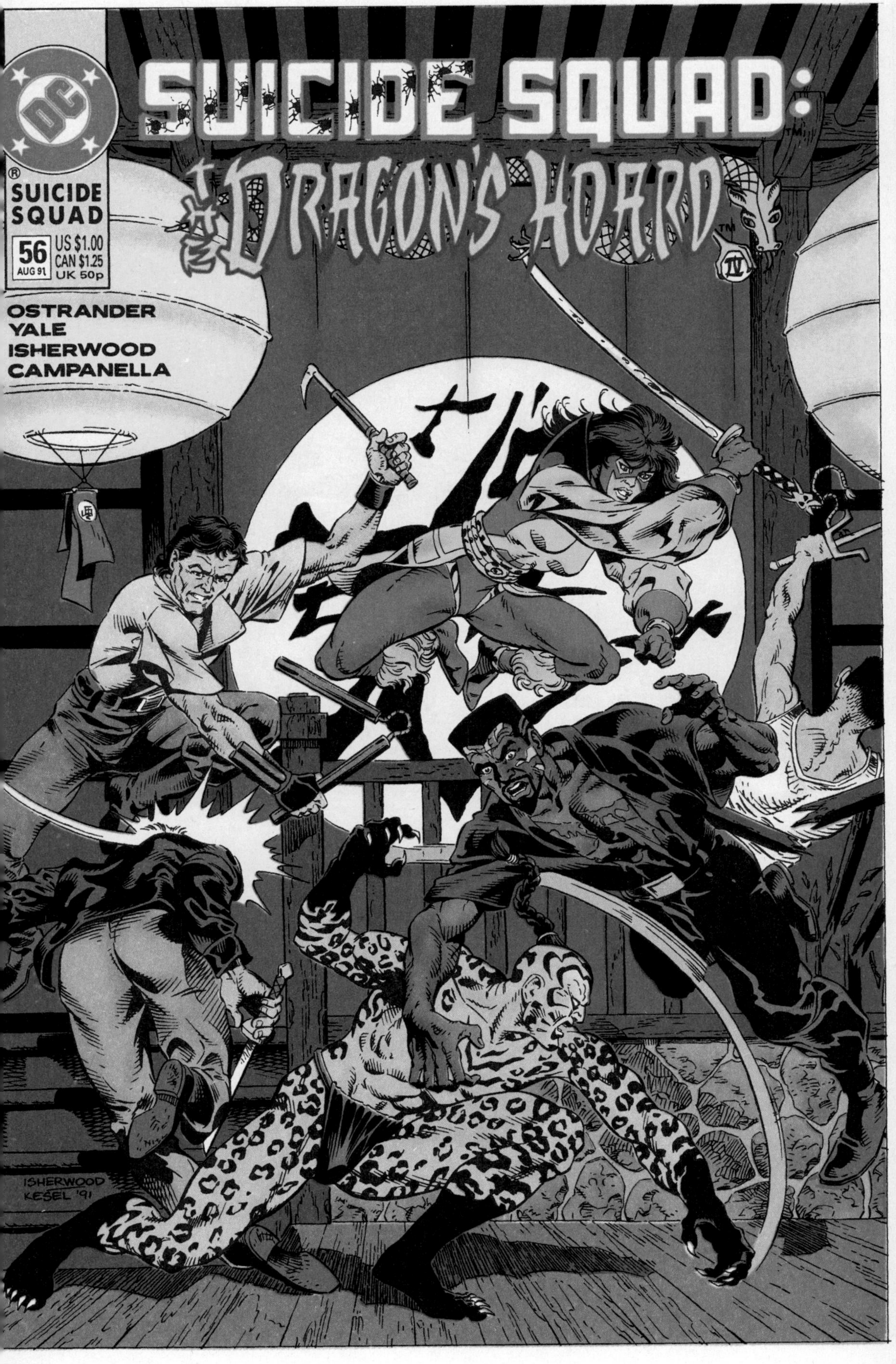

SUICIDE SQUAD:
DRAGON'S HOARD
SUICIDE SQUAD
56
AUG 91
US $1.00
CAN $1.25
UK 50p
OSTRANDER
YALE
ISHERWOOD
CAMPANELLA
ISHERWOOD
KESEL '91

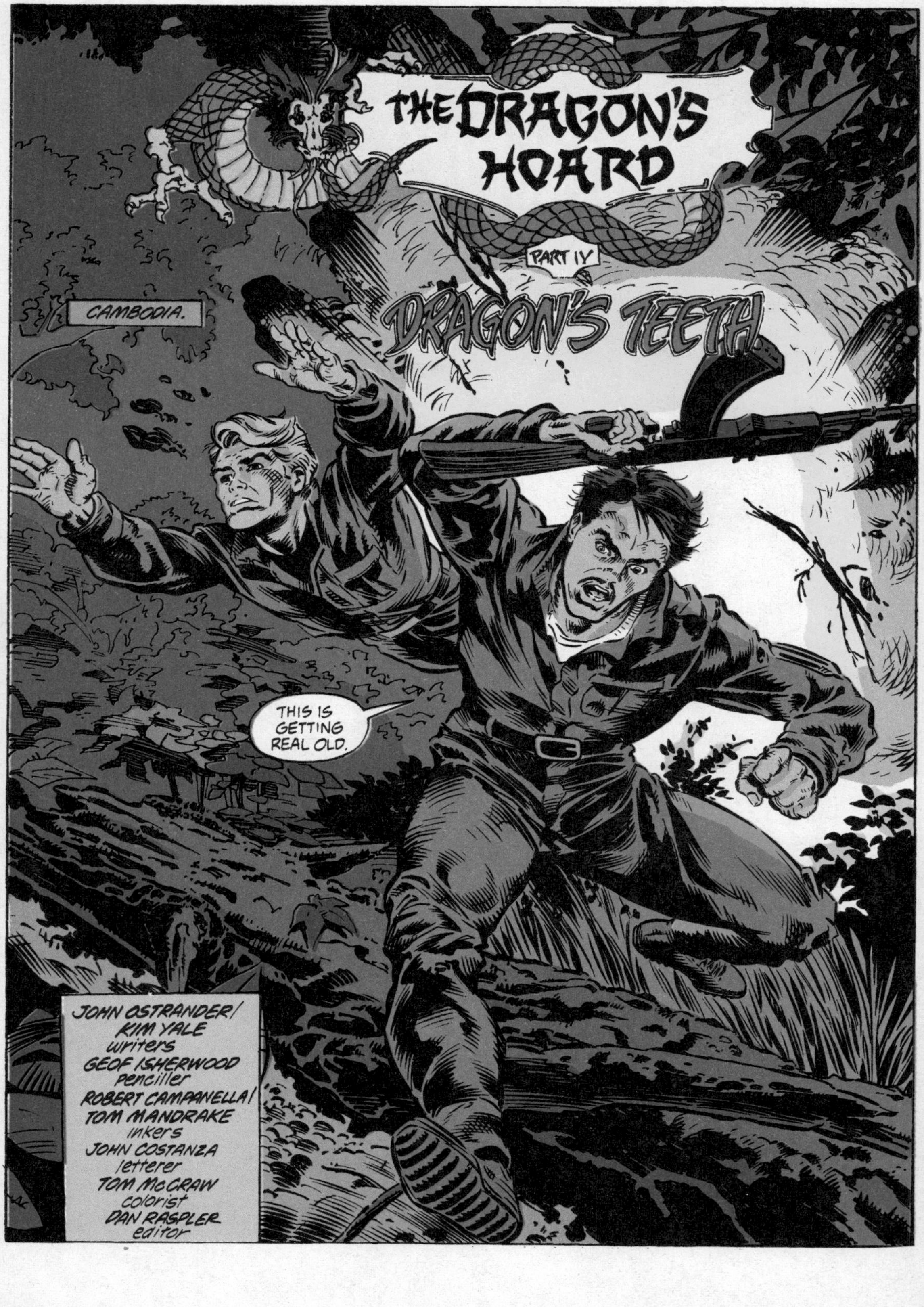
THE DRAGON'S HOARD
PART IV
DRAGON'S TEETH
CAMBODIA.
THIS IS GETTING REAL OLD.
JOHN OSTRANDER/ KIM YALE writers
GEOF ISHERWOOD penciller
ROBERT CAMPANELLA/ TOM MANDRAKE inkers
JOHN COSTANZA letterer
TOM McCRAW colorist
DAN RASPLER editor

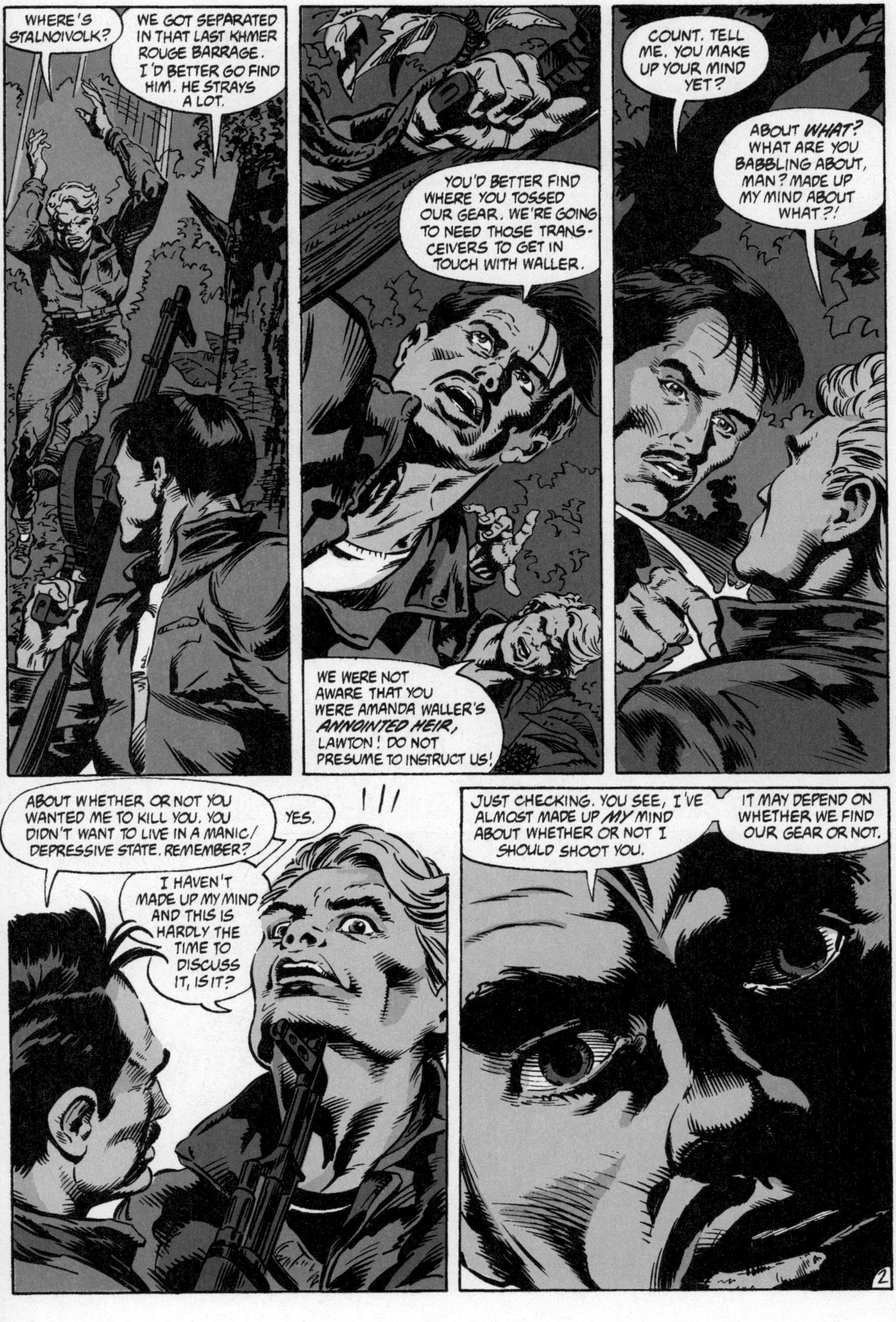
WHERE'S STALNOIVOLK?
WE GOT SEPARATED IN THAT LAST KHMER ROUGE BARRAGE. I'D BETTER GO FIND HIM. HE STRAYS A LOT.
YOU'D BETTER FIND WHERE YOU TOSSED OUR GEAR. WE'RE GOING TO NEED THOSE TRANS-CEIVERS TO GET IN TOUCH WITH WALLER.
WE WERE NOT AWARE THAT YOU WERE AMANDA WALLER'S ANNOINTED HEIR, LAWTON! DO NOT PRESUME TO INSTRUCT US!
COUNT. TELL ME. YOU MAKE UP YOUR MIND YET?
ABOUT WHAT? WHAT ARE YOU BABBLING ABOUT, MAN? MADE UP MY MIND ABOUT WHAT?!
ABOUT WHETHER OR NOT YOU WANTED ME TO KILL YOU. YOU DIDN'T WANT TO LIVE IN A MANIC/DEPRESSIVE STATE. REMEMBER?
I HAVEN'T MADE UP MY MIND AND THIS IS HARDLY THE TIME TO DISCUSS IT, IS IT?
YES.
JUST CHECKING. YOU SEE, I'VE ALMOST MADE UP MY MIND ABOUT WHETHER OR NOT I SHOULD SHOOT YOU.
IT MAY DEPEND ON WHETHER WE FIND OUR GEAR OR NOT.
2

FEEL LIKE LOOKING FOR IT?

WHOOM

I BEGIN TO *TIRE* OF THESE COMPANIONS.

<THERE IS ONE OF THEM!>

AH! LITTLE COMRADES! WELL MET! I AM FREE OF THE OTHERS' ANNOYING PRESENCE! STALNOIVOLK IS FREE TO JOIN YOU!

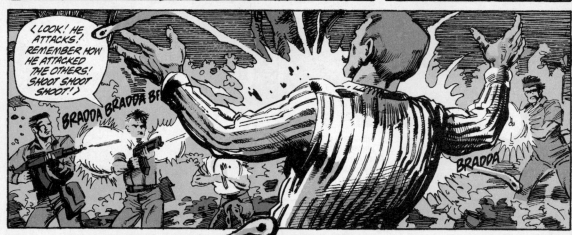

<LOOK! HE ATTACKS! REMEMBER HOW HE ATTACKED THE OTHERS! SHOOT SHOOT SHOOT!>

BRADDA BRADDA BR

BRADDA

GURK!

VIT VIT VIT

BRADDA BRADDA BRADDA

IS THIS HOW YOU WOULD GREET A COMRADE?

BRADDA BRA

3

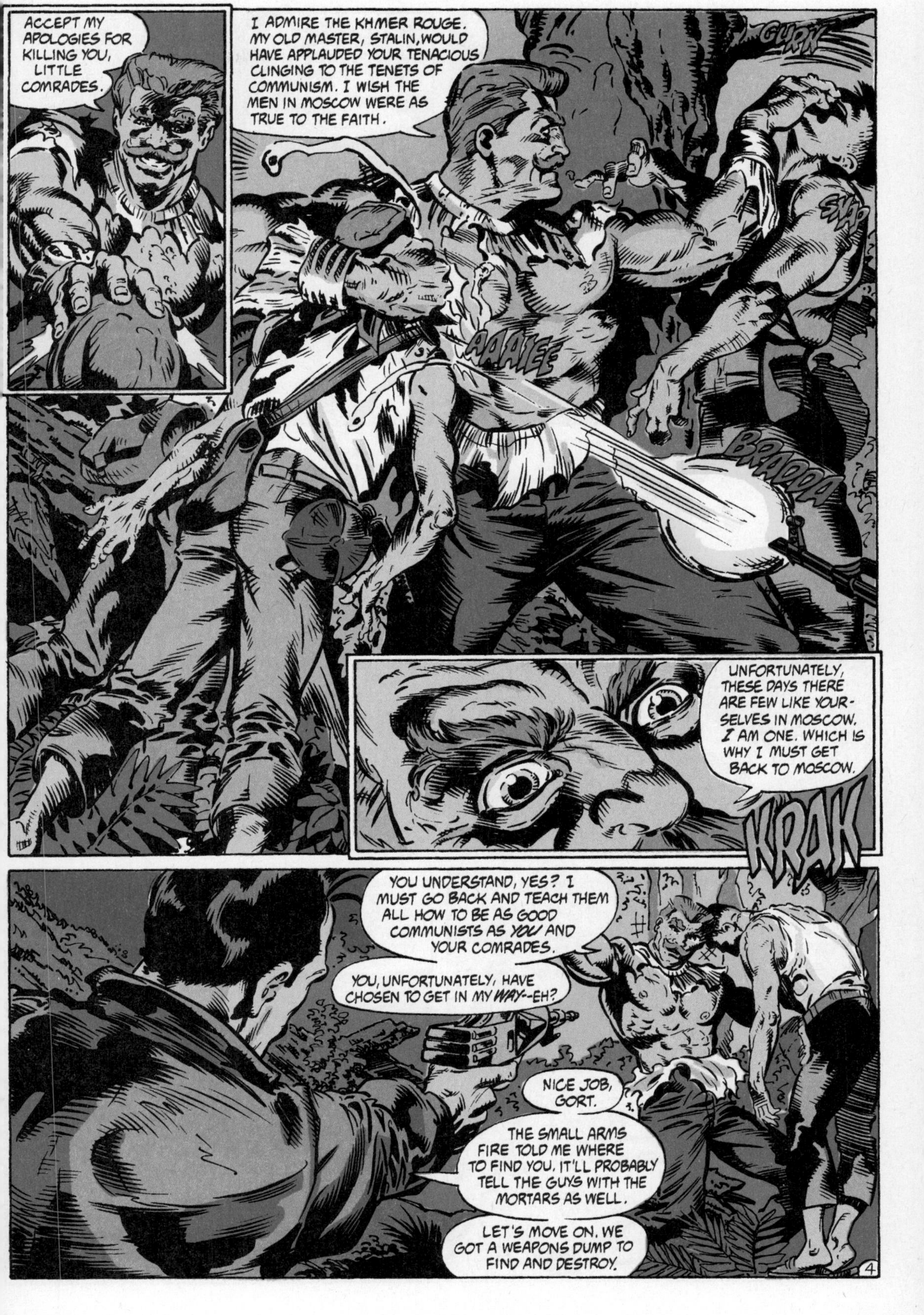

ACCEPT MY APOLOGIES FOR KILLING YOU, LITTLE COMRADES.
I ADMIRE THE KHMER ROUGE. MY OLD MASTER, STALIN, WOULD HAVE APPLAUDED YOUR TENACIOUS CLINGING TO THE TENETS OF COMMUNISM. I WISH THE MEN IN MOSCOW WERE AS TRUE TO THE FAITH.
GURK
SNAP
AAAIEE
BRADDA
UNFORTUNATELY, THESE DAYS THERE ARE FEW LIKE YOURSELVES IN MOSCOW. I AM ONE. WHICH IS WHY I MUST GET BACK TO MOSCOW.
KRAK
YOU UNDERSTAND, YES? I MUST GO BACK AND TEACH THEM ALL HOW TO BE AS GOOD COMMUNISTS AS YOU AND YOUR COMRADES.
YOU, UNFORTUNATELY, HAVE CHOSEN TO GET IN MY WAY--EH?
NICE JOB, GORT.
THE SMALL ARMS FIRE TOLD ME WHERE TO FIND YOU. IT'LL PROBABLY TELL THE GUYS WITH THE MORTARS AS WELL.
LET'S MOVE ON. WE GOT A WEAPONS DUMP TO FIND AND DESTROY.
4

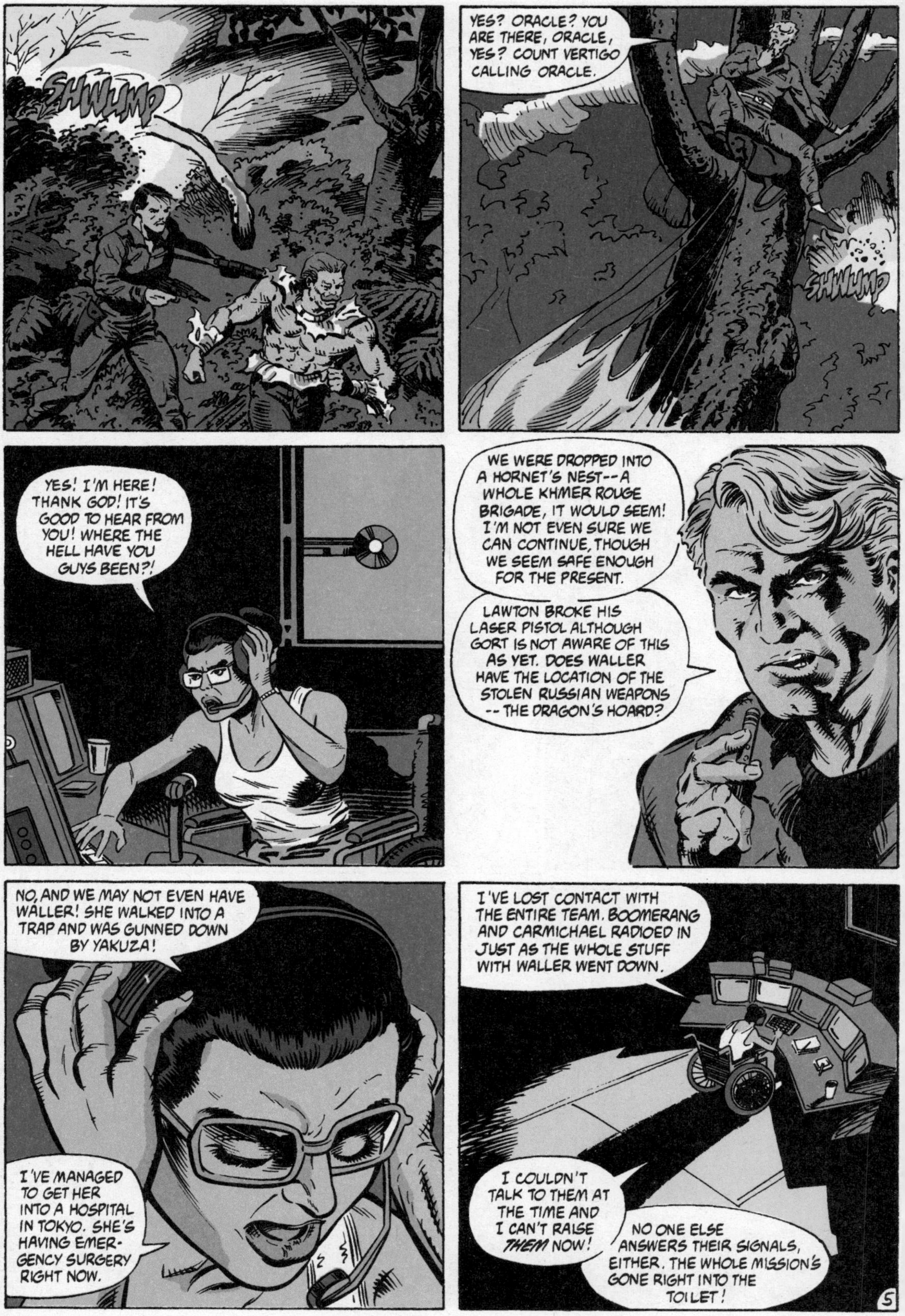
SHWUMP
YES? ORACLE? YOU ARE THERE, ORACLE, YES? COUNT VERTIGO CALLING ORACLE.
SHWUMP
YES! I'M HERE! THANK GOD! IT'S GOOD TO HEAR FROM YOU! WHERE THE HELL HAVE YOU GUYS BEEN?!
WE WERE DROPPED INTO A HORNET'S NEST--A WHOLE KHMER ROUGE BRIGADE, IT WOULD SEEM! I'M NOT EVEN SURE WE CAN CONTINUE, THOUGH WE SEEM SAFE ENOUGH FOR THE PRESENT.
LAWTON BROKE HIS LASER PISTOL ALTHOUGH GORT IS NOT AWARE OF THIS AS YET. DOES WALLER HAVE THE LOCATION OF THE STOLEN RUSSIAN WEAPONS --THE DRAGON'S HOARD?
NO, AND WE MAY NOT EVEN HAVE WALLER! SHE WALKED INTO A TRAP AND WAS GUNNED DOWN BY YAKUZA!
I'VE MANAGED TO GET HER INTO A HOSPITAL IN TOKYO. SHE'S HAVING EMERGENCY SURGERY RIGHT NOW.
I'VE LOST CONTACT WITH THE ENTIRE TEAM. BOOMERANG AND CARMICHAEL RADIOED IN JUST AS THE WHOLE STUFF WITH WALLER WENT DOWN.
I COULDN'T TALK TO THEM AT THE TIME AND I CAN'T RAISE *THEM* NOW!
NO ONE ELSE ANSWERS THEIR SIGNALS, EITHER. THE WHOLE MISSION'S GONE RIGHT INTO THE TOILET!
5

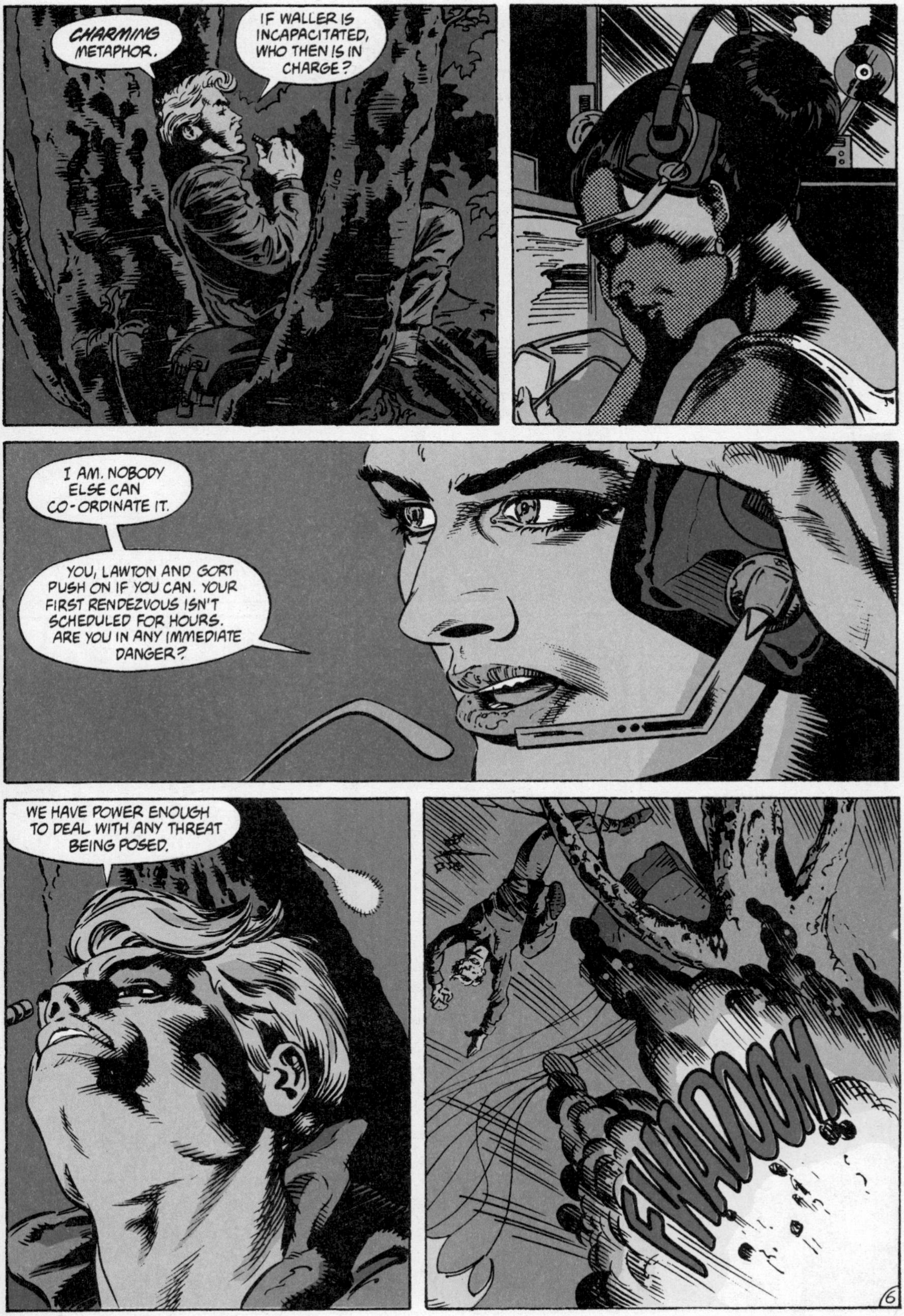
CHARMING METAPHOR.
IF WALLER IS INCAPACITATED, WHO THEN IS IN CHARGE?
I AM. NOBODY ELSE CAN CO-ORDINATE IT.
YOU, LAWTON AND GORT PUSH ON IF YOU CAN. YOUR FIRST RENDEZVOUS ISN'T SCHEDULED FOR HOURS. ARE YOU IN ANY IMMEDIATE DANGER?
WE HAVE POWER ENOUGH TO DEAL WITH ANY THREAT BEING POSED.
FWOOOM
6

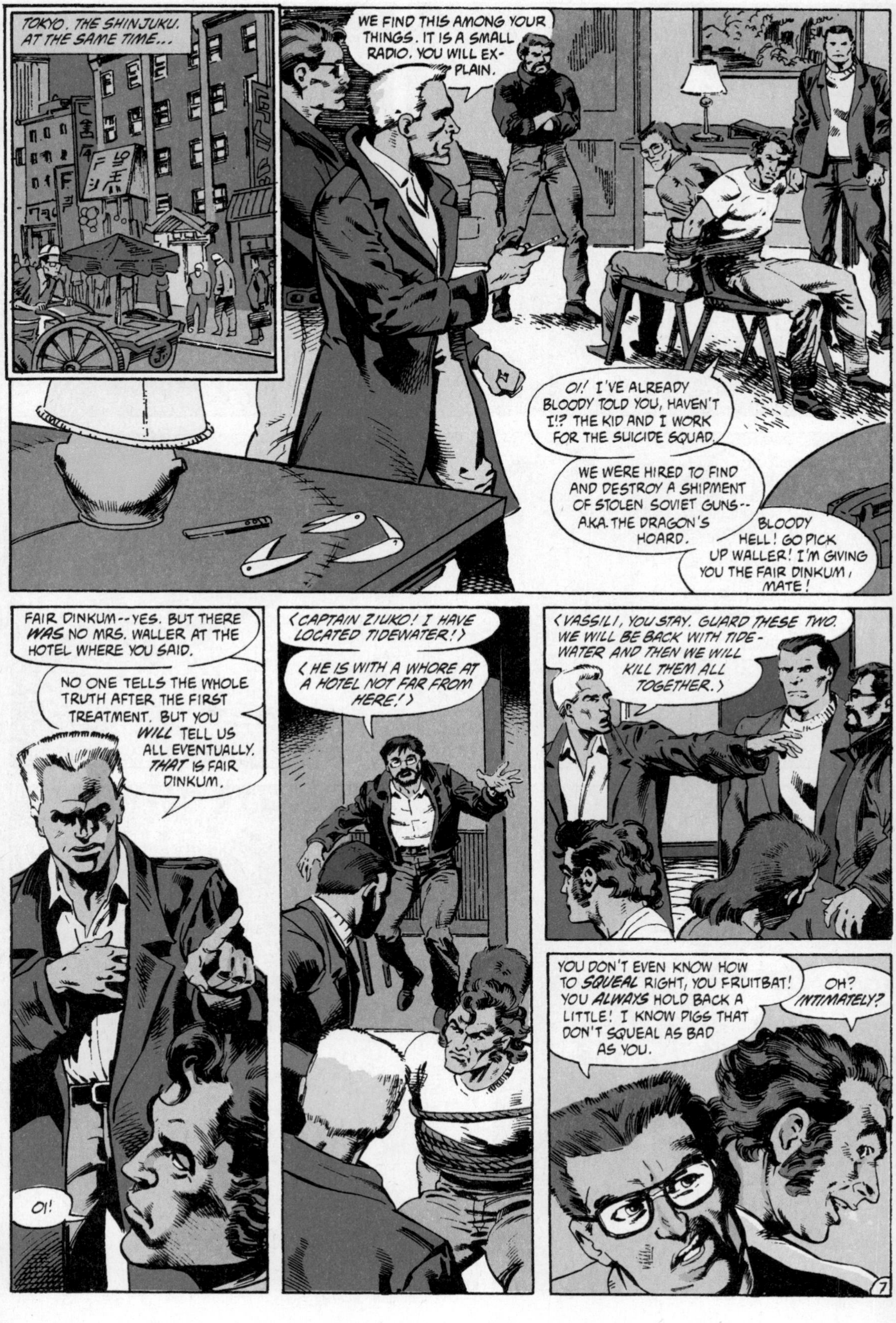
TOKYO. THE SHINJUKU. AT THE SAME TIME...
WE FIND THIS AMONG YOUR THINGS. IT IS A SMALL RADIO. YOU WILL EXPLAIN.
OI! I'VE ALREADY BLOODY TOLD YOU, HAVEN'T I!? THE KID AND I WORK FOR THE SUICIDE SQUAD.
WE WERE HIRED TO FIND AND DESTROY A SHIPMENT OF STOLEN SOVIET GUNS-- A.K.A. THE DRAGON'S HOARD.
BLOODY HELL! GO PICK UP WALLER! I'M GIVING YOU THE FAIR DINKUM, MATE!
FAIR DINKUM--YES. BUT THERE WAS NO MRS. WALLER AT THE HOTEL WHERE YOU SAID.
NO ONE TELLS THE WHOLE TRUTH AFTER THE FIRST TREATMENT. BUT YOU WILL TELL US ALL EVENTUALLY. THAT IS FAIR DINKUM.
OI!
<CAPTAIN ZIUKO! I HAVE LOCATED TIDEWATER!>
<HE IS WITH A WHORE AT A HOTEL NOT FAR FROM HERE!>
<VASSILI, YOU STAY. GUARD THESE TWO. WE WILL BE BACK WITH TIDEWATER AND THEN WE WILL KILL THEM ALL TOGETHER.>
YOU DON'T EVEN KNOW HOW TO SQUEAL RIGHT, YOU FRUITBAT! YOU ALWAYS HOLD BACK A LITTLE! I KNOW PIGS THAT DON'T SQUEAL AS BAD AS YOU.
OH? INTIMATELY?
7

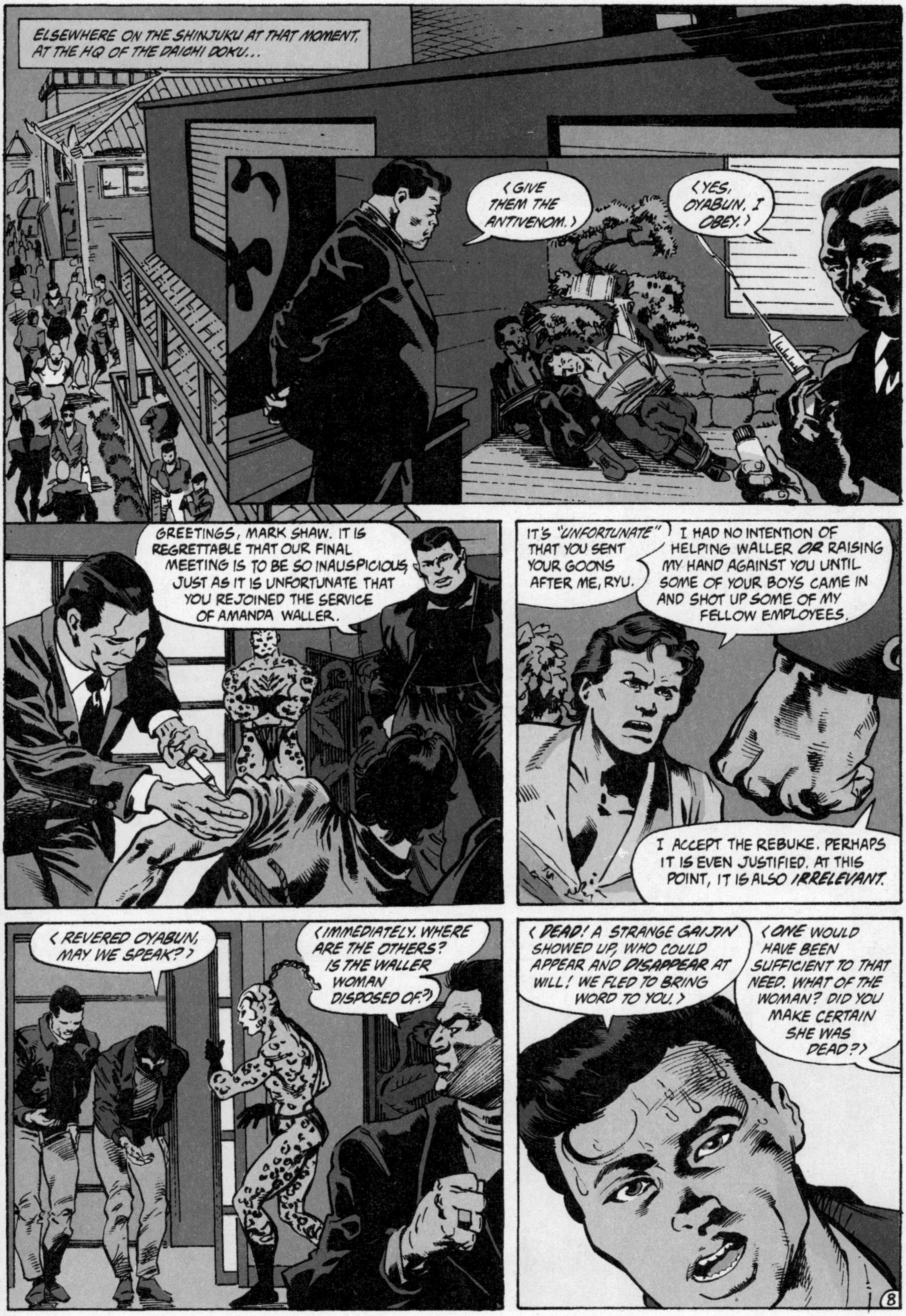

ELSEWHERE ON THE SHINJUKU AT THAT MOMENT, AT THE HQ OF THE DAICHI DOKU...
‹GIVE THEM THE ANTIVENOM.›
‹YES, OYABUN. I OBEY.›
GREETINGS, MARK SHAW. IT IS REGRETTABLE THAT OUR FINAL MEETING IS TO BE SO INAUSPICIOUS, JUST AS IT IS UNFORTUNATE THAT YOU REJOINED THE SERVICE OF AMANDA WALLER.
IT'S "UNFORTUNATE" THAT YOU SENT YOUR GOONS AFTER ME, RYU.
I HAD NO INTENTION OF HELPING WALLER OR RAISING MY HAND AGAINST YOU UNTIL SOME OF YOUR BOYS CAME IN AND SHOT UP SOME OF MY FELLOW EMPLOYEES.
I ACCEPT THE REBUKE. PERHAPS IT IS EVEN JUSTIFIED. AT THIS POINT, IT IS ALSO IRRELEVANT.
‹REVERED OYABUN, MAY WE SPEAK?›
‹IMMEDIATELY. WHERE ARE THE OTHERS? IS THE WALLER WOMAN DISPOSED OF?›
‹DEAD! A STRANGE GAIJIN SHOWED UP, WHO COULD APPEAR AND DISAPPEAR AT WILL! WE FLED TO BRING WORD TO YOU.›
‹ONE WOULD HAVE BEEN SUFFICIENT TO THAT NEED. WHAT OF THE WOMAN? DID YOU MAKE CERTAIN SHE WAS DEAD?›
8

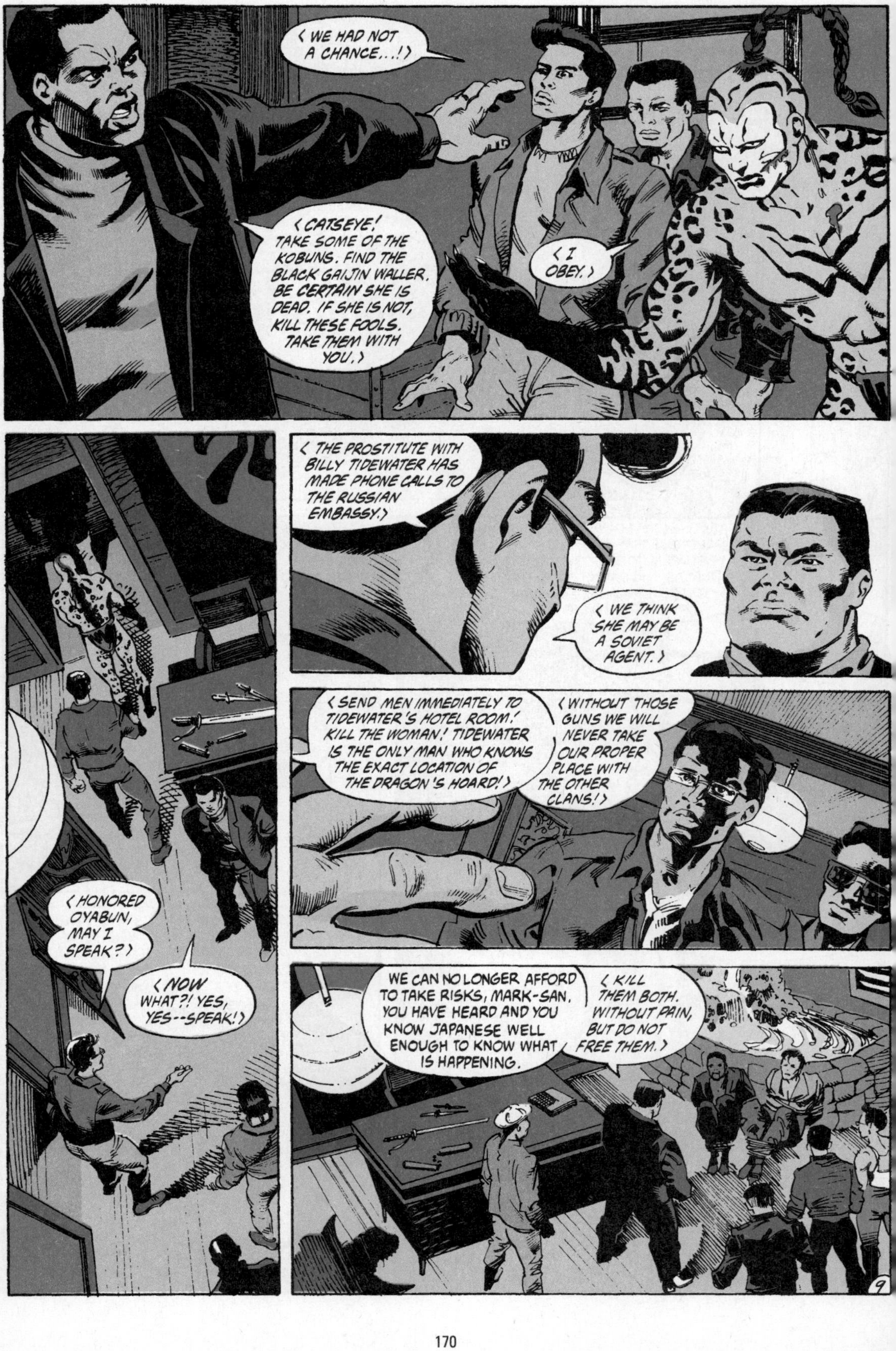

< WE HAD NOT A CHANCE...! >
< CATSEYE! TAKE SOME OF THE KOBUNS. FIND THE BLACK GAIJIN WALLER. BE CERTAIN SHE IS DEAD. IF SHE IS NOT, KILL THESE FOOLS. TAKE THEM WITH YOU. >
< I OBEY. >
< THE PROSTITUTE WITH BILLY TIDEWATER HAS MADE PHONE CALLS TO THE RUSSIAN EMBASSY. >
< WE THINK SHE MAY BE A SOVIET AGENT. >
< SEND MEN IMMEDIATELY TO TIDEWATER'S HOTEL ROOM! KILL THE WOMAN! TIDEWATER IS THE ONLY MAN WHO KNOWS THE EXACT LOCATION OF THE DRAGON'S HOARD! >
< WITHOUT THOSE GUNS WE WILL NEVER TAKE OUR PROPER PLACE WITH THE OTHER CLANS! >
< HONORED OYABUN, MAY I SPEAK? >
< NOW WHAT?! YES, YES--SPEAK! >
WE CAN NO LONGER AFFORD TO TAKE RISKS, MARK-SAN. YOU HAVE HEARD AND YOU KNOW JAPANESE WELL ENOUGH TO KNOW WHAT IS HAPPENING.
< KILL THEM BOTH. WITHOUT PAIN, BUT DO NOT FREE THEM. >
9

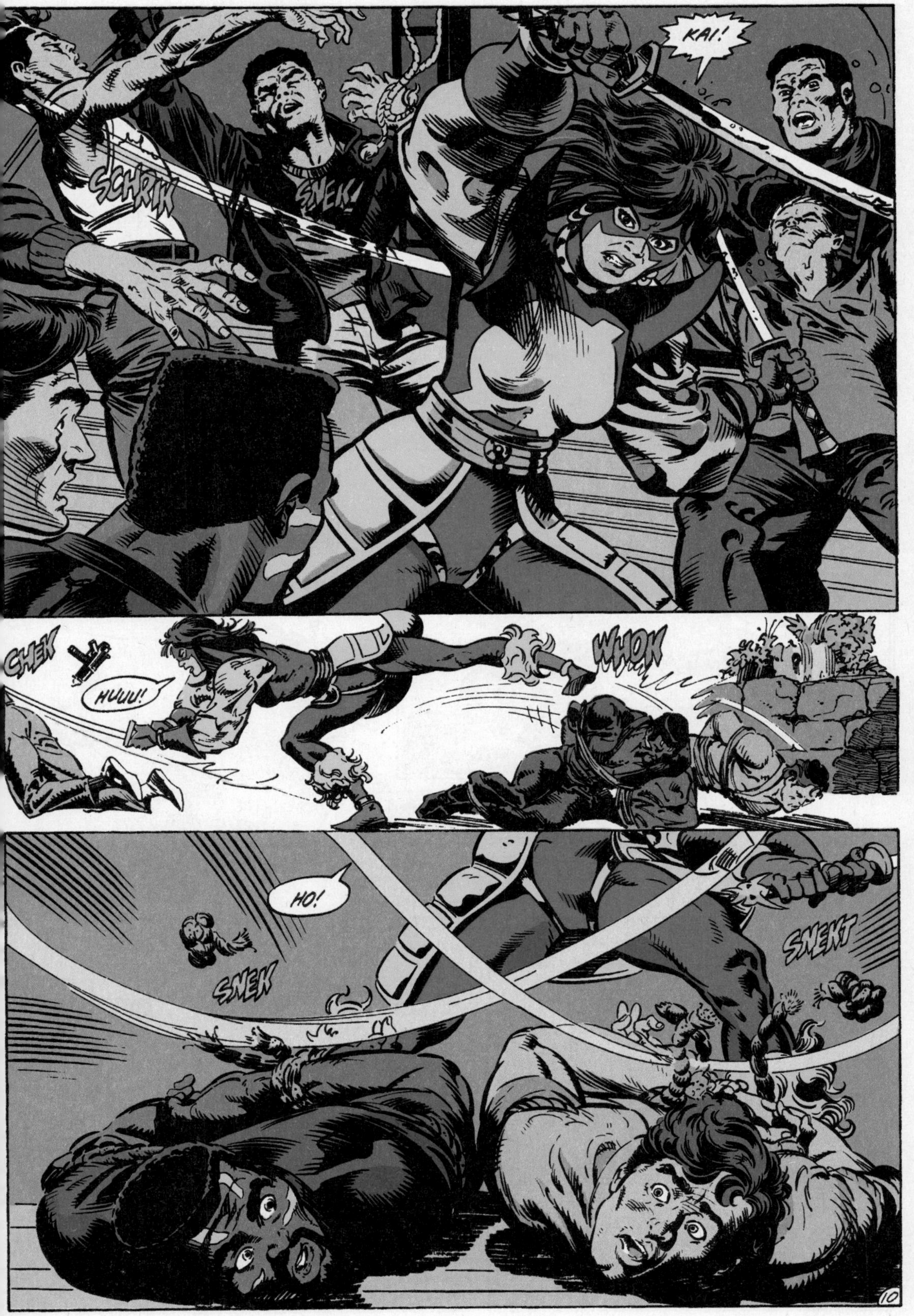
KAI!
SCHRIK
SNEK!
CHEK
HUUU!
WHOK
HO!
SNEK
SNEKT
10

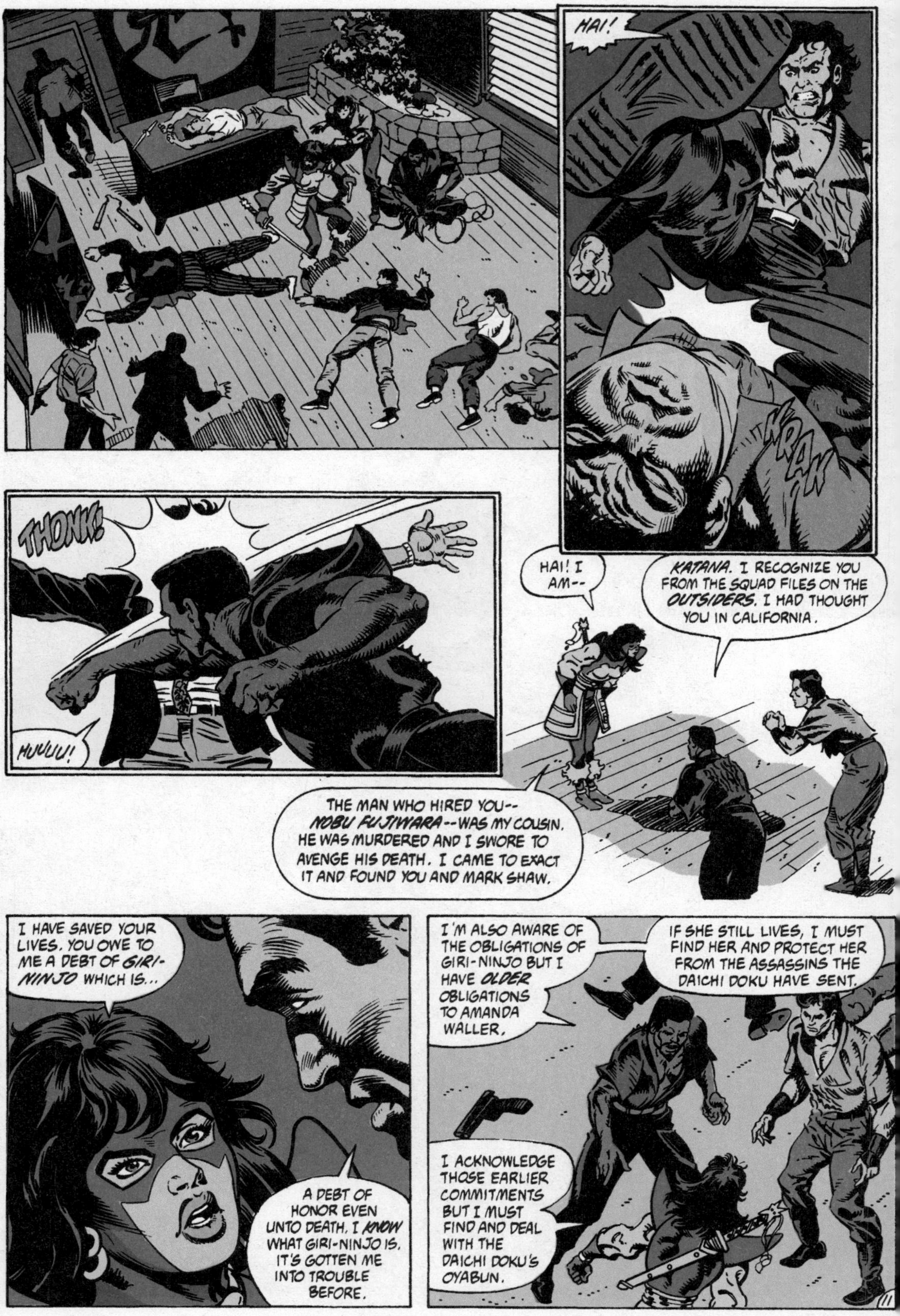
HAI!
KRAK
THONK!
HUUUU!
HAI! I AM--
KATANA. I RECOGNIZE YOU FROM THE SQUAD FILES ON THE OUTSIDERS. I HAD THOUGHT YOU IN CALIFORNIA.
THE MAN WHO HIRED YOU-- NOBU FUJIWARA--WAS MY COUSIN. HE WAS MURDERED AND I SWORE TO AVENGE HIS DEATH. I CAME TO EXACT IT AND FOUND YOU AND MARK SHAW.
I HAVE SAVED YOUR LIVES. YOU OWE TO ME A DEBT OF GIRI-NINJO WHICH IS...
A DEBT OF HONOR EVEN UNTO DEATH. I KNOW WHAT GIRI-NINJO IS. IT'S GOTTEN ME INTO TROUBLE BEFORE.
I'M ALSO AWARE OF THE OBLIGATIONS OF GIRI-NINJO BUT I HAVE OLDER OBLIGATIONS TO AMANDA WALLER.
IF SHE STILL LIVES, I MUST FIND HER AND PROTECT HER FROM THE ASSASSINS THE DAICHI DOKU HAVE SENT.
I ACKNOWLEDGE THOSE EARLIER COMMITMENTS BUT I MUST FIND AND DEAL WITH THE DAICHI DOKU'S OYABUN.
11

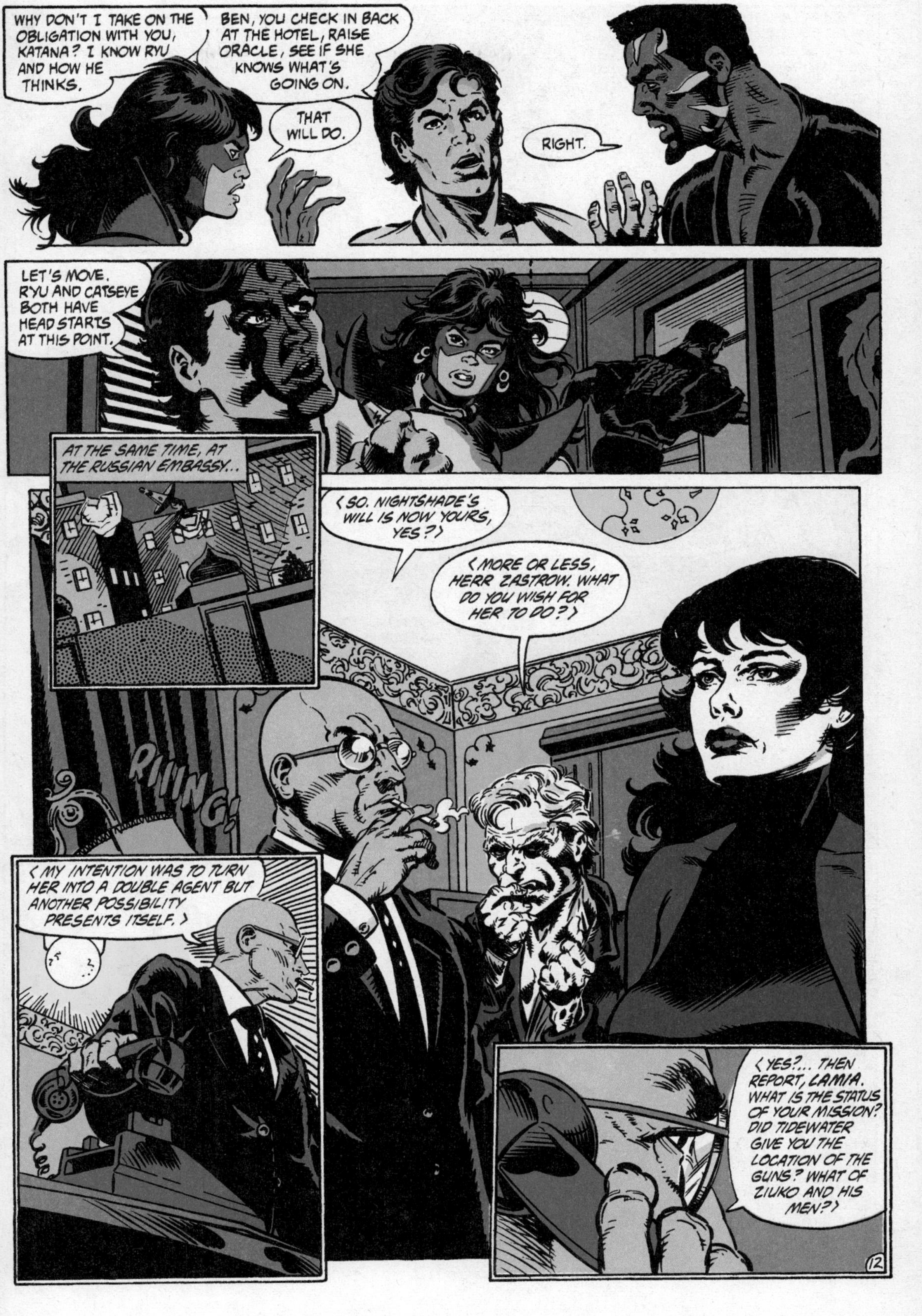
WHY DON'T I TAKE ON THE OBLIGATION WITH YOU, KATANA? I KNOW RYU AND HOW HE THINKS.
BEN, YOU CHECK IN BACK AT THE HOTEL, RAISE ORACLE, SEE IF SHE KNOWS WHAT'S GOING ON.
THAT WILL DO.
RIGHT.
LET'S MOVE. RYU AND CATSEYE BOTH HAVE HEAD STARTS AT THIS POINT.
AT THE SAME TIME, AT THE RUSSIAN EMBASSY...
<SO. NIGHTSHADE'S WILL IS NOW YOURS, YES?>
<MORE OR LESS, HERR ZASTROW. WHAT DO YOU WISH FOR HER TO DO?>
RIIING!
<MY INTENTION WAS TO TURN HER INTO A DOUBLE AGENT BUT ANOTHER POSSIBILITY PRESENTS ITSELF.>
<YES?... THEN REPORT, LAMIA. WHAT IS THE STATUS OF YOUR MISSION? DID TIDEWATER GIVE YOU THE LOCATION OF THE GUNS? WHAT OF ZIUKO AND HIS MEN?>
12

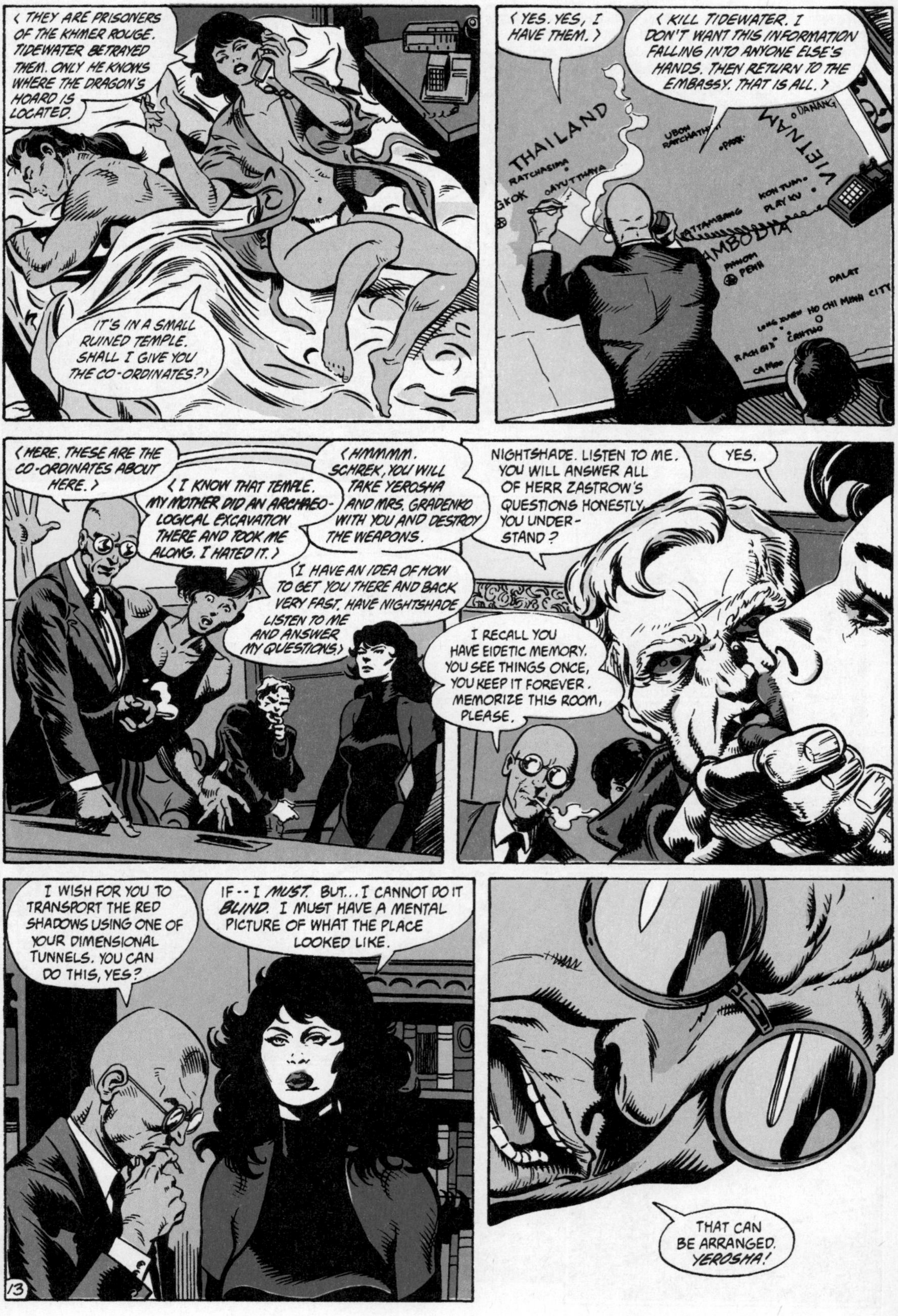
‹ THEY ARE PRISONERS OF THE KHMER ROUGE. TIDEWATER BETRAYED THEM. ONLY HE KNOWS WHERE THE DRAGON'S HOARD IS LOCATED.
IT'S IN A SMALL RUINED TEMPLE. SHALL I GIVE YOU THE CO-ORDINATES? ›
‹ YES. YES, I HAVE THEM. ›
‹ KILL TIDEWATER. I DON'T WANT THIS INFORMATION FALLING INTO ANYONE ELSE'S HANDS. THEN RETURN TO THE EMBASSY. THAT IS ALL. ›
THAILAND
VIETNAM
‹ HERE. THESE ARE THE CO-ORDINATES ABOUT HERE. ›
‹ I KNOW THAT TEMPLE. MY MOTHER DID AN ARCHAEO-LOGICAL EXCAVATION THERE AND TOOK ME ALONG. I HATED IT. ›
‹ HMMMM. SCHREK, YOU WILL TAKE YEROSHA AND MRS. GRADENKO WITH YOU AND DESTROY THE WEAPONS.
‹ I HAVE AN IDEA OF HOW TO GET YOU THERE AND BACK VERY FAST. HAVE NIGHTSHADE LISTEN TO ME AND ANSWER MY QUESTIONS. ›
NIGHTSHADE. LISTEN TO ME. YOU WILL ANSWER ALL OF HERR ZASTROW'S QUESTIONS HONESTLY. YOU UNDER-STAND?
YES.
I RECALL YOU HAVE EIDETIC MEMORY. YOU SEE THINGS ONCE, YOU KEEP IT FOREVER. MEMORIZE THIS ROOM, PLEASE.
I WISH FOR YOU TO TRANSPORT THE RED SHADOWS USING ONE OF YOUR DIMENSIONAL TUNNELS. YOU CAN DO THIS, YES?
IF -- I *MUST.* BUT... I CANNOT DO IT *BLIND.* I MUST HAVE A MENTAL PICTURE OF WHAT THE PLACE LOOKED LIKE.
13
THAT CAN BE ARRANGED. *YEROSHA!*

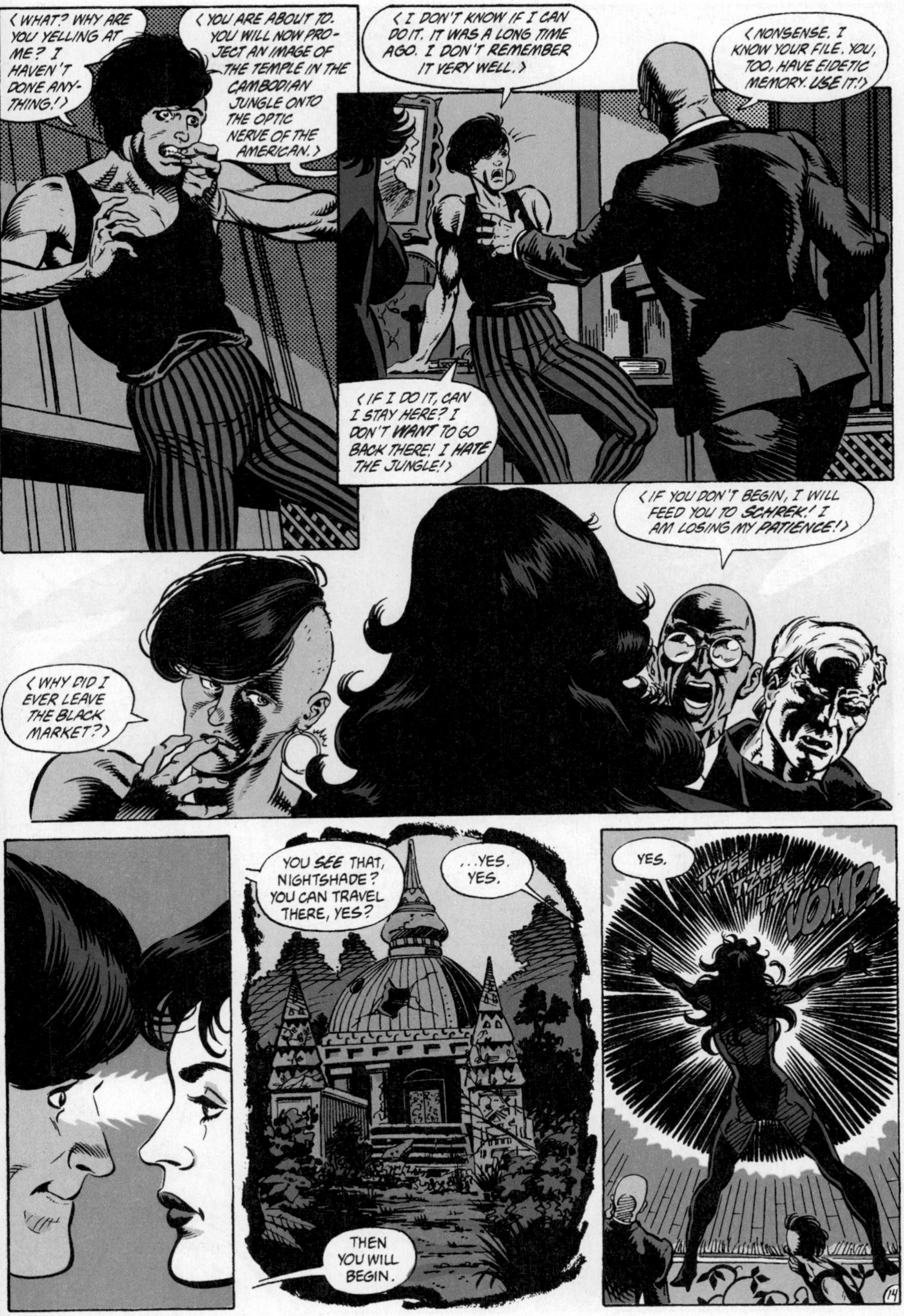
⟨WHAT? WHY ARE YOU YELLING AT ME? I HAVEN'T DONE ANYTHING!⟩
⟨YOU ARE ABOUT TO. YOU WILL NOW PROJECT AN IMAGE OF THE TEMPLE IN THE CAMBODIAN JUNGLE ONTO THE OPTIC NERVE OF THE AMERICAN.⟩
⟨I DON'T KNOW IF I CAN DO IT. IT WAS A LONG TIME AGO. I DON'T REMEMBER IT VERY WELL.⟩
⟨NONSENSE. I KNOW YOUR FILE. YOU, TOO, HAVE EIDETIC MEMORY. USE IT!⟩
⟨IF I DO IT, CAN I STAY HERE? I DON'T WANT TO GO BACK THERE! I HATE THE JUNGLE!⟩
⟨IF YOU DON'T BEGIN, I WILL FEED YOU TO SCHREK! I AM LOSING MY PATIENCE!⟩
⟨WHY DID I EVER LEAVE THE BLACK MARKET?⟩
YOU SEE THAT, NIGHTSHADE? YOU CAN TRAVEL THERE, YES?
...YES. YES.
THEN YOU WILL BEGIN.
YES.
TZZEE TZZEE TZZEE
VOMP!
14

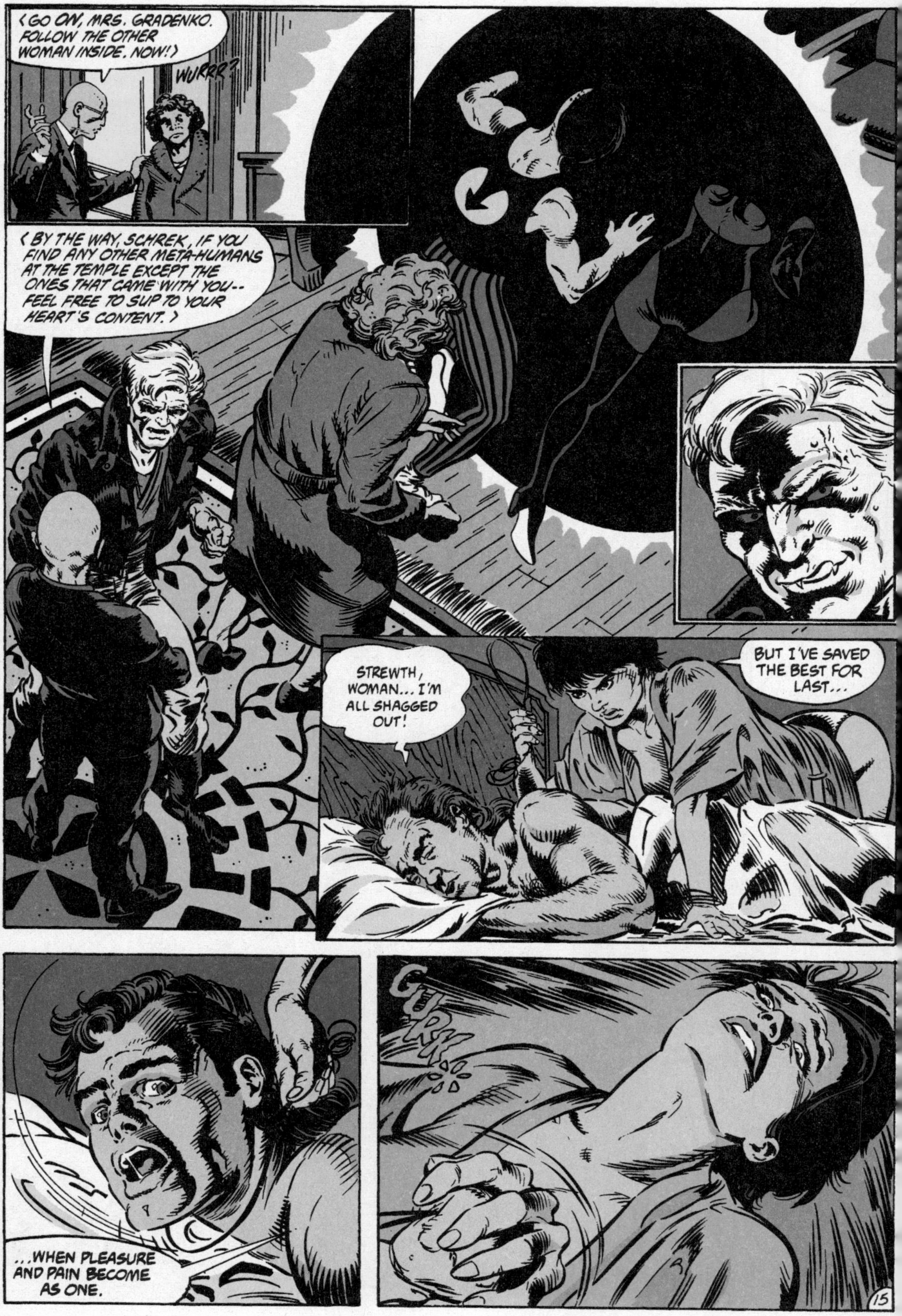
‹GO ON, MRS. GRADENKO. FOLLOW THE OTHER WOMAN INSIDE. NOW!›
WURRR?
‹BY THE WAY, SCHREK, IF YOU FIND ANY OTHER META-HUMANS AT THE TEMPLE EXCEPT THE ONES THAT CAME WITH YOU-- FEEL FREE TO SUP TO YOUR HEART'S CONTENT.›
STREWTH, WOMAN... I'M ALL SHAGGED OUT!
BUT I'VE SAVED THE BEST FOR LAST...
...WHEN PLEASURE AND PAIN BECOME AS ONE.
GURK
15

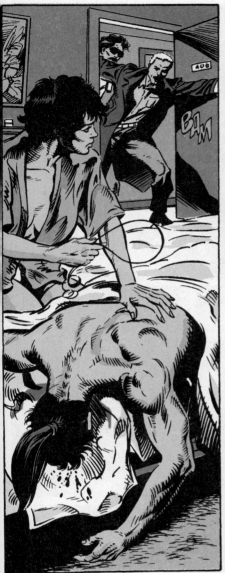

< HE'S BEEN GAROTTED. TIDEWATER'S DEAD, CAPTAIN! >

< OFF, CON! >

BAM

He paid for the thrill. Kinky, you know? It got out of hand. Happens.

< I AM NOT SO CERTAIN, MY LITTLE BIRD. ARE YOU A SWALLOW THAT SINGS PRETTILY FOR THE KGB, HMMM? >

< OH YES -- I KNOW ABOUT THEIR AGENT-WHORES. MAYBE YOU ARE ONE OF THOSE DAMNED RED SHADOWS, EH? >

< SHE WILL COME WITH US, VASSILI. >

< I AM NOT A SWALLOW. I AM A FIREBIRD -- PASSION INCARNATE. UMMM -- YOUR HAND. SO STRONG. SO -- >

16

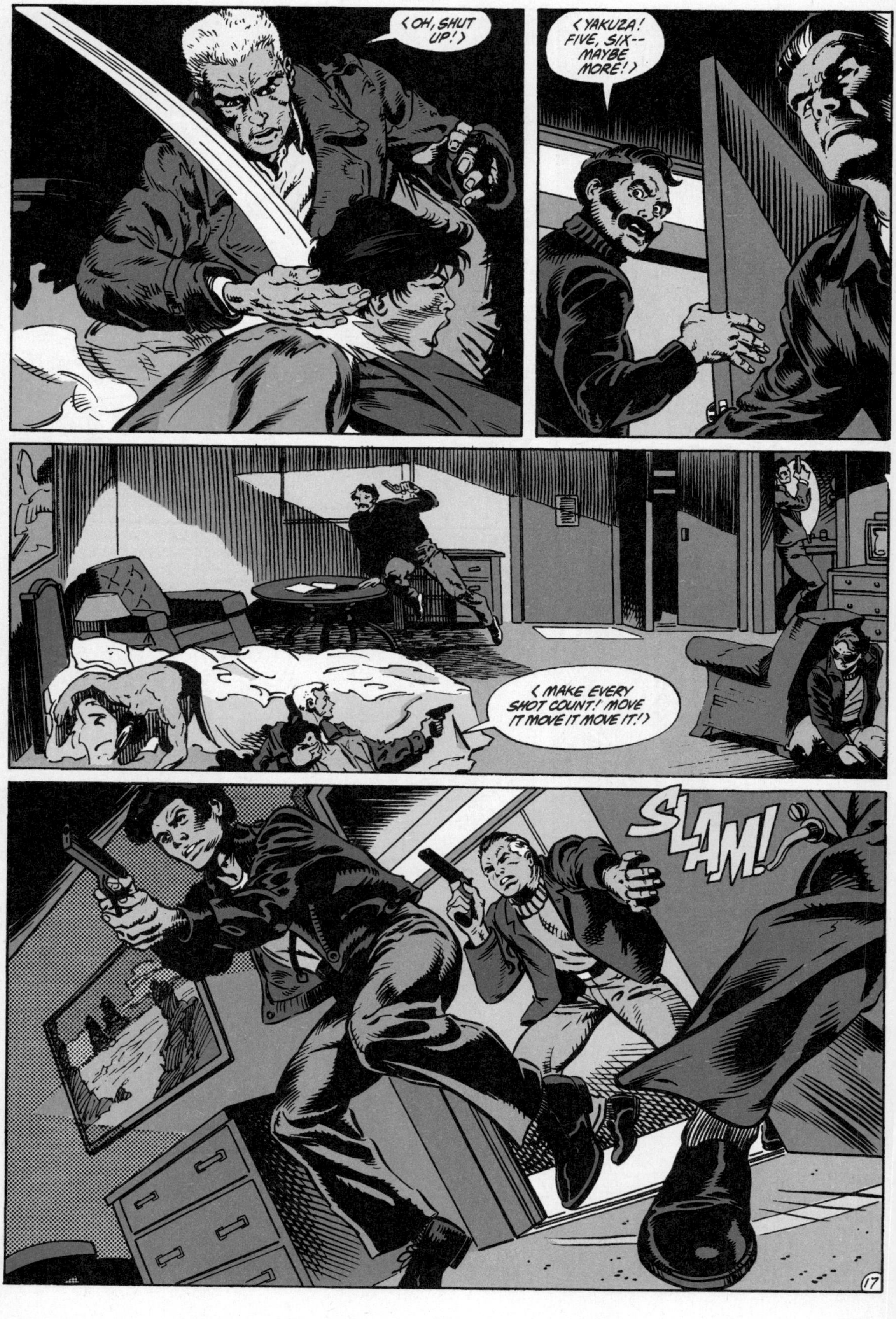

< OH, SHUT UP! >
< YAKUZA! FIVE, SIX-- MAYBE MORE! >
< MAKE EVERY SHOT COUNT! MOVE IT MOVE IT MOVE IT! >
SLAM!
17

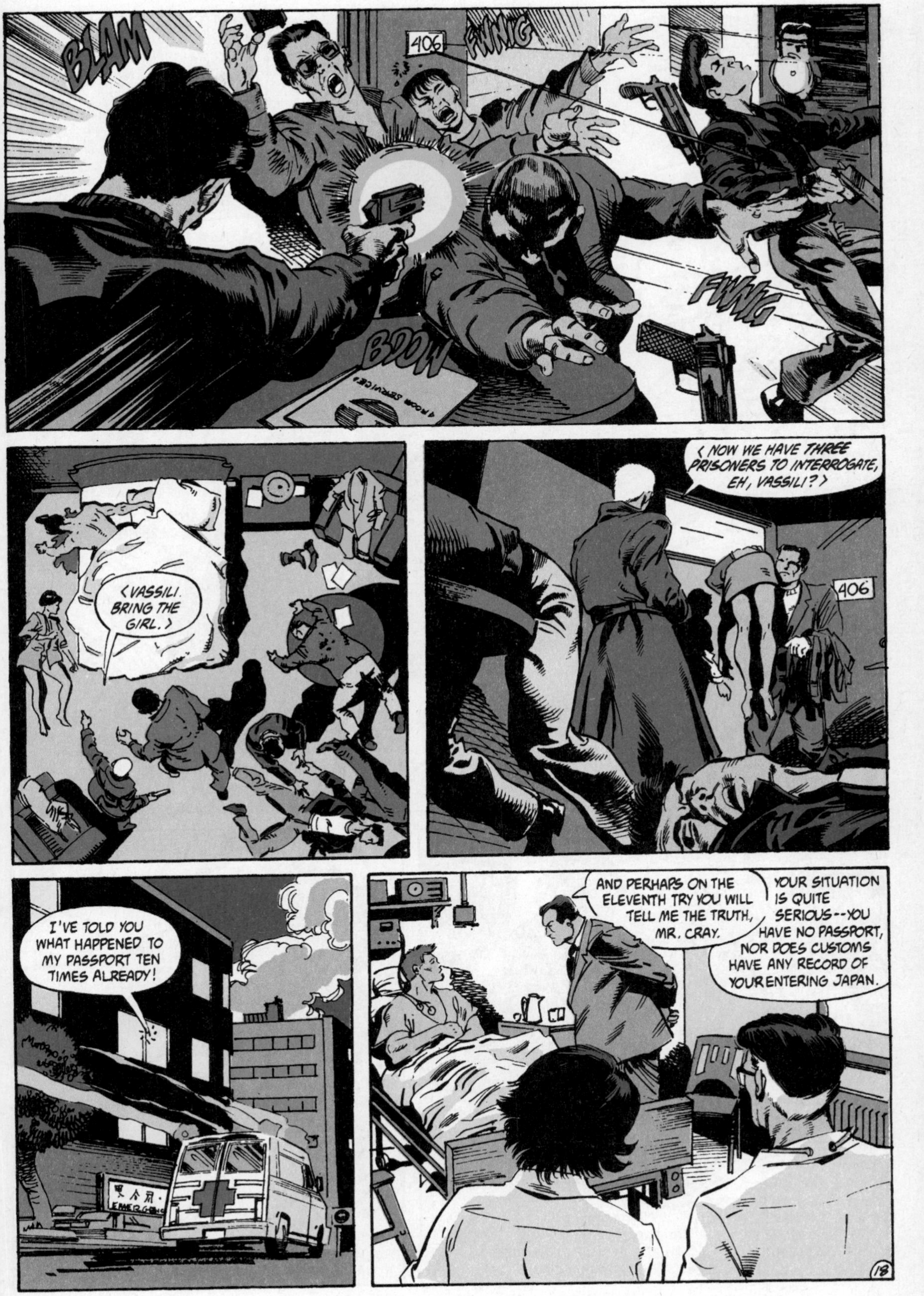
BLAM
406
FWNG
FWNG
BOOM
ROOM SERVICE
<VASSILI. BRING THE GIRL.>
<NOW WE HAVE THREE PRISONERS TO INTERROGATE, EH, VASSILI?>
406
I'VE TOLD YOU WHAT HAPPENED TO MY PASSPORT TEN TIMES ALREADY!
EMERGENCY
AND PERHAPS ON THE ELEVENTH TRY YOU WILL TELL ME THE TRUTH, MR. CRAY.
YOUR SITUATION IS QUITE SERIOUS--YOU HAVE NO PASSPORT, NOR DOES CUSTOMS HAVE ANY RECORD OF YOUR ENTERING JAPAN.
18

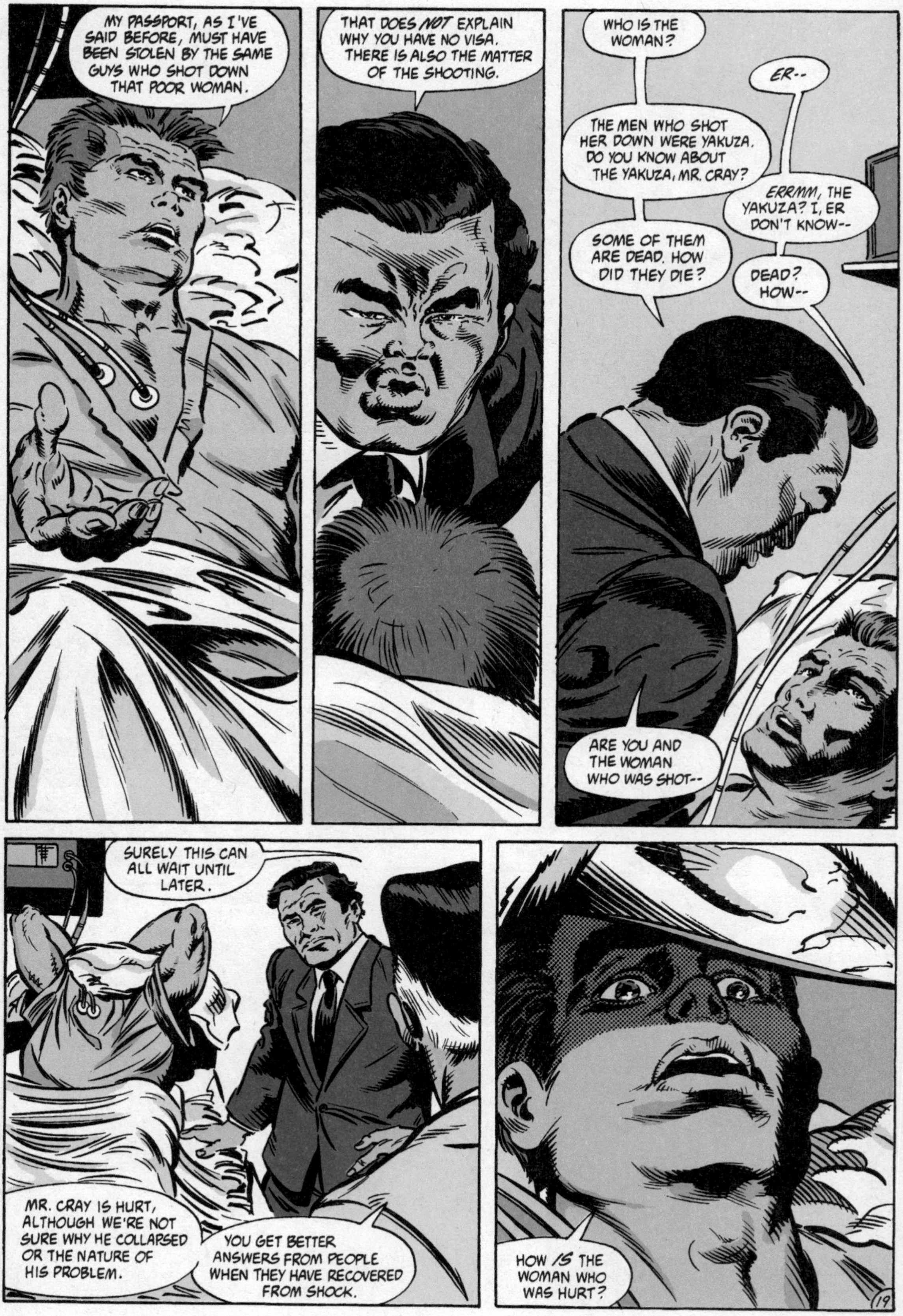
MY PASSPORT, AS I'VE SAID BEFORE, MUST HAVE BEEN STOLEN BY THE SAME GUYS WHO SHOT DOWN THAT POOR WOMAN.
THAT DOES NOT EXPLAIN WHY YOU HAVE NO VISA. THERE IS ALSO THE MATTER OF THE SHOOTING.
WHO IS THE WOMAN?
ER--
THE MEN WHO SHOT HER DOWN WERE YAKUZA. DO YOU KNOW ABOUT THE YAKUZA, MR. CRAY?
ERRMM, THE YAKUZA? I, ER DON'T KNOW--
SOME OF THEM ARE DEAD. HOW DID THEY DIE?
DEAD? HOW--
ARE YOU AND THE WOMAN WHO WAS SHOT--
SURELY THIS CAN ALL WAIT UNTIL LATER.
MR. CRAY IS HURT, ALTHOUGH WE'RE NOT SURE WHY HE COLLAPSED OR THE NATURE OF HIS PROBLEM.
YOU GET BETTER ANSWERS FROM PEOPLE WHEN THEY HAVE RECOVERED FROM SHOCK.
HOW IS THE WOMAN WHO WAS HURT?
19

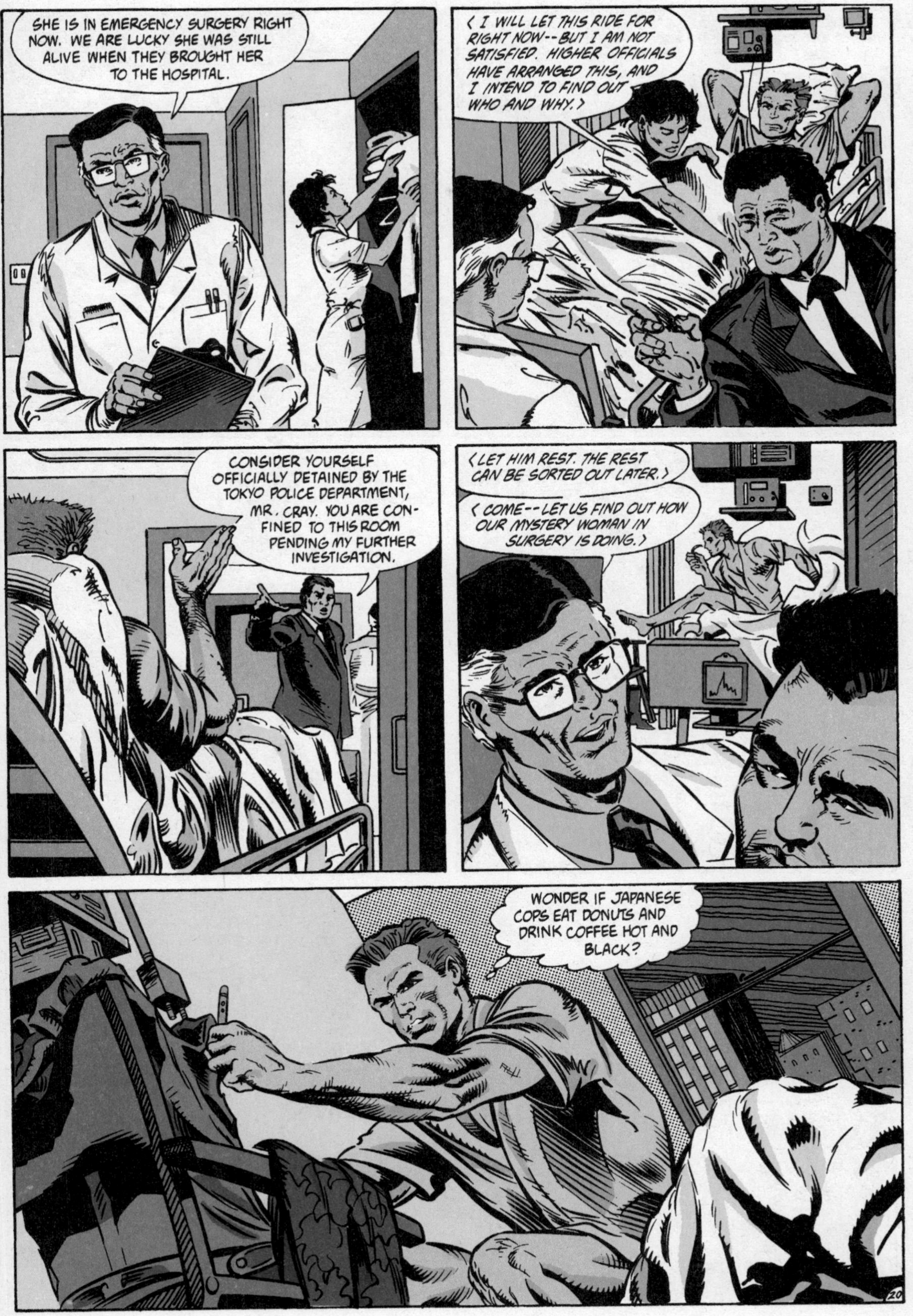
SHE IS IN EMERGENCY SURGERY RIGHT NOW. WE ARE LUCKY SHE WAS STILL ALIVE WHEN THEY BROUGHT HER TO THE HOSPITAL.
< I WILL LET THIS RIDE FOR RIGHT NOW-- BUT I AM NOT SATISFIED. HIGHER OFFICIALS HAVE ARRANGED THIS, AND I INTEND TO FIND OUT WHO AND WHY. >
CONSIDER YOURSELF OFFICIALLY DETAINED BY THE TOKYO POLICE DEPARTMENT, MR. CRAY. YOU ARE CONFINED TO THIS ROOM PENDING MY FURTHER INVESTIGATION.
< LET HIM REST. THE REST CAN BE SORTED OUT LATER. >
< COME-- LET US FIND OUT HOW OUR MYSTERY WOMAN IN SURGERY IS DOING. >
WONDER IF JAPANESE COPS EAT DONUTS AND DRINK COFFEE HOT AND BLACK?
20

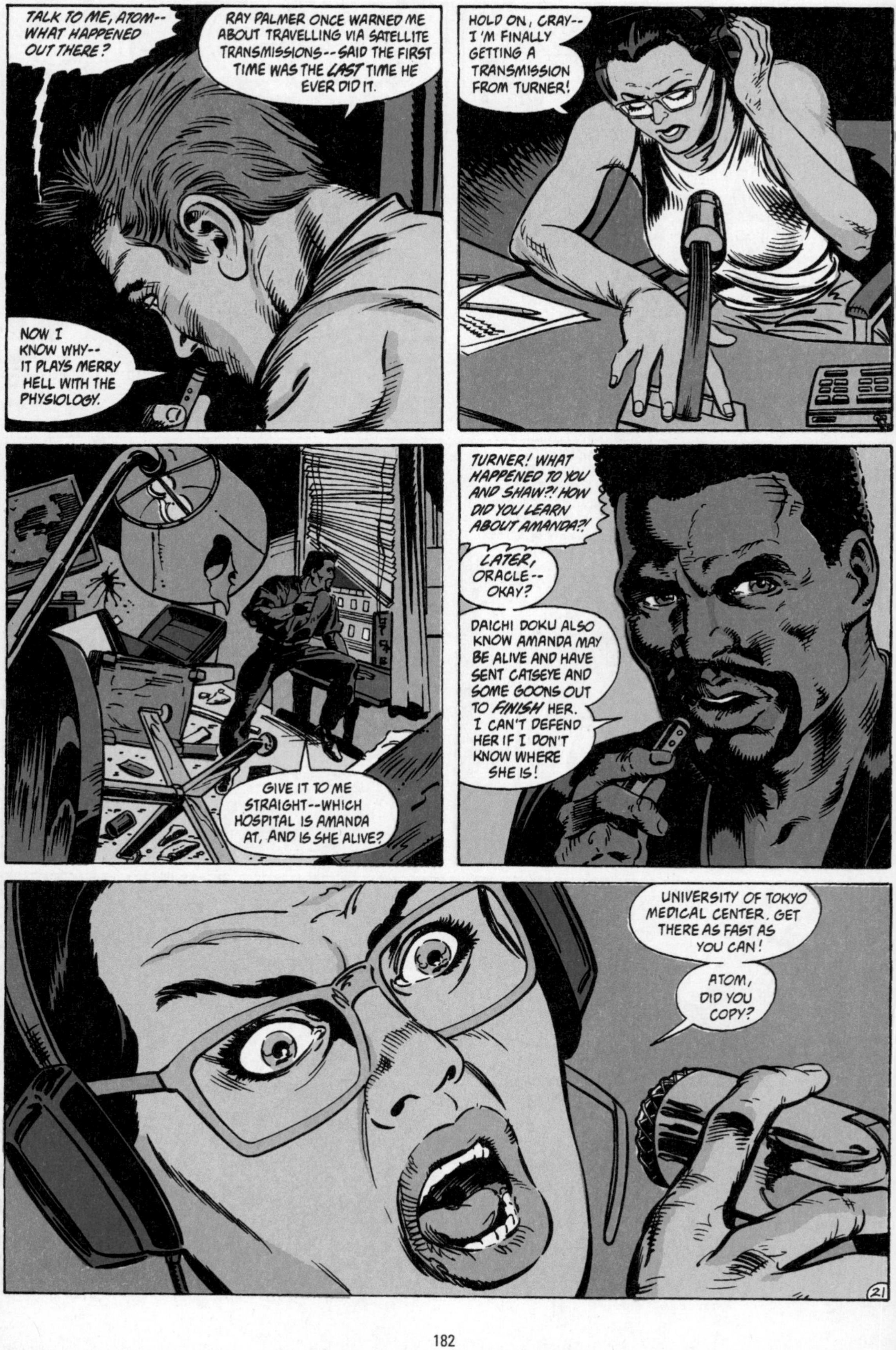
TALK TO ME, ATOM--WHAT HAPPENED OUT THERE?
RAY PALMER ONCE WARNED ME ABOUT TRAVELLING VIA SATELLITE TRANSMISSIONS--SAID THE FIRST TIME WAS THE LAST TIME HE EVER DID IT.
NOW I KNOW WHY--IT PLAYS MERRY HELL WITH THE PHYSIOLOGY.
HOLD ON, CRAY--I'M FINALLY GETTING A TRANSMISSION FROM TURNER!
GIVE IT TO ME STRAIGHT--WHICH HOSPITAL IS AMANDA AT, AND IS SHE ALIVE?
TURNER! WHAT HAPPENED TO YOU AND SHAW?! HOW DID YOU LEARN ABOUT AMANDA?!
LATER, ORACLE--OKAY?
DAICHI DOKU ALSO KNOW AMANDA MAY BE ALIVE AND HAVE SENT CATSEYE AND SOME GOONS OUT TO FINISH HER. I CAN'T DEFEND HER IF I DON'T KNOW WHERE SHE IS!
UNIVERSITY OF TOKYO MEDICAL CENTER. GET THERE AS FAST AS YOU CAN!
ATOM, DID YOU COPY?
21

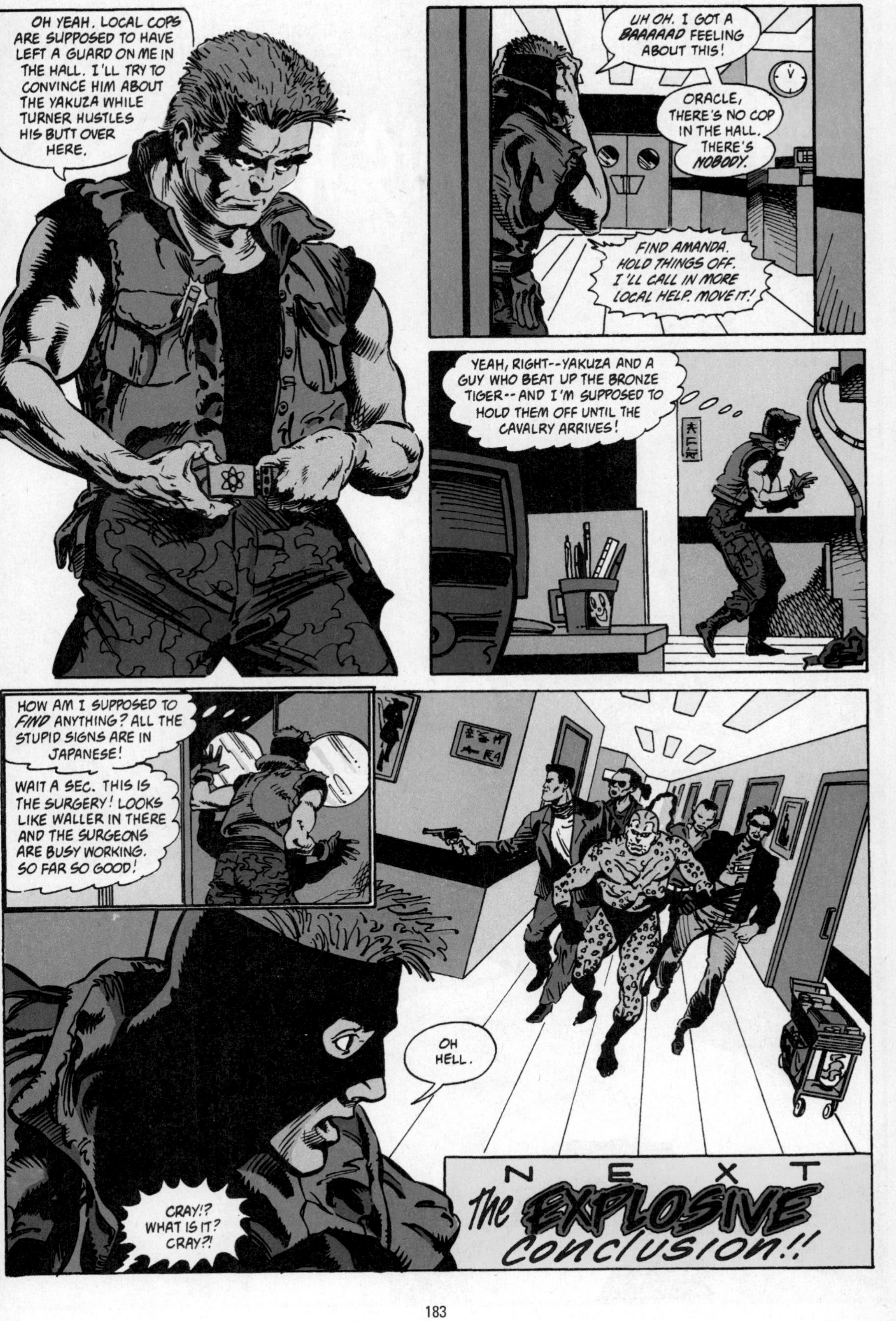
OH YEAH. LOCAL COPS ARE SUPPOSED TO HAVE LEFT A GUARD ON ME IN THE HALL. I'LL TRY TO CONVINCE HIM ABOUT THE YAKUZA WHILE TURNER HUSTLES HIS BUTT OVER HERE.
UH OH. I GOT A BAAAAAD FEELING ABOUT THIS!
ORACLE, THERE'S NO COP IN THE HALL. THERE'S NOBODY.
FIND AMANDA. HOLD THINGS OFF. I'LL CALL IN MORE LOCAL HELP. MOVE IT!
YEAH, RIGHT--YAKUZA AND A GUY WHO BEAT UP THE BRONZE TIGER--AND I'M SUPPOSED TO HOLD THEM OFF UNTIL THE CAVALRY ARRIVES!
HOW AM I SUPPOSED TO FIND ANYTHING? ALL THE STUPID SIGNS ARE IN JAPANESE!
WAIT A SEC. THIS IS THE SURGERY! LOOKS LIKE WALLER IN THERE AND THE SURGEONS ARE BUSY WORKING. SO FAR SO GOOD!
OH HELL.
CRAY!? WHAT IS IT? CRAY?!
NEXT
the EXPLOSIVE Conclusion!!

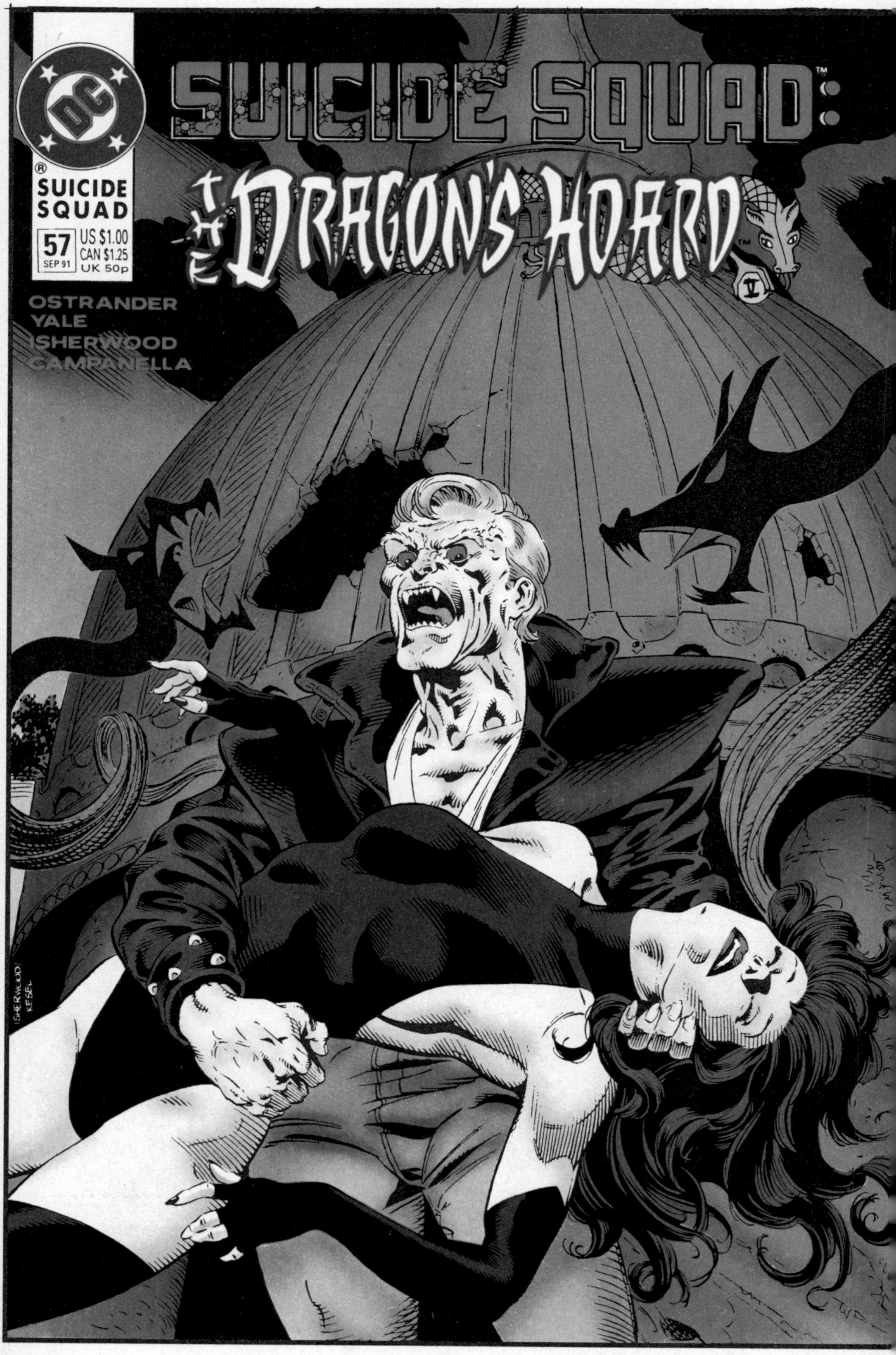
SUICIDE SQUAD:
THE DRAGON'S HOARD
V
DC
SUICIDE SQUAD
57
SEP 91
US $1.00
CAN $1.25
UK 50p
OSTRANDER
YALE
ISHERWOOD
CAMPANELLA
ISHERWOOD/KESEL

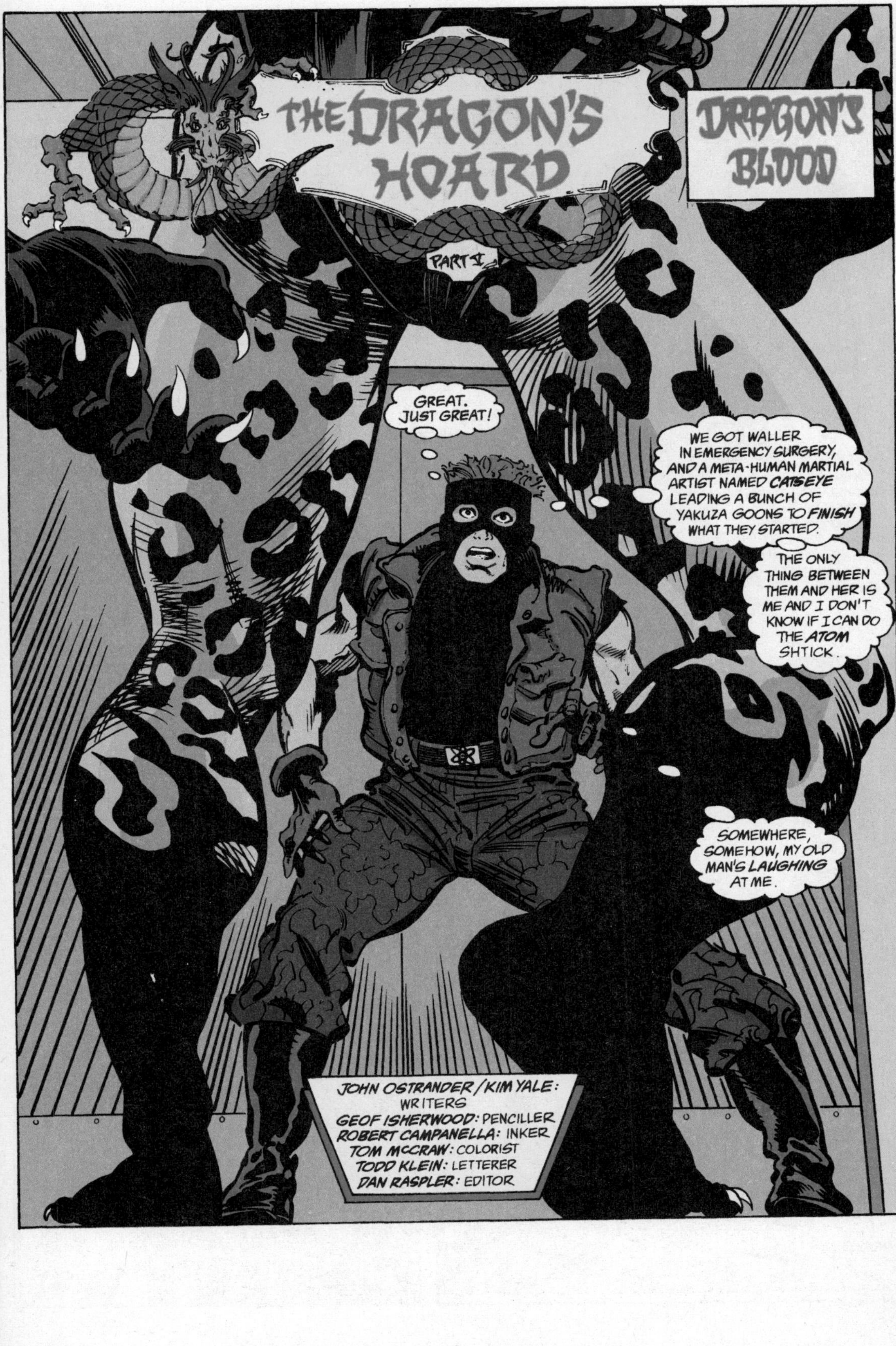
THE DRAGON'S HOARD
DRAGON'S BLOOD
PART V
GREAT. JUST GREAT!
WE GOT WALLER IN EMERGENCY SURGERY, AND A META-HUMAN MARTIAL ARTIST NAMED CATSEYE LEADING A BUNCH OF YAKUZA GOONS TO FINISH WHAT THEY STARTED.
THE ONLY THING BETWEEN THEM AND HER IS ME AND I DON'T KNOW IF I CAN DO THE ATOM SHTICK.
SOMEWHERE, SOMEHOW, MY OLD MAN'S LAUGHING AT ME.
JOHN OSTRANDER / KIM YALE: WRITERS
GEOF ISHERWOOD: PENCILLER
ROBERT CAMPANELLA: INKER
TOM McCRAW: COLORIST
TODD KLEIN: LETTERER
DAN RASPLER: EDITOR

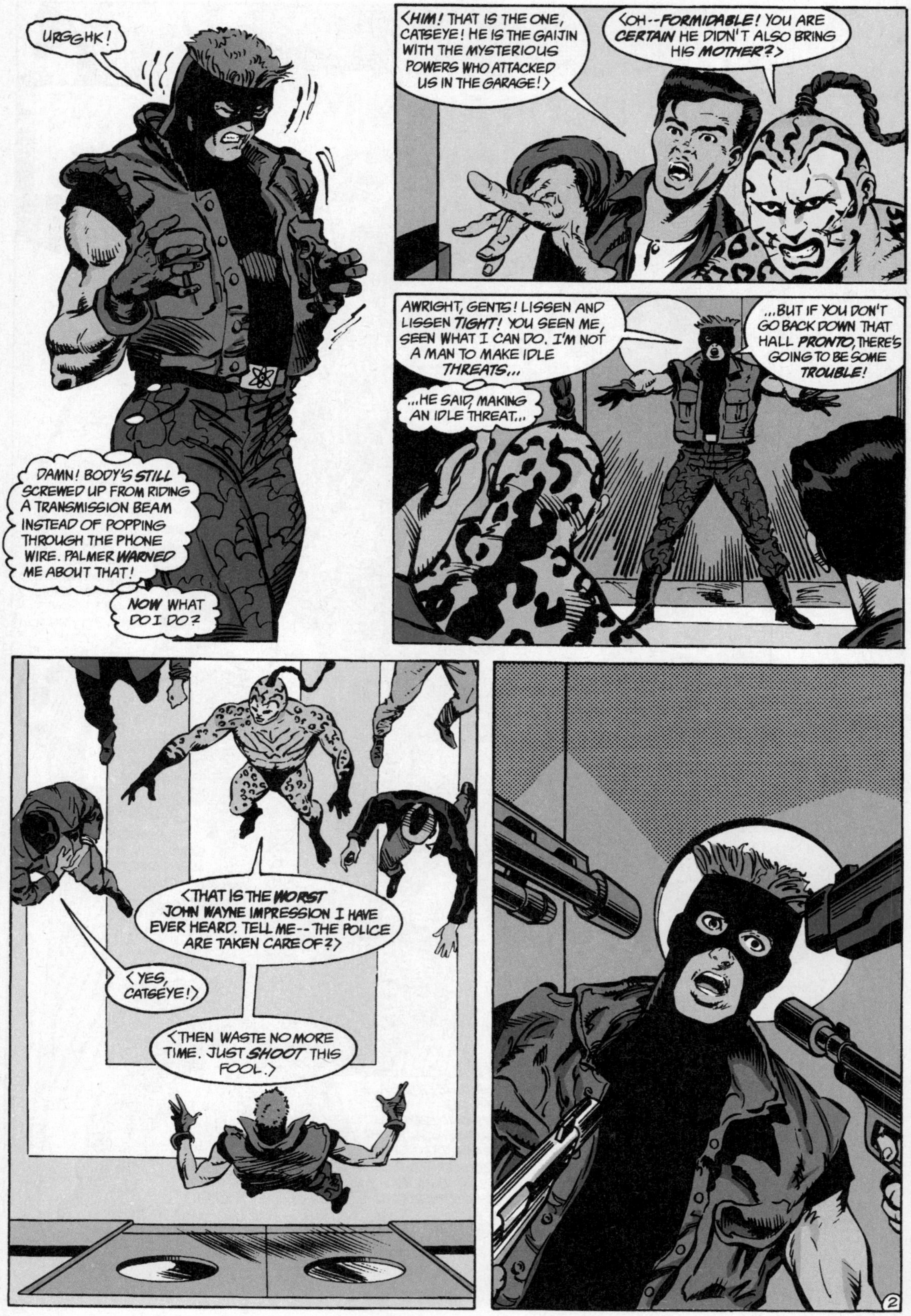
URGGHK!
DAMN! BODY'S STILL SCREWED UP FROM RIDING A TRANSMISSION BEAM INSTEAD OF POPPING THROUGH THE PHONE WIRE. PALMER WARNED ME ABOUT THAT!
NOW WHAT DO I DO?
<HIM! THAT IS THE ONE, CATSEYE! HE IS THE GAIJIN WITH THE MYSTERIOUS POWERS WHO ATTACKED US IN THE GARAGE!>
<OH--FORMIDABLE! YOU ARE CERTAIN HE DIDN'T ALSO BRING HIS MOTHER?>
AWRIGHT, GENTS! LISSEN AND LISSEN TIGHT! YOU SEEN ME, SEEN WHAT I CAN DO. I'M NOT A MAN TO MAKE IDLE THREATS...
...BUT IF YOU DON'T GO BACK DOWN THAT HALL PRONTO, THERE'S GOING TO BE SOME TROUBLE!
...HE SAID, MAKING AN IDLE THREAT...
<THAT IS THE WORST JOHN WAYNE IMPRESSION I HAVE EVER HEARD. TELL ME-- THE POLICE ARE TAKEN CARE OF?>
<YES, CATSEYE!>
<THEN WASTE NO MORE TIME. JUST SHOOT THIS FOOL.>
2

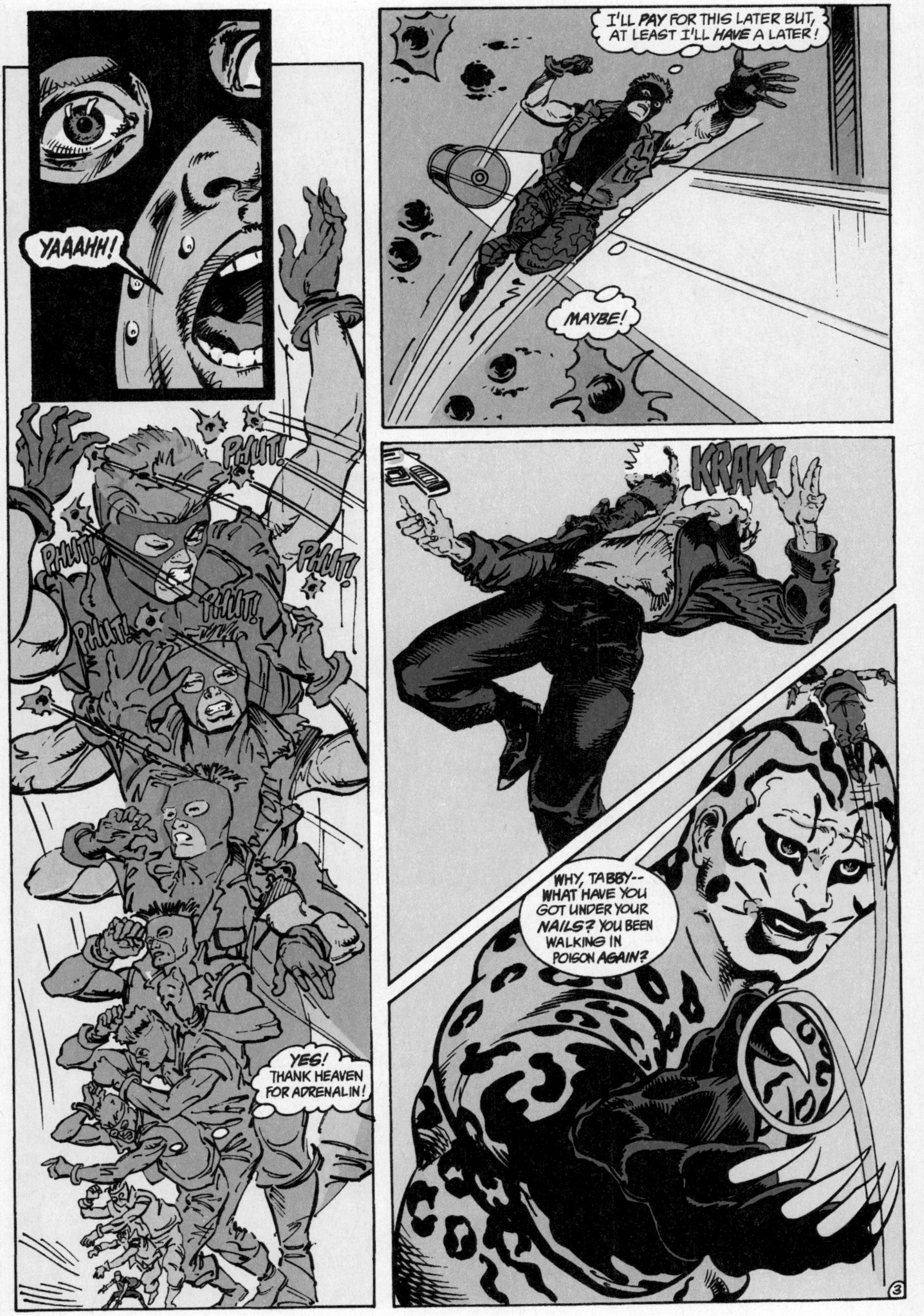
YAAAHH!
PHUT!
PHUT!
PHUT!
PHUT!
PHUT!
YES! THANK HEAVEN FOR ADRENALIN!
I'LL PAY FOR THIS LATER BUT, AT LEAST I'LL HAVE A LATER!
MAYBE!
KRAK!
WHY, TABBY-- WHAT HAVE YOU GOT UNDER YOUR NAILS? YOU BEEN WALKING IN POISON AGAIN?
3

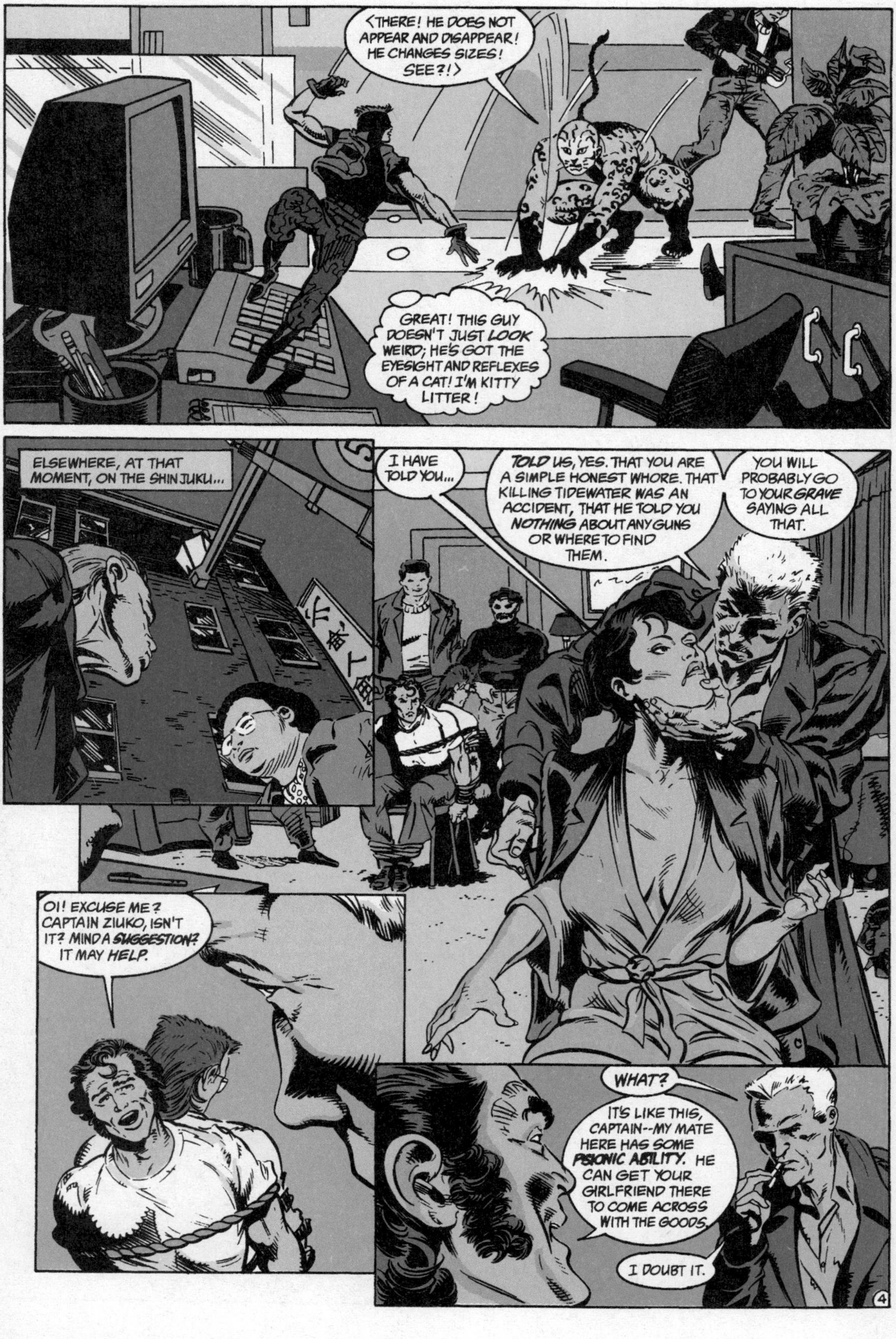

<THERE! HE DOES NOT APPEAR AND DISAPPEAR! HE CHANGES SIZES! SEE?!>
GREAT! THIS GUY DOESN'T JUST LOOK WEIRD; HE'S GOT THE EYESIGHT AND REFLEXES OF A CAT! I'M KITTY LITTER!
ELSEWHERE, AT THAT MOMENT, ON THE SHINJUKU...
I HAVE TOLD YOU...
TOLD US, YES. THAT YOU ARE A SIMPLE HONEST WHORE. THAT KILLING TIDEWATER WAS AN ACCIDENT, THAT HE TOLD YOU NOTHING ABOUT ANY GUNS OR WHERE TO FIND THEM.
YOU WILL PROBABLY GO TO YOUR GRAVE SAYING ALL THAT.
OI! EXCUSE ME? CAPTAIN ZIUKO, ISN'T IT? MIND A SUGGESTION? IT MAY HELP.
WHAT?
IT'S LIKE THIS, CAPTAIN--MY MATE HERE HAS SOME PSIONIC ABILITY. HE CAN GET YOUR GIRLFRIEND THERE TO COME ACROSS WITH THE GOODS.
I DOUBT IT.
4

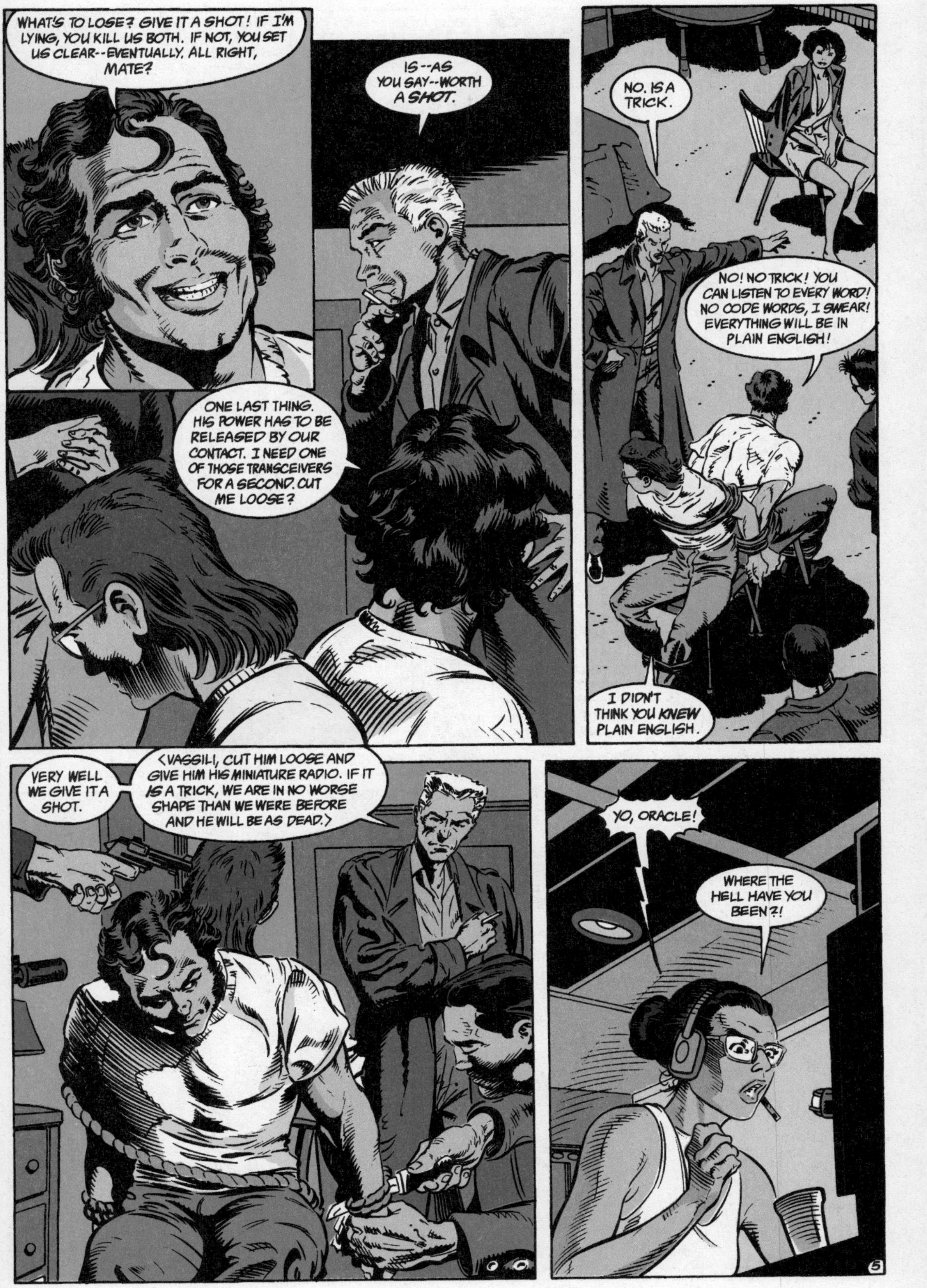
WHAT'S TO LOSE? GIVE IT A SHOT! IF I'M LYING, YOU KILL US BOTH. IF NOT, YOU SET US CLEAR--EVENTUALLY. ALL RIGHT, MATE?
IS--AS YOU SAY--WORTH A SHOT.
NO. IS A TRICK.
NO! NO TRICK! YOU CAN LISTEN TO EVERY WORD! NO CODE WORDS, I SWEAR! EVERYTHING WILL BE IN PLAIN ENGLISH!
ONE LAST THING. HIS POWER HAS TO BE RELEASED BY OUR CONTACT. I NEED ONE OF THOSE TRANSCEIVERS FOR A SECOND. CUT ME LOOSE?
I DIDN'T THINK YOU KNEW PLAIN ENGLISH.
VERY WELL WE GIVE IT A SHOT.
<VASSILI, CUT HIM LOOSE AND GIVE HIM HIS MINIATURE RADIO. IF IT IS A TRICK, WE ARE IN NO WORSE SHAPE THAN WE WERE BEFORE AND HE WILL BE AS DEAD.>
YO, ORACLE!
WHERE THE HELL HAVE YOU BEEN?!
5

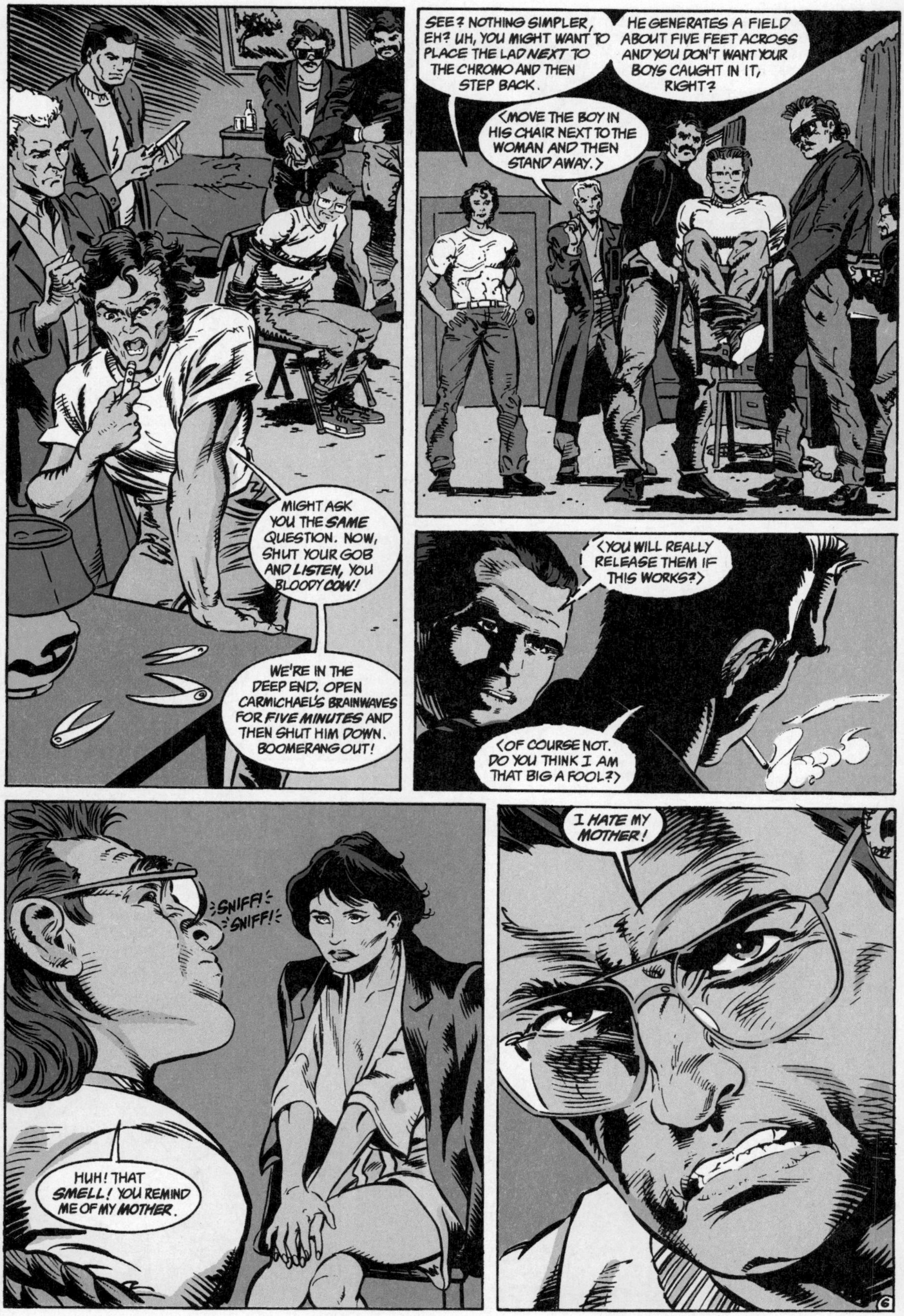
MIGHT ASK YOU THE SAME QUESTION. NOW, SHUT YOUR GOB AND LISTEN, YOU BLOODY COW!
WE'RE IN THE DEEP END. OPEN CARMICHAEL'S BRAINWAVES FOR FIVE MINUTES AND THEN SHUT HIM DOWN. BOOMERANG OUT!
SEE? NOTHING SIMPLER, EH? UH, YOU MIGHT WANT TO PLACE THE LAD NEXT TO THE CHROMO AND THEN STEP BACK.
HE GENERATES A FIELD ABOUT FIVE FEET ACROSS AND YOU DON'T WANT YOUR BOYS CAUGHT IN IT, RIGHT?
<MOVE THE BOY IN HIS CHAIR NEXT TO THE WOMAN AND THEN STAND AWAY.>
<YOU WILL REALLY RELEASE THEM IF THIS WORKS?>
<OF COURSE NOT. DO YOU THINK I AM THAT BIG A FOOL?>
SNIFF! SNIFF!
HUH! THAT SMELL! YOU REMIND ME OF MY MOTHER.
I HATE MY MOTHER!
6

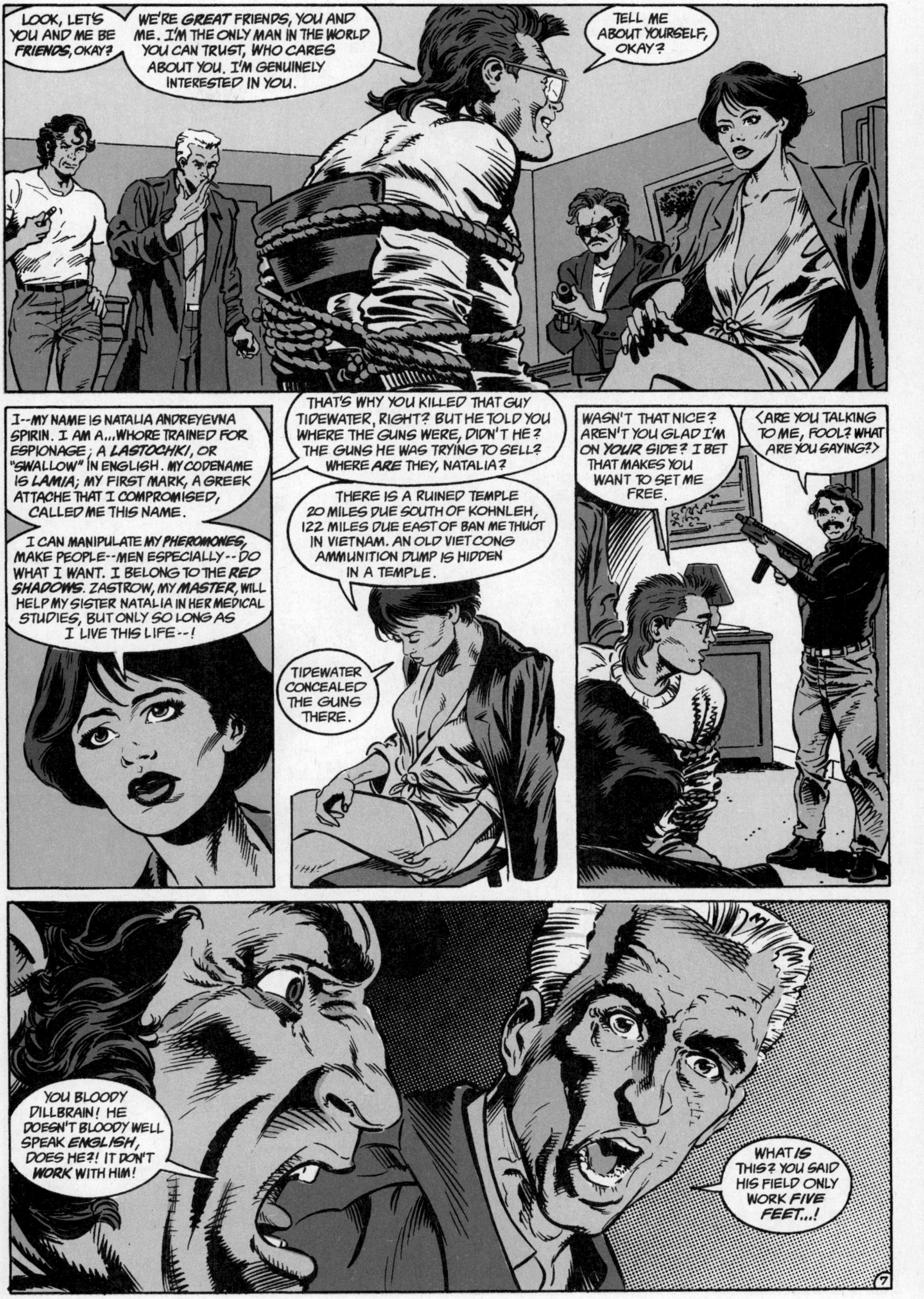
LOOK, LET'S YOU AND ME BE FRIENDS, OKAY?
WE'RE GREAT FRIENDS, YOU AND ME. I'M THE ONLY MAN IN THE WORLD YOU CAN TRUST, WHO CARES ABOUT YOU. I'M GENUINELY INTERESTED IN YOU.
TELL ME ABOUT YOURSELF, OKAY?
I--MY NAME IS NATALIA ANDREYEVNA SPIRIN. I AM A...WHORE TRAINED FOR ESPIONAGE; A LASTOCHKI, OR "SWALLOW" IN ENGLISH. MY CODENAME IS LAMIA; MY FIRST MARK, A GREEK ATTACHE THAT I COMPROMISED, CALLED ME THIS NAME.
I CAN MANIPULATE MY PHEROMONES, MAKE PEOPLE--MEN ESPECIALLY--DO WHAT I WANT. I BELONG TO THE RED SHADOWS. ZASTROW, MY MASTER, WILL HELP MY SISTER NATALIA IN HER MEDICAL STUDIES, BUT ONLY SO LONG AS I LIVE THIS LIFE--!
THAT'S WHY YOU KILLED THAT GUY TIDEWATER, RIGHT? BUT HE TOLD YOU WHERE THE GUNS WERE, DIDN'T HE? THE GUNS HE WAS TRYING TO SELL? WHERE ARE THEY, NATALIA?
THERE IS A RUINED TEMPLE 20 MILES DUE SOUTH OF KOHNLEH, 122 MILES DUE EAST OF BAN ME THUOT IN VIETNAM. AN OLD VIET CONG AMMUNITION DUMP IS HIDDEN IN A TEMPLE.
TIDEWATER CONCEALED THE GUNS THERE.
WASN'T THAT NICE? AREN'T YOU GLAD I'M ON YOUR SIDE? I BET THAT MAKES YOU WANT TO SET ME FREE.
<ARE YOU TALKING TO ME, FOOL? WHAT ARE YOU SAYING?>
YOU BLOODY DILLBRAIN! HE DOESN'T BLOODY WELL SPEAK ENGLISH, DOES HE?! IT DON'T WORK WITH HIM!
WHAT IS THIS? YOU SAID HIS FIELD ONLY WORK FIVE FEET...!
7

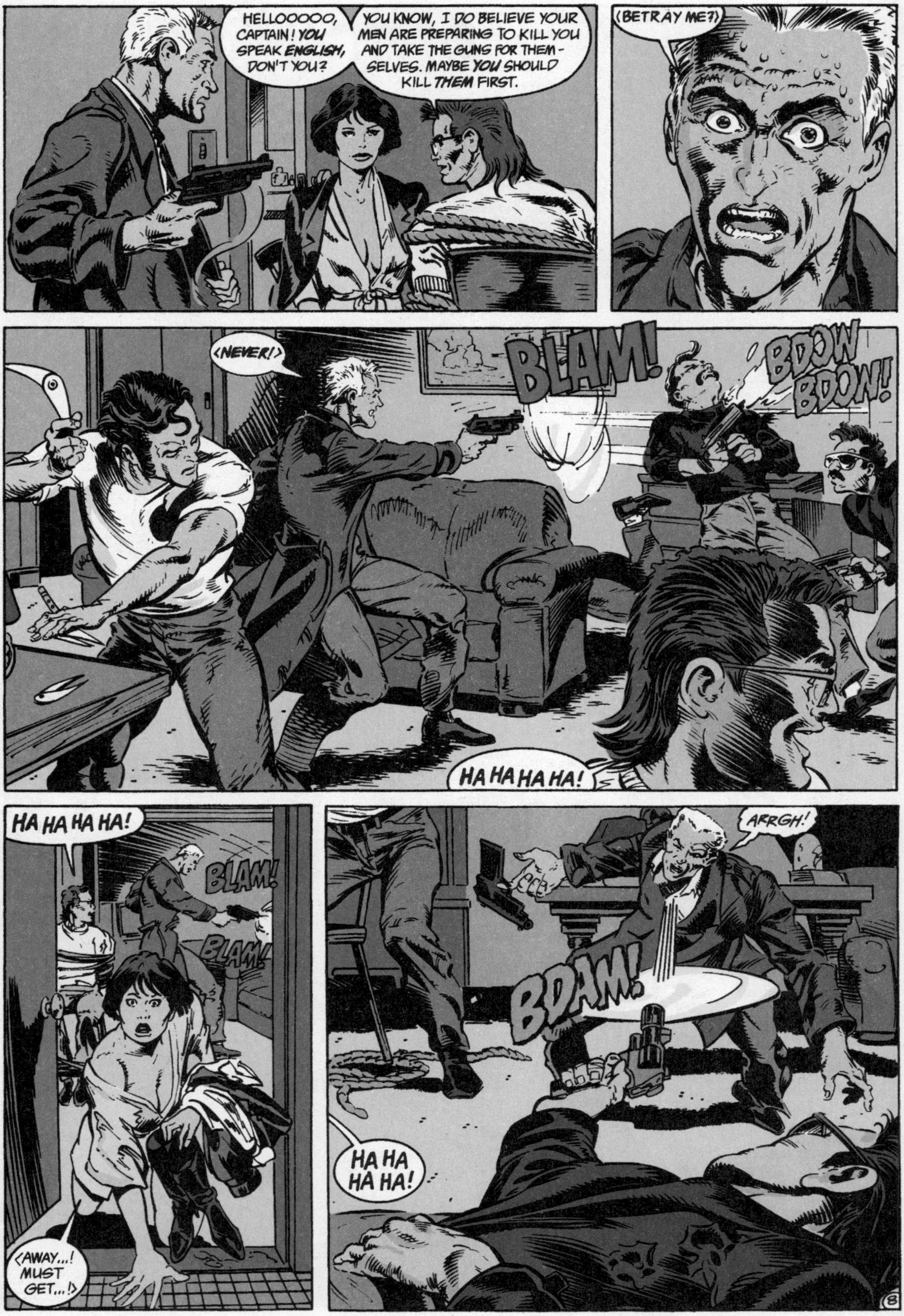
HELLOOOOO, CAPTAIN! YOU SPEAK ENGLISH, DON'T YOU?
YOU KNOW, I DO BELIEVE YOUR MEN ARE PREPARING TO KILL YOU AND TAKE THE GUNS FOR THEM-SELVES. MAYBE YOU SHOULD KILL THEM FIRST.
<BETRAY ME?>
<NEVER!>
BLAM!
BDOW BDOW!
HA HA HA HA!
HA HA HA HA!
BLAM!
BLAM!
<AWAY...! MUST GET...!>
ARRGH!
BDAM!
HA HA HA HA!
8

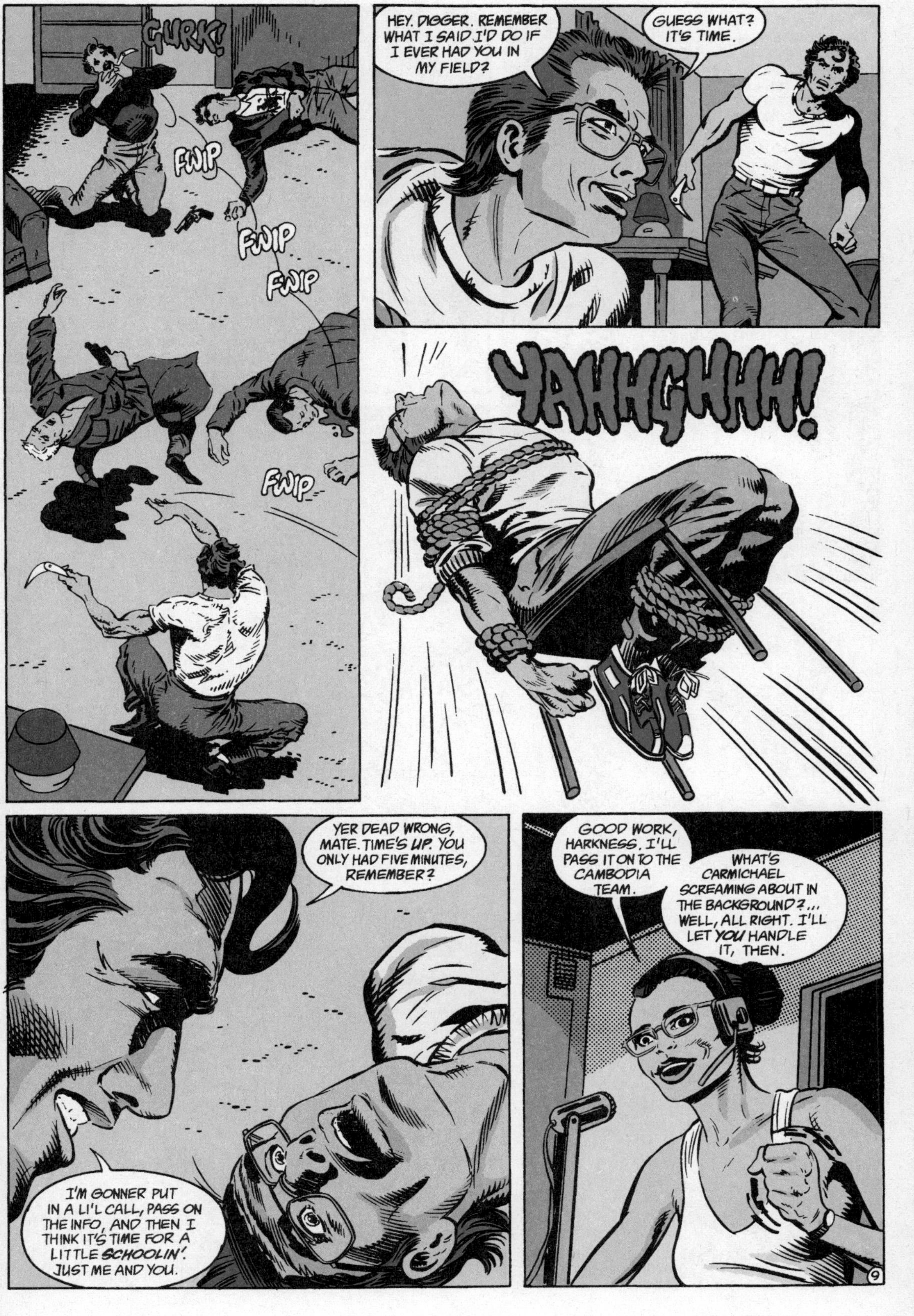
GURK!
FWIP
FWIP
FWIP
FWIP
HEY. DIGGER. REMEMBER WHAT I SAID I'D DO IF I EVER HAD YOU IN MY FIELD?
GUESS WHAT? IT'S TIME.
YAHHGHHH!
YER DEAD WRONG, MATE. TIME'S UP. YOU ONLY HAD FIVE MINUTES, REMEMBER?
I'M GONNER PUT IN A LI'L CALL, PASS ON THE INFO, AND THEN I THINK IT'S TIME FOR A LITTLE SCHOOLIN'. JUST ME AND YOU.
GOOD WORK, HARKNESS. I'LL PASS IT ON TO THE CAMBODIA TEAM.
WHAT'S CARMICHAEL SCREAMING ABOUT IN THE BACKGROUND?... WELL, ALL RIGHT. I'LL LET YOU HANDLE IT, THEN.
9

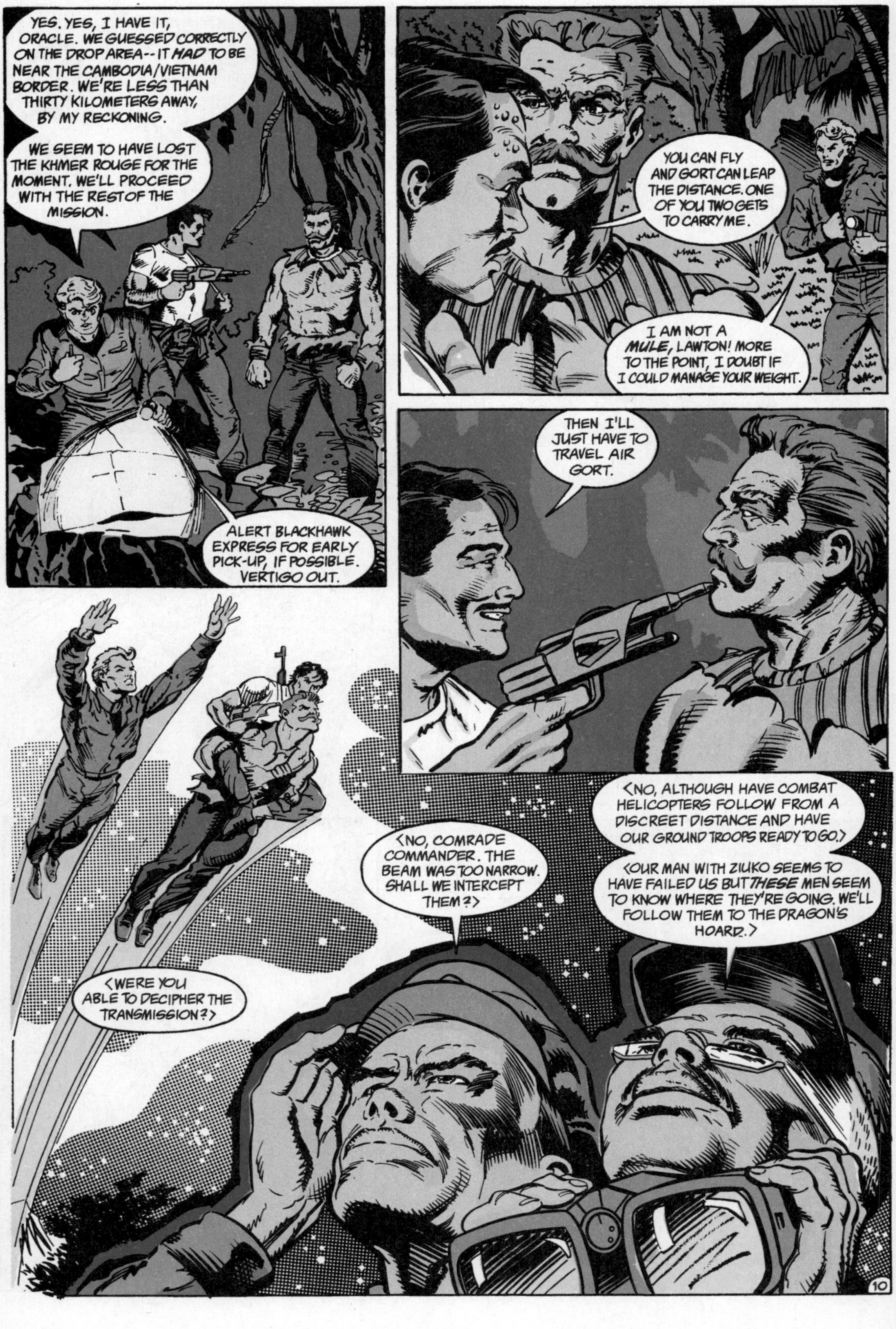
YES. YES, I HAVE IT, ORACLE. WE GUESSED CORRECTLY ON THE DROP AREA-- IT HAD TO BE NEAR THE CAMBODIA/VIETNAM BORDER. WE'RE LESS THAN THIRTY KILOMETERS AWAY, BY MY RECKONING.
WE SEEM TO HAVE LOST THE KHMER ROUGE FOR THE MOMENT. WE'LL PROCEED WITH THE REST OF THE MISSION.
ALERT BLACKHAWK EXPRESS FOR EARLY PICK-UP, IF POSSIBLE. VERTIGO OUT.
YOU CAN FLY AND GORT CAN LEAP THE DISTANCE. ONE OF YOU TWO GETS TO CARRY ME.
I AM NOT A MULE, LAWTON! MORE TO THE POINT, I DOUBT IF I COULD MANAGE YOUR WEIGHT.
THEN I'LL JUST HAVE TO TRAVEL AIR GORT.
<WERE YOU ABLE TO DECIPHER THE TRANSMISSION?>
<NO, COMRADE COMMANDER. THE BEAM WAS TOO NARROW. SHALL WE INTERCEPT THEM?>
<NO, ALTHOUGH HAVE COMBAT HELICOPTERS FOLLOW FROM A DISCREET DISTANCE AND HAVE OUR GROUND TROOPS READY TO GO.>
<OUR MAN WITH ZIUKO SEEMS TO HAVE FAILED US BUT THESE MEN SEEM TO KNOW WHERE THEY'RE GOING. WE'LL FOLLOW THEM TO THE DRAGON'S HOARD.>
10

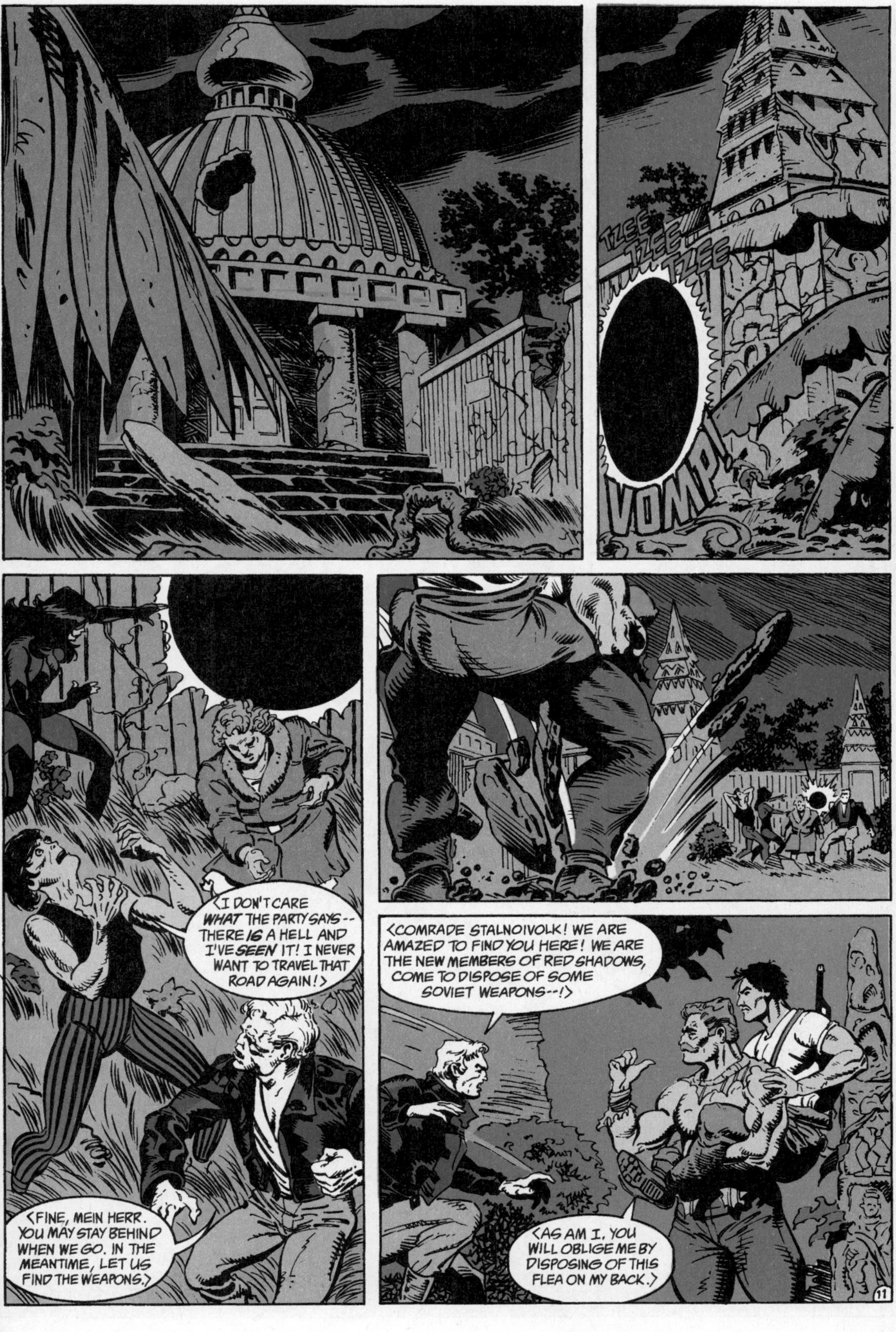
TZEE TZEE TZEE
VOMP!
<I DON'T CARE WHAT THE PARTY SAYS -- THERE IS A HELL AND I'VE SEEN IT! I NEVER WANT TO TRAVEL THAT ROAD AGAIN!>
<FINE, MEIN HERR. YOU MAY STAY BEHIND WHEN WE GO. IN THE MEANTIME, LET US FIND THE WEAPONS.>
<COMRADE STALNOIVOLK! WE ARE AMAZED TO FIND YOU HERE! WE ARE THE NEW MEMBERS OF RED SHADOWS, COME TO DISPOSE OF SOME SOVIET WEAPONS--!>
<AS AM I. YOU WILL OBLIGE ME BY DISPOSING OF THIS FLEA ON MY BACK.>
11

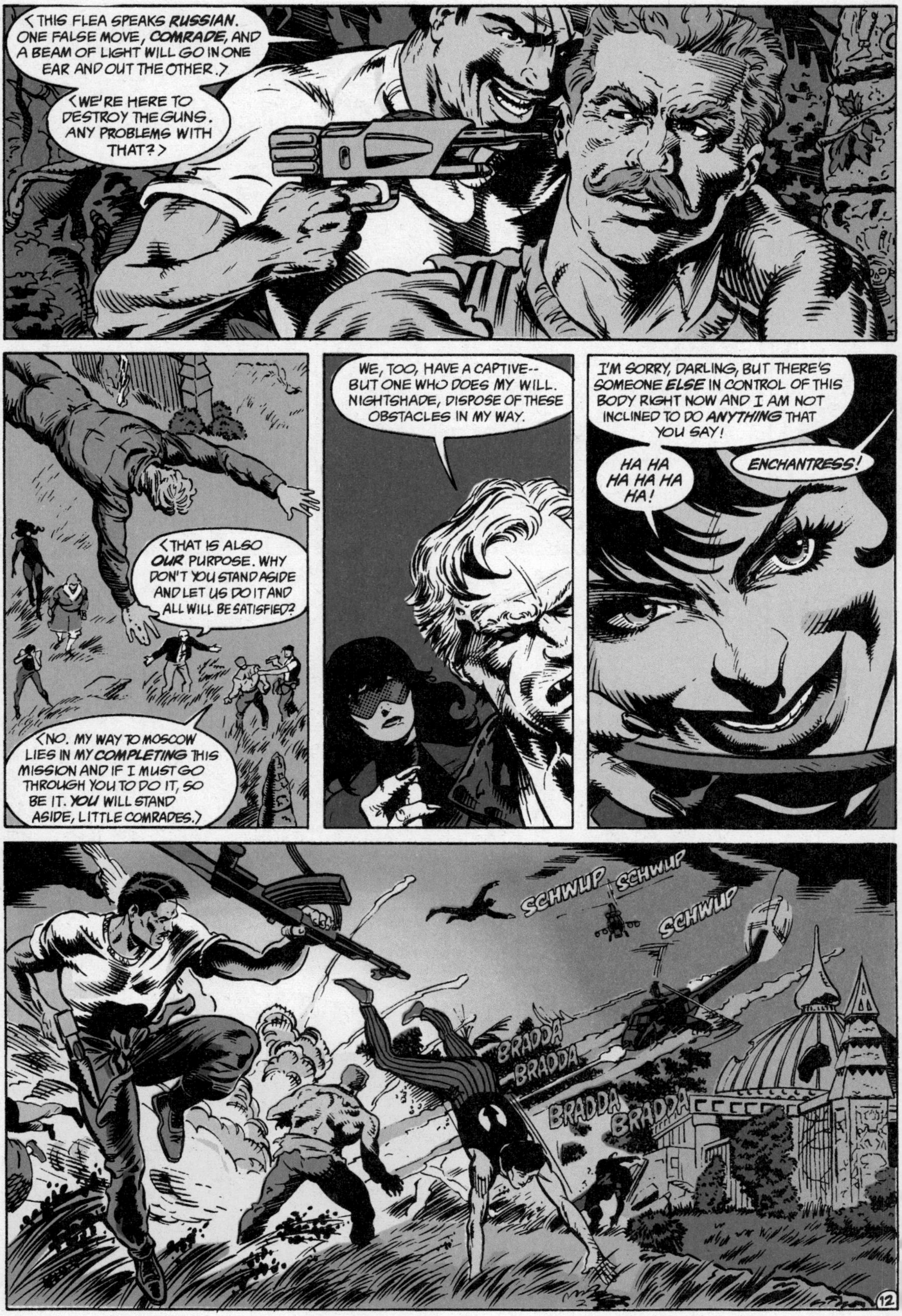

<THIS FLEA SPEAKS RUSSIAN. ONE FALSE MOVE, COMRADE, AND A BEAM OF LIGHT WILL GO IN ONE EAR AND OUT THE OTHER.>
<WE'RE HERE TO DESTROY THE GUNS. ANY PROBLEMS WITH THAT?>
<THAT IS ALSO OUR PURPOSE. WHY DON'T YOU STAND ASIDE AND LET US DO IT AND ALL WILL BE SATISFIED?
<NO. MY WAY TO MOSCOW LIES IN MY COMPLETING THIS MISSION AND IF I MUST GO THROUGH YOU TO DO IT, SO BE IT. YOU WILL STAND ASIDE, LITTLE COMRADES.>
WE, TOO, HAVE A CAPTIVE-- BUT ONE WHO DOES MY WILL. NIGHTSHADE, DISPOSE OF THESE OBSTACLES IN MY WAY.
I'M SORRY, DARLING, BUT THERE'S SOMEONE ELSE IN CONTROL OF THIS BODY RIGHT NOW AND I AM NOT INCLINED TO DO ANYTHING THAT YOU SAY!
HA HA HA HA HA HA!
ENCHANTRESS!
SCHWUP
SCHWUP
SCHWUP
BRADDA
BRADDA
BRADDA
BRADDA
12

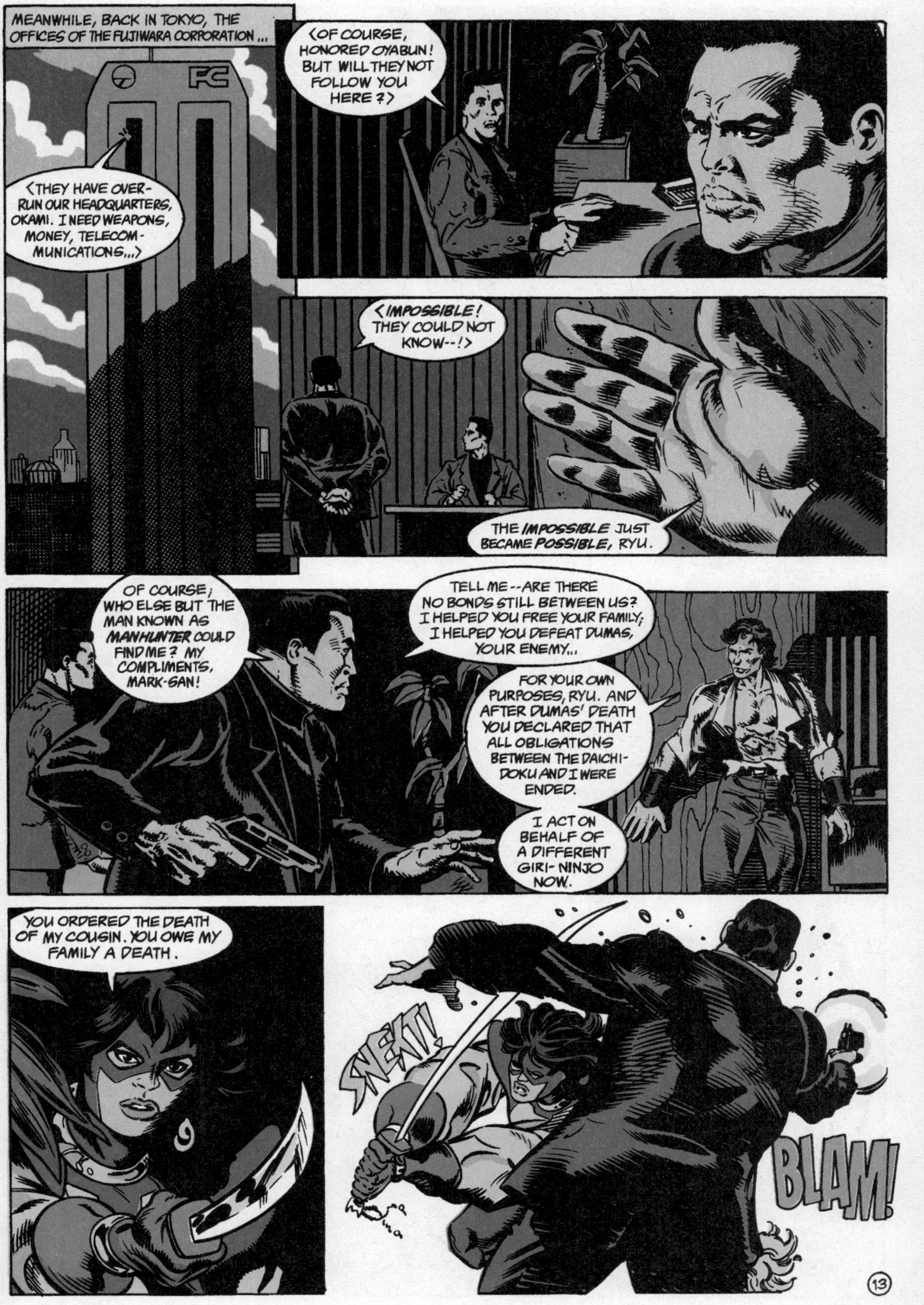

MEANWHILE, BACK IN TOKYO, THE OFFICES OF THE FUJIWARA CORPORATION...
FC
<THEY HAVE OVER-RUN OUR HEADQUARTERS, OKAMI. I NEED WEAPONS, MONEY, TELECOM-MUNICATIONS...>
<OF COURSE, HONORED OYABUN! BUT WILL THEY NOT FOLLOW YOU HERE?>
<IMPOSSIBLE! THEY COULD NOT KNOW--!>
THE IMPOSSIBLE JUST BECAME POSSIBLE, RYU.
OF COURSE; WHO ELSE BUT THE MAN KNOWN AS MANHUNTER COULD FIND ME? MY COMPLIMENTS, MARK-SAN!
TELL ME--ARE THERE NO BONDS STILL BETWEEN US? I HELPED YOU FREE YOUR FAMILY; I HELPED YOU DEFEAT DUMAS, YOUR ENEMY...
FOR YOUR OWN PURPOSES, RYU. AND AFTER DUMAS' DEATH YOU DECLARED THAT ALL OBLIGATIONS BETWEEN THE DAICHI-DOKU AND I WERE ENDED.
I ACT ON BEHALF OF A DIFFERENT GIRI-NINJO NOW.
YOU ORDERED THE DEATH OF MY COUSIN. YOU OWE MY FAMILY A DEATH.
SNEKT!
BLAM!
13

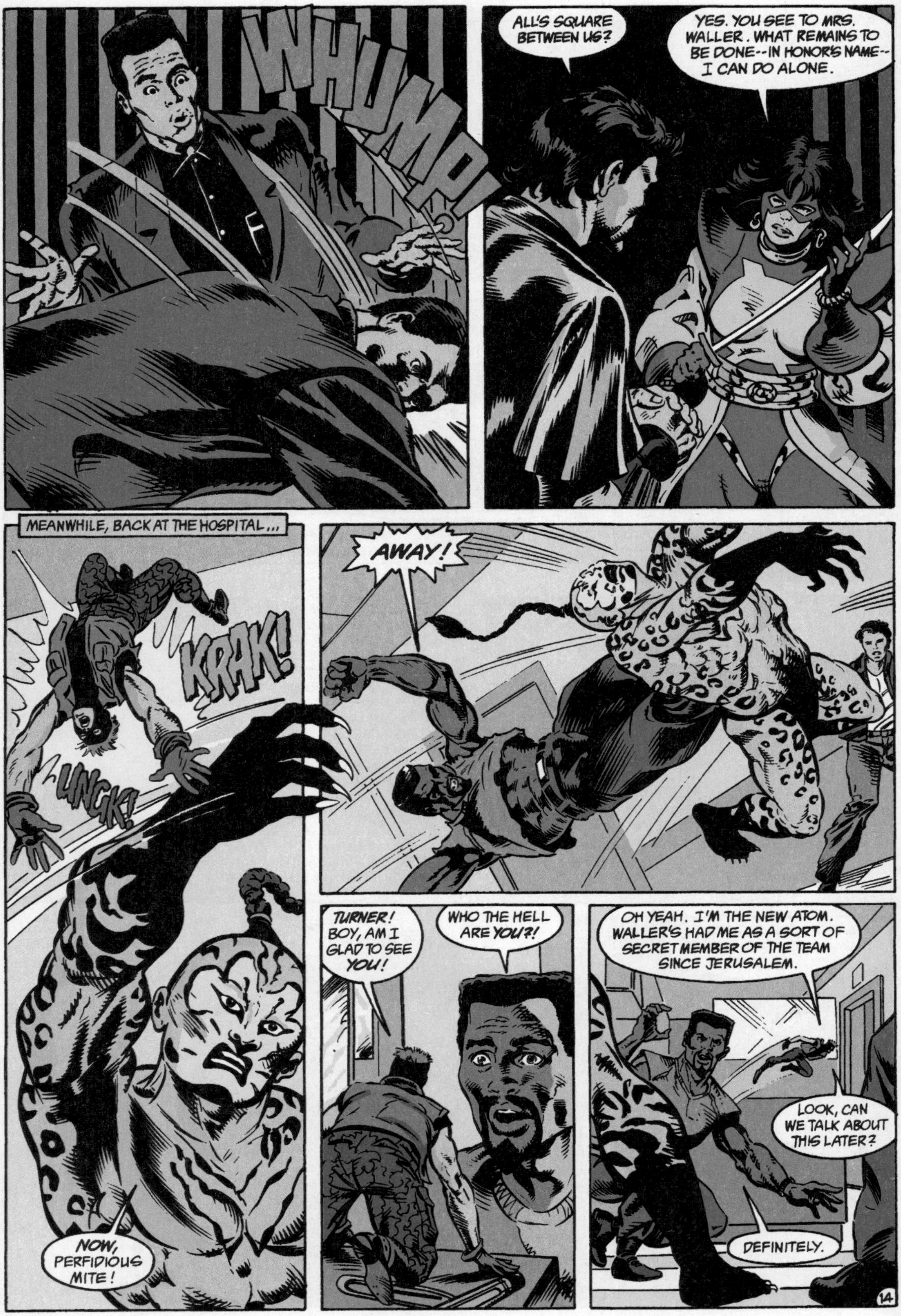
WHUMP!
ALL'S SQUARE BETWEEN US?
YES. YOU SEE TO MRS. WALLER. WHAT REMAINS TO BE DONE--IN HONOR'S NAME--I CAN DO ALONE.
MEANWHILE, BACK AT THE HOSPITAL...
KRAK!
UNGK!
NOW, PERFIDIOUS MITE!
AWAY!
TURNER! BOY, AM I GLAD TO SEE YOU!
WHO THE HELL ARE YOU?!
OH YEAH. I'M THE NEW ATOM. WALLER'S HAD ME AS A SORT OF SECRET MEMBER OF THE TEAM SINCE JERUSALEM.
LOOK, CAN WE TALK ABOUT THIS LATER?
DEFINITELY.
14

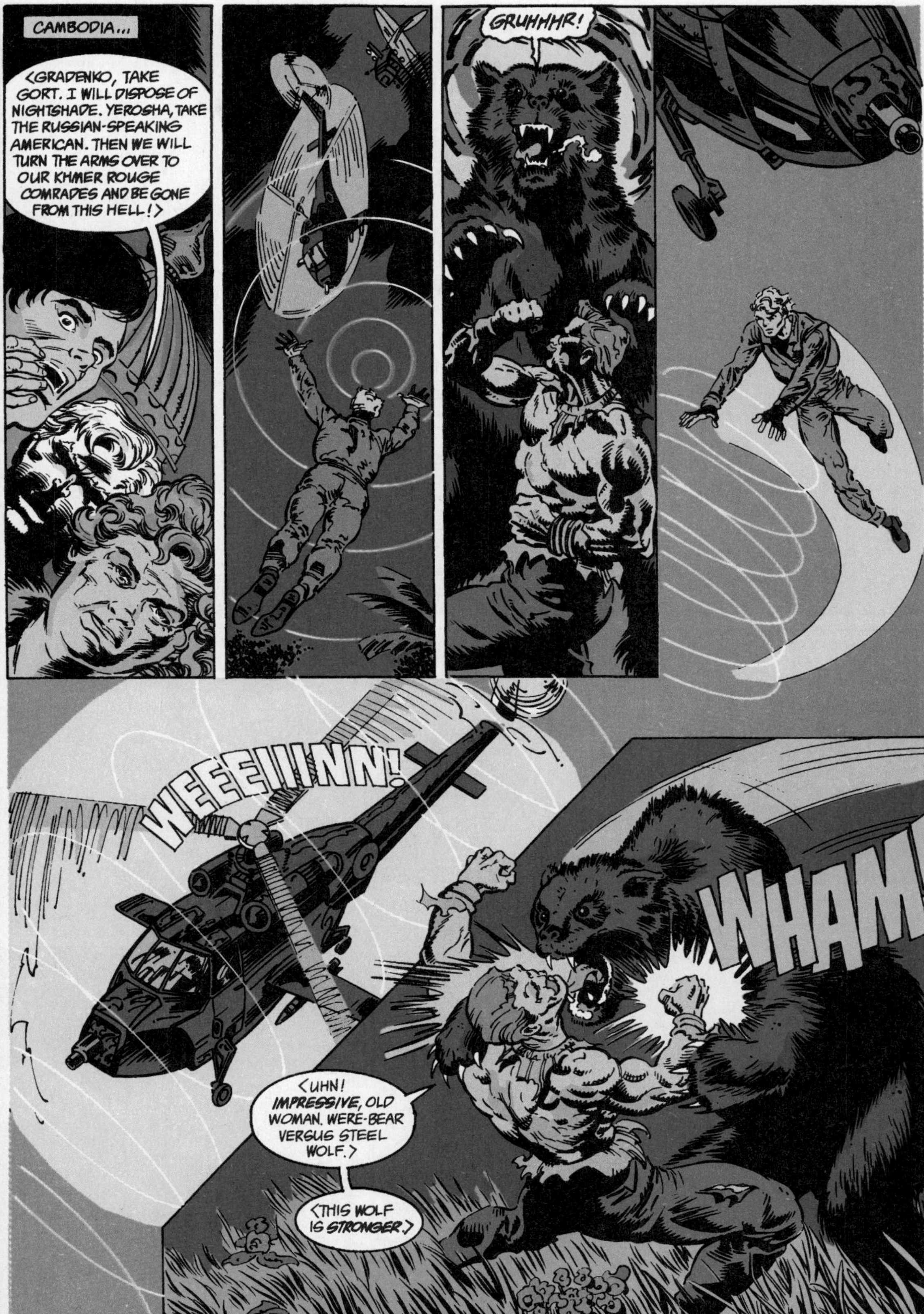
CAMBODIA...
<GRADENKO, TAKE GORT. I WILL DISPOSE OF NIGHTSHADE. YEROSHA, TAKE THE RUSSIAN-SPEAKING AMERICAN. THEN WE WILL TURN THE ARMS OVER TO OUR KHMER ROUGE COMRADES AND BE GONE FROM THIS HELL!>
GRUHHHR!
WEEEIIINN!
WHAM!
<UHN! IMPRESSIVE, OLD WOMAN. WERE-BEAR VERSUS STEEL WOLF.>
<THIS WOLF IS STRONGER.>
15

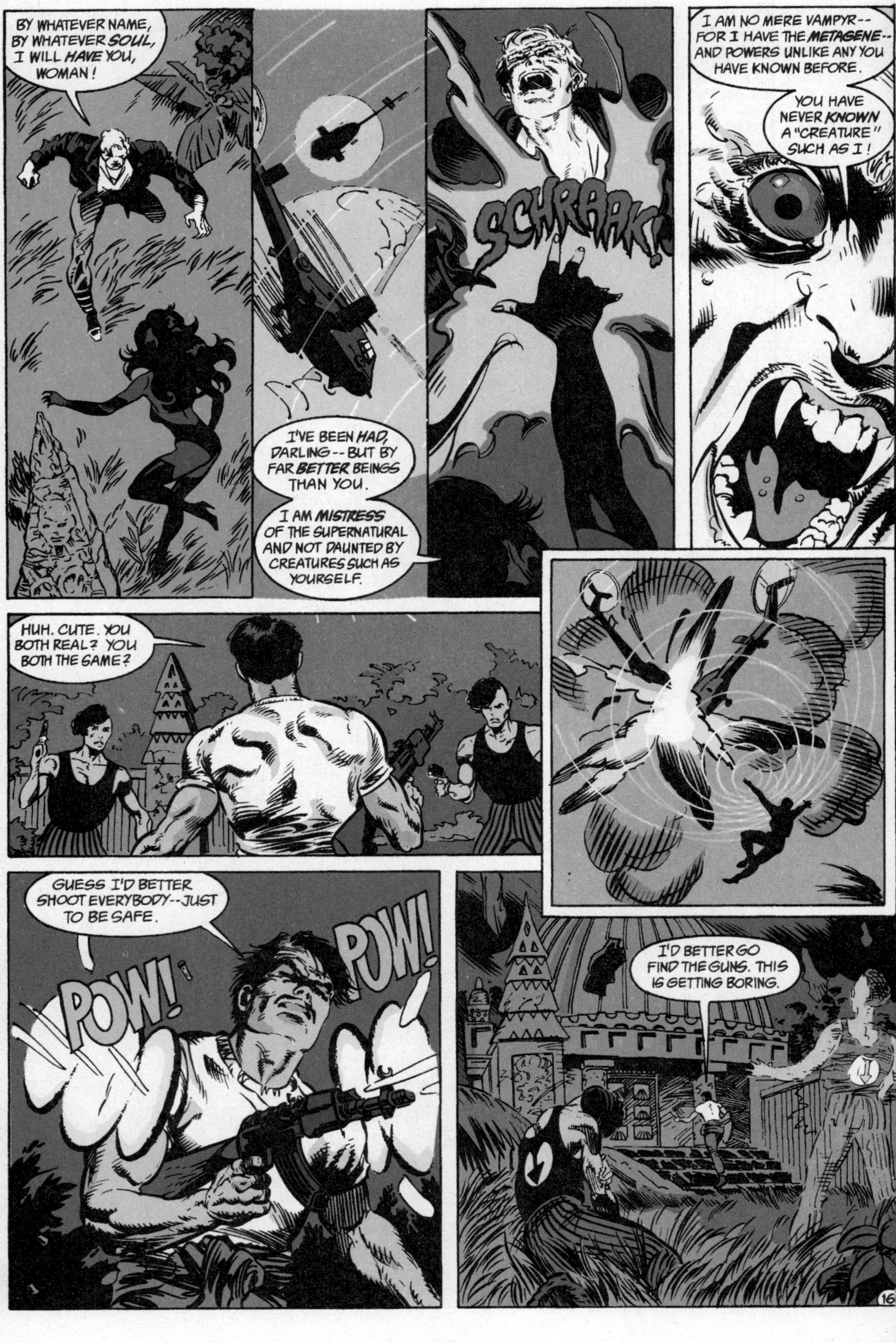
BY WHATEVER NAME, BY WHATEVER SOUL, I WILL HAVE YOU, WOMAN!
I'VE BEEN HAD, DARLING--BUT BY FAR BETTER BEINGS THAN YOU.
I AM MISTRESS OF THE SUPERNATURAL AND NOT DAUNTED BY CREATURES SUCH AS YOURSELF.
SCHRAAK!
I AM NO MERE VAMPYR--FOR I HAVE THE METAGENE--AND POWERS UNLIKE ANY YOU HAVE KNOWN BEFORE.
YOU HAVE NEVER KNOWN A "CREATURE" SUCH AS I!
HUH. CUTE. YOU BOTH REAL? YOU BOTH THE SAME?
GUESS I'D BETTER SHOOT EVERYBODY--JUST TO BE SAFE.
POW!
POW!
I'D BETTER GO FIND THE GUNS. THIS IS GETTING BORING.
16

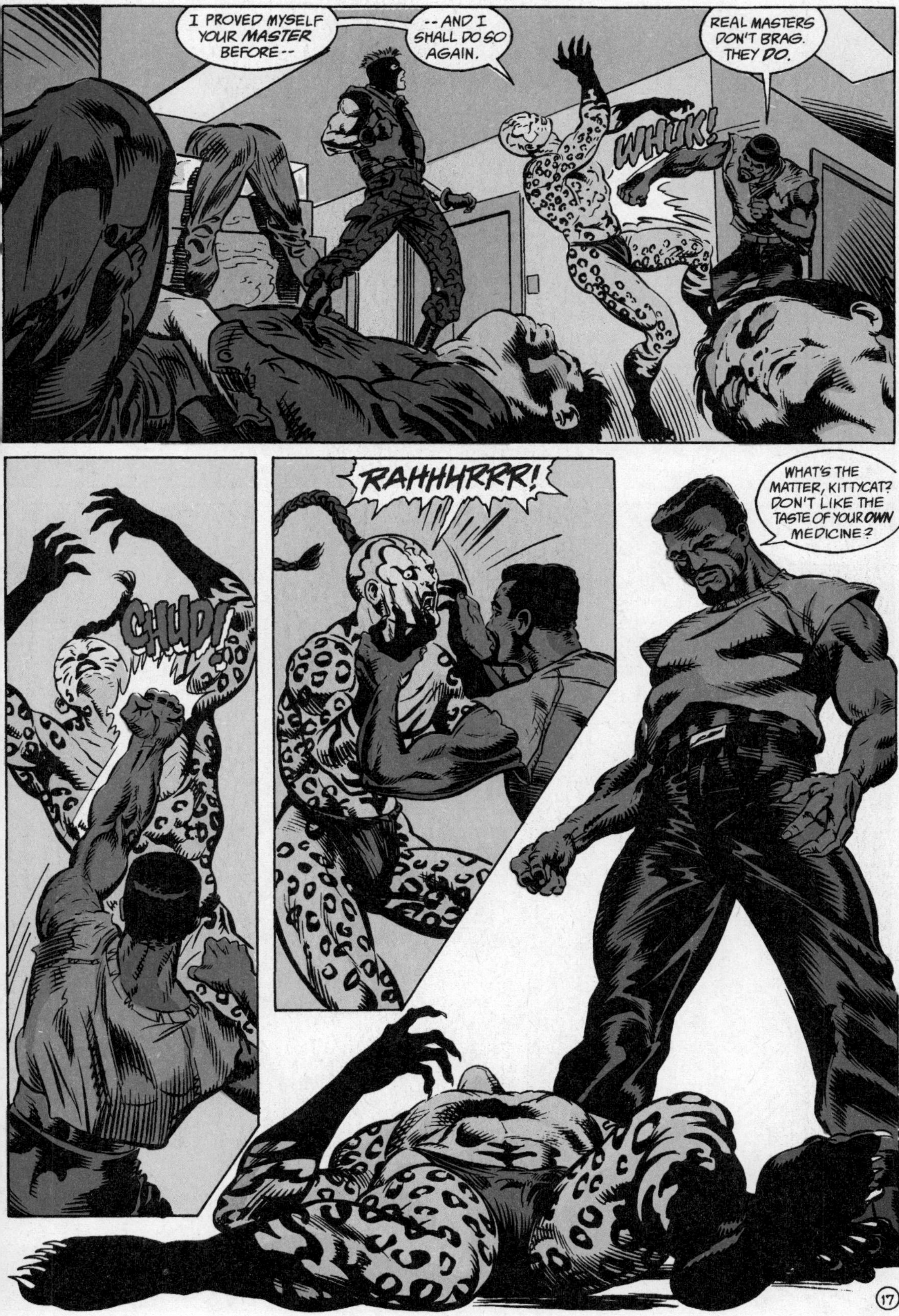
I PROVED MYSELF YOUR MASTER BEFORE --
-- AND I SHALL DO SO AGAIN.
REAL MASTERS DON'T BRAG. THEY DO.
WHUK!
CHUD!
RAHHHRRR!
WHAT'S THE MATTER, KITTYCAT? DON'T LIKE THE TASTE OF YOUR OWN MEDICINE?
17

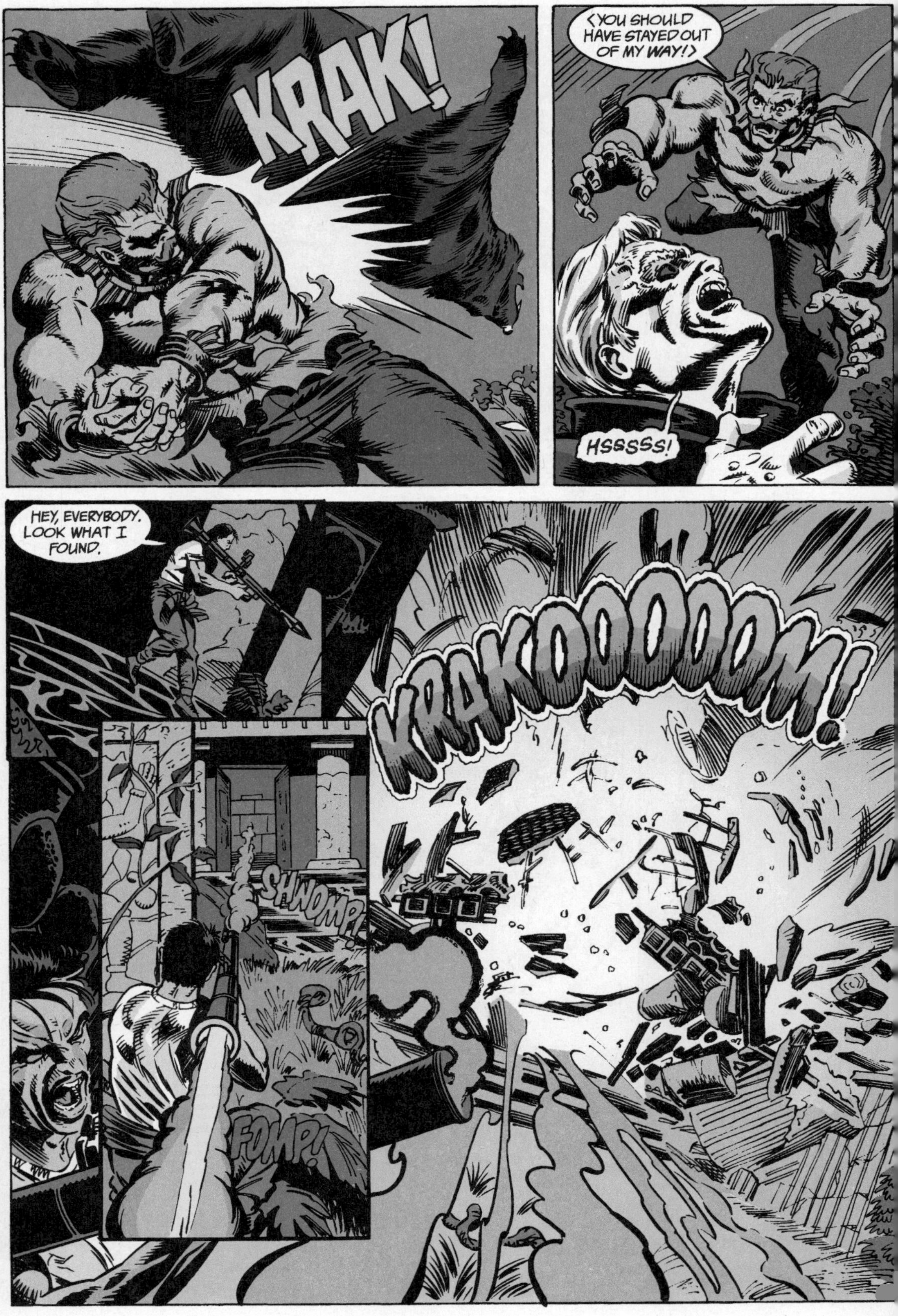
KRAK!
<YOU SHOULD HAVE STAYED OUT OF MY WAY!>
HSSSSS!
HEY, EVERYBODY. LOOK WHAT I FOUND.
SHWOMP!
FOMP!
KRAKOOOOOM!

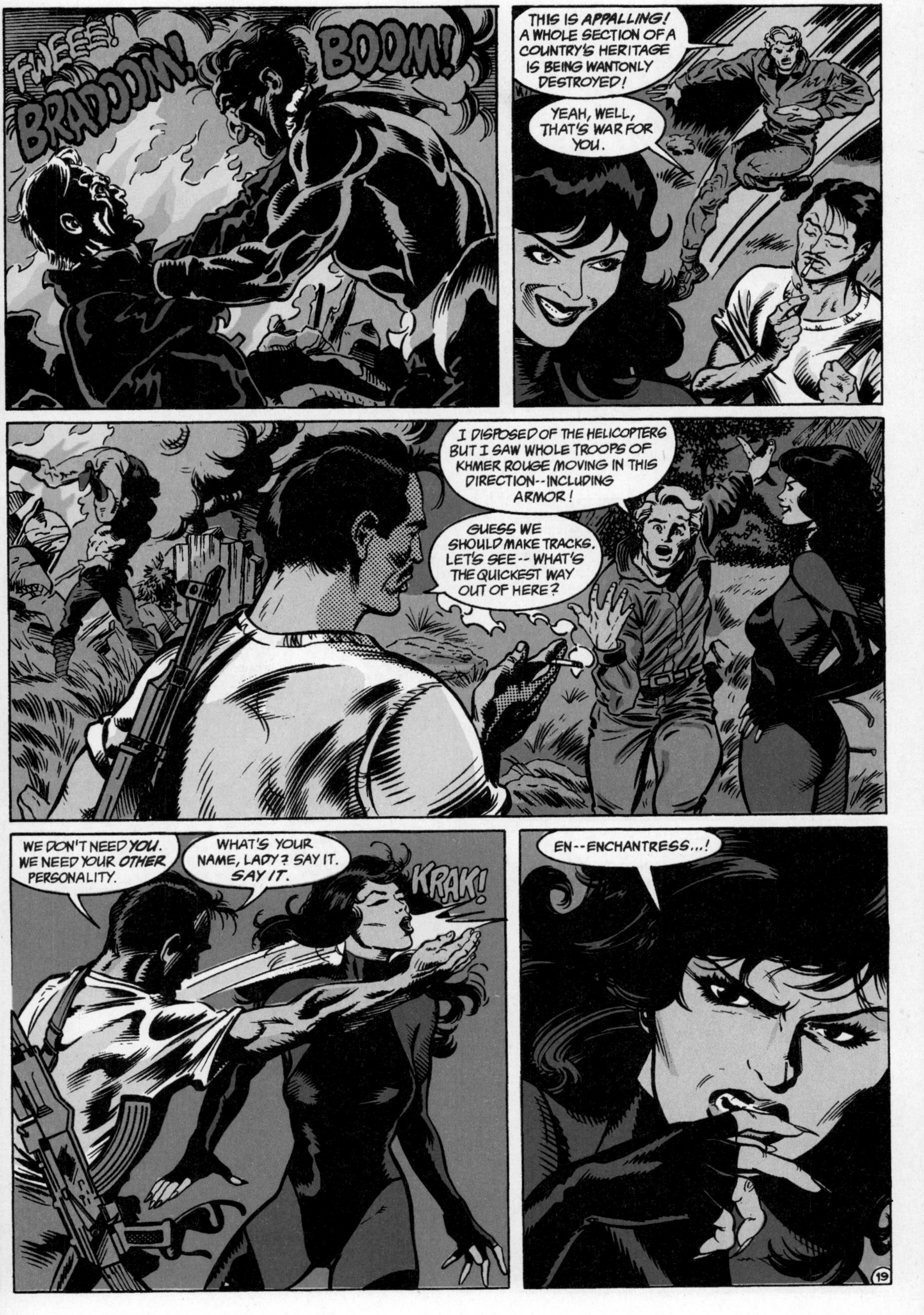
FWEEEE!
BRADOOOM!
BOOM!
THIS IS APPALLING! A WHOLE SECTION OF A COUNTRY'S HERITAGE IS BEING WANTONLY DESTROYED!
YEAH, WELL, THAT'S WAR FOR YOU.
I DISPOSED OF THE HELICOPTERS BUT I SAW WHOLE TROOPS OF KHMER ROUGE MOVING IN THIS DIRECTION--INCLUDING ARMOR!
GUESS WE SHOULD MAKE TRACKS. LET'S SEE--WHAT'S THE QUICKEST WAY OUT OF HERE?
WE DON'T NEED YOU. WE NEED YOUR OTHER PERSONALITY.
WHAT'S YOUR NAME, LADY? SAY IT. SAY IT.
KRAK!
EN--ENCHANTRESS...!
19

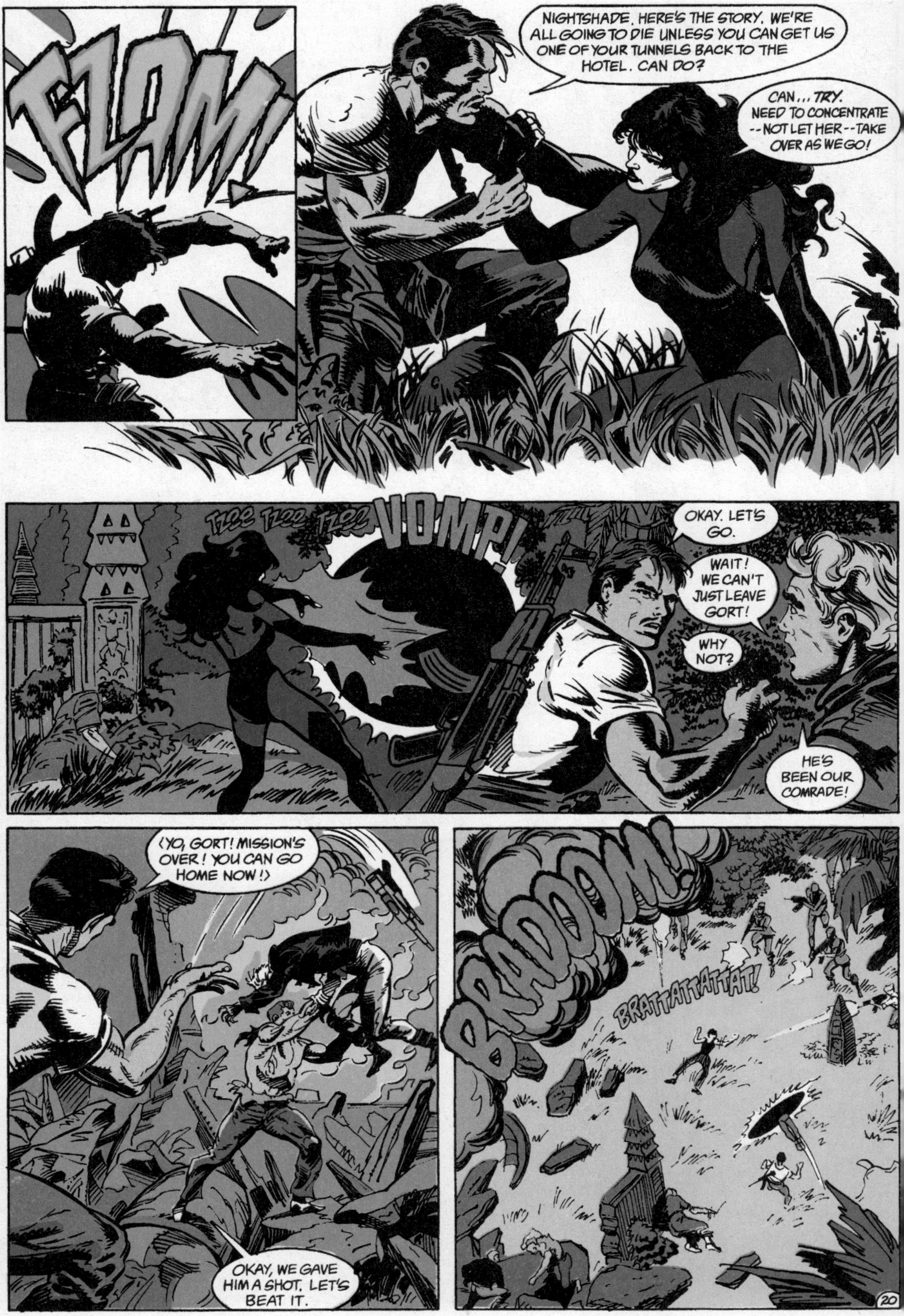
FZAM!
NIGHTSHADE. HERE'S THE STORY. WE'RE ALL GOING TO DIE UNLESS YOU CAN GET US ONE OF YOUR TUNNELS BACK TO THE HOTEL. CAN DO?
CAN... TRY. NEED TO CONCENTRATE --NOT LET HER--TAKE OVER AS WE GO!
TZEE TZEE TZEE
VOMP!
OKAY. LET'S GO.
WAIT! WE CAN'T JUST LEAVE GORT!
WHY NOT?
HE'S BEEN OUR COMRADE!
‹YO, GORT! MISSION'S OVER! YOU CAN GO HOME NOW!›
OKAY, WE GAVE HIM A SHOT. LET'S BEAT IT.
BRADOOOM!
BRATTATTATTAT!
20

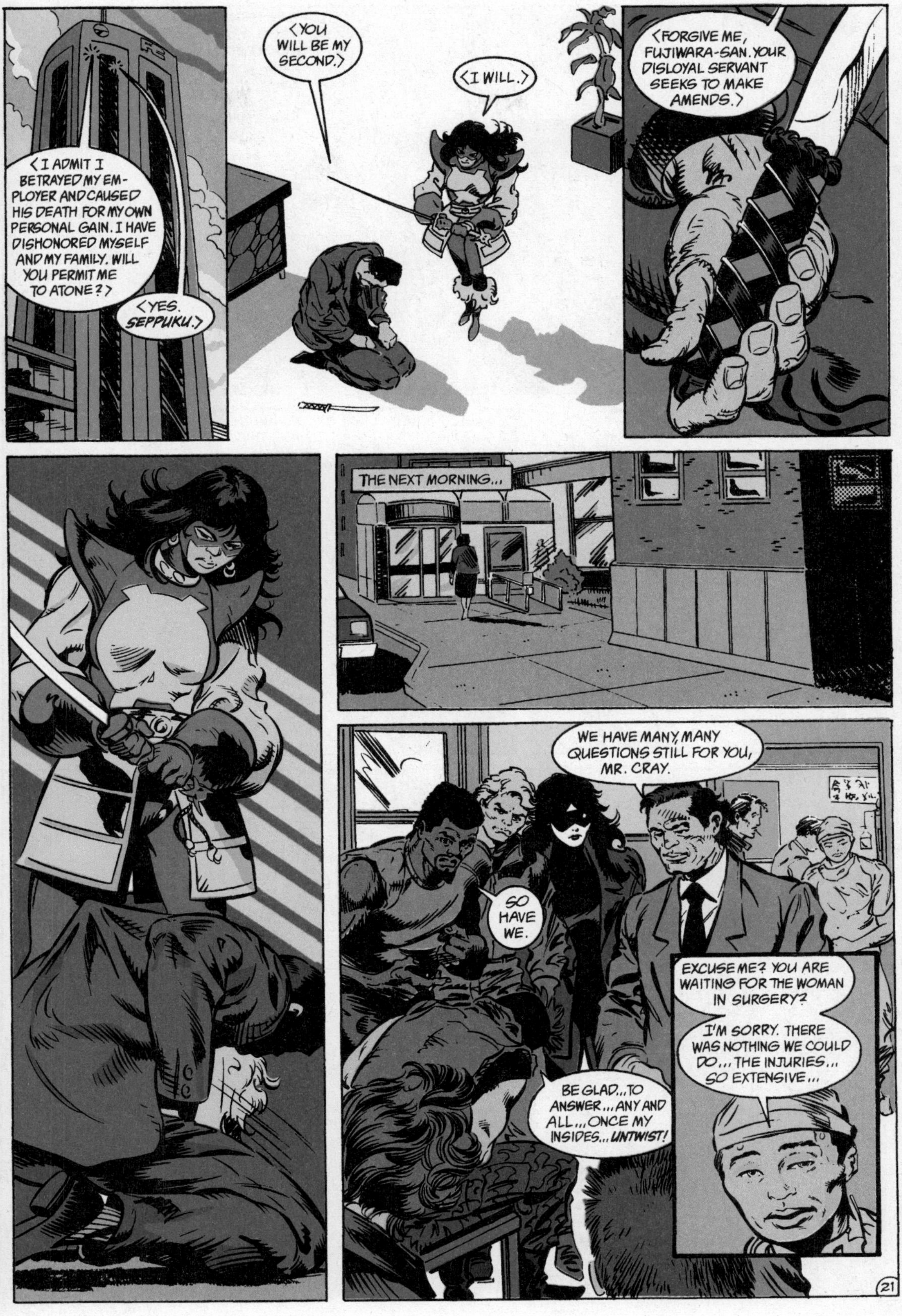

<I ADMIT I BETRAYED MY EMPLOYER AND CAUSED HIS DEATH FOR MY OWN PERSONAL GAIN. I HAVE DISHONORED MYSELF AND MY FAMILY. WILL YOU PERMIT ME TO ATONE?>
<YES. SEPPUKU.>
<YOU WILL BE MY SECOND.>
<I WILL.>
<FORGIVE ME, FUJIWARA-SAN. YOUR DISLOYAL SERVANT SEEKS TO MAKE AMENDS.>
THE NEXT MORNING...
WE HAVE MANY, MANY QUESTIONS STILL FOR YOU, MR. CRAY.
SO HAVE WE.
BE GLAD... TO ANSWER... ANY AND ALL... ONCE MY INSIDES... UNTWIST!
EXCUSE ME? YOU ARE WAITING FOR THE WOMAN IN SURGERY?
I'M SORRY. THERE WAS NOTHING WE COULD DO... THE INJURIES... SO EXTENSIVE...
21

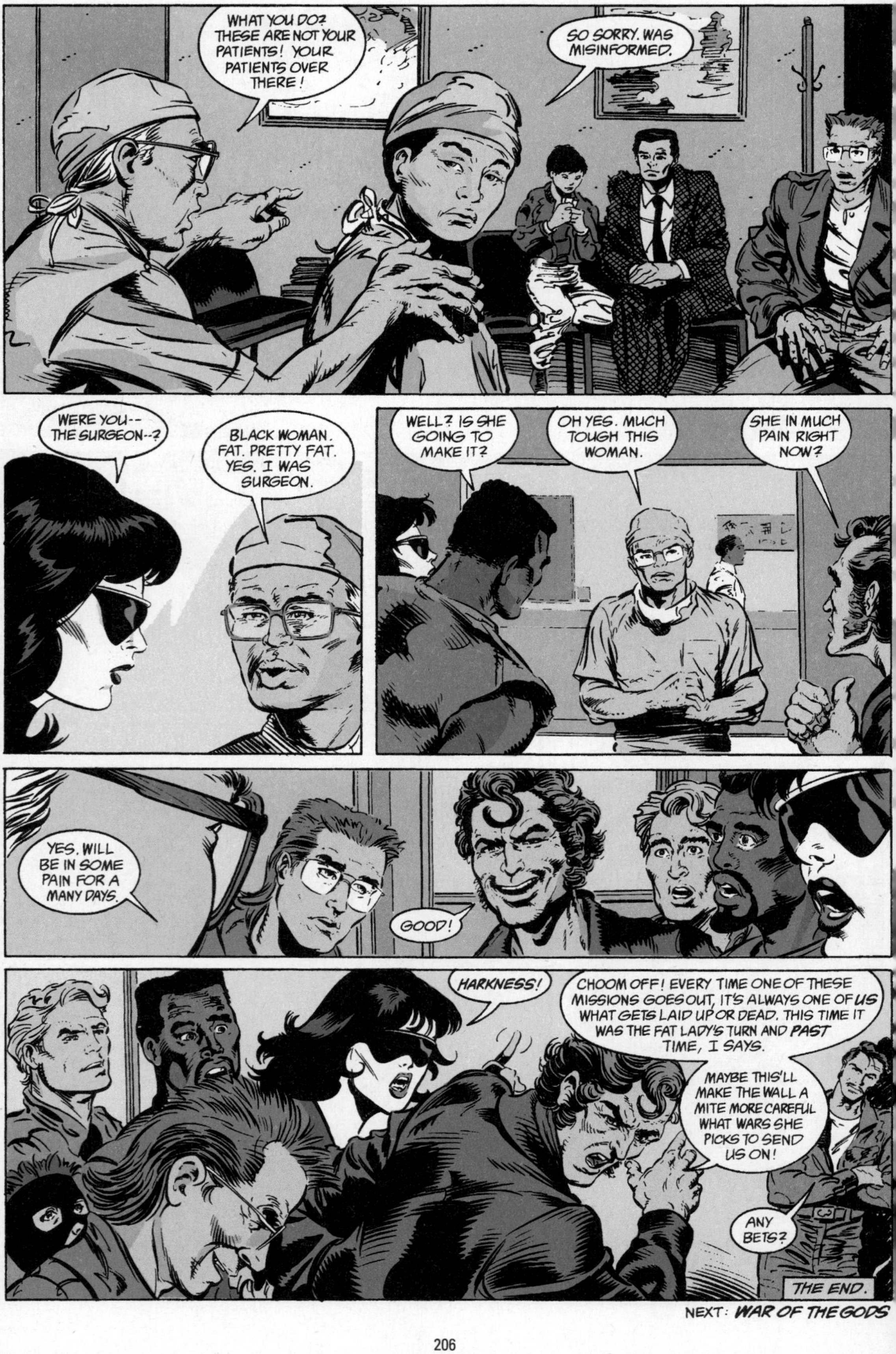
WHAT YOU DO? THESE ARE NOT YOUR PATIENTS! YOUR PATIENTS OVER THERE!
SO SORRY. WAS MISINFORMED.
WERE YOU-- THE SURGEON--?
BLACK WOMAN. FAT. PRETTY FAT. YES. I WAS SURGEON.
WELL? IS SHE GOING TO MAKE IT?
OH YES. MUCH TOUGH THIS WOMAN.
SHE IN MUCH PAIN RIGHT NOW?
YES. WILL BE IN SOME PAIN FOR A MANY DAYS.
GOOD!
HARKNESS!
CHOOM OFF! EVERY TIME ONE OF THESE MISSIONS GOES OUT, IT'S ALWAYS ONE OF US WHAT GETS LAID UP OR DEAD. THIS TIME IT WAS THE FAT LADY'S TURN AND PAST TIME, I SAYS.
MAYBE THIS'LL MAKE THE WALL A MITE MORE CAREFUL WHAT WARS SHE PICKS TO SEND US ON!
ANY BETS?
THE END.

NEXT: ***WAR OF THE GODS***

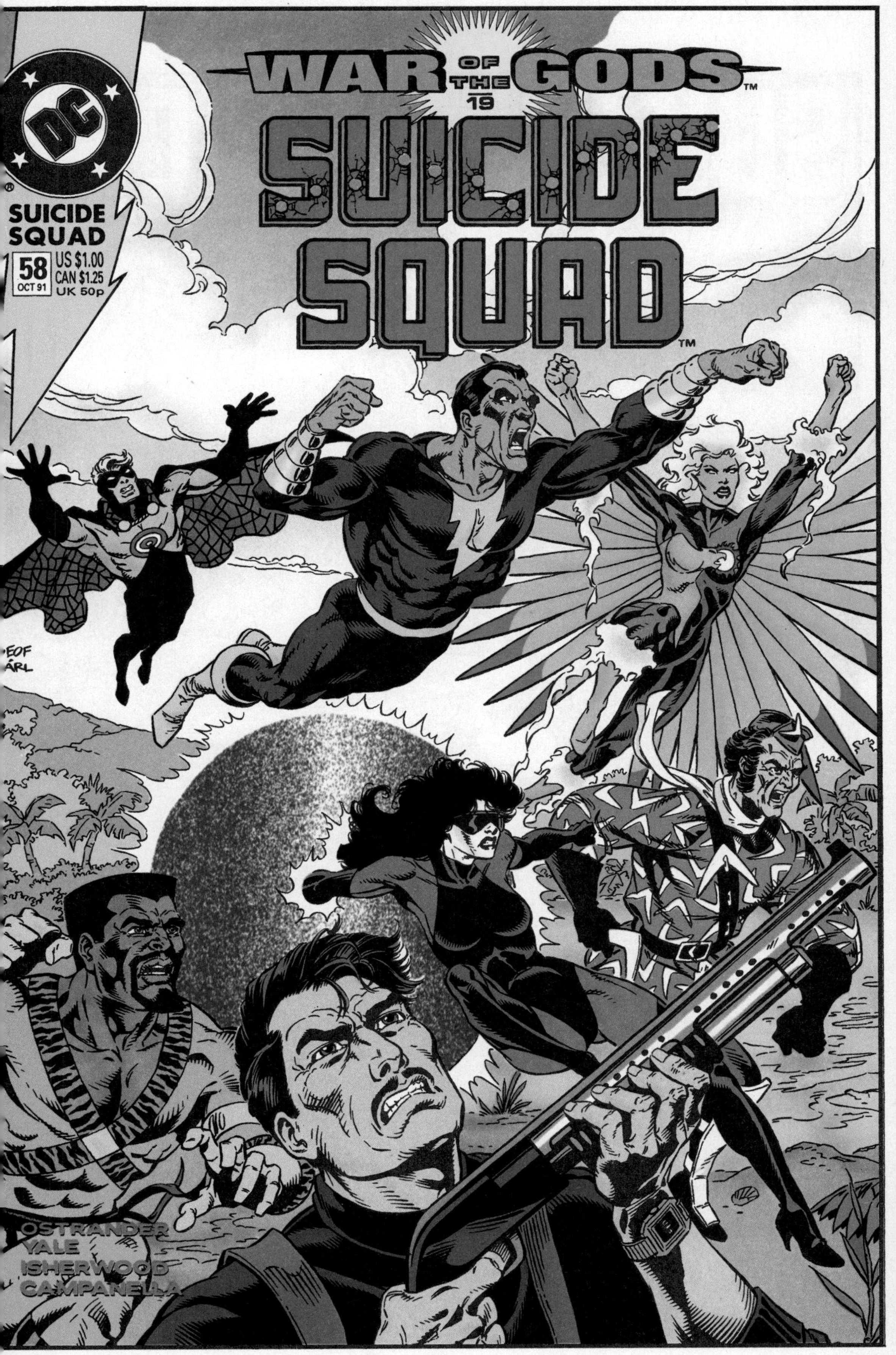

WAR OF THE GODS 19
SUICIDE SQUAD
SUICIDE SQUAD
58 OCT 91
US $1.00 CAN $1.25 UK 50p
OSTRANDER
YALE
ISHERWOOD
CAMPANELLA

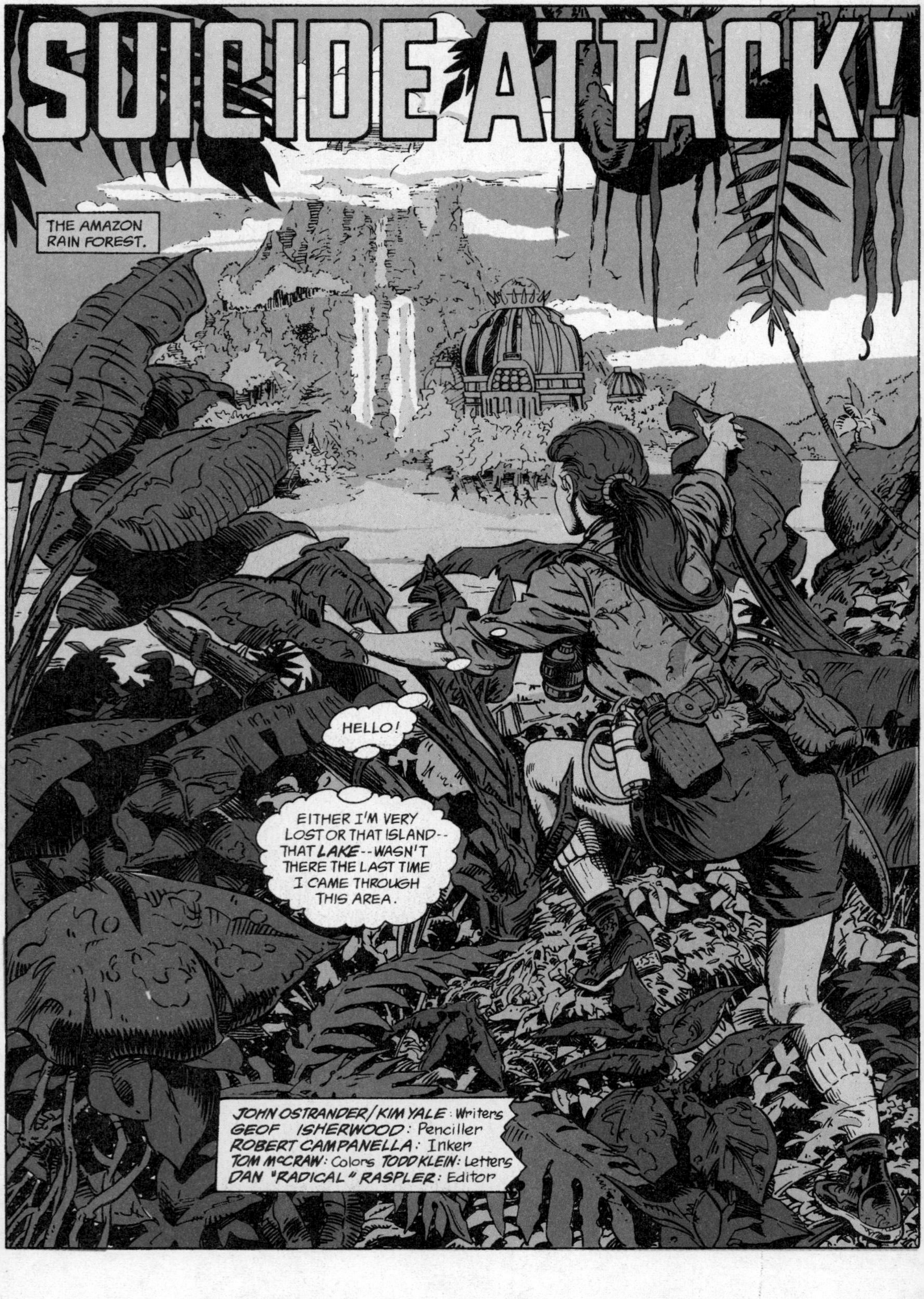
SUICIDE ATTACK!
THE AMAZON RAIN FOREST.
HELLO!
EITHER I'M VERY LOST OR THAT ISLAND-- THAT LAKE--WASN'T THERE THE LAST TIME I CAME THROUGH THIS AREA.
JOHN OSTRANDER/KIM YALE: Writers
GEOF ISHERWOOD: Penciller
ROBERT CAMPANELLA: Inker
TOM McCRAW: Colors TODD KLEIN: Letters
DAN "RADICAL" RASPLER: Editor

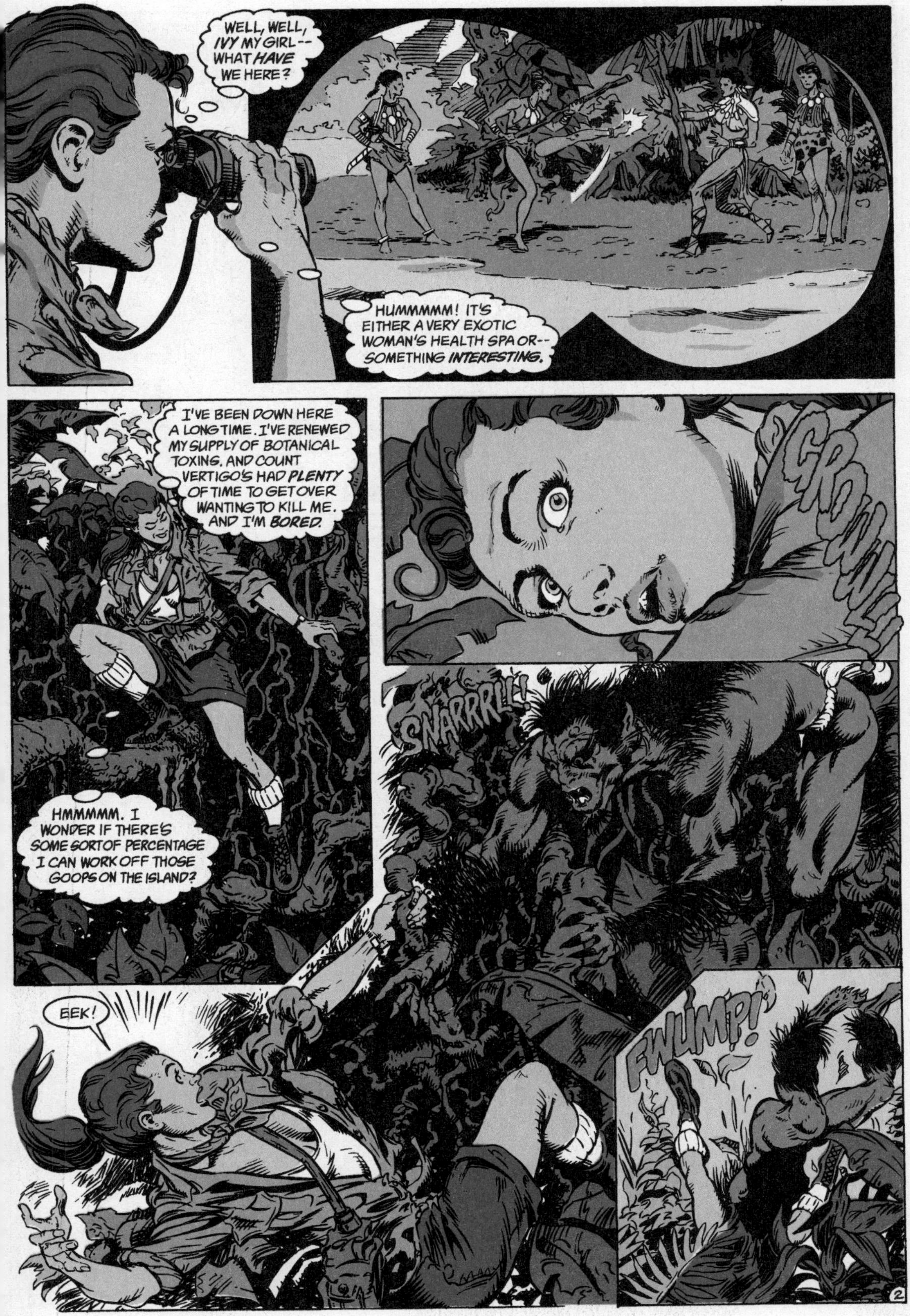
WELL, WELL, IVY MY GIRL-- WHAT HAVE WE HERE?
HUMMMMM! IT'S EITHER A VERY EXOTIC WOMAN'S HEALTH SPA OR-- SOMETHING INTERESTING.
I'VE BEEN DOWN HERE A LONG TIME. I'VE RENEWED MY SUPPLY OF BOTANICAL TOXINS. AND COUNT VERTIGO'S HAD PLENTY OF TIME TO GET OVER WANTING TO KILL ME. AND I'M BORED.
HMMMMM. I WONDER IF THERE'S SOME SORT OF PERCENTAGE I CAN WORK OFF THOSE GOOPS ON THE ISLAND?
GROWLLL!
SNARRRLL!
EEK!
FWUMP!
2

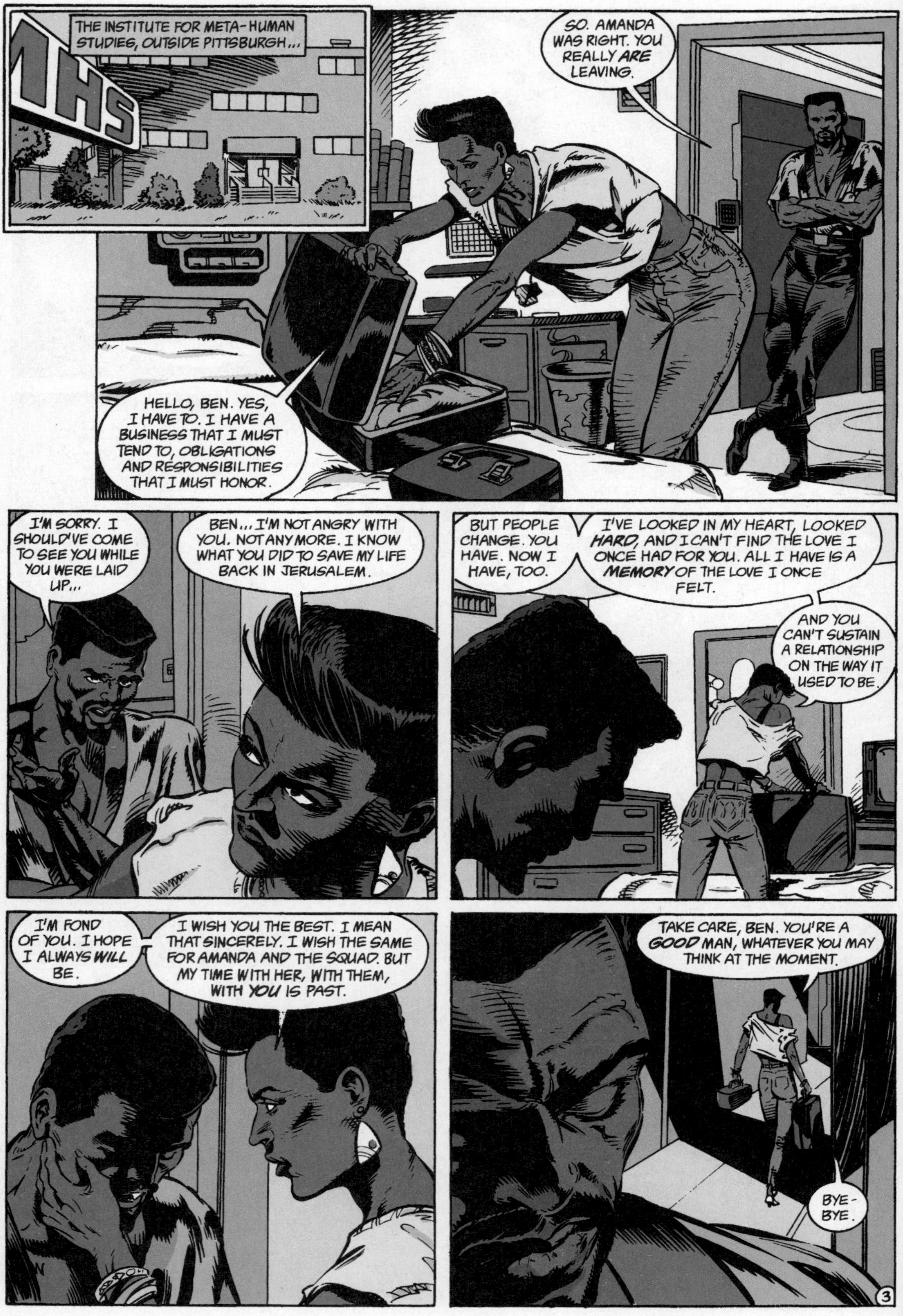
THE INSTITUTE FOR META-HUMAN STUDIES, OUTSIDE PITTSBURGH...
IHS
SO. AMANDA WAS RIGHT. YOU REALLY ARE LEAVING.
HELLO, BEN. YES, I HAVE TO. I HAVE A BUSINESS THAT I MUST TEND TO, OBLIGATIONS AND RESPONSIBILITIES THAT I MUST HONOR.
I'M SORRY. I SHOULD'VE COME TO SEE YOU WHILE YOU WERE LAID UP...
BEN... I'M NOT ANGRY WITH YOU. NOT ANYMORE. I KNOW WHAT YOU DID TO SAVE MY LIFE BACK IN JERUSALEM.
BUT PEOPLE CHANGE. YOU HAVE. NOW I HAVE, TOO.
I'VE LOOKED IN MY HEART, LOOKED HARD, AND I CAN'T FIND THE LOVE I ONCE HAD FOR YOU. ALL I HAVE IS A MEMORY OF THE LOVE I ONCE FELT.
AND YOU CAN'T SUSTAIN A RELATIONSHIP ON THE WAY IT USED TO BE.
I'M FOND OF YOU. I HOPE I ALWAYS WILL BE.
I WISH YOU THE BEST. I MEAN THAT SINCERELY. I WISH THE SAME FOR AMANDA AND THE SQUAD. BUT MY TIME WITH HER, WITH THEM, WITH YOU IS PAST.
TAKE CARE, BEN. YOU'RE A GOOD MAN, WHATEVER YOU MAY THINK AT THE MOMENT.
BYE-BYE.
3

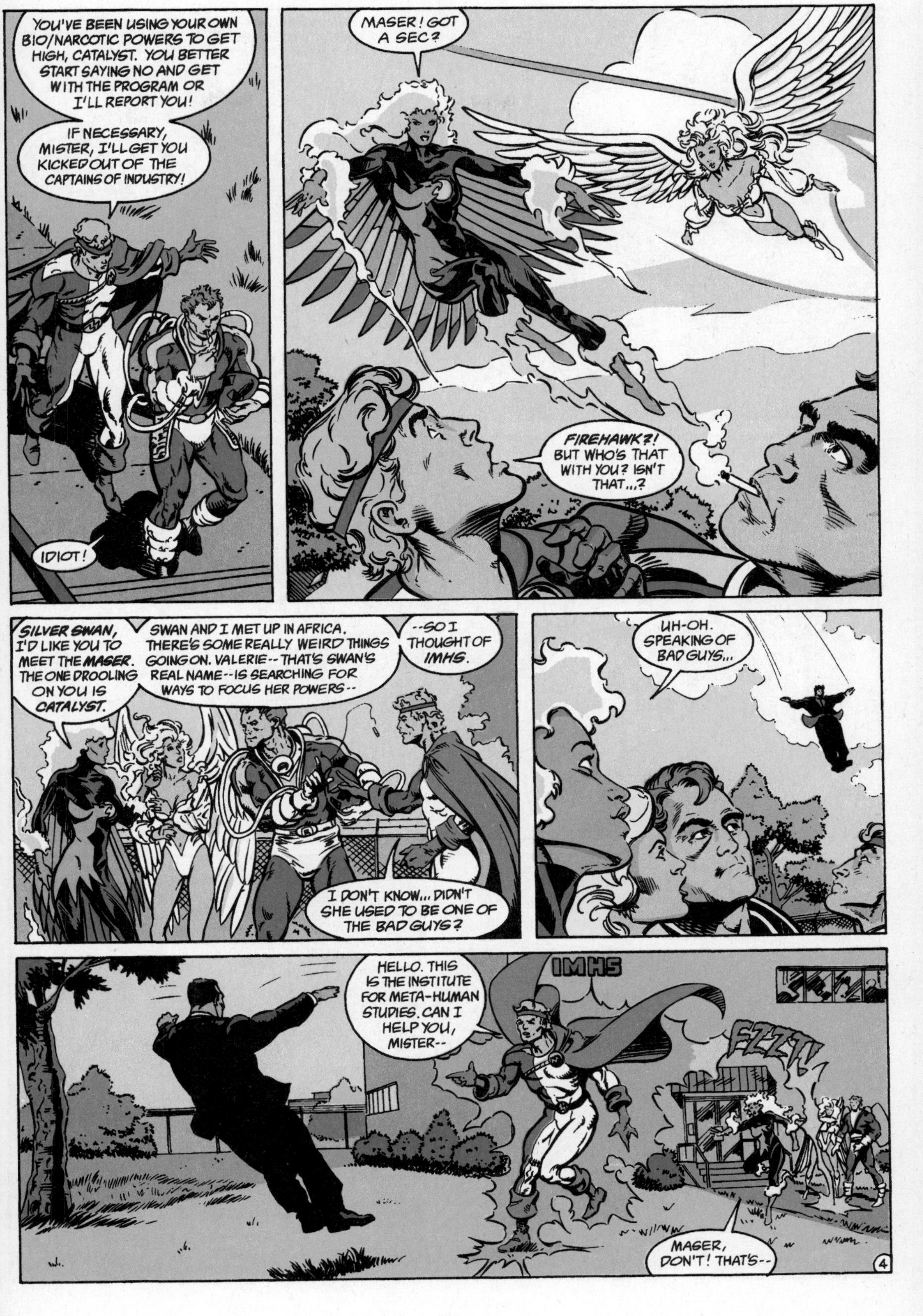

YOU'VE BEEN USING YOUR OWN BIO/NARCOTIC POWERS TO GET HIGH, CATALYST. YOU BETTER START SAYING NO AND GET WITH THE PROGRAM OR I'LL REPORT YOU!
IF NECESSARY, MISTER, I'LL GET YOU KICKED OUT OF THE CAPTAINS OF INDUSTRY!
IDIOT!
MASER! GOT A SEC?
FIREHAWK?! BUT WHO'S THAT WITH YOU? ISN'T THAT...?
SILVER SWAN, I'D LIKE YOU TO MEET THE MASER. THE ONE DROOLING ON YOU IS CATALYST.
SWAN AND I MET UP IN AFRICA. THERE'S SOME REALLY WEIRD THINGS GOING ON. VALERIE-- THAT'S SWAN'S REAL NAME--IS SEARCHING FOR WAYS TO FOCUS HER POWERS--
--SO I THOUGHT OF IMHS.
I DON'T KNOW... DIDN'T SHE USED TO BE ONE OF THE BAD GUYS?
UH-OH. SPEAKING OF BAD GUYS...
IMHS
HELLO. THIS IS THE INSTITUTE FOR META-HUMAN STUDIES. CAN I HELP YOU, MISTER--
FZZT!
MASER, DON'T! THAT'S--
4

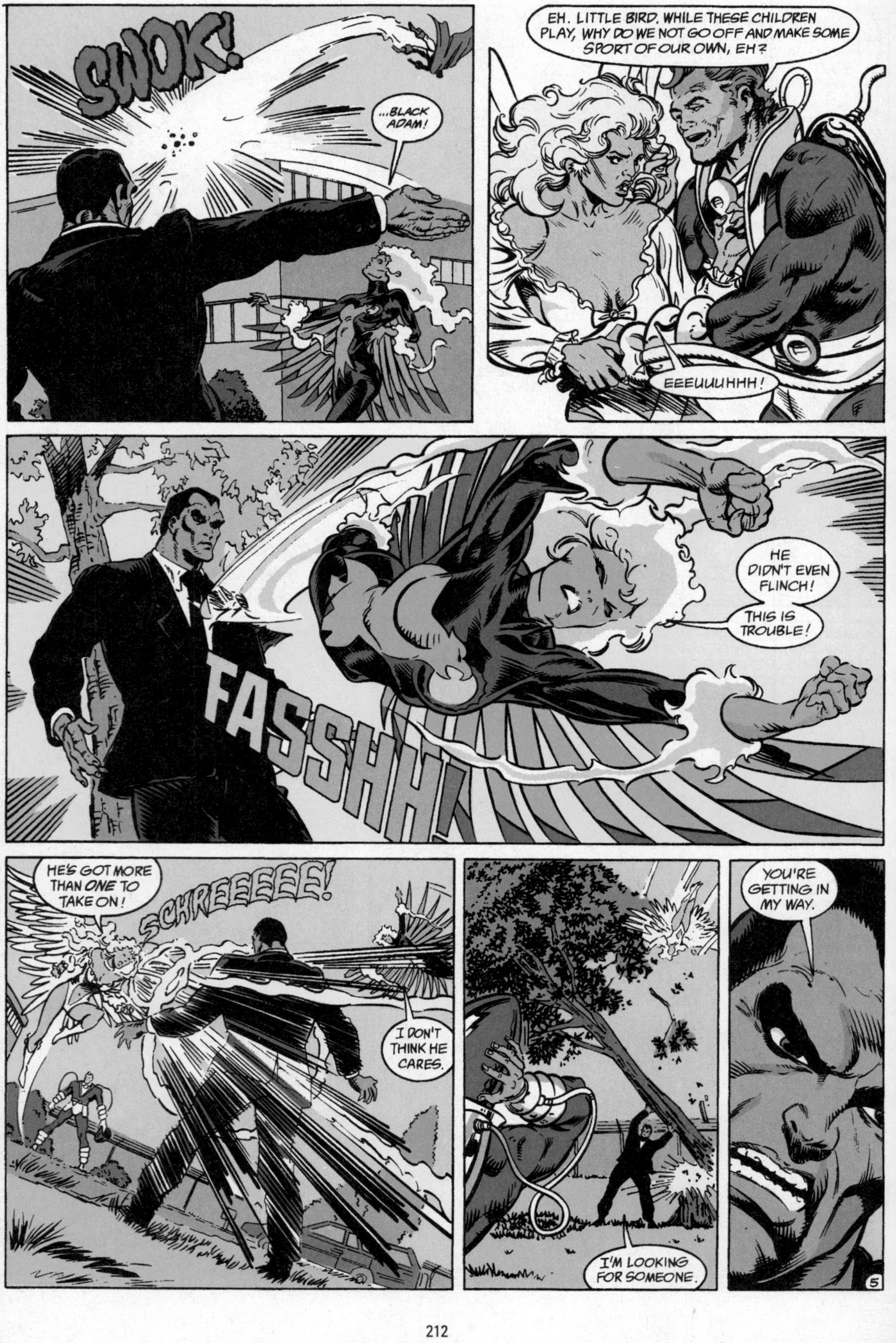
SWOK!
...BLACK ADAM!
EH. LITTLE BIRD, WHILE THESE CHILDREN PLAY, WHY DO WE NOT GO OFF AND MAKE SOME SPORT OF OUR OWN, EH?
EEEUUUHHH!
HE DIDN'T EVEN FLINCH!
THIS IS TROUBLE!
FASSHH!
HE'S GOT MORE THAN ONE TO TAKE ON!
SCHREEEEEE!
I DON'T THINK HE CARES.
I'M LOOKING FOR SOMEONE.
YOU'RE GETTING IN MY WAY.
5

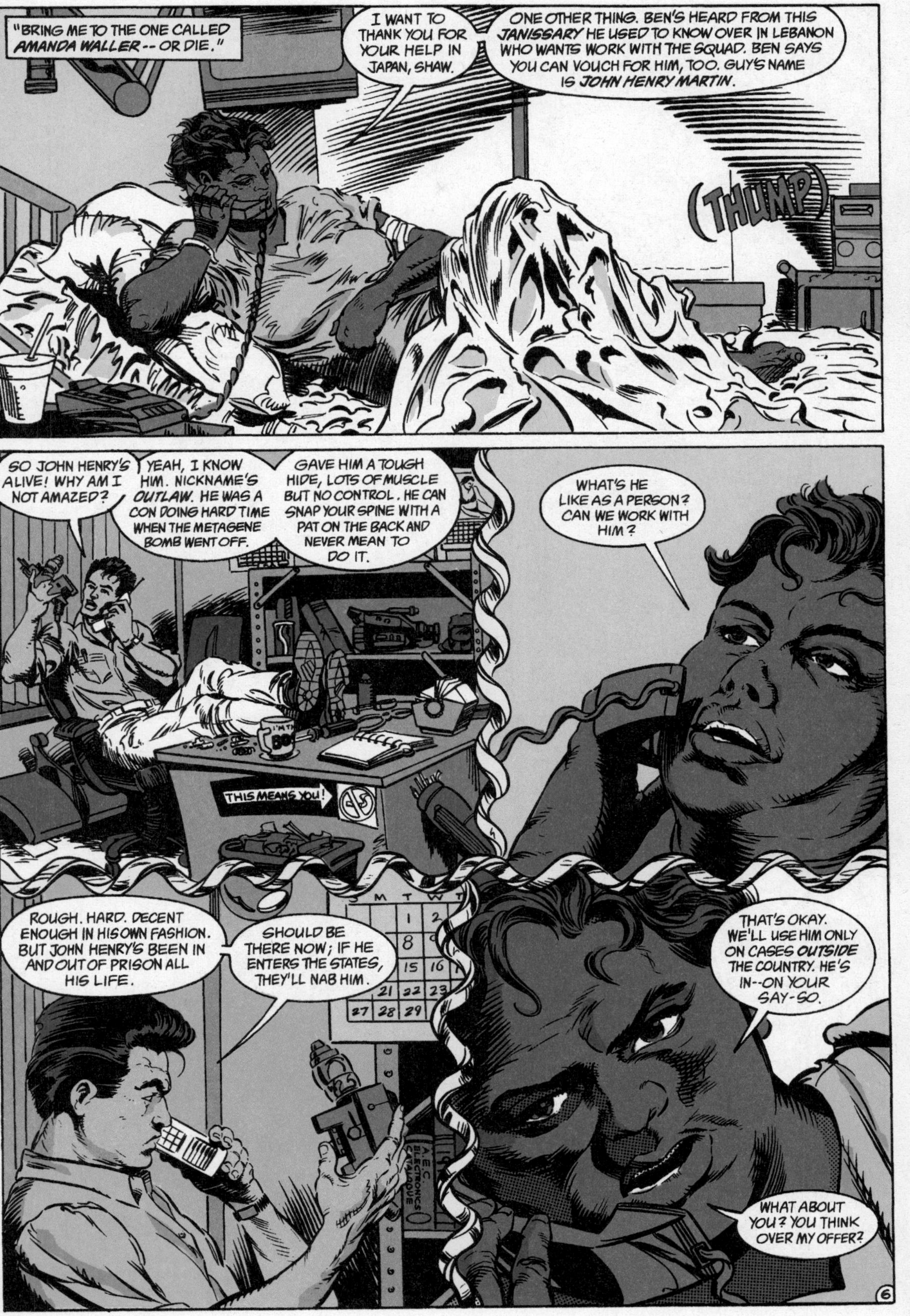
"BRING ME TO THE ONE CALLED AMANDA WALLER -- OR DIE."
I WANT TO THANK YOU FOR YOUR HELP IN JAPAN, SHAW.
ONE OTHER THING. BEN'S HEARD FROM THIS JANISSARY HE USED TO KNOW OVER IN LEBANON WHO WANTS WORK WITH THE SQUAD. BEN SAYS YOU CAN VOUCH FOR HIM, TOO. GUY'S NAME IS JOHN HENRY MARTIN.
(THUMP)
SO JOHN HENRY'S ALIVE! WHY AM I NOT AMAZED?
YEAH, I KNOW HIM. NICKNAME'S OUTLAW. HE WAS A CON DOING HARD TIME WHEN THE METAGENE BOMB WENT OFF.
GAVE HIM A TOUGH HIDE, LOTS OF MUSCLE BUT NO CONTROL. HE CAN SNAP YOUR SPINE WITH A PAT ON THE BACK AND NEVER MEAN TO DO IT.
WHAT'S HE LIKE AS A PERSON? CAN WE WORK WITH HIM?
THIS MEANS YOU!
ROUGH. HARD. DECENT ENOUGH IN HIS OWN FASHION. BUT JOHN HENRY'S BEEN IN AND OUT OF PRISON ALL HIS LIFE.
SHOULD BE THERE NOW; IF HE ENTERS THE STATES, THEY'LL NAB HIM.
THAT'S OKAY. WE'LL USE HIM ONLY ON CASES OUTSIDE THE COUNTRY. HE'S IN--ON YOUR SAY-SO.
WHAT ABOUT YOU? YOU THINK OVER MY OFFER?
6

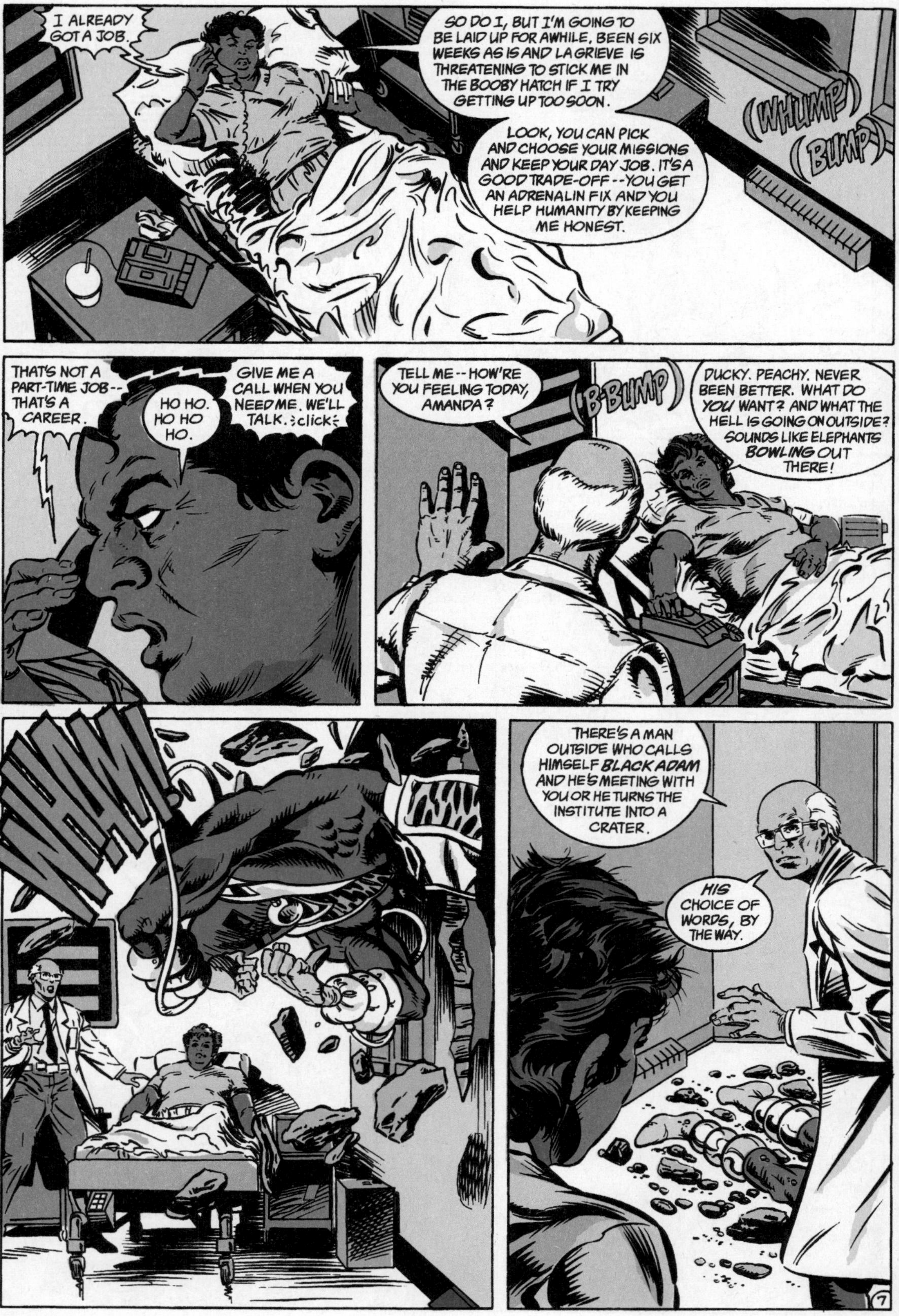
I ALREADY GOT A JOB.
SO DO I, BUT I'M GOING TO BE LAID UP FOR AWHILE. BEEN SIX WEEKS AS IS AND LA GRIEVE IS THREATENING TO STICK ME IN THE BOOBY HATCH IF I TRY GETTING UP TOO SOON.
LOOK, YOU CAN PICK AND CHOOSE YOUR MISSIONS AND KEEP YOUR DAY JOB. IT'S A GOOD TRADE-OFF--YOU GET AN ADRENALIN FIX AND YOU HELP HUMANITY BY KEEPING ME HONEST.
(WHUMP)
(BUMP)
THAT'S NOT A PART-TIME JOB--THAT'S A CAREER.
HO HO. HO HO HO HO.
GIVE ME A CALL WHEN YOU NEED ME. WE'LL TALK. ⋛click⋚
TELL ME--HOW'RE YOU FEELING TODAY, AMANDA?
(B-BUMP)
DUCKY. PEACHY. NEVER BEEN BETTER. WHAT DO YOU WANT? AND WHAT THE HELL IS GOING ON OUTSIDE? SOUNDS LIKE ELEPHANTS BOWLING OUT THERE!
WHAM!
THERE'S A MAN OUTSIDE WHO CALLS HIMSELF BLACK ADAM AND HE'S MEETING WITH YOU OR HE TURNS THE INSTITUTE INTO A CRATER.
HIS CHOICE OF WORDS, BY THE WAY.
7

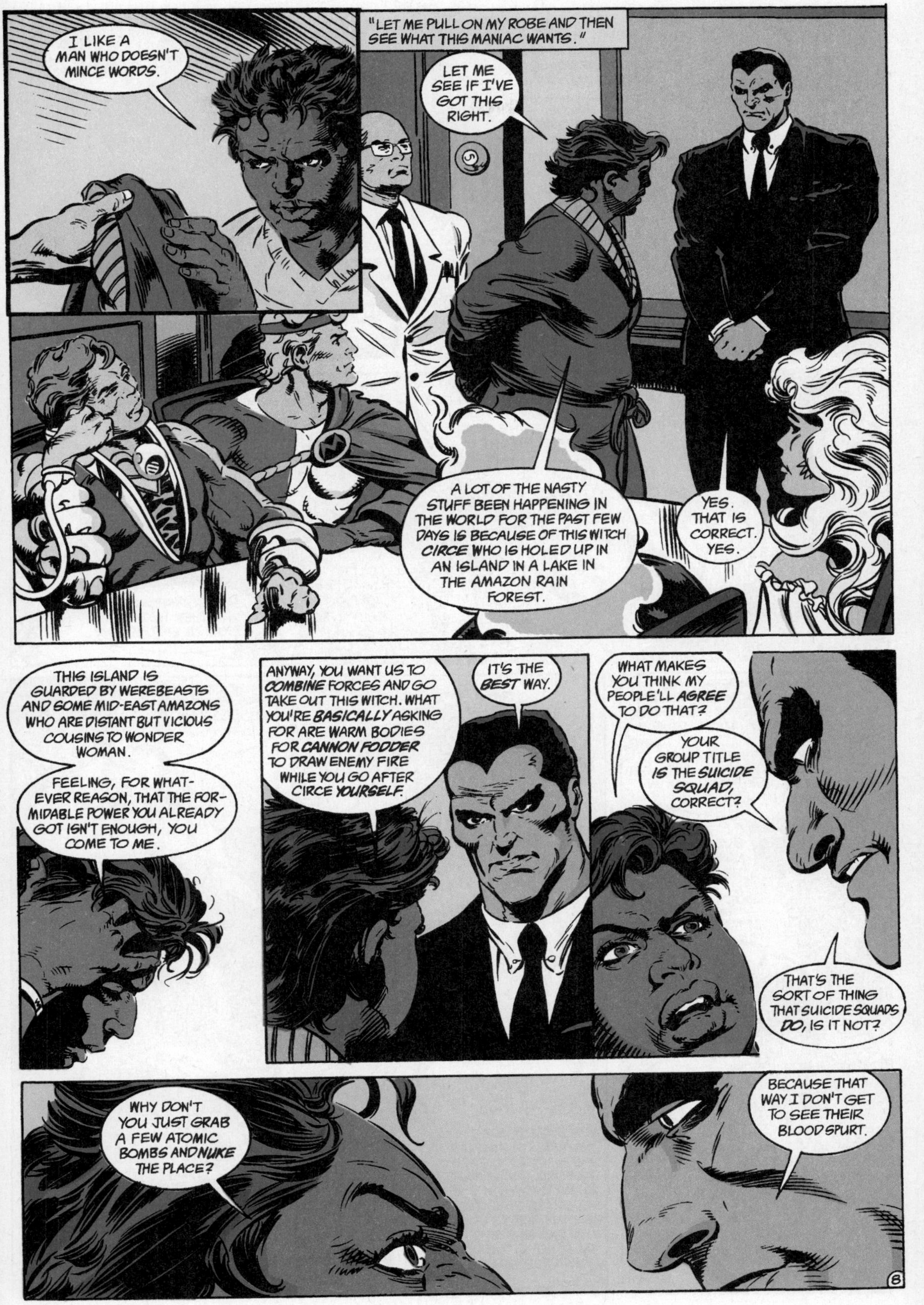
I LIKE A MAN WHO DOESN'T MINCE WORDS.
"LET ME PULL ON MY ROBE AND THEN SEE WHAT THIS MANIAC WANTS."
LET ME SEE IF I'VE GOT THIS RIGHT.
A LOT OF THE NASTY STUFF BEEN HAPPENING IN THE WORLD FOR THE PAST FEW DAYS IS BECAUSE OF THIS WITCH CIRCE WHO IS HOLED UP IN AN ISLAND IN A LAKE IN THE AMAZON RAIN FOREST.
YES. THAT IS CORRECT. YES.
THIS ISLAND IS GUARDED BY WEREBEASTS AND SOME MID-EAST AMAZONS WHO ARE DISTANT BUT VICIOUS COUSINS TO WONDER WOMAN.
FEELING, FOR WHATEVER REASON, THAT THE FORMIDABLE POWER YOU ALREADY GOT ISN'T ENOUGH, YOU COME TO ME.
ANYWAY, YOU WANT US TO COMBINE FORCES AND GO TAKE OUT THIS WITCH. WHAT YOU'RE BASICALLY ASKING FOR ARE WARM BODIES FOR CANNON FODDER TO DRAW ENEMY FIRE WHILE YOU GO AFTER CIRCE YOURSELF.
IT'S THE BEST WAY.
WHAT MAKES YOU THINK MY PEOPLE'LL AGREE TO DO THAT?
YOUR GROUP TITLE IS THE SUICIDE SQUAD, CORRECT?
THAT'S THE SORT OF THING THAT SUICIDE SQUADS DO, IS IT NOT?
WHY DON'T YOU JUST GRAB A FEW ATOMIC BOMBS AND NUKE THE PLACE?
BECAUSE THAT WAY I DON'T GET TO SEE THEIR BLOOD SPURT.
8

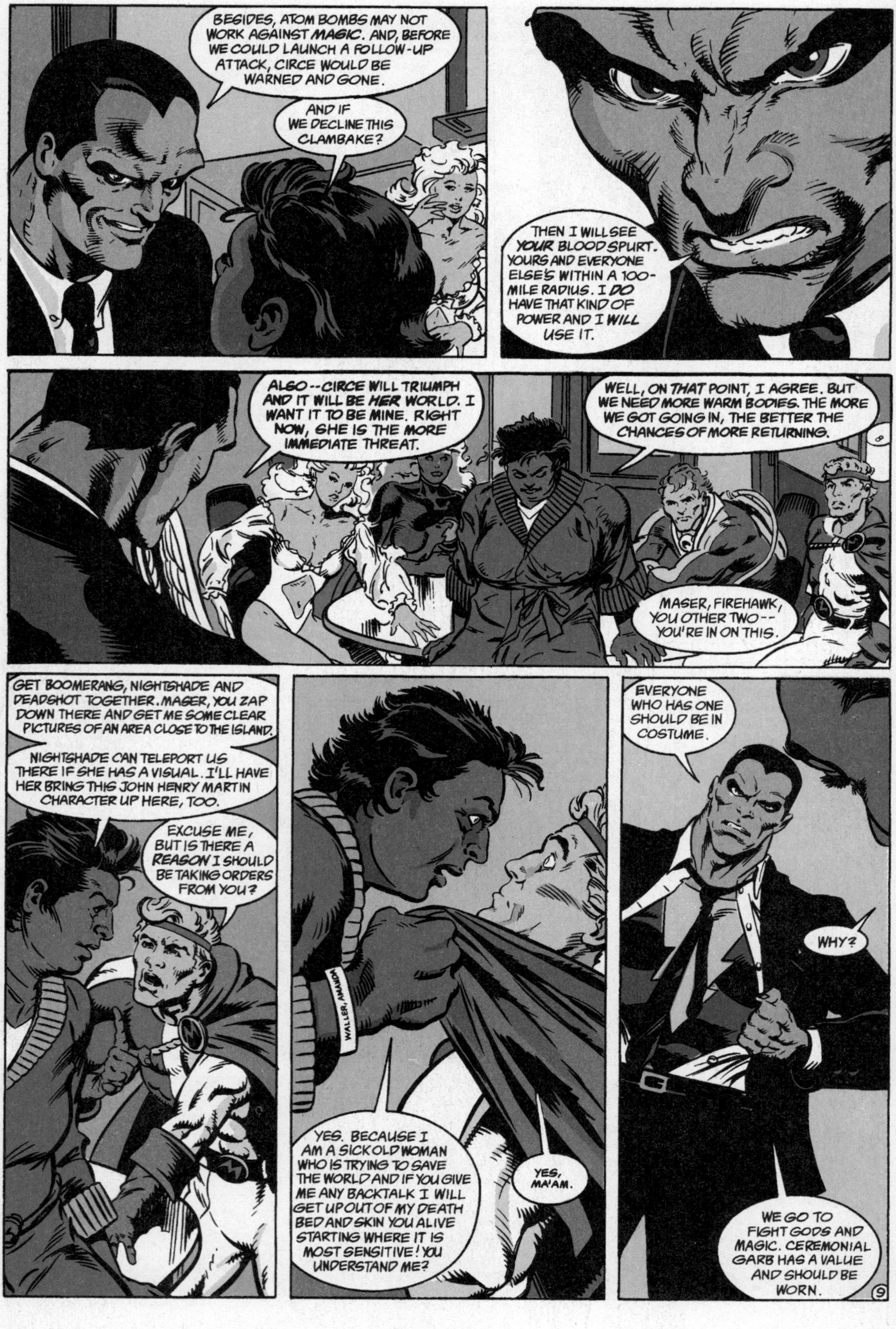

BESIDES, ATOM BOMBS MAY NOT WORK AGAINST MAGIC. AND, BEFORE WE COULD LAUNCH A FOLLOW-UP ATTACK, CIRCE WOULD BE WARNED AND GONE.
AND IF WE DECLINE THIS CLAMBAKE?
THEN I WILL SEE YOUR BLOOD SPURT. YOURS AND EVERYONE ELSE'S WITHIN A 100-MILE RADIUS. I DO HAVE THAT KIND OF POWER AND I WILL USE IT.
ALSO--CIRCE WILL TRIUMPH AND IT WILL BE HER WORLD. I WANT IT TO BE MINE. RIGHT NOW, SHE IS THE MORE IMMEDIATE THREAT.
WELL, ON THAT POINT, I AGREE. BUT WE NEED MORE WARM BODIES. THE MORE WE GOT GOING IN, THE BETTER THE CHANCES OF MORE RETURNING.
8
MASER, FIREHAWK, YOU OTHER TWO-- YOU'RE IN ON THIS.
GET BOOMERANG, NIGHTSHADE AND DEADSHOT TOGETHER. MASER, YOU ZAP DOWN THERE AND GET ME SOME CLEAR PICTURES OF AN AREA CLOSE TO THE ISLAND.
NIGHTSHADE CAN TELEPORT US THERE IF SHE HAS A VISUAL. I'LL HAVE HER BRING THIS JOHN HENRY MARTIN CHARACTER UP HERE, TOO.
EXCUSE ME, BUT IS THERE A REASON I SHOULD BE TAKING ORDERS FROM YOU?
WALLER, AMANDA
YES. BECAUSE I AM A SICK OLD WOMAN WHO IS TRYING TO SAVE THE WORLD AND IF YOU GIVE ME ANY BACKTALK I WILL GET UP OUT OF MY DEATH BED AND SKIN YOU ALIVE STARTING WHERE IT IS MOST SENSITIVE! YOU UNDERSTAND ME?
YES, MA'AM.
EVERYONE WHO HAS ONE SHOULD BE IN COSTUME.
WHY?
WE GO TO FIGHT GODS AND MAGIC. CEREMONIAL GARB HAS A VALUE AND SHOULD BE WORN.
9

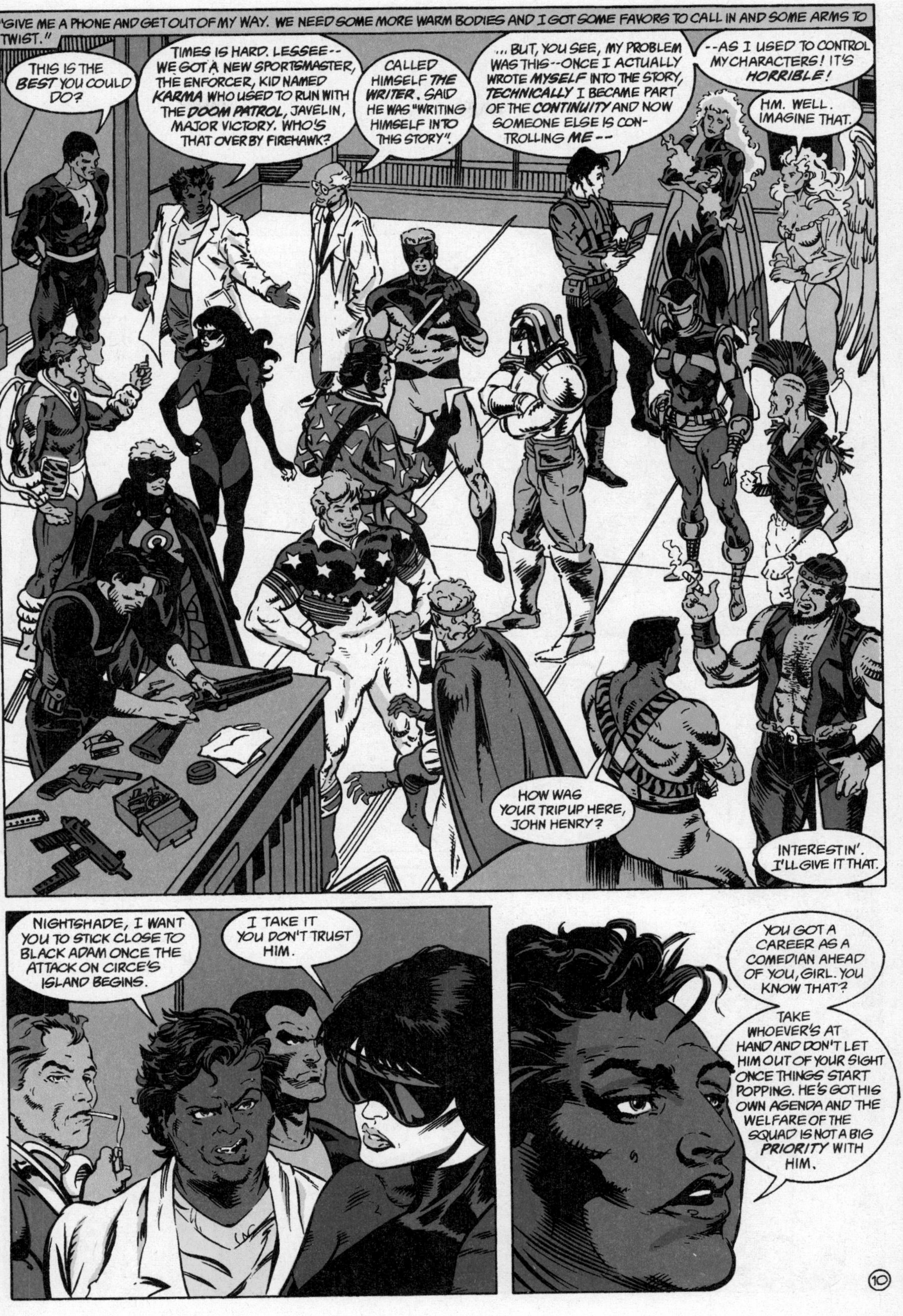
"GIVE ME A PHONE AND GET OUT OF MY WAY. WE NEED SOME MORE WARM BODIES AND I GOT SOME FAVORS TO CALL IN AND SOME ARMS TO TWIST."
THIS IS THE BEST YOU COULD DO?
TIMES IS HARD. LESSEE-- WE GOT A NEW SPORTSMASTER, THE ENFORCER, KID NAMED KARMA WHO USED TO RUN WITH THE DOOM PATROL, JAVELIN, MAJOR VICTORY. WHO'S THAT OVER BY FIREHAWK?
CALLED HIMSELF THE WRITER. SAID HE WAS "WRITING HIMSELF INTO THIS STORY".
...BUT, YOU SEE, MY PROBLEM WAS THIS--ONCE I ACTUALLY WROTE MYSELF INTO THE STORY, TECHNICALLY I BECAME PART OF THE CONTINUITY AND NOW SOMEONE ELSE IS CONTROLLING ME--
--AS I USED TO CONTROL MY CHARACTERS! IT'S HORRIBLE!
HM. WELL. IMAGINE THAT.
HOW WAS YOUR TRIP UP HERE, JOHN HENRY?
INTERESTIN'. I'LL GIVE IT THAT.
NIGHTSHADE, I WANT YOU TO STICK CLOSE TO BLACK ADAM ONCE THE ATTACK ON CIRCE'S ISLAND BEGINS.
I TAKE IT YOU DON'T TRUST HIM.
YOU GOT A CAREER AS A COMEDIAN AHEAD OF YOU, GIRL. YOU KNOW THAT?
TAKE WHOEVER'S AT HAND AND DON'T LET HIM OUT OF YOUR SIGHT ONCE THINGS START POPPING. HE'S GOT HIS OWN AGENDA AND THE WELFARE OF THE SQUAD IS NOT A BIG PRIORITY WITH HIM.
10

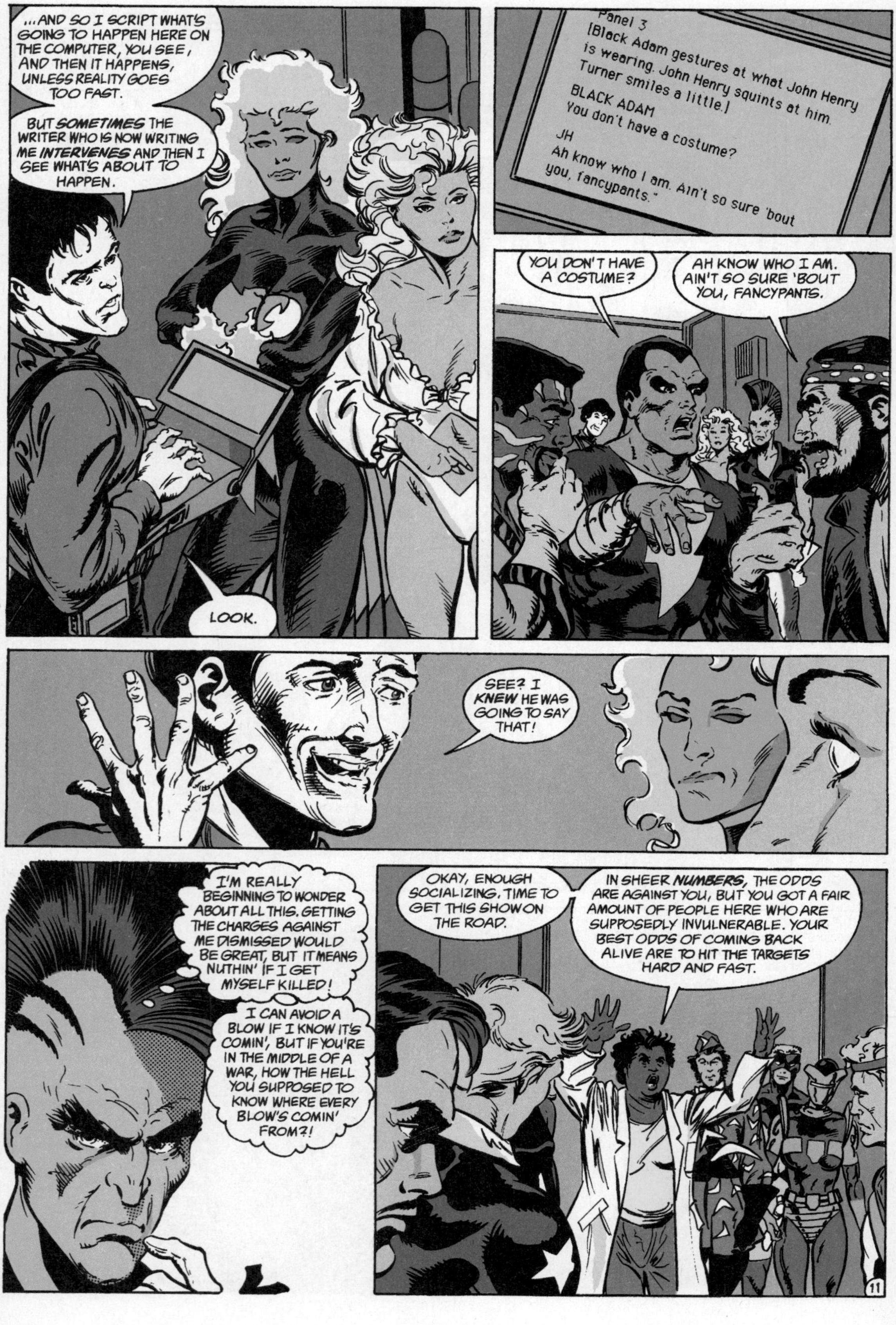
...AND SO I SCRIPT WHAT'S GOING TO HAPPEN HERE ON THE COMPUTER, YOU SEE, AND THEN IT HAPPENS, UNLESS REALITY GOES TOO FAST.
BUT SOMETIMES THE WRITER WHO IS NOW WRITING ME INTERVENES AND THEN I SEE WHAT'S ABOUT TO HAPPEN.
LOOK.
Panel 3
[Black Adam gestures at what John Henry is wearing. John Henry Turner smiles a little. John Henry squints at him.]
BLACK ADAM
You don't have a costume?
JH
Ah know who I am. Ain't so sure 'bout you, fancypants."
YOU DON'T HAVE A COSTUME?
AH KNOW WHO I AM. AIN'T SO SURE 'BOUT YOU, FANCYPANTS.
SEE? I KNEW HE WAS GOING TO SAY THAT!
I'M REALLY BEGINNING TO WONDER ABOUT ALL THIS. GETTING THE CHARGES AGAINST ME DISMISSED WOULD BE GREAT, BUT IT MEANS NUTHIN' IF I GET MYSELF KILLED!
I CAN AVOID A BLOW IF I KNOW IT'S COMIN', BUT IF YOU'RE IN THE MIDDLE OF A WAR, HOW THE HELL YOU SUPPOSED TO KNOW WHERE EVERY BLOW'S COMIN' FROM?!
OKAY, ENOUGH SOCIALIZING. TIME TO GET THIS SHOW ON THE ROAD.
IN SHEER NUMBERS, THE ODDS ARE AGAINST YOU, BUT YOU GOT A FAIR AMOUNT OF PEOPLE HERE WHO ARE SUPPOSEDLY INVULNERABLE. YOUR BEST ODDS OF COMING BACK ALIVE ARE TO HIT THE TARGETS HARD AND FAST.
11

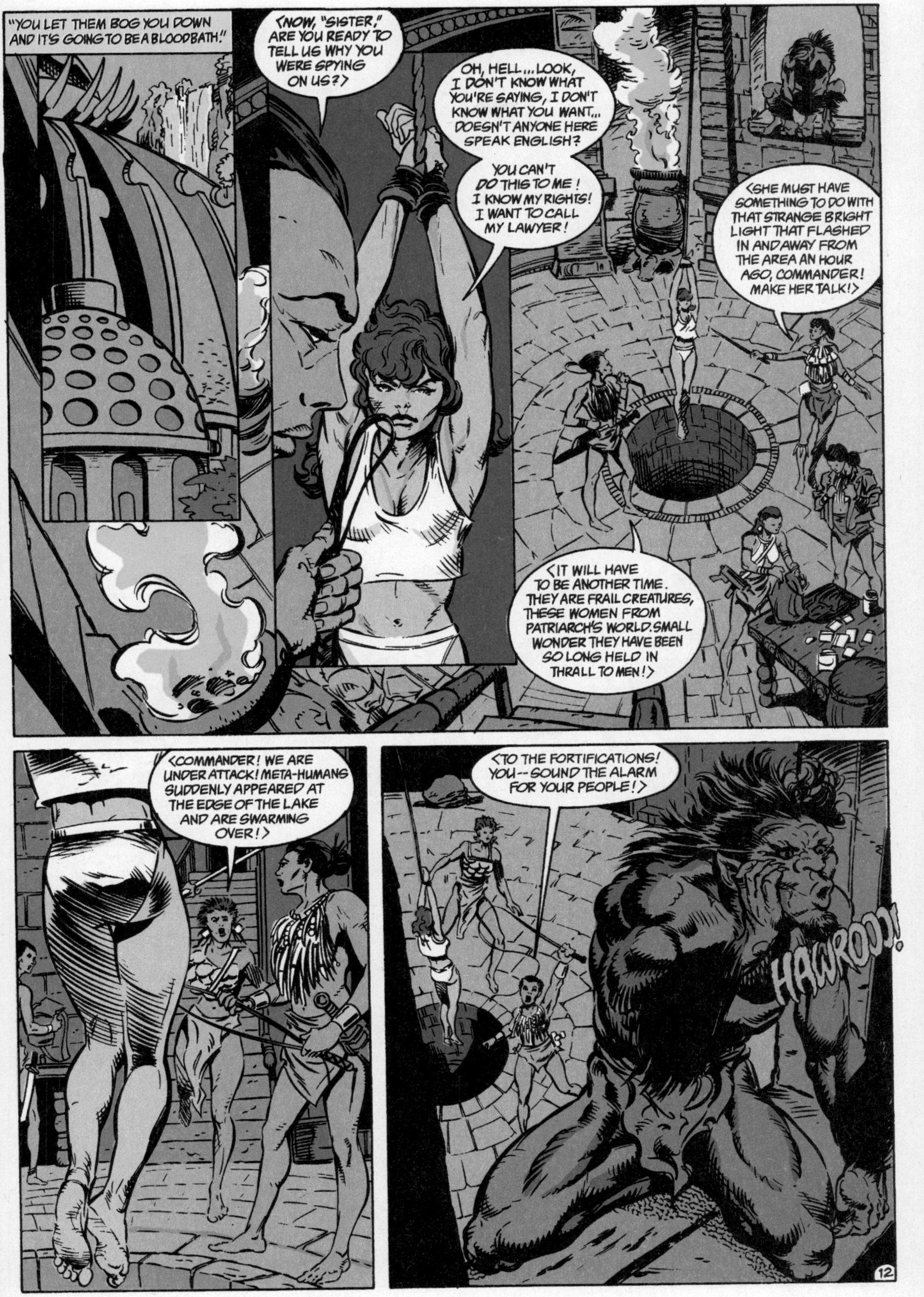
"YOU LET THEM BOG YOU DOWN AND IT'S GOING TO BE A BLOODBATH."
<NOW, "SISTER," ARE YOU READY TO TELL US WHY YOU WERE SPYING ON US?>
OH, HELL... LOOK, I DON'T KNOW WHAT YOU'RE SAYING, I DON'T KNOW WHAT YOU WANT... DOESN'T ANYONE HERE SPEAK ENGLISH?
YOU CAN'T DO THIS TO ME! I KNOW MY RIGHTS! I WANT TO CALL MY LAWYER!
<SHE MUST HAVE SOMETHING TO DO WITH THAT STRANGE BRIGHT LIGHT THAT FLASHED IN AND AWAY FROM THE AREA AN HOUR AGO, COMMANDER! MAKE HER TALK!>
<IT WILL HAVE TO BE ANOTHER TIME. THEY ARE FRAIL CREATURES, THESE WOMEN FROM PATRIARCH'S WORLD. SMALL WONDER THEY HAVE BEEN SO LONG HELD IN THRALL TO MEN!>
<COMMANDER! WE ARE UNDER ATTACK! META-HUMANS SUDDENLY APPEARED AT THE EDGE OF THE LAKE AND ARE SWARMING OVER!>
<TO THE FORTIFICATIONS! YOU -- SOUND THE ALARM FOR YOUR PEOPLE!>
HAWROOO!
12

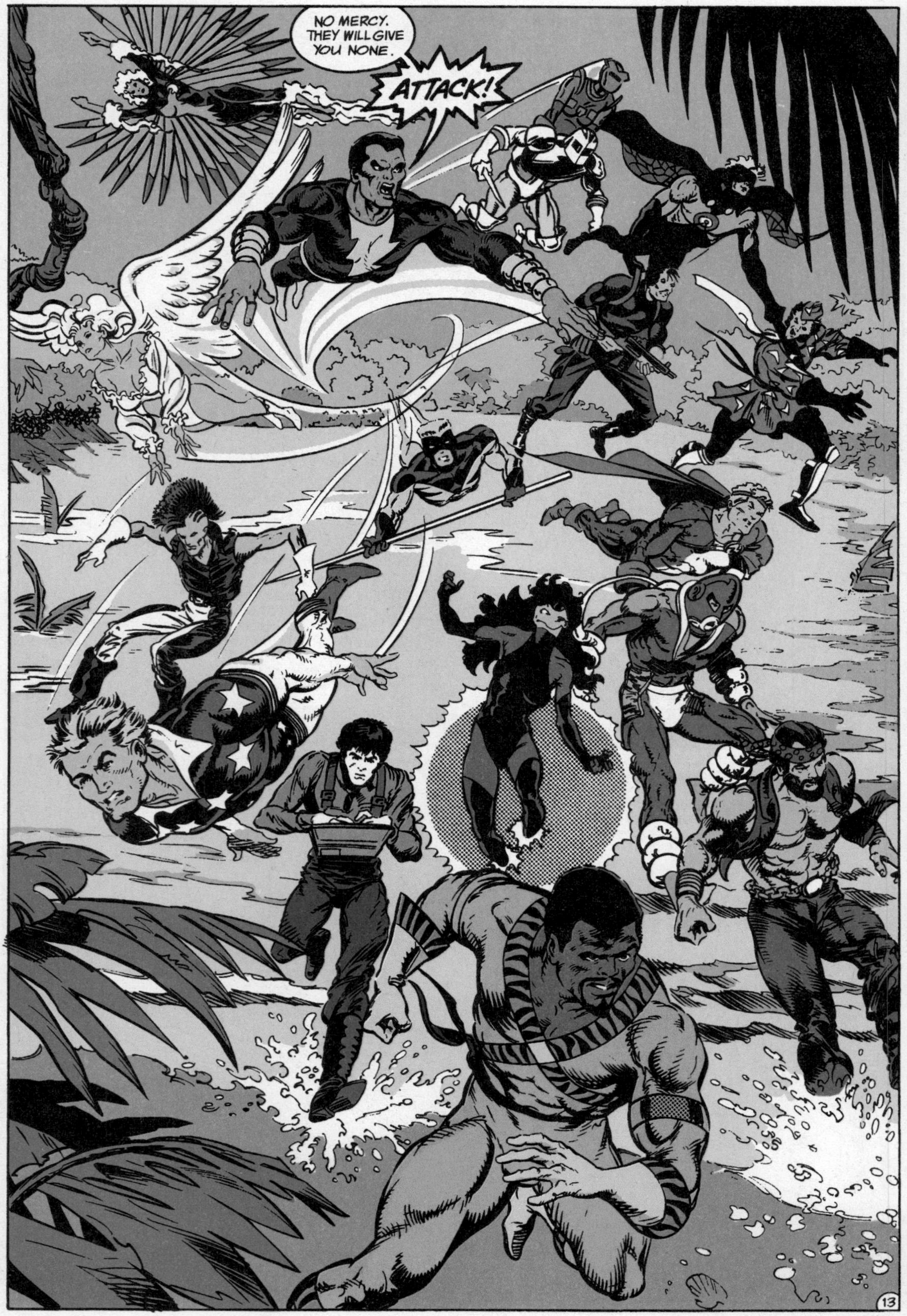
NO MERCY. THEY WILL GIVE YOU NONE.
ATTACK!
13

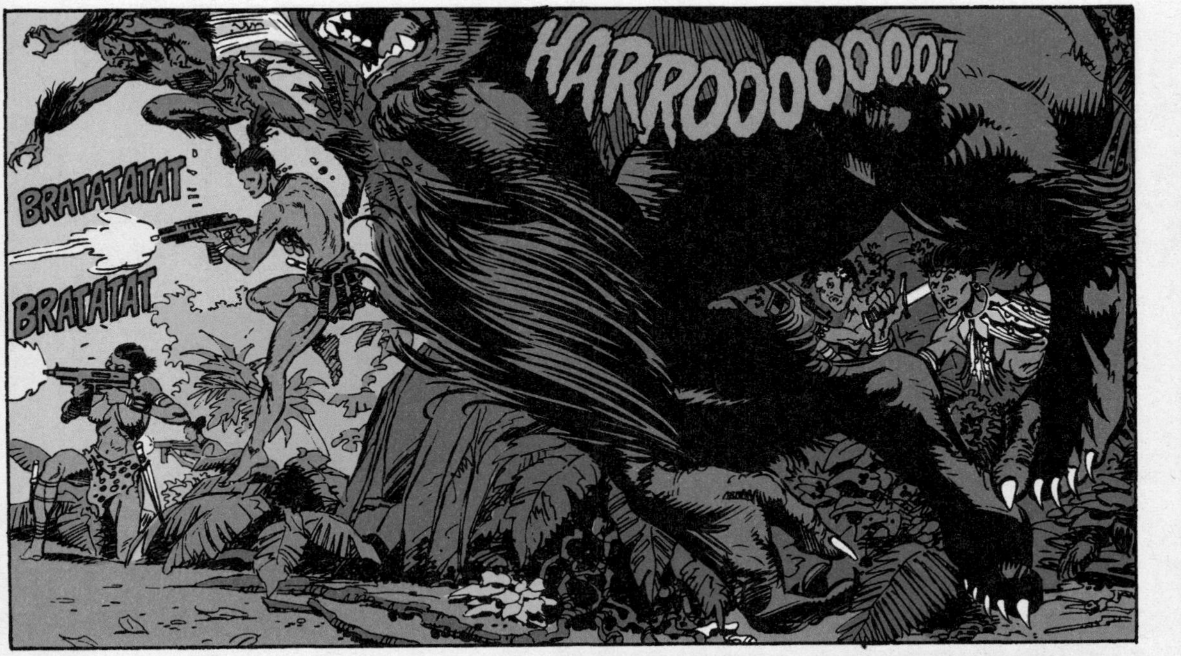
HARROOOOOOO!
BRATATATAT
BRATATAT

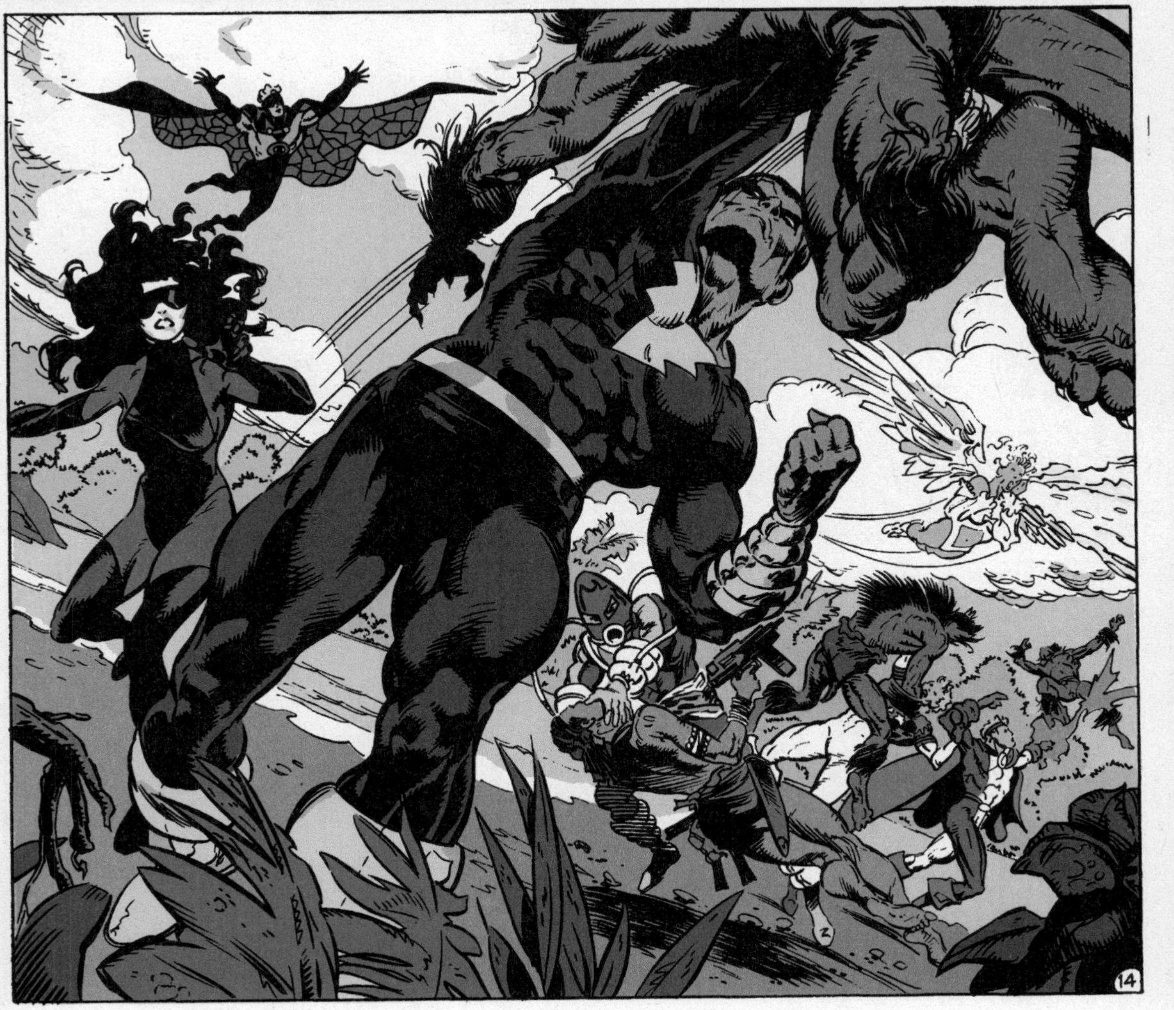
14

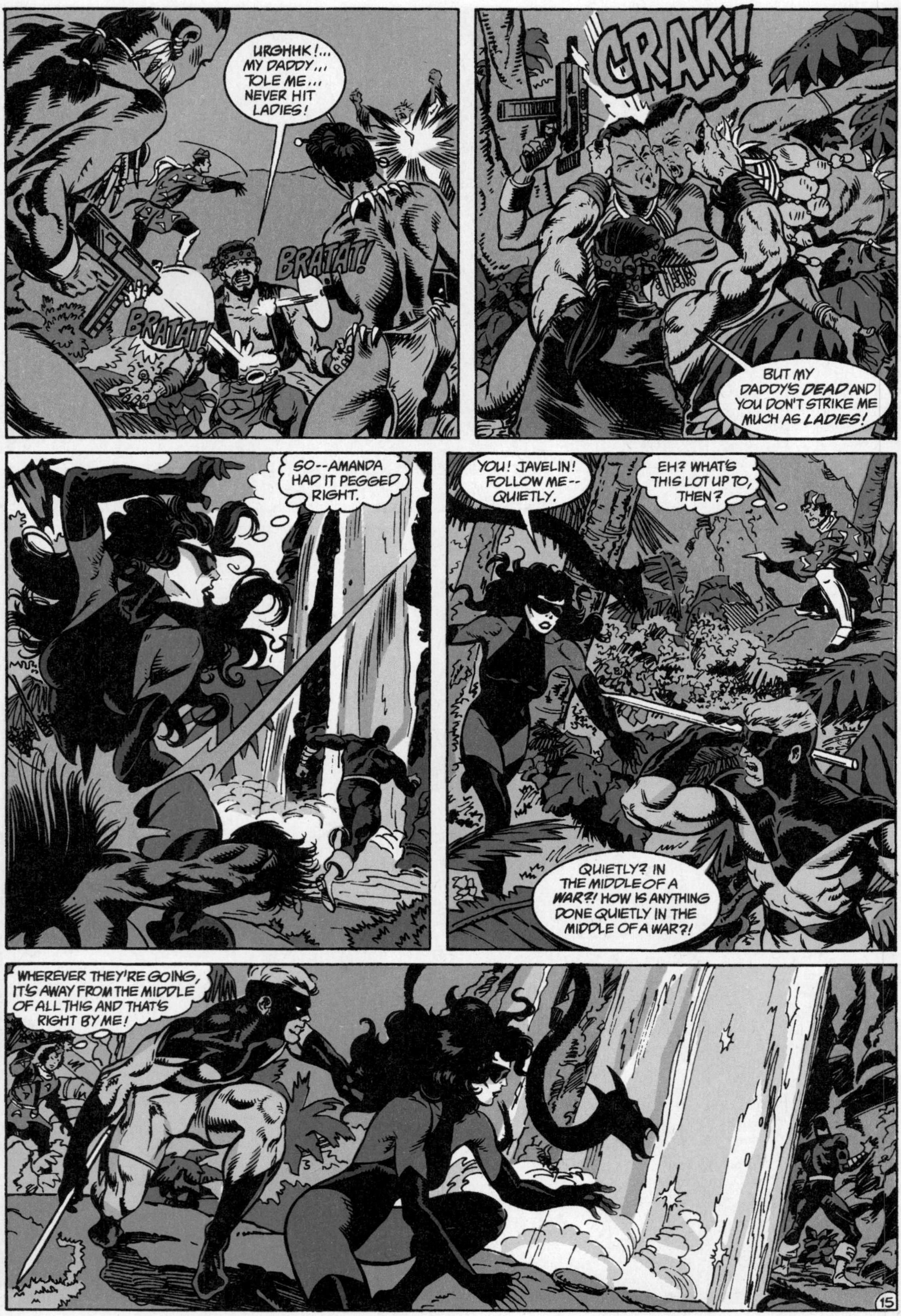
URGHHK!... MY DADDY... TOLE ME... NEVER HIT LADIES!
BRATAT!
BRATAT!
CRAK!
BUT MY DADDY'S DEAD AND YOU DON'T STRIKE ME MUCH AS LADIES!
SO--AMANDA HAD IT PEGGED RIGHT.
YOU! JAVELIN! FOLLOW ME-- QUIETLY.
EH? WHAT'S THIS LOT UP TO, THEN?
QUIETLY? IN THE MIDDLE OF A WAR?! HOW IS ANYTHING DONE QUIETLY IN THE MIDDLE OF A WAR?!
WHEREVER THEY'RE GOING, IT'S AWAY FROM THE MIDDLE OF ALL THIS AND THAT'S RIGHT BY ME!
15

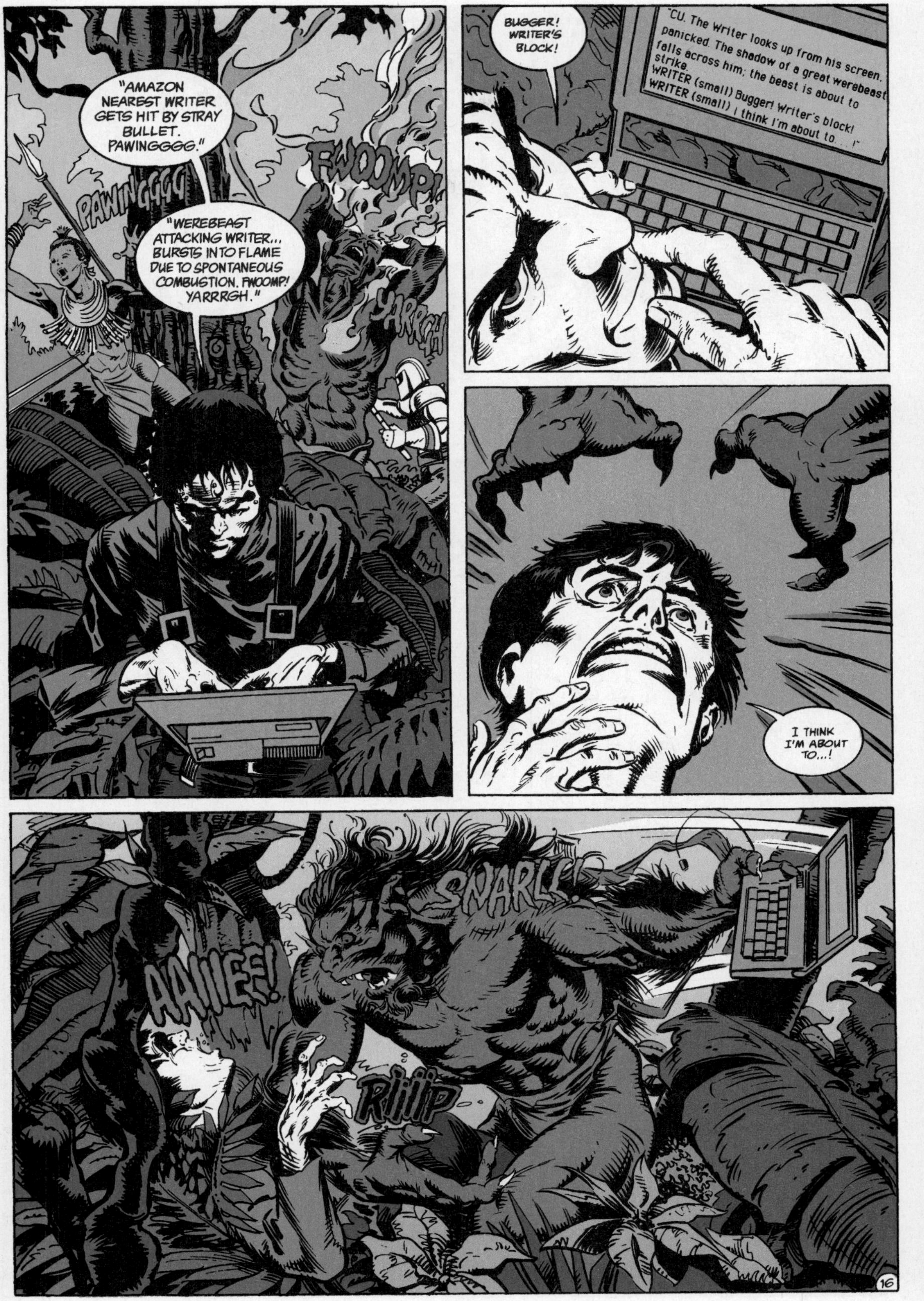
"AMAZON NEAREST WRITER GETS HIT BY STRAY BULLET. PAWINGGGG."
FWOOMP!
PAWINGGGG
"WEREBEAST ATTACKING WRITER... BURSTS INTO FLAME DUE TO SPONTANEOUS COMBUSTION. FWOOMP! YARRRGH."
YARRGH!
BUGGER! WRITER'S BLOCK!
"CU. The Writer looks up from his screen, panicked. The shadow of a great werebeast falls across him; the beast is about to strike.
WRITER (small) Bugger! Writer's block!
WRITER (small) I think I'm about to...!"
I THINK I'M ABOUT TO...!
SNARL!
AAIIEE!
RIIIP
16

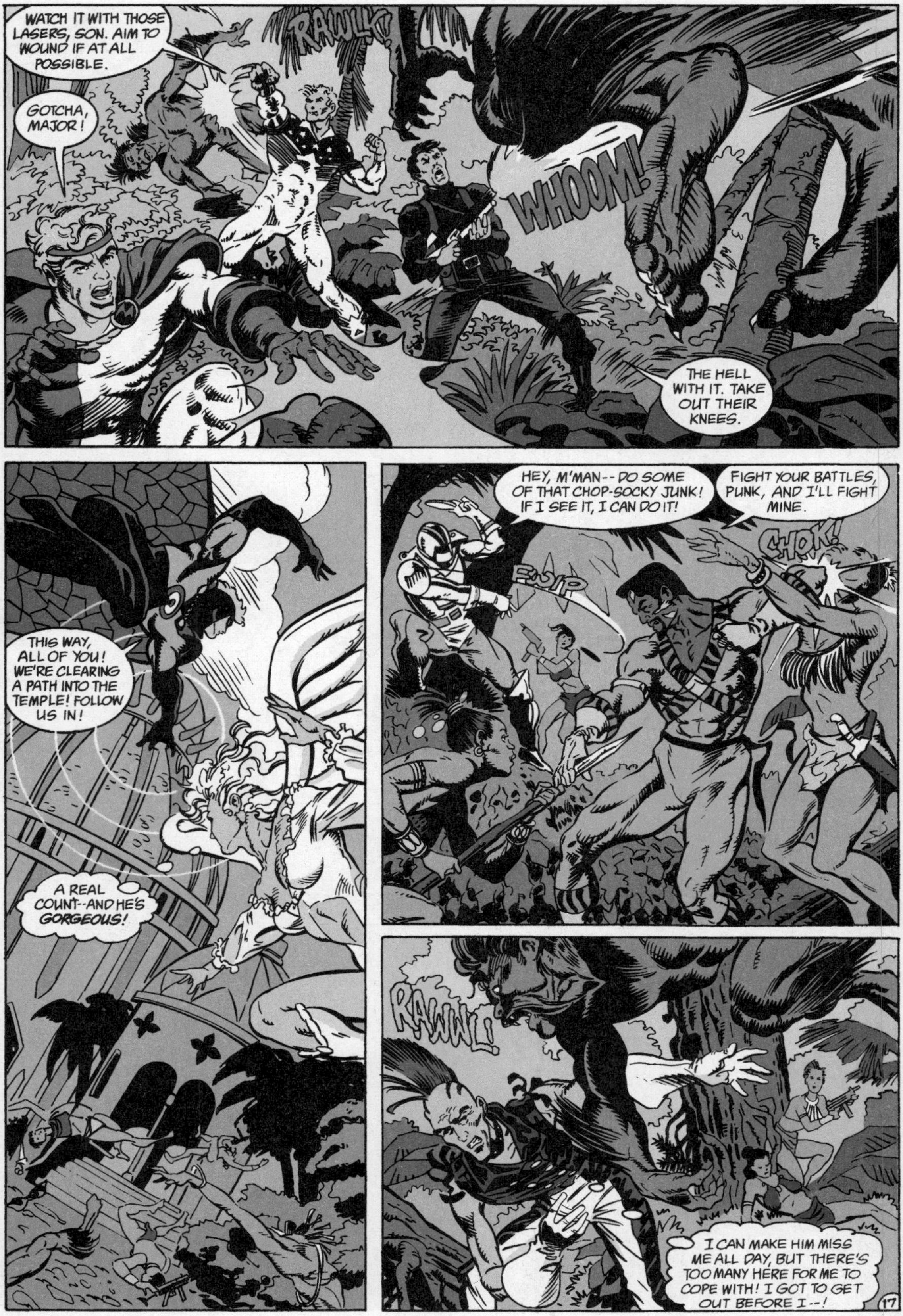
WATCH IT WITH THOSE LASERS, SON. AIM TO WOUND IF AT ALL POSSIBLE.
RAWLK!
GOTCHA, MAJOR!
WHOOM!
THE HELL WITH IT. TAKE OUT THEIR KNEES.
THIS WAY, ALL OF YOU! WE'RE CLEARING A PATH INTO THE TEMPLE! FOLLOW US IN!
A REAL COUNT--AND HE'S GORGEOUS!
HEY, M'MAN--DO SOME OF THAT CHOP-SOCKY JUNK! IF I SEE IT, I CAN DO IT!
FIGHT YOUR BATTLES, PUNK, AND I'LL FIGHT MINE.
CHOK!
RAWWL!
I CAN MAKE HIM MISS ME ALL DAY, BUT THERE'S TOO MANY HERE FOR ME TO COPE WITH! I GOT TO GET OUT BEFORE I--!
17

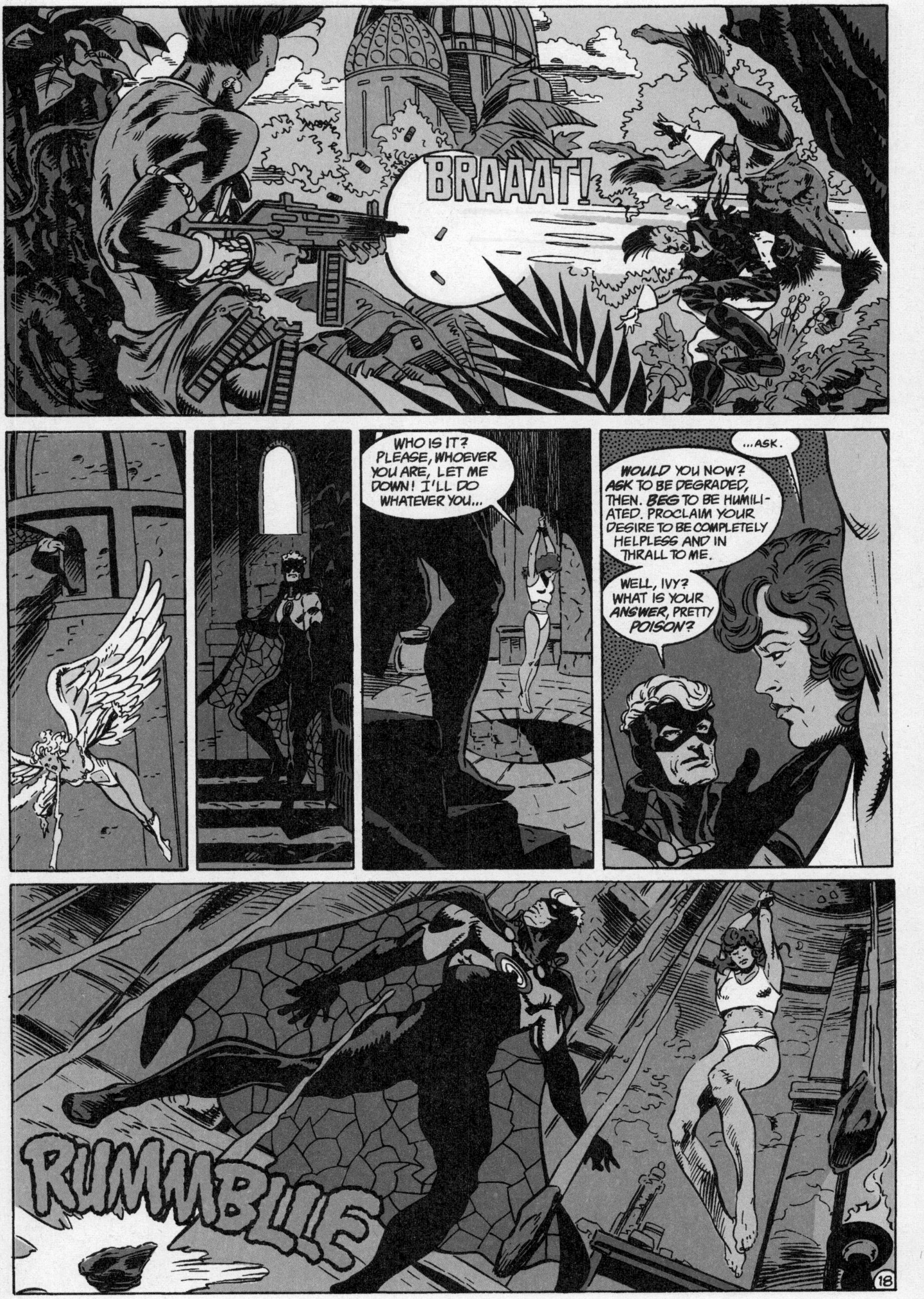
BRAAAT!
WHO IS IT? PLEASE, WHOEVER YOU ARE, LET ME DOWN! I'LL DO WHATEVER YOU...
...ASK.
WOULD YOU NOW? ASK TO BE DEGRADED, THEN. BEG TO BE HUMILIATED. PROCLAIM YOUR DESIRE TO BE COMPLETELY HELPLESS AND IN THRALL TO ME.
WELL, IVY? WHAT IS YOUR ANSWER, PRETTY POISON?
RUMMBLLE
18

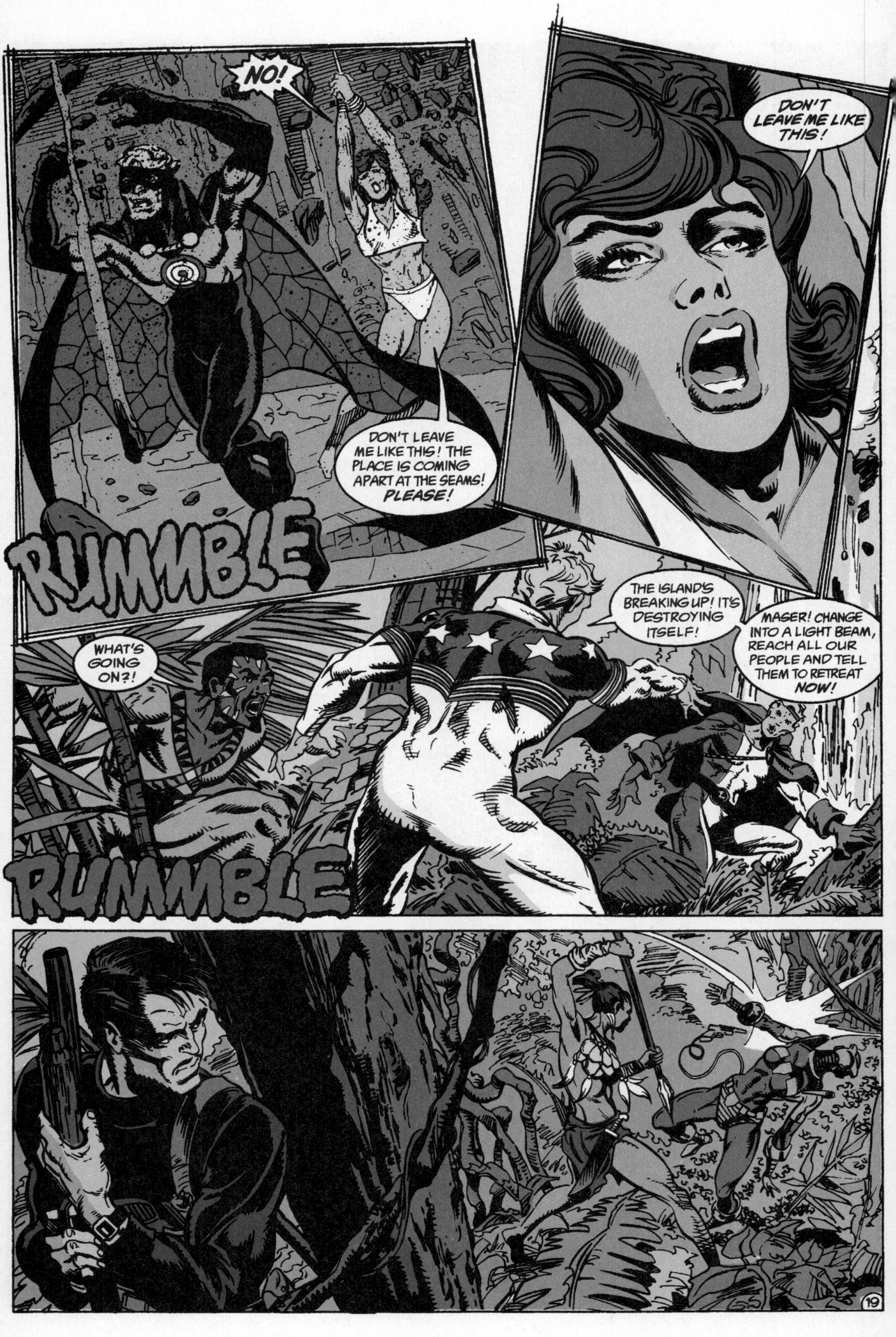
NO!
DON'T LEAVE ME LIKE THIS! THE PLACE IS COMING APART AT THE SEAMS! PLEASE!
DON'T LEAVE ME LIKE THIS!
RUMMBLE
THE ISLAND'S BREAKING UP! IT'S DESTROYING ITSELF!
MASER! CHANGE INTO A LIGHT BEAM, REACH ALL OUR PEOPLE AND TELL THEM TO RETREAT NOW!
WHAT'S GOING ON?!
RUMMBLE
19

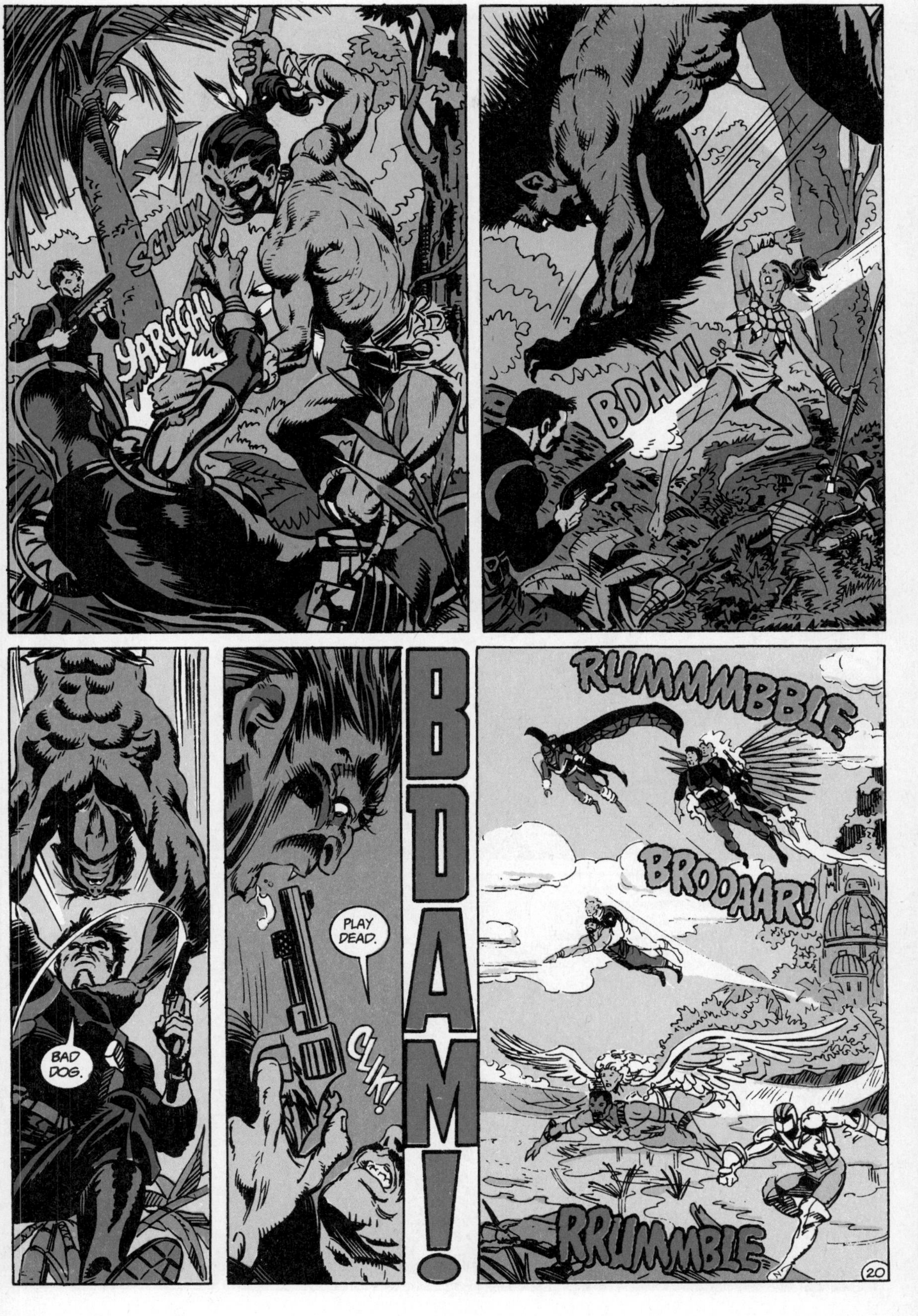
SCHLUK
YARGGH!
BDAM!
BAD DOG.
PLAY DEAD.
CLIK!
BDAM!
RUMMMMBBLE
BROOAAR!
RRUMMBLE
20

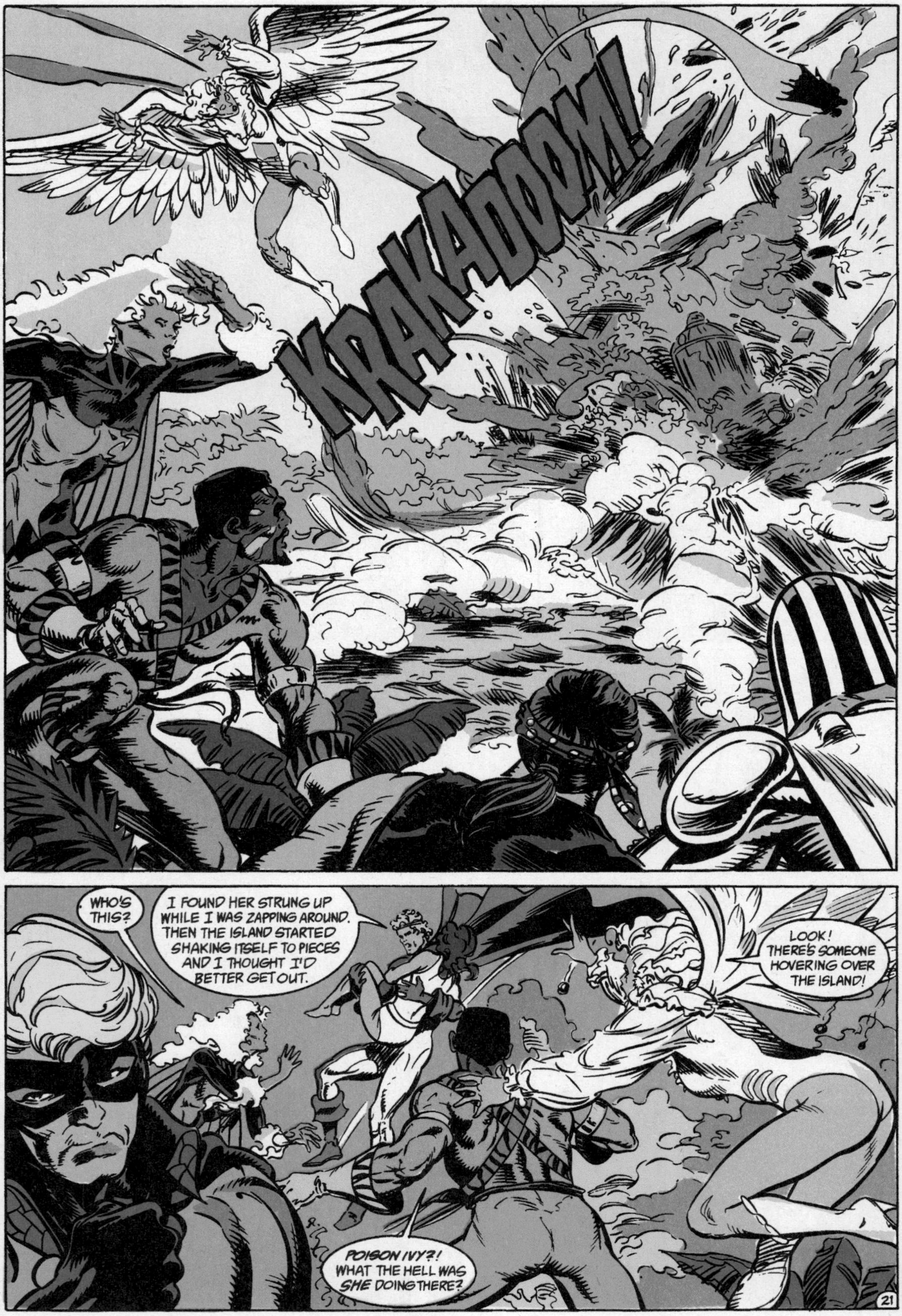
KRAKADOOM!
WHO'S THIS?
I FOUND HER STRUNG UP WHILE I WAS ZAPPING AROUND. THEN THE ISLAND STARTED SHAKING ITSELF TO PIECES AND I THOUGHT I'D BETTER GET OUT.
LOOK! THERE'S SOMEONE HOVERING OVER THE ISLAND!
POISON IVY?! WHAT THE HELL WAS SHE DOING THERE?
21

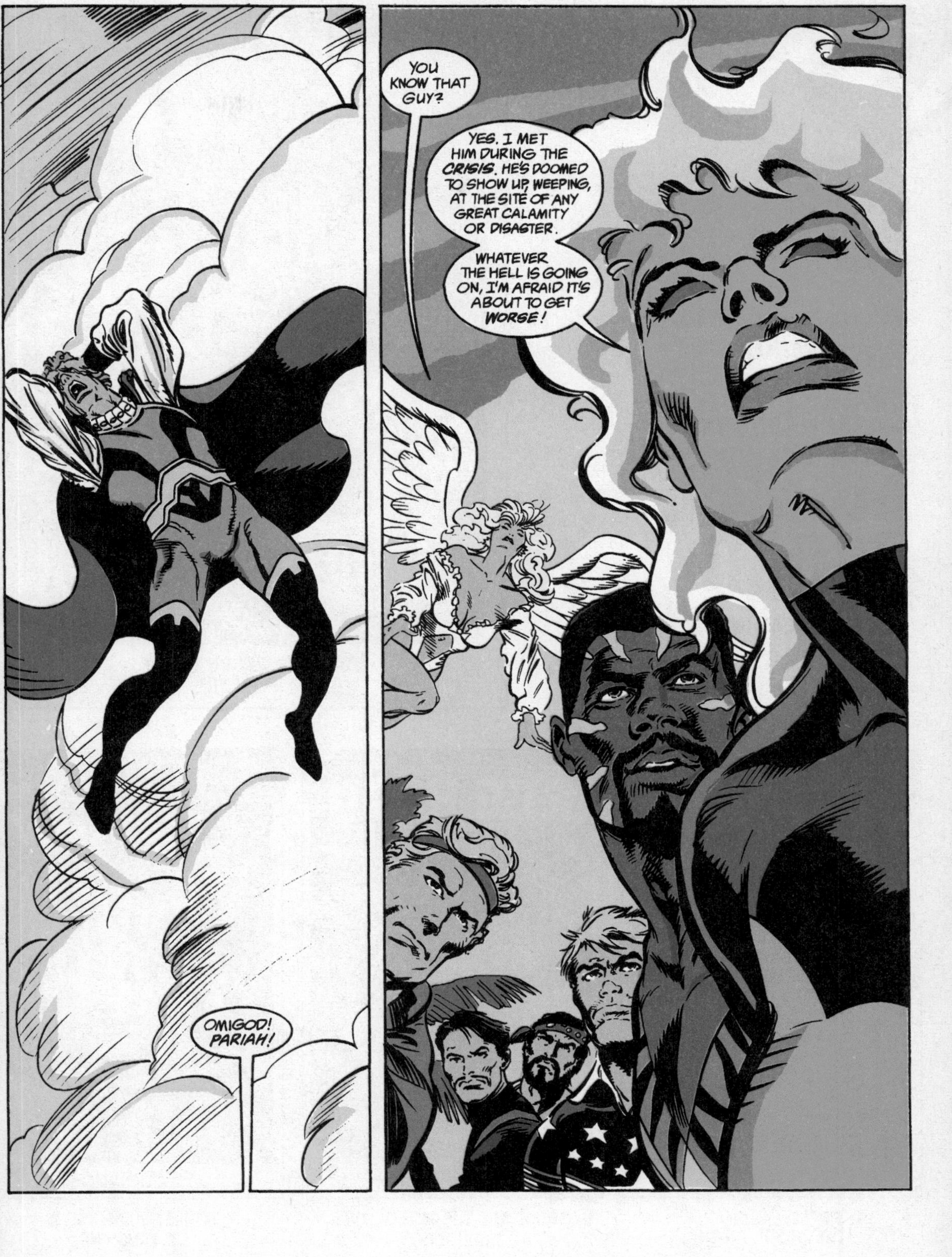
OMIGOD! PARIAH!
YOU KNOW THAT GUY?
YES. I MET HIM DURING THE CRISIS. HE'S DOOMED TO SHOW UP, WEEPING, AT THE SITE OF ANY GREAT CALAMITY OR DISASTER.
WHATEVER THE HELL IS GOING ON, I'M AFRAID IT'S ABOUT TO GET WORSE!

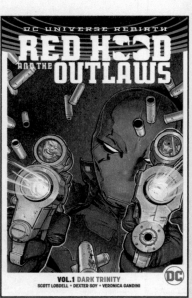

SUICIDE SQUAD

VOL. 1: KICKED IN THE TEETH

ADAM GLASS with FEDERICO DALLOCCHIO

THE NEW 52!

SUICIDE SQUAD

VOLUME 1
KICKED IN THE TEETH

ADAM **GLASS** FEDERICO **DALLOCCHIO** CLAYTON **HENRY**

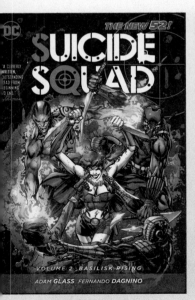

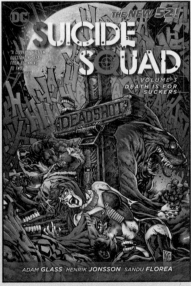

SUICIDE SQUAD
VOL. 2: BASILISK RISING

SUICIDE SQUAD
VOL. 3: DEATH IS FOR SUCKERS

READ THE ENTIRE EPIC!

"Chaotic and unabashedly fun."
– IGN

THE NEW YORK TIMES BESTSELLER
THE NEW 52!
HARLEY QUINN
VOLUME 1
HOT IN THE CITY
AMANDA CONNER JIMMY PALMIOTTI CHAD HARDIN
STEPHANE ROUX ALEX SINCLAIR PAUL MOUNTS

HARLEY QUINN

VOL. 1: HOT IN THE CITY

AMANDA CONNER
with JIMMY PALMIOTTI
& CHAD HARDIN

THE NEW YORK TIMES BEST-SELLING SERIES
HARLEY QUINN
VOLUME 2
POWER OUTAGE
AMANDA CONNER JIMMY PALMIOTTI
CHAD HARDIN JOHN TIMMS ALEX SINCLAIR

HARLEY QUINN
VOL. 2: POWER OUTAGE

THE #1 NEW YORK TIMES BEST-SELLING SERIES
HARLEY QUINN
VOLUME 3
KISS KISS
BANG STAB
AMANDA CONNER
JIMMY PALMIOTTI
CHAD HARDIN
JOHN TIMMS

HARLEY QUINN
VOL. 3: KISS KISS BANG STAB

READ THE ENTIRE EPIC

HARLEY QUINN VOL.
A CALL TO ARM

HARLEY QUINN VOL.
THE JOKER'S LAST LAUG

"I'm enjoying this a great deal;
it's silly, it's funny, it's irreverent."
– COMIC BOOK RESOURCES

Get more DC graphic novels wherever comics and books are sold!